HAESTAD METHODS

WATER DISTRIBUTION MODELING

First Edition

HAESTAD METHODS

WATER DISTRIBUTION MODELING

First Edition

THOMAS M. WALSKI, Ph.D., P.E.
Vice President of Engineering
Haestad Methods, Inc.

DONALD V. CHASE, Ph.D., P.E.
Lecturer
University of Dayton, U.S.A.

DRAGAN A. SAVIC, Ph.D., C.Eng.
Professor
University of Exeter, England

Managing Editor
Adam Strafaci

Peer Review Board
Lee Cesario, P.E., Denver Water
Bob Clark, Ph.D, P.E., D.E.E., U.S. EPA
Allen L. Davis, Ph.D, P.E., CH2MHill
Walter Grayman, Ph.D., P.E., Consulting Engineer
James W. Male, Ph.D, P.E., University of Portland
William M. Richards, P.E., WMR Engineering

Editors
Kristen Dietrich, Gregg Herrin, Peter Martin,
Houjung Rhee, Michael Tryby, Ben Wilson

HAESTAD PRESS
Waterbury, CT, U.S.A.

WATER DISTRIBUTION MODELING
First Edition
Reprinted with corrections June, 2001

Special thanks to the New Yorker Magazine for the cartoons throughout the book.

Page 17 - (1990) Peter Steiner
Page 54 - (1988) Sam Gross
Page 60 - (1999) Frank Cotham
Page 80 - (1990) Jack Ziegler
Page 110 - (1955) Joseph Mirachi
Page 126 - (1962) Robert Grossmanx
Page 144 - (1997) Warren Miller
Page 152 - (1999) Arnie Levin
Page 165 - (1999) Alex Gregory
Page 185 - (1999) Richard Cline
Page 201 - (1993) Dean Vietor
Page 216 - (1971) Chon Day
Page 236 - (1987) Arnie Levin
Page 255 - (1988) Ed Fisher
Page 285 - (1994) Leo Cultum
Page 320 - (2000) Charles Barsotti
Page 335 - (1990) Arnie Levin
Page 353 - (1994) Edward Koren
Page 373 - (1999) Barbara Smaller

Library of Congress Catalog Card No.: 98-87815
ISBN: 0-9657580-4-4

HAESTAD PRESS

Haestad Methods, Inc.
37 Brookside Rd.
Waterbury, CT 06708-1499
U.S.A.

Phone: +1-203-755-1666
Fax: +1-203-597-1488
e-mail: info@haestad.com
Internet: www.haestad.com

"In theory, there is no difference between theory and practice. But, in practice, there is."

-Jan L. A. van de Snepscheut

This book is dedicated to our dear friends and loved ones who suffer our intense passion for water resources and computer modeling. These are our companions in life who, though frequently puzzled by our devotion to these unfamiliar things, generously give us the time and support that we need to focus our attentions toward professional endeavors.

Through your trust, devotion, and tolerance, we found the freedom to solidify our passions in this book. We could never have made this book had you not been part of our lives - and part of our passions. We love you and thank you.

-The Authors

"…. provides an excellent coverage of a wide range of topics relating to water distribution system modeling, from acquisition of necessary data to model application and interpretation of results."

James M. Male, Ph. D., P. E.
University of Portland

"This book is a valuable addition to the reference library of water distribution system modelers. It covers a broad range of topics that must be addressed when modeling a pipe network."

Allen L. Davis, Ph. D., P. E.
CH2MHill

"Illustrations, problems, explanations, book content, and layout are excellent. This is what I would have wanted the second edition of my book to be. Excellent job. I am sure this will be a best seller."

Lee Cesario, P. E.
Denver Water

Acknowledgments

The completion of this book was truly a team effort and many deserve recognition. First and foremost, the thousands of engineers and operators that have made careers of ensuring the delivery of clean water to the world. Our discussions and meetings with you over the years have provided the inspiration to write this book.

While Don Chase, Dragan Savic, and Tom Walski wrote much of the first draft, many at Haestad Methods contributed to the final content and organization of the book. It is the synthesis of everyone's ideas that really made this book such a practical and helpful resource. Kristen Dietrich, Gregg Herrin, Michael Tryby, and Ben Wilson led this effort with countless hours of hard work and dedication.

Many developers, technical support representatives, and product specialists at Haestad Methods reviewed the chapters and accompanying examples and provided valuable input. These reviewers included Samuel Coran, Robert Mankowski, Fariborz Nouri, Jennifer Patty, Rajan Ray, Michael Rosh, Adam Simonsen, and Ben White. The contributions of Jack Cook and Keith Hodsden are particularly noteworthy.

The illustrations and graphs throughout the book were created and assembled by Peter Martin with the assistance of Emily Charles and Adam Simonsen of Haestad Methods and Cal Hurd and John Slate of Roald Haestad, Inc. Special thanks to the New Yorker Magazine for the cartoons throughout the book and to the Ductile Iron Pipe Research Association, Crane Valves, Peerless Pumps, Val-Matic, F.S. Brainard & Company, Badger Meter Inc., CMB Industries, Hersey Products, and the City of Waterbury Bureau of Water for providing us with additional illustrations. Houjung Rhee, Kristen Dietrich, Tom Walski, and Don Chase contributed greatly to the discussion topics and exercises at the end of each chapter.

Several people were involved in the final production and delivery of the book. Lissa Jennings proofread and handled publishing logistics. Rick Brainard and Jim O'Brien designed the cover. Jeanette August added her creative energy in the design of the review comment web site. Wes Cogswell managed the CD and software installation efforts.

We greatly appreciate the contributions of our peer reviewers Lee Cesario, Bob Clark, Allen Davis, Walter Grayman, Jim Male, and Bill Richards. They provided exceptional insights and shared practical experiences that added enormously to the depth of the work.

Finally, special thanks to our president John Haestad who provided the vision, as well as the resources and motivation, to make this collection of ideas a reality.

Adam Strafaci
Managing Editor

About the Authors

Water Distribution Modeling represents a collaborative effort combining the experiences and technical expertise of Dr. Tom Walski, Dr. Don Chase, Dr. Dragan Savic, and the engineers and software developers at Haestad Methods.

Thomas Walski, Ph.D., P.E.

Thomas M. Walski, Ph.D., P.E., is Vice President of Engineering for Haestad Methods, Inc. Over the past three decades, Dr. Walski has served as an expert witness; Research Civil Engineer for the U.S. Army Corps of Engineers; Engineer and Manager of Distribution Operation for the City of Austin, Texas; Executive Director of the Wyoming Valley Sanitary Authority; Associate Professor of Environmental Engineering at Wilkes University; and Engineering Manager for the Pennsylvania American Water Company. Over the past decade, he has also taught over 2,000 professionals in Haestad Methods' IACET accredited water distribution modeling course.

A widely published expert on water distribution modeling, Dr. Walski has written several books including *Analysis of Water Distribution Systems, Water Distribution Simulation and Sizing* (with Johannes Gessler and John Sjostrom), and *Water Distribution Systems - A Troubleshooting Manual* (with Jim Male). He was also editor and primary author of *Water Supply System Rehabilitation* and was chair of the AWWA Fire Protection Committee which produced the latest version of *Distribution Requirements for Fire Protection.*

He has served on numerous professional committees and chaired several including the ASCE Water Resources Systems Committee, ASCE Environmental Engineering Publications Committee, ASCE Environmental Engineering Awards Committee, and the ASCE Water Supply Rehabilitation Task Committee.

Dr. Walski has written over 50 peer reviewed papers and made roughly 100 conference presentations. He is three-time winner of the best paper award in Distribution and Plant Operation for the *Journal of the American Water Works Association*, and is past editor of the *Journal of Environmental Engineering*. He received his M.S. and Ph.D. in Environmental and Water Resources Engineering from Vanderbilt University. He is a registered professional engineer in two states and is a certified water and wastewater plant operator.

Donald V. Chase, Ph.D., P.E.

Donald V. Chase, Ph.D., P.E., is Assistant Professor of Civil & Environmental Engineering at the University of Dayton and a recognized authority in numerical modeling and computer simulation. Prior to receiving his Ph.D. from the University of Kentucky he was employed as a civil engineer by the U. S. Army Corps of Engineers Waterways Experiment Station (WES) in Vicksburg, Mississippi.

Dr. Chase is currently working on projects related to the fate and transport of contaminated dredged disposal material, energy costs of water supply systems, surges in large water transmission mains, operational characteristics of variable speed pumps, hydraulic characteristics of culverts, and using Geographic Information Systems (GIS) in wellhead protection. Dr. Chase is a registered professional engineer and a member of ASCE and AWWA. He has held several positions in these organizations, including chair of the ASCE Environmental Engineering Division Water Supply Committee.

Dragan Savic, Ph.D., C.Eng.

Dragan Savic, Ph.D., C. Eng., is a chartered (professional) engineer with over fifteen years of research, teaching, and consulting experience in various water-engineering disciplines. His interests include developing and applying computer modeling and optimization techniques to civil engineering systems, with particular application to the operation and design of water distribution networks, hydraulic structures, hydropower generation, and environmental protection and management.

Dr. Savic jointly heads the Center for Water Systems at the University of Exeter in England and is a founding member of Optimal Solutions, a consultancy service that specializes in using optimization technologies to plan, design, and operate water systems. He has published over 100 research/professional papers and reports and is internationally recognized as a research leader in modeling and optimization of pipe networks.

Foreword

Most of the popular network analysis programs let you solve the network using either the Hazen-Williams equation or some form of the Darcy-Weisbach equation. If you have carefully performed the modeling and calibration, you will find little difference in the output of these formulations for the same network.

Modeling can be successful using either the Hazen-Williams or the Darcy-Weisbach equation. (The Darcy-Weisbach formula is often described as the Colebrook-White equation or the Swamee-Jain equation, which are adaptations.) The real problem faced by anyone modeling a real system with existing pipe, regardless of which formula is used, is how to quantify the required coefficients and determine that they are reasonably accurate.

There are many approaches to network analysis, and probably no single approach satisfies all of the varied problems that can arise. You should become familiar with all of the well-tested methods and how the various equations were developed; then, you will be equipped to work with all of them and understand how others, using different methods, arrived at their conclusions.

Any good solution is preceded by a thorough investigation of the problem and its definition, and that investigation should include the determination that the problem falls within the constraints of the method used for analysis. No less important are inputting data correctly into the model and calibrating the model against well-developed and accurate field data. Don't forget to verify that the units used in the analysis are compatible. It is also extremely important that experienced engineering and technical personnel review the output of the analysis. A thorough engineering critique can save a lot of headaches later.

There is a great deal more to modeling a real water distribution system than painting the picture in the graphics section of an engineering analysis computer program. Some of the most important aspects are measuring flows, heads, pipe diameters, lengths and elevations; testing pump curves; checking SCADA systems and other system measuring devices for accuracy; and checking system anomalies that only system operators know.

Building the Model. You need to look at the end use of the network models you develop. Will they be used for water quality analyses, or will the output data be used for surge analyses? These are only two of the extended uses that need to be considered in current modeling practice.

In most cases, you will probably build a preliminary model before all the field data are collected; in fact, these processes should go hand in hand. A well-constructed model with reasonable assumed values can be used to determine where and how much field study will be required to satisfy the model calibration. A preliminary calibration of the model will also point out areas where the system itself may have problems such as closed valves, large leaks, or worn pump impellers. The worst modeling is done by those who believe that you can model an existing water system of reasonable complexity without some degree of field testing and accurate instrument calibration.

You should seriously question any data to be used in your model that has not been confirmed by good field measurements. There must be a reasonable number of field tests in order to provide a good statistical base for the application of various parameters to the rest of the physical system. However, in the face of time constraints, there are many instances in which these tests are not done. There have been engineering contracts lost to lower bidders who did not include the necessary field work in their estimates because their software "took care of it." You couldn't get away with sloppy lab work in college, and you can't in your professional life, either.

GIS systems do not ensure that data is more accurate than that contained in atlas books or paper filing systems—they are just more readily available. The real danger is that there are many who still believe that everything that is digitally stored is somehow magically reformed to a new accuracy. There are pitfalls to blindly using a GIS database to build a water distribution model for analysis if you don't take the time to review all the data.

Before you jump into any modeling software, you must think the process through and determine what it is that you want to do, and what you would expect to find under conditions that may exist in the real system you are modeling. Remember, you are the engineer and the modeling program is just another tool you are using to enhance your capabilities. If the tool is giving you answers that are unexpected, then you should question them until you are satisfied with their validity.

Calibrating Your Model. Keep an open mind when calibrating a model against actual system data. Many engineers struggle with trying to pinpoint a problem in the model, when what the model is really telling them is that there is a malfunction in the system. An unexpected head loss could be a closed or throttled valve, or a pipe that is a different size than that shown on a system map. An unexpected flow could be a large leak disappearing into a large storm sewer or a river, or an uncharted connection to the system. An unexpected discharge pressure at a pump station could point to a worn impeller that no longer conforms to the pump curve supplied by the manufacturer. These are only a few examples that many experienced modelers have faced.

Peak period demands are far more random than those for an average day. Peak hour demands may be influenced by community-specific factors that are difficult to assess, and that you may not want to design for. Examples of factors that can influence these demands are illegally opened fire hydrants and the excessive irrigation of private lawns. There is also the problem of large or wholesale users taking water at demand rates, rather than using equalizing storage to average out the demands over a 24-hour period. Depending on the factors influencing a given maximum day condition, the geographical distribution of the maximum day demand can vary significantly as well.

Average day demands, on the other hand, are much easier to predict and model, especially when you are trying to calibrate the model against actual system data. Certainly you must design the system for maximum day conditions, but determination of exactly what those conditions are involves decisions by the system's management regarding their approach to the factors discussed in the preceding paragraph. A well-calibrated model can be an excellent tool in helping management to make those decisions.

Once you have determined all of the above, the system should be analyzed and the output reviewed to determine where there might still be discrepancies with measurements in the real system. At this point, there is a question of whether the discrepancies indicate problems that exist in the model or the real system. This review should be done before any changes are made to rationally developed friction factors or pipe diameters, unless you're one of those rare people who enjoys getting really confused. It's amazing how many large leaks are discovered this way, or uncharted services, or previously undetected errors in the metered consumption, or errors in recorded pipe sizes, or unknown throttled or closed valves, or worn pump impellers, or old construction debris left in pipes. Certainly there may need to be changes in the model, but let's not calibrate it to an old system that's trying to tell us that it has some aches and pains. After this process is completed, and you have cleaned up both the system and the model, you can make whatever adjustments you feel are required to meet your needs—your client or boss will love you, and your old lab professor would be proud.

Enjoy the Results. A well-constructed model that is properly calibrated and updated on a regular basis is one of the more important tools in the engineer's bag for the design, maintenance and operation of today's modern water supply systems.

William M. Richards, P.E.
WMR Engineering

The process by which we analyze and design water distribution systems has gone through dramatic changes over the last 20 years. Most of these changes have paralleled the rapid growth in the speed and storage capabilities of computers. However, the fundamental principles that govern water flow and water quality remain the same.

Engineers must understand these underlying principles and know how they are applied; and they must use judgment accompanied by knowledge of the system to which they are applying computer models. Too frequently the easy use (relatively easy use, compared to the tasks of 20 years ago) of a computer model masks the complexities that exist in the real-world system. Engineers must not only understand the complexities of the water supply system being modeled, but also the capabilities of the model being used to assist them in making decisions about design, operation, rehabilitation, and maintenance.

James W. Male, Ph.D, P.E.
University of Portland

Table of Contents

Preface

Learning how to model a water distribution system is a complicated task. Understanding how to operate a modeling program is a minor part of the overall picture. To effectively use models, the engineer must be able to link knowledge of basic hydraulic theory and the mechanics of the program with that of the operation of real-world systems.

The purpose of this book is to provide a practical resource for engineers and modelers that goes well beyond being a how-to guide for typing data into a computer program. It contains straightforward answers to common questions related both to modeling and to distribution systems in general. The scope of this text includes such topics as:

- Definitions and industry standards
- Model assembly and verification
- Effective use of models as decision-support tools
- Recent innovations in modeling

The method in which these issues are approached is designed to be readily accessible for immediate application by practicing engineers, while sufficiently comprehensive for student use.

Overview. Chapter 1 of this book provides an overview of water distribution systems, water modeling application, and the modeling process. It also presents a history of water distribution from the first pipes used in Crete around 1500 B.C. to today's latest innovations.

Chapter 2 contains a review of basic hydraulic theory and its application to water distribution modeling. Chapter 3 then relates this theory to the basic physical elements found in typical water distribution systems and computer models.

Chapter 4 discusses computing customer demands and fire protection requirements and how water demands vary over time. Chapters 5 and 6 cover system testing and model calibration, respectively. These activities work together to minimize the gap between what the model computes and what occurs in the actual system, which is one of the chief goals of water distribution modeling.

More experienced modelers will probably find the latter portion of the book to be of the greatest benefit. Chapters 7, 8, and 9 help the engineer to apply the model to real-world problem solving in the areas of system design and operation. Developing a water model can be a big investment of time and money, and one of the main goals of this book is to help the modeler maximize that investment by finding efficient solutions to distribution system problems. In this area, we feel that this book goes beyond other works previously published on modeling.

Continuing Education and Problem Sets. Also included in this text are approximately 100 hydraulics and modeling problems to give students and professionals the opportunity to apply the material covered in each chapter. Some of these problems have short answers, while others require more thought and may have more than one solution. The accompanying CD-ROM in the back of the book contains an academic version of Haestad Methods' WaterCAD, which can be used to solve many of the problems, as well as data files with much of the given information in the problems pre-entered. However, we have endeavored to make this book a valuable resource to all modelers, including those who may be using other software packages, so these data files are merely a convenience, not a necessity.

If you would like to work the problems and receive continuing education credit in the form of Continuing Education Units (CEUs), you may do so by filling out the examination booklet available on the CD-ROM and submitting your work to Haestad Methods for grading.

For more information, see "Using this Book to Earn Continuing Education Credits" on page xiii and "CD-ROM Contents" in the back of this book.

Haestad Methods also publishes a solutions guide that is available for a nominal fee to instructors and professionals who are not submitting work for continuing education credit.

Feedback. The authors and staff of Haestad Methods have striven to make the content of this first edition of Water Distribution Modeling as useful, complete, and accurate as possible. However, we recognize that there is always room for improvement, and we invite you to help us make subsequent editions even better than the original.

If you have comments or suggestions regarding improvements to this textbook, or are interested in being one of our peer reviewers for future publications, we want to hear from you. We have established a forum for providing feedback at the following URL:

http://www.haestad.com/peer-review/

We hope that you find this culmination of our efforts and experience to be a core resource in your engineering library, and wish you the best with your modeling endeavors.

Thomas M. Walski, Ph.D., P.E.
Vice President of Engineering and Product Development
Haestad Methods, Inc.

Continuing Education Units

With the rapid technological advances taking place in the engineering profession today, continuing education is more important than ever for civil engineers. In fact, it is now mandatory for many, as an increasing number of engineering licensing boards are requiring Continuing Education Units (CEUs) or Professional Development Hours (PDHs) for annual license renewal.

Chapters 2 through 9 of this book contain exercises designed to reinforce the hydraulic principles and modeling techniques previously discussed in the text. Many of these problems provide an excellent opportunity to become further acquainted with software used in distribution systems modeling. Further, these exercises can be completed and submitted to Haestad Methods for grading and award of CEUs.

For the purpose of awarding CEUs, the chapters in this book have been grouped into several units. Complete the following steps to be eligible to receive credits as shown in the table on the following page. Note that you do not need to complete the units in order; you may skip units or complete only a single unit.

Unit	Topics Covered	Chapters Covered	CEUs Available (1 CEU = 10 PDHs)	Grading Fee* (US $)
1	Introduction and Modeling Theory	Chapters 1 & 2	1.5	$75
2	System Components and Demands	Chapters 3 & 4	1.5	$75
3	Testing and Calibration	Chapters 5 & 6	1.5	$75
4	Design of Utility & Customer Systems	Chapters 7 & 8	1.5	$75
5	System Operations	Chapter 9	3.0	$150
All Units	All	All	9.0	$400

*Prices subject to change without notice.

1. Print the exam booklet from the file *exam_booklet.pdf* located on the CD-ROM in the back of this book,

   - or -

   contact Haestad Methods by phone, fax, or mail to have an exam booklet sent to you.

   Haestad Methods
   37 Brookside Road
   Waterbury, CT 06708
   U.S.A.
   ATTN: Continuing Education

   Phone: +1 203 755 1666
   Fax: +1 203 597 1488
   e-mail: ceu@haestad.com

2. Read and study the material contained in the chapters covered by the Unit(s) you select.

3. Work the related questions at the end of the relevant chapters and complete the exam booklet.

4. Return your exam booklet and payment to Haestad Methods for grading.

5. A Haestad Methods engineer will review your work within 30 days and return your graded exam booklet to you. If you pass (70 percent is passing), you will receive a certificate documenting the CEUs (PDHs) earned for successfully completed units.

6. If you do not pass, you will be allowed to correct your work and resubmit it for credit within 30 days at no additional charge.

Notes on Completing the Exercises

- Some of the problems have both an English units version and an SI version. You need only complete one of these versions.

- Show your work where applicable to be eligible for partial credit.

- Many of the problems can be done manually with a calculator, while others are of a more realistic size and will be much easier if analyzed with a water distribution model.

- To aid in completing the exercises, a CD-ROM is included inside the back cover of this book. It contains an academic version of Haestad Methods' WaterCAD software, software documentation, and computer files with much of the given information from the problem statements already entered. For detailed information on the CD-ROM contents and the software license agreement, see the information pages in the back of the book.

- You are not required to use WaterCAD to work the problems.

Disclaimer

Grading is at the sole discretion of Haestad Methods. You are expected to answer all questions correctly; however, allowances are made for data entry errors and differing interpretations, provided you demonstrate knowledge of the underlying principles. Prices are subject to change and Haestad Methods reserves the right to modify the problems and other requirements with each edition of the book.

If you do not pass and wish to resubmit your work for re-grading after more than 30 days, or if you do not receive a passing grade on the resubmitted work and wish to correct it again, you will be charged an additional grading fee.

About Haestad Methods Continuing Education

When you submit your work to Haestad Methods, you are submitting it to the most highly accredited Continuing Education Department in the civil engineering community. Haestad Methods was the first in the industry to achieve Authorized Provider status with the International Association for Continuing Education and Training (IACET), and the courses meet the requirements of the National Council of Examiners for Engineering and Surveying (NCEES).

CHAPTER

1

Introduction to Water Distribution Modeling

Water distribution modeling is the latest technology in a process of advancement that began two millennia ago when the Minoans constructed the first piped water conveyance system. Today, it is a critical part of designing and operating water distribution systems that are capable of serving communities reliably, efficiently, and safely, both now and in the future. The availability of increasingly sophisticated and accessible models allows these goals to be realized more fully than ever before.

This book is structured to take the engineer through the entire modeling process, from gathering system data and understanding how a computer model works, through constructing and calibrating the model, to implementing the model in system design and operations. The text is designed to be a first course for the novice modeler or engineering student, as well as a reference for those more experienced with distribution system simulations.

This chapter introduces the reader to *water distribution modeling* (WDM) by giving an overview of the basic distribution system components, defining the nature and purposes of distribution system simulations, and outlining the basic steps in the modeling process. The last section of the chapter presents a chronology of advancements in water distribution.

1.1 ANATOMY OF A WATER DISTRIBUTION SYSTEM

Although the size and complexity of water distribution systems vary dramatically, they all have the same basic purpose - to deliver water from the source (or treatment facility) to the customer.

Sources of Potable Water

Untreated water (also called *raw* water) may come from groundwater sources or surface waters such as lakes, reservoirs, and rivers. The raw water is usually transported to a water treatment plant, where it is processed to produce *treated* water (also known as *potable* or *finished* water). The degree to which the raw water is processed to achieve potability depends on the characteristics of the raw water, relevant drinking water standards, treatment processes used, and the characteristics of the distribution system.

Before leaving the plant and entering the water distribution system, treated surface water usually enters a unit called a *clearwell*. The clearwell serves three main purposes in water treatment. First, it provides contact time for *disinfectants* such as chlorine that are added near the end of the treatment process. Adequate contact time is required to achieve acceptable levels of disinfection.

Second, the clearwell provides storage that acts as a buffer between the treatment plant and the distribution system. Distribution systems naturally fluctuate between periods of high and low water usage, thus the clearwell stores excess treated water during periods of low demand and delivers it during periods of peak demand. Not only does this storage make it possible for the treatment plant to operate at a more stable rate, but it also means that the plant does not need to be designed to handle peak demands. Rather, it can be built to handle more moderate treatment rates, which means lower construction and operational costs.

Third, the clearwell can serve as a source for backwash water for cleaning plant filters that, when needed, is used at a high rate for a short period of time.

In the case of groundwater, it is true that many sources offer up consistently high quality water that could be consumed without disinfection. However, the practice of maintaining a disinfectant residual is almost always adhered to for protection against accidental contamination and microbial regrowth in the distribution system. Disinfection at groundwater sources differs from sources influenced by surface water in that it is usually applied at the well itself.

Customers of Potable Water

Customers of a water supply system are easily identified since they are the reason that the system exists in the first place. Homeowners, factories, hospitals, restaurants, golf courses, and thousands of other types of customers depend on water systems to provide everything from safe drinking water to irrigation. As demonstrated throughout the book, customers and the nature in which they use water is the driving mechanism behind how a water distribution system behaves. Water use can vary over time both in the long-term (seasonally) and the short-term (daily), and over space. Good knowledge of how water use is distributed across the system is critical to accurate modeling.

Transport Facilities

Moving water from the source to the customer requires a network of *pipes*, *pumps*, *valves*, and other appurtenances. Storing water to accommodate fluctuations in demand due to varying rates of usage or fire protection needs requires storage facilities such as tanks and reservoirs. Piping, storage, and the supporting infrastructure are together referred to as the *water distribution system* (WDS).

Transmission and Distribution Mains. This system of piping is often categorized into *transmission/trunk mains* and *distribution mains*. Transmission mains consist of components that are designed to convey large amounts of water over great distances, typically between major facilities within the system. For example, a transmission main may be used to transport water from a treatment facility to storage tanks throughout several cities and towns. Individual customers are usually not served from transmission mains.

Distribution mains are an intermediate step toward delivering water to the end customers. Distribution mains are smaller in diameter than transmission mains, and typically follow the general topology and alignment of the city streets. *Elbows*, *tees*, *wyes*, *crosses*, and numerous other *fittings* are used to connect and redirect sections of pipe. *Fire hydrants*, *isolation valves*, *control valves*, *blow-offs*, and other maintenance and operational appurtenances are frequently connected directly to the distribution mains. *Services*, also called *service lines*, transmit the water from the distribution mains to the end customers.

Homes, businesses, and industries have their own internal plumbing systems to transport water to sinks, washing machines, hose bibbs, and so forth. Typically, the internal plumbing of a customer is not included in a WDS model; however, there are cases such as sprinkler systems where internal plumbing may be modeled.

System Configurations. Transmission and distribution systems can be either *looped* or *branched*, as shown in Figure 1.1. As the name suggests, in looped systems there may be several different paths that the water can follow to get from the source to a particular customer. In a branched system, also called a *tree* or *dendritic* system, the water has only one possible path from the source to a customer.

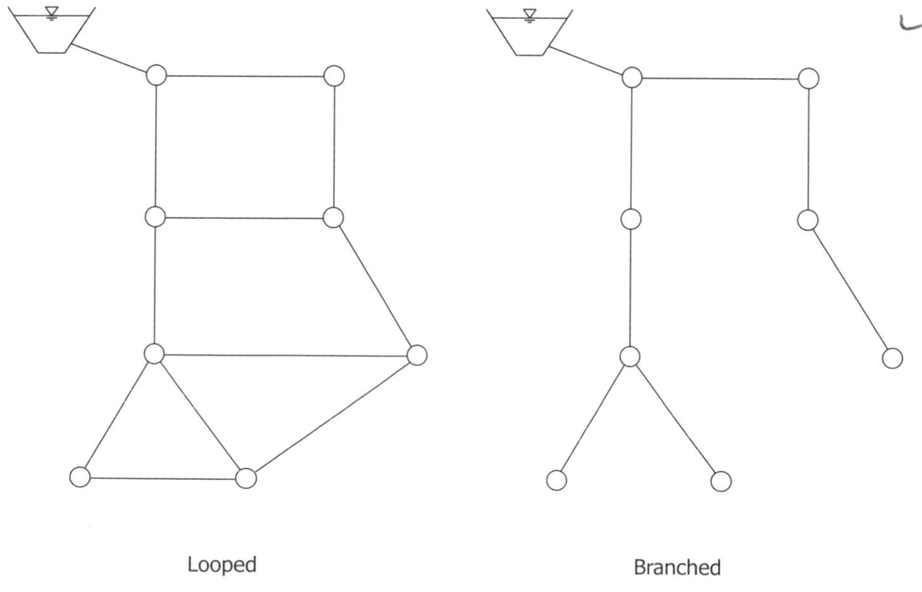

Figure 1.1 Looped and branched networks

Looped systems are generally more desirable than branched systems because, coupled with sufficient valving, they can provide an additional level of reliability. For example, consider a main break occurring near the *reservoir* in each system depicted in Figure 1.2. In the looped system, that break can be isolated and repaired with little impact on customers outside of that immediate area. In the branched system, however, all of the customers downstream from the break will have their water service interrupted until the repairs are finished. Another advantage of a looped configuration is that, because there is more than one path for water to reach the user, the velocities will be lower, and system capacity greater.

Figure 1.2
Looped and branched networks after network failure

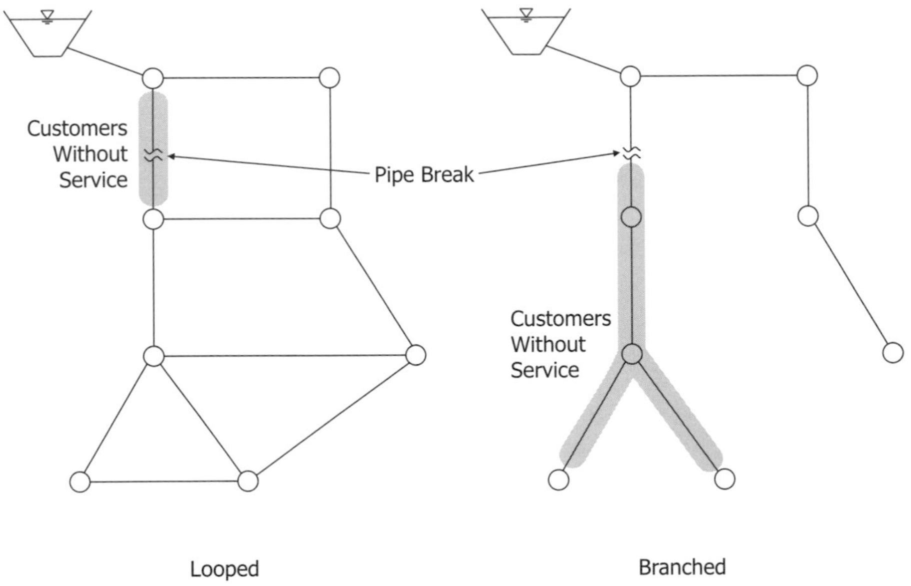

Most water supply systems are a complex combination of loops and branches, with a trade-off between loops for reliability (redundancy) and branches for infrastructure cost savings. In systems such as rural distribution networks, the low density of customers may make interconnecting the branches of the system prohibitive from both monetary and logistical standpoints.

1.2 WHAT IS A WATER DISTRIBUTION SYSTEM SIMULATION?

The term *simulation* generally refers to the process of imitating the behavior of one system through the functions of another. In this book, the term simulation will refer to the process of using a mathematical representation of the real system, or *model*. Network simulations, which replicate the dynamics of an existing or proposed system, are commonly performed when it is not practical for the real system to be directly subjected to experimentation, or for the purpose of evaluating a system before it is actually built. In addition, for situations in which water quality is an issue, directly testing a system may be costly and a potentially hazardous risk to public health.

Simulations can be used to predict system responses to events under a wide range of conditions without disrupting the actual system. Using simulations, problems can be anticipated in proposed or existing systems, and solutions can be evaluated before time, money, and materials are invested in a real-world project.

For example, a water utility might want to verify that a new subdivision can be provided with enough water to fight a fire without compromising the level of service to existing customers. The system could be built and tested directly, but if any problems were to be discovered, the cost of correction would be enormous. Regardless of project size, model-based simulation can provide valuable information to assist an engineer in making well-informed decisions.

Simulations can either be steady-state or extended period. *Steady-state* simulations represent a snapshot in time and are used to determine the operating behavior of a system under static conditions. This type of analysis can be useful in determining the short-term effect of fire flows or average demand conditions on the system. *Extended period simulations (EPS)* are used to evaluate system performance over time. This type of analysis allows the user to model tanks filling and draining, regulating valves opening and closing, and pressures and flow rates changing throughout the system in response to varying demand conditions and automatic control strategies formulated by the modeler.

Modern simulation software packages utilize a *graphical user interface* (GUI) that makes it easier to create models and visualize the results of simulations. Older-generation software relied exclusively on tabular input and output. A typical modern software interface with an annotated model drawing is shown in Figure 1.3.

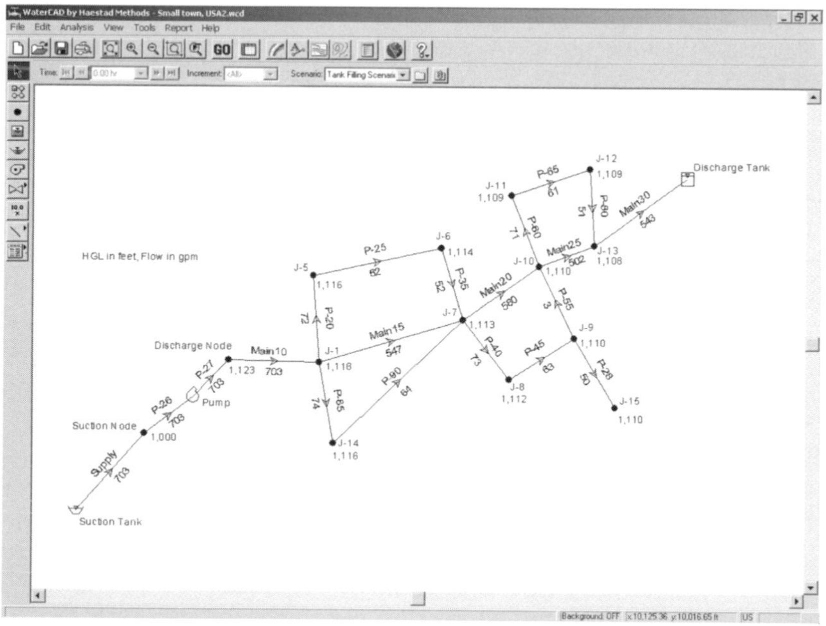

Figure 1.3
Software interface and annotated model drawing

1.3 APPLICATIONS OF WATER DISTRIBUTION MODELS

Most WDMs can be used to analyze a variety of other pressure piping systems, such as industrial cooling systems, oil pipelines, or any network carrying an incompressible, single-phase, Newtonian fluid in full pipes. Municipal water utilities, however, are by far the most common application of these models. Models are especially important for WDSs due to their complex topology, frequent growth and change, and sheer size. It is not uncommon for a system to supply hundreds of thousands of people (large networks supply millions); thus, the potential impact of a utility decision can be tremendous.

Water distribution network simulations are used for a variety of purposes, such as:

- Long-range master planning, including both new development and rehabilitation
- Fire protection studies
- Water quality investigations
- Energy management
- System design
- Daily operational uses including operator training, emergency response, and troubleshooting

Long-Range Master Planning

Planners carefully research all aspects of a water distribution system, and try to determine which major capital improvement projects are necessary to ensure the quality of service for the future. This process, called *master planning* (also referred to as *capital improvement planning* or *comprehensive planning*), may be used to project system growth and water usage for the next 5, 10, or 20 years. System growth may occur because of population growth, annexation, acquisition, or wholesale agreements between water supply utilities. The ability of the hydraulic network to adequately serve its customers must be evaluated whenever system growth is anticipated.

Not only can a model be used to identify potential problem areas (such as future low pressure areas or areas with water quality problems), but it can also be used to size and locate new transmission mains, pumping stations, and storage facilities to ensure that the predicted problems never occur. Maintaining a system at an acceptable level of service is preferable to having to rehabilitate a system that has become problematic.

Rehabilitation

As with all engineered systems, the wear and tear on a water distribution system may lead to the eventual need to rehabilitate portions of the system such as pipes, pumps, valves, and reservoirs. Pipes, especially older, unlined, metal pipes, may experience an internal buildup of deposits due to mineral deposits and chemical reactions within the water. This buildup can result in loss of carrying capacity, reduced pressures, and poorer water quality. To counter these effects of aging, a utility may choose to clean and reline a pipe. Alternatively, the pipe may be replaced with a new (possibly larger) pipe, or another pipe may be installed in parallel. Hydraulic simulations can be used to assess the impacts of such rehabilitation efforts, and to determine the most economical improvements.

Fire Protection Studies

Water distribution systems are often required to provide water for fire fighting purposes. Designing the system to meet the fire protection requirements is essential, and normally has a large impact on the design of the entire network. The engineer determines the fire protection requirements, and then uses a model to test the ability of the system to meet those requirements. If the system cannot provide certain flows and maintain adequate pressures, the model may also be used for sizing hydraulic elements (pipes, pumps, etc.) to correct the problem.

Water Quality Investigations

Some models provide *water quality modeling* in addition to hydraulic simulation capabilities. *Water age*, *source tracing*, and *constituent concentration analyses* can be modeled throughout a network. For example, chlorine residual maintenance can be studied and planned more effectively, *disinfection by-product formation* (DBP) in a network can be analyzed, or the impact of storage tanks on water quality can be evaluated. Water quality models are also used to study the modification of hydraulic operations to improve water quality.

Energy Management

Next to infrastructure maintenance and repair costs, energy usage for pumping is the largest operating expense of many water utilities (Figure 1.4). Hydraulic simulations can be used to study the operating characteristics and energy usage of pumps, along with the behavior of the system. By developing and testing different pumping strategies, the effects on energy consumption can be evaluated, and the utility can make an educated effort to save on energy costs.

Daily Operations

Individuals who operate water distribution systems are generally responsible for making sure that system-wide pressures, flows, and tank water levels remain within acceptable limits. The operator must monitor these indices and take action when a value falls outside of the acceptable range. By turning on a pump or adjusting a valve, for example, the operator can adjust the system so that it functions at an appropriate level of service. A hydraulic simulation can be used in daily operations to determine the impact of various possible actions, providing the operator with better information for decision-making.

Figure 1.4
Pumping is one of the largest operating expenses of many utilities

Operator Training. Most water distribution system operators do their jobs very well. As testimony to this fact, the majority of systems experience very few water outages, and those that do occur are rarely caused by operator error. Many operators, however, only gain experience and confidence in their ability to operate the system over a long period of time, and sometimes the most critical experience is only gained under conditions of extreme duress. Hydraulic simulations offer an excellent opportunity to train system operators in how their system will behave under different loading conditions, with various control strategies, and in emergency situations.

Emergency Response. Emergencies are a very real part of operating a water distribution system, and operators need to be prepared to handle everything from main breaks to power failures. Planning ahead for these emergencies by using a model may prevent service from being compromised, or may at least minimize the extent to which customers are influenced. Modeling is an excellent tool for emergency response planning and contingency.

System Troubleshooting. When hydraulic or water quality characteristics in an existing system are not up to standard, a model simulation can be used to identify probable causes. A series of simulations for a neighborhood that suffers from chronic low pressure, for example, may point toward the likelihood of a closed valve in the area. A field crew can then be dispatched to this area to check nearby valves.

1.4 THE MODELING PROCESS

Assembling, calibrating, and using a water distribution system model can seem like a foreboding task to someone confronted with a new program and stacks of data and maps of the actual system. As with any large task, the way to complete it is to break it down into its components and work through each step. Some tasks can be done in parallel while others must be done in series. The tasks that make up the modeling process are illustrated in Figure 1.5. Note that modeling is an iterative process.

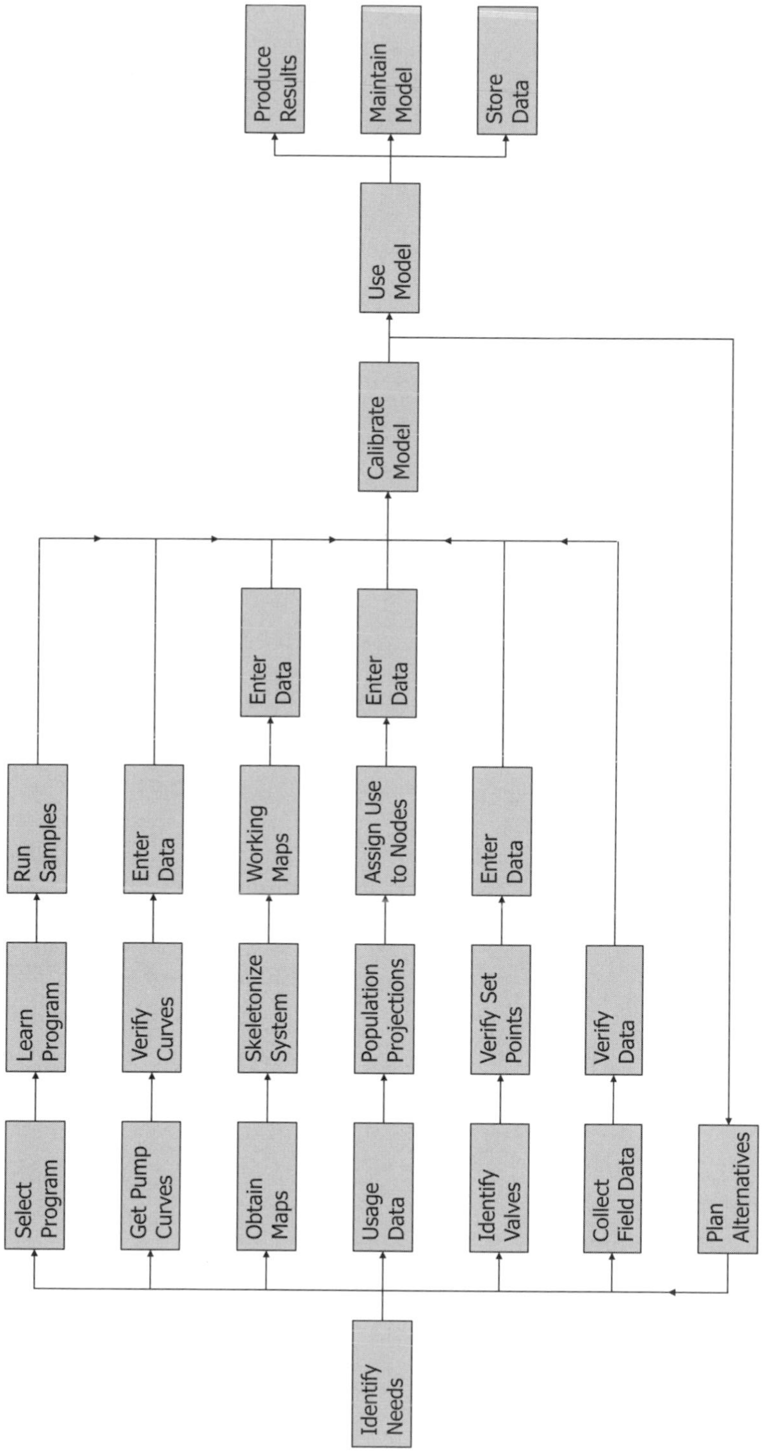

Figure 1.5
Flowchart of the modeling process

The first step in undertaking any modeling project is to develop a consensus within the water utility regarding the need for the model and the purposes for which the model will be used in both the near and long terms. It is important to have utility personnel, from upper management and engineering to operations and maintenance, commit to the model in terms of human resources, time, and funding. Modeling should not be viewed as an isolated endeavor by a single modeler, but rather a utility-wide effort with the modeler as the key worker. Once the vision of the model is accepted by the utility, decisions on such issues as extent of model skeletonization and accuracy of calibration will naturally follow.

Figure 1.5 shows that most of the work in modeling must be done before the model can be used to solve real problems. Therefore, it is important to budget sufficient time to use the model once it has been developed and calibrated. Too many modeling projects fall short of their goals for usage because the model-building process takes up all of the allotted time and resources. There is not enough time left to use the model to understand the full range of alternative solutions to the problems.

Modeling involves a series of abstractions. First, the real pipes and pumps in the system are represented in maps and drawings of those facilities. Then, the maps are converted to a model that represents the facilities as links and nodes. Another layer of abstraction is introduced as the behaviors of the links and nodes are described mathematically. The model equations are then solved, and the solutions are typically displayed on maps of the system or as tabular output. A model's value stems from the usefulness of these abstractions in facilitating efficient design of system improvements or better operation of an existing system.

1.5 A BRIEF HISTORY OF WATER DISTRIBUTION TECHNOLOGY

The practice of transporting water for human consumption has been around for several millennia. From the first pipes in Crete some 3,500 years ago, to today's complex hydraulic models, the history of water distribution technology is quite a story. The following highlights some of the key historical events that have shaped the field since its beginnings.

1500 B.C. - First water distribution pipes used in Crete. The Minoan civilization flourishes on the island of Crete. The City of Knossos develops an aqueduct system that uses tubular conduits to convey water. While other ancient civilizations have had surface water canals, these are probably the first pipes.

250 B.C. - Archimedes principle developed. Archimedes, best known for his discovery of π and for devising exponents, develops one of the earliest laws of fluids when he notices that any object in water displaces its own volume. Using this principle, he proves that a crown belonging to King Hiero of Syracuse is not made of gold. A legend will develop that he discovered this principle while bathing and became so excited that he ran naked through the streets shouting "Eureka" (I've found it).

100 A.D. - Roman aqueducts. The Romans bring water from great distances to their cities through aqueducts (Figure 1.6). While many of the aqueducts are above-ground, there are also enclosed conduits to supply public fountains and baths. Sextus Julius Frontinus, water commissioner of Rome, writes two books on the Roman water supply.

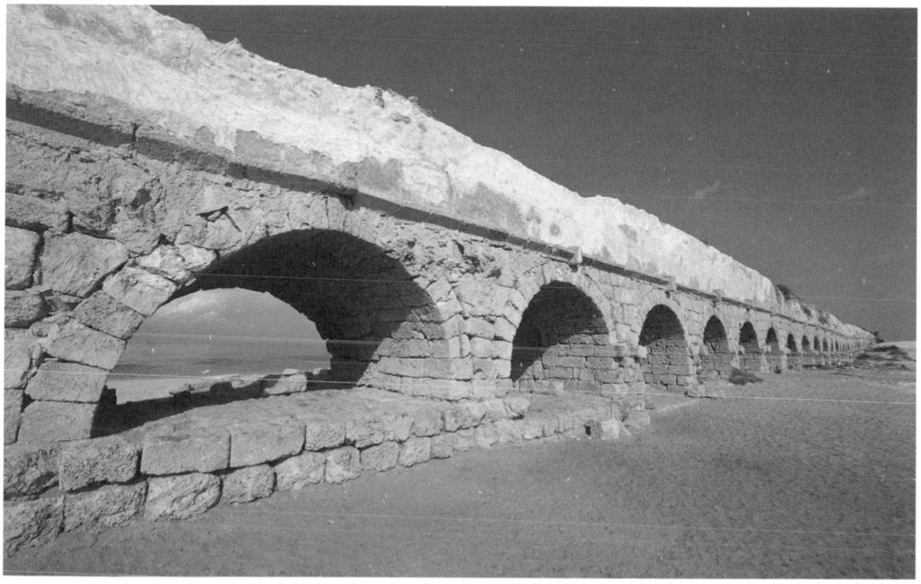

Figure 1.6
Roman aqueduct

1455 - First cast iron pipe. Casting of iron for pipe becomes practical, and the first installation of cast iron pipe, manufactured in Siegerland, Germany, is seen at Dillenburg Castle.

1652 - Piped water in Boston. The first water pipes in the U.S. are laid in Boston to bring water from springs to the Quincy Market area.

1664 - Palace of Versailles. King Louis XIV of France orders the construction of a 15-mile cast iron water main from Marly-on-Seine to the Palace of Versailles. This is the longest pipeline of its kind at this time, and portions of it remain in service into the 21st century. A section of the line, after being taken out of service, was shipped in the 1960s from France to the United States (Figure 1.7) where it is still on display.

Courtesy of the Ductile Iron Pipe Research Association

Figure 1.7
King Louis XIV of France and a section of the Palace of Versailles pipeline

1732 - Pitot invents a velocity-measuring device. Henri Pitot is tasked with measuring the velocity of water in the Seine River. He finds that by placing an L-shaped tube into the flow, water rises in the tube proportionally to the velocity squared, and the Pitot tube is born.

1738 - Bernoulli publishes *Hydrodynamica*. The Swiss Bernoulli family extends the early mathematics and physics discoveries of Newton and Leibniz to fluid systems. Daniel Bernoulli publishes *Hydrodynamica* while in St. Petersburg and Strasbourg, but there is a rivalry with his father Johann regarding who actually developed some of the principles presented in the book. These principles will become the key to energy principles used in hydraulic models and the basis for numerous devices such as the Venturi meter and, most notably, the airplane wing. In 1752, however, it will actually be their colleague, Leonard Euler, who develops the forms of the energy equations that will live on in years to come.

1754 - First U.S. water systems built. The earliest water distribution systems in the U.S. are constructed in Pennsylvania. The Moravian community in Bethlehem, Pennsylvania claims to have the first water system, and it is followed quickly by systems in Schaefferstown and Philadelphia, Pennsylvania. Horses drive the pumps in the Philadelphia system, and the pipes are made of bored logs. They will later be replaced with wood stave pipe made with iron hoops to withstand higher pressures. The first steam driven pumps will be used in Bethlehem ten years later.

1770 - Chezy develops head loss relationship. While previous investigators realized that energy was lost in moving water, it is Antoine Chezy who realizes that V^2/RS is reasonably constant for certain situations. This relationship will serve as the basis for head loss equations to be used for centuries.

1785 - Bell and spigot joint developed. The Chelsea Water Company in London begins using the first bell and spigot joints. The joint is first packed with yarn or hemp, and is then sealed with lead. Sir Thomas Simpson is credited with inventing this joint, which replaced the crude flanged joints previously used.

1839 - Hagen-Poiseuille equation developed. Gotthilf Hagen and Jean Louis Poiseuille independently develop the head loss equations for laminar flow in small tubes. Their work is experimental, and it is not until 1856 that Franz Neuman and Eduard Hagenbach will theoretically derive the Hagen-Poiseuille equation.

1843 - St. Venant develops equations of motion. Several researchers, including Louis Navier, George Stokes, Augustin de Cauchy, and Simeon Poisson, work toward the development of the fundamental differential equations describing the motion of fluids. They become known as the "Navier-Stokes equations." Jean-Claude Barre de Saint Venant develops the most general form of these equations, but the term "St. Venant equations" will be used to refer to the vertically and laterally averaged (that is, one-dimensional flow) form of equations.

1845 - Darcy-Weisbach head loss equation developed. Julius Weisbach publishes a three-volume set on engineering mechanics that includes the results of his experiments. The Darcy-Weisbach equation comes from this work, which is essentially an extension of Chezy's work, as Chezy's *C* is related to Darcy-Weisbach's *f* by $C^2=8g/f$. Darcy's name is also associated with Darcy's Law for flow through porous media, widely used in groundwater analysis.

1878 - First automatic sprinklers used. The first Parmelee sprinklers are installed. These are the first automatic sprinklers for fire protection.

1879 - Lamb's *Hydrodynamics* published. Sir Horace Lamb publishes his *Treatise on the Mathematical Theory of the Motion of Fluids*. Subsequent editions will be published under the title *Hydrodynamics*, with the last edition published in 1932.

1881 - AWWA formed. The 22 original members create the American Water Works Association. The first president is Jacob Foster from Illinois.

1883 - Laminar/turbulent flow distinction explained. While earlier engineers such as Hagen observed the differences between laminar and turbulent flow, Osborne Reynolds is the first to conduct the experiments that clearly define the two flow regimes. He identifies the dimensionless number, later referred to as the Reynolds Number, for quantifying the conditions in which each type of flow exists. He publishes "An Experimental Investigation of the Circumstances which Determine whether the Motion of Water shall be Direct or Sinuous and the Law of Resistance in Parallel Channels."

1896 - Cole invents Pitot tube for pressure pipe. Although numerous attempts were made to extend Henri Pitot's velocity measuring device to pressure pipes, Edward Cole develops the first practical apparatus using a Pitot tube with two tips connected to a manometer. The Cole Pitometer will be widely used for years to come, and Cole's company, Pitometer Associates, will perform flow measurement studies (among many other services) into the twenty-first century.

1906 - Hazen-Williams equation developed. A. Hazen and G.S. Williams develop an empirical formula for head loss in water pipes. While not as general or precise in rough, turbulent flow as the Darcy-Weisbach equation, the Hazen-Williams equation proves easy to use and will be widely applied in North America.

1900-1930 - Boundary Layer Theory developed. The interactions between fluids and solids are studied extensively by a series of German scientists lead by Ludwig Prandtl and his students Theodor von Karman, Johan Nikuradse, Heinrich Blasius, and Thomas Stanton. As a result of their research, they are able to theoretically explain and experimentally verify the nature of drag between pipe walls and a fluid. In particular, the experiments of Nikuradse, who glues uniform sand grains inside pipes and measures head loss, lead to a better understanding of the calculation of the *f* coefficient in the Darcy-Weisbach equation. Stanton develops the first graphical representation of the relationship between *f*, pipe roughness, and the Reynolds number, which later leads to the Moody diagram. This work is summarized in H. Schichting's book, *Boundary Layer Theory*.

1914 - First U.S. drinking water standards established. The U.S. Public Health Service publishes the first drinking water standards, which will continually evolve.

The U.S. Environmental Protection Agency (USEPA) will eventually assume the role of setting the water quality standards in the U.S.

1920s - Cement-mortar lining of water mains. Cement mortar lining of water mains is used to minimize corrosion and tuberculation. Procedures for cleaning and lining existing pipes in place will be developed by the 1930s.

1921 - First Hydraulic Institute Standards published. The first edition of *Trade Standards in the Pump Industry* is published as a 19-page pamphlet. These standards become the primary reference for pump nomenclature, testing, and rating.

1936 - Hardy Cross method developed. Hardy Cross, a structural engineering professor at the University of Illinois, publishes the Hardy Cross method for solving head loss equations in complex networks. This method is widely used for manual calculations and will serve as the basis for early digital computer programs for pipe network analysis.

1938 - Colebrook-White equation developed. Cyril Colebrook and Cedric White of Imperial College in London build upon the work of Prandtl and his students to develop the Colebrook-White equation for determining the Darcy-Weisbach f in commercial pipes.

1940 - Hunter Curves published. During the 1920s and 30s, Roy Hunter of the National Bureau of Standards conducts research on water use in a variety of buildings. His "fixture unit method" will become the basis for estimating building water use, even though plumbing fixtures will change over the years. His probabilistic analysis captured the mathematics of the concept that the more fixtures in a building, the less likely they are to be used simultaneously.

1944 - Moody diagram published. Lewis Moody of Princeton University publishes the Moody Diagram, which is essentially a graphical representation of the Colebrook-White equation in the turbulent flow range and the Hagen-Poisseuille equation in the laminar range. This diagram is especially useful because, at the time, there is no explicit solution for the Colebrook-White equation. Stanton had developed a similar chart 30 years earlier.

1950 - McIlroy network analyzer developed. The McIlroy network analyzer, an electrical analog computer, is developed to simulate the behavior of water distribution systems using electricity instead of water. The analyzer uses special elements called "fluistors" to reproduce head loss in pipes, because in the Hazen-Williams equation, head loss varies with flow raised to the 1.85 power, while normal resistors comply with Ohm's Law, in which voltage drop varies linearly with current.

1950s - Earliest digital computers developed. The Electronic Numerical Integrator and Computer (ENIAC) was assembled at the University of Pennsylvania. It contains approximately 18,000 vacuum tubes and fills a 30 x 50 ft (9 x 15 m) room. Digital computers such as the ENIAC and Univac show that computers can carry out numerical calculations quickly, opening the door for programs to solve complex hydraulic problems.

1956 - Push-on joint developed. The push-on pipe joint using a rubber gasket is developed. This type of assembly helps speed the construction of piping.

1960s and 70s - Earliest pipe network digital models created. With the coming of age of digital computers and the establishment of the Fortran programming language, researchers at universities begin to develop pipe network models and make them available to practicing engineers. Don Wood at the University of Kentucky, Al Fowler at the University of British Columbia, Roland Jeppson of Utah State University, Chuck Howard and Uri Shamir at MIT, and Simsek Sarikelle at the University of Akron all write pipe network models.

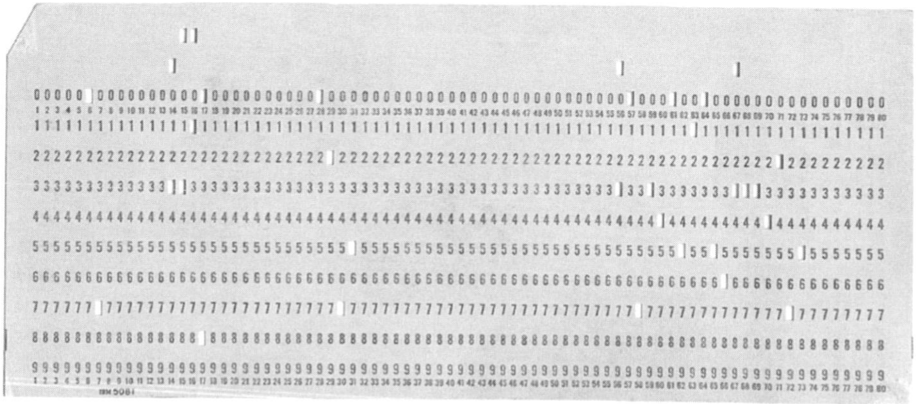

Figure 1.8
A computer punch card

1963 - First U.S. PVC pipe standards. The National Bureau of Standards accepts CS256-63 "Commercial Standard for PVC Plastic Pipes (SDR-PR and Class T)," which is the first U.S. standard for polyvinyl chloride water pipe.

1963 - URISA is founded. The Urban and Regional Information Systems Association is founded by Dr. Edgar Horwood. URISA becomes the premier organization for the use and integration of spatial information technology to improve the quality of life in urban and regional environments.

1960s and 70s - Water system contamination. Chemicals that can result in health problems when ingested or inhaled are dumped on the ground or stored in leaky ponds because of lack of awareness of their environmental impacts. Over the years, these chemicals will make their way into water distribution systems and lead to alleged contamination of water systems in places like Woburn, Massachusetts; Phoenix/Scottsdale, Arizona; and Dover Township, New Jersey. Water quality models of distribution systems will be used to attempt to recreate the dosages of chemicals received by customers. These situations lead to popular movies like "A Civil Action" and "Erin Brockavich."

1970s - Early attempts to optimize water distribution design. Dennis Lai and John Schaake at MIT develop the first approach to optimize water system design. Numerous papers will follow by researchers such as Arun Deb, Ian Goulter, Uri Shamir, Downey Brill, Larry Mays, and Kevin Lansey.

1970s - Models become more powerful. While the earliest pipe network models could only solve steady-state equations for simple systems, the seventies bring modeling features such as pressure regulating valves and extended period simulations.

1975 - Data files replace input cards. Modelers are able to remotely create data files on time-share terminals instead of using punched cards.

1975 - AWWA C-900 approved. The AWWA approves its first standard for PVC water distribution piping. C900 pipe is made to match old cast iron pipe outer diameters.

1976 - Swamee-Jain equation published. Dozens of approximations to the Colebrook-White equations have been published in an attempt to arrive at an explicit equation that would give the same results without the need for an iterative solution. Indian engineers P.K. Swamee and Akalnank Jain publish the most popular form of these approximations. The use of an explicit equation results in faster numerical solutions of pipe network problems.

1976 - Jeppson publishes *Analysis of Flow in Pipe Networks*. Roland Jeppson authors the book *Analysis of Flow in Pipe Networks*, which presents a summary of the numerical techniques used to solve network problems.

1980 - Personal computers introduced. Early personal computers make it possible to move hydraulic analysis to desktop systems. Initially, these desktop models are slow, but their power will grow exponentially over the next two decades.

Figure 1.9
Time-share terminal

Early 1980s - Water Quality Modeling First Developed. The concept of modeling water quality in distribution systems is first developed, and steady state formulations are proposed by Don Wood at the University of Kentucky and USEPA researchers in Cincinnati, Ohio.

1985 - "Battle of the Network Models." A series of sessions is held at the ASCE Water Resources Planning and Management Division Conference in Buffalo, New York, where researchers are given a realistic system called "Anytown" and are asked to optimize the design of that network. Comparison of results shows the strengths and weaknesses of these various models.

1986 - Introduction of Dynamic Water Quality Models. At the AWWA Distribution System Symposium, three groups independently introduced dynamic water quality models of distribution systems.

1988 - Gradient Algorithm. Ezio Todini and S. Pilati publish "A Gradient Algorithm for the Analysis of Pipe Networks" and R. Salgado, Todini and P. O'Connell publish "Comparison of the Gradient Method with some Traditional Methods of the Analysis of Water Supply Distribution Networks." The gradient algorithm serves as the basis for the WaterCAD model.

1989 - AWWA holds specialty conference. AWWA holds the *Computers and Automation in the Water Industry* conference. This conference will later grow into the popular IMTech event (Information Management and Technology).

1990s - Privatization of water utilities. The privatization of water utilities increases significantly as other utilities experience a greater push toward deregulation.

"Do you, Scofield Industries, take Amalgamated Pipe?"

1991 - Water Quality Modeling in Distribution Systems Conference held. The USEPA and the AWWA Research Foundation bring together researchers from around the world for a two-day meeting in Cincinnati. This meeting is a milestone in the establishment of water quality modeling as a recognized tool for investigators.

1991 - GPS technology becomes affordable. The cost of global positioning systems (GPS) drops to the point where a GPS can be an economical tool for determining coordinates of points in hydraulic models.

1993 - Introduction of water quality modeling tool. Water quality modeling comes of age with the development of EPANET by Lewis Rossman of the USEPA. Intended as a research tool, EPANET provides the basis for several commercial grade models.

1990 through present. Several commercial software developers release water distribution modeling packages. Each release brings new enhancements for data management and new abilities to interoperate with other existing computer systems.

1.6 WHAT NEXT?

Predicting the future is difficult, especially with rapidly changing fields such as the software industry. However, there are definite trends as data sharing continues to gain popularity, modeling spreads into operations, and automated design tools add to the modeler's arsenal.

The next logical question is, "When will network models eliminate the need for engineers?" The answer is, never. Though a word-processor can reduce the number of spelling and grammar mistakes, it cannot write a best-selling novel. Even as technology advances, there is still an essential need for a living, breathing, thinking human being. A network model is just another tool (albeit a very powerful, multi-purpose tool) for an experienced engineer or technician. It is still the responsibility of the user to understand the real system, understand the model, and make decisions based on sound engineering judgement.

REFERENCES

Mays, L. W. (2000). "Introduction." *Water Distribution System Handbook*, L. W. Mays ed., McGraw Hill, New York, New York.

Rouse, H. (1980). "Some Paradoxes in the History of Hydraulics." *Journal of Hydraulics Division*, ASCE, 106(6), 1077-1084.

CHAPTER

2

Modeling Theory

Model-based simulation is a method for mathematically approximating the behavior of real water distribution systems. To effectively utilize the capabilities of distribution system simulation software and interpret the results produced, the engineer or modeler must understand the mathematical principles involved. This chapter reviews the principles of hydraulics and water quality analysis that are frequently employed in water distribution network modeling software.

2.1 FLUID PROPERTIES

Fluids can be categorized as either gases or liquids. The most notable differences between the two states are that liquids are far denser than gases, and gases are highly compressible compared to liquids (liquids are relatively incompressible). The most important fluid properties taken into consideration in a water distribution simulation are specific weight, fluid viscosity, and (to a lesser degree) compressibility.

Density and Specific Weight

The *density* of a fluid is the mass of the fluid per unit volume. The density of water is 1.94 slugs/ft^3 (1000 kg/m^3) at standard pressure of 1 atm (1.013 bar) and standard temperature of 32.0 °F (0.0 °C). A change in temperature or pressure will affect the density, although the effects of minor changes are generally insignificant for water modeling purposes.

The property that describes the weight of a fluid per unit volume is called *specific weight*, and is related to density by gravitational acceleration:

$$\gamma = \rho g \tag{2.1}$$

where γ = fluid specific weight ($M/L^2/T^2$)
ρ = fluid density (M/L^3)
g = gravitational acceleration constant (L/T^2)

The specific weight of water, γ, at standard pressure and temperature is 62.4 lb/ft^3 (9,806 N/m^3).

Viscosity

Fluid *viscosity* is the property that describes the ability of a fluid to resist deformation due to shear stress. For many fluids, most notably water, viscosity is a proportionality factor relating the velocity gradient to the shear stress, as described by *Newton's Law of Viscosity*:

$$\tau = \mu \frac{dV}{dy} \tag{2.2}$$

where τ = shear stress ($M/L/T^2$)
μ = absolute (dynamic) viscosity ($M/L/T$)
$\frac{dV}{dy}$ = time rate of strain ($1/T$)

The physical meaning of this equation can be illustrated by considering the two parallel plates shown in Figure 2.1. The space between the plates is filled with a fluid, and the area of the plates is large enough that edge effects can be neglected. The plates are separated by a distance *y*, and the top plate is moving at a constant velocity *V* relative to the bottom plate. Liquids exhibit an attribute known as the no-slip condition, meaning that they adhere to surfaces they contact. Therefore, if the magnitude of *V* and *y* are not too large, then the velocity distribution between the two plates is linear.

From *Newton's Second Law of Motion*, for an object to move at a constant velocity, the net external force acting on the object must equal zero. Thus, the fluid must be exerting a force equal and opposite to the force *F* on the top plate. This force within the fluid is a result of the shear stress between the fluid and the plate. The velocity at which these forces balance is a function of the velocity gradient normal to the plate and the fluid viscosity, as described by Newton's Law of Viscosity.

Thick fluids, such as syrup and molasses, have high viscosities. Thin fluids, like water and gasoline, have low viscosities. For most fluids, the viscosity will remain constant regardless of the magnitude of the shear stress that is applied to it.

Returning to Figure 2.1, as the velocity of the top plate increases, the shear stresses in the fluid will increase at the same rate. Fluids that exhibit this property conform to Newton's Law of Viscosity, and are called *Newtonian fluids*. Water and air are examples of Newtonian fluids. Some types of fluids, like inks and sludge, undergo changes in viscosity as the shear stress changes. Fluids exhibiting this type of behavior are called *pseudo-plastic fluids*.

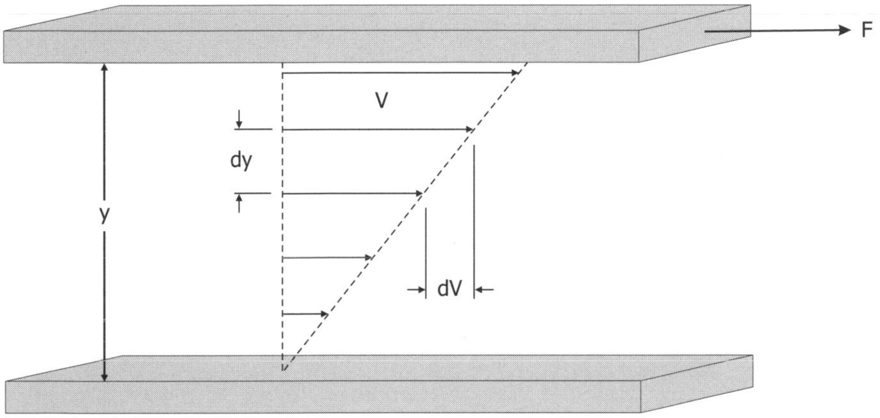

Figure 2.1
Physical interpretation of Newton's Law of Viscosity

Relationships between the shear stress and the velocity gradient for typical Newtonian and Non-Newtonian fluids are shown in Figure 2.2. Since most distribution system models are intended to simulate water, many of the equations used consider Newtonian fluids only.

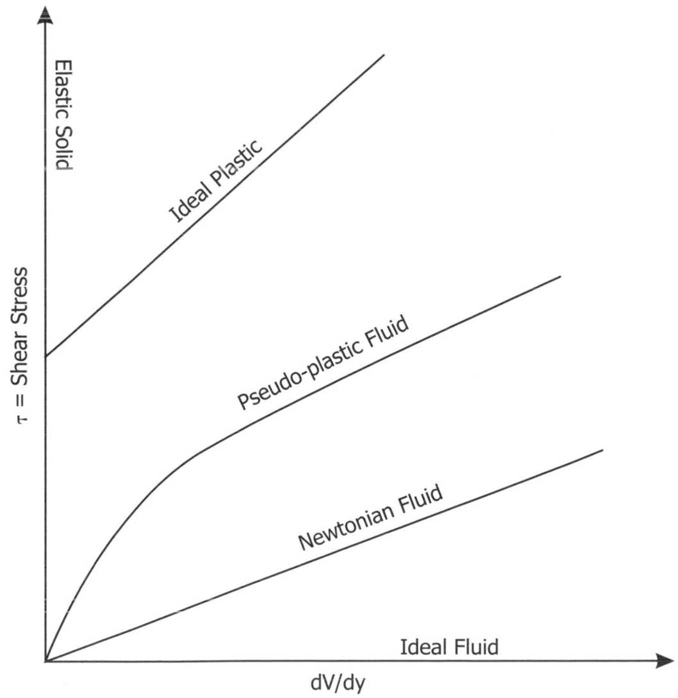

Figure 2.2
Stress versus strain for plastics and fluids

Viscosity is a function of temperature, but this relationship is different for liquids and gases. In general, viscosity decreases as temperature increases for liquids, and viscosity increases as temperature increases for gases. The temperature variation within water distribution systems, however, is usually quite small, and thus changes in water viscosity are considered negligible for this application. Generally, water distribution system modeling software treats viscosity as a constant [assuming a temperature of 68 °F (20 °C)].

The viscosity derived in Equation 2.2 is referred to as the *absolute viscosity* (or *dynamic viscosity*). For hydraulic formulas related to fluid motion, the relationship between fluid viscosity and fluid density is often expressed as a single variable. This relationship, called the *kinematic viscosity*, is expressed as:

$$\nu = \frac{\mu}{\rho} \tag{2.3}$$

where ν = kinematic viscosity (L^2/T)

Just as there are shear stresses between the plate and the fluid in Figure 2.1, there are shear stresses between the wall of a pipe and the fluid moving through the pipe. The higher the fluid viscosity, the greater the shear stresses that will develop within the fluid, and, consequently, the greater the friction losses along the pipe. Distribution system modeling software packages use fluid viscosity as a factor in estimating the friction losses along a pipe's length. Packages that can handle any fluid require the viscosity and density to be input by the modeler, while models that are developed only for water usually account for the appropriate value automatically.

Fluid Compressibility

Compressibility is a physical property of fluids that relates the volume occupied by a fixed mass of fluid to its pressure. In general, gases are much more compressible than liquids. An air compressor is a simple device that utilizes the compressibility of air to store energy. The compressor is essentially a pump that intermittently forces air molecules into the fixed volume tank attached to it. Each time the compressor turns on, the mass of air, and therefore the pressure within the tank, increases. Thus a relationship exists between fluid mass, volume, and pressure.

This relationship can be simplified by considering a fixed mass of a fluid. Compressibility is then described by defining the fluid's *bulk modulus of elasticity*:

$$E_v = -V_f \frac{dP}{dV} \tag{2.4}$$

where E_v = bulk modulus of elasticity ($M/L/T^2$)
P = pressure ($M/L/T^2$)
V_f = volume of fluid (L^3)

All fluids are compressible to some extent. The effects of compression in a water distribution system are very small, and thus the equations used in hydraulic simulations

Hydraulic Transients

When a pump starts or stops, or a valve is opened or closed, the velocity of water in the pipe changes. However, when flow accelerates or decelerates in a pipe, all of the water in that pipe does not change velocity instantly. It takes time for the water at one end of a pipe to experience the effect of a force applied some distance away. When flow decelerates, the water molecules in the pipe are compressed, and the pressure rises. Conversely, when the flow accelerates, the pressure drops. These changes in pressure travel through the pipe as waves referred to as "hydraulic transients." When a sudden change in velocity occurs, the resulting pressure waves can be strong enough to damage pipes and fittings. This phenomenon is known as water hammer.

The magnitude of the pressure change is determined by the pipe material and wall thickness, fluid compressibility and density, and—most importantly—the magnitude of the change in velocity. The Joukowski equation indicates that, in general, a change in velocity of 1 ft/s can result in a change in head of 100 ft (a 1 m/s change in velocity corresponds to 100 m change in head). Large positive pressures can burst pipes or separate joints, especially at bends. Negative pressure waves can reduce the pressure enough to cause vaporization of water in a process called "column separation." The collapse of these vapor pockets can damage piping. Negative pressures can also draw contaminated groundwater into the distribution system through pipe imperfections.

Transients are dampened by pipe friction and the effects of pipe loops that essentially cancel out the pressure waves. Surge tanks and air chambers also have dampening effects. Using slow-opening valves and flywheels on pumps can minimize transients before they occur by reducing the acceleration or deceleration of the water.

Fluid transients tend to be worse in long pipelines carrying water at high velocities. The worst transient effects in water systems are usually brought on by a sudden loss of power to a pump station. Transients can also be caused by a hydrant being shut off too quickly, rapid closing of an automated valve such as an altitude valve, pipe failure, and even normal starting and stopping of pumps.

The unsteady flow equations necessary to model transients are extremely difficult to solve manually in all but the simplest piping configurations. Mathematical models to solve these equations are available, but are considerably more complicated than the types of water distribution system models described in this book.

Transient analysis is a fairly specialized area of hydraulics, and there are several very good references available, including Almeida and Koelle (1992), Chaudhry (1987), Karney (2000), Martin (2000), Thorley (1991), and Wylie and Streeter (1993).

are based on the assumption that the liquids involved are incompressible. With a bulk modulus of elasticity of 410,000 psi (2.83×10^6 kPa) at 68 °F (20 °C), water can safely be treated as incompressible. For instance, a pressure change of over 2,000 psi (1.379×10^4 kPa) results in only a 0.5 percent change in volume.

Although the assumption of incompressibility is justifiable under most conditions, certain hydraulic phenomena are capable of generating pressures high enough that the compressibility of water becomes important. During field operations, a phenomenon known as *water hammer* can develop due to extremely rapid changes in flow (when, for instance, a valve suddenly closes, or a power failure occurs and pumps stop operating). The momentum of the moving fluid can generate pressures large enough that fluid compression and pipe wall expansion can occur, which in turn causes destructive transient pressure fluctuations to propagate throughout the network. Specialized network simulation software is necessary to analyze these transient pressure effects.

Vapor Pressure

Consider a closed container that is partly filled with water. The pressure in the container is measured when the water is first added, and again after some time has elapsed. These readings show that the pressure in the container increases during this period. The increase in pressure is due to the evaporation of the water, and the resulting increase in *vapor pressure* above the liquid.

Assuming that temperature remains constant, the pressure will eventually reach a constant value that corresponds to the *equilibrium* or *saturation vapor pressure* of water at that temperature. At this point, the rates of evaporation and condensation are equal.

The saturation vapor pressure increases with increasing temperature. This relationship demonstrates, for example, why the air in humid climates typically feels moister in summer than in winter, and why the boiling temperature of water is lower at higher elevations.

If a sample of water at a pressure of 1 atm and room temperature is heated to 212 °F (100 °C), the water will begin to boil since the vapor pressure of water at that temperature is equal to 1 atm. In a similar vein, if water is held at a temperature of 68 °F (20 °C), and the pressure is decreased to 0.023 atm, the water will also boil.

This concept can be applied in water distribution in cases in which the ambient pressure drops very low. Pump *cavitation* occurs when the fluid being pumped flashes into a vapor pocket, then quickly collapses. For this to happen, the pressure in the pipeline must be equal to or less than the vapor pressure of the fluid. When cavitation occurs it sounds as if gravel is being pumped, and severe damage to pipe walls and pump components can result.

2.2 FLUID STATICS AND DYNAMICS

Static Pressure

Pressure can be thought of as a force applied normal, or perpendicular, to a body that is in contact with a fluid. In the English system of units, pressure is expressed in pounds per square foot (lb/ft^2), but the water industry generally uses $lb/in.^2$, typically abbreviated as psi. In the SI system, pressure has units of N/m^2, also called a *Pascal*. However, because of the magnitude of pressures occurring in distribution systems, pressure is typically reported in kilo-Pascals (kPa), or 1,000 Pascals.

Pressure varies with depth as illustrated in Figure 2.3. For fluids at rest, the variation of pressure over depth is linear and is called the hydrostatic pressure distribution.

$$P = h\gamma \qquad (2.5)$$

where P = pressure ($M/L/T^2$)
h = depth of fluid above datum (L)
γ = fluid specific weight ($M/L^2/T^2$)

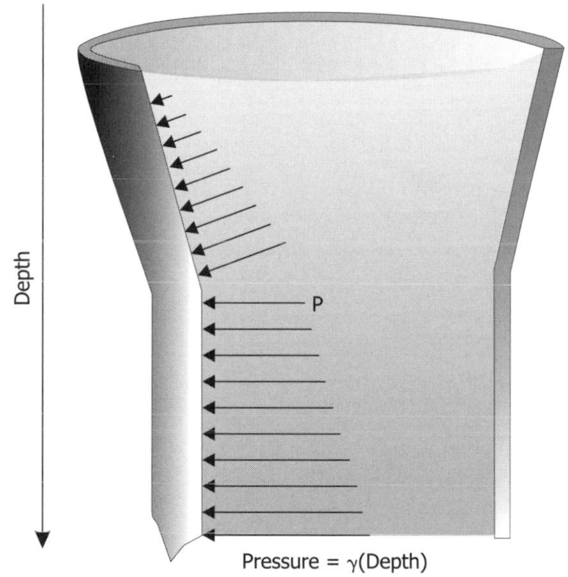

Figure 2.3
Static pressure in a standing water column

This equation can be rewritten to find the height of a column of water that can be supported by a given pressure:

$$h = \frac{P}{\gamma} \qquad (2.6)$$

The quantity P/γ is called the *pressure head*, which is the energy resulting from water pressure. Recognizing that the specific weight of water in English units is 62.4 lb/ft^3, a convenient conversion factor can be established for water as 1 psi = 2.31 ft (1 kPa = 0.102 m) of pressure head.

■ **Example - Pressure Calculation** Consider the storage tank in Figure 2.4 in which the water surface elevation is 120 ft above a pressure gage. The pressure at the base of the tank is due to the weight of the column of water directly above it, and can be calculated as follows:

$$P = \gamma h = \frac{62.4\frac{lb}{ft^3}(120ft)}{144\frac{in^2}{ft^2}}$$

$$P = 52\,psi$$

Figure 2.4
Storage tank

$P_{base} = 52$ psi

120 ft

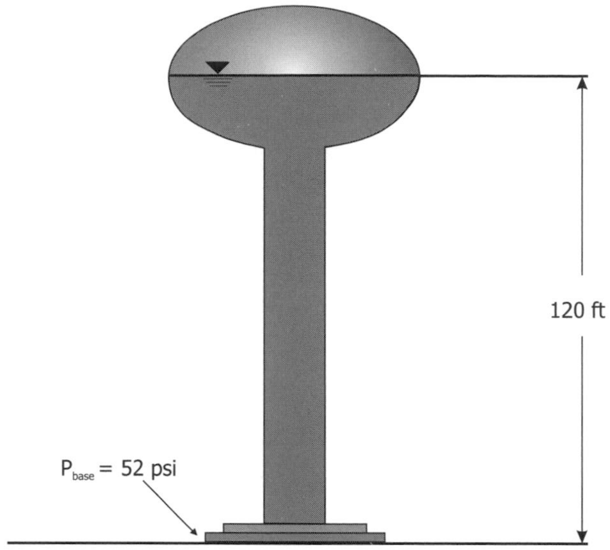

✓ **Absolute Pressure and Gage Pressure.** Pressure at a given point is due to the weight of the fluid above that point. The weight of the earth's atmosphere produces a pressure, referred to as *atmospheric pressure*. Although the actual atmospheric pressure will depend upon elevation and weather, standard atmospheric pressure at sea level is 1 atm (14.7 psi or 101 kPa).

Two types of pressure are commonly used in hydraulics, absolute pressure and gage pressure. *Absolute pressure* is the pressure measured with absolute zero (a perfect vacuum) as its datum, while *gage pressure* is the pressure measured with atmospheric pressure as its datum. The two are related to one another as shown in Equation 2.7. Note that when a pressure gage located at the earth's surface is open to the atmosphere, it registers zero on its dial. If the gage pressure is negative (that is, the pressure is below atmospheric), then the negative pressure is called a vacuum.

$$\checkmark \qquad P_{abs} = P_{gage} + P_{atm} \qquad\qquad (2.7)$$

where P_{abs} = absolute pressure (M/L/T^2)
$\quad\quad\quad\quad P_{gage}$ = gage pressure (M/L/T^2)
$\quad\quad\quad\quad P_{atm}$ = atmospheric pressure (M/L/T^2)

In most hydraulic applications, including water distribution systems analysis, gage pressure is used. Using absolute pressure has little value, since doing so would simply result in all the gage pressures being incremented by atmospheric pressure. Additionally, gage pressure is often more intuitive because people do not typically consider atmospheric effects when thinking about pressure.

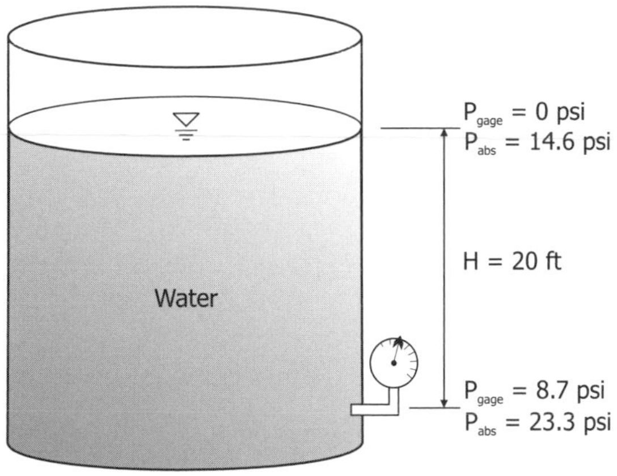

Figure 2.5
Gage versus absolute pressure

Velocity and Flow Regime

The velocity profile of a fluid as it flows through a pipe is not constant across the diameter. Rather, the velocity of a fluid particle depends upon where the fluid particle is located with respect to the pipe wall. In most cases, hydraulic models deal with the average velocity in a cross-section of pipeline, which can be found using the following formula:

$$V = \frac{Q}{A} \quad (2.8)$$

where V = average fluid velocity (L/T)
Q = pipeline flow rate (L^3/T)
A = cross-sectional area of pipeline (L^2)

The cross-sectional area of a circular pipe can be directly computed from the diameter D, so the velocity equation can be rewritten as:

$$V = \frac{4Q}{\pi D^2} \quad (2.9)$$

where D = diameter (L)

For water distribution systems in which diameter is measured in inches and flow is measured in gallons per minute, the equation simplifies to:

$$V = 0.41\frac{Q}{D^2} \quad (2.10)$$

where V = average fluid velocity (ft/s)
Q = pipeline flow rate (gpm)
D = diameter (in.)

Reynolds Number. In the late 1800s, an English scientist named Osborne Reynolds conducted experiments on fluid passing through a glass tube. His experimental setup looked much like the one in Figure 2.6 (Streeter, Wylie, and Bedford, 1998). The experimental apparatus was designed to establish the flow rate through a long glass tube (meant to simulate a pipeline) and to allow dye (from a smaller tank) to flow into the liquid. He noticed that at very low flow rates, the dye stream remained intact with a distinct interface between the dye stream and the fluid surrounding it. Reynolds referred to this condition as *laminar flow*. At slightly higher flow rates, the dye stream began to waver a bit, and there was some blurring between the dye stream and the surrounding fluid. He called this condition *transitional flow*. At even higher flows, the dye stream was completely broken up, and the dye mixed completely with the surrounding fluid. Reynolds referred to this regime as *turbulent flow*.

When Reynolds conducted the same experiment using different fluids, he noticed that the condition under which the dye stream remained intact not only varied with the flow rate through the tube, but also with the fluid density and viscosity, and the diameter of the tube.

Figure 2.6
Experimental apparatus used to determine Reynolds number

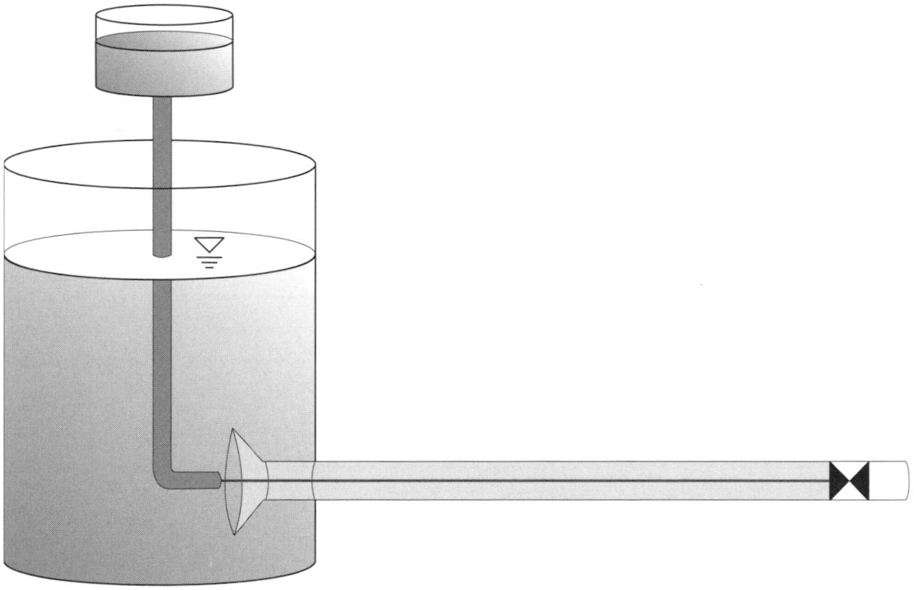

Based on experimental evidence gathered by Reynolds and dimensional analysis, a dimensionless number can be computed and used to characterize flow regime. Conceptually, the *Reynolds number* can be thought of as the ratio between inertial and viscous forces in a fluid. The Reynolds number for full flowing circular pipes can be found using the following equation:

$$Re = \frac{VD\rho}{\mu} = \frac{VD}{\nu} \qquad (2.11)$$

where Re = Reynolds Number
D = pipeline diameter (L)
ρ = fluid density (M/L^3)
μ = absolute viscosity (M/L/T)
ν = kinematic viscosity (L^2/T)

The ranges of the Reynolds Number that define the three flow regimes are shown in Table 2.1. The flow of water through municipal water systems is almost always turbulent, except in the periphery where water demand is low and intermittent, and may result in laminar and stagnant flow conditions.

Table 2.1 Reynolds Number for various flow regimes

Flow Regime	Reynolds Number
Laminar	< 2000
Transitional	2000-4000
Turbulent	> 4000

Velocity Profiles. Due to the shear stresses along the walls of a pipe, the velocity in a pipeline is not uniform over the pipe diameter. Rather, the fluid velocity is zero at the pipe wall. Fluid velocity increases with distance from the pipe wall, with the maximum occurring along the centerline of the pipe. Figure 2.7 illustrates the variation of fluid velocity within a pipe, also called the *velocity profile*.

The shape of the velocity profile will vary depending on whether the flow regime is laminar or turbulent. In laminar flow, the fluid particles travel in parallel layers or lamina, producing very strong shear stresses between adjacent layers, and causing the dye streak in Reynolds' experiment to remain intact. Mathematically, the velocity profile in laminar flow is shaped like a parabola as shown in Figure 2.7. In laminar flow, the head loss through a pipe segment is primarily a function of the fluid viscosity, not the internal pipe roughness.

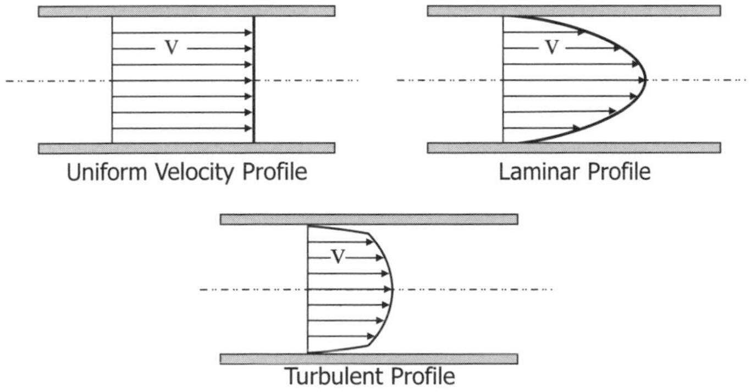

Figure 2.7
Velocity profiles for different flow regimes

Turbulent flow is characterized by eddies that produce random variations in the velocity profiles. Although the velocity profile of turbulent flow is more erratic than that of laminar flow, the mean velocity profile actually exhibits less variation across the pipe. The velocity profiles for both turbulent and laminar flows are shown in Figure 2.7.

2.3 ENERGY CONCEPTS

Fluids possess energy in three forms. The amount of energy depends upon the fluid's movement (*kinetic energy*), elevation (*potential energy*), and pressure (*pressure energy*). In a hydraulic system, a fluid can have all three types of energy associated with it simultaneously. The total energy associated with a fluid per unit weight of the fluid is called *head*. The kinetic energy is called *velocity head* ($V^2/2g$), the potential energy is called *elevation head* (Z), and the internal pressure energy is called *pressure head* (P/γ). While typical units for energy are foot-pounds (Joules), the units of total head are feet (meters).

$$H = Z + \frac{P}{\gamma} + \frac{V^2}{2g} \tag{2.12}$$

where
H = total head (L)
Z = elevation above datum (L)
P = pressure ($M/L/T^2$)
γ = fluid specific weight ($M/L^2/T^2$)
V = velocity (L/T)
g = gravitational acceleration constant (L/T^2)

Each point in the system has a unique head associated with it. A line plotted of total head versus distance through a system is called the *energy grade line* (EGL). The sum of the elevation head and pressure head yields the *hydraulic grade line* (HGL), which corresponds to the height that water will rise vertically in a tube attached to the pipe and open to the atmosphere. Figure 2.8 shows the EGL and HGL for a simple pipeline.

Figure 2.8
Energy and hydraulic grade lines

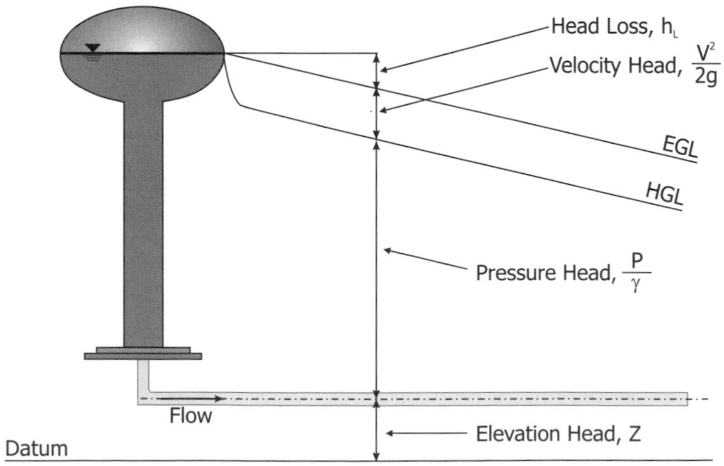

In most water distribution applications, the elevation and pressure head terms are much greater than the velocity head term. For this reason, velocity head is often ignored, and modelers work in terms of hydraulic grades rather than energy grades. Therefore, given a datum elevation and a hydraulic grade line, the pressure can be determined as:

$$P = \gamma(HGL - Z) \tag{2.13}$$

where HGL = hydraulic grade line (L)

Energy Losses

Energy losses, also called head losses, are generally the result of two mechanisms:

- Friction along the pipe walls
- Turbulence due to changes in streamlines through fittings and appurtenances

Head losses along the pipe wall are called *friction losses* or head losses due to friction, while losses due to turbulence within the bulk fluid are called *minor losses*.

2.4 FRICTION LOSSES

When a liquid flows through a pipeline, shear stresses develop between the liquid and the pipe wall. This shear stress is a result of friction, and its magnitude is dependent upon the properties of the fluid that is passing through the pipe, the speed at which it is moving, the internal roughness of the pipe, and the length and diameter of the pipe.

Consider, for example, the pipe segment shown in Figure 2.9. A force balance on the fluid element contained within a pipe section can be used to form a general expression describing the head loss due to friction. Note the forces in action:

- Pressure difference between Sections 1 and 2
- The weight of the fluid volume contained between Sections 1 and 2
- The shear at the pipe walls between Sections 1 and 2

Assuming the flow in the pipeline has a constant velocity (that is, acceleration is equal to zero), the system can be balanced based on the pressure difference, gravitational forces, and shear forces.

$$P_1A_1 - P_2A_2 - \bar{A}L\gamma\sin(\alpha) - \tau_o NL = 0 \tag{2.14}$$

where P_1 = pressure at section 1(M/L/T^2)
A_1 = cross-sectional area of section 1(L^2)
P_2 = pressure at section 2 (M/L/T^2)
A_2 = cross-sectional area of section 2 (L^2)
$\bar{A}$ = average area between section 1 and section 2 (L^2)

L = distance between section 1 and section 2 (L)
γ = fluid specific weight (M/L^2/T^2)
α = angle of the pipe to horizontal
τ_o = shear stress along pipe wall (M/L/T^2)
N = perimeter of pipeline cross-section (L)

Figure 2.9
Free body diagram of water flowing in an inclined pipe

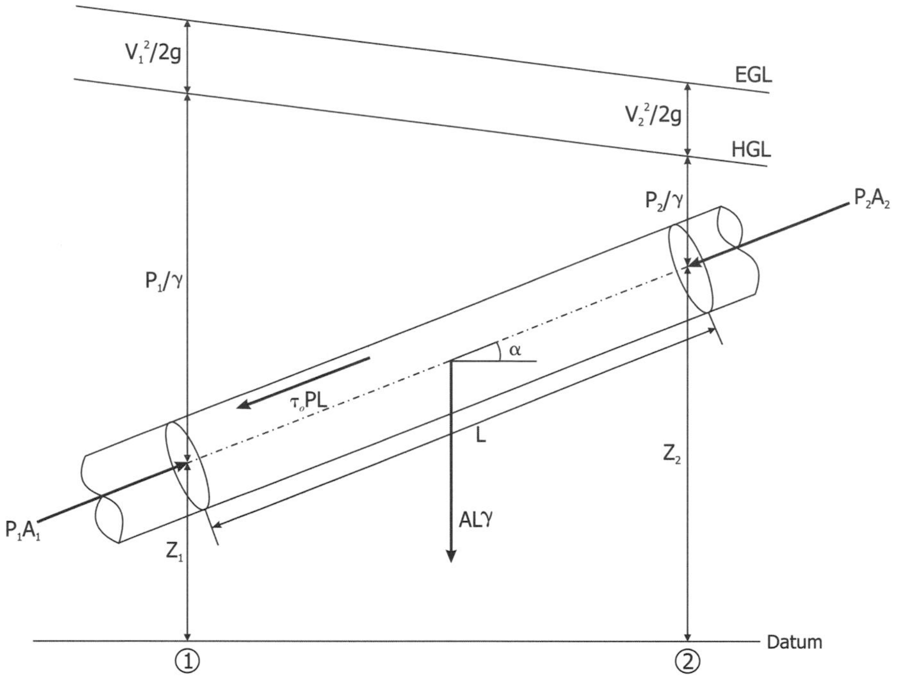

The last term on the left side of Equation 2.14 represents the friction losses along the pipe wall between the two sections. By recognizing that sin(α) = (Z_2-Z_1)/L, the equation for head loss due to friction can be rewritten to obtain the following equation. (Note that the velocity head is not considered in this case because the pipe diameters, and therefore the velocity heads, are the same.)

$$h_L = \tau_o \frac{NL}{\gamma A} = \left(\frac{P_1}{\gamma} + Z_1\right) - \left(\frac{P_2}{\gamma} + Z_2\right) \quad (2.15)$$

where h_L = head loss due to friction (L)
Z_1 = elevation of centroid of section 1 (L)
Z_2 = elevation of centroid of section 2 (L)

Recall that the shear stresses in a fluid can be found analytically for laminar flow using Newton's Law of Viscosity. Shear stress is a function of the viscosity and velocity gradient of the fluid, the fluid specific weight (or density), and the diameter of the pipeline. The roughness of the pipe wall is also a factor (that is, the rougher the pipe wall, the larger the shear stress). Combining all of these factors, it can be seen that:

$$\tau_o = F(\rho, \mu, V, D, \varepsilon) \tag{2.16}$$

where ρ = fluid density (M/L^3)
μ = absolute viscosity (M/L/T)
V = average fluid velocity (L/T)
D = diameter (L)
ε = index of internal pipe roughness (L)

Darcy-Weisbach

Using dimensional analysis, the *Darcy-Weisbach formula* was developed. The formula is an equation for head loss expressed in terms of the variables listed in Equation 2.16, as follows (note that head loss is expressed with units of length):

$$h_L = f\frac{LV^2}{D2g} = \frac{8fLQ^2}{gD^5\pi^2} \tag{2.17}$$

where f = Darcy-Weisbach friction factor
g = gravitational acceleration constant (L/T^2)
Q = pipeline flow rate (L^3/T)

The Darcy-Weisbach *friction factor*, *f*, is a function of the same variables as wall shear stress (Equation 2.16). Again using dimensional analysis, a functional relationship for the friction factor can be developed:

$$f = F\left(\frac{VD\rho}{\mu}, \frac{\varepsilon}{D}\right) = F\left(Re, \frac{\varepsilon}{D}\right) \tag{2.18}$$

where Re = Reynolds Number

The Darcy-Weisbach friction factor is dependent upon the velocity, density, and viscosity of the fluid; the size of the pipe in which the fluid is flowing; and the internal roughness of the pipe. The fluid velocity, density, viscosity, and pipe size are expressed in terms of the Reynolds Number. The internal roughness is expressed in terms of a variable called the *relative roughness*, which is the internal pipe roughness (ε) divided by the pipe diameter (D).

In the early 1930s, the German researcher Nikuradse performed an experiment that would become fundamental in head loss determination (Nikuradse, 1932). He glued uniformly sized sand grains to the insides of three pipes of different sizes. His experiments showed that the curve of f versus Re is smooth for the same values of ε/D. Partly because of Nikuradse's sand grain experiments, the quantity ε is called the *equivalent sand grain roughness* of the pipe. Table 2.2 provides values of ε for various materials.

Other researchers conducted experiments on artificially roughened pipes to generate data describing pipe friction factors for a wide range of relative roughness values.

Table 2.2 Equivalent sand grain roughness for various pipe materials

	Equivalent Sand Roughness, ε	
Material	(ft)	(mm)
Copper, brass	$1\text{x}10^{-4}$ - $3\text{x}10^{-3}$	$3.05\text{x}10^{-2}$ - 0.9
Wrought iron, steel	$1.5\text{x}10^{-4}$ - $8\text{x}10^{-3}$	$4.6\text{x}10^{-2}$ - 2.4
Asphalted cast iron	$4\text{x}10^{-4}$ - $7\text{x}10^{-3}$	0.1 - 2.1
Galvanized iron	$3.3\text{x}10^{-4}$ - $1.5\text{x}10^{-2}$	0.102 - 4.6
Cast iron	$8\text{x}10^{-4}$ - $1.8\text{x}10^{-2}$	0.2 - 5.5
Concrete	10^{-3} to 10^{-2}	0.3 to 3.0
Uncoated Cast Iron	$7.4\text{x}10^{-4}$	0.226
Coated Cast Iron	$3.3\text{x}10^{-4}$	0.102
Coated Spun Iron	$1.8\text{x}10^{-4}$	$5.6\text{x}10^{-2}$
Cement	$1.3\text{x}10^{-3}$ - $4\text{x}10^{-3}$	0.4 - 1.2s
Wrought Iron	$1.7\text{x}10^{-4}$	$5\text{x}10^{-2}$
Uncoated Steel	$9.2\text{x}10^{-5}$	$2.8\text{x}10^{-2}$
Coated Steel	$1.8\text{x}10^{-4}$	$5.8\text{x}10^{-2}$
Wood Stave	$6\text{x}10^{-4}$ - $3\text{x}10^{-3}$	0.2 - 0.9
PVC	$5\text{x}10^{-6}$	$1.5\text{x}10^{-3}$

Compiled from Lamont (1981), Moody (1944), and Mays (1999)

Colebrook-White Equation and the Moody Diagram. Numerous formulas exist that relate the friction factor to the Reynolds Number and relative roughness. One of the earliest and most popular of these formulas is the *Colebrook-White equation*:

$$\frac{1}{\sqrt{f}} = -0.86\ln\left(\frac{\varepsilon}{3.7D} + \frac{2.51}{Re\sqrt{f}}\right) \qquad (2.19)$$

The difficulty with using the Colebrook-White equation is that it is an implicit function of the friction factor (f is found on both sides of the equation). Typically, the equation is solved by iterating through assumed values of f until both sides are equal.

The *Moody diagram*, shown in Figure 2.10, was developed from the Colebrook-White equation as a graphical solution for the Darcy-Weisbach friction factor.

It is interesting to note that for laminar flow (low Re) the friction factor is a linear function of the Reynolds Number, while in the fully turbulent range (high ε/D and high Re) the friction factor is only a function of the relative roughness. This difference occurs because the effect of roughness is negligible for laminar flow, while for very turbulent flow the viscous forces become negligible.

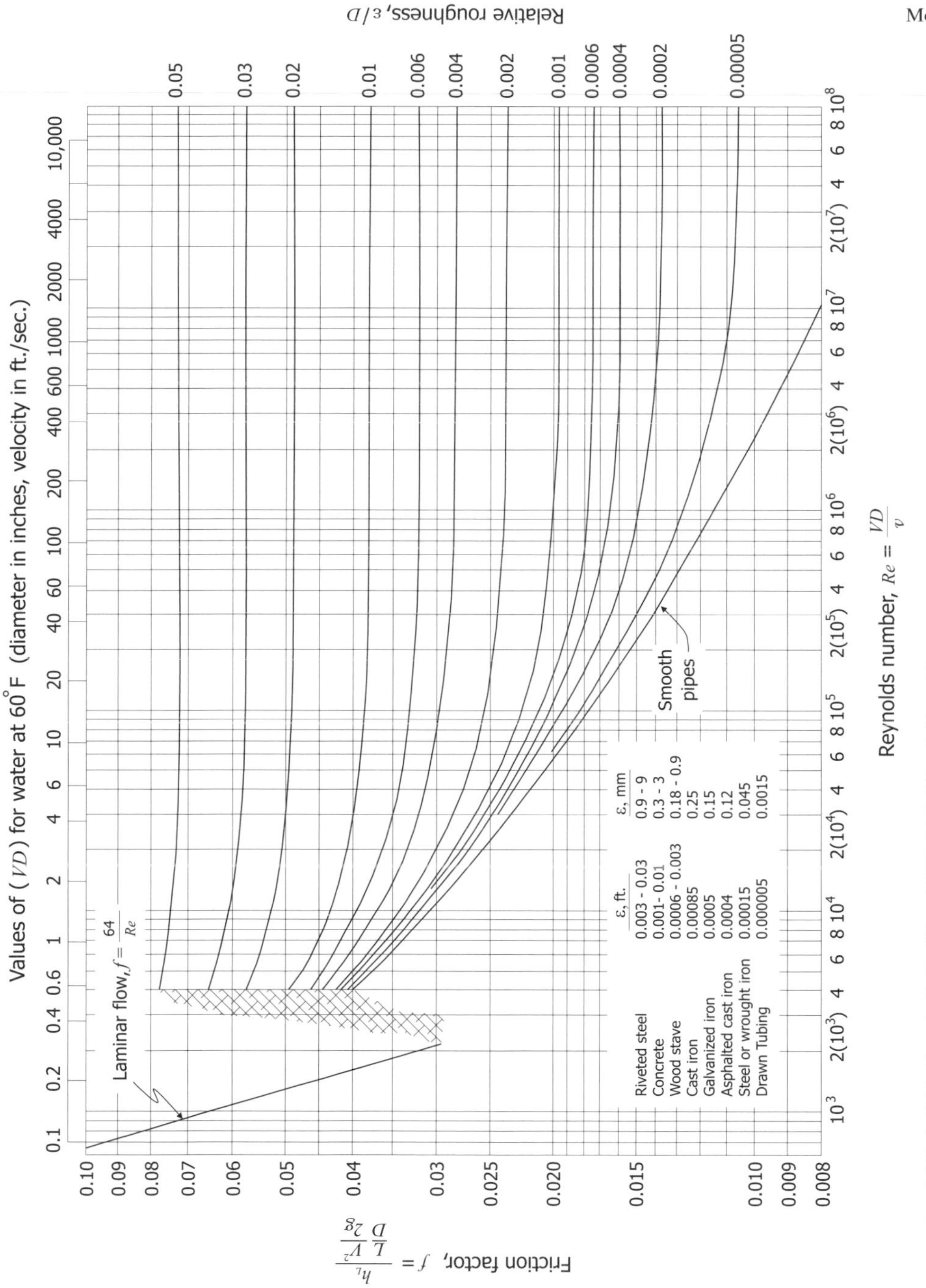

Figure 2.10
Moody diagram

From L. F. Moody, "Friction Factors for Pipe Flow," Trans. A.S.M.E., Vol. 66, 1944, used with permission.

Swamee-Jain Formula. Much easier to solve than the iterative Colebrook-White formula, the formula developed by Swamee and Jain (1976) also approximates the Darcy-Weisbach friction factor. This equation is an explicit function of the Reynolds Number and the relative roughness, and is accurate to within about one percent of the Colebrook-White equation over a range of:

$$4x10^3 \le Re \le 1x10^8 \text{ and}$$

$$1x10^{-6} \le \varepsilon/D \le 1x10^{-2}$$

$$f = \frac{1.325}{\left[\ln\left(\frac{\varepsilon}{3.7D} + \frac{5.74}{Re^{0.9}}\right)\right]^2} \qquad (2.20)$$

Because of its relative simplicity and reasonable accuracy, most water distribution system modeling software packages use the *Swamee-Jain formula* to compute the friction factor.

Hazen-Williams

Another frequently used head loss expression, particularly in North America, is the *Hazen-Williams formula* (Williams and Hazen, 1920; ASCE, 1992):

$$h_L = \frac{C_f L}{C^{1.852} D^{4.87}} Q^{1.852} \qquad (2.21)$$

where
h_L = head loss due to friction (ft, m)
L = distance between section 1 and 2 (ft, m)
C = Hazen-Williams C-factor
D = diameter (ft, m)
Q = pipeline flow rate (cfs, m^3/s)
C_f = unit conversion factor (4.73 English, 10.7 SI)

The Hazen-Williams formula uses many of the same variables as Darcy-Weisbach, but instead of using a friction factor, the Hazen-Williams formula uses a pipe carrying capacity factor, *C*. Higher C-factors represent smoother pipes (with higher carrying capacities) and lower C-factors describe rougher pipes. Table 2.3 shows typical C-factors for various pipe materials, based on Lamont (1981).

Lamont found that it was not possible to develop a single correlation between pipe age and C-factor and that instead, the decrease in C-factor also depended heavily on the corrosiveness of the water being carried. He developed four separate "trends" in carrying capacity loss depending on the "attack" of the water on the pipe. Trend 1, slight attack, corresponded to water that was only mildly corrosive. Trend 4, severe attack, corresponded to water that would rapidly attack cast iron pipe. As can be seen from Table 2.3, the extent of attack can significantly affect C-factor. Testing pipes to determine the loss of carrying capacity is discussed further on page 178.

From a purely theoretical standpoint, the C-factor of a pipe should vary with the flow velocity under turbulent conditions. Equation 2.22 can be used to adjust the C-factor

Table 2.3 C-factors for various pipe materials

Type of Pipe	C-factor Values for Discrete Pipe Diameters					
	1.0 in. (2.5 cm)	3.0 in. (7.6 cm)	6.0 in. (15.2 cm)	12 in. (30 cm)	24 in. (61 cm)	48 in. (122 cm)
Uncoated cast iron - smooth and new		121	125	130	132	134
Coated cast iron - smooth and new		129	133	138	140	141
30 years old						
Trend 1 - slight attack		100	106	112	117	120
Trend 2 - moderate attack		83	90	97	102	107
Trend 3 - appreciable attack		59	70	78	83	89
Trend 4 - severe attack		41	50	58	66	73
60 years old						
Trend 1 - slight attack		90	97	102	107	112
Trend 2 - moderate attack		69	79	85	92	96
Trend 3 - appreciable attack		49	58	66	72	78
Trend 4 - severe attack		30	39	48	56	62
100 years old						
Trend 1 - slight attack		81	89	95	100	104
Trend 2 - moderate attack		61	70	78	83	89
Trend 3 - appreciable attack		40	49	57	64	71
Trend 4 - severe attack		21	30	39	46	54
Miscellaneous						
Newly scraped mains		109	116	121	125	127
Newly brushed mains		97	104	108	112	115
Coated spun iron - smooth and new		137	142	145	148	148
Old - take as coated cast iron of same age						
Galvanized iron - smooth and new	120	129	133			
Wrought iron - smooth and new	129	137	142			
Coated steel - smooth and new	129	137	142	145	148	148
Uncoated Steel - smooth and new	134	142	145	147	150	150
Coated asbestos cement - clean		147	149	150	152	
Uncoated asbestos cement - clean		142	145	147	150	
Spun cement-lined and spun bitumen-lined - clean		147	149	150	152	153
Smooth pipe (including lead, brass, copper, polyethylene, and PVC) - clean	140	147	149	150	152	153
PVC wavy - clean	134	142	145	147	150	150
Concrete - Scobey						
Class 1 - Cs = 0.27; clean		69	79	84	90	95
Class 2 - Cs = 0.31; clean		95	102	106	110	113
Class 3 - Cs = 0.345; clean		109	116	121	125	127
Class 4 - Cs = 0.37; clean		121	125	130	132	134
Best - Cs = 0.40; clean		129	133	138	140	141
Tate relined pipes - clean		109	116	121	125	127
Prestressed concrete pipes - clean				147	150	150

Lamont (1981)

for different velocities, but the effects of this correction are usually minimal. A two-fold increase in the flow velocity correlates to an apparent five percent decrease in the roughness factor. This difference is usually within the error range for the roughness estimate in the first place, so most engineers assume the C-factor remains constant regardless of flow (Walski, 1984). However, if C-factor tests are done at very high velocities (e.g., >10 ft/s), then a significant error can result when the resulting C-factors are used to predict head loss at low velocities.

$$C = C_o\left(\frac{V_o}{V}\right)^{0.081} \tag{2.22}$$

where C = velocity adjusted C-Factor
C_o = reference C-Factor
V_o = reference value of velocity at which C_0 was determined (L/T)

Manning Equation

Another head loss expression more typically associated with open channel flow is the *Manning equation*:

$$h_L = \frac{C_f L (nQ)^2}{D^{5.33}} \tag{2.23}$$

where n = Manning roughness coefficient
C_f = unit conversion factor (4.66 English, 5.29 SI)

As with the previous head loss expressions, the head loss computed using Manning equation is dependent upon the pipe length and diameter, the discharge or flow through the pipe, and a *roughness coefficient*. In this case, a higher value of n represents a higher internal pipe roughness. Table 2.4 provides typical Manning's roughness coefficients for commonly used pipe materials.

Table 2.4 Manning's roughness values

Material	Manning Coefficient	Material	Manning Coefficient
Asbestos cement	.011	Corrugated metal	.022
Brass	.011	Galvanized iron	.016
Brick	.015	Lead	.011
Cast iron, new	.012	Plastic	.009
Concrete		Steel	
Steel forms	.011	Coal-tar enamel	.010
Wooden forms	.015	New unlined	.011
Centrifugally spun	.013	Riveted	.019
Copper	.011	Wood stave	.012

Comparison of Friction Loss Methods

Most hydraulic models have features that allow the user to select from the Darcy-Weisbach, Hazen-Williams, or Manning head loss formulas, depending on the nature of the problem and the user's preferences.

The Darcy-Weisbach formula is a more physically-based equation, derived from the basic governing equations of Newton's Second Law. With appropriate fluid viscosities and densities, Darcy-Weisbach can be used to find the head loss in a pipe for any Newtonian fluid in any flow regime.

The Hazen-Williams and Manning formulas, on the other hand, are empirically-based expressions (meaning that they were developed from experimental data), and generally only apply to water under turbulent flow conditions.

The Hazen-Williams formula is the predominant equation used in the U.S., while Darcy-Weisbach is predominant in Europe. The Manning formula is not typically used for water distribution modeling, however, it is sometimes used in Australia. Table 2.5 presents these three equations in several common unit configurations. These equations solve for the friction slope (S_f), which is the head loss per unit length of pipe.

Table 2.5 Friction loss equations in typical units

Equation	Q (m³/s); D (m)	Q (cfs); D (ft)	Q (gpm); D (in.)
Darcy-Weisbach	$S_f = \frac{0.083fQ^2}{D^5}$	$S_f = \frac{0.025fQ^2}{D^5}$	$S_f = \frac{0.031fQ^2}{D^5}$
Hazen-Williams	$S_f = \frac{10.7}{D^{4.87}}\left(\frac{Q}{C}\right)^{1.852}$	$S_f = \frac{4.73}{D^{4.87}}\left(\frac{Q}{C}\right)^{1.852}$	$S_f = \frac{10.5}{D^{4.87}}\left(\frac{Q}{C}\right)^{1.852}$
Manning	$S_f = \frac{10.3(nQ)^2}{D^{5.33}}$	$S_f = \frac{4.66(nQ)^2}{D^{5.33}}$	$S_f = \frac{13.2(nQ)^2}{D^{5.33}}$

Compiled from ASCE (1975) and ASCE/WEF (1982)

2.5 MINOR LOSSES

Head losses also occur at valves, tees, bends, reducers, and other *appurtenances* within the piping system. These losses, called *minor losses*, are due to turbulence within the bulk flow as it moves through fittings and bends. Figure 2.11 illustrates the turbulent eddies that develop within the bulk flow as it travels through a valve and a 90-degree bend.

Head loss due to minor losses can be computed by multiplying a *minor loss coefficient* by the velocity head as shown in Equation 2.24.

Figure 2.11
Valve and bend cross-sections generating minor losses

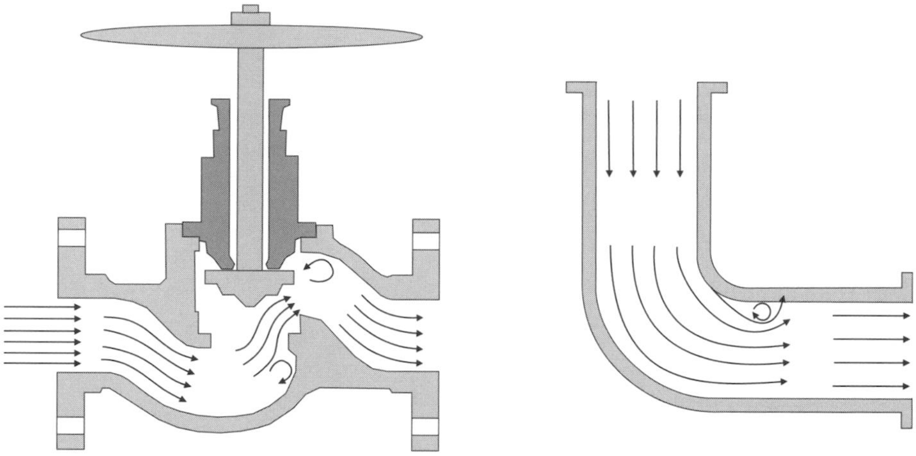

$$h_m = K_L\frac{V^2}{2g} = K_L\frac{Q^2}{2gA^2} \quad (2.24)$$

where
h_m = head loss due to minor losses (L)
K_L = minor loss coefficient
V = velocity (L/T)
g = gravitational acceleration constant (L/T^2)
A = cross-sectional area (L^2)
Q = flow rate (L^3/T)

Minor loss coefficients are found experimentally, and data are available for many different types of fittings and appurtenances. Table 2.6 provides a list of minor loss coefficients associated with several of the most commonly used fittings. More thorough treatments of minor loss coefficients can be found in Crane (1972), Miller (1978), and Idelchik (1999).

For water distribution systems, minor losses are generally much smaller than the head losses due to friction (hence the term "minor" loss). For this reason, many modelers frequently choose to neglect minor losses. In some cases, however, such as at pump stations or valve manifolds where there may be more fittings and higher velocities, minor losses can play a significant role in the piping system under consideration.

Like pipe roughness coefficients, minor head loss coefficients will vary somewhat with velocity. For most practical network problems, however, the minor loss coefficient is treated as constant.

Table 2.6 Minor loss coefficients

Fitting	K_L	Fitting	K_L
Pipe Entrance		90° smooth bend	
Bellmouth	0.03-0.05	Bend radius/D = 4	0.16-0.18
Rounded	0.12-0.25	Bend radius/D = 2	0.19-0.25
Sharp Edged	0.50	Bend radius/D = 1	0.35-0.40
Projecting	0.78	Mitered bend	
Contraction - sudden		$\theta = 15°$	0.05
D_2/D_1=0.80	0.18	$\theta = 30°$	0.10
D_2/D_1=0.50	0.37	$\theta = 45°$	0.20
D_2/D_1=0.20	0.49	$\theta = 60°$	0.35
Contraction - conical		$\theta = 90°$	0.80
D_2/D_1=0.80	0.05	Tee	
D_2/D_1=0.50	0.07	Line flow	0.30-0.40
D_2/D_1=0.20	0.08	Branch flow	0.75-1.80
Expansion - sudden		Cross	
D_2/D_1=0.80	0.16	Line flow	0.50
D_2/D_1=0.50	0.57	Branch flow	0.75
D_2/D_1=0.20	0.92	45° Wye	
Expansion - conical		Line flow	0.30
D_2/D_1=0.80	0.03	Branch flow	0.50
D_2/D_1=0.50	0.08	Check valve - conventional	4.0
D_2/D_1=0.20	0.13	Check valve - clearway	1.5
Gate valve - open	0.39	Check valve - ball	4.5
3/4 open	1.10	Butterfly valve - open	1.2
1/2 open	4.8	Cock - straight through	0.5
1/4 open	27	Foot valve - hinged	2.2
Globe valve - open	10	Foot valve - poppet	12.5
Angle valve - open	4.3		

Walski (1984)

Valve Coefficient

Most valve manufacturers can provide a chart of percent opening versus valve coefficient (C_v), which can be related to the minor loss (K_L) using the following formula.

$$K_L = C_f D^4 / C_v^2 \qquad (2.25)$$

where
D = diameter (in., m)
C_v = valve coefficient [gpm/(psi)$^{0.5}$, (m^3/s)/(kPa)$^{0.5}$]
C_f = unit conversion factor (880 English, 1.22 SI)

Figure 2.12
48-in. elbow fitting

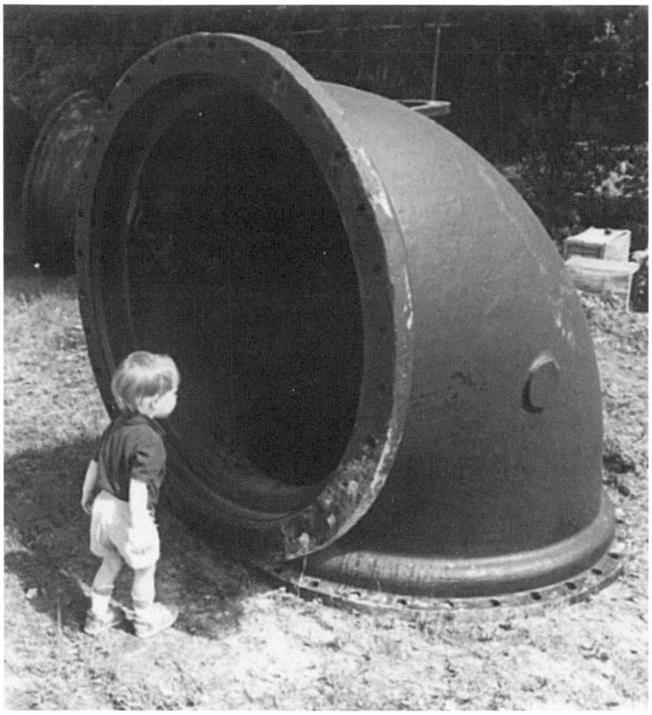

Equivalent Pipe Length

Rather than including minor loss coefficients directly, a modeler may choose to adjust the modeled pipe length to account for minor losses by adding an equivalent length of pipe for each minor loss. Given the minor loss coefficient for a valve or fitting, the equivalent length of pipe to give the same head loss can be calculated as:

$$L_e = \frac{K_L D}{f} \tag{2.26}$$

where L_e = equivalent length of pipe (L)
D = diameter of equivalent pipe (L)
f = Darcy-Weisbach friction factor

The practice of assigning equivalent pipe lengths was typically used when hand calculations were more common, because it could save time for the overall analysis of a pipeline. With modern computer modeling techniques, this is no longer a widespread practice. Because it is now so easy to use minor loss coefficients directly within a hydraulic model, the process of determining equivalent lengths is actually less efficient. In addition, use of equivalent pipe lengths can unfavorably affect the travel time predictions that are important in many water quality calculations.

2.6 RESISTANCE COEFFICIENTS

Many related expressions for head loss have been developed. They can be mathematically generalized with the introduction of a variable referred to as a *resistance coefficient*. This format allows the equation to remain essentially the same regardless of which friction method is used, making it ideal for hydraulic modeling.

$$h_L = K_P Q^z \tag{2.27}$$

where h_L = head loss due to friction (L)
K_P = pipe resistance coefficient (T^z/L^{3z-1})
Q = pipeline flow rate (L^3/T)
z = exponent on flow term

Equations for computing K_P with the various head loss methods are given below.

Darcy-Weisbach

$$K_P = f\frac{L}{2gA^zD} \tag{2.28}$$

where f = Darcy-Weisbach friction factor
L = length of pipe (L)
D = pipe diameter (L)
A = cross-sectional area of pipeline (L^2)
z = 2

Hazen-Williams

$$K_P = \frac{C_f L}{C^z D^{4.87}} \tag{2.29}$$

where K_P = pipe resistance coefficient (s^z/ft^{3z-1}, s^z/m^{3z-1})
L = length of pipe (ft, m)
C = C-factor with velocity adjustment
z = 1.852
D = pipe diameter (ft, m)
C_f = unit conversion factor (4.73 English, 10.7 SI)

Manning

$$K_P = \frac{C_f L n^z}{D^{5.33}} \tag{2.30}$$

where n = Manning's roughness coefficient
z = 2
C_f = unit conversion factor [4.64 English, 10.3 SI (ASCE/WEF, 1982)]

Minor Losses

A resistance coefficient can also be defined for minor losses, as shown in the equation below. Like the pipe resistance coefficient, the resistance coefficient for minor losses is a function of the physical characteristics of the fitting or appurtenance and the discharge.

$$h_m = K_M Q^2 \tag{2.31}$$

where h_m = head loss due to minor losses (L)
K_M = minor loss resistance coefficient (T^2/L^5)
Q = pipeline flow rate (L^3/T)

Solving for the minor loss resistance coefficient by substituting Equation 2.24, results in:

$$K_M = \frac{\sum K_L}{2gA^2} \tag{2.32}$$

where $\sum K_L$ = sum of individual minor loss coefficients

2.7 ENERGY GAINS - PUMPS

There are many occasions when energy needs to be added to a hydraulic system to overcome elevation differences, friction losses, and minor losses. A pump is a device to which mechanical energy is applied and transferred to the water as total head. The head added is called *pump head*, and is a function of the flow rate through the pump. The following discussion is oriented toward *centrifugal pumps* since they are the most frequently used pumps in water distribution systems. Additional information about pumps can be found in Bosserman (2000), Hydraulic Institute Standards (2000), Karassik (1976), and Sanks (1998).

Pump Head-Discharge Relationship

The relationship between pump head and pump discharge is given in the form of a *head versus discharge curve* (also called a head characteristic curve) similar to the one shown in Figure 2.13. This curve defines the relationship between the head that the pump adds and the amount of flow that the pump passes. The pump head versus discharge relationship is nonlinear, and as one would expect, the more water the pump passes, the less head it can add. The head that is plotted in the head characteristic curve is the head difference across the pump, called the *total dynamic head* (TDH).

This curve must be described as a mathematical function to be used in a hydraulic simulation. Some models fit a polynomial curve to selected data points, but a more common approach is to describe the curve using a power function in the following form:

$$h_P = h_o - cQ_P^m \tag{2.33}$$

where
h_P = pump head (L)
h_o = cutoff (shutoff) head (pump head at zero flow) (L)
Q_P = pump discharge (L/T³)
c, m = coefficients describing pump curve shape

More information on pump performance testing is available in Chapter 5 (see page 179).

Figure 2.13
Pump head characteristic curve

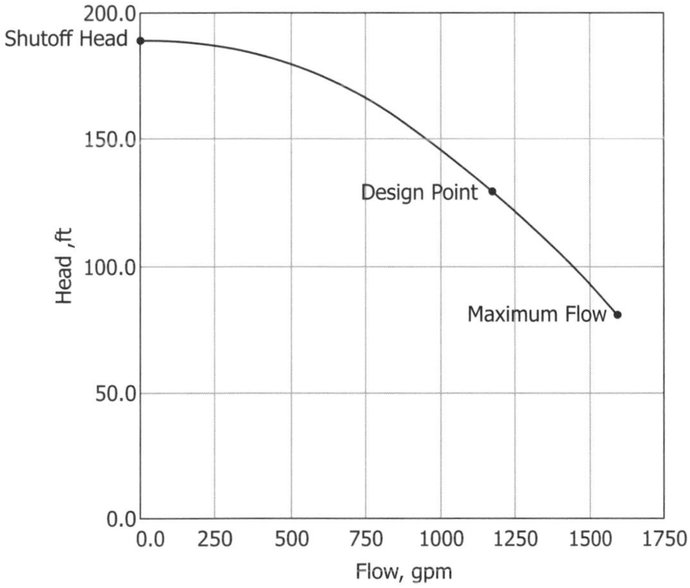

Affinity Laws for Variable-Speed Pumps. A centrifugal pump's characteristic curve is fixed for a given motor speed and impeller diameter, but can be determined for any speed and any diameter by applying relationships called the *affinity laws*. For variable-speed pumps, these affinity laws are presented as:

$$Q_{P1}/Q_{P2} = n_1/n_2 \tag{2.34}$$

$$h_{P1}/h_{P2} = (n_1/n_2)^2 \tag{2.35}$$

where $Q_{P1, P2}$ = pump flow rate (L^3/T)
$n_{1, 2}$ = pump speed (1/T)
$h_{P1, P2}$ = pump head (L)

Thus, pump discharge rate is directly proportional to pump speed, and pump discharge head is proportional to the square of the speed. Using this relationship, once the pump curve at any one speed is known, then the curve at another speed can be predicted. Figure 2.14 illustrates the affinity laws for variable-speed pumps where the line through the pump head characteristic curves represents the locus of best efficiency points.

Figure 2.14
Relative speed factors for variable-speed pumps

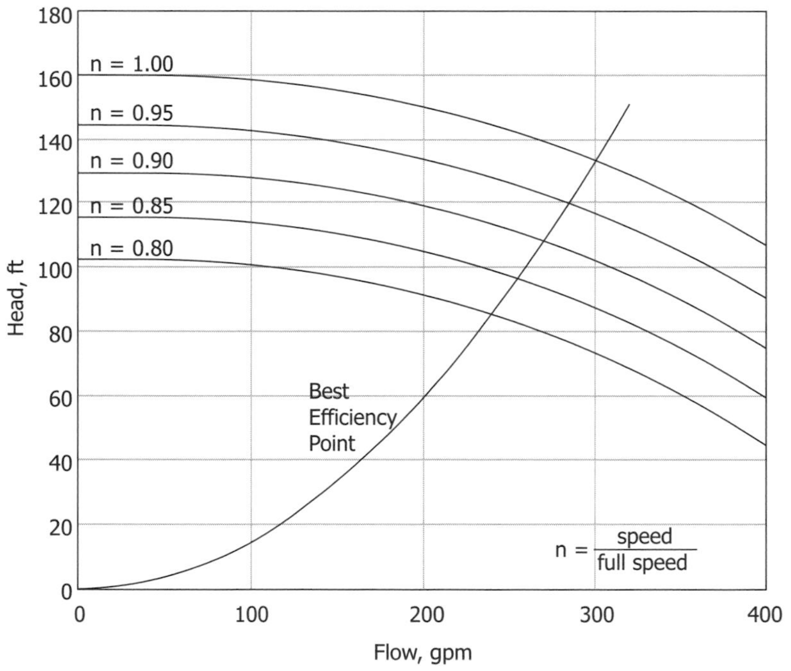

System Head Curves

The purpose of a pump is to overcome elevation differences and head losses due to pipe friction and fittings. The amount of head the pump must add to overcome elevation differences is dependent on system characteristics and topology (and independent of the pump discharge rate), and is referred to as *static head* or *static lift*. Friction and minor losses, however, are highly dependent on the rate of discharge through the pump. When these losses are added to the static head for a series of discharge rates, the resulting plot is called a *system head curve* (Figure 2.15).

The pump characteristic curve is a function of the pump and independent of the system, while the system head curve is dependent on the system and is independent of the pump. Unlike the pump curve, which is fixed for a given pump at a given speed, the system head curve is continually sliding up and down as tank water levels change and demands change. Rather than there being a unique system head curve, there is actually a family of system head curves forming a band on the graph.

For the case of a single pipeline between two points, the system head curve can be described in equation form as:

$$H = h_l + \sum K_P Q^z + \sum K_M Q^2 \qquad (2.36)$$

where H = total head (L)
h_l = static lift (L)
K_P = pipe resistance coefficient (T^z/L^{3z-1})
Q = pipe discharge (L^3/T)
z = coefficient
K_M = minor loss resistance coefficient (T^2/L^5)

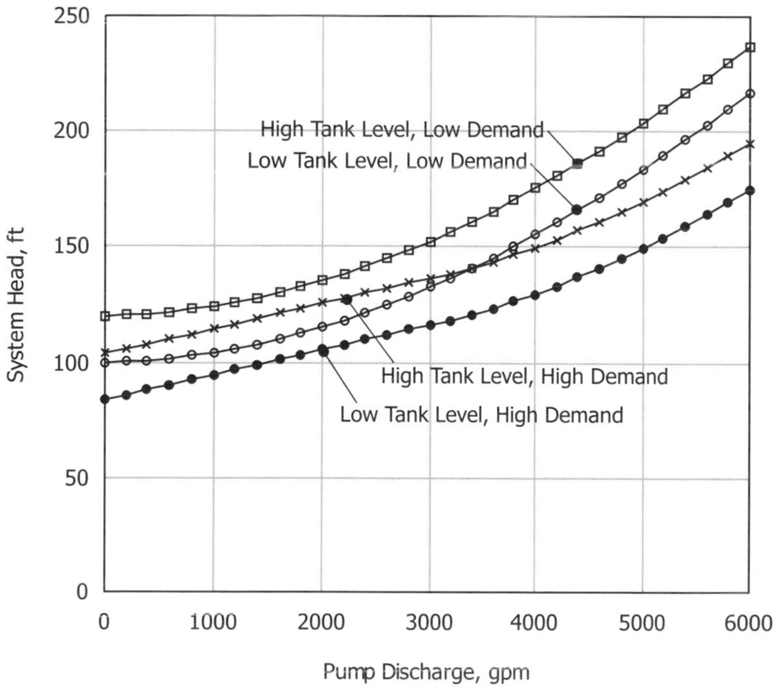

Figure 2.15
A family of system head curves

Thus, the head losses and minor losses associated with each segment of pipe are summed along the total length of the pipeline. When the system is more complex, the interdependencies of the hydraulic network make it impossible to write a single equation to describe a point on the system curve. In these cases, hydraulic analysis using a hydraulic model may be needed. It is helpful to visualize the hydraulic grade line as increasing abruptly at a pump and sloping downward as the water flows through pipes and valves (Figure 2.16).

Figure 2.16
Schematic of hydraulic grade line for a pumped system

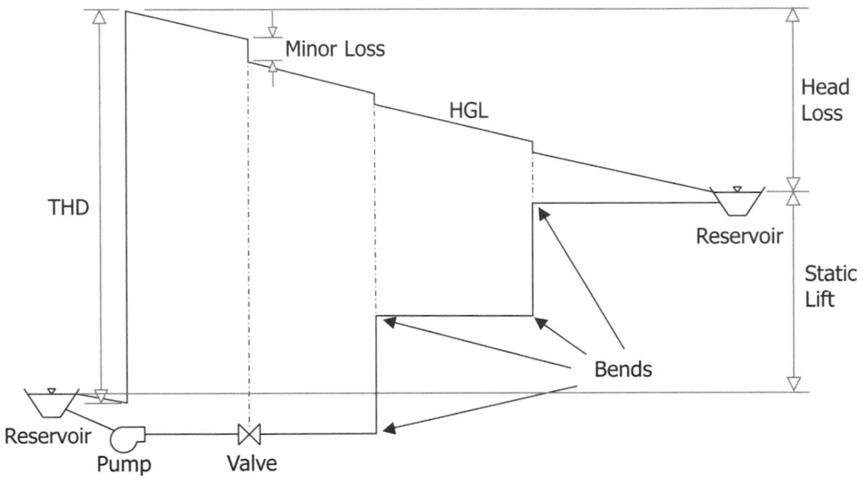

Pump Operating Point

When the pump head discharge curve and the system head curve are plotted on the same axes (Figure 2.17), there is only one point that lies on both the pump characteristic curve and the system head curve. This intersection defines the pump *operating point*, which represents the discharge that will pass through the pump and the head that the pump will add. This head is equal to the head needed to overcome the static head and other losses in the system.

Other Uses of Pump Curves

In addition to the pump head-discharge curve, other curves representing pump behavior describe power, water horsepower, and efficiency (Figure 2.18), and are discussed further in Chapter 3 (see page 93) and Chapter 5 (see page 179). Since utilities want to minimize the amount of energy necessary for system operation, the engineer should select pumps that run as efficiently as possible. Pump operating costs are discussed further in Chapter 9 (see page 353).

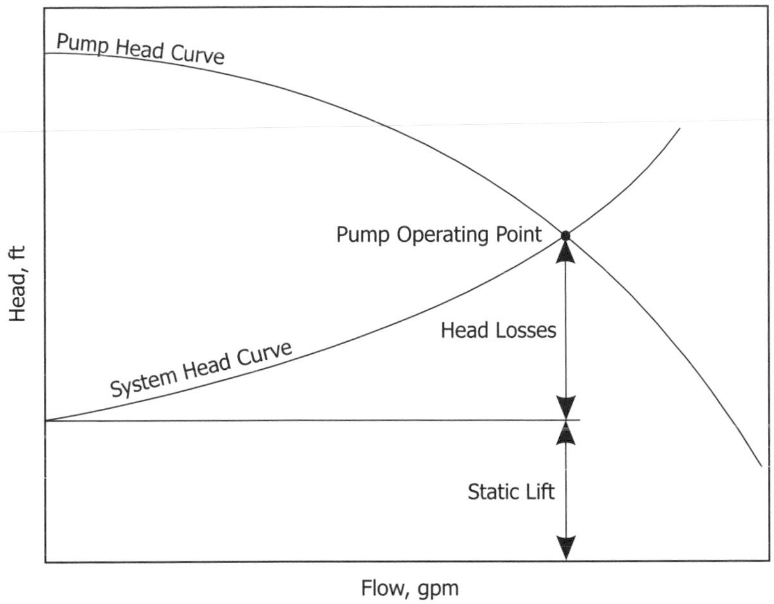

Figure 2.17
System operating point

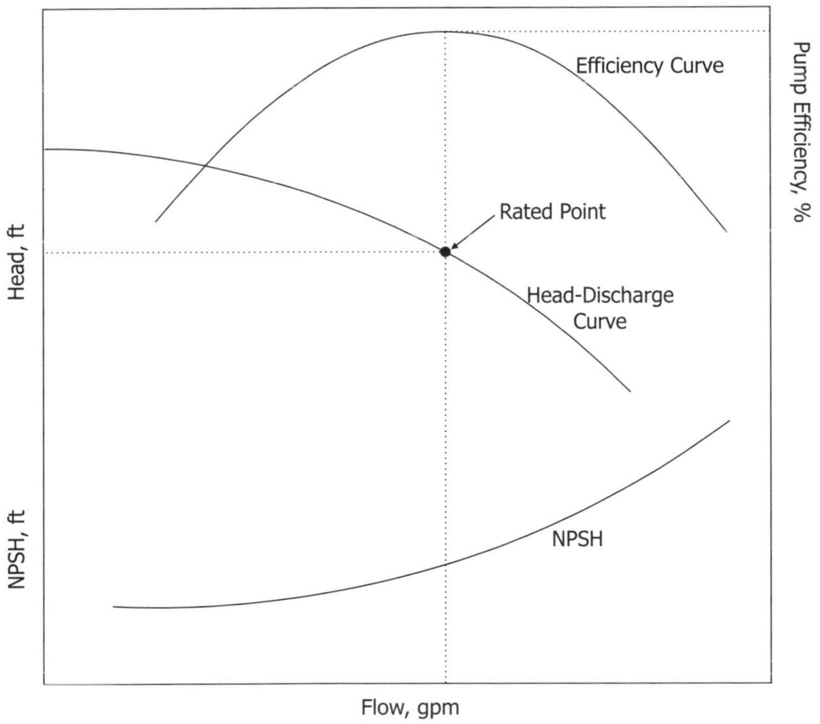

Figure 2.18
Pump efficiency curve

Another issue when designing a pump is the *net positive suction head* (NPSH) required (see page 260). NPSH is the head that is present at the suction side of the pump. Each pump requires that the available NPSH exceed the required NPSH to ensure that local pressures within the pump do not drop below the vapor pressure of the fluid, causing cavitation. As discussed on page 24, cavitation is essentially a boiling of the liquid within the pump, and it can cause tremendous damage. The NPSH required is unique for each pump model, and is a function of flow rate. The use of a calibrated hydraulic model in determining available net positive suction head is discussed further on page 260.

2.8 NETWORK HYDRAULICS

In networks of interconnected hydraulic elements, every element is influenced by each of its neighbors; the entire system is interrelated in such a way that the condition of one element must be consistent with the condition of all other elements. Two concepts define these interconnections:

- Conservation of mass
- Conservation of energy

Conservation of Mass

The principle of *Conservation of Mass* (Figure 2.19) dictates that the fluid mass that enters any pipe will be equal to the mass leaving the pipe (since fluid is typically neither created nor destroyed in hydraulic systems). In network modeling, all outflows are lumped at the nodes or junctions.

$$\sum_{pipes} Q_i - U = 0 \tag{2.37}$$

where Q_i = inflow to node in i-th pipe (L^3/T)
U = water used at node (L^3/T)

Note that for pipe outflows from the node, the sign of Q is negative.

When extended period simulations are considered, water can be stored and withdrawn from tanks, thus a term is needed to describe the accumulation of water at certain nodes:

$$\sum_{pipes} Q_i - U - \frac{dS}{dt} = 0 \tag{2.38}$$

where $\frac{dS}{dt}$ = change in storage (L^3/T)

The conservation of mass equation is applied to all junction nodes and tanks in a network, and one equation is written for each of them.

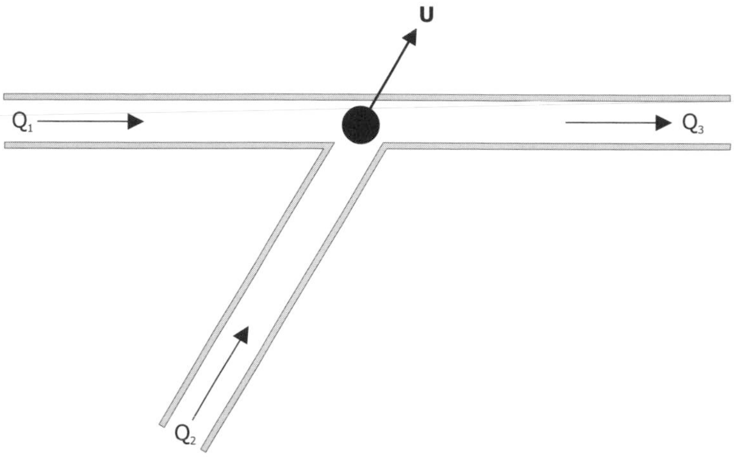

Figure 2.19
Conservation of Mass principle

Conservation of Energy

The principle of *Conservation of Energy* dictates that the difference in energy between two points must be the same regardless of the path that is taken (Bernoulli, 1738). For convenience within the hydraulic analysis, the equation is written in terms of head as:

$$Z_1 + \frac{P_1}{\gamma} + \frac{V_1^2}{2g} + \sum h_P = Z_2 + \frac{P_2}{\gamma} + \frac{V_2^2}{2g} + \sum h_L + \sum h_m \tag{2.39}$$

where
Z = elevation (L)
P = pressure (M/L/T^2)
γ = fluid specific weight (M/L^2/T^2)
V = velocity (L/T)
g = gravitational acceleration constant (L/T^2)
h_P = head added at pumps (L)
h_L = head loss in pipes (L)
h_m = head loss due to minor losses (L)

Thus the difference in energy at any two points connected in a network is equal to the energy gains from pumps and energy losses in pipes and fittings that occur in the path between them. This equation can be written for any open path between any two points. Of particular interest are paths between reservoirs or tanks (where the difference in head is known), or paths around loops since the changes in energy must sum to zero as illustrated in Figure 2.20.

Figure 2.20
The sum of head losses around a pipe loop is equal to zero

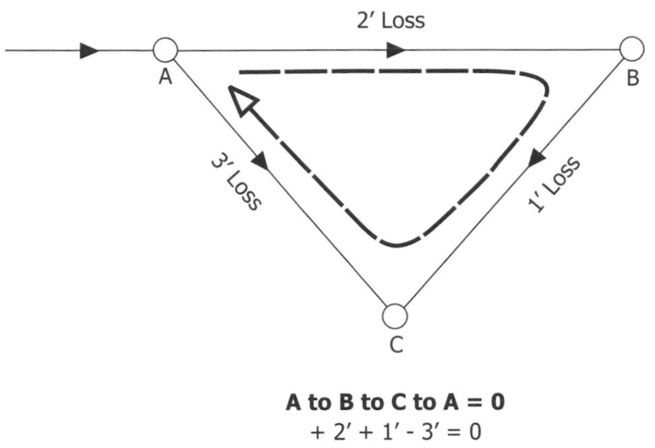

Solving Network Problems

Real water distribution systems do not consist of a single pipe and cannot be described by a single set of continuity and energy equations. Instead, one continuity equation must be developed for each node in the system, and one energy equation must be developed for each pipe (or loop), depending on the method used. For real systems, these equations can number in the thousands.

The first systematic approach for solving these equations was developed by Hardy Cross (1936). The invention of digital computers, however, allowed more powerful numerical techniques to be developed. These techniques set up and solve the system of equations describing the hydraulics of the network in matrix form. Because the energy equations are non-linear in terms of flow and head, they cannot be solved directly. Instead, these techniques estimate a solution and then iteratively improve it until the difference between solutions falls within a specified tolerance. At this point, the hydraulic equations are considered solved.

Some of the methods used in network analysis are described in Bhave (1991); Lansey and Mays (2000); Larock, Jeppson, and Watters (1999); and Todini and Pilati (1987).

2.9 WATER QUALITY MODELING

Water quality modeling is a direct extension of hydraulic network modeling and can be used to perform many useful analyses. Developers of hydraulic network simulation models recognized the potential for water quality analysis and began adding water quality calculation features to their models in the mid 1980s. *Transport*, mixing, and *decay* are the fundamental physical and chemical processes typically represented in water quality models. Water quality simulations also use the network hydraulic solution as part of their computations. Flow rates in pipes and the flow paths that define how water travels through the network are used to determine mixing, *residence times*, and other hydraulic characteristics affecting disinfectant transport and decay. The results of an extended period hydraulic simulation can be used as a starting point in performing a water quality analysis.

The equations describing transport through pipes, mixing at nodes, and storage and mixing in tanks are adapted from Boccelli, et al. (1998), and those describing chemical formation and decay reactions are developed in each of the following sections. Additional information on water quality models can be found in Clark and Grayman (1998) and Grayman, Rossman, and Geldreich (2000).

Transport in Pipes

Most water quality models make use of one-dimensional advective-reactive transport to predict the changes in constituent concentrations due to transport through a pipe, and to account for formation and decay reactions. Equation 2.40 shows concentration within a pipe i as a function of distance along its length (x) and time (t).

$$\frac{\partial C_i}{\partial t} = \frac{Q_i}{A_i}\frac{\partial C_i}{\partial x} + \theta(C_i),\ i = 1 \ldots P \tag{2.40}$$

where C_i = concentration in pipe i (M/L^3)
Q_i = flow rate in pipe i (L^3/T)
A_i = cross-sectional area of pipe i (L^2)
$\theta(C_i)$ = reaction term (M/L^3/T)

Equation 2.40 must be combined with two boundary condition equations (concentration at $x = 0$ and $t = 0$) to obtain a solution. Equation 2.40 is typically solved, however, by converting it to a standard first-order differential equation using a finite-difference scheme as shown in Equation 2.41.

$$\frac{dC_{i,l}}{dt} = \frac{Q_i}{A_i}\frac{(C_{i,l} - C_{i,l-1})}{\Delta x_i} + \theta(C_{i,l}),\ i = 1 \ldots P,\ l = 1 \ldots n_i \tag{2.41}$$

where $C_{i,l}$ = concentration in pipe i at finite difference node l (M/L^3)
Δx_i = distance between finite difference nodes (L)
$\theta(C_{i,l})$ = reaction term (M/L^3/T)
n_i = number of finite difference nodes in pipe i

The equation for *advective transport* is a function of the flow rate in the pipe divided by the cross-sectional area, which is equal to the mean velocity of the fluid. Thus, the bulk fluid is transported down the length of the pipe with a velocity that is directly proportional to the average flow rate. The equation is based on the assumption that longitudinal dispersion in pipes is negligible, and the bulk fluid is completely mixed (a valid assumption under turbulent conditions). Furthermore, the equation can also account for the formation or decay of a substance during transport with the substitution of a suitable equation into the reaction term. Such an equation will be developed later. First, however, the nodal mixing equation is presented.

Mixing at Nodes

Water quality simulation uses a nodal mixing equation to combine concentrations from individual pipes described by the advective transport equation, and to define the boundary conditions for each pipe as referred to above. The equation is written by performing a mass balance on concentrations entering a junction node.

$$C_{OUT_j} = \frac{\sum_{i \in IN_j} Q_i C_{i,n_i} + U_j}{\sum_{i \in OUT_j} Q_i} \qquad (2.42)$$

where C_{OUT_j} = concentration leaving the junction node j (M/L^3)
OUT_j = set of pipes leaving node j
IN_j = set of pipes entering node j
Q_i = flow rate entering the junction node from pipe i (L^3/T)
C_{i,n_i} = concentration entering junction node from pipe i (M/L^3)
U_j = concentration source at junction node j (M/T)

The nodal mixing equation describes the concentration leaving a network node (either by advective transport into an adjoining pipe or by removal from the network as a demand) as a function of the concentrations that enter it. The equation describes the flow-weighted average of the incoming concentrations. If a source is located at a junction, constituent mass can also be added and combined in the mixing equation

"My wife doesn't understand me."

with the incoming concentrations. Figure 2.21 illustrates how the nodal mixing equation is used at a pipe junction. Concentrations enter the node with pipe flows. The incoming concentrations are mixed according to Equation 2.42, and the resulting concentration is transported through the outgoing pipes and as demand leaving the system. The nodal mixing equation assumes that incoming flows are completely and instantaneously mixed. The basis for the assumption is the turbulence occurring at the junction node, which is usually sufficient for good mixing.

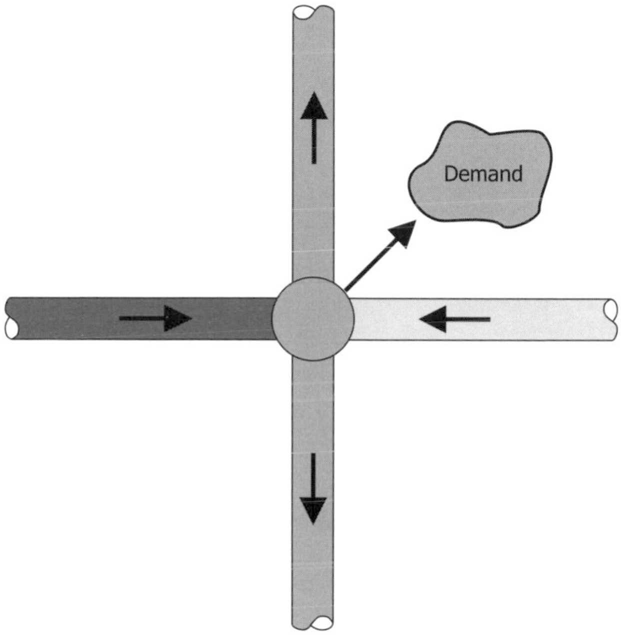

Figure 2.21
Nodal mixing

Mixing in Tanks

Pipes are sometimes connected to reservoirs and tanks as opposed to junction nodes. Again, a mass balance of concentrations entering or leaving the tank or reservoir can be performed.

$$\frac{dC_k}{dt} = \frac{Q_i}{V_k}(C_{i,np}(t) - C_k) + \theta(C_k) \tag{2.43}$$

where C_k = concentration within tank or reservoir k (M/L^3)
Q_i = flow entering the tank or reservoir from pipe i (L^3/T)
V_k = volume in tank or reservoir k (L^3)
$\theta(C_k)$ = reaction term ($M/L^3/T$)

Equation 2.43 applies when a tank is filling. During a hydraulic time step in which the tank is filling, the water entering from upstream pipes mixes with water that is already in storage. If the concentrations are different, blending occurs. The tank mixing equation accounts for blending and any reactions that occur within the tank volume during the hydraulic step. During a hydraulic step in which draining occurs, terms can be dropped and the equation simplified.

$$\frac{dC_k}{dt} = \theta(C_k) \tag{2.44}$$

Specifically, the dilution term can be dropped since it does not occur. Thus, the concentration within the volume is only subject to chemical reactions. Furthermore, the concentration draining from the tank becomes a boundary condition for the advective transport equation written for the pipe connected to it.

Equations 2.43 and 2.44 assume that concentrations within the tank or reservoir are completely and instantaneously mixed. This assumption is frequently applied in water quality models. There are, however, other useful mixing models for simulating flow processes in tanks and reservoirs (Grayman, et al., 1996). For example, contact basins or clear wells designed to provide sufficient contact time for disinfectants are frequently represented as simple plug-flow reactors using a *"first in first out" (FIFO)* model. In a FIFO model, the first volume of water to enter the tank during a filling cycle is the first to leave during the drain cycle.

If severe short-circuiting is occurring within the tank, a *"last in first out" (LIFO)* model should be applied, in which the first volume entering the tank during filling is the last to leave while draining. More complex tank mixing behavior can be captured using more generalized "compartment" models. *Compartment models* have the ability to represent mixing processes and time delays within tanks more accurately. Figure 2.22 illustrates a three-compartment model for a tank with a single pipe for filling and draining. Good quality water entering the tank occupies the first compartment, and a mixing zone and poor quality water are found in compartments two and three, respectively. The model simulates the exchange of water between different compartments, and in doing so, mimics complex tank mixing dynamics. All of the models mentioned above can be used to simulate a non-reactive (conservative) constituent, as well as decay or formation reactions for substances that react over time.

Chemical Reaction Terms

Equations 2.41, 2.42, 2.43, and 2.44 compose the linked system of first-order differential equations solved by typical water quality simulation algorithms. This set of equations and the algorithms for solving them can be used to model different chemical reactions known to impact water quality in distribution systems. Chemical reaction terms are present in Equations 2.41, 2.43, and 2.44. Concentrations within pipes, storage tanks, and reservoirs are a function of these reaction terms. Once water leaves the treatment plant and enters the distribution system, it is subject to many complex physical and chemical processes, some of which are poorly understood, and most of which are not modeled. Three chemical processes that are frequently modeled, however, are bulk fluid reactions, reactions that occur on a surface (typically the pipe wall), and formation reactions involving a limiting reactant. First, an expression for bulk fluid reactions is presented, and then a reaction expression that incorporates both bulk and pipe wall reactions is developed.

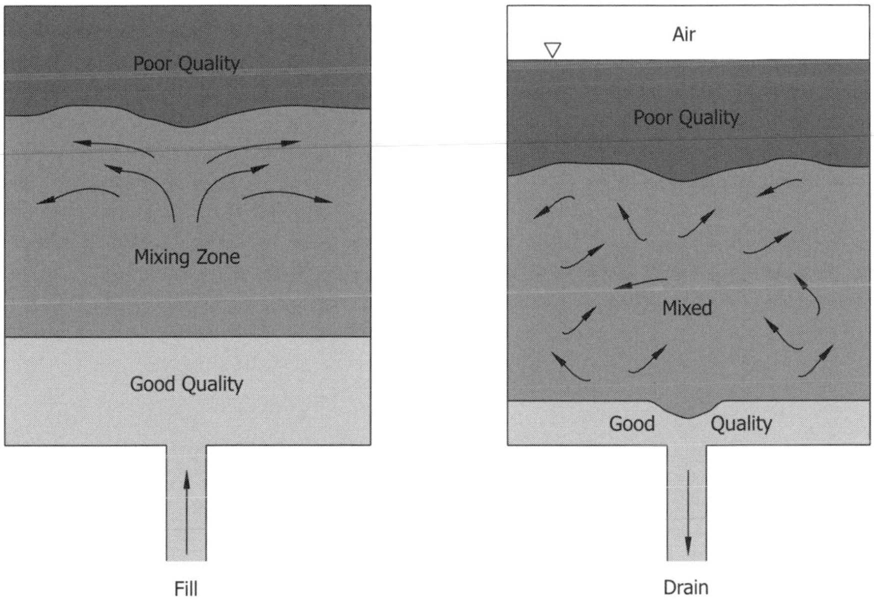

Figure 2.22
Three-compartment tank mixing model

Bulk Reactions. *Bulk fluid reactions* occur within the fluid volume and are a function of constituent concentrations, reaction rate and order, and concentrations of the formation products. A generalized expression for n^{th} order bulk fluid reactions is developed in Equation 2.45 (Rossman, 2000).

$$\theta(C) = \pm kC^n \qquad (2.45)$$

where $\theta(C)$ = reaction term ($M/L^3/T$)
k = reaction rate coefficient [$(L^3/M)^{n-1}/T$]
C = concentration (M/L^3)
n = reaction rate order constant

Equation 2.45 is the generalized bulk reaction term most frequently used in water quality simulation models. The rate expression only accounts for a single reactant concentration, tacitly assuming that any other reactants (if they participate in the reaction) are available in excess of the concentration necessary to sustain the reaction. The sign of the *reaction rate coefficient*, *k*, signifies that a *formation reaction* (positive) or a *decay reaction* (negative) is occurring. The units of the reaction rate coefficient depend on the order of the reaction. The order of the reaction depends on the composition of the reactants and products that are involved in the reaction. The reaction rate order is frequently determined experimentally.

Zero-, first-, and second-order decay reactions are commonly used to model chemical processes that occur in distribution systems. Figure 2.23 is a conceptual illustration showing the change in concentration versus time for these three most common reaction rate orders. Using the generalized expression in Equation 2.45, these reactions can be modeled by allowing *n* to equal 0, 1, or 2, and then performing a regression analysis to experimentally determine the rate coefficient.

Figure 2.23
Conceptual illustration of concentration vs. time for zero, first, and second-order decay reactions

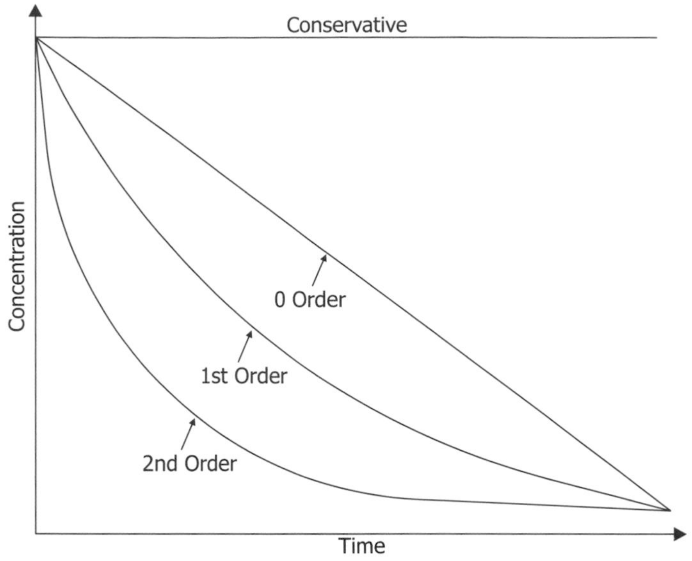

Bulk and Wall Reactions. *Disinfectants* are the most frequently modeled constituents in water distribution systems. Upon leaving the plant and entering the distribution system, disinfectants are subject to a poorly characterized set of potential chemical reactions. Figure 2.24 illustrates the flow of water through a pipe and the types of chemical reactions with disinfectants that can occur along its length. Chlorine (the most common disinfectant) is shown reacting in the bulk fluid with *natural organic matter* (NOM), and at the pipe wall, where oxidation reactions with biofilms and the pipe material (a cause of corrosion) can occur.

Figure 2.24
Disinfectant reactions occurring within a typical distribution system pipe

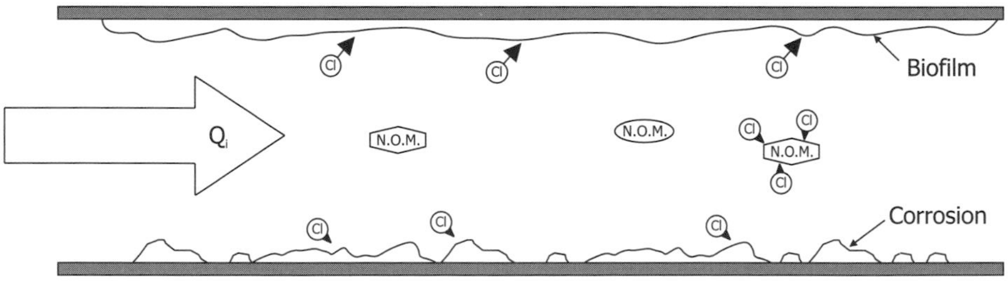

Many disinfectant decay models have been developed to account for these reactions. The first-order decay model has been shown to be sufficiently accurate for most distribution system modeling applications and is well established. Rossman, Clark, and Grayman (1994) proposed a mathematical framework for combining the complex reactions occurring within distribution system pipes. This framework accounts for the physical transport of the disinfectant from the bulk fluid to the pipe wall (mass transfer effects) and the chemical reactions occurring there.

$$\theta(C) = \pm KC \qquad (2.46)$$

where K = overall reaction rate constant (1/T)

Equation 2.46 is a simple first-order reaction ($n = 1$). The reaction rate coefficient K, however, is now a function of the bulk reaction coefficient and the wall reaction coefficient, as indicated in the following equation.

$$K = k_b + \frac{k_w k_f}{R_H(k_w + k_f)} \qquad (2.47)$$

where k_b = bulk reaction coefficient (1/T)
k_w = wall reaction coefficient (L/T)
k_f = mass transfer coefficient, bulk fluid to pipe wall (L/T)
R_H = hydraulic radius of pipeline (L)

The rate that disinfectant decays at the pipe wall depends on how quickly disinfectant is transported to the pipe wall and the speed of the reaction once it is there. The mass transfer coefficient is used to determine the rate at which disinfectant is transported using the dimensionless *Sherwood Number*, along with the molecular diffusivity coefficient (of the constituent in water) and the pipeline diameter.

$$k_f = \frac{S_H d}{D} \qquad (2.48)$$

where S_H = Sherwood number
d = molecular diffusivity of constituent in bulk fluid (L^2/T)
D = pipeline diameter (L)

For stagnant flow conditions ($Re < 1$), the Sherwood number, S_H, is equal to 2.0. For turbulent flow ($Re > 2{,}300$), the Sherwood Number is computed using Equation 2.49.

$$S_H = 0.023 Re^{0.83}\left(\frac{\nu}{d}\right)^{0.333} \qquad (2.49)$$

where Re = Reynolds number
ν = kinematic viscosity of fluid (L^2/T)

For laminar flow conditions ($1 < Re < 2{,}300$), the average Sherwood Number along the length of the pipe can be used. To have laminar flow in a 6-in. (150-mm) pipe, the flow would need to be less than 5 gpm (0.3 l/s) with a velocity of 0.056 ft/s (0.017 m/s). At such flows, head loss would be negligible.

$$S_H = 3.65 + \frac{0.0668\left(\frac{D}{L}\right)(Re)\left(\frac{\nu}{d}\right)}{1 + 0.04\left[\left(\frac{D}{L}\right)Re\left(\frac{\nu}{d}\right)\right]^{2/3}} \qquad (2.50)$$

where L = pipe length (L)

Using the first-order reaction framework developed immediately above, both bulk fluid and pipe wall disinfectant decay reactions can be accounted for. Bulk decay coefficients can be determined experimentally. *Wall decay coefficients*, however, are more difficult to measure and are frequently estimated using disinfectant concentration field measurements and water quality simulation results.

"I don't think it's sanitary to drink from the same footprint."

Formation Reactions. One shortcoming of the first-order reaction model is that it only accounts for the concentration of one reactant. This model is sufficient if only one reactant is being considered. For example, when chlorine residual concentrations are modeled, chlorine is assumed to be the limiting reactant and the other reactants - material at the pipe walls and *natural organic matter* (NOM) - are assumed to be present in excess. The behavior of some *disinfection by-product* (DBP) formation reactions, however, differs from this assumption. NOM, not chlorine, is frequently the limiting reactant. DBP formation is just one example of a generalized class of reactions that can be modeled using a limiting reactant. The reaction term for this class of formation and decay reactions as proposed by Rossman (2000) is shown in Equation 2.51.

$$\theta(C) = \pm k(C_{lim} - C)C^{n-1} \tag{2.51}$$

where C_{lim} = limiting concentration of the reaction (M/L^3)

Other Types of Water Quality Simulations

While the water quality features of individual software packages vary, the most common types of water quality simulations, in addition to the constituent analysis already described, are source trace and water age analyses. The solution methods used in both of these simulations are actually specific applications of the method used in constituent analysis.

Source Trace Analysis. For the sake of reliability, or to simply provide sufficient quantities of water to customers, a utility often uses more than one water supply source. Suppose, for instance, that two treatment plants serve the same distribution system. One plant draws water from a surface source, and the other pulls from an underground aquifer. The raw water qualities from these sources are likely to differ significantly, resulting in quality differences in the finished water as well.

Using a *source trace analysis*, the areas within the distribution system influenced by a particular source can be determined, and, more importantly, areas where mixing of water from different sources has occurred can be identified. The significance of source mixing is dependent upon the quality characteristics of the waters. Sometimes, mixing can reduce the aesthetic qualities of the water (for example, creating cloudiness as solids precipitate, or causing taste and odor problems to develop), and can contribute to disinfectant residual maintenance problems. Source trace analyses are also useful in tracking water quality problems related to storage tanks by tracing water from storage as it is transported through the network.

A source trace analysis is a useful tool for better management of these situations. Specifically, it can be used to determine the percentage of water originating from a particular source for each junction node, tank, and reservoir in the distribution system model. The procedure the software uses for this calculation is a special case of constituent analysis in which the trace originates from the source as a conservative constituent with an output concentration of 100 units. The constituent transport and mixing equations introduced in the beginning of this section are then used to simulate the transport pathways through the network and the influence of transport delays and dilution on the trace constituent concentration. The values computed by the simulation are then read directly as the percentage of water arriving from the source location.

Water Age Analysis. The chemical processes that can affect distribution system water quality are a function of water chemistry and the physical characteristics of the distribution system itself (for example, pipe material and age). More generally, however, these processes occur over time, making residence time in the distribution system a critical factor influencing water quality. The cumulative residence time of water in the system, or *water age*, has come to be regarded as a reliable surrogate for water quality. Water age is of particular concern when quantifying the effect of storage tank turnover on water quality. It is also beneficial for evaluating the loss of disinfectant residual and the formation of disinfection by-products in distribution systems.

The chief advantage of a water age analysis when compared to a constituent analysis is that once the hydraulic model has been calibrated, no additional water quality calibration procedures are required. The water age analysis, however, will not be as precise as a constituent analysis in determining water quality; nevertheless, it is an easy way to leverage the information imbedded in the calibrated hydraulic model. Consider a project in which a utility is analyzing mixing in a tank and its effect on water quality in an area of a network experiencing water quality problems. If a hydraulic model has been developed and adequately calibrated, it can immediately be used to evaluate water age. The water age analysis may indicate that excessively long residence times within the tank are contributing to water quality degradation. Using this information, a more precise analysis can be planned (such as an evaluation of tank hydraulic dynamics and mixing characteristics, or a constituent analysis to determine the impact on disinfectant residuals), and preliminary changes in design or operation can be evaluated.

The water age analysis reports the cumulative residence time for each parcel of water moving through the network. Again, the algorithm the software uses to perform the analysis is a specialized case of constituent analysis. Water entering a network from a source is considered to have an age of zero. The constituent analysis is performed assuming a zero-order reaction with a k value equal to +1 [(l/mg)/s]. Thus, constituent concentration growth is directly proportional to time, and the cumulative residence time along the transport pathways in the network is numerically summed.

Using the descriptions of water quality transport and reaction dynamics provided here, and the different types of water quality-related simulations available in modern software packages, water quality in the distribution system can be accurately predicted. Water quality modeling can be used to help improve the performance of distribution system modifications meant to reduce hydraulic residence times, and as a tool for improving the management of disinfectant residuals and other water quality-related operations. Continuing advancements in technology combined with more stringent regulations on quality at the customer's tap are motivating an increasing number of utilities to begin using the powerful water quality modeling capabilities already available to them.

REFERENCES

Almeida, A. B., and Koelle, E. (1992). *Fluid Transients in Pipe Networks*. Elsevier Applied Science, Southampton, UK.

ASCE. (1975). *Pressure Pipeline Design for Water and Wastewater*. ASCE, New York, New York.

ASCE/WEF. (1982). *Gravity Sanitary Sewer Design and Construction*. ASCE, Reston, Virginia.

ASCE Committee on Pipeline Planning. (1992). *Pressure Pipeline Design for Water and Wastewater*. ASCE, Reston, Virginia.

Bernoulli, D. (1738). *Hydrodynamica*. Argentorati.

Bhave, P. R. (1991). *Analysis of Flow in Water Distribution Networks*. Technomics, Lancaster, Pennsylvania.

Boccelli, D. L., Tryby, M. E., Uber, J. G., Rossman, L. A., Zierolf, M. L., and Polycarpou, M. M. (1998). "Optimal Scheduling of Booster Disinfection in Water Distribution Systems." *Journal of Water Resources Planning and Management*, ASCE, 124(2), 99.

Bosserman, B. E., (2000). "Pump System Hydraulic Design." *Water Distribution System Handbook*, Mays, L. W., ed., McGraw-Hill, New York, New York.

Chaudhry, M. H. (1987). *Applied Hydraulic Transients*. Van Nostrand Reinhold, New York.

Clark, R. M., and Grayman, W. M. (1998). *Modeling Water Quality in Distribution Systems*. AWWA, Denver, Colorado.

Crane Company (1972). *Flow of Fluids through Valves and Fittings*. Crane Co., New York, New York.

Cross, H. (1936). "Analysis of Flow in Networks of Conduits or Conductors." *Univ. Of Illinois Experiment Station Bulletin No. 286*, Department of Civil Engineering, University of Illinois, Champaign Urbana, Illinois.

Grayman, W. M., Deininger, R. A., Green, A., Boulos, P. F., Bowcock, R. W., and Godwin, C. C. (1996). "Water Quality and Mixing Models for Tanks and Reservoirs." *Journal of the American Water Works Association*, 88(7).

Grayman, W. M.; Rossman, L. A., and Geldreich, E. E. (2000). "Water Quality." *Water Distribution Systems Handbook*, Mays, L. W., ed., McGraw-Hill, New York, New York.

Hydraulic Institute (2000). *Pump Standards*. Parsippany, New Jersey.

Idelchik, I. E. (1999). *Handbook of Hydraulic Resistance*. 3rd edition. Begell House, New York, New York.

Karney, B. W. (2000). "Hydraulics of Pressurized Flow." *Water Distribution Systems Handbook*, Mays, L.W., ed., McGraw-Hill, New York.

Lamont, P. A. (1981). "Common Pipe Flow Formulas Compared with the Theory of Roughness." *Journal of the American Water Works Association*, 73(5), 274.

Lansey, K., and Mays, L. W. (2000). "Hydraulics of Water Distribution Systems." *Water Distribution Systems Handbook*, Mays, L. W., ed., McGraw-Hill, New York, New York.

Larock, B. E., Jeppson, R. W., and Watters, G. Z. (1999). *Handbook of Pipeline Systems*. CRC Press, Boca Raton, Florida.

Karassik, I. J., ed. (1976). *Pump Handbook*. McGraw-Hill, New York, New York.

Martin, C. S. (2000). "Hydraulic Transient Design for Pipeline Systems." *Water Distribution Systems Handbook*, Mays, L.W., ed., McGraw-Hill, New York, New York.

Mays, L. W., ed. (1999). *Hydraulic Design Handbook*. McGraw-Hill, New York, New York.

Miller, D. S. (1978). *Internal Flow Systems*. BHRA Fluid Engineering, Bedford, United Kingdom.

Moody, L. F. (1944). "Friction Factors for Pipe Flow." *Transactions of the American Society of Mechanical Engineers*, Vol. 66.

Nikuradse (1932). "Gestezmassigkeiten der Turbulenten Stromung in Glatten Rohren." *VDI-Forschungsh*, No. 356 (in German).

Rossman, L. A., Clark, R. M., and Grayman, W. M. (1994). "Modeling Chlorine Residuals in Drinking Water Distribution Systems." *Journal of Environmental Engineering*, ASCE, 1210(4), 803.

Rossman, L.A. (2000). *EPANET Users Manual*. Risk Reduction Engineering Laboratory, U.S. Environmental Protection Agency, Cincinnati, Ohio.

Sanks, R. L., ed. (1998). *Pumping Station Design*. 2nd edition, Butterworth, London, UK.

Streeter, V. L., Wylie, B. E., and Bedford, K. W. (1998). *Fluid Mechanics*. 9th edition, WCB/McGraw-Hill, Boston, Massachusetts.

Swamee, P. K., and Jain, A. K. (1976). "Explicit Equations for Pipe Flow Problems." *Journal of Hydraulic Engineering*, ASCE, 102(5), 657.

Thorley, A. R. D. (1991). *Fluid Transients in Pipeline Systems*. D&L George Ltd., UK.

Todini, E., and Pilati, S. (1987). "A Gradient Method for the Analysis of Pipe Networks." *Proceedings of the International Conference on Computer Applications for Water Supply and Distribution*, Leicester Polytechnic, UK.

Walski, T. M. (1984). *Analysis of Water Distribution Systems*. Van Nostrand Reinhold, New York, New York.

Williams, G. S., and Hazen, A. (1920). *Hydraulic Tables*. John Wiley & Sons, New York, New York.

Wylie, E. B., and Streeter, V. L. (1993). *Fluid Transients in Systems*. Prentice-Hall, New York.

DISCUSSION TOPICS AND PROBLEMS

Earn CEUs

Read Chapters 1 and 2 and complete the problems. Submit your work to Haestad Methods and earn up to 1.5 CEUs. See *Continuing Education Units* on page xiii for more information, or visit www.haestad.com/wdm-ceus/.

2.1 Find the viscosity of the fluid contained between the two square plates shown in Figure 2.25. The top plate is moving at a velocity of 3 ft/s.

Figure 2.25

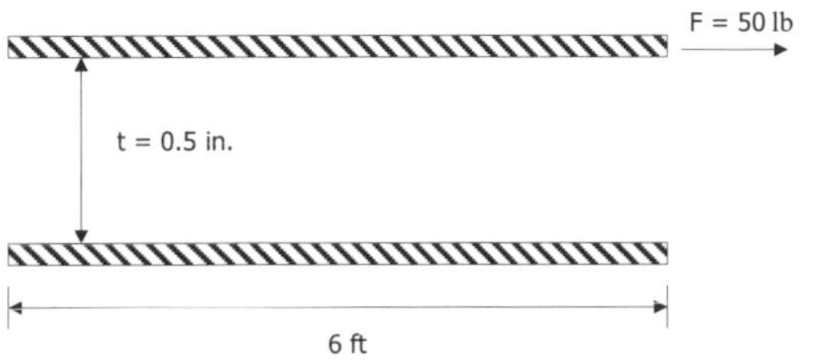

2.2 Find the force P required to pull the 150 mm circular shaft in Figure 2.26 through the sleeve at a velocity of 1.5 m/s. The fluid between the shaft and the sleeve is water at a temperature of 15°C.

Figure 2.26

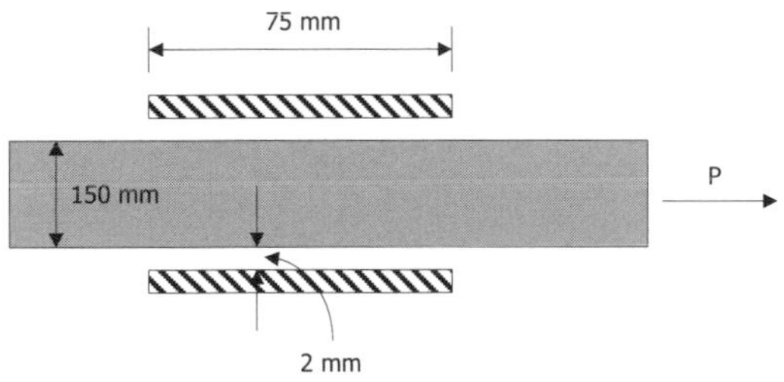

2.3 Find the pressure at the base of a container of water having a depth of 15 m.

2.4 How high is the water level from the base of an elevated storage tank if the pressure at the base of the tank is 45 psi?

2.5 Water having a temperature of 65°F is flowing through a 6-in. ductile iron main at a rate of 300 gpm. Is the flow laminar, turbulent, or transitional?

2.6 What type of flow do you think normally exists in water distribution systems: laminar, turbulent, or transitional? Justify your selection with sound reasoning.

2.7 What is the total head at point A in the system shown in Figure 2.27 if the flow through the pipeline is 1,000 gpm? What is the head loss in feet between point A and point B?

Figure 2.27

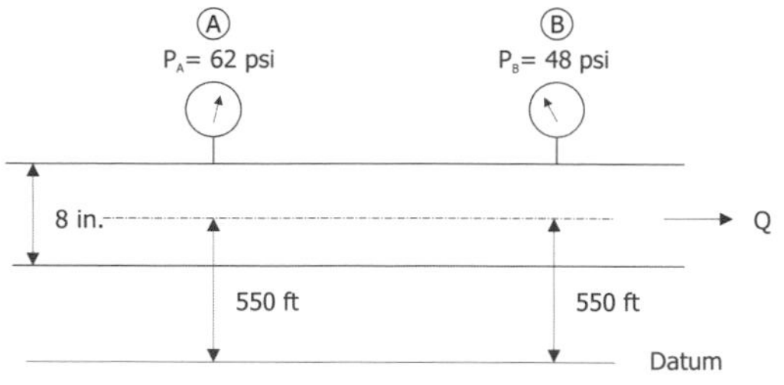

2.8 For the piping system shown in Figure 2.27, what would the elevation at point B have to be in order for the reading on the two pressure gages to be the same?

2.9 Assuming that there are no head losses through the Venturi meter shown in Figure 2.28, what is the pressure reading in the throat section of the Venturi? Assume that the discharge through the meter is 158 l/s.

Figure 2.28

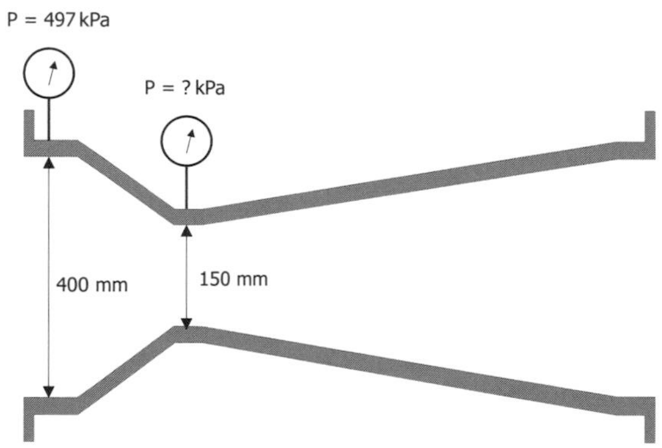

2.10 What is the head loss through a 10-in. diameter concrete water main 2,500 ft in length if water at 60°F is flowing through the line at a rate of 1,250 gpm? Solve using the Darcy-Weisbach formula.

2.11 For Problem 2.10, what is the flow through the line if the head loss is 32 ft? Solve using the Darcy-Weisbach formula.

2.12 Find the length of a pipeline that has the following characteristics: Q=41 l/s, D=150 mm, Hazen Williams C=110, H_L=7.6 m.

2.13 For the pipeline shown in Figure 2.27, what is the Hazen-Williams C-factor if the distance between the two pressure gages is 725 ft and the flow is 1,000 gpm?

2.14 *English Units* - Compute the pipe resistance coefficient, K_P, for the following pipelines.

Length (ft)	Diameter (in.)	Hazen-Williams C-factor	Pipe Resistance Coefficient (K_P)
1,200	12	120	
500	4	90	
75	3	75	
3,500	10	110	
1,750	8	105	

SI Units - Compute the pipe resistance coefficient, K_P, for the following pipelines.

Length (m)	Diameter (mm)	Hazen-Williams C-factor	Pipe Resistance Coefficient (K_P)
366	305	120	
152	102	90	
23	76	75	
1067	254	110	
533	203	105	

2.15 *English Units* - Compute the minor loss term, K_M, for the fittings shown in the table below.

Type of Fitting/Flow Condition	Minor Loss Coefficient	Pipe Size (in.)	Minor Loss Term (K_M)
Gate Valve - 50% Open	4.8	8	
Tee - Line Flow	0.4	12	
90° Mitered Bend	0.8	10	
Fire Hydrant	4.5	6	

SI Units - Compute the minor loss term, K_M, for the fittings shown in the table below.

Type of Fitting/Flow Condition	Minor Loss Coefficient	Pipe Size (mm)	Minor Loss Term (K_M)
Gate Valve - 50% Open	4.8	200	
Tee - Line Flow	0.4	300	
90° Mitered Bend	0.8	250	
Fire Hydrant	4.5	150	

2.16 *English Units* - Determine the pressures at the following locations in a water distribution system, assuming that the HGL and ground elevations at the locations are known.

Node Label	HGL (ft)	Elevation (ft)	Pressure (psi)
J-1	550.6	423.5	
J-6	485.3	300.5	
J-23	532.6	500.0	
J-5	521.5	423.3	
J-12	515.0	284.0	

SI Units - Determine the pressures at the following locations in a water distribution system, assuming that the HGL and ground elevations at the locations are known.

Node Label	HGL (m)	Elevation (m)	Pressure (kPa)
J-1	167.8	129.1	
J-6	147.9	91.6	
J-23	162.3	152.4	
J-5	159.0	129.0	
J-12	157.0	86.6	

2.17 Using the concept of Conservation of Mass, is continuity maintained at the junction node shown in Figure 2.29?

Figure 2.29

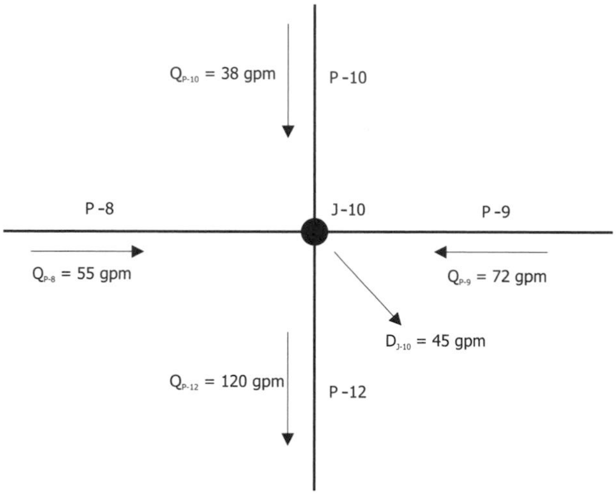

2.18 Find the magnitude and direction of the flow through pipe P-9 so that continuity is maintained at node J-10 in Figure 2.30.

Figure 2.30

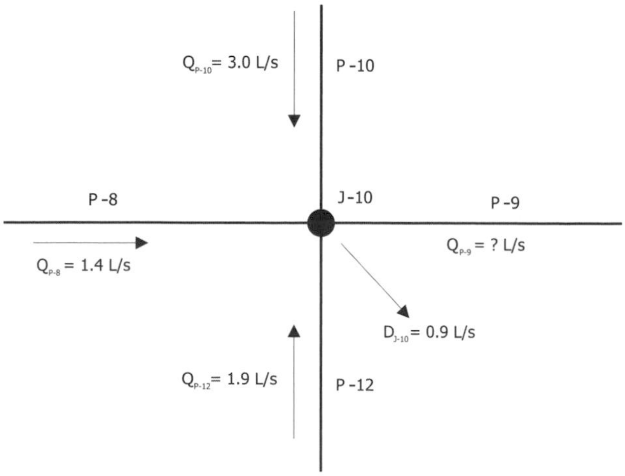

2.19 Does Conservation of Energy around a loop apply to the loop shown in the Figure 2.31? Why or why not? The total head loss (sum of friction losses and minor losses) in each pipe and the direction of flow are shown in the figure.

Figure 2.31

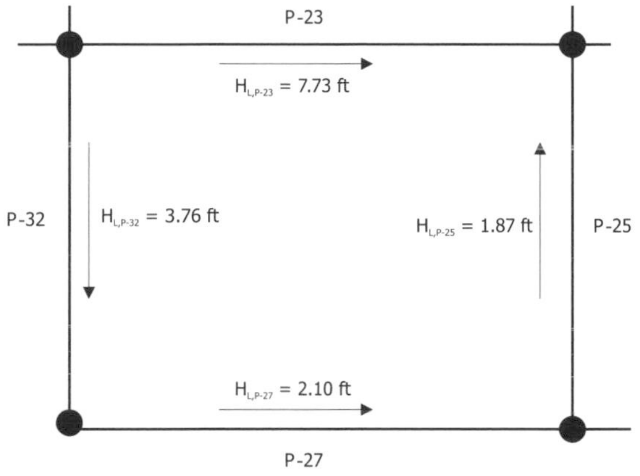

2.20 Does Conservation of Energy apply to the system shown in the Figure 2.32? Data describing the physical characteristics of each pipe are presented in the table below. Assume that there are no minor losses in this loop.

Figure 2.32

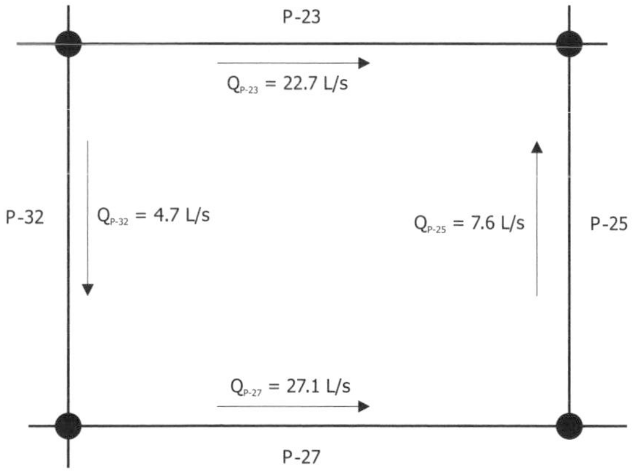

Pipe Label	Length (m)	Diameter (mm)	Hazen-Williams C-factor
P-23	381.0	305	120
P-25	228.6	203	115
P-27	342.9	254	120
P-32	253.0	152	105

2.21 Find the discharge through the system shown in Figure 2.33. Compute friction loss using the Hazen-Williams equation.

Figure 2.33

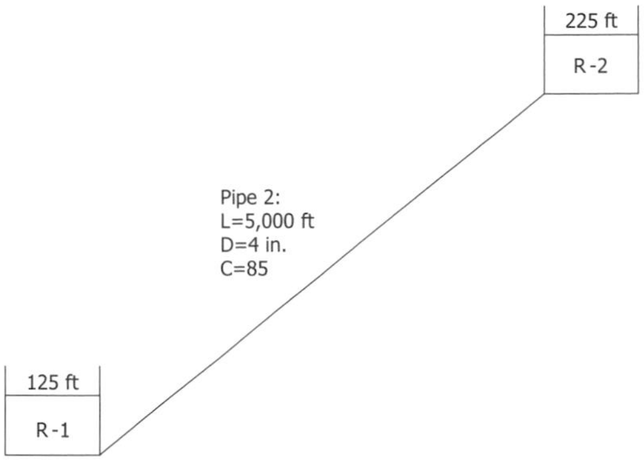

2.22 Find the pump head needed to deliver water from reservoir R-1 to reservoir R-2 in Figure 2.34 at a rate of 70.8 l/s. Compute friction losses using the Hazen-Williams equation.

Figure 2.34

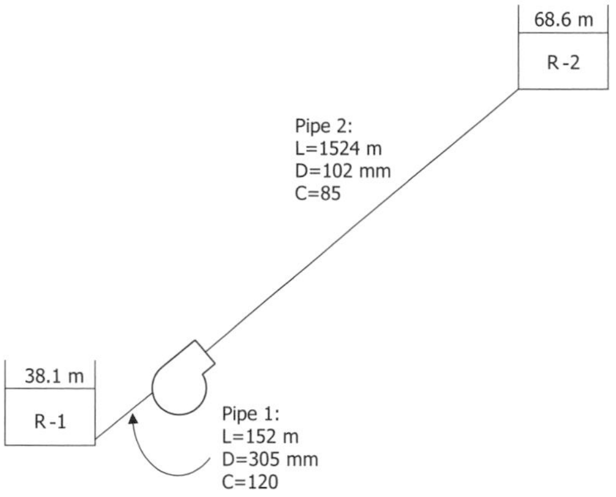

2.23 Compute the age of water at the end of a 12-in. pipe that is 1,500 ft in length and has a flow of 900 gpm. The age of the water when it enters the pipeline is 7.2 hours.

2.24 Suppose that a 102-mm pipe is used to serve a small cluster of homes at the end of a long street. If the length of the pipe is 975 m, what is the age of water leaving it if the water had an age of 6.3 hours when entering the line? Assume that the water use is 1.6 l/s.

2.25 Given the data in the tables below, what is the average age of the water leaving junction node J-4 shown in Figure 2.25? What is the flow rate through pipe P-4? What is the average age of the water arriving at node J-5 through pipe P-4? Fill in your answers in the tables provided.

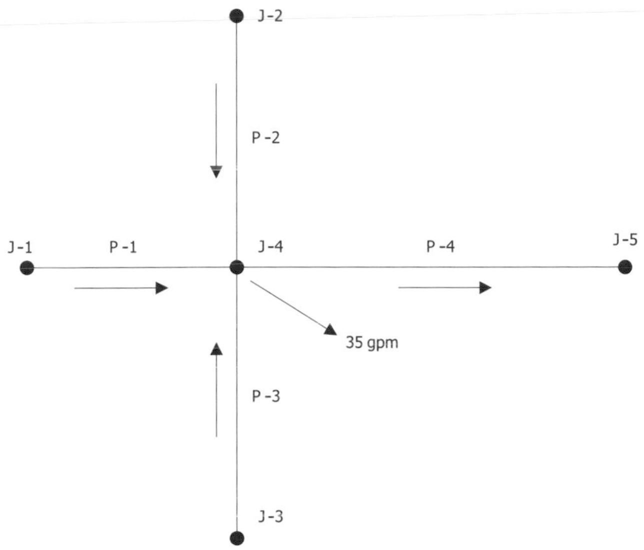

Pipe Label	Flow (gpm)	Length (ft)	Diameter (in)
P-1	75	1,650	10
P-2	18	755	8
P-3	23	820	6
P-4		2,340	10

Node Label	Average Age (hours)
J-1	5.2
J-2	24.3
J-3	12.5
J-4	
J-5	

2.26 What will be the concentration of chlorine in water samples taken from a swimming pool after 7 days if the initial chlorine concentration in the pool was 1.5 mg/l? Bottle tests performed on the pool water indicate that the first-order reaction rate is -0.134 day^{-1}.

2.27 Do you think that the actual reaction rate coefficient for water in the swimming pool described above (i.e., the water being considered remains in the pool, and is not being stored under laboratory conditions) would be equal to -0.134 day^{-1}? Suggest some factors that might cause the actual reaction rate to differ. Would these factors most likely cause the actual reaction rate to be greater than or less than -0.134 day^{-1}?

2.28 For the system presented in Problem 2.25, what is the concentration of a constituent leaving node J-4 (assume it is a conservative constituent)? The constituent concentration is 0.85 mg/L in pipe P-1, 0.50 mg/l in pipe P-2, and 1.2 mg/l in pipe P-3.

2.29 What is the fluoride concentration at the end of a 152-mm diameter pipeline 762 m in length if the fluoride concentration at the start of the line is 1.3 mg/l? Fluoride is a conservative species; that is, it does not decay over time. Ignoring dispersion, if there is initially no fluoride in the pipe and it is introduced at the upstream end at a 2.0 mg/l concentration, when will this concentration be reached at the end of the line if the flow through the pipe is 15.8 l/s? Assume that there are no other junction nodes along the length of this pipe.

CHAPTER

3

Assembling a Model

As discussed in Chapter 1, a water distribution model is a mathematical description of a real-world system. Before building a model, it is necessary to gather information describing the network. In this chapter, we will introduce and discuss sources of data used in constructing models.

The latter part of the chapter covers model skeletonization. *Skeletonization* is the process of simplifying the real system for model representation, and it involves making decisions about the level of detail to be included.

3.1 MAPS AND RECORDS

There are many potential sources for obtaining the data required to generate a water distribution model, and the availability of these sources varies dramatically from utility to utility. Some of the most commonly used resources, including system maps, as-built drawings, and electronic data files, are discussed in the following sections.

System Maps

System maps are typically the most useful documents for gaining an overall understanding of a water distribution system, since they illustrate a wide variety of valuable system characteristics. System maps may include such information as:

- Pipe alignment, connectivity, material, diameter, etc.
- The locations of other system components, such as tanks and valves
- Pressure zone boundaries
- Elevations

- Miscellaneous notes or references for tank characteristics
- Background information, such as the locations of roadways, streams, planning zones, etc.
- Other utilities

Topographic Maps

A *topographic map* uses sets of lines called *contours* to indicate elevations of the ground surface. Contour lines represent a contiguous set of points that are at the same elevation, and can be thought of as the outline of a horizontal "slice" of the ground surface. Figure 3.1 illustrates the cross-sectional and topographic views of a sphere, and Figure 3.2 shows a portion of an actual topographic map. Topographic maps are often referred to by the contour interval that they present, such as a 20-foot topographic map or a 1-meter contour map.

Figure 3.1
Topographic representation of a hemisphere

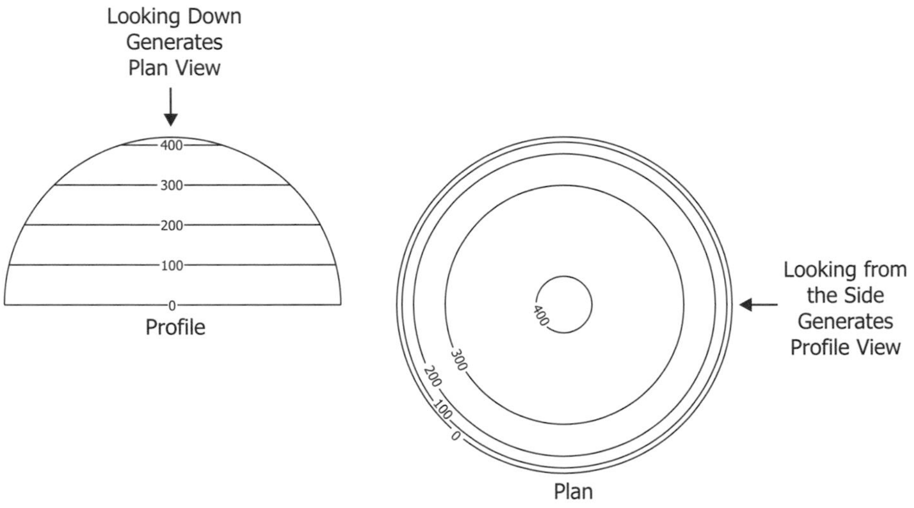

By superimposing a topographic map on a map of the network model, it is possible to interpolate the ground elevations at junction nodes and other locations throughout the system. Of course, the smaller the contour interval, the more precisely the elevations can be estimated. If available topographic maps cannot provide the level of precision needed, other sources of elevation data need to be considered.

Topographic maps are also available in the form of *Digital Elevation Models (DEMs)*, which can be used to electronically interpolate elevations. The results of the DEM are only as accurate as the underlying topographic data on which they are based; thus, it is possible to calculate elevations to a large display precision but with no additional accuracy.

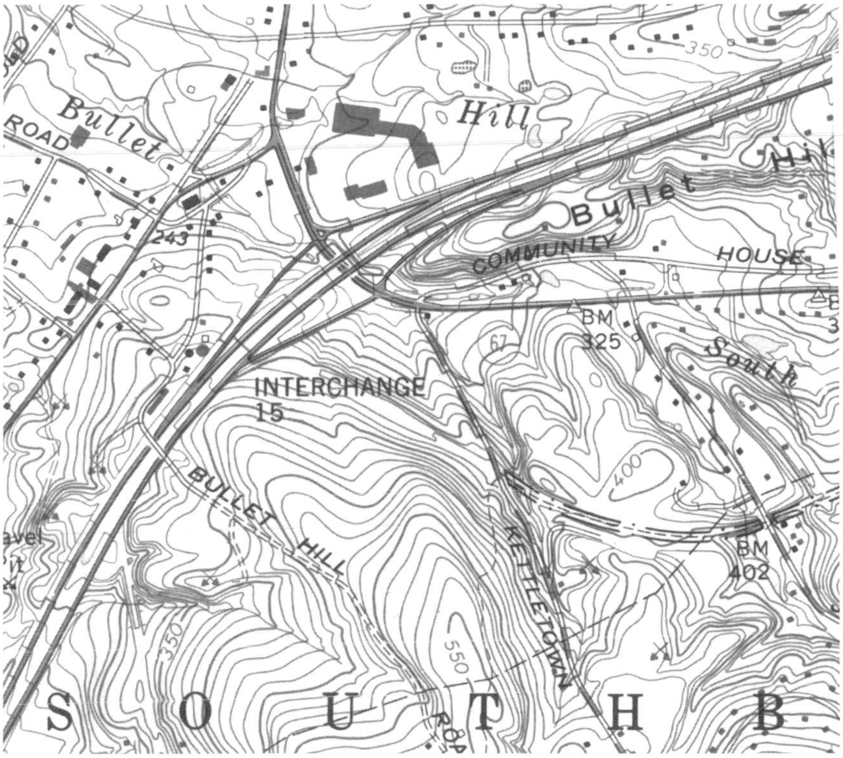

Figure 3.2
Typical topographic map

As-Built Drawings

Site restrictions and on-the-fly changes often result in differences between original design plans and the actual constructed system. As a result, most utilities perform post-construction surveys and generate a set of *as-built* or *record drawings* for the purpose of documenting the system exactly as it was built. In some cases, an inspector's notes may even be used as a supplemental form of documentation. As-built drawings can be especially helpful in areas where a fine level of precision is required for pipe lengths, fitting types and locations, elevations, and so forth.

As-built drawings can also provide reliable descriptions of other system components such as storage tanks and pumping stations. There may be a complete set of drawings for a single tank, or the tank plans could be included as part of a larger construction project.

Electronic Maps and Records

Many water distribution utilities have some form of electronic representation of their systems in formats that may vary from a non-graphical database, to a graphics-only *Computer Aided Drafting (CAD)* drawing, to a *Geographic Information System (GIS)* that combines graphics and data.

Non-Graphical Data. It is common to find at least some electronic data in non-graphical formats, such as a tracking and inventory database, or even a legacy text-based model. These sources of data can be quite helpful in expediting the process of model construction. Even so, care needs to be taken to ensure that the network topology is correct, since a simple typographic error in a non-graphical network can be difficult to detect.

Computer-Aided Drafting. The rise of computer technology has led to many improvements in all aspects of managing a water distribution utility, and mapping is no exception. CAD systems make it much easier to plug in survey data, combine data from different sources, and otherwise maintain and update maps faster and more reliably than ever before.

Even for systems having only paper maps, many utilities go through the process of *digitizing* those maps to convert them to an electronic drawing format. Traditionally, digitizing has been a process of tracing over paper maps with special computer peripherals, called a digitizing tablet and puck (Figure 3.3). A paper map is attached to the tablet, and the drafts person uses crosshairs on the puck to point at locations on the paper. Through magnetic or optical techniques, the tablet creates an equivalent point at the appropriate location in the CAD drawing. As long as the tablet is calibrated correctly, it will automatically account for rotation, skew, and scale.

Figure 3.3
A typical digitizing tablet

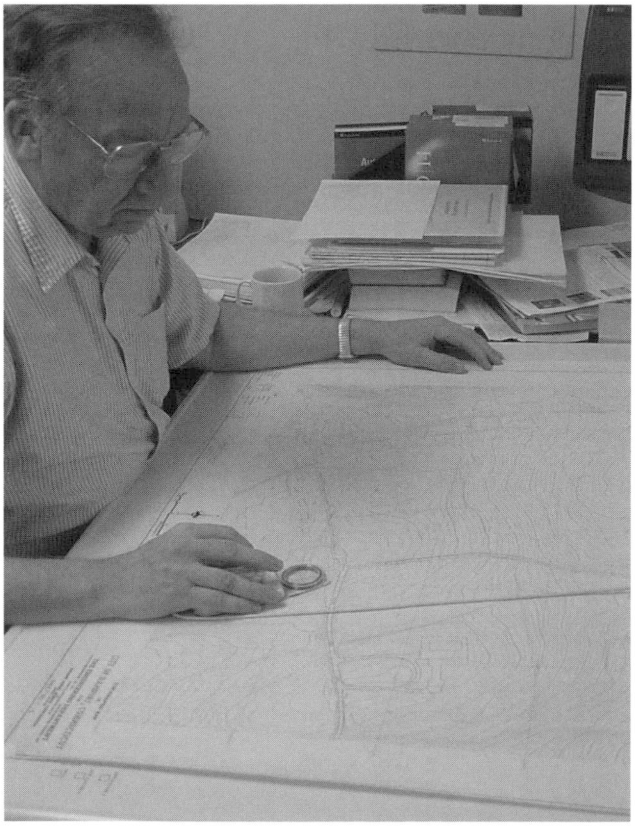

Another form of digitizing is called *heads-up digitizing* (Figure 3.4). This method involves scanning a paper map into a raster electronic format (such as a bitmap), bringing it into the background of a CAD system, and electronically tracing over it on a different layer. The term "heads-up" is used because the draftsman remains focused on the computer screen rather than a digitizing tablet.

Figure 3.4
Network model overlaid on aerial photograph

Geographic Information Systems. A Geographic Information System (GIS) is a computer-based tool for mapping and analyzing objects and events that happen on earth. GIS technology integrates common database operations such as query and statistical analysis with the unique visualization and geographic analysis benefits offered by maps (ESRI, 2001). Because a GIS stores data on thematic layers linked together geographically, disparate data sources can be combined to determine relationships between data and to synthesize new information.

GIS can be used for tasks such as *proximity analysis* (identifying customers within a certain distance of a particular node), *overlay analysis* (determining all junctions that are completely within a particular zoning area), *network analysis* (identifying all households impacted by a water main break), and *visualization* (displaying and communicating master plans graphically). With a hydraulic model that links closely to a GIS, the benefits can extend well beyond just the process of building the model, and can include skeletonization, demand generalization, and numerous other operations.

3.2 MODEL REPRESENTATION

The concept of a *network* is fundamental to a water distribution model. The network contains all of the various components of the system, and defines how those elements are interconnected. Networks are comprised of *nodes*, which represent features at specific locations within the system, and *links*, which define relationships between nodes.

Network Elements

Water distribution models have many different types of nodal elements, including junction nodes where pipes connect, storage tank and reservoir nodes, pump nodes, and control valve nodes. Models use link elements to describe the pipes connecting these nodes. Also, elements such as valves and pumps are sometimes classified as links rather than nodes. Table 3.1 lists each model element, the type of element used to represent it in the model, and the primary modeling purpose.

Table 3.1 Common network modeling elements

Element	Type	Primary Modeling Purpose
Reservoir	Node	Provides water to the system
Tank	Node	Stores excess water within the system, and releases that water at times of high usage
Junction	Node	Removes (demand) or adds (inflow) water from/to the system
Pipe	Link	Conveys water from one node to another
Pump	Node or Link	Raises the hydraulic grade to overcome elevation differences and friction losses
Control Valve	Node or Link	Controls flow or pressure in the system based on specified criteria

Naming Conventions (Element Labels). Since models may contain tens of thousands of elements, naming conventions are an important consideration in making the relationship between real-world components and model elements as obvious as possible (Figure 3.5). Some models only allow numeric numbering of elements, but most modern models support at least some level of alphanumeric labeling (for example "J-1," "Tank 5," or "West Side Pump A").

Naming conventions should mirror the way the modeler thinks about the particular network by using a mixture of prefixes, suffixes, numbers, and descriptive text. In general, labels should be as short as possible to avoid cluttering a drawing or report, but should include enough information to identify the element. For example, a naming convention might include a prefix for the element type, another prefix to indicate the pressure zone or map sheet, a sequential number, and a descriptive suffix.

Of course, modelers can choose to use some creativity, but it is important to realize that a name that seems obvious today may be baffling to future users.

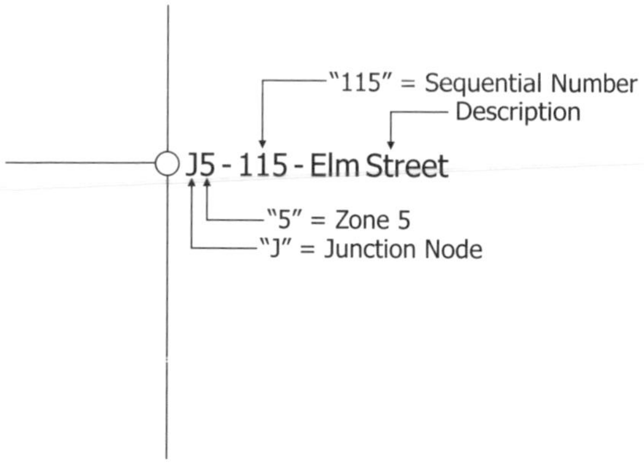

Figure 3.5
Schematic junction with naming convention

Boundary Nodes. A *boundary node* is a network element used to represent locations with known hydraulic grade elevations. A boundary condition imposes a requirement within the network that simulated flows entering or exiting the system agree with that hydraulic grade. Reservoirs (also called *fixed grade nodes*) and tanks are common examples of boundary nodes.

Every model must have at least one boundary node so that there is a reference point for the hydraulic grade. In addition, every node must maintain at least one path back to a boundary node so that its hydraulic grade can be calculated. When a node becomes disconnected from a boundary (as when pipes and valves are closed), it can result in an error condition that needs to be addressed by the modeler.

Network Topology

The most fundamental data requirement is to have an accurate representation of the network *topology*, which details what the elements are and how they are interconnected. If a model does not faithfully duplicate real-world layout (for example, the model pipe connects two nodes that are not really connected), then the model will never accurately depict real-world performance, regardless of the quality of the remaining data.

System maps are generally good sources of topological information, typically including data on pipe diameters, lengths, materials, and connections with other pipes. There are situations in which the modeler must use caution, however, because maps may be imperfect or unclear.

False Intersections. Just because mains appear to cross on a map does not necessarily mean that there is a hydraulic connection at that location. As illustrated in Figure 3.6, it is possible for one main to pass over the other (called a *crossover*). Modeling this location as an intersecting junction node would be incorrect, and could result in serious model inaccuracies. Note that some GISs automatically assign nodes where pipes cross, which may not be hydraulically correct.

When pipes are connected in the field via a *bypass* (as illustrated in Figure 3.6), the junction node should only be included in the model if the bypass line is open. Since the choice to include or omit a junction in the model based on the open or closed status of a bypass in the field is somewhat difficult to control, it is recommended that the bypass itself be included in the model. As a result, the modeler can more easily open or close the bypass in accordance with the real system.

Figure 3.6
Pipe crossover and crossover with bypass

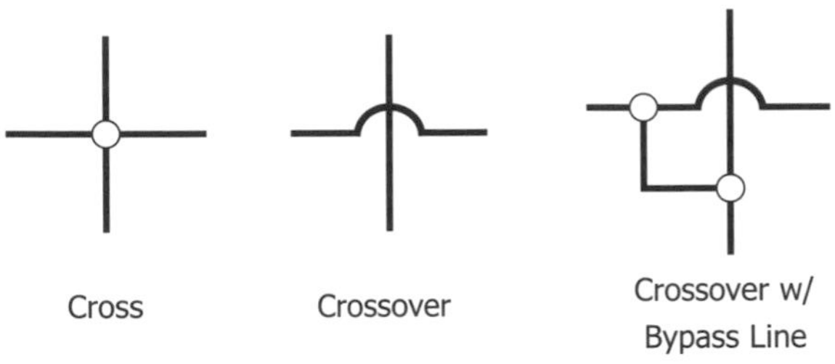

Converting CAD Drawings into Models. While paper maps can sometimes falsely make it appear as though there is a pipe intersection, CAD maps can have the opposite problem. CAD drawings are often not created with a hydraulic model in mind; thus, lines representing pipes may visually appear to be connected on a large-scale plot, but upon closer inspection of the CAD drawing, the lines are not actually touching. Consider Figure 3.7, which demonstrates three distinct conditions that may result in a misinterpretation of the topology:

- **T-intersections -** Are there supposed to be three intersecting pipes or two non-intersecting pipes? The drawing indicates that there is no intersection, but this could easily be a drafting error.

- **Crossing pipes -** Are there supposed to be four intersecting pipes, or two non-intersecting pipes?
- **Nearly connecting line endpoints -** Are the two pipes truly non-intersecting?

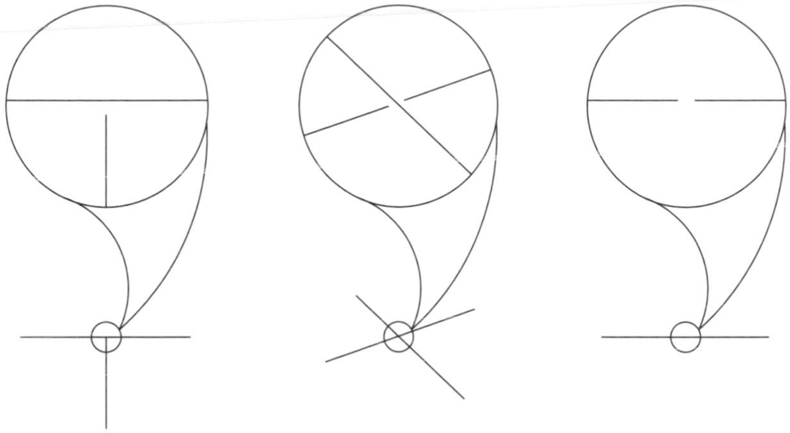

Figure 3.7
Common CAD conversion errors

Automated conversion from CAD drawing elements to model elements can save time, but (as with any automated process) the modeler needs to be aware of the potential pitfalls involved and should review the end result. Some models assist in the review process by highlighting areas with potential connectivity errors. The possibility of difficult to detect errors still remains, however, persuading some modelers to trace over CAD drawings when creating model elements.

3.3 RESERVOIRS

The term *reservoir* has a specific meaning with regard to water distribution system modeling that may differ slightly from the use of the word in normal water distribution construction and operation. A reservoir represents a boundary node in a model that can supply or accept water with such a large capacity that the hydraulic grade of the reservoir is unaffected and remains constant. It is an infinite source, which means that it can theoretically handle any inflow or outflow rate, for any length of time, without running dry or overflowing. In reality, there is no such thing as a true infinite source. For modeling purposes, however, there are situations where inflows and outflows have little or no effect on the hydraulic grade at a node.

Reservoirs are used to model any source of water where the hydraulic grade is controlled by factors other than the water usage rate. Lakes, groundwater wells, and clearwells at water treatment plants are often represented as reservoirs in water distribution models. For modeling purposes, a municipal system that purchases water from a bulk water vendor may model the connection to the vendor's supply as a reservoir (assuming that the vendor maintains a constant hydraulic grade at the connection regardless of demands, which is frequently not the case).

For a reservoir, the two pieces of information required are the hydraulic grade line (water surface elevation) and the water quality. By model definition, storage is not a concern for reservoirs, so no volumetric storage data is needed.

3.4 TANKS

A *storage tank* is also a boundary node, but unlike a reservoir, the hydraulic grade line of a tank fluctuates according to the inflow and outflow of water. Tanks have a finite storage volume, and it is possible to completely fill or completely exhaust that storage (although most real systems are designed and operated to avoid such occurrences). Storage tanks are present in most real-world distribution systems, and the relationship between an actual tank and its model counterpart is typically straightforward.

Figure 3.8
Storage tanks

For steady-state runs, the tank is viewed as a known hydraulic grade elevation, and the model calculates how fast water is flowing into or out of the tank given that HGL. Given the same HGL setting, the tank is hydraulically identical to a reservoir for a steady-state run. In extended period simulation (EPS) models, the water level in the tank is allowed to vary over time. To track how a tank's HGL changes, the relationship between water surface elevation and storage volume must be defined. Figure 3.9 illustrates this relationship for various tank shapes. For cylindrical tanks, developing this relationship is a simple matter of identifying the diameter of the tank, but for non-cylindrical tanks it can be more challenging to express the tank's characteristics.

Some models do not support non-cylindrical tanks, forcing the modeler to approximate the tank by determining an equivalent diameter based on the tank's height and capacity. This approximation, of course, has the potential to introduce significant errors in hydraulic grade. Fortunately, most models do support non-cylindrical tanks, although the exact set of data required varies from model to model.

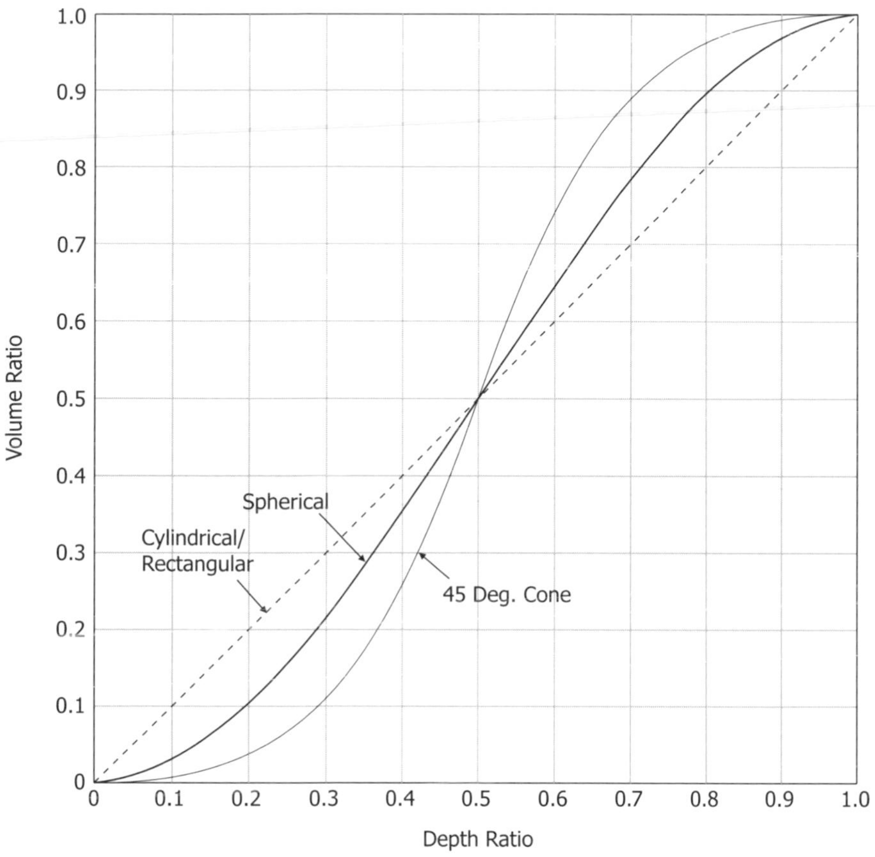

Figure 3.9
Volume versus level curves for various tank shapes

Regardless of the shape of the tank, several elevations are important for modeling purposes. The *maximum* elevation represents the highest fill level of the tank, and is usually determined by the setting of the altitude valve if the tank is equipped with one. The *overflow* elevation, the elevation at which the tank begins to overflow, is slightly higher. Similarly, the *minimum* elevation is the lowest the water level in the tank should ever be. A *base* or *reference* elevation is a datum from which tank levels are measured.

The HGL in a tank can be referred to as an absolute *elevation* or a relative *level*, depending on the datum used. For example, a modeler working near the "Mile High" city of Denver, Colorado could specify a tank's base elevation as the datum, and then work with HGLs that are relative to that datum. Alternatively, the modeler could work with absolute elevations that are in the thousands of feet. The choice of whether to use absolute elevations or relative tank levels is a matter of personal preference. Figure 3.10 illustrates these important tank elevation conventions when modeling tanks. Notice that when using relative tank levels, it is possible to have different values for the same level, depending on the datum selected.

Water storage tanks can be classified by construction material (welded steel, bolted steel, reinforced concrete, prestressed concrete), shape (cylindrical, spherical, torroidal, rectangular), style (elevated, standpipe, ground, buried), and ownership (utility, private) (Walski, 2000). However, for pipe network modeling, the most important classification is whether or not the tank "floats on the system." A tank is said to *float* on the system if the hydraulic grade elevation inside the tank is the same as the HGL in the water distribution system immediately outside of the tank. With tanks, there are really three situations that a modeler can encounter:

1. Tank that floats on the system with a free surface;
2. Pressure (hydropneumatic) tank that floats on the system;
3. *Pumped storage* in which water must be pumped from a tank.

Figure 3.10
Important tank elevations

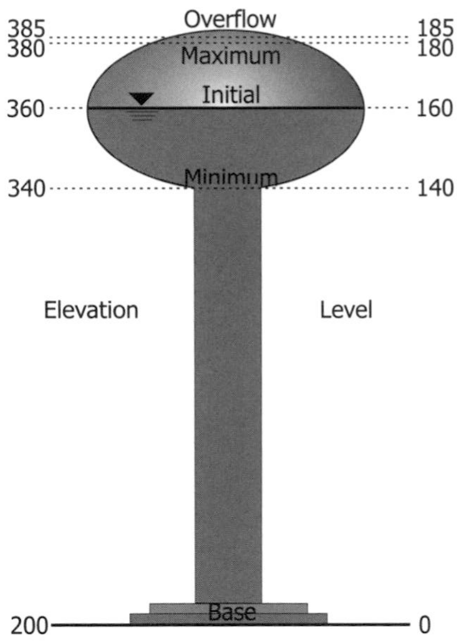

Figure 3.11 shows that elevated tanks, standpipes, and hydropneumatic tanks float on the system because their HGL is the same as that of the system. Ground tanks and buried tanks may or may not float on the system, depending on their elevation. If the HGL in one of these tanks is below the HGL in the system, water must be pumped from the tank, resulting in pumped storage.

A tank with a free surface floating on the system is the simplest and most common type. The pumped storage tank needs a pump to deliver water from the tank to the distribution system and a control valve (usually modeled as a pressure sustaining valve) to gradually fill the tank without seriously affecting pressure in the surrounding system.

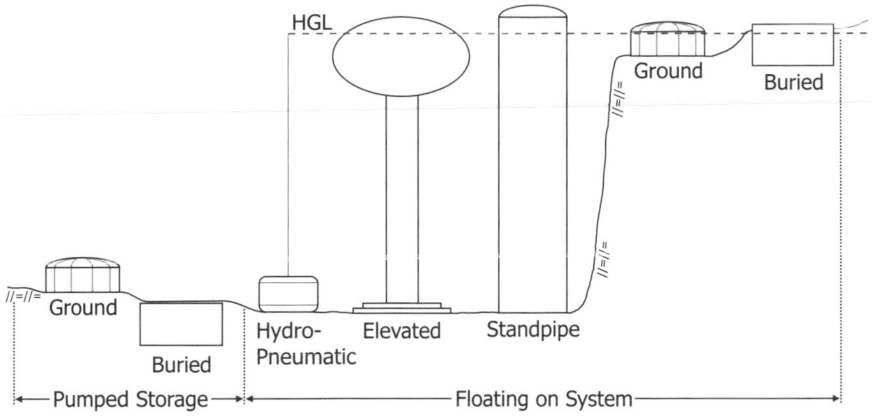

Figure 3.11
Relationship between floating, pressurized, and pumped tanks

Hydropneumatic Tanks. In most tanks, the water surface elevation in the tank equals the HGL in the tank. In the case of a pressure tank, however, the HGL is higher than the tank's water surface. Pressure tanks, also called *hydropneumatic tanks,* are partly full of compressed air. Because the water in the tank is pressurized, the HGL is higher than the water surface elevation, as reflected in Equation 3.1.

$$HGL = C_f P + Z \tag{3.1}$$

where HGL = HGL of water in tank (ft, m)
P = pressure recorded at tank (psi, kPa)
Z = elevation of pressure gage (ft, m)
C_f = unit conversion factor (2.31 English, 0.102 SI)

In steady-state models, a hydropneumatic tank can be represented by a tank or reservoir having this HGL. In EPS models, the tank must be represented by an equivalent free surface tank floating on the system. Because of the air in the tank, a hydropneumatic tank has an effective volume that is less than 30 to 50 percent of the total volume of the tank. Modeling the tank involves first determining the minimum and maximum pressures occurring in the tank and converting them to HGL values using Equation 3.1. The cross-sectional area (or diameter) of this equivalent tank can be determined using:

$$A_{eq} = \frac{V_{eff}}{HGL_{max} - HGL_{min}} \tag{3.2}$$

where A_{eq} = area of equivalent tank (ft², m²)
V_{eff} = effective volume of tank (ft³, m³)
HGL_{max} = maximum HGL in tank (ft, m)
HGL_{min} = minimum HGL in tank (ft, m)

The relationship between the actual hydropneumatic tank and the model tank is shown in Figure 3.12.

Figure 3.12
Relationship between a hydropneumatic tank and a model tank

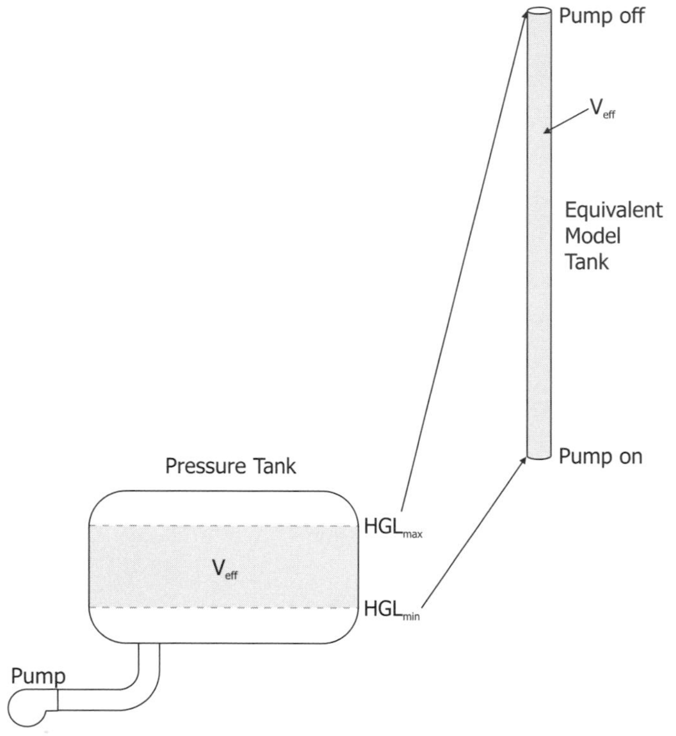

Using this technique, the EPS model of the tank will track HGL at the tank and volume of water in the tank, but not the actual water level.

3.5 JUNCTIONS

As the term implies, one of the primary uses of a *junction node* is to provide a location for two or more pipes to meet. Junctions, however, do not need to be elemental intersections, as a junction node may exist at the end of a single pipe (typically referred to as a *dead-end*). The other chief role of a junction node is to provide a location to withdraw water demanded from the system or inject inflows (sometimes referred to as negative demands) into the system.

Junction nodes typically do not directly relate to real-world distribution components, since pipes are usually joined with fittings, and flows are extracted from the system at any number of customer connections along a pipe. From a modeling standpoint, the importance of these distinctions varies, as discussed in the section on skeletonization on page 109. Most water users have such a small individual impact that their withdrawals can be assigned to nearby nodes without adversely affecting a model.

Junction Elevation

The only physical characteristic defined at a junction node is its elevation. While this may seem like a simple attribute to define, there are some considerations that need to be taken into account before assigning elevations to junction nodes. Since pressure is determined by the difference between calculated hydraulic grade and elevation, the most important consideration is, at what elevation is the pressure most important?

Selecting an Elevation. Figure 3.13 represents a typical junction node, illustrating that there are at least four possible choices for elevation that could be used in the model. The elevation could be taken as Point A, the centerline of the pipe. Alternatively, the ground elevation above the pipe (Point B), or the elevation of the hydrant (Point C), may be selected. As a final option, the ground elevation at the highest service point, point D, could be used. Each of these possibilities has associated benefits, so the determination of which elevation to use needs to be made on a case-by-case basis. Regardless of which elevation is selected, it is good practice to be consistent within a given model to avoid confusion.

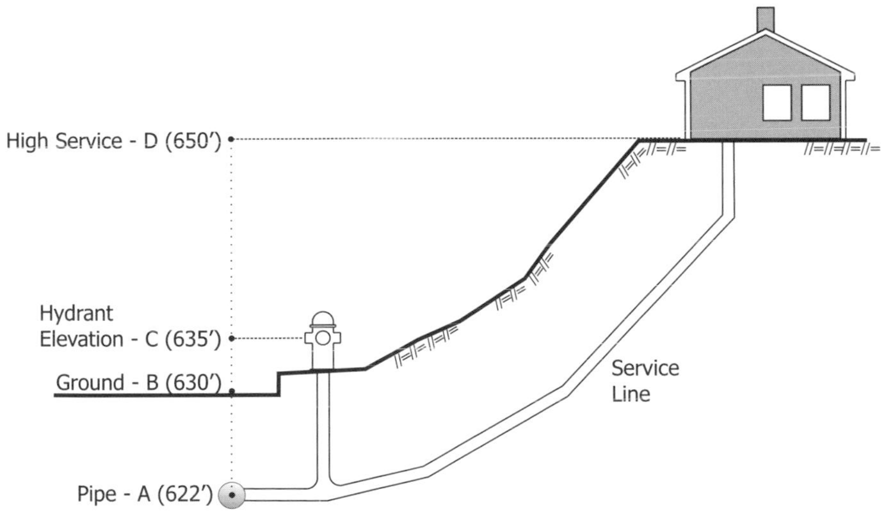

Figure 3.13
Elevation choices for a junction node

The elevation of the centerline of the pipe may be useful for determining pressure for leakage studies, or may be appropriate when modeling above-ground piping systems (such as systems used in chemical processing). Ground elevations may be the easiest data to obtain, and will also overlay more easily onto mapping systems that use ground elevations. They are frequently used for models of municipal water distribution systems. Both methods, however, have the potential to overlook poor service pressures, since the model could incorrectly indicate acceptable pressures for a customer that is notably higher than the ground or pipe centerline. In such cases, it may be more appropriate to select the elevation based on the highest service elevation required.

In the process of model calibration (see Chapter 6 for more about calibration), accurate node elevations are crucial. If the elevation chosen for the modeled junction is not the same as the elevation associated with recorded field measurements, then direct pressure comparisons are meaningless. Methods for obtaining good node elevation data are described in Walski (1999).

3.6 PIPES

A *pipe* conveys flow as it moves from one junction node to another in a network. In the real world, individual pipes are usually manufactured in lengths of around 18 or 20 feet (6 meters), which are then assembled in series as a pipeline. Real-world pipelines may also have various fittings, such as elbows, to handle abrupt changes in direction, or isolation valves to close off flow through a particular section of pipe.

Figure 3.14
Ductile iron pipe sections

For modeling purposes, individual segments of pipe and associated fittings can all be combined into a single pipe element. A model pipe should have the same characteristics (size, material, etc.) throughout its length.

Length

The length assigned to a pipe should represent the full distance that water flows from one node to the next, not necessarily the straight-line distance between the end nodes of the pipe.

Scaled vs. Schematic. Most simulation software enables the user to indicate either a scaled length or a user-defined length for pipes. Scaled lengths are automatically determined by the software, or scaled from the alignment along an electronic background map. User-defined lengths, applied when scaled electronic maps are not available, require the user to manually enter pipe lengths based on some other measurement method. A model using user-defined lengths is a *schematic* model. The overall connectivity of a schematic model should be identical to that of a scaled model, but the quality of the planimetric representation is more similar to a caricature than a photograph.

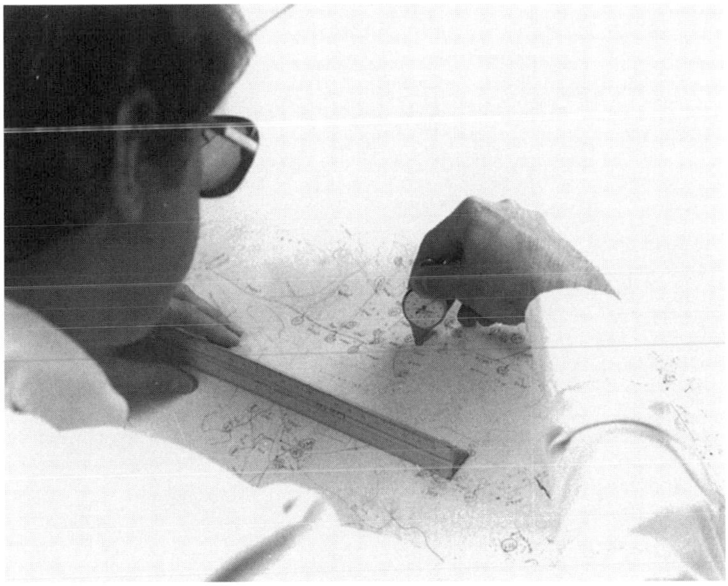

Figure 3.15
Use of a map measuring wheel for measuring pipe lengths

Even in some scaled models, there may be areas where there are simply too many nodes in close proximity to work with them easily at the model scale (such as at a pump station). In these cases, the modeler may want to selectively depict that portion of the system schematically (Figure 3.16).

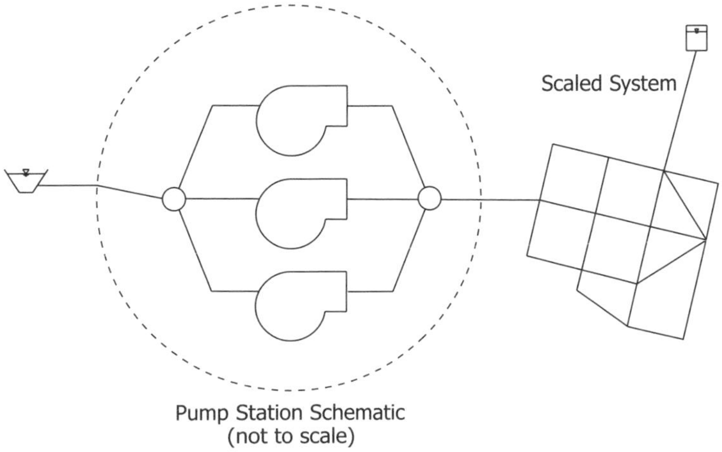

Figure 3.16
Scaled system with a schematic of a pump station

Diameter

As with junction elevations, determining a pipe's diameter is not as straightforward as it might seem. A pipe's *nominal diameter* refers to its common name, such as a 16-in. (400-mm) pipe. The pipe's *internal diameter*, the distance from one inner wall of the pipe to the opposite wall, may differ from the nominal diameter because of manufacturing standards. Most new pipes have internal diameters that are actually larger than the nominal diameters, although the exact measurements depend on the class (pressure rating) of pipe.

For example, Figure 3.17 depicts a new ductile iron pipe with a 16-in. nominal diameter (ND) and a 250-psi pressure rating that has an outside diameter (OD) of 17.40 in. and a wall thickness (Th) of 0.30 in., resulting in an internal diameter (ID) of 16.80 in. (AWWA, 1996).

Figure 3.17
Cross section of a 16-in. pipe

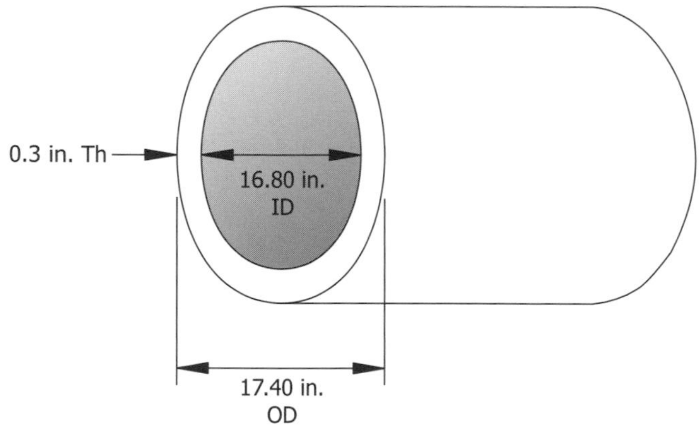

To add to the confusion, the ID may change over time as corrosion, tuberculation, and scaling occur within the pipe. Corrosion and tuberculation are related in iron pipes. As corrosion reactions occur on the inner surface of the pipe, the reaction by-products expand to form an uneven pattern of lumps (or tubercules) in a process called *tuberculation*. *Scaling* is a chemical deposition process that forms a material build-up along the pipe walls due to chemical conditions in the water. For example, lime scaling is caused by the precipitation of calcium carbonate. Scaling can actually be used to control corrosion, but when it occurs in an uncontrolled manner it can significantly reduce the ID of the pipe.

Of course, no one is going to refer to a pipe as a 16.80-in. (426.72-mm) pipe, and because of the process just described, it is difficult to measure a pipe's actual internal diameter. As a result, a pipe's nominal diameter is commonly used in modeling, in combination with a roughness value that accounts for the diameter discrepancy. However, using nominal rather than actual diameters can cause significant differences when water quality modeling is performed. Because flow velocity is related to flow rate by the internal diameter of a pipe, the transport characteristics of a pipe are affected. These calibration issues are discussed further in Chapter 6 (see page 202). Typical roughness values can be found in Section 2.4.

Minor Losses

Including separate modeling elements to represent every fitting and appurtenance present in a real-world system would be an unnecessarily tedious task. Instead, the minor losses caused by those fittings are typically associated with pipes (that is, minor losses are assigned as a pipe property).

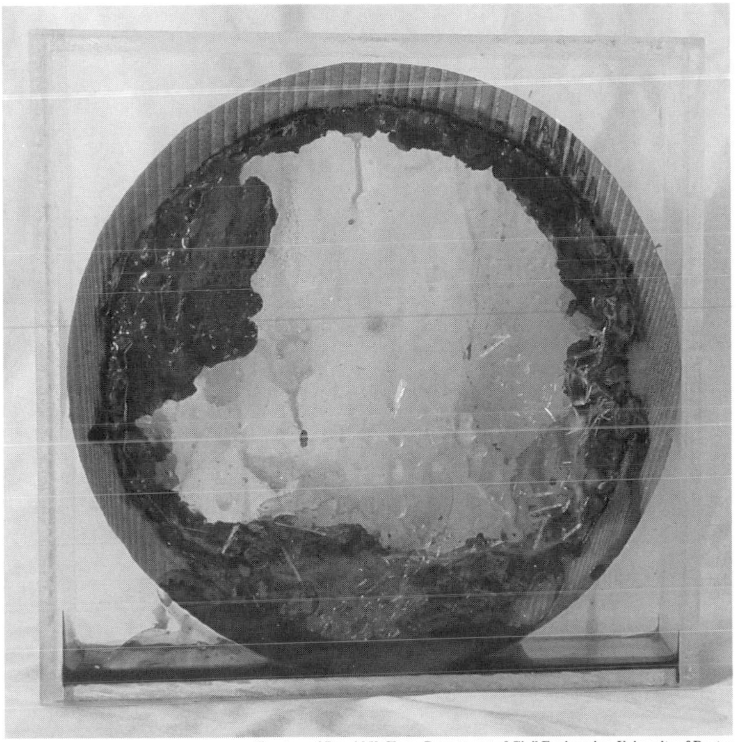

Courtesy of Donald V. Chase, Department of Civil Engineering, University of Dayton

Figure 3.18
Pipe corrosion and tuberculation

In many hydraulic simulations, minor losses are ignored because they do not contribute substantially to the overall head loss throughout the system. In some cases, however, flow velocities within a pipe and the configuration of fittings can cause minor losses to be considerable (for example, at a pump station). The term "minor" is relative, so the impact of these losses varies for different situations.

Composite Minor Losses. At any instant in time, velocity in the model is constant throughout the length of a particular pipe. Since individual minor losses are related to a coefficient multiplied by a velocity term, the overall headloss from several minor losses is mathematically equivalent to having a single composite minor loss coefficient. This *composite coefficient* is equal to the simple sum of the individual coefficients.

Red Water

Distribution systems with unlined iron or steel pipes can be subject to water quality problems related to corrosion, referred to as red water. Red water is treated water containing a colloidal suspension of very small, oxidized iron particles that originated from the surface of the pipe wall. Over a long period of time, this form of corrosion weakens the pipe wall and leads to the formation of tubercles. The most obvious and immediate impact, however, is that the oxidized iron particles give the water a murky, reddish-brown color. This reduction in the aesthetic quality of the water prompts numerous customer complaints.

Several alternative methods are available to control the pipe corrosion that causes red water. The most traditional approach is to produce water that is slightly supersaturated with calcium carbonate. When the water enters the distribution system, the dissolved calcium carbonate slowly precipitates on the pipe walls, forming a thin, protective scale (Caldwell and Lawrence, 1953; Merrill and Sanks, 1978). The *Langelier Index* (an index of the corrosive potential of water) can be used as an indication of the potential of the water to precipitate calcium carbonate, allowing better management of the precipitation rate (Langelier, 1936). A positive saturation index indicates that the pipe should be protected, provided that sufficient alkalinity is present.

More recently, corrosion inhibitors such as zinc orthophosphate and hexametaphosphate have become popular in red water prevention (Benjamin, Reiber, Ferguson, Vanderwerff, and Miller, 1990; Mullen and Ritter, 1974; Volk, Dundore, Schiermann, and LeChevallier, 2000). Several different theories exist concerning the predominant mechanism by which these inhibitors prevent corrosion.

The effectiveness of corrosion control measures can be dependent on the hydraulic flow regime occurring in the pipe. Several researchers have reported that corrosion inhibitors and carbonate films do not work well in pipes with low velocities (Maddison and Gagnon, 1999; McNeil and Edwards, 2000). Water distribution models provide a way to identify pipes with chronic low velocities, and therefore more potential for red water problems. The effect of field operations meant to control red water (for example, flushing and blow-offs) can also be investigated using hydraulic model simulations.

3.7 PUMPS

A *pump* is an element that adds energy to the system in the form of an increased hydraulic grade. Since water flows "downhill" (that is, from higher energy to lower energy), pumps are used to boost the head at desired locations to overcome piping head losses and physical elevation differences. Unless a system is entirely operated by gravity, pumps are an integral part of the distribution system.

In water distribution systems, the most frequently used type of pump is the *centrifugal pump*. A centrifugal pump has a motor that spins a piece within the pump called an *impeller*. The mechanical energy of the rotating impeller is imparted to the water, resulting in an increase in head. Figure 3.19 illustrates a cross-section of a centrifugal pump and the flow path water takes through it. Water from the intake pipe enters the pump through the eye of the spinning impeller (1), where it is then thrown outward between vanes and into the discharge piping (2).

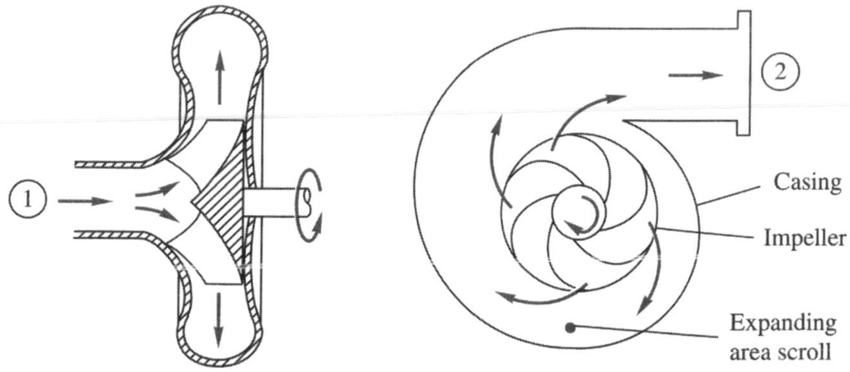

Frank M. White, Fluid Mechanics, 1994, McGraw-Hill, Inc. Reproduced by permission of the McGraw-Hill Companies.

Figure 3.19
Cross-section of a centrifugal pump

Pump Characteristic Curves

With centrifugal pumps, pump performance is a function of flow rate. The performance is described by the following four parameters, which are plotted versus discharge.

- **Head** - total dynamic head added by pump in units of length (see page 45)
- **Efficiency** - overall pump efficiency (wire-to-water efficiency) in units of percent (see page 181 and 357)
- **Brake horsepower** - power needed to turn pump (in power units)
- **Net positive suction head (NPSH) required** - head above vacuum (in units of length) required to prevent cavitation (see page 50)

Only the head curve is an energy equation necessary for solving pipe network problems. The other curves are used once the network has been solved to identify power consumption (energy), motor requirements (brake horsepower), and suction piping (NPSH).

Fixed-Speed and Variable-Speed Pumps. A pump characteristic curve is related to the speed at which the pump motor is operating. With *fixed-speed pumps*, the motor remains at a constant speed regardless of other factors. *Variable-speed pumps*, on the other hand, have a motor or other device that can change the pump speed in response to the system conditions.

A variable-speed pump is not really a special type of pump, but rather a pump connected to a variable-speed drive or controller. The most common type of variable-speed drive controls the flow of electricity to the pump motor, and therefore controls the rate at which the pump rotates. The difference in pump speed, in turn, produces different head and discharge characteristics. Variable-speed pumps are useful in applications requiring operational flexibility, such as when flow rates change rapidly, but the desired pressure remains constant. An example of such a situation would be a network with little or no storage available.

Positive Displacement Pumps

Virtually all water distribution system pumps are centrifugal pumps. However, pipe network models are used in other applications—such as chemical feeds, low-pressure sanitary sewer collection systems, and sludge pumping—in which positive displacement pumps (for example, diaphragm, piston, plunger, lobe and progressive cavity pumps) are used. Unlike centrifugal pumps, these pumps produce a constant flow, regardless of the head supplied, up to a very high pressure.

The standard approximations to pump curves used in most models do not adequately address positive displacement pumps because the head characteristic curve for such pumps consists of a virtually straight, vertical line. Depending on the model, forcing a pump curve to fit this shape usually results in warning messages.

An easy way to approximate a positive displacement pump in a model is to not include a pump at all, but rather to use two nodes—a suction node and a discharge node—that are not connected. The suction side node would have a demand set equal to the pump flow, while the discharge node would have an inflow set equal to this flow. The model will then give the suction and discharge HGLs and pressures at the nodes. (Custom extended curve options can also be used.)

Because the suction and discharge systems are separated, it is important for the modeler to include a tank or reservoir on both the suction and discharge sides of the pump. Otherwise, the model will not be able to satisfy the Law of Conservation of Mass. For example, if the demands on the discharge side do not equal the inflow to the discharge side, the model may not give a valid solution. Because most models assume demands as independent of pressure, inflows must equal system demands, plus or minus any storage effects. If no storage is present, the model cannot solve unless inflows and demands are equal.

Power and Efficiency. The term *power* may have one of several meanings when dealing with a pump. These possible meanings are listed below:

- **Input power -** the amount of power that is delivered to the motor, usually in electric form.
- **Brake power -** the amount of power that is delivered to the pump from the motor.
- **Water power -** the amount of power that is delivered to the water from the pump.

Of course, there are losses as energy is converted from one form to another (electricity to motor, motor to pump, pump to water), and every transfer has an *efficiency* associated with it. The efficiencies associated with these transfers may be expressed either as percentages (100 percent is perfectly efficient) or as decimal values (1.00 is perfectly efficient), and are typically defined as follows:

- **Motor efficiency -** the ratio of brake power to input power.
- **Pump efficiency -** the ratio of water power to brake power.
- **Wire-to-water (overall) efficiency -** the ratio of water power to input power.

Pump efficiency tends to vary significantly with flow, while motor efficiency remains relatively constant over the range of loads imposed by most pumps. Note that there may also be an additional efficiency associated with a variable-speed drive. Some engineers refer to the combination of the motor and any speed controls as the *driver*.

Figure 3.20 shows input power and wire-to-water efficiency curves overlaid on a typical pump head curve. Notice that the input power increases as discharge increases, and head decreases as discharge increases. For each impeller size, there is a flow rate corresponding to maximum efficiency. At higher or lower flows, the efficiency increases. This maximum point on the efficiency curve is called the *best efficiency point* (BEP).

Figure 3.20
Pump curves with efficiency, NPSH, and horsepower overlays

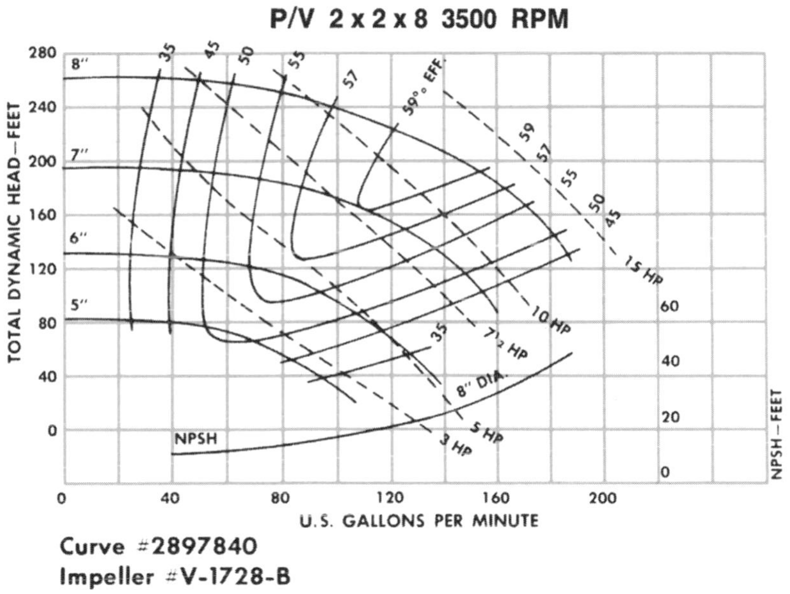

Courtesy of Peerless Pumps

Obtaining Pump Data. Ideally, a water utility will have pump operating curves on file for every pump in the system. These are usually furnished to the utility with the shop drawings of the pump stations, or as part of the manufacturer's submittals when replacing pumps. If the pump curve cannot be located, a copy of the curve can usually be obtained from the manufacturer (provided the model and serial numbers for the pump are available).

To perform energy cost calculations, pump efficiency curves should also be obtained. Note that the various power and efficiency definitions can be confusing, and it is important to distinguish which terms are being referred to in any particular document.

Every pump differs slightly from its catalog model, and normal wear and tear will cause a pump's performance to change over time. Thus, pumps should be checked to verify that the characteristic curves on record are in agreement with field performance. If an operating point does not agree with a characteristic curve, a new curve can be developed to reflect the actual behavior. More information is available on this subject in Chapter 5 (see page 181).

Even though a pump curve on record may not perfectly match the actual pump characteristics, many utilities accept that the cataloged values for the pump curve are sufficiently accurate for the purposes of the model, and forgo any performance testing or field verification. This decision is dependent on the specific situation.

Model Representation

In order to model a pump's behavior, some mathematical expression describing its pump head curve must be defined. Different models support different definitions, but most are centered on the same basic concept, furnishing the model with sufficient sample points to define the characteristic head curve.

Selecting Representative Points. As discussed previously, the relationship between pump head and discharge is nonlinear. For most pumps, three points along the curve are usually enough to represent the normal operating range of the pump. These three points include:

1. The zero-discharge point, also known as the *cutoff* or *shutoff* point;
2. The *normal operating point*, which should typically be close to the best efficiency point of the pump; and
3. The point at the maximum expected discharge value.

It is also possible to provide some models with additional points along the pump curve, but not all models treat these additional data points in the same way. Some models perform linear interpolation between points, some fit a polynomial curve between points, and others determine an overall polynomial or exponential curve that fits the entire data set.

Constant Power Pumps. Many models also support the concept of a *constant power pump*. With this type of pump, the water power produced by the pump remains constant, regardless of how little or how much flow the pump passes.

Water power is a product of discharge and head, which means that a curve depicting constant water power is asymptotic to both the discharge and head axes, as shown in Figure 3.21.

Some modelers use a constant power pump definition to define a curve simply because it is easier than providing several points from the characteristic curve, or because the characteristic curve is not available. The results generated using this definition, however, can be unreliable and sometimes counter-intuitive. As can be seen in Figure 3.21, the constant power approximation will be accurate for a specific range of flows, but not at very high or low flows. For very preliminary studies when all the modeler knows is the approximate size of the pump, this approximation can be used to get into pipe sizing quickly. However, it should not be used for pump selection.

The modeler must remember that the power entered for the constant power pump is not the rated power of the motor but the water power added. For example, a 50 hp motor that is 90 percent efficient, running at 80 percent of its rated power, and connected to a pump that is operating at 70 percent efficiency will result in a water power of roughly 25 hp (that is, $50 \times 0.9 \times 0.8 \times 0.7$). The value 25 hp, not 50 hp, should be entered into the model.

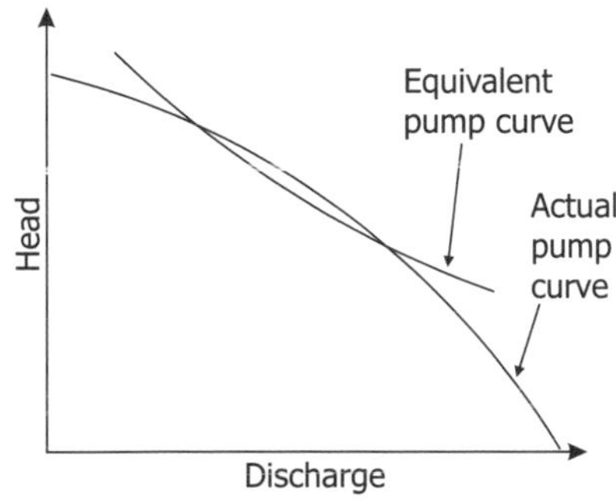

Figure 3.21
Characteristic pump curve for a constant power pump

Node vs. Link Representation. A pump can be represented as a node or a link element, depending on the software package. In software that symbolizes pumps as links, the pump connects upstream and downstream nodes in a system the same way a pipe would. A link symbolization more closely reflects the internal mathematical representation of the pump, but it can introduce inaccuracies. For example, Figure 3.22 illustrates how the pump intake and discharge piping may be ignored, and the head losses occurring in them neglected.

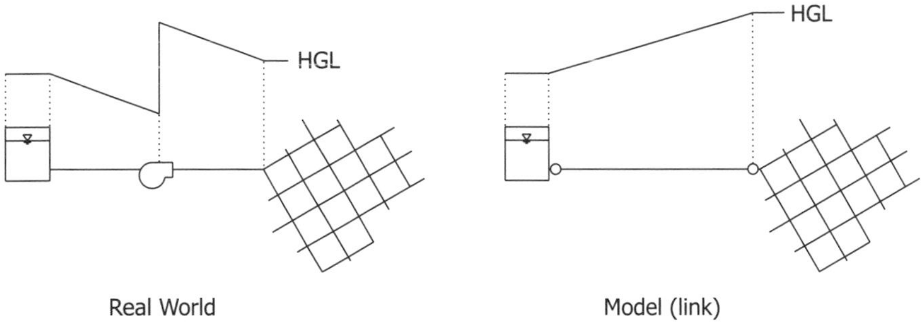

Figure 3.22
Comparison of an actual pump and a pump modeled as a link element

Other models represent pumps as nodes, typically with special connectivity rules (for example, only allowing a single downstream pipe). This nodal representation is less error-prone, more realistic, and easier for the modeler to implement. Nodal representation may also be more intuitive, since a real-world pump is usually thought of as being in a single location with two distinct hydraulic grades (one on the intake side and one on the discharge side). Figure 3.23 illustrates a nodal representation of a pump.

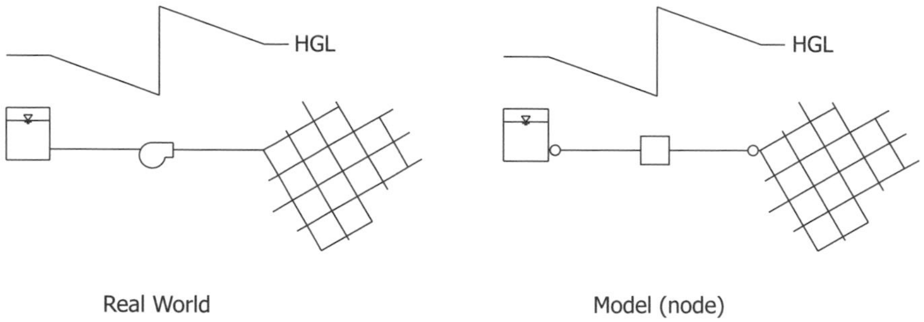

Figure 3.23
Comparison of an actual pump and a pump modeled as a node element

3.8 VALVES

A *valve* is an element that can be opened and closed to different extents (called *throttling*) to vary its resistance to flow, thereby controlling the movement of water through a pipeline (Figure 3.24). Valves can be classified into the following five general categories:

- Isolation valves
- Directional valves
- Altitude valves
- Air release and vacuum breaking valves
- Control valves

Some valves are intended to automatically restrict the flow of water based on pressures or flows, while others are operated manually and used to completely turn off portions of the system. The behaviors of different valve types vary significantly depending on the software used. This section provides an introduction to some of the most common valve types and applications.

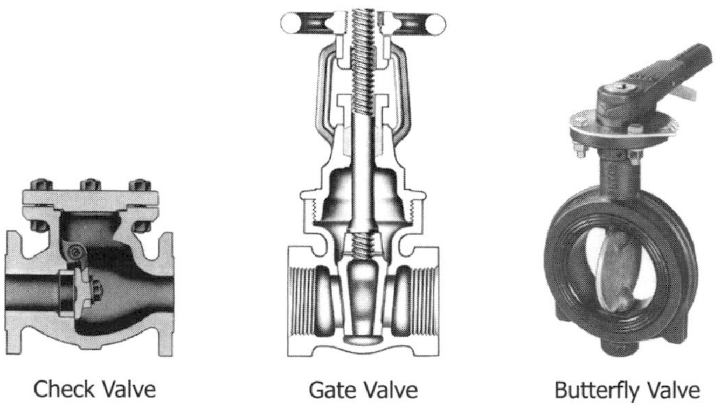

Figure 3.24
Different valve types

Isolation Valves

Perhaps the most common type of valve in water distribution systems is the *isolation valve*, which can be manually closed to block the flow of water. As the term "isolation" implies, the primary purpose of these valves is to provide a field crew with a means of turning off a portion of the system to, for example, replace a broken pipe or a leaky joint. Well-designed water distribution systems have isolation valves throughout the network, so that maintenance and emergencies affect as few customers as possible. In some systems, isolation valves may be intentionally kept in a closed position to control pressure zone boundaries, for example.

There are several types of isolation valves that may be used, including *gate valves* (the most popular type), *butterfly valves*, *globe valves*, and *plug valves*.

In most hydraulic models, the inclusion of each and every isolation valve would be an unnecessary level of detail. Instead, the intended behavior of the isolation valve (minor loss, the ability to open and close, etc.) can be defined as part of a pipe.

A common question in constructing a model is whether to explicitly include minor losses due to open gate valves, or to account for the effect of such losses in the Hazen-Williams C-factor. If the C-factor for the pipe with no minor losses is known, an equivalent C-factor that accounts for the minor losses is given by:

$$C_e = C\left(\frac{L}{L + D\left(\frac{\Sigma K_L}{f}\right)}\right)^{0.54} \tag{3.3}$$

where
C_e = equivalent Hazen-Williams C-factor accounting for minor losses
C = Hazen-Williams C-factor
L = length of pipe segment (ft, m)
D = diameter (ft, m)
f = Darcy-Weisbach friction factor
ΣK_L = sum of minor loss coefficients in pipe

For example, consider a 400-ft (122-m) segment of 6-in. (152-mm) pipe with a C-factor of 120 and an f of 0.02. From Equation 3.3, the equivalent C-factor for the pipe including a single open gate valve (K_L = 0.39) is 118.4. For two open gate valves, the equivalent C-factor is 116.9. Given that C-factors are seldom known to within plus or minus 5, these differences are generally negligible. Note that if a model is calibrated without explicitly accounting for many minor losses, then the C-factor resulting from the calibration is the equivalent C-factor, and no further adjustment is needed.

Directional Valves

Directional valves, also called *check valves*, are used to ensure that water can flow in one direction through the pipeline, but cannot flow in the opposite direction (*backflow*). Any water flowing backwards through the valve causes it to close, and it remains closed until the flow once again begins to go through the valve in the forward direction.

Simple check valves commonly utilize a hinged disk or flap to prevent flow from traveling in the undesired direction. For example, the discharge piping from a pump may include a check valve to prevent flow from passing through the pump backwards (which could damage the pump). Most models automatically assume that every pump has a built-in check valve, so there is no need to explicitly include one (Figure 3.25). If a pump does not have a check valve on its discharge side, water can flow backwards through the pump when the power is off. This situation can be modeled with a pipe parallel to the pump that only opens when the pump is off. The pipe must have an equivalent length and minor loss coefficient that will generate the same head loss as the pump running backwards.

Figure 3.25
A check valve operating at a pump

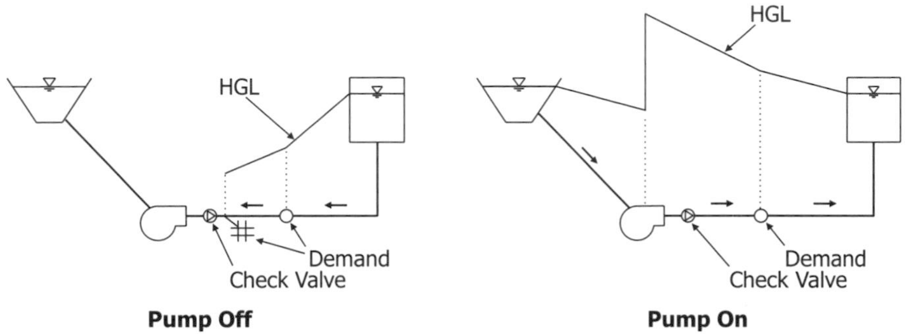

Mechanically, some check valves require a certain differential in head before they will seat fully and seal off any backflow. They may allow small amounts of reverse flow, which may or may not have noteworthy consequences. When potable water systems are hydraulically connected to non-potable water uses, a reversal of flow could be disastrous. These situations, called *cross-connections*, are a serious danger for water distributors, and the possibility of such occurrences warrants the use of higher quality check valves. Figure 3.26 illustrates a seemingly harmless situation that is a potential cross-connection. A device called a *backflow preventer* is designed to be highly sensitive to flow reversal, and frequently incorporates one or more check valves in series to prevent backflow.

As far as most modeling software is concerned, there is no difference in sensitivity between different types of check valves (all are assumed to close completely even for the smallest of attempted reverse flows). As long as the check valve can be represented using a minor loss coefficient, the majority of software packages allow them to be modeled as an attribute associated with a pipe, rather than requiring that a separate valve element be created.

Figure 3.26
A potential cross-connection

Altitude Valves

Many water utilities employ devices called *altitude valves* at the point where a pipeline enters a tank (Figure 3.27). When the tank level rises to a specified upper limit, the valve closes to prevent any further flow from entering, thus eliminating overflow. When the flow trend reverses, the valve reopens and allows the tank to drain to supply the usage demands of the system.

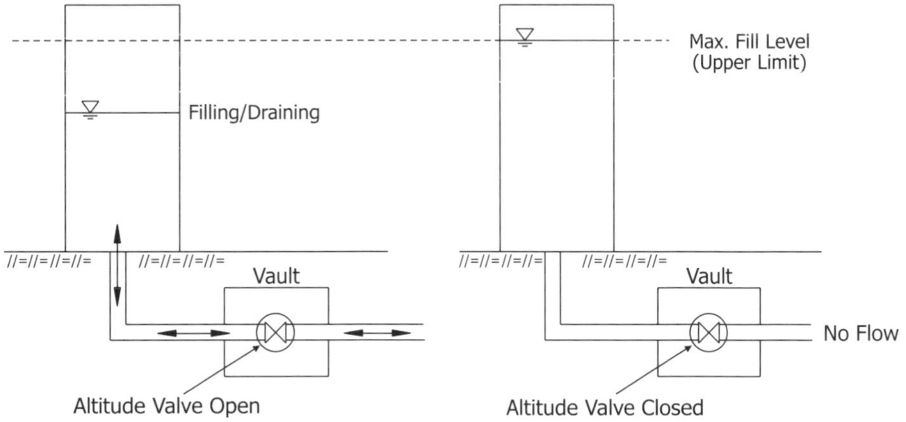

Figure 3.27
Altitude valve controlling the maximum fill level of a tank

Most software packages, in one form or another, automatically incorporate the behavior of altitude valves at both the minimum and maximum tank levels, and do not require explicit inclusion of them. If, however, an altitude valve does not exist at a tank, tank overflow is possible, and steps must be taken to include this behavior in the model.

Air Release Valves and Vacuum Breaking Valves

Most systems include special *air release valves* to release trapped air during system operation, and *air/vacuum* valves that discharge air upon system start-up and admit air into the system in response to negative gage pressures (Figure 3.28). These types of valves are often found at system high points, where trapped air settles, and at changes in grade, where pressures are most likely to drop below ambient or atmospheric conditions. Combination air valves that perform the functions of both valve types are often used as well.

Figure 3.28
Air release and air/vacuum valves

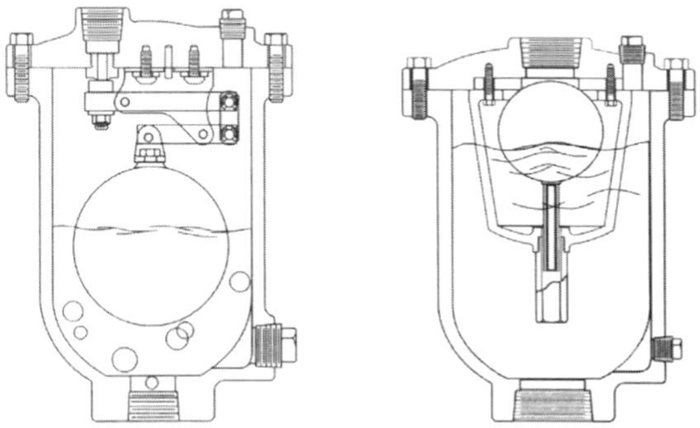

Courtesy of Val-Matic Valve and Manufacturing Corporation, Elmhurst, Illinois.

Air release and air/vacuum valves are typically not included in standard water distribution system modeling. The importance of such elements is significant, however, for advanced studies such as transient analyses.

Control Valves

For any *control valve*, also called *regulating valve*, the setting is of primary importance. For a flow control valve, this setting refers to the flow setting, and for a throttle control valve, it refers to a minor loss coefficient. For pressure-based controls, however, the setting may be either the hydraulic grade or the pressure that the valve tries to maintain. Models are driven by hydraulic grade, so if a pressure setting is used, it is critically important to have not only the correct pressure setting, but also the correct valve elevation.

Given the setting for the valve, the model calculates the flow through the valve and the inlet and outlet HGL (and pressures). A control valve is complicated in that, unlike a pump, which is either on or off, it can be in any one of the several states described below. Note that the terminology may vary slightly between models.

- **Active -** automatically controlling flow
  - **Open -** opened fully
  - **Closed (1) -** closed fully
  - **Throttling -** throttling flow and pressure
- **Closed (2) -** manually shut, as when an isolating valve located at the control valve is closed
- **Inactive -** ignored

Because of the many possible control valve states, valves are often points where model convergence problems exist.

Pressure Reducing Valves (PRVs). *Pressure reducing valves* (PRVs) throttle automatically to prevent the downstream hydraulic grade from exceeding a set value, and are used in situations where high downstream pressures could cause damage. For example, Figure 3.29 illustrates a connection between pressure zones. Without a PRV, the hydraulic grade in the upper zone could cause pressures in the lower zone to be high enough to burst pipes or cause relief valves to open.

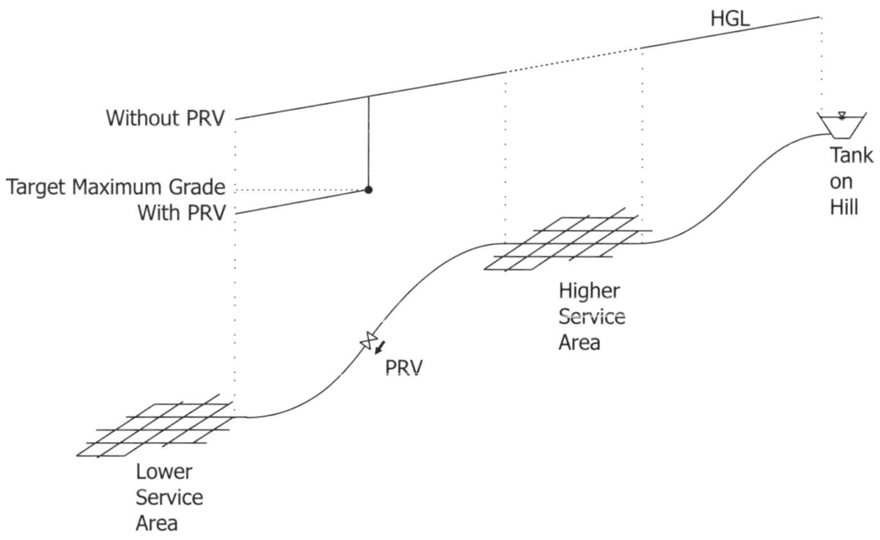

Figure 3.29
Schematic network illustrating the use of a pressure reducing valve

Unlike the isolation valves discussed earlier, PRVs are not associated with a pipe, but are explicitly represented within a hydraulic model. A PRV is characterized in a model by the downstream hydraulic grade that it attempts to maintain, its controlling status, and its minor loss coefficient. Since the valve intentionally introduces losses to meet the required grade, a PRV's minor loss coefficient is really only a concern when the valve is wide open (not throttling).

Similar to pumps, PRVs connect two pressure zones and have two associated hydraulic grades, so some models represent them as links and some represent them as nodes. The pitfalls of link characterization of PRVs are the same as those described previously for pumps (see page 97).

Pressure Sustaining Valves (PSVs). A *pressure sustaining valve* (PSV) throttles the flow automatically to prevent the upstream hydraulic grade from dropping below a set value. This type of valve can be used in situations in which unregulated flow would result in inadequate pressures for the upstream portion of the system (Figure 3.30). They are frequently used to model pressure relief valves (see page 249).

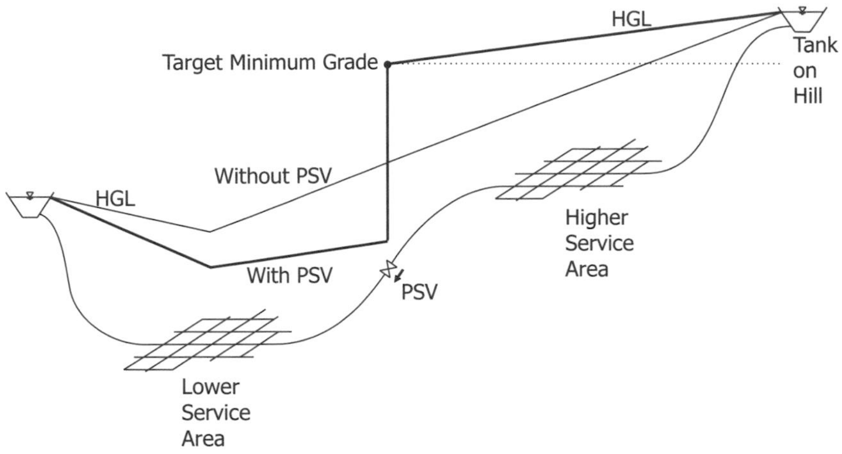

Figure 3.30
Schematic network illustrating the use of a pressure sustaining valve

Like PRVs, a PSV is typically represented explicitly within a hydraulic model, and is characterized by the upstream pressure it tries to maintain, its status, and its minor loss coefficient.

Flow Control Valves (FCVs). *Flow control valves* (FCVs) automatically throttle to limit the rate of flow passing through the valve to a user-specified value. This type of valve can be employed anywhere that flow-based regulation is appropriate, such as when a water distributor has an agreement with a customer regarding maximum usage rates. FCVs do not guarantee that the flow will not be less than the setting value, only that the flow will not exceed the setting value. If the flow does not equal the setting, modeling packages will typically indicate so with a warning.

Similar to PRVs and PSVs, most models directly support FCVs, which are characterized by their maximum flow setting, status, and minor loss coefficient.

Throttle Control Valves (TCVs). Unlike an FCV where the flow is specified directly, a *throttle control valve* (TCV) throttles to adjust its minor loss coefficient based on the value of some other attribute of the system (such as the pressure at a critical node or a tank water level). Often the throttling effect of a particular valve position is known, but the minor loss coefficients as a function of position are unknown. This relationship can frequently be provided by the manufacturer.

Valve Books

Many water utilities maintain *valve books*, which are sets of records that provide details pertaining to the location, type, and status of isolation valves and other fittings throughout a system. From a modeling perspective, valve books can provide valuable insight into the pipe connectivity at hydraulically complex intersections, especially in areas where system maps may not show all of the details.

3.9 CONTROLS (SWITCHES)

Operational *controls*, such as *pressure switches*, are used to automatically change the status or setting of an element based on the time of day, or in response to conditions within the network. For example, a switch may be set to turn on a pump when pressures within the system drop below a desired value. Or, a pump may be programmed to turn on and refill a tank in the early hours of the morning.

Without operational controls, conditions would have to be monitored and controlled manually. This type of operation would be expensive, mistake-prone, and sometimes impractical. Automated controls enable operators to take a more supervisory role, focusing on issues larger than the everyday process of turning on a pump at a given time or changing a control valve setting to accommodate changes in demand. Consequently, the system can be run more affordably, predictably, and practically.

Models can represent controls in different ways. Some consider controls to be separate modeling elements, while others consider them to be an attribute of the pipe, pump, or valve being controlled.

Pipe Controls

For a pipe, the only status that can really change is whether the pipe (or, more accurately, an isolation valve associated with the pipe) is open or closed. Most pipes will always be open, but some pipes may be opened or closed to model a valve that automatically or manually changes based on the state of the system. If a valve in the pipe is being throttled, it should be handled either through the use of a minor loss directly applied to the pipe, or by inserting a throttle control valve in the pipe and adjusting it.

Pump Controls

The simplest type of pump control turns a pump on or off. For variable-speed pumps, controls can also be used to adjust the pump's relative speed factor to raise or lower the pressures and flow rates that it delivers. For more information about pump relative speed factors, see Chapter 2 (page 46).

The most common way to control a pump is by tank water level. Pumps are classified as either "lead" pumps, which are the first to turn on, or "lag" pumps, the second to turn on. *Lead pumps* are set to activate when tanks drain to a specified minimum level, and shut off when tanks refill to a specified maximum level, usually just below the tank overflow point. *Lag pump*s only turn on when the tank continues to drain below the minimum level, even with the lead pump still running. They turn off when the tank fills to a point below the shut off level for the lead pump. Controls get much more complicated when there are other considerations such as time of day control rules, or parallel pumps that are not identical.

Regulating Valve Controls

Similar to a pump, a control valve can change both its status (open, closed, or active) and its setting. For example, an operator may want a flow control valve to restrict flow more when upstream pressures are poor, or a pressure reducing valve to open completely to accommodate high flow demands during a fire event.

Indicators of Control Settings

If a pressure switch setting is unknown, examining tank level charts and pumping logs may provide a clue. As shown in Figure 3.31, pressure switch settings can be determined by looking at tank level charts and correlating them to the times when pumps are placed into or taken out of service. Operations staff can also be helpful in the process of determining pressure switch settings.

Figure 3.31
Correlation between tank levels and pump operation

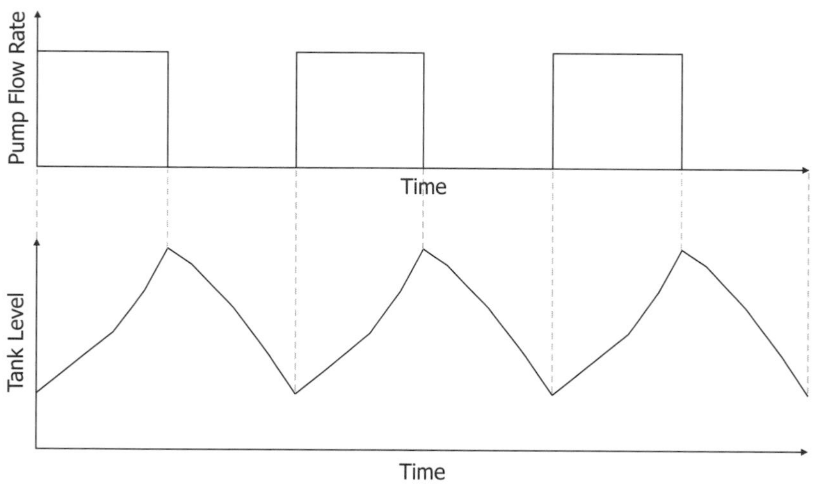

3.10 TYPES OF SIMULATIONS

Once the basic elements and the network topology have been defined, further refinement of the model can be done depending on its intended purpose. There are various types of simulations that a model may perform, depending on what the modeler is trying to observe or predict. The two most basic types are:

- **Stead- state simulation -** computes the state of the system (flows, pressures, pump operating attributes, valve position, etc.) assuming that hydraulic demands and boundary conditions do not change with respect to time.
- **Extended period simulation (EPS) -** determines the quasi-dynamic behavior of a system over a period of time, computing the state of the system as a series of steady-state simulations in which hydraulic demands and boundary conditions do change with respect to time.

Steady-State Simulation

As the term implies, steady-state refers to a state of a system that is unchanging in time, essentially the long-term behavior of a system once it has achieved equilibrium. Tank and reservoir levels, hydraulic demands, and pump and valve operation remain constant and define the boundary conditions of the simulation. A steady-state simulation provides information regarding the equilibrium flows, pressures, and other variables defining the state of the network for a unique set of hydraulic demands and boundary conditions.

Real water distribution systems are seldom in a true steady state. Therefore, the notion of a steady state is a mathematical construct. Demands and tank water levels are continuously changing, and pumps are routinely cycling on and off. A steady-state hydraulic model is more like a blurred photograph of a moving subject than a sharp photo of a still one. However, by enabling designers to predict the response to a unique set of hydraulic conditions (for example, peak hour demands or a fire at a particular node), the mathematical construct of a steady state can be a very useful tool.

Steady-state simulations are the building blocks for other types of simulations. Once the steady-state concept is mastered, it is easier to understand more advanced topics such as extended period simulation, water quality analysis, and fire protection studies (these topics are discussed in later chapters).

Steady-state models are generally used to analyze specific worst-case conditions such as peak demand times, fire protection usage, and system component failures in which the effects of time are not particularly significant.

Extended Period Simulation

The results provided by a steady-state analysis can be extremely useful for a wide range of applications in hydraulic modeling. There are many cases, however, for which assumptions of a steady-state simulation are not valid, or a simulation is required that allows the system to change over time. For example, to understand the effects of changing water usage over time, fill and drain cycles of tanks, or the response of pumps and valves to system changes, an *extended period simulation (EPS)* is needed.

It is important to note that there are many inputs required for an extended period simulation. Due to the volume of data and the number of possible actions that a modeler can take during calibration, analysis, and design, it is highly recommended that a model be examined under steady-state situations prior to working with extended period simulations. Once satisfactory steady-state performance is achieved, it is much easier to proceed into EPSs.

EPS Calculation Process. Similar to the way a film projector flashes a series of still images in sequence to create a moving picture, the hydraulic time steps of an extended period simulation are actually steady-state simulations that are strung together in sequence. After each steady-state step, the system boundary conditions are reevaluated and updated to reflect changes in junction demands, tank levels, pump operations, etc. Then, another hydraulic time step is taken, and the process continues until the end of the simulation.

Why Use a Scenario Manager?

When water distribution models were first created, data was input into the computer program using punched cards, which were submitted and processed as a batch run. In this type of run, a separate set of input data was required to generate each set of results. Since a typical modeling project requires analysis of many alternative situations, large amounts of time were spent creating and debugging multiple sets of input cards.

When data files replaced punch cards, the batch approach to data entry was carried over. The modeler could now edit and copy input files more easily, but there was still the problem of trying to manage a large number of model runs. Working with many data files or a single data file with dozens of edits was confusing, inefficient, and error-prone.

The solution to this problem is to keep alternative data sets within a single model data file. For example, data for current average day demands, maximum day demands with a fire flow at node 37, and peak hour demands in 2020 can be created, managed, and stored in a central database. Once this structure is in place, the user can then create many runs, or scenarios, by piecing together alternative data sets.

For example, a scenario may consist of the peak hour demands in 2020 paired with infrastructure data that includes a proposed tank on Washington Hill and a new 16-in. (400 mm) pipe along North Street. This idea of building model runs from alternative data sets created by the user is more intuitive than the batch run concept, and is consistent with the object-oriented paradigm found in modern programs. Further, descriptive naming of scenarios and alternative data sets provides internal documentation of the user's actions.

Since alternative plans in water modeling tend to grow out of previous alternatives, a good scenario manager will use the concept of inheritance to create new child alternatives from existing parent alternatives. Combining this idea of inheritance with construction of scenarios from alternative data sets gives the model user a self-documenting way to quickly create new and better solutions based on the results of previous model runs.

A user accustomed to performing batch runs may find some of the terminology and concepts employed in scenario management a bit of a challenge at first. But, with a little practice, it becomes difficult to imagine building or maintaining a model without this versatile feature.

Simulation Duration. An extended period simulation can be run for any length of time, depending on the purpose of the analysis. The most common simulation duration is typically a multiple of 24 hours, since the most recognizable pattern for demands and operations is a daily one. When modeling emergencies or disruptions occur over the short-term, however, it may be desirable to model only a few hours into the future to predict immediate changes in tank level and system pressures. For water quality applications, it may be more appropriate to model a duration of several days in order for quality levels to stabilize.

Even with established daily patterns, a modeler may want to look at a simulation duration of a week or more. For example, consider a storage tank with inadequate capacity operating within a system. The water level in the tank may be only slightly less at the end of each day than it was at the end of the previous day, which may go unnoticed when reviewing model results. If a duration of one or two weeks is used, the trend of the tank level dropping more and more each day will be more evident. Even in systems that have adequate storage capacity, a simulation duration of 48 hours or longer can be helpful in better determining the tank draining and filling characteristics.

Hydraulic Time Step. An important decision when running an extended period simulation is the selection of the *hydraulic time step*. The time step is the length of time for one steady-state portion of an EPS, and it should be selected such that changes in system hydraulics from one increment to the next are gradual. A time step that is too large may cause abrupt hydraulic changes to occur, making it difficult for the model to give good results.

For any given system, it is difficult to predict in advance how small the time increment should be, although experience is certainly beneficial in this area. Typically, modelers begin by assuming one-hour time steps, unless there are considerations that point to the need for a different time step.

When junction demands and tank inflow/outflow rates are highly variable, decreasing the time step can improve the accuracy of the simulation. The sensitivity of a model to time increment changes can be explored by comparing the results of the same analysis using different increments. This sensitivity can also be evaluated during the calibration process. Ultimately, finding the correct balance between calculation time and accuracy is up to the modeler.

Intermediate Changes. Of course, changes within a system don't always occur at even time increments. When it is determined that an element's status changes between time steps (such as a tank completely filling or draining, or a control condition being triggered), many models will automatically report a status change and results at that intermediate point in time. The model then steps ahead in time to the next even increment until another intermediate time step is required. If calculations are frequently required at intermediate times, the modeler should consider decreasing the time increment.

Other Types of Simulations

Using the fundamental concepts of steady-state and extended period simulations, more advanced simulations can be built. *Water quality simulations* are used to ascertain chemical or biological constituent levels within a system or to determine the age or source of water (see page 61). *Automated fire flow analyses* establish the suitability of a system for fire protection needs. *Cost analyses* are used for looking at the monetary impact of operations and improvements. *Transient analyses* are used to investigate the short-term fluctuations in flow and pressure due to sudden changes in the status of pumps or valves.

With every advance in computer technology and each improvement in software methods, hydraulic models become a more integral part of designing and operating safe and reliable water distribution systems.

3.11 SKELETONIZATION

Skeletonization is the process of selecting for inclusion in the model only the parts of the hydraulic network that have a significant impact on the behavior of the system. Attempting to include each individual service connection, gate valve, and every other component of a large system in a model could be a huge undertaking without a significant impact on the model results. Capturing every feature of a system would also result in tremendous amounts of data; enough to make managing, using, and troubleshooting the model an overwhelming and error-prone task. Skeletonization is a more practical approach to modeling that allows the modeler to produce reliable, accurate results without investing unnecessary time and money.

Eggener and Polkowski (1976) did the first study of skeletonization when they systematically removed pipes from a model of Menomonie, Wisconsin, to test the sensitivity of model results. They found that under normal demands they could remove a large number of pipes and still not affect pressure significantly. Shamir and Hamberg (1988a, 1988b) investigated rigorous rules for reducing the size of models.

Skeletonization should not be confused with the omission of data. The portions of the system that are not modeled during the skeletonization process are not discarded; rather, their effects are accounted for within parts of the system that are included in the model.

Skeletonization Example

Consider the following proposed subdivision, which is to tie into an existing water system model. Figures 3.32, 3.33, 3.34, and 3.35 show how demands can be aggregated from individual customers to nodes with larger and larger nodal service areas. Although a modeler would almost never include the individual connections as shown in Figure 3.32, this example, which can be extrapolated to much larger networks, shows the steps that are followed to achieve various levels of skeletonization.

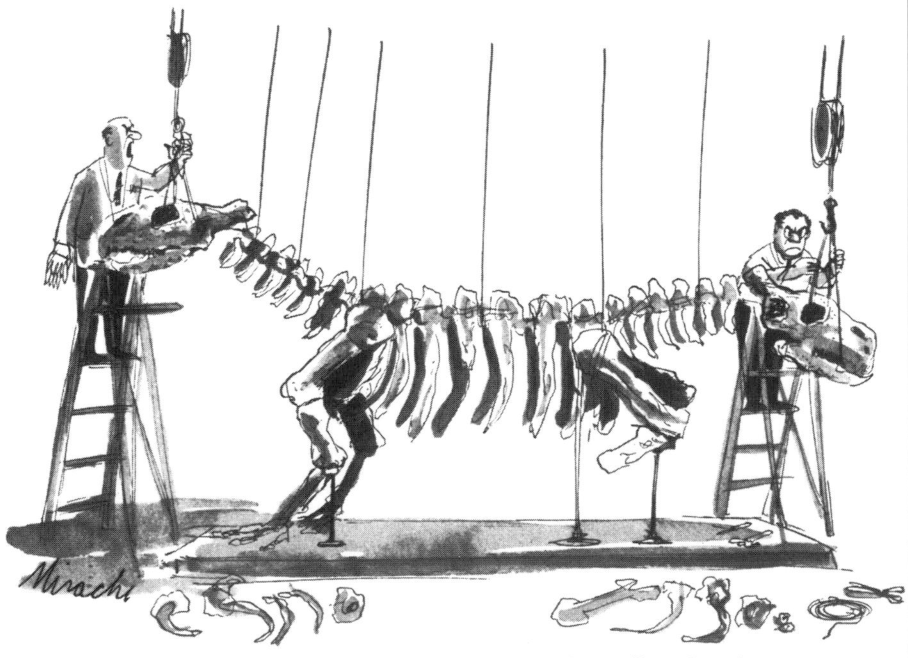

Yeah? Well, I've forgotten more about paleontology than you'll ever know."

As depicted in the network segment in Figure 3.32, it is possible to not skeletonize at all. In this case, there is a junction at each service tap, with a pipe and junction at each house. There are also junctions at the main intersections, resulting in a total of nearly fifty junctions (not including those required for fire hydrants).

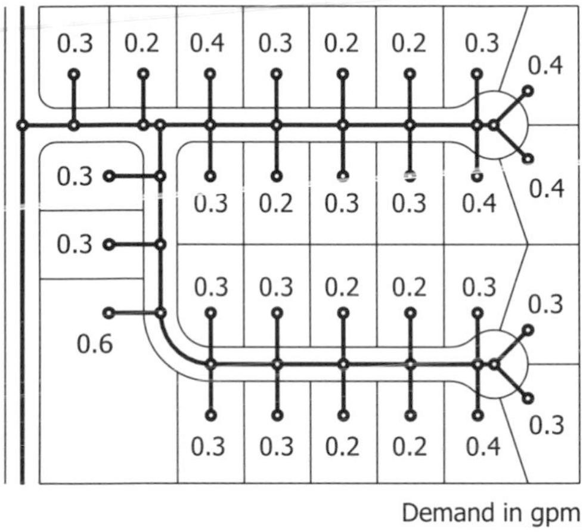

Figure 3.32
An all-link network

The same subdivision could be modeled again, but slightly more skeletonized. Instead of explicitly including each household, only the tie-ins and main intersections are included. This level of detail results in a junction count of less than twenty (Figure 3.33). Note that in this level of skeletonization, hydraulic results for the customer service lines would not be available since they were not included in the model. If results for service lines are not important, then the skeletal model shown in Figure 3.33 represents an adequate level of detail.

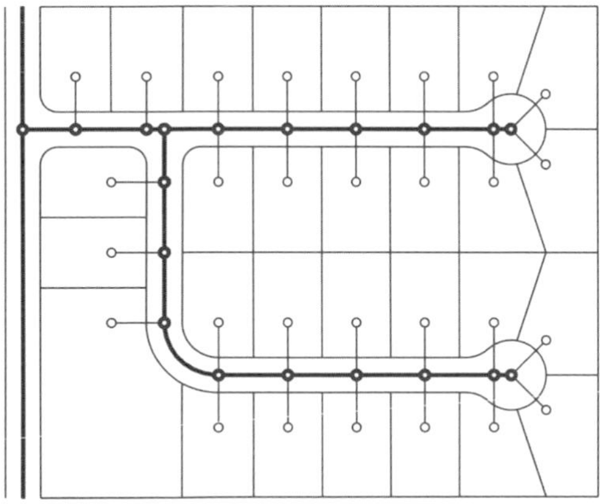

Figure 3.33
Minimal skeletonization

The system can be skeletonized even more, modeling only the ends of the main piping and the major intersections (Figure 3.34). Attributing the demands to the junctions becomes a little trickier since a junction is not being modeled at each tap location.

The demands for this model are attributed to the junction nearest to the service (following the pipeline). The dashed boundary areas indicate the contributing area for each model junction. For example, the junction in the upper right will be assigned the demand for eight houses, while the lower right junction has demands for ten houses, and so forth.

Figure 3.34
Moderate skeletonization

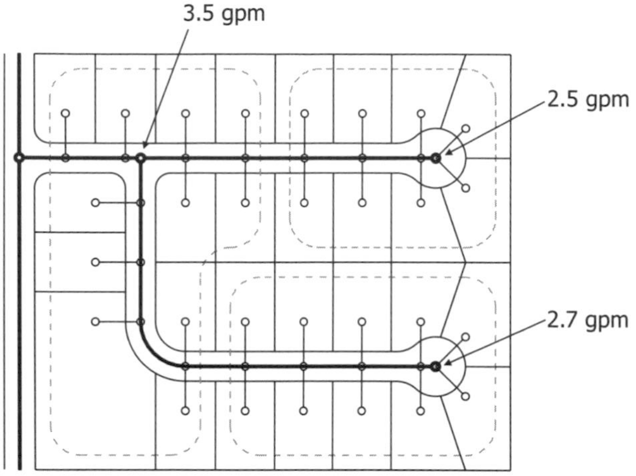

An even greater level of skeletonization can be achieved using just a single junction node where the subdivision feeds from the existing system. The piping within the entire subdivision has been removed, with all demands being attributed to the remaining junction (Figure 3.35). In this case, the model will indicate the impact of the demands associated with the subdivision on the overall hydraulic network. However, the modeler will not be able to determine how pressures and flows vary within the subdivision.

Figure 3.35
Maximum skeletonization

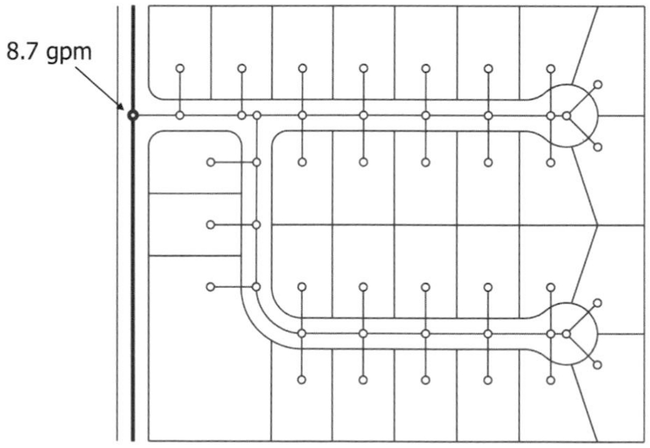

An even broader level of skeletonization is possible in which even the junction node where the subdivision piping ties into the main line is excluded. The subdivision demands would simply be added to a nearby junction, where other effects may be combined with several other subdivisions that also have not been included in detail.

As this example demonstrates, the extent of skeletonization depends on the intended use of the model, and to a large degree is subject to the modelers discretion.

Skeletonization Guidelines

There are no absolute criteria for determining whether a pipe should be included in the model, but it is safe to say that all models are most likely skeletonized to some degree. Water distribution networks vary drastically from one system to another, and modeling judgment plays a large role in the creation of a solution. For a small-diameter system, such as household plumbing or a fire sprinkler system, small differences in estimated flow rate may have perceptible effects on the system head losses. For a large city system, however, the effects of water demanded by an entire subdivision may be insignificant.

Opposing Philosophies. There are definitely opposing philosophies regarding skeletonization that stem from different modeling perspectives. Some modelers assert that a model should never be bigger than a few hundred elements, because no one can possibly digest all of the data that pours out of a larger model. Others contend that a model should include all the pipes, so that data entry can be done by less skilled personnel (since they will not need to exercise judgment about whether or not an element should be included). Followers of this approach then use database queries, automated consolidation algorithms, and demand allocation procedures (see page 126) to generate skeletonized models for individual applications.

Somewhere in the Middle. Most network models, however, fall somewhere between the two extremes. The level of skeletonization used depends on the intended use of the model. At one extreme, energy operation studies require minimal detail, while determining available fire flow at individual hydrants requires the most. For master planning or regional water studies, a broader level of skeletonization will typically suffice. For detailed design work or water quality studies, however, much more of the system needs to be included to accurately model the real-world system.

The responsibility really comes back to the modeler, who must have a good understanding of the model's intended use, and must select a level of detail appropriate for that purpose. Most modelers choose to develop their own skeletonization guidelines.

Elements of High Importance

Any elements that are important to the system or can potentially influence system behavior should be included in the model. For most models this criterion includes:

- Large water consumers
- Points of known conditions, such as sampling points
- Critical points with unknown conditions

- Large-diameter pipes
- Pipes that complete important loops
- Pumps, control valves, tanks, and other controlling elements

Elements of Unknown Importance

If the modeler is unsure what the effects of including or excluding specific elements may be, there is a very simple method that can be used to find out exactly what the effects are on the system. Run the model and see what happens.

A base skeleton can be created using experience and judgment, with pipes of questionable importance included. The model should be run over a range of study conditions and the results noted. One or more questionable pipes can then be closed (preventing them from conveying water) and the model run again. If the modeler determines that the results from the two analyses are essentially the same, then the pipes apparently did not have a significant effect on the system and can be removed from the skeleton.

If a pipe's level of significance cannot be determined, or is questionable, it is usually better to leave the pipe in the model. With older, non-graphical interfaces, it was often desirable to limit the number of pipes as much as possible to prevent becoming lost in the data. With the advanced computers and easy-to-use software tools of today, however, there are fewer reasons to exclude pipes from the model.

Skeletonization Conclusions

There are no hard and fast rules regarding skeletonization. It all depends on perspective and the intended use of the model. For a utility that operates large transmission mains and sells water to community networks, a model may be skeletonized to include only the source and large-diameter pipes. For a community that receives water from that utility, the opposite may be true. While most planning and analysis activities can be performed successfully with a moderately skeletonized model, local fire flow evaluations and water quality analyses call for little to no skeletonization.

3.12 MODEL MAINTENANCE

Once a water distribution model is constructed and calibrated, it can be modified to simulate and predict system behavior under a range of conditions. The model represents a significant investment on the part of the utility, and that investment should be maximized by carefully maintaining the model for use well into the future.

Good record keeping that documents model runs and history is necessary to ensure that the model is used correctly by others or at a later date, and that time is not wasted in deciphering and reconstructing what was done previously. There should be notes in the model files or paper records indicating the state of the system in the various model versions. These explanations will help subsequent users to determine the best model run to use as a starting point in future analyses.

While the initial calibrated model reflects conditions in the current system, the model is frequently used to test future conditions and alternative piping systems. The scenario manager features in modeling software (see page 108) enable the user to maintain the original model while keeping track of numerous proposed changes to the system, some of which are never constructed. Eventually, a model file may contain many "proposed" facilities and demands that fall into the following categories:

- Installed
- Under design or construction
- To be installed later
- Never to be installed

The user needs to periodically update the model file so that installed piping is accurately distinguished from proposed facilities, and that facilities that will most likely never be installed are removed from the model. The modeler also needs to be in regular contact with operations personnel to determine when new piping is placed into service. Note that there may be a substantial lag between the time that a pipe or other facility is placed into service, and the time that facility shows up in the system map or GIS.

Once a master plan or comprehensive planning study is completed, model use typically becomes sporadic, though the model will still be used to respond to developer inquiries, address operations problems, and verify project designs. Each of these special studies involves creating and running additional scenarios. A single model eventually becomes cluttered with extraneous data on alternatives not selected.

A good practice in addressing these special studies is to start from the existing model and create a new data file that will be used to study alternative plans. Once the project design is complete, the facilities and demands associated with the selected plan should be placed into the main model file as future facilities and demands. The version of the model used for operational studies should not be updated until the facilities are actually placed into service.

REFERENCES

American Water Works Association. (1996). "Ductile Iron Pipe and Fitting." *AWWA Manual M-41*, Denver, Colorado.

Benjamin, M. M., Reiber, S. H., Ferguson, J. F., Vanderwerff, E. A., and Miller, M. W. (1990). *Chemistry of corrosion inhibitors in potable water.* AWWARF, Denver, Colorado.

Caldwell, D. H., and Lawrence, W. B. (1953). "Water Softening and Conditioning Problems." *Industrial Engineering Chemistry*, 45(3), 535.

Eggener, C. L., and Polkowski, L. (1976). "Network Modeling and the Impact of Modeling Assumptions. *Journal of the American Water Works Association*, 68(4), 189.

ESRI. (2001). "What is a GIS?" http://www.esri.com/library/gis/abtgis/what_gis.html.

Langelier, W. F. (1936). "The Analytical Control of Anti-Corrosion in Water Treatment." *Journal of the American Water Works Association*, 28(10), 1500.

Maddison, L. A., and Gagnon, G. A. (1999). "Evaluating Corrosion Control Strategies for a Pilot-Scale Distribution System." *Proceedings of the Water Quality Technology Conference*, American Water Works Association, Denver, Colorado.

McNeil, L. S., and Edwards, M. (2000). "Phosphate Inhibitors and Red Water in Stagnant Iron Pipes." *Journal of Environmental Engineering*, ASCE, 126(12), 1096.

Merrill, D. T. and Sanks, R. L. (1978). *Corrosion Control by Deposition of $CaCO_3$ Films*. AWWA, Denver, Colorado.

Mullen, E. D., and Ritter, J. A. (1974). "Potable-Water Corrosion Control." *Journal of the American Water Works Association*, 66(8), 473.

Shamir, U. and Hamberg, D. (1988a). "Schematic Models for Distribution Systems Design I: Combination Concept." *Journal of Water Resources Planning and Management*, ASCE, 114(2), 129.

Shamir, U. and Hamberg, D. (1988b). "Schematic Models for Distribution Systems Design II: Continuum Approach." *Journal of Water Resources Planning and Management*, ASCE, 114(2), 141.

Volk, C., Dundore, E., Schiermann, J., LeChevallier, M. (2000). "Practical Evaluation of Iron Corrosion Control in a Drinking Water Distribution System." *Water Research*, 34(6), 1967.

Walski, T. M. (1999). "Importance and Accuracy of Node Elevation Data." *Essential Hydraulics and Hydrology*, Haestad Press, Waterbury, Connecticut.

Walski, T. M. (2000). "Hydraulic Design of Water Distribution Storage Tanks." *Water Distribution System Handbook*, Mays L. W., ed., McGraw Hill, New York, New York.

DISCUSSION TOPICS AND PROBLEMS

Earn CEUs — Read Chapters 3 and 4 and complete the problems. Submit your work to Haestad Methods and earn up to 1.5 CEUs. See *Continuing Education Units* on page xiii for more information, or visit www.haestad.com/wdm-ceus/.

3.1 Manually find the flow rate through the system shown in Figure 3.36 and compute the pressure at node J-1. Also, find the suction and discharge pressures of the pump if it is at an elevation of 115 ft. Use the Hazen-Williams equation to compute friction losses. Assume h_p is in ft and Q is in cfs.

Figure 3.36

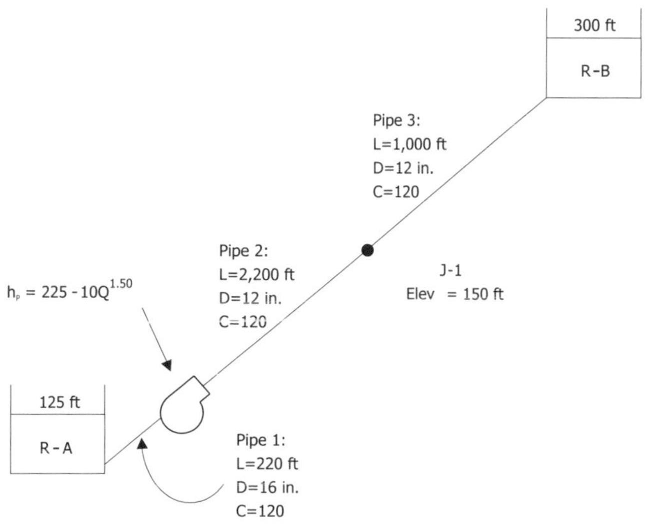

3.2 Manually find the flow in each pipeline and the pressure at node J-1 for the system shown in Figure 3.37. Assume that h_p is in m and Q is in m^3/s and note the demand at junction J-1 of 21.2 l/s. Use the Hazen-Williams equation to compute friction losses.

Hint: Express the flow in Pipe 3 in terms of the flow in Pipe 1 or Pipe 2.

Figure 3.37

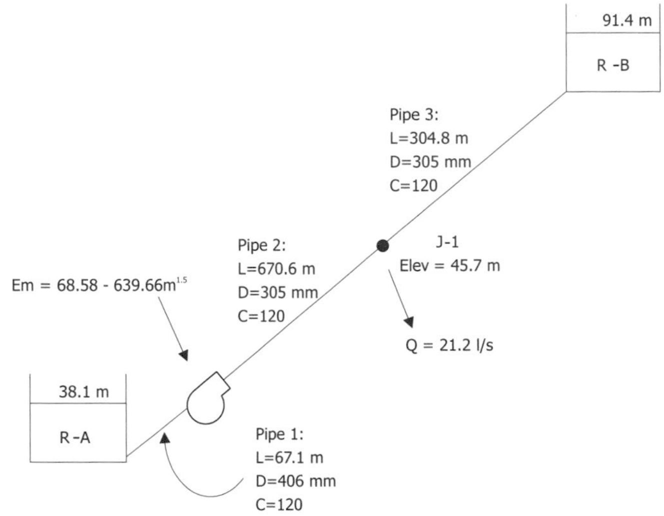

3.3 *English Units* - Manually find the discharge through each pipeline and the pressure at each junction node of the rural water system shown in Figure 3.38. Physical data for this system are given in the tables that follow. Fill in the tables at the end of the problem.

Figure 3.38

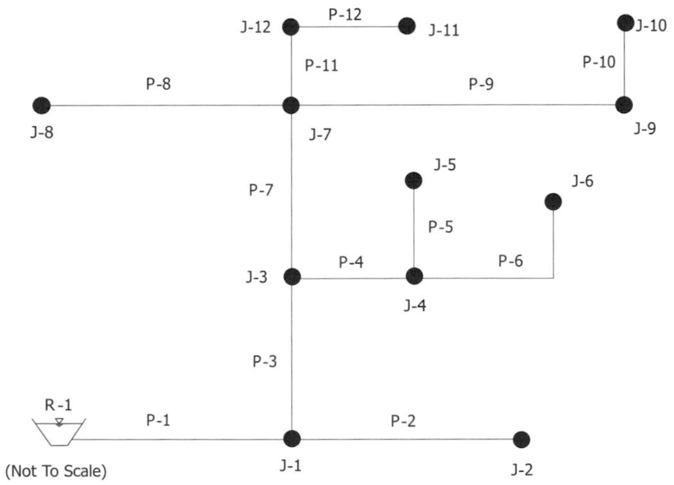

Pipe Label	Length (ft)	Diameter (in.)	Hazen-Williams C-factor
P-1	500	10	120
P-2	1,200	6	120
P-3	4,200	10	120
P-4	600	6	110
P-5	250	4	110
P-6	500	4	100
P-7	5,200	8	120
P-8	4,500	4	100
P-9	5,500	3	90
P-10	3,000	6	75
P-11	570	6	120
P-12	550	4	80

Node Label	Elevation (ft)	Demand (gpm)
R-1	1050	N/A
J-1	860	40
J-2	865	15
J-3	870	30
J-4	875	25
J-5	880	5
J-6	885	12
J-7	880	75
J-8	850	25
J-9	860	0
J-10	860	18
J-11	850	15
J-12	845	10

Pipe Label	Flow (gpm)	Head loss (ft)
P-1		
P-2		
P-3		
P-4		
P-5		
P-6		
P-7		
P-8		
P-9		
P-10		
P-11		
P-12		

Node Label	HGL (ft)	Pressure (psi)
J-1		
J-2		
J-3		
J-4		
J-5		
J-6		
J-7		
J-8		
J-9		
J-10		
J-11		
J-12		

SI Units - Manually find the discharge through each pipeline and the pressure at each junction node of the rural water system shown Figure 3.38. Physical data for this system are given in the tables that follow. Fill in the tables at the end of the problem.

Pipe Label	Length (m)	Diameter (mm)	Hazen-Williams C-factor
P-1	152.4	254	120
P-2	365.8	152	120
P-3	1,280.2	254	120
P-4	182.9	152	110
P-5	76.2	102	110
P-6	152.5	102	100
P-7	1,585.0	203	120
P-8	1,371.6	102	100
P-9	1,676.4	76	90
P-10	914.4	152	75
P-11	173.7	152	120
P-12	167.6	102	80

Node Label	Elevation (m)	Demand (l/s)
R-1	320.0	N/A
J-1	262.1	2.5
J-2	263.7	0.9
J-3	265.2	1.9
J-4	266.7	1.6
J-5	268.2	0.3
J-6	269.7	0.8
J-7	268.2	4.7
J-8	259.1	1.6
J-9	262.1	0
J-10	262.1	1.1
J-11	259.1	0.9
J-12	257.6	0.6

Pipe Label	Flow (l/s)	Head loss (m)
P-1		
P-2		
P-3		
P-4		
P-5		
P-6		
P-7		
P-8		
P-9		
P-10		
P-11		
P-12		

Node Label	HGL (m)	Pressure (kPa)
J-1		
J-2		
J-3		
J-4		
J-5		
J-6		
J-7		
J-8		
J-9		
J-10		
J-11		
J-12		

3.4 Determine the effect of placing demands at points along a pipe rather than at the end node (point D) for the 300-m long pipe segment A-D shown in Figure 3.39. The pipe has a diameter of 150 mm and a roughness height of 0.0001 m, and the kinematic viscosity of water at the temperature of interest is 1x10-6 m^2/s. The total head at Point A is 200 m, and the ground elevation along the pipe is 120 m. The flow past point A is 9 l/s. Points A, B, C, and D are equidistant from each other.

Figure 3.39

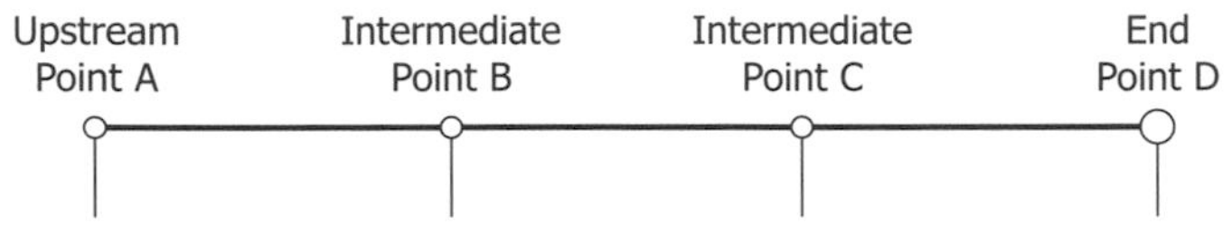

a) Assume that there is no water use along the pipe (that is, flow is 9 l/s in all segments). Determine the head loss in each segment and the pressure head (in meters) at points B, C, and D.

b) Assume that a small amount of water is used at points B and C (typical of a pipe in a residential neighborhood), such that the flow in the second and third segments decreases to 8 and 7 l/s, respectively. Determine the pressures at points B, C, and D.

c) Assume that the water is withdrawn evenly along the pipe, such that the flows in the second and third segments are 6 and 3 l/s, respectively. Find the pressures at points B, C, and D.

d) At these flows, do the pressures in the pipe vary significantly when the water use is lumped at the endpoint versus being accounted for along the length of the pipe? Would you expect a similar outcome at much higher flows?

Pressure in meters of water

Point	Part (a)	Part (b)	Part (c)
B			
C			
D			

CHAPTER

4

Water Consumption

The consumption or use of water, also known as *water demand*, is the driving force behind the hydraulic dynamics occurring in water distribution systems. Anywhere that water can leave the system represents a point of consumption, including a customer's faucet, a leaky main, or an open fire hydrant.

There are three questions related to water consumption that must be answered when building a hydraulic model: (1) How much water is being used? (2) Where are the points of consumption located? and (3) How does the usage change as a function of time? This chapter addresses these questions for each of the three basic demand types described below.

- *Customer demand* is the water required to meet the non-emergency needs of users in the system. This demand type typically represents the metered portion of the total water consumption.
- *Unaccounted-for water* is the portion of total consumption that is "lost" due to system leakage, theft, unmetered services, or other causes.
- *Fire flow demand* is a computed system capacity requirement for ensuring adequate protection is provided during fire emergencies.

Determining demands is not a straightforward process like collecting data on the physical characteristics of a system. Some data, such as billing and production records, can be collected directly from the utility but are usually not in a form that can be directly entered into the model. For example, metering data are not broken down by nodes. Once this information has been collected, establishing consumption rates is a process requiring study of past and present usage trends, and, in some cases, the projection of future ones.

After consumption rates are determined, the water use is spatially distributed as demands, or *loads*, assigned to model nodes. This process is referred to as *loading* the model. Loading is usually a multi-step process that may vary depending upon the problem being considered. The steps below outline a typical example of the process the modeler might follow.

1. Allocate average day demands to nodes.
2. Develop peaking factors for steady-state runs (page 135) or diurnal curves for EPS runs (page 137).
3. Estimate fire and other special demands.
4. Project demands under future conditions for planning and design.

This chapter presents some of the methods to follow when undertaking the process of loading a water distribution system model.

4.1 BASELINE DEMANDS

Most modelers start by determining baseline demands to which a variety of peaking factors and demand multipliers can be applied, or to which new land developments and customers can be added. Baseline demands typically include both customer demands and unaccounted-for water. Usually, the average day demand in the current year is the baseline from which other demand distributions are built.

Data Sources

Pre-Existing Compiled Data. The first step in finding demand information for a specific utility should always be to research the utility's existing data. Previous studies, and possibly even existing models, may have a wealth of background information that can save many hours of investigation.

However, many utilities do not have existing studies or models, or may have only limited resources to collect this type of information. Likewise, models that do exist may be outdated, not reflecting recent expansion and growth.

System Operational Records. There are various types of operational records that can offer insight into the demand characteristics of a given system. Treatment facility logs may provide data regarding long-term usage trends such as seasonal pattern changes or general growth indications. Pumping logs and tank level charts (such as the one shown in Figure 4.1) contain data on daily system usage, as well as the changing pattern of demand and storage levels over time.

Water distribution systems may measure and record water usage in a variety of forms, including:

- Flow information, such as the rate of production of a treatment or well facility
- Volumetric information, such as the quantity of water consumed by a customer
- Hydraulic grade information, such as the water level within a tank

The data described above are frequently collected in differing formats and require conversion before they can be used. For example, tank physical characteristics can be used to convert tank level data to volumes. If data describing the temporal changes in tank levels is incorporated, volumes can be directly related to flow rates.

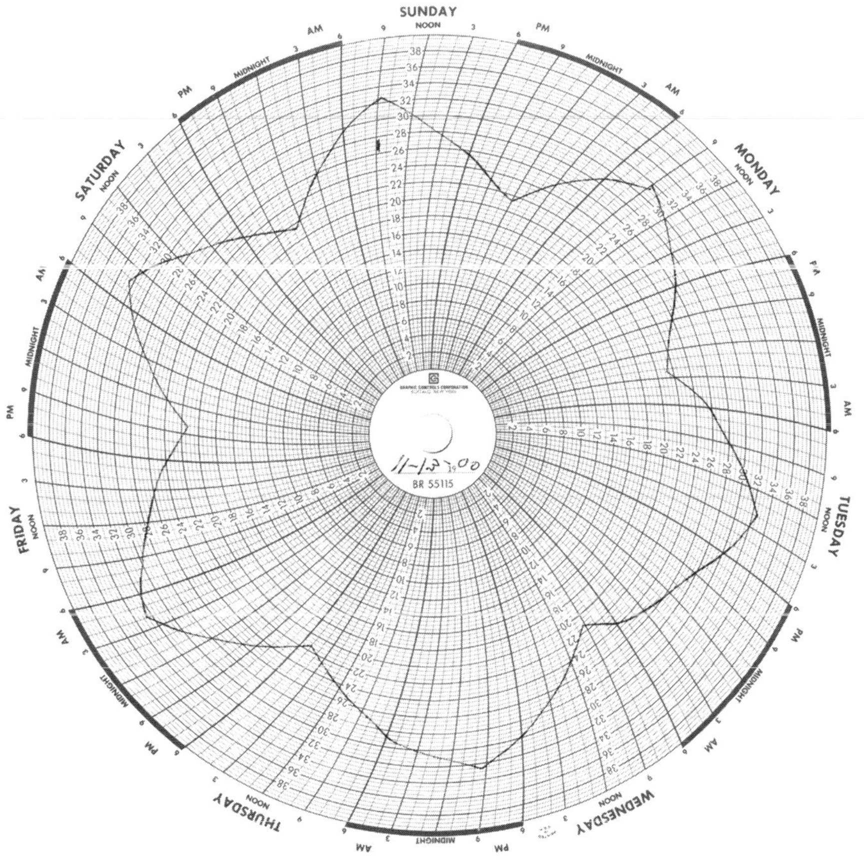

Figure 4.1
Tank level chart

Courtesy of the City of Waterbury, CT Bureau of Water

Customer Meters and Billing Records. If meters are employed throughout a system, they can be the best source of data for determining customer demands. Customers are typically billed on a volumetric measure of usage, with meter readings taken on a monthly or quarterly cycle. Using these periodically recorded usage volumes, customers' average usage rates can be computed. Billing records, therefore, provide enough information to determine a customer's baseline demand, but not enough to determine fluctuations in demand on a finer time scale such as that required for extended period simulations.

Ideally, the process of loading demand data into a model from another source would be relatively automatic. Cesario and Lee (1980) describe an early approach to automate model loading. Coote and Johnson (1995) developed a system in Valparaiso, Indiana in which each customer account was tied to a node in their hydraulic model. With the increasing popularity of Geographic Information Systems (GIS) among water utilities, more modelers are turning to GIS to store and manipulate demand data to be imported into the model. Stern (1995) described how Cybernet data were loaded from a GIS in Los Angeles, while Basford and Sevier (1995) and Buyens, Bizier, and Combee (1996) describe similar applications in Newport News, Virginia, and Lakeland, Florida, respectively. As GIS usage becomes more widespread, more utilities will construct automated links between customer data, GIS, and hydraulic models.

Spatial Allocation of Demands

While water utilities make a large number of flow measurements, such as at customer meters for billing, and at treatment plants and wells for production monitoring, data are usually not compiled on the node-by-node basis needed for modeling. The modeler is thus faced with the task of spatially aggregating data in a useful way and assigning the appropriate usage to model nodes.

The most common method of allocating baseline demands is a simple unit loading method. This method involves counting the number of customers [or acres (hectares) of a given land use, number of fixture units, or number of equivalent dwelling units] that contribute to the demand at a certain node, and then multiplying that number by the unit demand [for instance, number of gallons (liters) per capita per day] for the applicable load classification. For example, if a junction node represents a population of 200, and the average usage is 100 gal/day/person (380 l/day/person), the total baseline demand for the node would be 20,000 gal/day (75,710 l/day).

In applying unit demands, the user must be careful to understand what is accounted for by that measure. Equations 4.1, 4.2, and 4.3 show three different unit demands that can be determined for a utility (Male and Walski, 1990).

"Ammonia! Ammonia!"

Demands in the United Kingdom

Not all water systems are universally metered as is customary in North America. For example, in the United Kingdom, only roughly 10 percent of the domestic customers are metered.

Instead of metering individual customers, distribution systems in the UK are divided up into smaller zones, called District Metered Areas (DMAs), which are isolated by valving and are fed through a smaller number of inlet and outlet meters (WRc, 1985). The number of properties in a DMA is known fairly precisely, and usually varies from 500 to 5,000 properties but can go as high as 10,000. The flows are recorded using data logging technology or telemetered to a central location.

Per capita consumption at the unmetered residences is estimated to be on the order of 150 liters per capita per day, although there is considerable variation (Ofwat, 1998). Some of the variation is attributed to different socioeconomic classes as accounted for by ACORN (A Classification of Residential Neighborhoods), which classifies properties in England and Wales into categories such as "modern family housing with higher income" to "poorest council estates."

Demand patterns in the UK are similar to most other developed nations, and the patterns can be established by DMA or groups of DMAs. Data logging is used to determine individual demand patterns only for the largest users.

Because most residences are not metered, unaccounted-for water in the UK is large, but most of this water is delivered to legitimate users and can be estimated fairly reasonably. The amount of actual leakage depends on pressure, burst frequency, leakage control policy, and age of pipes.

Despite the differences in metering practice between the UK and North America, loading of the model still involves many of the same steps, and the system metering data collected in the UK can make calibration easier than in locations without pervasive distribution metering.

$$\textit{system-wide use} = (\textit{production}) / (\textit{domestic customers}) \tag{4.1}$$

$$\textit{non-industrial use} = (\textit{production - industrial use}) / (\textit{domestic customers}) \tag{4.2}$$

$$\textit{domestic use} = (\textit{domestic metered consumption}) / (\textit{domestic customers}) \tag{4.3}$$

All three unit demands can be determined on a per capita or per account basis. While all three can be referred to as unit demands, each will yield a different result, and it is important that the modeler understand which unit demand is being used. The first unit demand includes all non-emergency uses and will be the largest numerical value; the second excludes industrial uses; the third excludes industrial use and unaccounted-for water and will be the smallest. If the third unit demand is used, then unaccounted-for water and industrial use must be handled separately from the unit demands. This approach may be advantageous where industrial use is concentrated in one portion of the network.

Another approach to determining the baseline demand for individual customers involves the use of billing records. However, rarely does a system have enough recorded information to directly define all aspects of customer usage. Even in cases where both production records and full billing records are available, there may be disagreements between the two that need to be resolved.

There are two basic approaches for filling in the data gaps between water production and computed customer usage: *top-down* and *bottom-up*. Both of these methods are based on general mass balance concepts, and are shown schematically in Figure 4.2.

Figure 4.2
Approaches to model loading

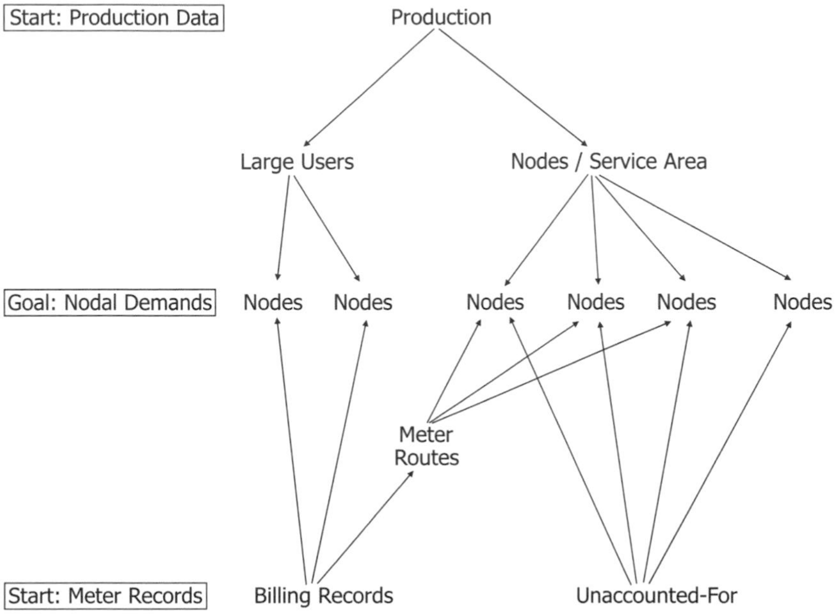

Top-down demand determination involves starting from the water sources (at the "top") and working down to the nodal demands. With knowledge about the production of water and any large individual water customers, the remainder of the demand is disaggregated among the rest of the customers. Bottom-up demand determination is exactly the opposite, starting with individual customer billing records and summing their influences using meter routes as an intermediate level of aggregation to determine the nodal demands.

Most methods for loading models are some variation or combination of the top-down and bottom-up approaches, and tend to be system-specific depending on the availability of data, the resources for data entry, and the need for accuracy in demands. For some systems, the decision to use top-down or bottom-up methods can be made on a zone-by-zone basis.

Cesario (1995) uses the terms *estimated consumption method* and *actual consumption method* to describe the two approaches above. However, both methods involve a certain level of estimation. An intermediate level of detail can be achieved by applying the top-down approach with usage data on a meter-route-by-meter-route basis (AWWA, 1989).

Most design decisions, especially for smaller pipes, are controlled by fire flows, so modest errors in loading have very little impact on pipe sizing. The case in which loading becomes critical is in the tracking of water quality constituents through a system, because fire flows are not typically considered in such cases.

■ **Example - Top-Down Demand Determination** Consider a system that serves a community of 1,000 people and a single factory, which is metered. Over the course of a year, the total production of potable water is 30,000,000 gallons (114,000 m^3). The factory meter registered a usage of 10,000,000 gallons (38,000 m^3). Determining the average per capita residential usage in this case is straightforward:

Total volume of residential usage	=	(Total usage) - (Non-residential usage)
	=	30,000,000 gallons - 10,000,000 gallons
	=	20,000,000 gallons
Residential volume usage per capita	=	(Total volume of residential usage) / (no. of residents)
	=	20,000,000 gallons / 1,000 capita
	=	20,000 gallons/capita

Residential usage rate per capita (given that prior volume calculations were for a period of one year)

	=	(Residential volume usage per capita) / time
	=	(20,000 gallons/capita/year) x (1 year / 365 days)
	=	55 gallons/capita/day = 210 liters/capita/day

Models usually require demands in gallons per minute or liters per second, which gives:

0.038 gpm/capita = 0.0024 l/s/capita

Next, the approximate number of people (or houses) per node (e.g., 25 houses with 2.5 residents per house = 62.5 residents/node) is determined to give average nodal demand of:

2.37 gpm/node =0.15 l/s/node

These average residential nodal demands can be adjusted for different parts of town based on population density, amount of lawn irrigation, or other factors.

■ **Example - Bottom-Up Demand Determination** Each customer account is assigned an x-y coordinate in a GIS. Then, each account can be assigned to a node in the model based on polygons around each node in the GIS. (If a GIS is not available, customer accounts can be directly assigned to a node in the customer service information system used for billing purposes.) Then, each account in the customer information database records can be assigned to a model node. By querying the customer information database, the average demand at each node for any billing period can be determined.

The billing data must now be corrected for unaccounted-for water. Consider a user who decides to allocate unaccounted-for water uniformly to each node. The daily production is 82,000 gpd, while metered sales are 65,000 gpd. For each node, the demand must be corrected for unaccounted-for water. One approach is to assign uncounted-for water in proportion to the demand at a node using:

Corrected demand = (Node consumption) x [(Production) / (Metered Sales)]

For a node with a consumption of 4.2 gpm, the corrected demand is:

Corrected demand = (4.2 gpm) x (82,000/65,000) = 5.3 gpm = 0.33 l/s

---

As can be seen in the examples above, bottom-up demand allocation requires a great deal of initial effort to set up links between accounts and nodes, but once this work is done, the loads can be recalculated easily. Of course, the corrections due to unaccounted-for water and the fact that instantaneous demands are most likely not equal to average demands suggest that both approaches are subject to error.

■ **Example - Demand Allocation** In a detailed demand allocation, a key step is determining the customers assigned to each node. Figure 4.3 demonstrates the allocation of customer demands to modeled junction nodes. The dashed lines represent the boundaries between junction associations. For example, the junction labeled *J-1* should have demands that represent nine homes and two commercial establishments. Likewise, *J-4* represents the school, six homes, and one commercial building.

Figure 4.3
Allocating demands to network junctions

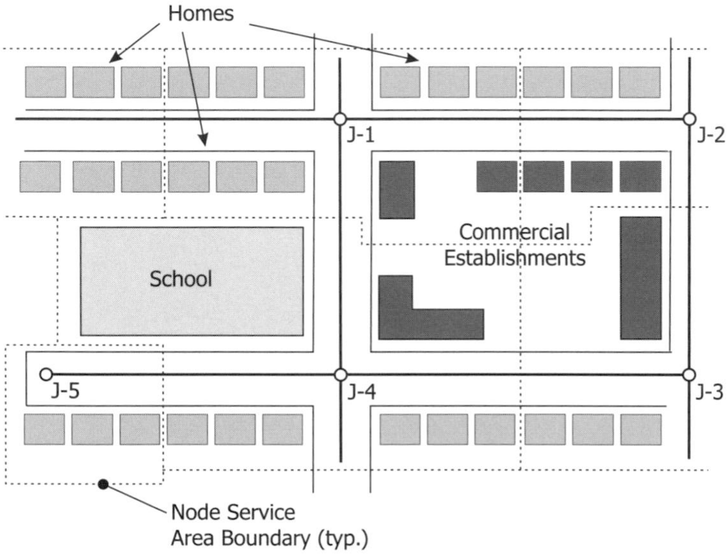

Following demand allocation, the modeler must ensure that demands have been assigned to junction nodes in such a way that (1) the sums of the nodal demands system-wide and in each pressure zone are in agreement with production records, and (2) the spatial allocation of demands closely approximates actual demands.

When working with high quality GIS data, the modeler can much more precisely assign demands to nodes. Nodal demands can be loaded using several GIS-related methodologies, ranging from a simple inverse pipe-diameter allocation model to a comprehensive polygon overlay. The inverse pipe-diameter approach assumes that demands are associated with small-diameter pipes, whereas large-diameter pipes are mainly used for transmission and thus should have less "weight" associated with them. More detailed methods make use of extensive statistical data analysis and GIS processing by combining layers of data that account for variables such as population changes over time, land use, seasonal changes, planning, and future development rates. Davis and Brawn (2000) describe an approach they employed to allocate demands using a GIS.

Categorizing Demands

Sometimes water users at a single node fall into several categories, and the modeler would like to keep track of these categories within the model. Composite demands enable the modeler to do this type of tracking. The modeler can selectively search for all demands of a certain type (for example, residential or industrial) and make adjustments. The modeler can also make changes to the characteristics of an entire category, and all of the customers of that type will automatically be modified.

Composite Demands. Whether a unit-loading or a billing-record-based method is used to generate the baseline demand, the user may need to convert it into a composite demand at a particular node. This conversion is necessary since a junction node does not always supply a single customer type. When more than one demand type is served by a particular junction, the demand is said to be a *composite*. Determining the total rate of consumption for a junction node with a composite demand is a simple matter of summing the individual components. Composite demands are also a way of keeping track of unaccounted-for water independent of the other demands at a node.

When temporal patterns are applied to composite demands, the total demand for a junction at any given time is equal to the sum of each baseline demand times its respective pattern multiplier. It is also possible with most software packages to assign a different pattern to the different components of the composite demand.

$$Q_{i,t} = \sum_{j} B_{i,j} P_{i,j,t} \tag{4.4}$$

where $Q_{i,t}$ = total demand at junction i at time t (cfs, m³/s)
$B_{i,j}$ = baseline demand for demand type j at junction i (cfs, m³/s)
$P_{i,j,t}$ = pattern multiplier for demand type j at junction i at time t

Nomenclature. Depending on the scale of the model, the demand type may consist of such broad categories as "residential," "commercial," and "industrial," or be broken down into a finer level of detail with categories such as "school," "restaurant," "multi-family dwelling," etc.

An issue that arises when discussing demands is that each utility classifies customers differently. For example, an apartment may be a "residential" account at one utility, a "commercial" account at another, and a "multi-family residential" at yet another. Schools may be classified as "institutional", "commercial", "public", or simply "schools". A modeler working for a utility can easily adapt to the naming conventions, but a consultant who works with many utilities may have a difficult time keeping track of the nomenclature when moving from one system to another.

Mass Balance Technique

Regardless of whether a modeler is studying the entire system, one particular pressure zone, or an individual customer, mass balance techniques are useful for determining changes in demand occurring on finer time scales than a monthly billing cycle. For a water distribution system, a mass balance simply indicates that whatever goes into the system must be equal to what comes out of the system or zone (accounting for changes in storage). In equation form, this can be stated as:

$$Q_{demand} = Q_{inflow} - Q_{outflow} + \Delta V_{storage}/\Delta t \qquad (4.5)$$

where Q_{inflow} = average rate of production (cfs, m^3/s)
Q_{demand} = average rate of demand (cfs, m^3/s)
$Q_{outflow}$ = average outflow rate (cfs, m^3/s)
$\Delta V_{storage}$ = change in storage within the system (ft^3, m^3)
Δt = time between volume measurements (sec)

Note that the rates of production and demand in the above equation are representative of the average flow rates over the time period. The change in storage, however, is found by taking the difference between storage volumes at the beginning and end of the time period for each tank, as follows:

$$\Delta V_{storage} = \sum_i (V_{i,t+\Delta t} - V_{i,t}) \qquad (4.6)$$

where $V_{i,t+\Delta t}$ = storage volume of tank i at time $t+\Delta t$ (ft^3, m^3)
$V_{i,t}$ = storage volume of tank i at time t (ft^3, m^3)

When calculating volume changes in storage, a sign convention must apply. If the volume in storage decreased during the time interval, then that volume is added to the inflows, and if it increased over the time period, then it is subtracted from inflows.

For upright cylindrical tanks (or any tank with vertical sides), the change in storage can be determined directly from the change in tank level, as follows:

$$\Delta V_{storage} = \sum_i (H_{i,t+\Delta t} - H_{i,t})A_{i,t} \qquad (4.7)$$

where $H_{i,t+\Delta t}$ = water level at beginning of times step $t+\Delta t$ at tank i (ft, m)
$H_{i,t}$ = water level at beginning of times step t at tank i (ft, m)
$A_{i,t}$ = surface area of tank i during time step t (ft^2, m^2)

■ **Example - Mass Balance** Consider a pressure zone with a single cylindrical tank having a diameter of 40 feet. At the beginning of a daily monitoring interval, the water level is at 28.3 feet, and at the beginning of the next day it is 29.1 feet. During that time, the total flow into that zone is determined to be 455 gallons per minute, and there is no outflow to other zones. What is the total average daily demand within the zone?

Knowing the tank's diameter, its area is found to be:

$$A = \frac{\pi D^2}{4} = \frac{\pi(40)^2}{4} = 1256 ft^2$$

The change in storage is then found as:

$$dV = A(H_{i+1} - H_i) = 1256\, ft^2\, (29.1\, ft - 28.3\, ft) \times 7.48\, gal/ft^3 = 7{,}516\, gal$$

Storage in the tank increased over the monitoring period, thus the sign convention dictates that the flows to storage be subtracted from the total inflow. With the change in storage and the average inflow, the average zone demand occurring over the hourly monitoring period is:

$$Q = 455 - \frac{7516}{60 \times 24} = 449.8 \text{ gpm}$$

This answer makes sense since the average zone demand must be smaller than the average inflow for the tank to fill during the monitoring period.

Unaccounted-For Water

Ideally, if individual meter readings are taken at every customer, they should exactly equal the amount of water that is measured leaving the treatment facility. In practice, however, this is not the case. Although inflow does indeed equal outflow, not all of the outflows are metered. These "lost" flows are referred to as unaccounted-for water (UFW).

There are many possible reasons why the sum of all metered customer usage may be less than the total amount of water produced by the utility. The most common reasons for discrepancies are leakage, errors in measurement, and unmetered usage. Ideally, customer demands and unaccounted-for water should be estimated separately. In this way, a utility can analyze the benefits of reducing unaccounted-for water.

Unaccounted-for water must be loaded into the model just like any other demand. However, the fact that it is unaccounted-for means that the user does not know where to place it. Usually, the user simply calculates total unaccounted-for water and divides that quantity equally among all nodes. If the modeler knows that one portion of a system has a greater likelihood of leakage because of age, then more unaccounted-for water can be placed within that section.

Leakage. Leakage is frequently the largest component of UFW and includes distribution losses from supply pipes, distribution and trunk mains, services up to the meter, and tanks. The amount of leakage varies from system to system, but there is a general correlation between the age of a system and the amount of UFW. Newer systems may have as little as 5% leakage, while older systems may have 40% leakage or higher. Leakage tends to increase over time unless a leak detection and repair program is in place. Use of leak acoustic detection equipment to listen for leaks is shown in Figure 4.4.

Other factors affecting leakage include system pressure (the higher the pressure, the more leakage), burst frequencies of mains and service pipes, and leakage detection and control policies. These factors make leakage very difficult to estimate, even without the complexity of approximating other UFW causes. If better information is not available, UFW is usually assigned uniformly around the system.

Figure 4.4
Use of leak detection equipment

Meter Under Registration. Flow measurement errors also contribute to UFW. Flow measurements are not always exact, and thus metered customer usage may contain inaccuracies. Some flow meters under-register usage at low flow rates, especially as they get older.

Unmetered Usage. Systems may have illegal connections or other types of unmetered usage. Not all unmetered usage is indicative of water theft. Fire hydrants, blow-offs, and other maintenance appurtenances are typically not metered.

4.2 DEMAND MULTIPLIERS

By definition, baseline demands during a steady-state simulation do not change over time. However, in reality, water demand varies continuously over time according to several time scales, including:

- **Daily -** Water use varies with activities over the course of a day.
- **Weekly -** Weekend patterns are different from weekdays.
- **Seasonal -** Depending on the extent of outdoor water use or seasonal changes, such as tourism, consumption can vary significantly from one season to another.

- **Long-term -** Demands can grow due to increases in population and the industrial base, changes in unaccounted-for water, annexation of areas previously without service, and regionalization of neighboring water systems.

The modeler needs to be cognizant of the impacts of temporal changes on all of these scales. These time-varying demands are handled in the model by either:

- steady-state runs for a particular condition; or
- extended period model runs.

For extended period simulations, the model requires both baseline demand data and information on how demands vary over time. Modeling of these temporal variations is described in the next section.

In steady-state runs, the user can build on the baseline demand by using multipliers and/or assigning different demands to specific nodes. Fortunately, the entire demand allocation need not be redone.

Some examples of demand events frequently considered are listed below.

- **Average Day Demand -** the average rate of demand for an average day (past, present, or future)
- **Maximum Day Demand -** the average rate of use on the maximum usage day (past, present, or future)
- **Peak Hour Demand -** the average rate of usage during the maximum hour of usage (past, present, or future)
- **Maximum Day of Record -** the highest average rate of demand for the historical record

Peaking Factors

For some consumption conditions (especially predicted consumption conditions), demands can be determined by applying a multiplication factor or a *peaking factor.* For example, a modeler might determine that future maximum day demands will be double the average day demands for a particular system. The peaking factor is calculated as the ratio of discharges for the various conditions. For example, the peaking factor applied to average day demands to obtain maximum day demands can be found using Equation 4.8.

$$PF = Q_{max}/Q_{avg} \tag{4.8}$$

where PF = peaking factor between maximum day and average day demands
Q_{max} = maximum day demands (cfs, m^3/s)
Q_{avg} = average day demands (cfs, m^3/s)

Determining system-wide peaking factors is fairly easy because most utilities keep good records on production and tank levels. However, peaking factors for different types of demands applied at individual nodes are more difficult to determine, since individual nodes do not necessarily follow the same demand pattern as the system as a whole.

Peaking factors from average day to maximum day tend to range from 1.2 to 3.0, and factors from average day to peak hour are typically between 3.0 and 6.0. Of course, these values are system-specific, so they must be determined based on the demand characteristics of the system at hand.

Fire flows represent a special type of peaking condition, and they are described on page 147. Fire flows are usually added to maximum day flow when evaluating the capacity of the system for fire fighting.

Demands in Systems with High Unaccounted-For Water. Using global demand multipliers for projections in systems with high unaccounted-for water is based on the assumption that the relative size of unaccounted-for water will remain constant in the future. Unaccounted-for water can also be treated as one of the parts of a composite demand, as discussed on page 131. If unaccounted-for water is reduced, then the utility will see higher peaking factors because unaccounted-for water tends to flatten out the diurnal demand curve. Walski (1999) describes a method for correcting demand multipliers for systems where leakage is expected to change over time.

$$\frac{M}{A} = \frac{\left(\frac{M}{A}\right)_c Q_c + L}{Q_c + L} \tag{4.9}$$

where M/A = corrected multiplier
$(M/A)_c$ = multiplier for consumptive users only
Q_c = water use through customer meters in future (cfs, m^3/s)
L = leakage in future (cfs, m^3/s)

■ **Example - Peaking Factors** For example, if the multiplier for metered customers (M/A_c) is 2.1, and the metered demand (Q_c) is projected to be 2.4 MGD in a future condition, then the overall multiplier can be determined based on estimated future leakage as shown below.

Leakage (MGD)	M/A
0.0	2.1
0.5	1.9
1.0	1.8

Because leakage contributes the same to average and peak demands, the peak demand multipliers increase as leakage decreases. The numerical value of $(M/A)_c$ can be calculated using current year data and Equation 4.10.

$$\left(\frac{M}{A}\right)_c = \frac{\frac{M}{A}(Q_c + L) - L}{Q_c} \tag{4.10}$$

The L and Q values are based on current year actual values. For example, in this problem, say that the current year overall multiplier is 1.8, the metered demand is 1.5 MGD, and the leakage is 0.6 MGD. The multiplier for metered consumption is then:

$$\left(\frac{M}{A}\right)_c = \frac{1.8(1.5 + 0.6) - 0.6}{1.5} = 2.1$$

Commercial Building Demands. A means of estimating design demands for proposed commercial buildings is called the *Fixture Unit Method*. If the nature of the customer/buildings is known, and the number and types of water fixtures (toilets, dish washers, drinking fountains, etc.) can be calculated, then the peak design flow can be determined. The fixture unit method accounts for the fact that it is very unlikely that all of the fixtures in a building will be operated simultaneously. More information on using this method is included in Chapter 8 (see page 318).

4.3 TIME-VARYING DEMANDS

Water usage in municipal water distribution systems is inherently unsteady due to continuously varying demands. In order for an extended period simulation to accurately reflect the dynamics of the real system, these demand fluctuations must be incorporated into the model.

The temporal variations in water usage for municipal water systems typically follow a 24-hour cycle called a *diurnal* demand pattern. However, system flows experience changes not only on a daily basis, but also weekly and annually. As one might expect, weekend usage patterns often differ from weekday patterns. Seasonal differences in water usage have been related to climatic variables such as temperature and precipitation, but are also related to the changing habits of customers, such as outdoor recreational and agricultural activities occurring in the summer months.

Diurnal Curves

Each city has its own unique level of usage that is a function of recent climatic conditions and the time of day. (Economic growth also influences demands, but its effect occurs over periods longer than the typical modeling time horizon, and it is accounted for using future demand projections.) Figure 4.5 illustrates a typical diurnal curve for a residential area. There is relatively low usage at night when most people sleep, increased usage during the early morning hours as people wake up and prepare for the day, decreased usage during the middle of the day, and finally, increased usage again in the early evening as people return home.

For other water utilities and other types of demands, the usage pattern may be very different. For example, in some areas, residential irrigation occurs overnight to minimize evaporation, which may cause peak usage to occur during the pre-dawn hours.

For small towns that are highly influenced by a single industry, the diurnal pattern may be much more pronounced because the majority of the population follows a similar schedule. For example, if a large water-using industry runs 24 hours per day, the overall demand pattern for the system may appear relatively flat since the steady industrial usage is much larger than peaks in the residential patterns.

Figure 4.5
A typical diurnal curve

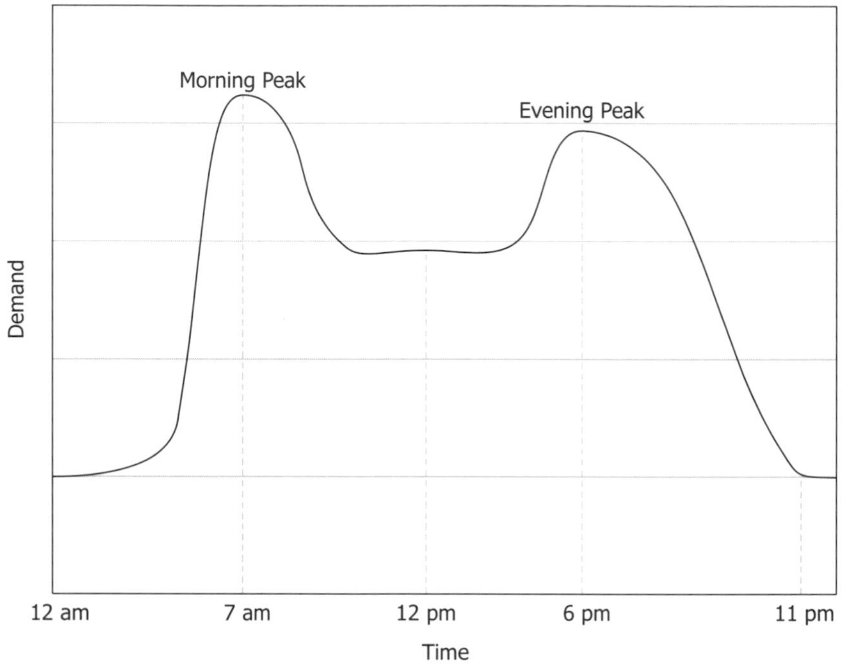

Developing System-Wide Diurnal Curves

A system-wide diurnal curve can be constructed using the same mass balance techniques discussed earlier in this chapter. The only elaboration is that the mass balance is performed as a series of calculations, one for each hydraulic step of an EPS simulation.

Time Increments. The amount of time between measurements has a direct correlation to the resolution and precision of the constructed diurnal curve. If measurements are only available once per day, then only a daily average can be calculated. Likewise, if measurements are available in hourly increments, then hourly averages can be used to define the pattern over the entire day.

If the modeler tries to use a time step that is too small, small errors in tank water level can lead to large errors in water use calculations. This type of error is explained further in Walski, Lowry, and Rhee (2000). Modeling of hydraulic time steps smaller than one hour is usually only justified in situations in which tank water levels change rapidly. Even if facility operations (such as pump cycling) occur frequently, it may still be acceptable for the demand pattern time interval to be longer than the hydraulic time step.

The modeler should be aware that incremental measurements can still overlook a peak event. For example, consider something as simple as determining the peak-hour demand (the highest average demand over any continuous one-hour period). If measurements are taken every hour on the hour, then the computed peak will only be accurate if the actual peak begins and ends right on an even hour increment (such as 7:00 to 8:00 a.m.). The modeler will underestimate peak hour usage if the true peak occurs from 7:15 to 8:15 a.m., or from 6:30 to 7:30 a.m. The diurnal demand curve in Figure 4.6 illustrates this point. In this example, as time increments become smaller, peak flows become higher (for instance, the 15-minute peak is higher than the one-hour peak).

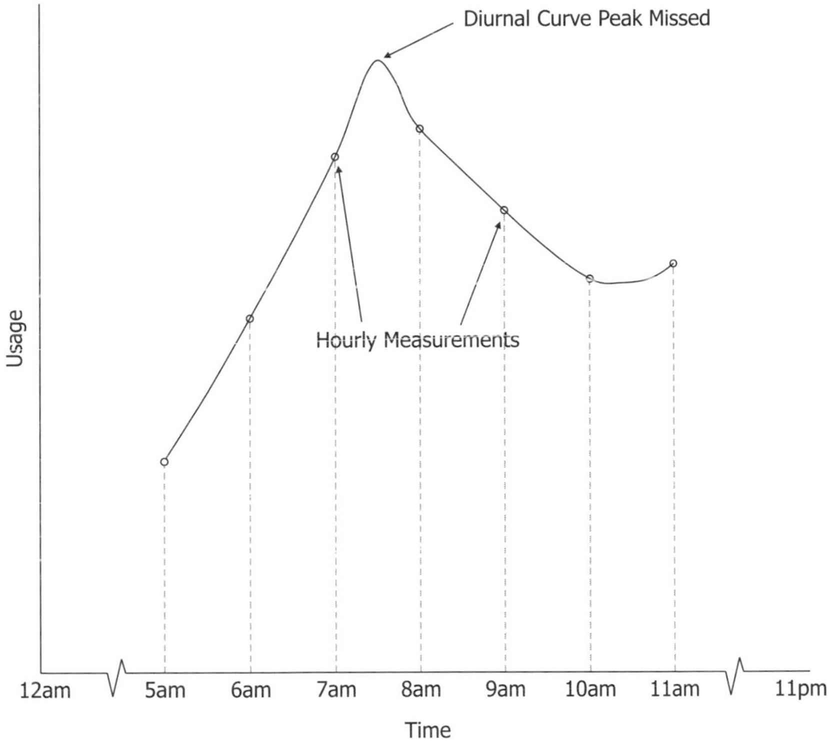

Figure 4.6
Missed peak on a diurnal curve due to model time step

Developing Customer Diurnal Curves

Frequently, developing a diurnal curve for a specific customer requires more information than can be extracted from typical billing records. In these situations more intensive data collection methods are needed to portray the time variant nature of the demands.

Data Logging for Customer Usage. Manually reading a customer's water meter at frequent intervals would obviously be a tedious and expensive undertaking. The process of *data-logging* refers to the automated gathering of raw data in the field. This data is later compiled and analyzed for a variety of purposes, among them the creation of diurnal demand curves. Various applications of data logging are described in papers by Brainard (1994); Rhoades (1995); and DeOreo, Heaney, and Mayer (1996).

There have been many recent advances in data-logging technology, making it a reliable and fairly inexpensive way to record customer water usage. Figure 4.7 illustrates a typical meter/data logger setup. Utilities can now easily place a data logger on a customer meter and determine that customer's consumption pattern. While it would be nice to have such a detailed level of data on all customers, the cost of obtaining the information is only justifiable for large customers and a sampling of smaller ones.

Figure 4.7
A typical meter/data logger setup

Meter-Master Model 100EL Flow Recorder manufactured by F.S. Brainard & Company

Representative Customers. Although it is possible to study a few customers in detail and extend the conclusions of that study to the rest of the system, this type of data extrapolation has some inherent dangers. The probability of selecting the "perfect" average customer is small, and any deviation from the norm or error in measurement will be compounded when it is applied to an entire community. As with all statistical data collection methods, the smaller the sample size, the less confidence there can be in the results.

There are also applications in which use of a representative customer is inappropriate under any circumstances. With large industries, for example, there may be no relationship at all between the volumes and patterns of usage just because they share a similar zoning classification. Therefore, demands for large consumers (industries, hospitals, hotels, etc.) and their diurnal variations should be individually determined.

Even if data logging cannot be applied to all customers, studying the demands of large consumers and applying the top-down demand determination concept to the smaller consumers can still yield reasonable demand calculations. The large customer data is subtracted from the overall system or zone usage, and the difference in demand is attributable to the smaller customers.

It is impossible to know with absolute certainty when water will be used or how much water is used in a short period of time, even though usage per billing period is known exactly. Bowen, Harp, Baxter, and Shull (1993) collected data from single and multi-family residential customers in several U.S. cities. These demand patterns can be used as a starting point for assigning demand patterns to residential nodes.

Buchberger and Wu (1995) and Buchberger and Wells (1996) developed a stochastic model for residential water demands and verified it by collecting extensive data on individual residential customers. The model is particularly useful for evaluating the hydraulics of dead-ends and looped systems in the periphery of distribution networks. The researchers found that the demand at an individual house cannot simply be multiplied by the number of houses to determine the demand in a larger area. The methods that they developed provide a way of combining the individual stochastic demands from individual customers who are brushing their teeth or running their washing machines, etc. into the aggregate for use in a larger area over a larger time interval.

In general, hotels and apartments have demand patterns similar to those of residential customers, office buildings have demand patterns corresponding to 8 a.m. to 5 p.m. operations, and retail area demand patterns reflect 9 a.m. to 9 p.m. operations. Every large industry that uses more than a few percentage points of total system production should have an individual demand pattern developed for it.

Defining Usage Patterns Within a Model

Usage could be defined directly by describing a series of actual flow versus time points for each junction in the system. One shortcoming of this type of definition is that it does not offer much data reuse for nodes with similar usage patterns. Consequently, most hydraulic models express demands by using a constant baseline demand multiplied by a dimensionless demand pattern factor at each time increment. The series of demand pattern multipliers models the diurnal variation in demand, and can be reused at nodes with similar usage characteristics. The baseline demand is often chosen to be the average daily demand (although peak day demand or some other value can be used). Assuming a baseline demand of 200 gpm, Table 4.1 illustrates how nodal demands are computed using a base demand and pattern multipliers.

Table 4.1 Calculation of Nodal Demands Using Pattern Multipliers

Time	Pattern Multiplier	Demand
0:00	0.7	200 gpm x 0.7 = 140 gpm
1:00	1.1	200 gpm x 1.1 = 220 gpm
2:00	1.8	200 gpm x 1.8 = 360 gpm

As one can imagine, usage patterns are as diverse as the customers themselves. Figure 4.8 illustrates just how different diurnal demand curves for various classifications can be. A broad zoning classification, such as commercial, may contain differences significant enough to warrant the further definition of subcategories for the different types of businesses being served. For instance, a hotel may have a demand pattern that resembles that of a residential customer. A dinner restaurant may have its peak usage during the late afternoon and evening. A clothing store may use very little water, regardless of the time of day. Water usage in an office setting may coincide with coffee breaks and lunch hours.

Figure 4.8
Diurnal curve for different user categories

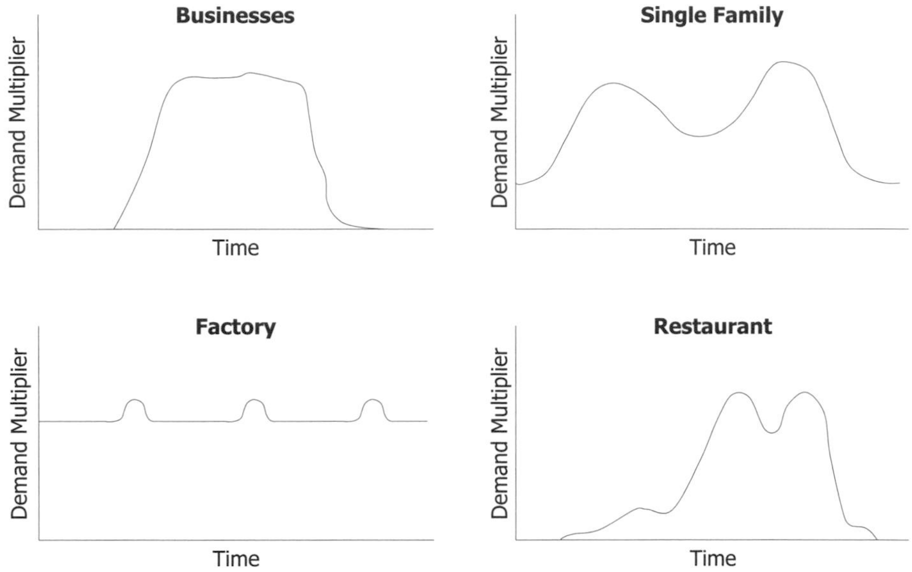

There will sometimes be customers within a demand classification whose individual demand patterns may differ significantly from the typical demand pattern assigned to the classification as a whole. For most types of customers, the impact such differences have on the model is insignificant. For other customers, such as industrial users, errors in the usage pattern may have a large impact on the model. In general, the larger the individual usage of a customer, the more important it is to ensure the accuracy of the consumption data.

Stepwise and Continuous Patterns. In a *stepwise* demand pattern, demand multipliers are assumed to remain constant over the duration of the pattern time step. A *continuous* pattern, on the other hand, refers to a pattern that is defined independently of the pattern time step. Interpolation methods are used to compute multiplier values at intermediate time steps. If the pattern time step is reset to a smaller or larger value, the pattern multipliers are automatically recalculated. The pattern multiplier value is updated by linearly interpolating between values occurring along the continuous curve at the new time step interval. The result is a more precise curve fit that is independent of the time step specified (as shown in Figure 4.9).

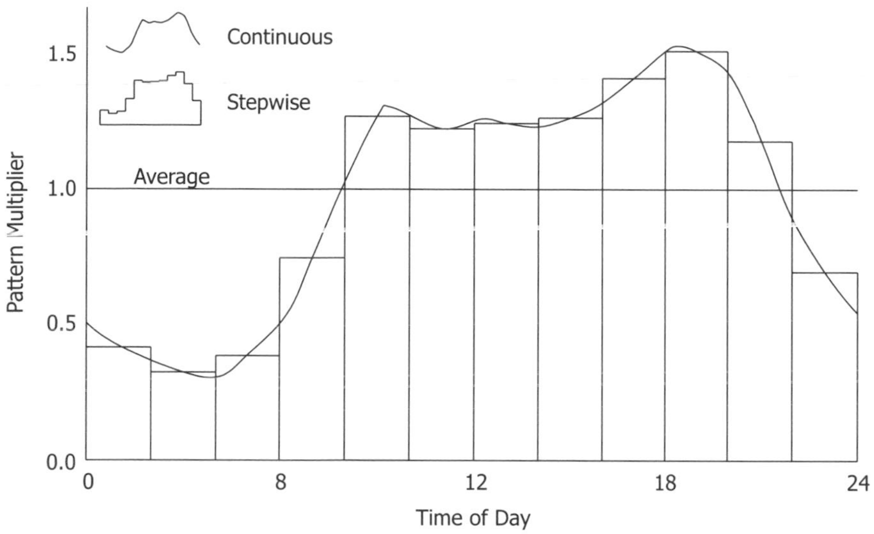

Figure 4.9
Stepwise and continuous pattern variation

For example, the pattern from Table 4.1 can be extended to show how a typical model might determine multipliers after the time step had been changed from 1 hour to 15 minutes over the time period 0:00 to 1:00. As Table 4.2 shows, a pattern multiplier for an intermediate time increment in a continuous pattern can differ significantly from its stepwise pattern counterpart.

Table 4.2 Interpolated stepwise and continuous pattern multipliers

Time	Pattern Multiplier	Stepwise Multiplier	Continuous Multiplier
0:00	0.7	0.7	0.7
0:15	0.7	0.7	0.8
0:30	0.7	0.7	0.9
0:45	0.7	0.7	1.0
1:00	1.1	1.1	1.1

Pattern Start Time and Repetition. When defining and working with patterns, it is important to understand how the pattern start time is referenced. Does pattern hour 2 refer to 2:00 a.m., or does it refer to the second hour from the beginning of a simulation? If a model simulation begins at midnight, then there is no difference between military time and time step number. If the model is intended to start at some other time (such as 6:00 a.m., when many systems have refilled all their tanks), then the patterns may need to be adjusted, advancing or retarding them in time accordingly.

Most modelers accept that demand patterns repeat every 24 hours with only negligible differences, and are willing to use the same pattern each day, in such a way that hours 25 and 49 use the same demands as the first hour. For a factory with three shifts, a pattern may repeat every eight hours. Other patterns may not repeat at all. Each software package handles pattern repetition in its own way; thus, some research and experimentation may be required to produce the desired behavior for a particular application.

4.4 PROJECTING FUTURE DEMANDS

Water distribution models are created not only to solve the problems of today, but also to prevent problems in the future. With almost any endeavor, the future holds a lot of uncertainty, and demand projection is no exception. Long-range planning may include the analysis of a system for 5-, 10-, and 20-year time frames. When performing long-term planning analyses, estimating future demands is an important factor influencing the quality of information provided by the model.

The uncertainty of this process puts the modeler in the difficult position of trying to predict the future. The complexity of such analyses, however, can be reduced to some extent with software that supports the creation and comparison of a series of possible alternative futures. Testing alternative future projections provides a way for the modeler to understand the sensitivity of decisions regarding demand projections. Scenario

"Those who do not learn from the future are destined to make mistakes in it."

management tools in models help make this process easier. Even the most comprehensive scenario management, however, is just another tool that needs to be applied intelligently to obtain reasonable results.

Historical Trends

Since the growth of cities and industries is hard to predict, it follows that it is also difficult to predict future water demands. Demand projections are only as accurate as the assumptions made and the methods used to extrapolate development. While some cities have relatively stagnant demands, others experience volatile growth that challenges engineers designing water systems.

How will the economy affect local industries? Will growth rates continue at their current rate, or will they level off? Will regulations requiring low-flow fixtures actually result in a drop in water usage? What will be the combined result of increased population and greater interest in water conservation? These questions are all difficult to answer, and no method exists that can answer them with absolute certainty.

In general, the decision about which alternative future projection should be used is not so much a modeling decision as a utility-wide planning decision. The modeler alone should not try to predict the future, but rather facilitate the utility decision-makers' process of coming to a consensus on likely future demands.

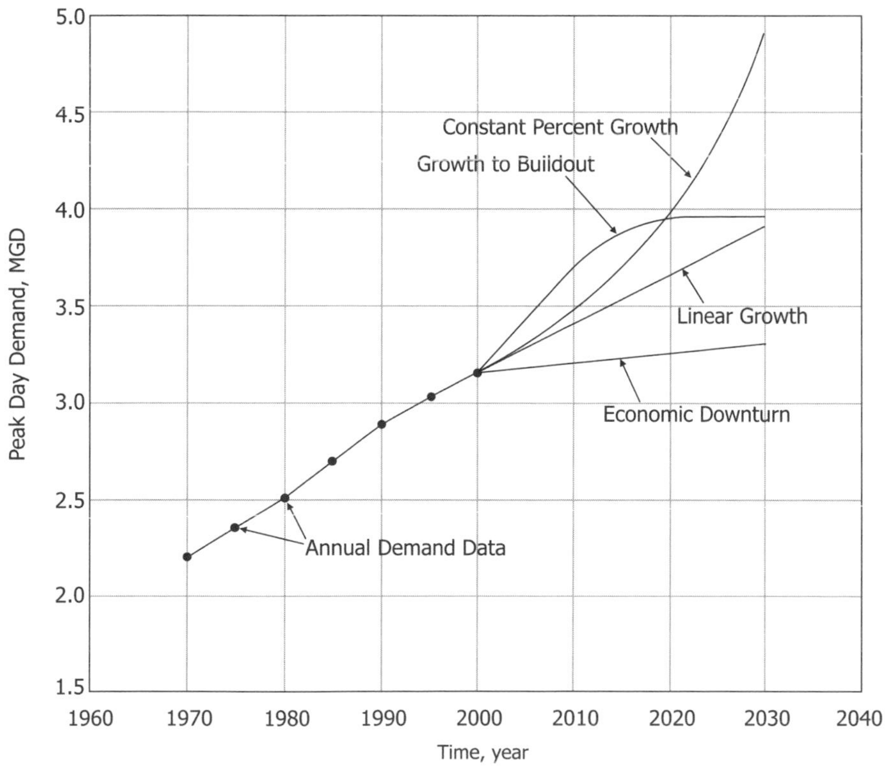

Figure 4.10
Several methods for projecting future demands

Figure 4.10 illustrates some possible alternative futures given a historical demand pattern. In spite of its shortcomings, the most commonly used method for predicting demands is to examine historical demand trends and to extrapolate them into the future under the assumption that they will continue.

Spatial Allocation of Future Demands

Planning departments and other groups may provide population projections for future years and associate these population estimates with census tracts, traffic analysis zones, planning districts, or other areas. The data must then be manipulated to determine the spatial allocation of nodal demands for the water model.

This manipulation requires a good deal of judgment on the modeler's part, reflecting the uncertainty of the process. Predictions concerning the future, by their nature, contain varying degrees of uncertainty. If the significant factors affecting community growth have been identified, the modeler can usually save time by making good judgments about how the current baseline demand allocation can be modified and reused for planning purposes. It is also important for the modeler to consider the future fire protection requirements. Since fire protection demands are often much larger than baseline demands, they are usually a major factor in future pipe-sizing decisions.

Disaggregated Projections

Rather than basing projections on extrapolation of flow rate data, it is somewhat more rational to examine the causes of demand changes and then project that data into the future. This technique is called *disaggregated projection*. Instead of predicting demands, the user will predict such things as industrial production, number of hotel rooms, and cost of water, and then use a forecasting model to predict demand.

The simplest type of disaggregated demand projection involves projecting population and per capita demand separately. In this way, for example, the modeler can separate the effects of population growth from the effects of a decrease in per capita consumption due to low volume fixtures and other water conservation measures.

These types of approaches attempt to account for many variables that influence future demands, including population projections, water pricing, land use, industrial growth, and the effects of water conservation (Vickers, 1991; and Macy, 1991). The IWR-Main model (Opitz et al., 1998; Dziegielewski and Boland, 1989) is a sophisticated model that uses highly disaggregated projections to forecast demands.

The most difficult factor to predict when performing a projection is drastic change in the economy of an area (for example, a military base closure or the construction of a factory). Using disaggregated projections, population projections can be modified more rationally than flow projections to develop demand forecasts that reflect these types of events.

Population Estimates. Planning commissions often have population studies and estimates that predict the future growth of a city or town. Though population estimates usually contain uncertainties, they can be used as a common starting point for any model requiring future estimates, such as water distribution models, sewer plans, and traffic models.

Starting with current per capita usage rates or projections of per capita usage trends, future demands can be estimated by taking the product of the future population and the future per capita usage. In areas that are already densely populated, the growth may be only slightly positive, or even negative.

The United States Geological Survey (USGS) publishes per capita consumption rates for each state, but these values include non-municipal uses such as water used for power generation and agriculture. A per capita consumption rate developed in this manner, however, cannot be widely applied, since there are large differences in water consumption between customers in different areas within a particular state.

Land Use. Sometimes water demands can be estimated based upon land use designations, such as single-family residential, high-density residential, commercial, light industrial, heavy industrial, and so on. Information regarding a representative water usage rate based on land use can then aid in planning for other areas that are in the same category.

As with population estimates, using land use designation requires some level of prediction regarding future growth in every area from residential land use to industrial and commercial operations. For example, the loss or gain of a single large industry can have a tremendous effect on the overall consumption in the system.

4.5 FIRE PROTECTION DEMANDS

When a fire is in progress, fire protection demands can represent a huge fraction of the total demand for the system. The effects of fire demands are difficult to derive precisely, since fires occur with random frequency in different areas, with each area having unique fire protection requirements. Generally, the amount of water needed to adequately fight a fire depends upon the size of the burning structure, its construction materials, the combustibility of its contents, and the proximity of adjacent buildings.

For some systems, fire protection is a lower priority than water quality or construction costs. To reduce costs in situations in which customers are very spread out, such as in rural areas, the network may not be designed to provide fire protection. Instead, the fire departments rely on water tanker trucks or other sources for water to combat fires (for example, ponds constructed specifically for that purpose).

One of the primary benefits of providing water for fire protection is a reduction in the insurance rates of residents and businesses in the community. In the U.S., community fire protection infrastructure (the fire-fighting capabilities of the fire departments and the capacity of the water distribution network) is audited and rated by the Insurance Services Office (ISO) using the *Fire Protection Rating System* (ISO, 1998). In Canada, the Insurers Advisory Organization (IAO) evaluates water supply systems using the *Grading Schedule for Municipal Fire Protection* (IAO, 1974). The ISO evaluation process is summarized in AWWA M-31 (1998).

In Europe, there are no fire prevention standards that apply to all European countries; therefore, each country must develop or adopt their own fire flow requirements. For example, the flow rates that the UK Fire Services ideally require to fight fires are based on the national guidance document on the provision of water for fire fighting (Water UK and LGA, 1998). Similarly, the German standards (DVGW, 1978), the French standards (Circulaire, 1951, 1957, and 1967), the Russian standards (SNIP, 1985), and others, are based on fire risk categories that assign the level of risk according to the type of premises to be protected, fire-spread risk, and/or installed fire proofing.

Because systems will be evaluated using ISO methods, engineers in the U.S. usually base design of fire protection systems on the ISO rating system, which includes determining fire flow demands according to the ISO approach. While the actual water needed to fight a fire depends on the structure and the fire itself, the ISO method yields a *Needed Fire Flow (NFF)* that can be used for design and evaluation of the system. Different calculation methods are used for different building types, such as residential, commercial, or industrial.

For one and two family residences, the needed fire flow is determined based on the distance between structures, as shown in Table 4.3.

Table 4.3 Needed fire flow for residences two stories and less

Distance Between Buildings (ft)	Fire Flow (gpm)
More than 100	500
31-100	750
11-30	1000
Less than 11	1500

For commercial and industrial structures, the needed fire flow is based on building area, *construction class* (i.e., frame or masonry construction), *occupancy* (like a department store or chemical manufacturing plant), *exposure* (distance to and type of nearest building), and *communication* (types and locations of doors and walls). The formula can be summarized as:

$$NFF = 18FA^{0.5}O(X+P) \tag{4.11}$$

where NFF = needed fire flow (gpm)
F = class of construction coefficient
A = effective area (ft^2)
O = occupancy factor
X = exposure factor
P = communication factor

The procedure for determining NFF is documented in the *Fire Protection Rating System* (1998) and AWWA M-31 (1998). The minimum needed fire flow is not less than 500 gpm (32 l/s), and the maximum is no more than 12,000 gpm (757 l/s). Most frequently, the procedure produces values less than 3,500 gpm (221 l/s). Values are rounded off to the nearest 250 gpm (16 l/s) for NFFs less than 2,500 gpm (158 l/s), and to the nearest 500 gpm (32 l/s) for values greater than 2,500 gpm (158 l/s). Values are also adjusted if a building is equipped with sprinklers.

In addition to a flow rate requirement, there is also a requirement for the duration over which the flow can be supplied. According to ISO (1998), fires requiring 3,500 gpm (221 l/s) or less are referred to as receiving "Public Fire Suppression," while those requiring greater than 3,500 gpm (221 l/s) are classified as receiving "Individual Property Fire Suppression." For fires requiring 2,500 gpm (158 l/s) or less, a two-hour duration is sufficient; for fires needing 3,000 to 3,500 gpm (190 to 221 l/s), a three-hour duration is used; and for fires needing greater than 3,500 gpm (221 l/s), a four-hour duration is used along with slightly different rules for evaluation.

Methods for estimating sprinkler demands are based on the area covered and a flow density in gpm/ft^2 as described in NFPA 13 (1999) for commercial and industrial structures, and in NFPA 13D (1999) for single- and two-family residential dwellings. For residences, the sprinklers shall provide at least 18 gpm (1.14 l/s) when one sprinkler operates, and no less than 13 gpm (0.82 l/s) per sprinkler when more than one operates. For commercial and industrial buildings, the flow density can vary from 0.05 to 0.35 gpm/ft^2 (2 to 14 l/min/m^2), depending on the hazard class associated with the building and the floor area. Sprinkler design is covered in detail on page 320.

NFPA 13 provides a chart for determining flow density based on whether occupancy is light, ordinary hazard, or extra hazard. There is also a hose stream requirement for water used to supplement the sprinkler flows. These values range from 100 to 1000 gpm (6.3 to 63 l/s), depending on the hazard classification.

REFERENCES

American Water Works Association. (1989). "Distribution Network Analysis for Water Utilities." *AWWA Manual M-32*, Denver, Colorado.

American Water Works Association. (1998). "Distribution System Requirements for Fire Protection." *AWWA Manual M-31*, Denver, Colorado.

Basford, C., and Sevier, C. (1995). "Automating the Maintenance of Hydraulic Network Model Demand Database Utilizing GIS and Customer Billing Records." *Proceedings of the AWWA Computer Conference*, American Water Works Association, Norfolk, Virginia.

Bowen, P. T., Harp, J., Baxter, J., and Shull, R. (1993). *Residential Water Use Patterns*. AWWARF, Denver, Colorado.

Brainard, B. (1994). "Using Electronic Rate of Flow Recorders." *Proceeding of the AWWA Distribution System Symposium*, American Water Works Association, Omaha, Nebraska.

Buchberger, S. G., and Wu, L. (1995). "A Model for Instantaneous Residential Water Demands." *Journal of Hydraulic Engineering*, ASCE, 54(4), 232.

Buchberger, S. G., and Wells, G. J. (1996). "Intensity, Duration, and Frequency of Residential Water Demands." *Journal of Water Resources Planning and Management*, ASCE, 122(1), 11.

Buyens, D. J., Bizier, P. A., and Combee, C. W. (1996). "Using a Geographical Information System to Determine Water Distribution Model Demands." *Proceedings of the AWWA Annual Conference*, American Water Works Association, Toronto, Canada.

Cesario, A. L., and Lee T. K. (1980). "A Computer Method for Loading Model Networks." *Journal of the American Water Works Association*, 72(4), 208.

Cesario, A. L. (1995). *Modeling, Analysis, and Design of Water Distribution Systems*. American Water Works Association, Denver, Colorado.

Circulaire des Ministreres de l'Intériur et de l'Agriculture du Février. (1957). *Protection Contre l'incendie dnas les Communes Rurales*. Paris, France

Circulaire du Ministrere de l'Agriculture du Auout. (1967). *Réserve d'eau Potable. Protection Contre l'incendie dans les Communes Rurales*. Paris, France.

Circulaire Interministérielle du Décembre. (1951). *Alimentation des communes en eau potable - Lutte contre l'incendie*. Paris, France.

Coote, P. A., and Johnson, T. J. (1995). "Hydraulic Model for the Mid-Size Utility." *Proceedings of the AWWA Computer Conference*, American Water Works Association, Norfolk, Virginia.

Davis, A. L., and Brawn, R. C. (2000). "General Purpose Demand Allocator (DALLOC)." *Proceedings of the Environmental and Water Resources Institute Conference*, American Society of Civil Engineers, Minneapolis, Minnesota.

DeOreo, W. B., Heaney, J. P., and Mayer, P. W. (1996). "Flow Trace Analysis to Assess Water Use." *Journal of the American Water Works Association*, 88(1), 79.

DVGW. (1978). "DVGW W405 Bereitstellung von Löschwasser durch die Öffentliche Trinkwasserversorgung." *Deutscher Verein des Gas - und Wasserfaches*, Franfurt, Germany.

Dziegielewski, B., and Boland J. J. (1989). "Forecasting Urban Water Use: the IWR-MAIN Model." *Water Resource Bulletin*, 25(1), 101-119.

Insurance Advisory Organization (IAO). (1974). *Grading Schedule for Municipal Fire Protection*. Toronto, Canada.

Insurance Services Office (ISO). (1998). *Fire Suppression Rating Schedule*. New York, New York.

Macy, P. P. (1991). "Integrating Construction and Water Master Planning." *Journal of the American Water Works Association*, 83(10), 44 - 47.

Male, J. W., and Walski, T. M. (1990). *Water Distribution: A Troubleshooting Manual*. Lewis Publishers, Chelsea, Florida.

National Fire Protection Association (NFPA). (1999). "Sprinkler Systems in One- and Two-Family Dwellings and Manufactured Homes." *NFPA 13D*, Quincy, Massachusetts.

National Fire Protection Association (NFPA). (1999). "Standard for Installation of Sprinkler Systems." *NFPA 13*, Quincy, Massachusetts.

Office of Water Services (Ofwat). (1998). *1997-98 Report on Leakage and Water Efficiency*. http://www.open.gov.uk/ofwat/leak97.pdf, United Kingdom.

Opitz, E. M., et al. (1998). "Forecasting Urban Water Use: Models and Application." *Urban Water Demand Management and Planning*, Baumann D., Boland, J. and Hanemann, W. H., eds., McGraw Hill. New York, New York, 350.

Rhoades, S. D. (1995). "Hourly Monitoring of Single-Family Residential Areas." *Journal of the American Water Works Association*, 87(8), 43.

SNIP. (1985). *Water Supply Standards* (in Russian). 2.04.02-84, Moscow, Russia.

Stern, C. T. (1995). "The Los Angeles Department of Water and Power Hydraulic Modeling Project." *Proceedings of the AWWA Computer Conference*, American Water Works Association, Norfolk, Virginia.

Vickers, A. L. (1991). "The Emerging Demand Side Era in Water Conservation." *Journal of the American Water Works Association*, 83(10), 38.

Walski, T. M. (1999). "Peaking Factors for Systems with Leakage." *Essential Hydraulics and Hydrology*, Haestad Methods Press, Waterbury, Connecticut.

Walski, T. M., Lowry, S. G., and Rhee, H. (2000). "Pitfalls in Calibrating an EPS Model." *Proceedings of the Environmental and Water Resource Institute Conference*, American Society of Civil Engineers, Minneapolis, Minnesota.

Water Research Centre (WRc). (1985). *District Metering, Part I - System Design and Installation*. Report ER180E, United Kingdom.

Water UK and Local Government Association. (1998). *National Guidance Document on the Provision of Water for Fire Fighting*. London, United Kingdom.

"Oh no, not homework again."

DISCUSSION TOPICS AND PROBLEMS

Earn CEUs — Read Chapters 3 and 4 and complete the problems. Submit your work to Haestad Methods and earn up to 1.5 CEUs. See *Continuing Education Units* on page xiii for more information, or visit www.haestad.com/wdm-ceus/.

4.1 Develop a steady-state model of the water distribution system shown in Figure 4.11. Data describing the system and average daily demands are provided in the tables below.

Figure 4.11

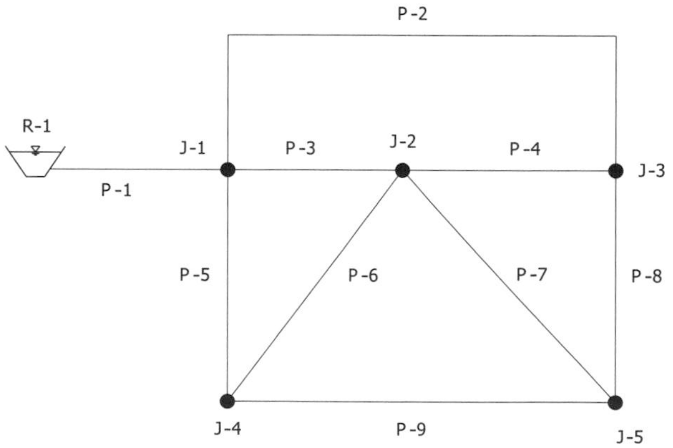

Pipe Label	Length (ft)	Diameter (in.)	Hazen-Williams C-factor	Minor Loss Coefficient
P-1	500	12	120	10
P-2	2,600	10	120	0
P-3	860	8	120	0
P-4	840	8	120	5
P-5	710	6	120	0
P-6	1,110	4	120	0
P-7	1,110	4	120	0
P-8	710	6	120	0
P-9	1,700	6	120	0

Node Label	Elevation (ft)	Demand (gpm)
R-1	750	N/A
J-1	550	250
J-2	520	75
J-3	580	125
J-4	590	50
J-5	595	0

a) Fill in the tables below with the pipe and junction node results.

Pipe Label	Flow (gpm)	Hydraulic Gradient (ft/1000 ft)
P-1		
P-2		
P-3		
P-4		
P-5		
P-6		
P-7		
P-8		
P-9		

Node Label	Hydraulic Grade (ft)	Pressure (psi)
J-1		
J-2		
J-3		
J-4		
J-5		

b) Complete the tables below assuming that all demands are increased to 225% of average day demands.

Pipe Label	Flow (gpm)	Hydraulic Gradient (ft/1000 ft)
P-1		
P-2		
P-3		
P-4		
P-5		
P-6		
P-7		
P-8		
P-9		

Node Label	Hydraulic Grade (ft)	Pressure (psi)
J-1		
J-2		
J-3		
J-4		
J-5		

c) Complete the tables below assuming that, in addition to average day demands, there is a fire flow demand of 1,850 gpm added at node J-3.

Pipe Label	Flow (gpm)	Hydraulic Gradient (ft/1000 ft)
P-1		
P-2		
P-3		
P-4		
P-5		
P-6		
P-7		
P-8		
P-9		

Node Label	Hydraulic Grade (ft)	Pressure (psi)
J-1		
J-2		
J-3		
J-4		
J-5		

4.2 *English Units* - Perform a 24-hour extended period simulation with a one-hour time step for the system shown in Figure 4.12. Data necessary to conduct the simulation are provided in the tables below. Alternatively, the pipe and junction node data has already been entered into Prob4-02.wcd. Use a stepwise format for the diurnal demand pattern. Answer the questions presented at the end of this problem.

Figure 4.12

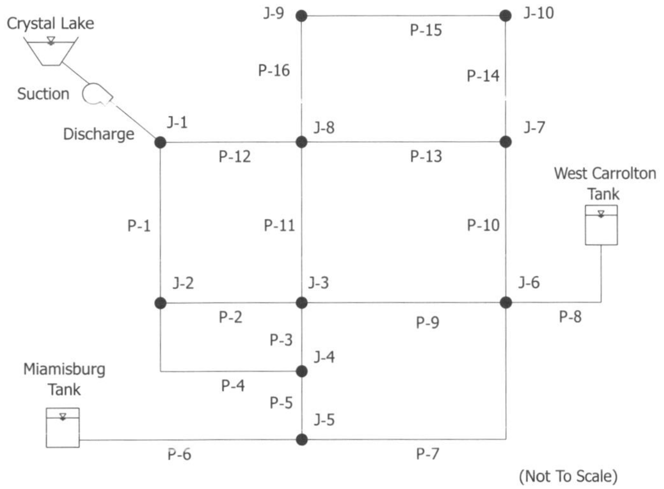

Pipe Label	Length (ft)	Diameter (in.)	Hazen-Williams C-factor
Suction	25	24	120
Discharge	220	21	120
P-1	1,250	6	110
P-2	835	6	110
P-3	550	8	130
P-4	1,010	6	110
P-5	425	8	130
P-6	990	8	125
P-7	2,100	8	105
P-8	560	6	110
P-9	745	8	100
P-10	1,100	10	115
P-11	1,330	8	110
P-12	890	10	115
P-13	825	10	115
P-14	450	6	120
P-15	690	6	120
P-16	500	6	120

Node Label	Elevation (ft)	Demand (gpm)
Crystal Lake	320	N/A
J-1	390	120
J-2	420	75
J-3	425	35
J-4	430	50
J-5	450	0
J-6	445	155
J-7	420	65
J-8	415	0
J-9	420	55
J-10	420	20

Pump Curve Data

	Head (ft)	Flow (gpm)
Shutoff	245	0
Design	230	1,100
Max Operating	210	1,600

Elevated Tank Information

	Miamisburg Tank	West Carrolton Tank
Base Elevation (ft)	0	0
Minimum Elevation (ft)	535	525
Initial Elevation (ft)	550	545
Maximum Elevation (ft)	570	565
Tank Diameter (ft)	49.3	35.7

Diurnal Demand Pattern

Time of Day	Multiplication Factor
Midnight	1.00
6:00 am	0.75
Noon	1.00
6:00 pm	1.20
Midnight	1.00

a) Produce a plot of the HGL in the Miamisburg and West Carrolton tanks as a function of time.

b) Produce a plot of the pressures at node J-3 vs. time.

SI Units - Perform a 24-hour extended period simulation with a one-hour time step for the system shown in Figure 4.12. Data necessary to conduct the simulation are provided in the tables below. Alternatively, the pipe and junction node data has already been entered into Prob4-02m.wcd. Use a stepwise format for the diurnal demand pattern. Answer the questions presented at the end of this problem.

Pipe Label	Length (m)	Diameter (mm)	Hazen-Williams C-factor
Suction	7.6	610	120
Discharge	67.1	533	120
P-1	381.0	152	110
P-2	254.5	152	110
P-3	167.6	203	130
P-4	307.8	152	110
P-5	129.5	203	130
P-6	301.8	203	125
P-7	640.1	203	105
P-8	170.7	152	110
P-9	227.1	203	100
P-10	335.3	254	115
P-11	405.4	203	110
P-12	271.3	254	115
P-13	251.5	254	115
P-14	137.2	152	120
P-15	210.3	152	120
P-16	152.4	152	120

Node Label	Elevation (m)	Demand (l/s)
Crystal Lake	97.5	N/A
J-1	118.9	7.6
J-2	128.0	4.7
J-3	129.5	2.2
J-4	131.1	3.2
J-5	137.2	0
J-6	135.6	9.8
J-7	128.0	4.1
J-8	126.5	0
J-9	128.0	3.5
J-10	128.0	1.3

Pump Curve Data

	Head (m)	Flow (l/s)
Shutoff	74.6	0
Design	70.1	69
Max Operating	64.0	101

Elevated Tank Information

	Miamisburg Tank	West Carrolton Tank
Base Elevation (m)	0	0
Minimum Elevation (m)	163.1	160.0
Initial Elevation (m)	167.6	166.1
Maximum Elevation (m)	173.7	172.2
Tank Diameter (m)	15.0	10.9

Diurnal Demand Pattern

Time of Day	Multiplication Factor
Midnight	1.00
6:00 am	0.75
Noon	1.00
6:00 pm	1.20
Midnight	1.00

a) Produce a plot of the HGL in the Miamisburg and West Carrolton tanks as a function of time.

b) Produce a plot of the pressures at node J-3 vs. time.

4.3 Develop a steady-state model for the system shown in Figure 4.13 and answer the questions that follow. Data necessary to conduct the simulation are provided in the tables below. Alternatively, the pipe and junction node data has already been entered into Prob4-03.wcd. Note that there are no minor losses in this system. The PRV setting is 74 psi.

Figure 4.13

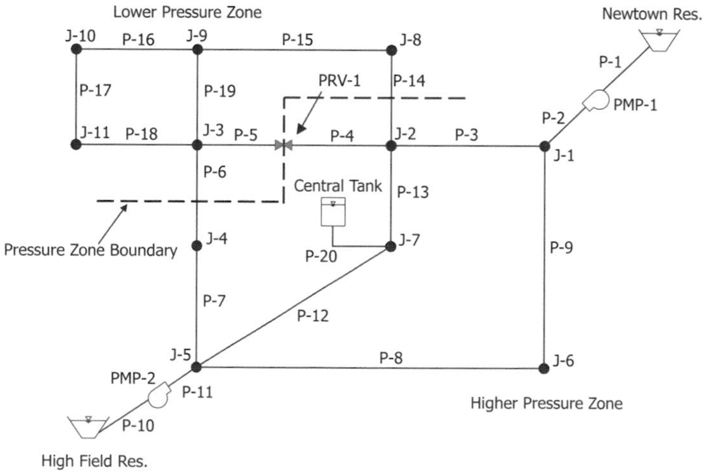

Pipe Label	Length (ft)	Diameter (in.)	Hazen-Williams C-factor
P-1	120	24	120
P-2	435	16	120
P-3	2,300	12	120
P-4	600	10	110
P-5	550	10	110
P-6	1,250	12	110
P-7	850	12	110
P-8	4,250	12	120
P-9	2,100	12	120
P-10	50	24	105
P-11	250	16	105
P-12	1,650	10	115
P-13	835	8	110
P-14	800	8	100
P-15	1,300	6	95
P-16	1,230	6	95
P-17	750	6	95
P-18	1,225	8	95
P-19	725	6	100
P-20	155	4	75

Node Label	Elevation (ft)	Demand (gpm)
High Field Reservoir	1,230	N/A
Newtown Reservoir	1,050	N/A
Central Tank	1,525	N/A
J-1	1,230	0
J-2	1,275	0
J-3	1,235	120
J-4	1,250	35
J-5	1,300	55
J-6	1,250	325
J-7	1,260	0
J-8	1,220	100
J-9	1,210	25
J-10	1,210	30
J-11	1,220	45
PRV-1	1,180	N/A
PMP-1	1,045	N/A
PMP-2	1,225	N/A

Pump Curve Data

	PMP-1		PMP-2	
	Head (ft)	Flow (gpm)	Head (ft)	Flow (gpm)
Shutoff	550	0	320	0
Design	525	750	305	1,250
Max Operating	480	1,650	275	2,600

a) Fill in the tables for pipe and junction node results.

Pipe Label	Flow (gpm)	Hydraulic Gradient (ft/1000 ft)
P-1		
P-2		
P-3		
P-4		
P-5		
P-6		
P-7		
P-8		
P-9		
P-10		
P-11		
P-12		
P-13		
P-14		
P-15		
P-16		
P-17		
P-18		
P-19		
P-20		

Node Label	Hydraulic Grade (ft)	Pressure (psi)
J-1		
J-2		
J-3		
J-4		
J-5		
J-6		
J-7		
J-8		
J-9		
J-10		
J-11		

Analyze the following demand conditions for this system using the average day demands as your base demands.

b) Increase all demands to 150% of average day demands. What are the pressures at nodes J-2 and J-10?

c) Add a fire flow demand of 1,200 gpm to node J-4. What is the discharge from the Newtown pump station? What is the pressure at node J-4?

d) Replace the demand of 120 gpm at node J-3 with a demand of 225 gpm. How does the pressure at node J-3 change between the two demand cases?

e) Replace the existing demands at nodes J-3, J-9, J-10, and J-11 with 200 gpm, 50 gpm, 90 gpm, and 75 gpm, respectively. Is Central Tank filling or draining? How does the tank condition compare with the original simulation before demands were changed?

4.4 Perform an extended period simulation on the system from part (a) of Problem 4.3. However, first add a PRV to pipe P-6 and close pipe P-14. Note that pipe P-6 must split into two pipes when the PRV is inserted. Specify the elevation of the PRV as 1,180 ft and the setting as 74 psi.

The simulation duration is 24 hours and starts at midnight. The hydraulic time step is 1 hour. The capacity and geometry of the elevated storage tank and the diurnal demand pattern are provided below. Assume that the diurnal demand pattern applies to each junction node and that the demand pattern follows a continuous format. Assume that the High Field pump station does not operate.

Central Tank Information

Base Elevation (ft)	1,260
Minimum Elevation (ft)	1,505
Initial Elevation (ft)	1,525
Maximum Elevation (ft)	1,545
Tank Diameter (ft)	46.1

Diurnal Demand Pattern

Time of Day	Multiplication Factor
Midnight	0.60
3:00 a.m.	0.75
6:00 a.m.	1.20
9:00 a.m.	1.10
Noon	1.15
3:00 p.m.	1.20
6:00 p.m.	1.33
9:00 p.m.	0.80
Midnight	0.60

a) Produce a plot of HGL vs. time for Central Tank.

b) Produce a plot of the discharge from the Newtown pump station vs. time.

c) Produce a plot of the pressure at node J-3 vs. time.

d) Does Central Tank fill completely? If so, at what time does the tank completely fill? What happens to a tank when it becomes completely full or completely empty?

e) Why does the discharge from the Newtown pump station increase between midnight and 6:00 a.m.? Why does the discharge from the pump station decrease particularly after 3:00 p.m.?

f) Does the pressure at node J-3 vary significantly over time?

4.5 Given a pressure zone with one pump station pumping into it and a smaller one pumping out of it, and a single 40-ft diameter cylindrical tank, develop a diurnal demand pattern. The pumping rates and tank water levels are given in the table below. The pumping rates are the average rates during the hour, while the tank levels are the values at the beginning of the hour.

What is the average use in this pressure zone? What is the average flow to the higher pressure zone?

Hour	Pump In (gpm)	Pump Out (gpm)	Tank Level (ft)
0	650	0	35.2
1	645	210	38.5
2	645	255	40.4
3	652	255	42.1
4	310	255	43.5
5	0	255	42.8
6	0	255	39.6
7	0	0	36.0
8	0	0	33.4
9	225	0	30.3
10	650	0	28.9
11	650	0	30.5
12	650	0	32.1
13	650	0	33.8
14	650	45	35.8
15	645	265	37.5
16	645	260	37.5
17	645	260	37.2
18	645	260	36.5
19	645	260	36.4
20	645	255	36.7
21	645	150	37.2
22	115	0	38.7
23	0	0	38.3
24	0	0	37.1

CHAPTER

5

Testing Water Distribution Systems

Verifying that a water distribution model replicates field conditions requires an intimate knowledge of how the system performs over a wide range of operating conditions. For example, can the model reproduce the flow patterns and pressures that occur during periods of peak summertime usage, or can the model accurately simulate chlorine decay? Collecting water distribution system data in the field will provide valuable insight into system performance, and is also an essential part of calibration.

Data collection, the first step in the model calibration process, is discussed in depth within this chapter. The chapter begins with a brief discussion of system testing, including descriptions of some simple tests for measuring flow and pressure, as well as some of the pitfalls that may be encountered. The details of performing fire hydrant flow tests, head loss tests, pump performance tests, and water quality tests are discussed as well.

5.1 TESTING FUNDAMENTALS

Pressure Measurement

Pressures are measured throughout the water distribution system to monitor the level of service and to collect data for use in model calibration. Pressure readings are commonly taken at fire hydrants (Figure 5.1), but can also be read at hose bibs; home faucets; pump stations (both suction and discharge sides); tanks; reservoirs; and blow-off, air release, and other types of valves.

If the measurements are taken at a location other than a direct connection to a water main [for example, at a house hose bib (spigot)], the head loss between the supply main and the site where pressure is measured must be considered. Of course, the best solution is to have no flow (and hence no head loss) between the main and the gage. To check if flow into the building is occurring, listen at the hose bib for the sound of rushing water.

Figure 5.1
Pressure gages on a fire hydrant

When measuring pressure, slight fluctuations may be seen on the gage due to changing flows in the system. Devices such as *pressure snubbers* and liquid-filled pressure gages can be used to dampen the pressure fluctuations, unless the fluctuations themselves are a source of interest.

Pressure gages are most accurate when measuring pressures within 50 to 75% of the maximum value on the scale. Using several pressure gages of varying pressure ranges is advisable when working with a water distribution system. A pressure gage with a range of 0 to 100 psi (690 kPa) is commonly used; however, a pressure gage that can read up to 200 psi (1,380 kPa) may be necessary for measurements taken at a pump discharge or at a low elevation. If pressure measurements are taken on the suction side of a pump, then a pressure gage capable of reading negative pressures, called a *pressure-vacuum gage*, may be required. Remember that it is the elevation of the gage, not the elevation of the node, that is used in calculating the elevation of the HGL (see page 198).

Flow Measurement

Flow is measured at key locations throughout a system to provide insight into flow patterns and system performance, develop consumption data, and determine flow rates for calibration.

Many of the tests described in this chapter require measuring flow in pipes. A variety of flow meters are available for this purpose, including *venturi meters*, *magnetic flowmeters*, and *ultrasonic meters*. Pressure and flow metering and recording equipment should be calibrated regularly and undergo routine performance checks to ensure that it is in good working order. Furthermore, even if a flow meter is accurate and calibrated, the monitoring station may use an analog gage or dial readout that has a coarse level of precision, which limits the overall precision.

The extent of flow measurement employed varies from system to system. Usually, flow is measured continuously at only a few key locations in the distribution system such as treatment plants and pump stations. Data from these sites should be used to the greatest extent possible in system calibration. More rarely, systems employ in-line flow meters at key points throughout the network and transmit the flow rates back to a control center using *Supervisory Control and Data Acquisition (SCADA)* systems and *telemetry.* This type of comprehensive flow monitoring is not typically done in the United States; however, more utility managers and operators are starting to see the value of in-line flow information (see page 369).

Temporary flow metering may be a cost-effective option to check pump discharges or to see if in-line flow measurements are required throughout the system. Field measurement using a Pitot rod is shown in Figure 5.2. The rod is inserted into the pipe to measure total head and pressure head, which can then be converted into velocity (Walski, 1984a). The Pitot rod should not be confused with the Pitot gage, which measures velocity head only. Clamp-on or insertion electromagnetic or ultrasonic meters may also be used.

Placement of the flow-measuring device is important. To be sure that disturbances caused by any bends or obstructions do not influence the readings, the device should be placed far enough downstream of the disturbance (usually at a distance of approximately 10 times the pipe diameter) that the effects will have completely dissipated.

Under certain cases it may be desirable to isolate one end of the pipe such that all of the flow through the pipe is diverted through a hydrant for measurement. The hydrant flow can then be measured with a hydrant Pitot gage as described in Section 5.2.

Net flow in and out of a tank during a time period can be measured by monitoring water level in the tank and then calculating the flow based on cross-sectional area in the tank.

Potential Pitfalls in System Measurements

While flow measurement tests can be beneficial, there are potential drawbacks to keep in mind. Testing may result in disruption of service to some customers. For example, fire flow tests typically cause lower than normal pressures and higher than normal velocities, particularly in residential areas. Higher velocities can entrain sediments in pipes, or shear against tuberculation on pipe walls, causing customers to experience discolored water.

Customers may, either by accident or necessity, be disconnected from the system when valves are operated to facilitate flow tests. As described in the following sections, head loss tests require the operation of system valves to isolate sections of water main. Valve operation needs to be carefully planned when conducting such tests to avoid inadvertently disconnecting customers from the system. To avoid surprises, customers should be notified prior to the tests.

Figure 5.2
Tip of Pitot rod inserted into clear pipe

5.2 FIRE HYDRANT FLOW TESTS

Obtaining data for a wide range of operating conditions, including peak (high) demand periods, would be difficult without *fire hydrant flow tests*. These tests can be used to simulate high flow conditions (see page 199), and allow the system behavior to be analyzed under extreme conditions. Fire hydrant flow tests are primarily used to measure the fire flow capacity of the system. They also provide data on pressures within the system under static conditions (no hydrants flowing) and stressed conditions (high flows occurring at the hydrants) and can be used in conjunction with the hydraulic model to calibrate parameters such as pipe roughness (Walski, 1988). Procedures for conducting fire hydrant flow tests are described in AWWA (1989) and ISO (1963).

Two or more hydrants are required to perform a fire hydrant flow test as illustrated in Figure 5.3. One hydrant is identified as the *residual hydrant(s)* where all pressure measurements are taken, and the other as the *flowed hydrant(s)*, where all flow measurements are taken. When the flowed hydrant(s) is closed, referred to as static conditions, the pressure at the residual hydrant is called the *static pressure*. When one or more of the flowed hydrants are open, referred to as flowed conditions, the pressure at the residual hydrant is called the *residual pressure*.

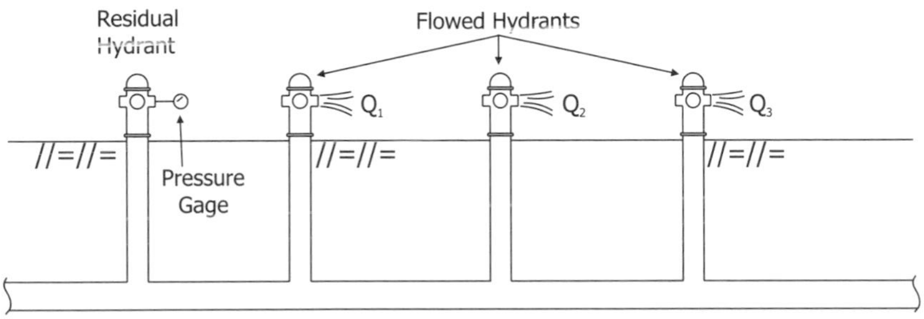

Figure 5.3
Hydrant flow test

Conducting a fire hydrant flow test is a simple procedure, and a number of these tests can be conducted throughout the system in a day's time. While not essential, many utilities have a policy requiring that the residual hydrant is opened and allowed to flow prior to connecting the pressure gage. This precaution helps remove any particles that have accumulated in the hydrant lateral and barrel since it was last exercised. After that, a pressure gage is connected to the residual hydrant and a static pressure reading taken.

Next, the first of the flowed hydrants is opened and flowed. Once the readings stabilize, a reading is taken at the flowed hydrant using a hand-held or clamp-on *Pitot gage* (Figure 5.4) or a *Pitot diffuser* (see Figure 5.6). Meanwhile, another pressure reading is taken at the residual hydrant. Once the residual pressure is taken and the discharge rate of the flowed hydrant is recorded, the same procedure can be repeated for additional hydrants if needed.

The number of hydrants that should be flowed during a test is determined by the pressure drop observed at the residual hydrant. Usually, a drop of at least 10 psi (70 kPa) is needed to give good results. In a 6- to 8-in. pipe (15 to 20 cm), flowing a single hydrant is sufficient. For larger pipes, more hydrants may need to be flowed.

Pitot Gages and Diffusers

Because a Pitot gage (Figure 5.4) converts virtually all of the velocity head associated with the flow stream to pressure head, the Pitot gage pressure reading can be converted to a hydrant discharge rate using the orifice relationship in Equation 5.1.

Figure 5.4
Hand-held Pitot gage

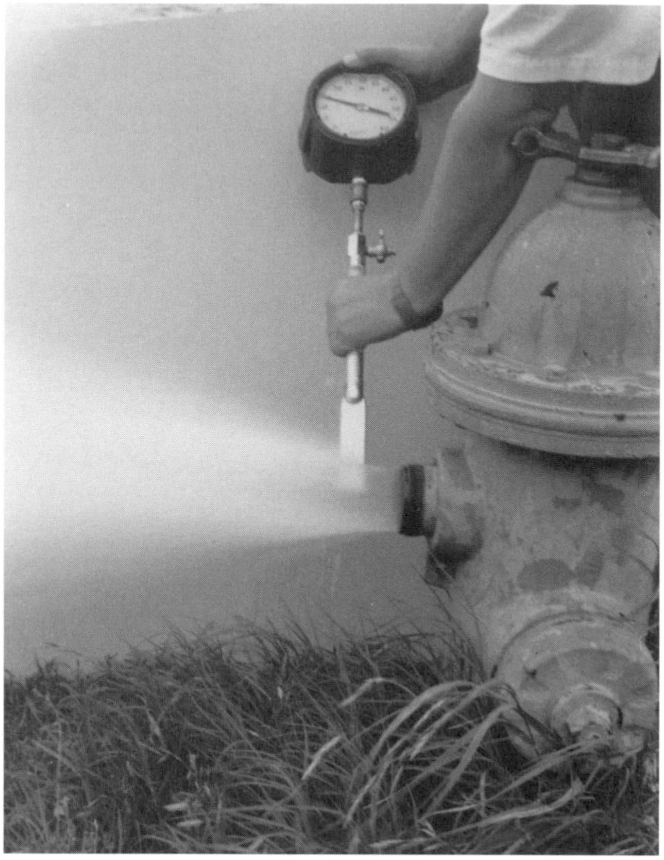

$$Q = C_f C_d D^2 \sqrt{P} \quad (5.1)$$

where Q = hydrant discharge (gpm, l/s)
C_d = discharge coefficient
D = outlet diameter (in., cm)
P = pressure reading from Pitot gage (psi, kPa)
C_f = unit conversion factor (29.8 English, 0.111 SI)

For a typical 2.5 in. outlet with a discharge coefficient of 0.9, Equation 5.1 can be reduced to:

$$Q = 167\sqrt{P}$$

The discharge coefficient in Equation 5.1 accounts for the decrease in the diameter of flow that occurs between the hydrant opening and the end of the Pitot gage, as well as the head losses through the opening. The coefficient depends upon the geometry of the inside of the hydrant opening, and can be determined by feeling the inside of the *hydrant nozzle* (Figure 5.5).

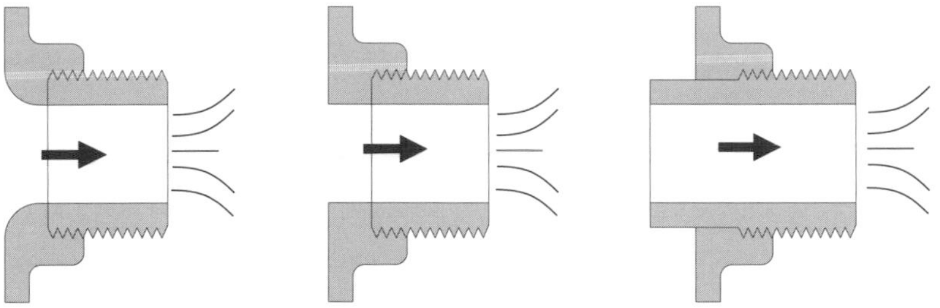

Figure 5.5
Discharge coefficients at hydrant openings

The Pitot diffuser is similar to a Pitot gage except that it incorporates a nozzle that redirects the flow from the hydrant, reducing its momentum and thus the potential for erosion. Because the velocity head sensor is measuring inside the diffuser at a point where the pressure is not equal to zero, a slightly modified formula is required to compute flow. This formula varies with the manufacturer of the diffuser (Walski and Lutes, 1990; and Morin and Rajaratnam, 2000). For example, for the Pitot diffuser shown in Figure 5.6, the coefficient of 167 given previously reduces to 140.

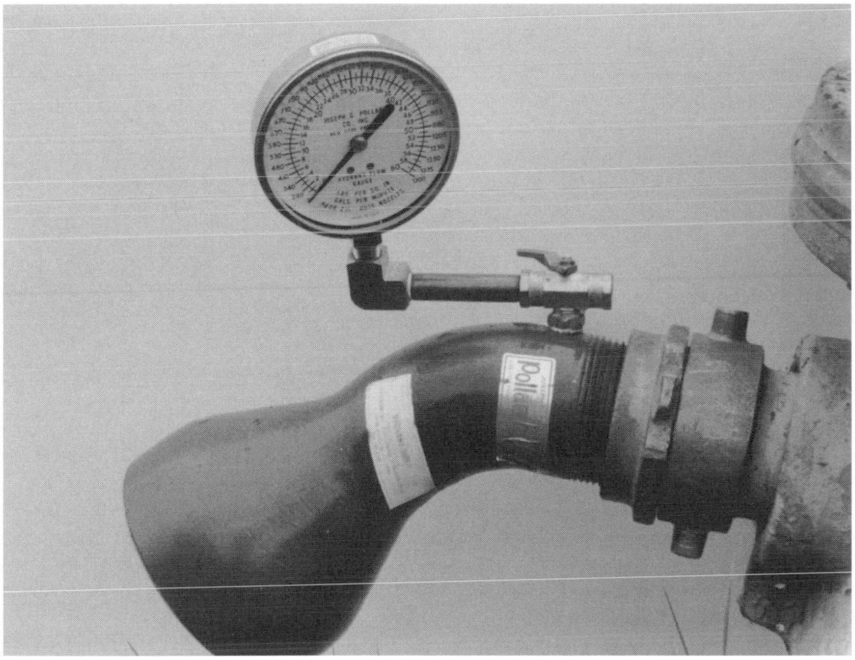

Figure 5.6
Pitot diffuser

To briefly review, the procedure for conducting a fire hydrant flow test is as follows:

1. Place a pressure gage on the residual hydrant and record static pressure.
2. Take the 2 ½-in. cap off of the flowed hydrant.

3. Feel the inside of the hydrant opening to determine its geometry for C_d.
4. Slowly start the flow.
5. Once readings stabilize, take a Pitot gage reading at the flowed hydrant(s).
6. Simultaneously measure the residual pressure(s) at the residual hydrant(s).
7. Slowly close the hydrants.
8. Assign the discharge coefficient according to the geometry of the hydrant opening.
9. Determine the hydrant discharge rate by using Equation 5.1 or the equation provided by the Pitot diffuser manufacturer.

Once all of the data have been collected, a table similar to Table 5.1 can be constructed to present the results of the fire hydrant flow test.

Table 5.1 Results of fire hydrant flow test

Number of Hydrants Flowing	Residual Pressure (psi)	Hydrant #1 Discharge (gpm)	Hydrant #2 Discharge (gpm)	Hydrant #3 Discharge (gpm)	Total Discharge (gpm)
0	78	N/A	N/A	N/A	0
1	72	1,360	N/A	N/A	1360
2	64	1,150	975	N/A	2125
3	49	850	745	600	2195

When sufficient resources are available, additional residual pressure measurements can be taken during the fire hydrant flow test at various locations throughout the system. Taking these additional pressure readings will provide more information on how the hydraulic grade changes across the system. Depending on the nature of the water distribution system, the pressure drop may be localized to the vicinity of the flowed hydrants.

If the hydrant flow test is conducted to provide data for model calibration, it is extremely important to note the boundary conditions at the time of the test. Recall that boundary conditions reflect the water levels in tanks and reservoirs, as well as the operational status of any high-service pumps, booster pumps, or control valves (for example, PRVs) for both static and flowed conditions. As will be discussed in Chapter 6 (see page 208), these boundary conditions must also be defined in the hydraulic model.

In addition, system demands in place at the time of the test need to be replicated in the model. It is important to note the time of day and the weather conditions when the test was performed to assist in establishing the demands and boundary conditions.

Potential Problems With Fire Flow Tests

Fire hydrant flow tests are a useful tool. They do, however, present some areas of concern. Because the discharges from fire hydrants can be quite large, the following suggestions can reduce potential problems associated with these flows.

1. Minimize the period of time over which hydrants are flowed to limit flooding potential.
2. Direct the flow through the 2 ½-in. nozzle opening instead of the 4 ½-in. opening. This will help to reduce street flooding while still producing flow velocities sufficient for calibration.
3. Use hydrant diffusors to reduce the high velocity of the hydrant stream. This will help to avoid erosion problems and damage to vegetation.
4. Conduct fire hydrant flow tests during warm weather to eliminate ice problems.
5. Notify customers that may be impacted by the test beforehand. In some systems, hydrant flow tests can stir up sediments and rust, causing temporary water quality problems.

Evaluating Distribution Capacity with Hydrant Tests

The results of hydrant flow tests described in this chapter are used primarily to evaluate the distribution system's capacity to provide water for fighting fires. The standard formula for converting the test flow to the distribution capacity at some desired residual pressure—usually 20 psi (135 kPa)—was developed by the Insurance Services Office (1963), and is given in AWWA M-17 (1989) as:

$$Q_r = Q_t\left(\frac{P_s - P_r}{P_s - P_t}\right)^{0.54}$$

where Q_r = fire flow at residual pressure P_r (gpm, l/s)
Q_t = hydrant discharge during test (gpm, l/s)
P_s = static pressure (psi, kPa)
P_r = desired residual pressure (psi, kPa)
P_t = residual pressure during test (psi, kPa)

The value of Q_r is referred to as the distribution main capacity in that location, and is used in evaluation of water systems for insurance purposes.

Assumptions made when using the above equation are as follows:

1. Head loss is negligible during static conditions.
2. Demands correspond to maximum day demands.
3. All pumps and regulating valves that would open during an actual fire are open and operating during the test.
4. There is sufficient water quantity to supply the fire throughout the duration of the fire event.
5. Tank level is at normal day low level.
6. The residual and flowed hydrants are close to one another (Walski, 1984b).

Water system models can explicitly account for these factors, and are a more accurate and flexible way of assessing available fire flow at a given residual pressure. However, this equation is still widely used.

The previous equation can also be rearranged to provide a rough estimate of residual pressure for some future flow, given hydrant flow test results, according to:

$$P_r = P_s - (P_s - P_t)\left(\frac{Q_r}{Q_t}\right)^{1.85}$$

In this case, Q_r is the estimated flow, and P_r is the pressure that will exist at that flow rate, given that all other conditions remain the same.

6. Make sure to open and close the hydrants gradually, as sudden changes in flow can induce dangerous pressure surges in the system.

7. Make sure that the residual and flowed hydrants are hydraulically close to one another. It is possible to have two hydrants that are near each other at the street but are fed by different mains that may not be hydraulically connected for several blocks. Ideally, the flowed and residual hydrants would be located side-by-side on the same pipeline, but since this will almost never be the case, accuracy can instead be improved by minimizing the flow between the hydrants. (The flow can often be reduced by bracketing the residual hydrant between two flowed hydrants.)

Using Fire Flow Tests for Calibration

In addition to measuring the fire protection capacity of the network, fire hydrant flow tests can provide valuable data for hydraulic model calibration. To use the results of a test, a demand equivalent to the hydrant discharge should be assigned to the junction node in the model that corresponds to the flowed hydrant. When the hydraulic simulation is conducted, the HGL at the junction node representing the residual hydrant should agree with the HGL measured in the field. Note that comparisons between field measurements and model results should be done in terms of HGL, not pressure (see page 198). Although this section refers to pressure comparisons, remember that in practice, the field pressures should be converted to the equivalent HGL before comparing them to the model results.

Consider the system shown in Figure 5.7 and the results of the fire hydrant flow test presented in Table 5.1. The top half of the figure illustrates the model representation of a series of hydrants where nodes J-23, J-24, and J-25 correspond to Hydrants 1, 2, and 3 respectively; and J-22 corresponds to the residual hydrant. The hydrant flow test results outlined in Table 5.1 can be described in 4 unique scenarios:

1. Static conditions where none of the hydrants are flowing;

2. Hydrant 1 is flowing;

3. Hydrants 1 and 2 are flowing simultaneously; and

4. Hydrants 1, 2, and 3 are flowing simultaneously.

The scenario in which only Hydrant 1 is flowing results in a discharge of 1,360 gpm (40 m^3/s) and a residual pressure of 72 psi (497 kPa). Therefore, a demand of 1,360 gpm will be placed at model node J-23, and when the hydraulic simulation is conducted, the pressure computed at node J-22 will be compared to the residual pressure of 72 psi measured in the field. If the pressure at J-22 is close to that figure, the model will be nearly calibrated; at least for this one condition.

On the other hand, if the pressure at J-22 is not close to the measured pressure, adjustments need to be made to the model to bring it into better agreement. Identifying the actual adjustments that need to be made depends upon the cause of the discrepancy. Chapter 6 has more information regarding reasons why differences might occur, as well as details on modeling the results of flow tests. The procedure described above is repeated for each of the flowed conditions, and the parameters are changed as necessary to obtain a suitable match between observed and computed pressures.

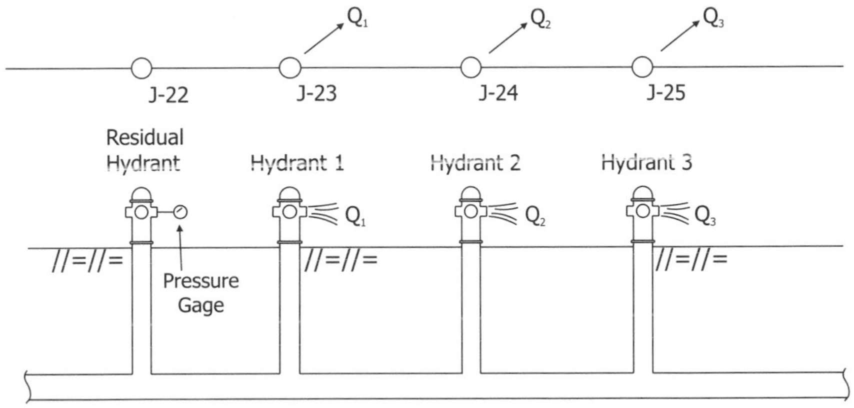

Figure 5.7
Field measured flows are modeled as demands in a network simulation

It is critical that the modeling nodes used to represent the hydrants are placed in exactly the same location as the hydrants in the field. Accurate placement is particularly important for calibration purposes, as illustrated in the following example.

In Figure 5.8a, the pressure measurements are taken at the residual hydrant, while the model representation of the hydrant is at J-35 (Figure 5.8b), a few hundred feet away. The modeler may have justified this simplification by reasoning that the locations of the residual hydrant and node J-35 are relatively close together, and that the pressures should be similar because the elevations are approximately the same. During calibration, the modeler then (mistakenly) compares the field-measured pressure at the residual hydrant to the modeled pressure at J-35, and adjusts the model to achieve an acceptable match.

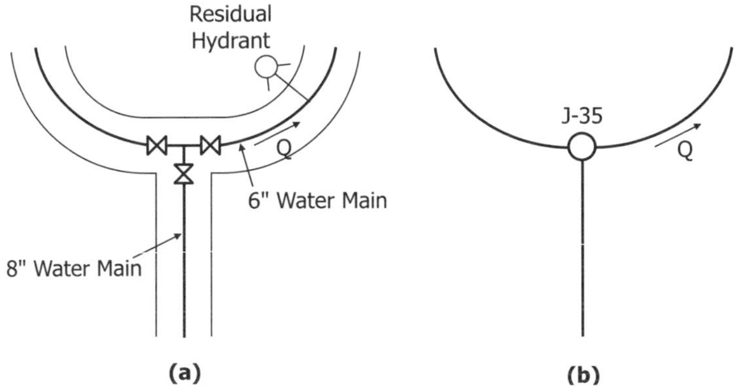

Figure 5.8
Importance of node location

What the modeler has failed to consider in this situation is the head loss between the two points (J-35 and the actual hydrant location) during the fire hydrant flow test. If the head loss is significant, the computed pressure at node J-35 would be higher than the computed pressure at the residual hydrant. By trying to match pressures at different locations, the modeler could introduce inaccuracies into the model. The subject of model calibration and the use of fire hydrant flow tests for that purpose are treated in greater detail in Chapter 6.

5.3 HEAD LOSS TESTS

The purpose of a head loss test is to directly measure the head loss and discharge through a length of pipe, information that can then be used to compute the pipe roughness. Head loss tests can be performed using either the two-gage or the parallel-pipe method. The *two-gage method* uses pressure readings from two standard pressure gages to determine the head loss over the pipe length, while the *parallel-pipe method* uses a single pressure differential gage to find the head loss.

The length of water main being tested is typically located between two fire hydrants. During a head loss test, valves are closed downstream of the length of test pipe to hydraulically isolate the test section. Thus, all flow through the section is directed to the downstream fire hydrant for measurement. Assuming that the internal pipe diameter is known, head loss, pipe length, and flow rate are then measured between the two points and used to compute the internal pipe roughness using the expressions for the Hazen-Williams C-factor and the Darcy-Weisbach friction factor (Equations 5.2 and 5.3).

$$C = \left(\frac{C_f L Q^{1.852}}{h_L D^{4.87}}\right)^{1/1.852} \tag{5.2}$$

where
C = Hazen-Williams C-factor
L = length of test section (ft, m)
Q = flow through test section (cfs, m^3/s)
h_L = head loss due to friction (ft, m)
D = diameter of test section (ft, m)
C_f = unit conversion factor (4.73 English, 10.7 SI)

$$f = h_L \frac{D2g}{LV^2} \tag{5.3}$$

where
f = Darcy-Weisbach friction factor
g = gravitational acceleration constant (32.2 ft/s^2, 9.81 m/s^2)
V = velocity through test section (ft/s, m/s)

The velocity is determined from the flow and diameter using Equation 2.9 repeated below.

$$V = \frac{4Q}{\pi D^2}$$

To apply the friction factor to other pipes, it is necessary to convert f to absolute roughness. Equation 5.4 is the Colebrook-White formula solved for roughness.

$$\frac{\varepsilon}{D} = 3.7\left[\exp\left(\frac{1}{-0.86\sqrt{f}}\right) - \frac{2.51}{Re\sqrt{f}}\right] \tag{5.4}$$

where ε = absolute roughness
Re = Reynolds number

For smooth pipes, the above equation can occasionally yield negative numbers, which should be converted to zero roughness (that is, hydraulically smooth pipe).

Two-Gage Test

For the two-gage test (Figure 5.9), the test section is located between two fire hydrants and is isolated by closing the downstream valves. The pressures at both of the fire hydrants are measured using standard pressure gages, and these pressures are then converted to HGLs. The head loss over the test section is then computed as the difference between the HGLs at the 2 fire hydrants, as shown in Equation 5.5. McEnroe, Sharp, and Chase (1989) found that to overcome uncertainties in measuring length, diameter, and flow, a pressure drop of 15-20 psi should be attained.

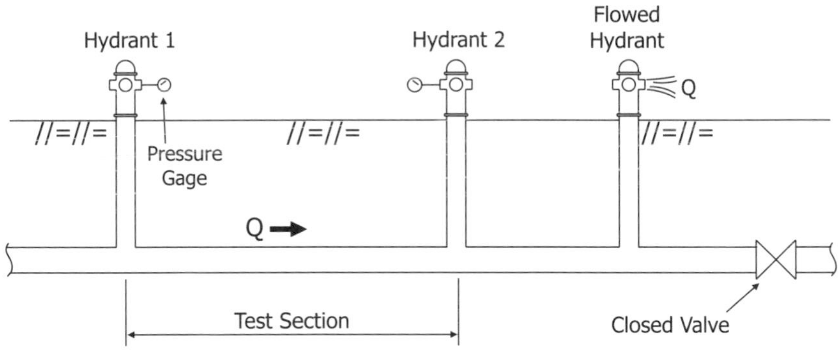

Figure 5.9
The two-gage head loss test

$$h_L = HGL_U - HGL_D \tag{5.5}$$

where HGL_U = hydraulic grade at upstream fire hydrant (ft, m)
HGL_D = hydraulic grade at downstream fire hydrant (ft, m)

Realizing that the HGL can be more generally described using the difference in pressure and elevation between the upstream and downstream hydrants, Equation 5.5 can be rearranged to yield:

$$h_L = C_f(P_U - P_D) + (Z_U - Z_D) \tag{5.6}$$

where P_U = pressure at upstream fire hydrant (psi, kPa)
P_D = pressure at downstream fire hydrant (psi, kPa)

Z_U = elevation at upstream fire hydrant (ft, m)
Z_D = elevation at downstream fire hydrant (ft, m)
C_f = unit conversion factor (2.31 English, 0.102 SI)

Head loss occurs only when there is a flow; therefore, if no flow is passing through the test section, the HGL values at the upstream and downstream hydrants will be the same. Even so, the pressures at the upstream and downstream hydrants may be different as a result of the elevation difference between them. Assuming a no-flow condition, the head loss in Equation 5.6 is set to zero and the elevation difference can be expressed through the use of pressures, as shown in the following equation.

$$Z_U - Z_D = -C_f(P_{US} - P_{DS}) \tag{5.7}$$

where P_{US} = pressure at upstream hydrant, static conditions (psi, kPa)
P_{DS} = pressure at downstream hydrant, static conditions (psi, kPa)
C_f = unit conversion factor (2.31 English, 0.102 SI)

Substituting Equation 5.7 into 5.6 provides a new expression for determining the head loss between two hydrants. This expression eliminates the need to obtain the elevation of the pressure gages by using two sets of pressure readings, static and flowed.

$$h_L = C_f[(P_{UT} - P_{DT}) - (P_{US} - P_{DS})] \tag{5.8}$$

where P_{UT} = pressure at upstream hydrant, flowed conditions (psi, kPa)
P_{DT} = pressure at downstream hydrant, flowed conditions (psi, kPa)
C_f = unit conversion factor (2.31 English, 0.102 SI)

In some situations, the test section may be located near a permanent system meter, such as at the discharge of a pump station, and thus the flow meters at the pump station can be used instead of a hydrant. A pressure gage located on the pipe just before it leaves the pump station can give the upstream pressure. The downstream pressure must be measured sufficiently far away such that the head loss will be much greater than the error associated with measuring it. It may be necessary to close valves at tees and crosses along the pipeline to obtain this long run of pipe with constant flow. Walski and O'Farrell (1994) described how head loss testing equipment can be installed with important transmission mains to assist routine head loss testing.

Parallel-Pipe Test

The concept of the parallel-pipe head loss test is illustrated in Figure 5.10. As with the two-gage test, a test section is isolated between two hydrants by closing the downstream valves. Then, a hose equipped with a differential pressure gage is connected between the two hydrants in parallel with the pipe test section. Since there is no flow, and consequently no head loss, through the hose or gage, the hydraulic grade on each side of the gage will be equal to the hydraulic grade of the hydrant on that same side. Therefore, the measured pressure differential can be used in the expression below to calculate the head loss through the pipe.

$$h_L = C_f \times \Delta P \qquad (5.9)$$

where ΔP = differential pressure reading (psi, kPa)
C_f = unit conversion factor (2.31 English, 0.102 SI)

The head loss, or pressure head difference, over the test section can be found for any fluid by dividing the differential pressure (ΔP) by the specific weight of the fluid (γ). Because the pressure readings are taken at one location (at the pressure differential gage), there is no need to consider the elevation of either hydrant. However, if water in the parallel hose is allowed to change temperature from the water in the pipes, errors can occur (Walski, 1985). Accordingly, water in the hose should be kept moving whenever a reading is not being taken. This can be accomplished by opening a small valve (pit-cock) at the differential pressure gage.

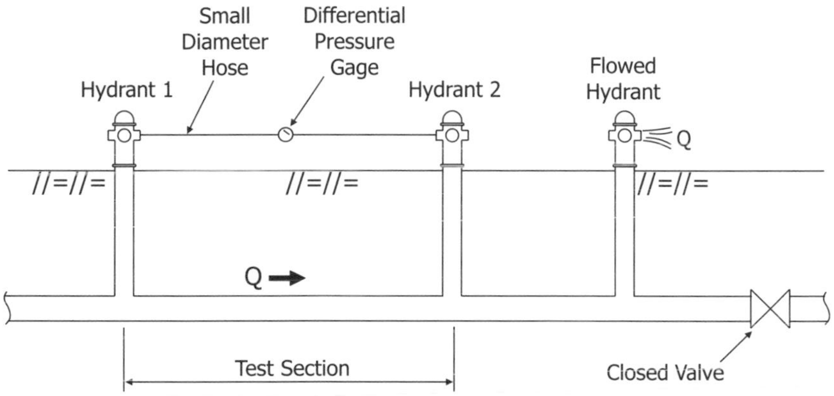

Figure 5.10
Parallel-pipe head loss test

The procedure for finding the discharge through the test section is similar to the one used for fire hydrant flow tests. A Pitot gage is used to measure the velocity head at the flowed hydrant, assuming the flow out of the hydrant equals the flow through the test section. The orifice formula (Equation 5.1) is then used to convert the Pitot gage reading into the discharge from the hydrant (McEnroe, Chase, and Sharp, 1989).

McEnroe, Sharp, and Chase (1989) found that to overcome uncertainties in measuring length, diameter, and flow, a pressure drop of 2-3 psi for the parallel-pipe method should be attained.

Potential Problems With Head Loss Tests

Regardless of the method used for measuring head loss, all flow that passes through the test section is directed out of a flowed hydrant by closing the valve downstream of the flowed hydrant. When working with a looped system, isolation valves on some side mains may also be closed, as shown in Figure 5.11. To ensure that no customers are taken out of service when closing valves, the utility should examine system maps to verify that alternate flow paths (loops) are available within the system. As a check, have one individual watch the pressure gage as the valve is being closed and be ready to give a signal if the pressure drops to zero.

Figure 5.11
Use of isolation valves during a head loss test

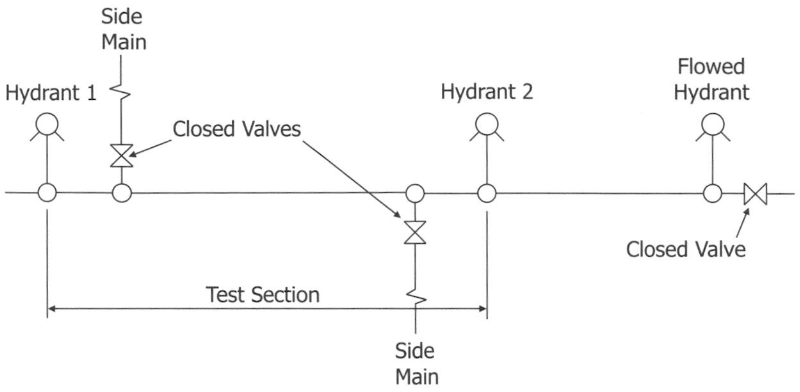

Frequently, there will be customers connected to the test section between the two hydrants. To obtain accurate results, the customer water usage during the head loss tests should be negligible compared to the amount of water discharged through the flowed hydrant. Recall from Equations 5.2 and 5.3 that the discharge is assumed to reflect the total amount of water that passes through the test section. Therefore, if the amount of water that passes through the test section is significantly different from the measured discharge due to withdrawals at other points in the system, then a correction must be made.

Using Head Loss Test Results for Calibration

The process of using the results of a head loss test is fairly straightforward. Head loss tests provide information on the internal roughness of a pipe; therefore, once the head loss tests are complete, the calculated roughness values can simply be supplied to the computer model. The extent of head loss testing, however, is dependent upon the project budget. Some projects are planned such that a sample of mains that are representative of the system are selected for testing. Then, the results are extrapolated to the rest of the system.

One way to limit the amount of head loss testing that must be done to get valid data is to perform head loss tests for a wide variety of pipe sizes, types, and ages. This data can then be placed in chart form, showing pipe roughness values as a function of pipe and size (Ormsbee and Lingireddy, 1997). Roughness values are then selected based upon the age and size of the selected main.

Systems in which pipe roughness varies over a wide range usually contain a significant amount of unlined cast iron pipe. Sharp and Walski (1988) showed that equivalent sand grain roughness heights in unlined, commercial, cast iron pipe increased linearly with time. Therefore, in terms of absolute roughness:

$$\varepsilon = \varepsilon_o + at \qquad (5.10)$$

where ε = roughness height at age t (in., mm)

ε_o = roughness height when pipe was new (t=0) (in., mm)

a = rate of change in roughness height (in./year, mm/year)

t = age of pipe (years)

Roughness height for new cast iron pipe is usually on the order of 0.008 in. (0.18 mm).

By measuring the roughness height for a few pipes in a head loss test, it is possible to determine the coefficient in Equation 5.10 (the rate of change of roughness, *a*) and use the value for other pipes of that type, provided that the corrosive characteristics of the water have not changed significantly. Walski, Edwards, and Hearne (1989) developed a method for adjusting values when water quality had changed during the life of a pipe.

For those using Hazen-Williams C-factor instead of equivalent sand grain roughness height, the relationship between C and age is related to the base 10 log of the roughness height and diameter.

$$C = 18.0 - 37.2\log\left(\frac{\varepsilon_o + at}{D}\right) \qquad (5.11)$$

where D = diameter (in., mm)

Using data from Lamont (1981) and Hudson (1966), Sharp and Walski (1988) performed a regression analysis using Equation 5.10, relating the corrosivity of the water using the *Langelier Index*, shown in Table 5.2. It should be noted that values for any water system are specific to that system.

Table 5.2 Correlation between Langelier Index and the roughness growth rate

Description	a (in./year)	a (mm/year)	Langelier Index
Slight attack	0.00098	0.025	0.0
Moderate attack	0.003	0.076	-1.3
Appreciable attack	0.0098	0.25	-2.6
Severe attack	0.030	0.76	-3.9

5.4 PUMP PERFORMANCE TESTS

There are four types of pump characteristic curves: head, brake horsepower, efficiency, and NPSH required (see page 49). Although modelers can usually rely on pump characteristic curves that are provided by the manufacturer, it is good practice to check these curves against pump performance data collected in the field. The following section discusses how to determine points for the head characteristic curve. It is followed by a discussion of measuring efficiency, which is needed for pump energy analysis.

Head Characteristic Curve

As presented in Chapter 2 (see page 45), the head characteristic curve gives total dynamic head as a function of discharge through the pump. Consider the pump shown in Figure 5.12. If the energy equation is applied between the discharge (Section 2) and suction (Section 1) sides of the pump, the following expression is obtained.

$$h_{dis} + \frac{V_{dis}^2}{2g} = h_{suc} + h_P - h_L - h_m + \frac{V_{suc}^2}{2g} \tag{5.12}$$

where h_{dis} = pump discharge head (m, ft)
V_{dis} = velocity at point where discharge head is measured (ft/s, m/s)
g = gravitational acceleration constant (32.2 ft/sec², 9.81 m/sec²)
h_{suc} = pump suction head (m, ft)
h_P = head added at pump (m, ft)
h_L = head loss due to friction (m, ft)
h_m = minor head losses due to fittings and appurtenances (m, ft)
V_{suc} = velocity at point where suction head is measured (ft/s, m/s)

Figure 5.12
Pump performance test

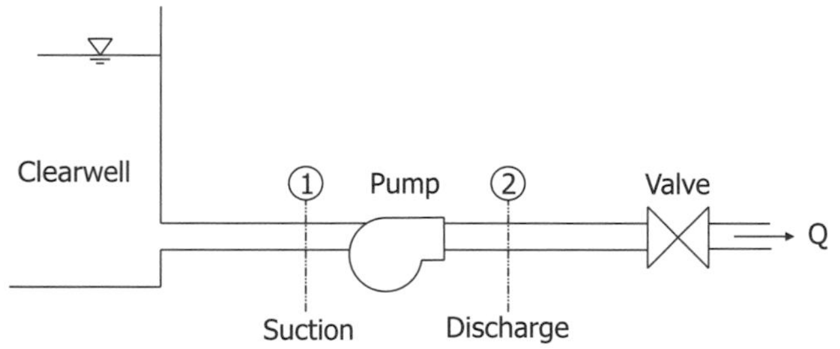

Because Sections 1 and 2 are close together, any head losses due to friction, h_L, will usually be negligible. In addition, the minor losses that occur within the pump due to changing streamlines are not directly considered through the h_m term. Accordingly, the head loss terms are usually set to zero, and the minor losses within the pump are addressed through the pump head term, h_P.

Assuming that sections 1 and 2 have the same elevation, Equation 5.12 can be rewritten as shown below:

$$h_P = \left(\frac{P_{dis}}{\gamma} - \frac{P_{suc}}{\gamma}\right) + \left(\frac{V_{dis}^2}{2g} - \frac{V_{suc}^2}{2g}\right) + h_L + h_m \tag{5.13}$$

where P_{dis} = discharge pressure (psi, kPa)
P_{suc} = suction pressure (psi, kPa)

A pump head characteristic curve is a plot of h_p vs. flow. As shown in Equation 5.13, suction and discharge pressures and the suction and discharge velocity heads are needed to develop the curve. The velocity heads can be calculated based on the flow through the pump (most pump stations are equipped with flow meters) and the suction and discharge pipe diameters. Because the suction and discharge pipe diameters are usually not significantly different for water distribution pumps, the difference between velocity head terms is often negligible.

If the pump is equipped with pressure gages on the suction and discharge lines, the pressure information can also be easily collected. In some instances, however, a pump will have a pressure gage on the discharge side only. In this case, the suction head can be found by applying the energy equation to the suction side of the pump, making sure that all head losses between a hydraulic boundary condition and the pump are accounted for. If the pump does not have a discharge pressure gage, then the energy equation can be applied between the pump discharge and a point of known head (a boundary condition). Again, all head losses between the two points must be considered.

The pump head characteristic curve is developed by finding the pump heads for a series of corresponding pump flows. To do so, the operator varies pump flows through the use of a valve on the discharge side of the pump. With the discharge valve wide open, the pump is turned on and allowed to arrive at full speed. Next, the suction pressure, discharge pressure, and pump flow are measured. The result of substituting these measured values into Equation 5.13 is a point on the pump curve. Then, the valve is adjusted slightly, and another set of pressure and flow data is collected. This process is repeated, closing the valve a little more each time until the desired number of data points have been obtained. The key to developing a useful curve is to vary the discharge over the entire range, from shutoff head to maximum flow. In some cases, it may be necessary to operate hydrants or blow-offs to get sufficiently high flows.

Pump Efficiency Testing

Typically, only the head characteristic curve is needed for modeling; however, some models determine energy usage at pump stations as well as flow and head. To determine energy usage, the model must convert the water power produced by the pump into electric power used by the pump. This conversion is done using the efficiency relationships summarized below.

$$e_p = (water\ power_{out}) / (pump\ power_{in}) \tag{5.14}$$

$$e_m = (pump\ power_{in}) / (electric\ power_{in}) \tag{5.15}$$

where e_p = pump efficiency (%)
e_m = motor efficiency (%)

Pump power refers to the brake horsepower on the pump shaft, and it is difficult to measure in the field. Therefore, all that can be calculated is the *overall* (*wire-to-water*) *efficiency*.

$$e_{w\text{-}w} = e_p \times e_m = (water\ power_{out}) / (electric\ power_{in}) \quad (5.16)$$

where $e_{w\text{-}w}$ = wire-to-water efficiency (%)

While efficiency is expressed as a decimal in the above equations and in most calculations, it is generally discussed in terms of percentages. Waterpower is computed from the following relationship:

$$WP = C_f Q h_P \gamma \quad (5.17)$$

where
WP = water power (hp, Watts)
Q = flow rate (gpm, l/s)
h_P = head added at pump (ft, m)
γ = specific weight of water (lb/ft^3, N/m^3)
C_f = unit conversion factor (4.058E-06 English, 0.0098 SI)

The measurement of electric power depends upon the instrumentation available at the pump station. Large stations may have a direct readout of kilowatts, thus the wire-to-water efficiency can be easily computed by converting the waterpower and electric power to the same units. In other cases, it may be possible to measure the current drawn in amps. Knowing the voltage, power factor, and number of phases, the electric power drawn can be determined as:

$$EP = VI\sqrt{N}(PF) \quad (5.18)$$

where
EP = electrical power (watts)
V = voltage (volts)
I = current averaged over all legs (amps)
N = number of phases
PF = power factor

Except for the motors driving the smallest pumps, pump motors are generally three-phase. The power factor is a function of the motor size and the load for three phase motors. Additional information can be found in WEF (1997).

At some pump stations, there may be no instrumentation available for measuring electric power, and it may be difficult for electricians to directly determine amperage. In these situations, it is necessary to measure the energy usage at the building power meter and divide the energy use by time to determine power. If the meter is being read directly, be sure to account for other sources of power consumption.

Similar to the head characteristic curve, the efficiency curve can be developed by setting a flow rate, measuring the necessary parameters, and then adjusting the flow until sufficient points to form a curve are determined.

Potential Problems with Pump Performance Tests

A key piece of information needed for the model representation of the pump is the shutoff head (the head at zero flow). To find this point, the discharge valve is closed and measurements are taken while the pump is operating. It is important to note that if the pump operates with the valve closed for an extended period of time, the water in the pump may begin to heat, potentially damaging the pump and seals. Thus, the measurements must be taken quickly.

Another potential area of concern is electric billing rates. Some water utilities include an electric *demand charge* in their billing structure that is typically based on the highest 15 or 30 minute peak power usage period for the pump station. This demand charge, which can be quite high ($14/kW for example), is applied to all of the current billing period, and may be applied to subsequent billing periods for up to a year. It is important to note that pump testing may require large amounts of energy, and care should be taken that a new and expensive demand charge is not set for the utility.

Using Pump Performance Test Data for Calibration

The data obtained from a pump performance test is used to generate the pump head vs. discharge and efficiency curves, which are used to mathematically model the performance of the pumps. The pump test data collected is input into the model, which then uses curve-fitting techniques to create the relationships describing the pump efficiency and head curves.

5.5 WATER QUALITY SAMPLING

When extending a calibrated hydraulic model to include water quality, parameters describing the chemical reaction dynamics occurring in a network must be measured. Some tests require bench scale experiments that can easily be conducted in a modestly outfitted water quality laboratory.

Constituent Analysis Data Requirements

A calibrated extended period network hydraulic model can be used as a starting point to perform water quality simulations. Using a steady-state hydraulic analysis, however, will not account for the effect of storage and mixing in tanks and reservoirs, a factor known to contribute to the degradation of water quality. As described in Chapter 2 (see page 52), transport, mixing, and chemical reactions depend on the pipe flows, transport pathways, and residence times of water in the network (all are network characteristics determined by the hydraulic simulation). Therefore, a calibrated extended period hydraulic model is a prerequisite for any water quality modeling project. Once a hydraulic model has been prepared, some types of water quality modeling analyses can be conducted with little additional effort.

Constituent analysis, the modeling of disinfectant residuals or *disinfection by-product (DBP)* formation reactions, requires the determination of bulk and wall reaction coefficients, boundary conditions, and initial conditions. Determining bulk and wall reaction coefficients involves laboratory analysis and field studies as discussed in the following section. The determination of boundary and initial conditions is simpler and is addressed in Section 6.5.

Laboratory Testing

For constituent analysis, reaction dynamics can be specified using bulk and wall reaction coefficients. Bulk reaction coefficients can be associated with individual pipes and storage tanks or applied globally. Wall reaction coefficients can be associated with individual pipes, applied globally, or assigned to groups of pipes with similar characteristics. Unlike bulk reaction coefficients, which can be determined through laboratory testing, wall reaction coefficients are more a product of calibration and are discussed on page 223.

Bulk Reaction Coefficients. Recall that the parameter used to express the rate of the reaction occurring within the bulk fluid is called the bulk reaction coefficient. Bulk reaction coefficients can be determined using a simple experimental procedure called a *bottle test*. A bottle test allows the bulk reactions to be separated from other processes that affect water quality, and thus the bulk reaction can be evaluated solely as a function of time. Conceptually, the volume of water in a bottle can be thought of as a water parcel being transported down a pipe (see page 53). A bottle test allows for the evaluation of the impact of transport time on water quality, and for an experimental determination of the parameters necessary to model this process accurately.

Determining the length of the bottle test and the frequency of sampling is the first and most critical decision. The duration and frequency of sampling will influence the error associated with the experimental determination of the rate coefficient. The duration of the experiment should reflect the transport times occurring in the network. If, for example, a water age analysis using the calibrated hydraulic model indicates that residence times range from 5 to 7 days, conducting a 7-day test would provide bulk reaction data over the entire range.

The frequency of the sampling should be proportional to the rate of the reaction. Typically, the sampling frequency should be more rapid at the start of the experiment (every 30 minutes for a fast reaction and once every two hours for a slow one) and can gradually decrease to a lower level (once or twice a day). Once a schedule of samples has been determined, bottles, reagents, and other experimental equipment can be gathered.

Bottle tests can be used to determine bulk reaction rates for different types of reactions; for example, disinfectant decay or DBP formation. The size of the bottles depends on the volume of water required by the experimental procedure. Methods for determining disinfectant concentrations can require anywhere from 20 to 100 ml. Methods for determining DBP formation typically require a smaller sample volume. In either case, the volume and number of bottles should also include any duplicates taken.

It is important for the modeler to appreciate the precision (or lack thereof) when measuring disinfectant residual concentrations. Each analytical method has its own minimum and maximum detection limits, and each person performing a method may have a bias or error associated with them as well. For example, attempting to measure concentrations of 0.08 mg/l when the analytical method is only accurate to 0.20 mg/l can produce misleading data. Duplicates and replicates can be used to quantify these types of errors.

Bottles should be washed prior to the experiment in accordance with the experimental procedure. Frequently, bottles are prepared improperly and the experiment yields worthless data. For example, if disinfectant decay is being measured, the bottle should be prepared so that it does not contribute to the decay reaction. This can be accomplished by soaking the bottles for 24 hours in a strong solution of the disinfectant (10 mg/l) and then rinsing with laboratory clean water (Summers, Hooper, Shukairy, Solarik, and Owen, 1996). Reagents should be gathered and prepared in accordance with the experimental procedure specific to the constituent being measured. Once the experiment has been planned and the laboratory prepared, the test can begin.

"Who does your water?"

For the purposes of determining rates of reaction in the distribution system, water is typically collected as it leaves the clearwell and enters the network, though this need not always be the case. The water should be gathered and the bottles quickly filled and capped with no airspace in the bottle. The experiment starts when the last bottle is capped. At scheduled times, samples should be pulled and tested using the constituent-specific experimental procedure. Between sampling times, samples should be stored in complete darkness and at a constant temperature, because reaction rates (and thus reaction coefficients) are temperature dependent, and some reactions are influenced by ambient light.

■ **Example - Bottle Test Data Analysis** Once all measurements have been taken and the experiment is over, the data will describe the constituent concentration for each of the samples as a function of time. The data can then be graphed. The constituent concentrations are charted along the Y-axis (the dependent variable), and the time is charted along the X-axis (the independent variable). Table 5.3 and Figure 5.13 show an example of data collected from a bottle test for which the constituent was chlorine.

Table 5.3 Bottle test results

Time (hours)	Observed Concentration (mg/l)	Time (hours)	Observed Concentration (mg/l)
0	2.2	54	0.9
6	2.1	60	0.9
12	2.0	66	0.8
18	1.7	72	0.7
24	1.4	78	0.6
30	1.3	84	0.5
36	1.2	90	0.5
42	1.0	96	0.5
48	1.0		

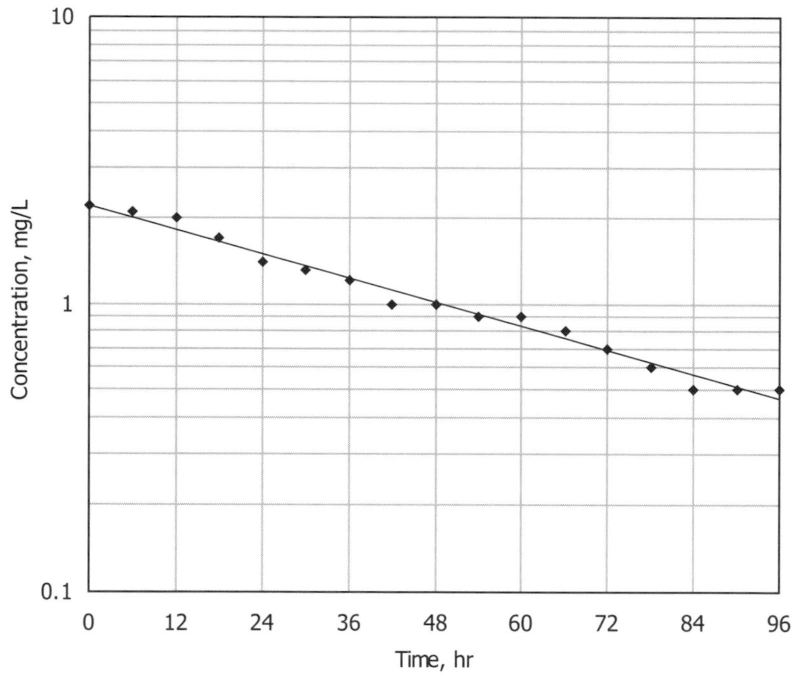

Figure 5.13
A best-fit straight line drawn through the charted results where the slope of the line is the bulk reaction coefficient

If the substance in the bulk fluid exhibits a first-order reaction, then the reaction rate coefficient can be found using linear regression techniques. A best-fit straight line is drawn through the data collected from the bottle test, with concentration plotted on a log axis as illustrated in Figure 5.13. The slope of the line for the data presented above, -0.0165 hr^{-1}, becomes the bulk reaction coefficient. Note that the reaction coefficient is negative since the constituent concentration decays over time.

Bottle Test Procedure

1. Preparation:
   - -Plan the length of the experiment.
   - -Collect materials needed for the experiment.
   - -Wash bottles and prepare them using the chlorine demand-free procedure.
   - -Prepare reagents for experimental methods and work area.
   - -Prepare laboratory notebook for recording experimental conditions and results.
2. Sample Collection:
   - -Collect water from the clearwell as it enters the distribution system.
   - -Fill and cap bottles headspace-free.
   - -Start the master clock.
3. Sample Testing:
   - -Store samples in complete darkness with the temperature held constant (a water bath or BOD incubator may be used).
   - -Pull samples at designated times and measure using experimental procedure.
   - -Record time and result of the experimental procedure.
4. Processing Data:
   - -Plot data.
   - -Process data to determine rate coefficient.

(Summers, Hooper, Shukairy, Solarik, and Owen, 1996; Rossman, Clark, and Grayman, 1994; and Vasconcelos, Rossman, Grayman, Boulos, and Clark, 1996)

The straight line shown in Figure 5.13 produces a very nice fit with the observed data. A more likely scenario is that the data will not fit as well as that shown. In fact, there may be a few data points that are widely scattered. *Outliers*, as these points are called, should be carefully examined and possibly discarded if they are found to negatively influence the results of the data analysis. If there is a large amount of scatter, another bottle test may be performed in an attempt to collect more reliable data.

Bottle tests can be performed on any water sample, regardless of where the sample is collected. Samples from treatment plants and other entry points to the distribution system are particularly important because these facilities act as water sources, and therefore have a strong influence on water quality. Raw water quality influences finished water quality as well. Therefore, if a system has multiple treatment facilities each with a different raw water source, the bulk reaction rates for each of the finished waters are likely to differ. Although storage tanks are not sources of finished water, under some circumstances, the bulk decay rate can be different in tanks than in the distribution system. As a result, a separate bulk reaction coefficient should be considered for tanks and reservoirs. Booster disinfection (when disinfectant is reapplied to previously disinfected water) is another circumstance in which bulk reaction coefficients are likely to change.

Bulk reaction coefficients are associated with pipes for purposes of a simulation, and are assumed to remain constant throughout the simulation for a particular pipe. Since the bulk reaction coefficient is, in reality, associated with the fluid itself, the bulk reaction rate can change throughout the actual system as water from different sources becomes mixed at nodes. When assigning bulk reaction coefficients for pipes, the mixing can be considered by designing and conducting bottle tests with representative source mixtures. A source tracing analysis can assist in determining the degree of mixing in a system. Source blending can change over the course of the day for a particular pipe, thus the predominant source or mix of sources should be used in assigning the bulk reaction coefficient.

For example, suppose that a tracing analysis is performed on a system that has two treatment plants. Through the bottle tests, a bulk reaction coefficient is established for each treatment facility and each storage tank. Through a source tracing analysis of a junction node, it is found that 90 percent of the water for that node comes from a specific treatment plant. Accordingly, the bulk reaction rate coefficient for those pipes that make up the path between the plant and the node would be equal to, or nearly equal to, the rate coefficient for the plant. For a single-source network, it is useful to remember that the bulk reaction coefficient is really a function of the water passing through a pipe or stored in a tank, and not a function of the pipe or tank itself. Thus, specifying a global bulk reaction coefficient is frequently the simplest and the best method for modeling bulk reactions occurring in such networks.

REFERENCES

American Water Works Association. (1989). "Installation, Field Testing, and Maintenance of Fire Hydrants." *AWWA Manual M-17*, Denver, Colorado.

Hudson, W. D. (1966). "Studies of Distribution System Capacity in Seven Cities." *Journal of the American Water Works Association*, 58(2), 157.

Insurance Service Office (ISO). (1963). *Fire Flow Tests*. New York, New York.

Lamont, P. A. (1981). "Common Pipe Flow Formulas Compared with the Theory of Roughness." *Journal of the American Water Works Association*, 73(5), 274.

McEnroe, B. M., Chase, D. V., and Sharp, W. W. (1989). "Field Testing Water Mains to Determine Carrying Capacity." *Miscellaneous Paper EL-89*, U.S., Army Engineer Waterways Experiment Station, Vicksburg, Mississippi.

Morin, M., and Rajaratnam, I. V. (2000). *Testing and Calibration of Pitot Diffusers*. University of Alberta Hydraulics Laboratory, Alberta, Canada.

Ormsbee, L. E., and Lingireddy, S. (1997). "Calibrating Hydraulic Network Models." *Journal of the American Water Works Association*, 89(2), 44.

Rossman, L. A., Clark, R. M., and Grayman, W. M. (1994). "Modeling Chlorine Residuals in Drinking-Water Distribution Systems." *Journal of Environmental Engineering*, ASCE, 120(4), 803.

Sharp, W. W., and Walski, T. M. (1988). "Predicting Internal Roughness in Water Mains." *Journal of the American Water Works Association*, 80(11), 34.

Summers, R. S., Hooper, S. M., Shukairy, H. M., Solarik, G., and Owen, D. (1996). "Assessing DBP Yield: Uniform Formation Conditions." *Journal of the American Water Works Association*, 88(6), 80.

Vasconcelos, J. J., Rossman, L. A., Grayman, W. M., Boulos, P. F., and Clark, R. M. (1996). *Characterization and Modeling of Chlorine Decay in Distribution Systems.* AWWA Research Foundation, Denver, Colorado.

Walski, T. M. (1984a). *Analysis of Water Distribution Systems*. Van Nostrand Reinhold, New York, New York.

Walski, T. M. (1984b). "Hydrant Flow Test Results." *Journal of Hydraulic Engineering*, ASCE, 110(6), 847.

Walski, T. M. (1985). "Correction of Head Loss Measurements in Water Mains." *Journal of Transportation Engineering*, ASCE, 111(1), 75.

Walski, T. M. (1988). "Conducting and Reporting Hydrant Flow Tests." *WES Video Report*, U.S. Army Engineer Waterways Experiment Station, Vicksburg, Mississippi.

Walski, T. M., Edwards, J. D., and Hearne, V. M. (1989). "Loss of Carrying Capacity in Pipes Transporting Softened Water with High pH." *Proceedings of the National Conference on Environmental Engineering*, American Society of Civil Engineers, Austin, Texas.

Walski, T. M., and Lutes, T. L. (1990). "Accuracy of Hydrant Flow Tests Using a Pitot Diffuser." *Journal of the American Water Works Association*, 82(7), 58.

Walski, T. M., and O'Farrell, S. J. (1994). "Head Loss Testing in Transmission Mains." *Journal of the American Water Works Association*, 86(7), 62.

Water and Environment Federation (WEF). (1997). "Energy Conservation in Wastewater Treatment Facilities." *WEF Manual of Practice MFD-2*, Alexandria, Virginia.

DISCUSSION TOPICS AND PROBLEMS

Earn CEUs Read Chapters 5 and 6 and complete the problems. Submit your work to Haestad Methods and earn up to 1.5 CEUs. See *Continuing Education Units* on page xiii for more information, or visit www.haestad.com/wdm-ceus/.

5.1 *English Units* - Compute the HGL at each of the fire hydrants for the pressure readings presented below and complete the table.

Location	Elevation (ft)	Pressure Reading (psi)	HGL (ft)
FH-1	235	57	
FH-5	321	42	
FH-34	415	15	
FH-10	295	68	
FH-19	333	45	
FH-39	412	27	

SI Units - Compute the HGL at each of the fire hydrants for the pressure readings presented below and complete the table.

Location	Elevation (m)	Pressure Reading (kPa)	HGL (m)
FH-1	71.6	393	
FH-5	97.8	290	
FH-34	126.5	103	
FH-10	89.9	469	
FH-19	101.5	310	
FH-39	125.6	186	

5.2 *English Units* - A tank is used to capture the flow from a fire hydrant as illustrated in Figure 5.14. The tank is 50 ft long, 30 ft wide, and 12 ft high. What is the average discharge from the fire hydrant if the container is filled to a depth of 10 ft in 90 minutes?

Figure 5.14

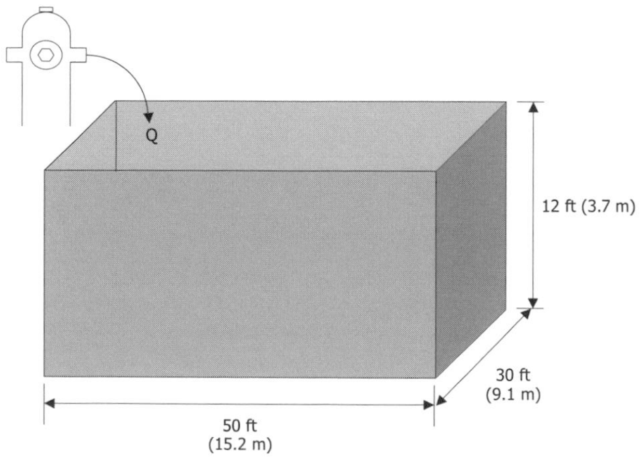

SI Units - A tank is used to capture the flow from a fire hydrant as illustrated in Figure 5.14. The tank is 15.2 m long, 9.1 m wide, and 3.7 m high. What is the average discharge from the fire hydrant if the container is filled to a depth of 3.0 m in 90 minutes?

5.3 *English Units* - A fire flow test was conducted using the four fire hydrants shown in Figure 5.15. Before flowing the hydrants, the static pressure at the residual hydrant was recorded as 93 psi. Given the data for the flow test in the tables below, find the discharges from each hydrant and finish filling out the tables. Flow was directed out of the 2 ½-in. nozzle, and each hydrant has a rounded entrance where the nozzle meets the hydrant barrel.

a) Would you consider the data collected for this fire flow test to be acceptable for use with a hydraulic simulation model? Why or why not?

b) Based on the results of the fire flow tests, do you think that the hydrants are located on a transmission line or a distribution line?

c) Would these results typically be more consistent with a test conducted near a water source (such as a storage tank), or at some distance away from a source?

d) If the needed fire flow is 3,500 gpm with a minimum residual pressure of 20 psi, is this system capable of delivering sufficient fire flows at this location?

Figure 5.15

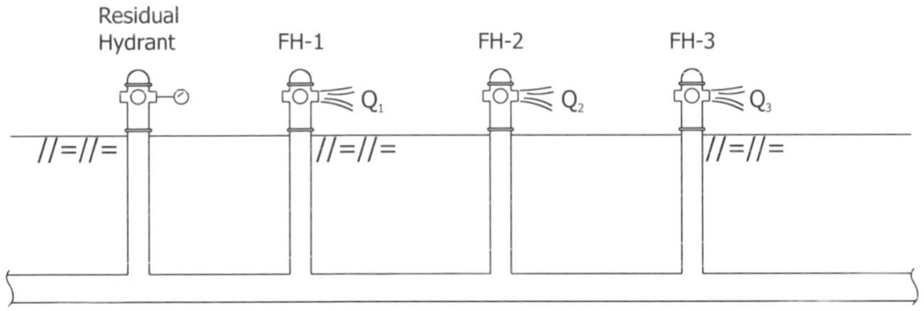

Flowed Hydrant	Residual Pressure (psi)	Pitot Reading (psi)	Hydrant Discharge (gpm)
Residual Hydrant	91	N/A	
FH-1	N/A	65	
FH-2	N/A	Closed	
FH-3	N/A	Closed	

Flowed Hydrant	Residual Pressure (psi)	Pitot Reading (psi)	Hydrant Discharge (gpm)
Residual Hydrant	88	N/A	
FH-1	N/A	58	
FH-2	N/A	52	
FH-3	N/A	Closed	

Flowed Hydrant	Residual Pressure (psi)	Pitot Reading (psi)	Hydrant Discharge (gpm)
Residual Hydrant	83	N/A	
FH-1	N/A	53	
FH-2	N/A	51	
FH-3	N/A	48	

SI Units - A fire flow test was conducted using the four fire hydrants shown in Figure 5.15. Before flowing the hydrants, the static pressure at the residual hydrant was recorded as 641 kPa. Given the data for the flow test in the tables below, find the discharges from each hydrant and finish filling out the tables. Flow was directed out of the 64 mm nozzle, and each hydrant has a rounded entrance where the nozzle meets the hydrant barrel.

a) Would you consider the data collected for this fire flow test to be acceptable for use with a hydraulic simulation model? Why or why not?

b) Based on the results of the fire flow tests, do you think that the hydrants are located on a transmission line or a distribution line?

c) Would these results typically be more consistent with a test conducted near a water source (such as a storage tank), or at some distance away from a source?

d) If the needed fire flow is 220 l/s with a minimum residual pressure of 138 kPa, is this system capable of delivering sufficient fire flows at this location?

Flowed Hydrant	Residual Pressure (kPa)	Pitot Reading (kPa)	Hydrant Discharge (l/s)
Residual Hydrant	627	N/A	
FH-1	N/A	448	
FH-2	N/A	Closed	
FH-3	N/A	Closed	

Flowed Hydrant	Residual Pressure (kPa)	Pitot Reading (kPa)	Hydrant Discharge (l/s)
Residual Hydrant	607	N/A	
FH-1	N/A	400	
FH-2	N/A	359	
FH-3	N/A	Closed	

Flowed Hydrant	Residual Pressure (kPa)	Pitot Reading (kPa)	Hydrant Discharge (l/s)
Residual Hydrant	572	N/A	
FH-1	N/A	365	
FH-2	N/A	352	
FH-3	N/A	331	

5.4 *English Units* - A two-gage head loss test was conducted over 650 ft of 8-in. PVC pipe as shown in Figure 5.16. The pipe was installed in 1981. The discharge from the flowed hydrant was 1,050 gpm. The data obtained from the test are presented in the table below.

	Elevation (ft)	Pressure (psi)
Fire Hydrant 1	500	62
Fire Hydrant 2	520	57

a) Can the results of the head loss test be used to determine the internal roughness of the pipe? Why or why not?

b) If the test results cannot be used, what is most likely causing the problem?

Figure 5.16

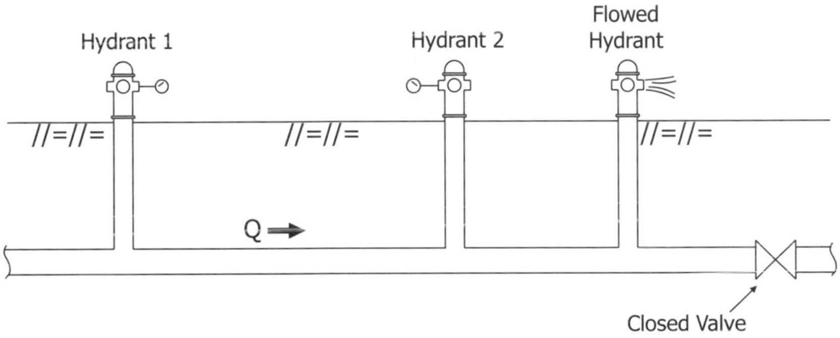

SI Units - A two-gage head loss test was conducted over 198 m of 203-mm PVC pipe as shown in Figure 5.16. The pipe was installed in 1981. The discharge from the flowed hydrant was 66.2 l/s. The data obtained from the test are presented in the table below.

	Elevation (m)	Pressure (kPa)
Fire Hydrant 1	152	428
Fire Hydrant 2	158	393

a) Can the results of the head loss test be used to determine the internal roughness of the pipe? Why or why not?

b) If the test results cannot be used, what is most likely causing the problem?

5.5 *English Units* - A different two-gage head loss test was conducted over the same 650 ft of 8-in. PVC pipe shown in Figure 5.16. In this test, the pressure at Fire Hydrant 1 was 65 psi, and the pressure at Fire Hydrant 2 was 40 psi. The discharge through the flowed hydrant was 1,350 gpm.

a) Can the results of the head loss test be used to determine the internal roughness of the pipe? Why or why not?

b) What is the Hazen-Williams C-factor for this line?

c) How can the results of this test be used to help calibrate the water distribution system?

d) Is this a realistic roughness value for PVC?

SI Units - A different two-gage head loss test was conducted over the same 198 m of 203-mm PVC pipe shown in Figure 5.16. In this test, the pressure at Fire Hydrant 1 was 448 kPa, and the pressure at Fire Hydrant 2 was 276 kPa. The discharge through the flowed hydrant was 85.2 l/s.

a) Can the results of the head loss test be used to determine the internal roughness of the pipe? Why or why not?

b) What is the Hazen-Williams C-factor for this line?

c) How can the results of this test be used to help calibrate the water distribution system?

d) Is this a realistic roughness value for PVC?

5.6 The table below presents the results of a chlorine decay bottle test. Compute the bulk reaction rate coefficient for this water sample.

Time (hr)	Concentration (mg/L)
0	1.5
3	1.4
6	1.2
9	1.0
12	1.0
15	0.9
18	0.7
21	0.7
24	0.6
27	0.5
30	0.5
33	0.5
36	0.4
39	0.4
42	0.3
45	0.3
48	0.3
51	0.3
54	0.2
57	0.2
60	0.2

5.7 *English Units* - Data from a pump test are presented in the table below. Fortunately, this pump had a pressure tap available on both the suction and discharge sides. The diameter of the suction line is 12 in. and the diameter of the discharge line is 8 in. Plot the pump head-discharge curve for this unit.

Suction Pressure (psi)	Discharge Pressure (psi)	Pump Discharge (gpm)
10.5	117	0
10.1	116	260
9.3	114	500
8.7	111	725
7.2	101	1,250
5.7	93	1,500
4.4	85	1,725
3.0	76	2,000
1.6	65	2,300
-0.2	53	2,500
-2.0	41	2,700

SI Units - Data from a pump test are presented in the table below. Fortunately, this pump had a pressure tap available on both the suction and discharge sides. The diameter of the suction line is 300 mm, and the diameter of the discharge line is 200 mm. Plot the pump head-discharge curve for this unit.

Suction Pressure (kPa)	Discharge Pressure (kPa)	Pump Discharge (l/s)
72.4	803	0
69.6	798	16.4
64.1	784	31.5
60.0	764	45.7
49.6	694	78.9
39.3	644	94.6
30.3	586	108.8
20.7	522	126.2
11.0	451	145.1
-1.4	366	157.7
-13.8	283	170.3

5.8 A C-factor test is conducted in a 350 ft length of 12-in. pipe. The upstream pressure gage is at elevation 520 ft, and the downstream gage is at 524 ft.

a) The Hazen-Williams equation can be rearranged to solve for C as

$$C = KQ/h_L^{0.54}$$

where
C = Hazen-Williams roughness coefficient
K = constant
Q = flow (gpm)
h_L = head loss due to friction (ft)

What is the expression for K if length (L) is in feet and diameter (D) is in inches? All of the terms in K are constant for this problem, so determine the numerical value for K.

b) What is the expression for head loss between the upstream and downstream pressure gages if the head loss (h) and elevations (z_1 and z_2) are in feet, and the pressures (P_1 and P_2) are in psi?

c) The elevations are surveyed to the nearest 0.01 ft and the pressure gage is accurate to +/- 1 psi. Opening a downstream hydrant resulted in a flow of 800 gpm (accurate to +/- 50 gpm) with a measured upstream pressure of 60 psi and a measured downstream pressure of 57 psi. Determine the possible range of actual Hazen-Williams C-factors and fill in the table below.

Hint: For the roughest possible C-factor, use 800 – 50 gpm for flow and h + 5 ft for head loss. For the smoothest possible C-factor, use 800 + 50 gpm for flow and h – 5 ft for head loss.

	Measured values	Roughest possible C	Smoothest possible C
Q (gpm)			
h (ft)			
C			

d) What can you conclude about the C-factor from this test?

e) Which measurement contributed more to the error in this problem, head loss or flow?

f) What could you do to improve the results if you ran the test over again?

5.9 *English Units* - A hydrant flow test was performed on a main line where a new industrial park is to tie in. The following hydrant flow test values were obtained from a 2 ½-in. nozzle in the field. First, use Equation 5.1 to determine the hydrant discharge for a discharge coefficient of 0.90.

Determine if the existing system is able to handle 1,200 gpm of fire flow demand for the new industrial park by using the equation given in the sidebar on page 171 entitled *Evaluating Distribution Capacity with Hydrant Tests.*

Fire Hydrant Number	Static Pressure	Residual Pressure	Pitot Pressure
200	48 psi	33 psi	12 psi

SI Units - A hydrant flow test was performed on a main line where a new industrial park is to tie in. The following hydrant flow test values were obtained from 64-mm nozzle in the field. First, use Equation 5.1 to determine the hydrant discharge for a discharge coefficient of 0.90.

Determine if the existing system is able to handle 75.7 l/s of fire flow demand for the new industrial park by using the equation given in the sidebar on page 171 entitled *Evaluating Distribution Capacity with Hydrant Tests.*

Fire Hydrant Number	Static Pressure	Residual Pressure	Pitot Pressure
200	331 kPa	227.5 kPa	82.7 kPa

CHAPTER

6

Calibrating Hydraulic Network Models

Even though the required data have been collected and entered into a hydraulic simulation software package, the modeler cannot assume that the model is an accurate mathematical representation of the system. The hydraulic simulation software simply solves the equations of continuity and energy using the supplied data; thus, the quality of the data will dictate the quality of the results. The accuracy of a hydraulic model depends upon how well it has been calibrated, so a calibration analysis should always be performed before a model is used for decision-making purposes.

Calibration is the process of comparing the model results to field observations, and, if necessary, adjusting the data describing the system until model-predicted performance reasonably agrees with measured system performance over a wide range of operating conditions. The process of calibration may include changing system demands, fine-tuning the roughness of pipes, altering pump operating characteristics, and adjusting other model attributes that affect simulation results.

The calibration process is necessary for the following reasons:

- **Confidence -** Results provided by a computer model are frequently used to aid in making decisions regarding the operation or improvement of a hydraulic system. Calibration demonstrates the model's ability to reproduce existing conditions, thereby increasing the confidence the engineer will have in the model to predict system behavior.

- **Understanding -** The process of calibrating a hydraulic model provides excellent insight into the behavior and performance of the hydraulic system. In particular, it can show which input values the model is most sensitive to, so the modeler knows to be more careful in determining those values. With a better understanding of the system, the modeler will have an idea of the possible impact of various capital improvements or operational changes.

- **Troubleshooting -** One area of calibration that is often overlooked is the ability to uncover missing or incorrect data describing the system, such as incorrect pipe diameters, missing pipes, or closed valves. Thus, another benefit of calibration is that it will help in identifying errors caused by mistakes made during the model-building process.

This chapter begins with a discussion of data requirements and the reasons for discrepancies between computer-predicted behavior and actual field performance of a water distribution system. Variations can stem from the cumulative effects of errors, approximations, and simplifications in the way the system is modeled; site-specific reasons such as outdated system maps; and more difficult-to-quantify causes like the inherent variability of water consumption.

Next, the chapter addresses some of the specific methods used to calibrate models, including both manual and automated approaches like genetic algorithms. The chapter concludes with a discussion on the limits of calibration and how to know when the model is sufficiently calibrated.

6.1 MODEL-PREDICTED VS. FIELD-MEASURED PERFORMANCE

In making comparisons between model results and field observations, the user must ensure that the field data are correct and useful. While the details of field-testing were explained in Chapter 5, this section focuses on identifying useful data for calibration.

Comparisons Based on Head

When comparisons are made between field and model results, there is no mathematical reason to use pressures instead of hydraulic grades, or vice versa. Because pressure is just a converted representation of the height of the HGL relative to the ground elevation datum, the two are essentially equivalent for comparison purposes. For calibration purposes, however, there are several compelling arguments for working with hydraulic grades rather than pressures (Herrin, 1997).

- Hydraulic grades provide the modeler with a sense of the accuracy and reliability of the data. If computed and measured hydraulic grade values are drastically different from one another, it should immediately signal the modeler that a particular value may be in error. For example, an elevation may have been entered incorrectly.
- Hydraulic grades give an indication of the direction of flow—insight that pressures do not provide.
- Working with hydraulic grade makes it easier to work with pressure measurements not taken exactly at node locations within the model, because it is the elevation of the pressure gage, not the node, that is used to convert measured pressure into HGL.

Although HGL or pressure comparisons will both lead to the same results if all other factors are equal, pressure comparisons make it much easier to overlook errors and much harder to track down inconsistencies between real-world observations and the model results. Accordingly, the first step the modeler should do upon collection of field data is to convert pressure and tank water level data into the equivalent HGLs. Subsequent comparisons should be made between observed and modeled HGL.

Quality of Calibration Data

Users will sometimes try to calibrate models where the velocity and head loss are very low, and thus the hydraulic grade line is essentially flat. Under such conditions, the heads in the system are essentially the same as those at the boundary conditions and virtually any value of the roughness coefficient or demand can be used to produce similar results (Walski, 2000). McBean, Al-Nassari, and Clarke (1983) used first-order analysis to determine the accuracy of pressure measurements needed for field data to be useful for model calibration.

Referring back to the head loss equations presented in Chapter 2 (see page 36), the head loss depends heavily on the flow and the C-factor. Most model calibration eventually comes down to adjustments in a parameter like the C-factor, according to the equation:

$$C = \frac{k(Q \pm \Delta Q)}{(h_L \pm \Delta h_L)^{0.54}} \qquad (6.1)$$

where
C = Hazen-Williams C-factor
k = factor depending on units and distribution system
Q = estimated flow (gpm, m^3/s)
ΔQ = error in measuring Q (gpm, m^3/s)
h_L = estimated head loss due to friction (ft, m)
Δh_L = error in measuring head loss due to friction (ft, m)

If the flows and heads are small, errors in measuring these quantities will be the same order of magnitude as the quantities themselves, making them of little use in the calibration process. Furthermore, the value of parameters found by calibration will be poor.

The key to successful calibration is to increase the flows and the head losses such that these values are significantly greater than errors in measurement. The best way to do this is by conducting hydrant flow tests as described in the previous chapter. If the model can match conditions under normal demands and fire flow tests, then the user can feel confident that the model can be applied to other conditions.

In larger pipes [e.g., greater than 16 in. (400 mm)], hydrant flow tests will not generate significant velocities. For these larger pipes, the engineer needs to create head loss by measuring it over very long lengths of pipe, or by artificially increasing flow by allowing tank water levels to drop significantly, and then filling the tank quickly.

Figure 6.1
Hydrant Flow Test

Location of Data Collection

Errors in roughness coefficients and demand affect the slope of the hydraulic grade line. If data are collected near the boundary nodes, the differences between the model and the field data may appear to be small because of the short distance even though the slope of the HGLs (and hence the roughness coefficient and demand) are significantly in error. Head data for model calibration should generally be collected a significant distance away from known boundary heads. Data should also be collected for pipes that have not been removed from the model during skeletonization.

There should be at least one flow test conducted in each pressure zone, and the number of flow tests should be roughly proportional to the size of the pressure zone. In general, more tests will increase the confidence the user will have in the model. One approach to selecting sampling locations uses a special procedure to select locations that minimize the uncertainty of the model's predictions (Bush and Uber, 1998). Another uses genetic algorithms to determine the best locations to conduct fire hydrant flow tests to maximize the coverage of the pipe network (Meier and Barkdoll, 2000).

Data collection can be classified as either point reading (grab samples) or continuous monitoring. *Point reading* involves collecting data for a single location at a specific point in time, while *continuous monitoring* involves collecting data at a single location over time. For point readings, samples should be collected at locations where the parameter being measured is steady, so that the sample measurement is representative of the location over a fairly long period of time. To get the most out of continuous monitoring, the data should be collected from locations where the parameter being measured is dynamic. In situations where a point reading must be made at a dynamic location, it is critical to carefully note the time and boundary conditions corresponding to the data point.

6.2 SOURCES OF ERROR IN MODELING

The primary objective of a simulation is to reproduce the behavior of a real system and its spatial and dynamic characteristics in a useful way. To accomplish this goal, data are supplied that depict the physical characteristics of the system, the loads placed on the system, and the boundary conditions in effect. Even if all of the data gathered describing the model match the real system exactly, it is unlikely that the pressures and flows computed by the simulation model will absolutely agree with observed pressures and flows. There are significant mathematical assumptions employed by the simulation software to make the simulation computationally tractable, yet allow the simulated results to be meaningful and useful. Thus, modeling is essentially a balance between reality, a simulated reality, and the effort necessary to make the two agree. This section explores some of the sources of error in input data, as well as the causes for discrepancies between field conditions and modeling results.

Some may assume that calibration can be accomplished by only adjusting internal pipe roughness values or estimates of nodal demands until an agreement between observed and computed pressures and flows is obtained. Generally speaking, the basis for this claim is that unlike pipe lengths, diameters, and tank levels, which are directly measured, pipe roughness values and nodal demands are typically estimated, and thus have room for adjustment. Numerous factors, however, can contribute to disagreement between model and field observations (Walski, 1990). Any and all input data that have uncertainty associated with them are candidates for adjustment during calibration to obtain reasonable agreement between model-predicted behavior and actual field behavior.

A discrepancy found during the calibration process can also mean that the system itself may have problems. A review of the system should be done before any changes are made to rationally developed model data. Possible system problems are large leaks, unchartered services, previously undetected errors in the metered consumption, errors in recorded pipe sizes, unknown throttled or closed valves, worn pump impellers, or old construction debris left in pipes.

Types of Errors

Errors in input data can be broken down into two main categories, typographical errors and measurement errors. *Typographical errors*, although simple to correct, can be very difficult to uncover (for example, a pipe length of 2,250 ft is accidentally entered as 250 ft). Fortunately, some of today's graphically-based hydraulic network models have tools that can help reduce the potential for typographical errors. For example, some models include automatic validation of input values and/or the ability to determine pipe lengths and vertices automatically by measuring the distance between two nodes based on the drawing scale.

Unfortunately, these tools do not completely eliminate the possibility for human error. After data entry is completed, it is recommended that the model be reviewed for possible typographical errors. One tip is to use the sorting and color-coding capabilities available in many models to quickly identify very large or very small values for pipe length, diameter, or internal roughness. At a minimum, such values should be verified as accurate.

Compared to typographical errors, *measurement errors* can be much more difficult to identify and correct. One example of such an error may result from variations in scale on system maps. For instance, if a length of a pipe is measured with an engineering scale from a system map that has a scale of 1 in (2.54 cm) = 1000 ft (304.8 m), the measured length may only be within ± 50 ft (15.24 m) of the actual length. Depending on the application of the model, this level of accuracy may or may not be sufficient for calibration purposes.

Nominal vs. Actual Pipe Diameters

As discussed in Chapter 3 (see page 90), the nominal and actual diameters of a pipe typically differ. Determining the actual diameter of a pipe is further complicated by the chemical processes of corrosion and deposition that occur over time after the pipe has been installed. Therefore, for lack of a better value, nominal pipe diameters are generally used for model development, and the roughness coefficient is adjusted to compensate for the change in diameter due to pipe wall build-up.

With severe tuberculation, a Hazen-Williams C-factor as low as 20 or 30 may be necessary to obtain a suitable calibration. Conversely, high roughness coefficients may be needed for calibration of new piping. Since the actual diameter of new pipe is usually greater than the nominal diameter, an increased roughness coefficient may be used to account for the difference.

The pipe diameter has a much greater influence on the head loss through a pipe than the pipe roughness value does. According to the Hazen-Williams equation, the head loss is a function of the pipe diameter raised to nearly the fifth power, while it is a function of the roughness value raised to only the second power. The result is that a 10 percent increase in the pipe diameter will decrease head loss by nearly 40 percent, while a 10 percent increase in the roughness coefficient will decrease head loss by about 20 percent.

There is little advantage to be gained in adjusting both the roughness coefficient and diameter in a model. For example, a 6-in. (150-mm) pipe with a roughness coefficient of 100 gives the same head loss as a 5-in. (130-mm) pipe with a coefficient of 161. In calibration, the user wants to minimize the number of variables to adjust, and considering diameter as an unknown would double the number of variables that must be determined for each pipe. Accordingly, making adjustments to roughness coefficients is the preferable means of fine-tuning a model calibration (except for certain situations in water quality calibration, as explained later in this chapter).

Roughness coefficient values can help identify other problems in a model. In general, if C-factors less than 40 or greater than 150 are needed to calibrate the model, then chances are that some other condition, such as a partially closed valve, may be causing the difference between observed and modeled heads. The status of the valve may then be changed within the model, or the valve in the real system may require adjusting. Either alternative is a valuable result of the calibration process.

Internal Pipe Roughness Values

A great deal of research has been done in the area of estimating pipe roughness values. Colebrook and White (1937) developed the theory behind the loss of carrying capacity with age. Full-scale testing of pipes was done in several cities to document the effect in real systems (California Section AWWA, 1962; and Hudson, 1966). Later, Lamont (1981) compiled an extensive table documenting pipe C-factors for a wide variety of pipe materials, sizes, and ages. The increase in pipe roughness as a function of water quality was also evaluated (Walski, Edwards, and Hearne, 1989). They found that two pipes of the same size, material, and age can have different effective diameters and roughness based on the quality of the water historically flowing through the pipe.

Compensating Errors. Despite all of these variables, pressure data collected in the field can be used to select appropriate roughness values for the pipes. However, in calibrating a model, it is important to consider the potential for compensating errors; that is, fixing one inaccuracy by introducing another one into the network. When calibrating, the adjustments made to the variables should be appropriate for a range of operating conditions, and not just the individual case being considered.

■ **Example - Compensating Errors** Consider the simple parallel pipe system shown in Figure 6.2 for which the internal roughness values of each pipe are unknown. Suppose that pressure measurements have been taken at the nodes on each end of the pipe segments, the total flow through the system is known, and the elevations of the nodes on each end of the pipe loop are the same. Knowing that the head loss through Pipe 1 and Pipe 2 is the same, the expressions for head loss in

Pipes 1 and 2 can be equated. (Note that the pressure drop of 7 psi translates into a head loss of 16.2 ft).

Figure 6.2
Simple parallel pipe system

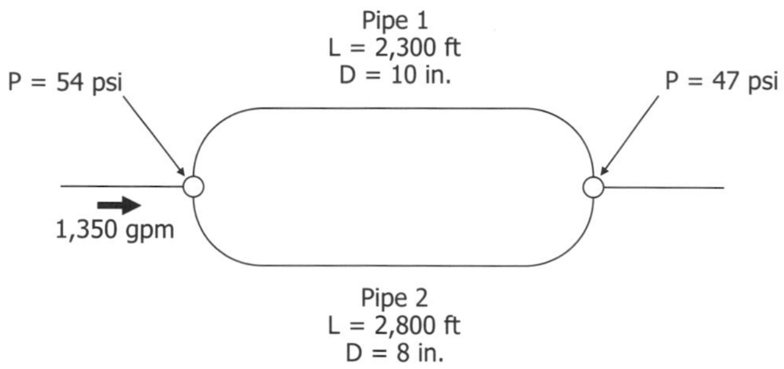

$$\frac{L_1}{D_1^{4.87}}\left(\frac{Q_1}{C_1}\right)^{1.852} = \frac{L_2}{D_2^{4.87}}\left(\frac{Q_2}{C_2}\right)^{1.852}$$

where L = pipe length (ft)
D = pipe diameter (ft)
Q = pipe discharge (cfs)
C = Hazen-Williams C-factor

Table 6.1 shows the results of a simple analysis performed on this system. Column 1 provides a range of assumed C-factor values for Pipe 1. The flow through Pipe 1 resulting from the assumed C-factor, known head loss, pipe length, and diameter is shown in Column 2. Column 3 provides the flow in Pipe 2 assuming a total system flow of 1,350 gpm. Column 4 shows the C-factor for Pipe 2 back-calculated from the head loss, pipe characteristics, and pipe flow.

Table 6.1 Flow rate versus pipe roughness values for parallel pipe system

Pipe #1 Roughness	Pipe #1 Flow (gpm)	Pipe #2 Flow (gpm)	Pipe #2 Roughness
80	660	689	166
90	743	606	146
100	825	524	126
110	908	441	106
120	991	358	86
130	1073	276	66
140	1156	193	46

Clearly, there are multiple C-factor choices for Pipes 1 and 2 that will produce the same head loss across the system. While one set of C-factors may be correct for a particular case, the selection may introduce error into the model for another case, a clue useful in identifying the presence of compensating errors. The question then becomes, which is the correct set of C-factors? The flow in one of the pipes must be measured to answer this question and establish the correct C-factors.

This problem illustrates compensating errors for a simple two-pipe system. Assume, for the same system, that the flow into the system and the pressure at the upstream node are both unknown. The various combinations of flow, pipe roughness values, and upstream pressures that would match the single pressure measurement taken at the downstream node are now essentially infinite. As more parallel paths from point A to point B are added, the problem grows in complexity. This simple example illustrates that compensating errors are often hidden behind seemingly valid data. As the problems get larger and hydraulic measurements become more sparse, they become increasingly more difficult to find.

When velocities are low, it is possible to make a model appear to be calibrated even when C-factors contain significant errors (Walski, 1986). The best way to reduce the likelihood of compensating errors in pipe roughness values is to take head measurements under a range of demand conditions. Because the head loss equations are nonlinear, it will be difficult for compensating errors to make the model look calibrated when it is not.

Flow measurements provide another way to reduce the likelihood that the wrong parameter is adjusted. For instance, in the previous example, knowledge of the total flow through the system eliminated one degree of freedom. Obviously, it is not practical to measure flows for each pipe in the field that corresponds to a pipe in the model. Nevertheless, to minimize the potential for compensating errors and to aid in the calibration process, as many flow measurements should be made as possible, particularly at critical locations such as pipelines connected to treatment plants, pump stations, tanks, reservoirs, and other water sources. Tests should also be conducted along major transmission mains that carry a large portion of the total system flow and along distribution lines that are considered to be representative of the overall system (Ormsbee and Lingireddy, 1997).

Determining roughness coefficients for a representative sampling of pipes of varying ages and sizes provides a good check on the reasonableness of the coefficients used in calibration. The measurement of flow and roughness coefficients is discussed in greater detail in Chapter 5, Testing Water Distribution Systems.

Distribution of System Demands

The water distribution modeling equations are based on the simplifying assumption that water is withdrawn at a junction node. In reality, however, water usage occurs along the entire length of a pipe, as shown in Figure 6.3. Spatially redistributing water usages that occur along a length of pipe to the junction nodes in the model is known as demand allocation. The demand allocation process is a possible source of error that should be considered when calibrating a model. Another, and often more significant source of error with regard to demands, is related to how the demands change over time (an important issue when doing EPS). Both of these sources of error and their impact on calibration are discussed below. [They are also discussed more generally in Chapter 4 (see page 126).]

It is conceivable that a model could incorporate all of the locations where water is withdrawn from the system by placing junction nodes where the service lines are connected to the water main. This approach, however, would significantly increase the number of pipes required in the model, thereby increasing its complexity. Model simplification is achieved through spatial demand allocation (see the example on page 130). For example, in Figure 6.3, the sum of the water use associated with the eight homes closest to J-23 can be assigned to J-23, and the sum of the water use for the 10 homes closest to J-24 can be assigned to J-24. By placing the demands properly, they will be accounted for in the model even if the pipe between nodes J-23 and J-24 is removed during skeletonization. However, the modeler must realize that the simulated pressures at the model nodes are only an approximation of the actual pressures at the homes.

Figure 6.3
Spatial demand allocation

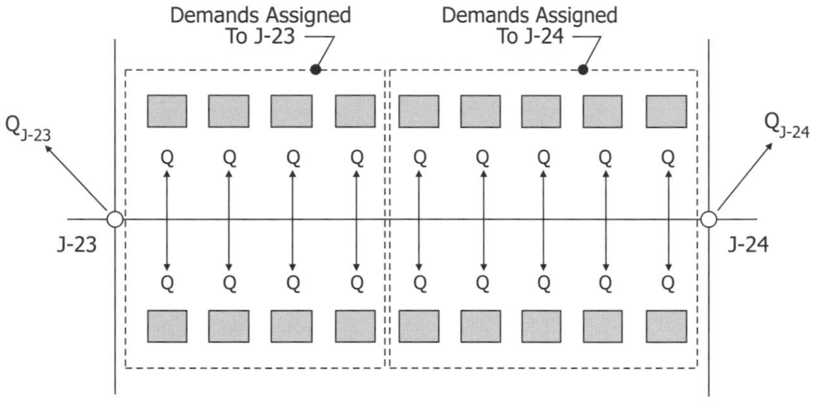

Several expressions have been developed that equate uniform water withdrawal along a pipe to point loads at junction nodes. In the early stages of modeling, a method was developed for correcting head loss equations with multiple service lines when performing manual calculations (Muss, 1960). Another method uses a step-wise combination of elements and a nonlinear representation of the entire network (Shamir and Hamberg, 1988).

Grouping water usage at the junction nodes instead of at the actual locations where water is withdrawn from the system produces relatively minor differences between computer-predicted and actual field performance, if the actual location of the customer demand is in close proximity to the assigned node. Incorrect spatial demand allocation usually becomes problematic when demands from large customers are missed or assigned to nodes in the wrong pressure zones. In most cases, however, errors in allocating demands to exactly the right node are insignificant, especially when fire flows used in design are significantly greater than normal demands.

When making comparisons between the model and field measurements, it is important that the demands in the model correspond to the time that the field measurements were taken. A common mistake is to compare model HGL for an average day demand with a field HGL taken at an hour when the demand is actually larger.

Just as a modeler should be skeptical of needing to assign unrealistic pipe roughness values to obtain a calibrated model, he or she should also be skeptical of needing to use unrealistically high or low nodal demands to achieve calibration. If demand values that are significantly different from historical records are needed to calibrate the model, then a logical explanation for this deviation should be provided. For example, maybe the community swimming pool was being filled on the day pressures were measured; or maybe a large water-using industry was temporarily shut down by a strike during pressure testing. In conclusion, demands should be adjusted within reason to match actual field conditions.

System Maps

As discussed in Chapter 3, water system maps (Figure 6.4) are the primary source of data for the physical characteristics of the distribution network. Network topology, pipe/node connectivity, pipeline lengths, nominal diameters, and information on fittings and appurtenances can all be determined from water system maps.

As new pipelines are installed and new connections are made, the maps of a system should be updated to reflect the changes. The quality and format of water system maps, however, can range from highly detailed and regularly updated CAD or GIS systems, to sets of rolled-up plans that have not been maintained in years. In some cases, the full extent of system mapping actually resides in the head of the system caretaker. Regardless of the medium on which they are available, it is important to realize that system maps do not necessarily reflect real-world conditions.

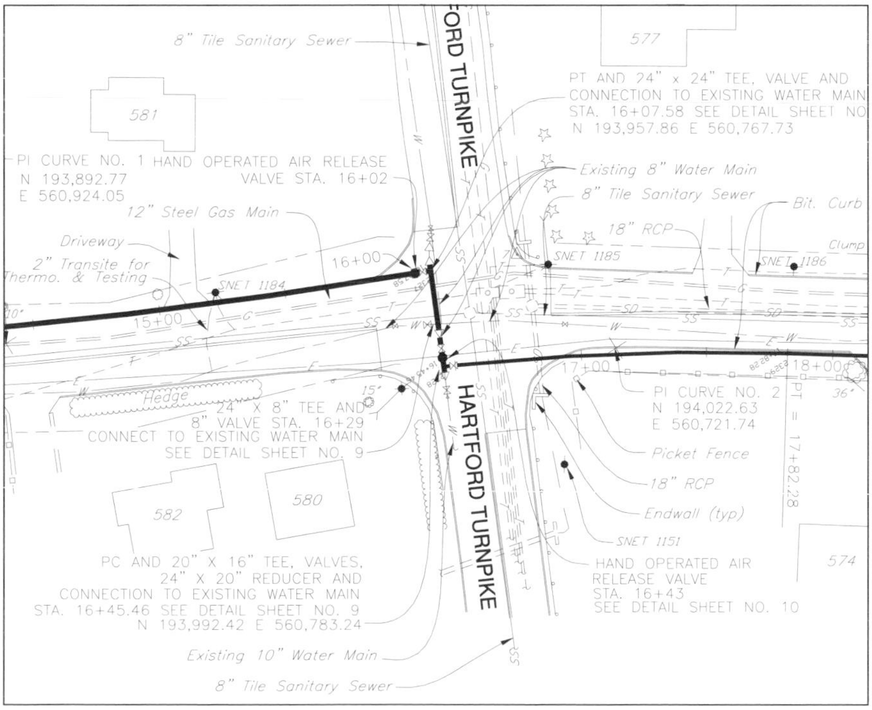

Figure 6.4
Portion of as-built system map

If the differences in pressures and flows between actual conditions and predicted conditions are so great that unrealistic and unexplainable pipe roughness values (less than 30 or more than 150) or major adjustments in demands must be used to achieve calibration, then chances are good that the discrepancy is the result of a closed or partially closed valve or errors in system mapping. For example, suppose that during calibration the observed pressure at a location is consistently about 20 psi (138 kPa) higher than simulated pressure, regardless of the pipe roughness values used. This result is an indication that there are problems with the model. A pipeline in the service area where the pressure measurement was taken may not be included in the model, or a junction elevation may be incorrect.

If errors in the connectivity of the model are suspected, then it may be necessary to look at detailed intersection maps to determine how pipes are connected, or to talk with system operators and maintenance personnel to determine the location and status of valves in the system. It may even be necessary to locate the original as-built drawings or field construction notes.

Temporal Boundary Condition Changes

The effect of time can have a significant impact on calibration efforts because many of the parameters describing a water system, such as demands and boundary conditions, are time-dependant. As was the case with demands, synchronizing times at which field measurements are taken and the calculation time step used for simulations will improve the accuracy of the calibration.

When a simulation is conducted for the purpose of calibration, it is critical that the model's loading and boundary conditions reflect the actual conditions at the time that pressure measurements were taken. For example, consider that on a particular day, pressure measurements were taken throughout the system at 6:00 a.m., 10:00 a.m., 12:00 p.m., 3:00 p.m., and 7:00 p.m. Because the demands, tank levels, control valve settings, and pump and pipe statuses can change over time, a unique set of boundary conditions reflecting system conditions for each point in time that measurements are taken needs to be created. For this example, five separate steady-state simulations must be performed, with each set of system conditions corresponding to a time when pressures were measured.

Information on how tank water levels change over time is often collected from circular chart recorders (Figure 4.1) or a SCADA system (Figure 6.5). This type of information is frequently used for steady-state calibration, and is particularly useful for extended period simulation (EPS) calibration (see page 219). Based on data from these sources, the flow rate to or from the tank can be determined using Equation 6.2.

$$Q_i = A\frac{H_{i+1} - H_i}{\Delta t} \tag{6.2}$$

where Q_i = flow into tank in i-th time step (cfs, m^3/s)

A = cross-sectional area of tank (ft^2, m^2)

H_i = water level in tank at beginning of i-th time step (ft, m)
Δt = length of i-th time step (s)

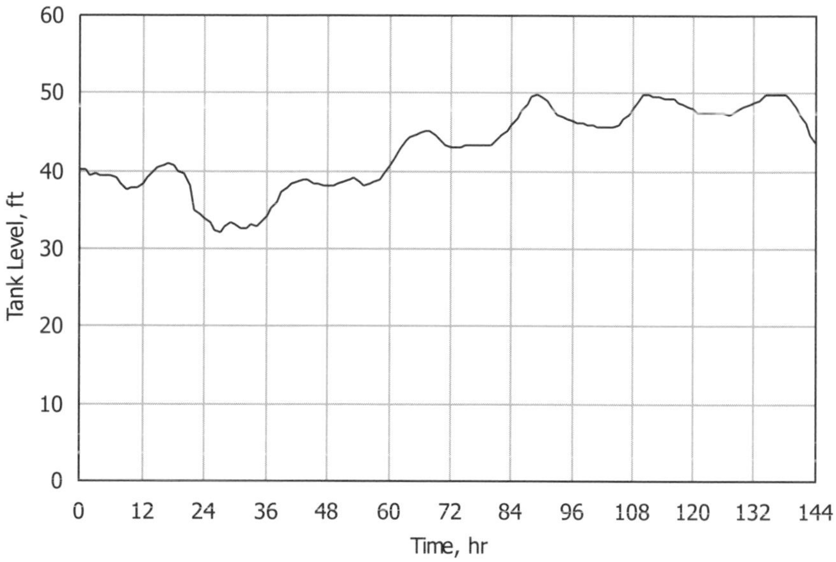

Figure 6.5
SCADA data showing tank water levels

Model Skeletonization

When a computer model of an existing system is constructed, a skeletonized version of the system will often be analyzed. As discussed previously in Chapter 3 (see page 109), a skeletonized model may remove certain types of fittings and appurtenances, and typically does not include small-diameter pipes or those lines that do not have a significant influence on the system hydraulics. Ideally, a skeletonized model should provide a simplified but accurate representation of the system. Accordingly, it is very important that the integrity of the network connectivity (or topology) is maintained during skeletonization.

The level to which a model is skeletonized can have a significant impact on calibration. It is possible to over skeletonize a model, leaving out critical links in the system. In these cases, details that have been removed may need to be added back to the skeletonized model to improve accuracy, especially in the vicinity of fire flow tests. Consider a system that includes a dense grid of small-diameter mains. Excluding those mains from a model based solely on diameter may be inappropriate if, as a group, they have a significant hydraulic impact on the system. This specific type of condition can be identified by the unrealistically large C-factors required in the remaining pipes to achieve calibration, especially during high flows.

Geometric Anomalies

Even if the modeler supplies high quality information on the physical attributes of the system and provides good estimates of nodal demands, the degree of calibration still may not be satisfactory. In these cases, anomalies in the geometry of the system are usually to blame.

Placing a node at the intersection of two pipes in the model when they are not hydraulically connected would obviously have the potential to cause problems with calibration because the model would not match the actual system. The modeler should pay particular attention to this type of situation when extracting data from CAD and GIS systems (see page 80 for additional information).

Pump Characteristic Curves

Recall that hydraulic simulation models require data concerning the pump head vs. discharge relationship. Generally, these models use some type of interpolation routine that fits a curve through selected points from the manufacturer's pump head characteristic curve. Because a curve-fitting method is used, the true head and discharge of the pump may differ somewhat from the curve, and error is introduced into the model. Numerical curve-fitting errors can be identified by comparing the manufacturer's curve with the curve produced by the hydraulic model.

A more likely cause of error when modeling pumps results from the use of old or outdated pump curves. For instance, suppose you are modeling a system that uses 25-year-old centrifugal pumps, but the head vs. discharge relationship shown on the manufacturer's pump curves reflects the performance of the pump when it was new. Normal wear and tear on a pump as it ages can cause the field performance to deviate from the performance illustrated on the pump characteristic curve. In fact, the pump impellers may have been changed several times since the pumps were originally installed. If so, the original pump curves will have little value since the head/discharge relationship of a pump is dependent upon the characteristics of the pump impeller. In such cases, new curves should be determined based on field tests.

Hydraulic network model calibration involves more than just adjusting pipe roughness values and nodal demands until suitable simulation results are obtained. Model calibration can involve a significant amount of detective work (such as locating closed and partially closed valves) as clues are tracked down and errors between field and simulation results are investigated (Walski, 1990). Some leads may yield results, others may not.

6.3 CALIBRATION APPROACHES

Identifying and addressing large discrepancies between predicted and observed behavior is critical in the calibration effort. This step, referred to as *rough-tuning* or *macro-calibration*, is necessary to bring predicted and observed system parameters into closer agreement with one another. After larger discrepancies are corrected, effort can be focused on *fine-tuning* or *micro-calibration*. Fine-tuning involves adjusting the pipe roughness values and nodal demand estimates, and is the final step in the calibration process.

The most challenging part of calibrating a model is making judgments regarding the adjustments that must be made to the model to bring it into agreement with field results. This section introduces methods for making these calibration judgments.

The following is a seven-step approach that can be used as a guide to model calibration (Ormsbee and Lingireddy, 1997).

1. Identify the intended use of the model.
2. Determine estimates of model parameters.
3. Collect calibration data.
4. Evaluate model results based on initial estimates of model parameters.
5. Perform a rough-tuning or macro-calibration analysis.
6. Perform a sensitivity analysis.
7. Perform a fine-tuning or micro-calibration analysis.

Identifying the intended use of the model is the first and most important step because it helps the designer establish the level of detail needed in the model, the nature of the data collection, and the acceptable level of tolerance for errors between field measurements and simulation results.

Once the intended use of the model is established, the modeler can begin estimating model parameters and collecting calibration data as discussed in the previous sections. The model can then be evaluated, and large discrepancies can be addressed simply by looking at the nature and location of differences between the model results and the field data.

Next, a sensitivity analysis can be conducted to judge how performance of the calibration changes with respect to parameter adjustments. For example, if pipe roughness values are globally adjusted by 10 percent, the modeler may notice that pressures do not change much in the system, thus indicating that the system is insensitive to roughness for that demand pattern. Alternatively, nodal demands may be changed by 15 percent for the same system, causing pressures and flows to change significantly. In this case, time may be more wisely spent focusing on establishing good estimates of system demands. If neither roughness coefficients nor demands have a significant impact on system heads, then the velocity in the system may be too low for the data to be useful for this purpose.

The final step in the calibration process, fine-tuning, can be time consuming, particularly if there are a large number of pipes or nodes that are candidates for adjustment. Compensating errors, as discussed on page 203, can further complicate the fine-tuning stage.

Manual Calibration Approaches

The trial and error, or manual process, generally involves the modeler supplying estimates of pipe roughness values and nodal demands, conducting the simulation, and comparing predicted performance to observed performance. If the agreement is unacceptable, then a hypothesis explaining the cause of the problem should be developed, modifications made to the model, and the process repeated again.

The process is conducted iteratively until a satisfactory match is obtained between modeled and observed values. If no satisfactory match can be obtained, then the model is not a true representation of the part of the real system where discrepancies remain. In such cases, further site investigations are usually made to identify discrepancies between the model and the real system, such as incorrectly modeled valve settings and unrecorded connections. The overlay of computed values on a contour map can provide insight into this process.

Models can be calibrated using one steady-state simulation, but the more steady-state simulations for which calibration is achieved, the more closely the model will represent the behavior of the real system. At a minimum, a steady-state calibration should be performed for a range of demand conditions. To improve results further, the model should be calibrated for time-varying conditions using an extended period simulation. In an EPS, calibration is performed until there is a reasonable agreement between modeled and observed pressures, flows, and tank water levels. EPS calibration is discussed later in this chapter on page 219.

What Should be Adjusted. Depending on the flow conditions being simulated, the model will have different reactions to different types of data changes. The following provides some general guidelines.

- **Average and low flows** - For most water distribution systems, the HGL throughout the system (also referred to as the piezometric surface) is fairly flat during average day demand conditions. The reason for these small head losses is that most systems are designed to operate at an acceptable level of service during maximum day demands while accommodating fire flows. As a result, the pipe sizes are usually large enough that average day head losses are small. For this reason, calibration during average conditions does not provide much information on roughness coefficients and water use. Average conditions do, however, provide insights into boundary conditions and node elevations.

- **High flows** - During periods when flows through the system are high, such as fire flow conditions or peak hour flows, pipe roughness and demand values play a much larger role in determining system-wide pressures. Therefore, pipe roughness values, and to a lesser extent demands, should be adjusted during periods of high flow to achieve model calibration.

Relatively speaking, when pipe flow or roughness is greater, there will be more head loss. Based on this relationship, the following are some recommendations for making adjustments to models (Herrin, 1997).

- If the model HGLs are higher than field-recorded values (Figure 6.6) then the model is not predicting enough head loss. To produce larger head losses, try reducing the Hazen-Williams C-factor and/or increasing the junction demands in the area of the measurements.

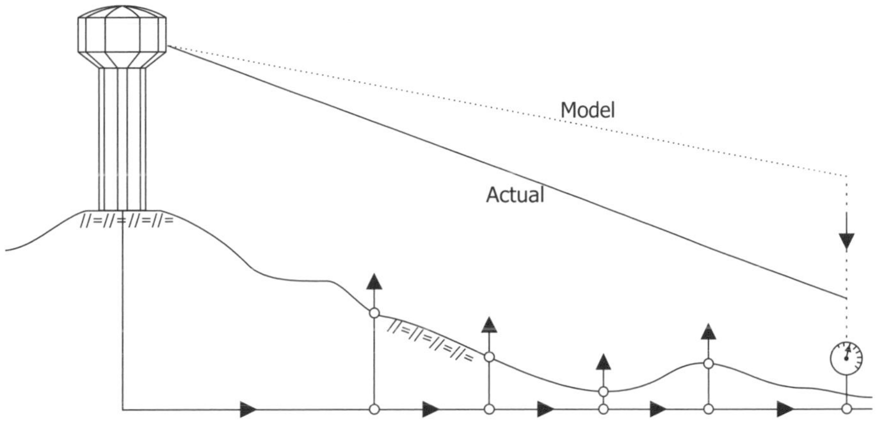

Figure 6.6
Model HGLs are higher than field values

- If the model HGLs are lower than field-recorded values (Figure 6.7) then the model is probably predicting too much head loss. To produce smaller head losses, try increasing the Hazen-Williams C-factor and/or decreasing the junction demands in the area of the measurements.

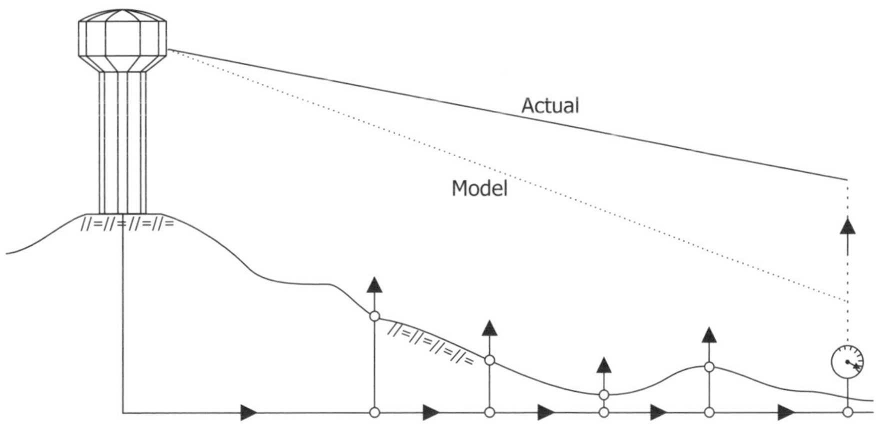

Figure 6.7
Model HGLs are lower than field values

Occasionally, an agreement in head is obtained for all but one node in the model. In these cases, the elevation for that location should be questioned and verified. During high-flow conditions, the system's increased head loss can mask pressure discrepancies caused by poor elevation data. Thus, inaccurate elevations are more easily identified during low-flow conditions, when the system's head losses are smaller.

Adjusting Roughness Coefficients. In trying to determine whether to adjust roughness or water use, the following procedure (Walski, 1983) can be helpful. Using the pressure and flow results from a fire flow test, the modeler can simulate the hydrant flow test with the model and develop estimates of head loss during the static and test conditions. The user can then calculate correction factors A and B as follows:

$$A = \frac{F}{(b/a)(Q_e + F) - Q_e} \tag{6.3}$$

$$B = \frac{F}{b(Q_e + F) - aQ_e} \tag{6.4}$$

where
A = correction factor
B = correction factor
F = fire flow (gpm, m^3/s)
$b = \left(\frac{h_2}{h_4}\right)^{0.54}$
$a = \left(\frac{h_1}{h_3}\right)^{0.54}$
Q_e = estimate of demand in area of test (gpm, m^3/s)
h_1 = measured head loss over test section, static conditions (ft, m)
h_2 = measured head loss over test section, flowed conditions (ft, m)
h_3 = modeled head loss over test section, static conditions (ft, m)
h_4 = modeled head loss over test section, flowed conditions (ft, m)

The correction factors are then applied to the estimated Hazen-Williams C-factor and water use to develop better estimates.

$$Q_c = AQ_e \tag{6.5}$$

$$C_c = BC_e \tag{6.6}$$

where
Q_c = corrected value for demands (gpm, m^3/s)
C_c = corrected value for C-factors
C_e = initial estimated value for C-factors

Note that the above equations are true for any units as long as the flows and heads are kept in consistent units.

■ **Example - Corrected Demand and Roughness** Given that the head at the nearest tank is 970 ft, the demands in the vicinity of the fire flow test are 200 gpm, the test flow is 750 gpm, and the C-factors in the vicinity of the test are estimated as 85, find the corrected values for demand and C-factor based on the fire flow test observation shown in the following table.

	Field Test HGL (ft)	Model-predicted HGL (ft)
Static Condition	962	958
Fire Flow Test	927	910

Computing the correction factors introduced above results in:

$$a = \left(\frac{970-962}{970-958}\right)^{0.54} = 0.80$$

$$b = \left(\frac{970-927}{970-910}\right)^{0.54} = 0.83$$

$$A = \frac{750}{(0.83/0.80)(200+750)-200} = 0.95$$

$$B = \frac{750}{0.83(200+750)-0.80(200)} = 1.20$$

$$Q_c = 0.95(200) = 190$$

$$C_c = 1.20(85) = 101$$

Accordingly, the user would decrease the demands to 190 gpm and increase the C-factors to 101 for the next model run. Evaluating the table above, these computed adjustments are consistent with what would be intuitively expected.

Automated Calibration Approaches

Unlike solving the network hydraulic equations where n equations can be written for n unknowns, calibration problems usually involve solving for more unknowns than there are equations. For example, the demands at nodes and roughness values for pipes are the unknowns, and only a relatively small number of observed heads and flows can be used to write equations. The problem is referred to as "under-constrained" (having many more unknowns than equations), and straightforward numerical solutions cannot be used.

One symptom of the under-constrained nature of calibration problems is that there are an infinite number of roughness values and demands that can make a model appear calibrated. Optimization techniques, however, can be used to successfully solve such problems. Optimization-based methods have worked well in making model heads agree with observed heads, but they should be used with caution since the user cannot be certain that the roughness and demand values are correct even though the heads may agree. One solution to this problem is to constrain the range of acceptable roughness coefficients. This task can be accomplished by grouping pipes using characteristics that affect the roughness coefficient, such as material and age. Furthermore, grouping pipes with similar characteristics reduces the number of unknowns in the calibration problem.

The optimization approaches used include gradient-based and stochastic search methods. *Gradient-based methods* are generally faster, but more difficult to formulate because either an analytical expression must be derived, or the gradient must be approximated. *Stochastic search methods* are more robust and simpler to formulate and use, but are generally slower.

Most of the published optimization methods treat roughness as the unknown, regardless of whether it is the parameter that is causing the model to be out of sync with reality. Indeed, a user can spend hours using optimization routines to obtain better and better estimates of roughness coefficients when the error is really due to incorrect pump curves, elevations, or demands. Thus, as with all optimization procedures, automated calibration can save enormous amounts of time, but it is not infallible and is not a substitute for engineering judgement. The user must oversee the analysis and identify and correct errors to achieve a well-calibrated model. When used properly, automatic calibration can be a powerful tool for saving time and improving model performance.

"The machine then selects the likely equations from a complicated pattern of theoretical probables. It calculates these, and the correct answer is printed on a card. Then our Miss Swenson files them God knows where, and we can never find the damn things again."

The optimization methods search for a solution describing the unknown calibration parameters that minimize an objective function, while simultaneously satisfying constraints that describe the range over which parameters are allowed to vary. The objective function usually involves minimization of the sum of the squares of differences between observed and model-predicted heads and flow. The exact formulation depends on the optimization method used. A typical objective function (Ormsbee and Lingireddy, 2000) is shown in Equation 6.7.

$$f(X) = a\sum_{n=1}^{N} W_n(OH_n - PH_n)^2 + b\sum_{p=1}^{P} W_p(OQ_p - PQ_p)^2 \qquad (6.7)$$

where
f = objective function to be minimized
X = vector of unknowns (roughness, demands, and elevations)
a, b = objective function unit conversion factors
$W_{n,p}$ = weighting factor for nodes and pipes
N = number of nodes at which head is known
OH_n = observed head at n-th node (ft, m)
PH_n = model-predicted head at n-th node (ft, m)
P = number of pipes for which flow is known
OQ_p = observed flow in p-th pipe (gpm, m^3/s)
PQ_p = model-predicted flow at p-th pipe (gpm, m^3/s)

Using Genetic Algorithm Optimization for Calibration

The selection of a satisfactory set of roughness values can be a tedious and time-consuming business when undertaken using a traditional trial-and-error approach. If one is willing to assume that most of the model error is due to roughness, this process can be largely automated using an optimization approach that is well suited to the problem. The method that is found to be particularly useful is the *genetic algorithm* (GA) closely coupled with a network solver for maximum efficiency (Savic and Walters, 1995, 1997; and Walters, et al., 1998).

The term GA refers to a type of optimization that attempts to find the best solution to a problem by mimicking the natural selection process in genetics. A trial solution consists of a set of assumed values for the *decision variables*, which are the variables in the model that the GA is permitted to adjust. The trial solution is then used to solve an objective function that evaluates the solution's *fitness*. Based on the solution's fitness, the assumed values for decision variables are either combined with those from other solution trials (called *crossover*), or they are adjusted slightly (*mutated*), to arrive at a new trial solution. However, the GA process does not rely on just one trial solution, but rather is based on considering a set of solutions (*a population*) at any one time. The process is continued until the GA eventually arrives at a solution that cannot readily be improved. While this solution is not guaranteed to be optimal, it is usually a very good solution to the objective function as defined.

When applying a GA to a network calibration problem, the decision variables are generally defined to be the roughness values for the pipes in the system. These roughness values can be the values used in the Colebrook-White formulation, or Hazen-Williams C-factors. All pipes can have individually variable roughness values, or groups of pipes can be pre-selected to have a common roughness based on similarities such as diameter, age, material, and/or location. Variables other than pipe roughness can also be used in the calibration. For instance, neither demands nor pipe diameters may be known precisely, so it may make sense to allow these values to vary to some extent to achieve a good modeling fit. However, use of variables other than roughness is not commonly practiced.

When using GAs to calibrate water distribution models, it is important to make sure that the optimized solution is appropriate under different system conditions. Multiple steady-state simulations must be used, and should at least include average, minimum, and maximum demand times during a 24-hour cycle.

At each measurement point and for each simulation, the differences between simulated and observed data (head and/or flow) are calculated and used to compute an overall error value for the network and determine the fitness of the solution. Several different forms of error function can be used, but normally a root mean square formulation is adopted. Different weightings between head and flow measurements can also be incorporated into the error expression. As this simulation is performed many thousands of times during the evolution of the best calibration, it is important that the GA and the analysis modules are fully integrated.

There are usually anomalies in the data or in the basic model representing the physical network that need resolution. Initial data inspection and model analysis followed by several preliminary runs of the GA are generally required to eliminate misleading data originating from faulty loggers, and to correct model features such as wrongly closed valves. Without these corrections, an accurate calibration is impossible.

Application of the GA approach to model calibration is in its infancy, but it has already demonstrated an ability to assist the modeler in the task of deriving a good network model for complex water distribution systems. As well as removing most of the routine and tedious aspects of the job, it will generally achieve better fits to the available data than can be achieved manually. Further, it uses a consistent, unbiased approach that is more likely to highlight real inconsistencies and problems. However, the input of experienced modeling staff is still required to validate data and interpret results within an essentially iterative process.

The earliest paper on this subject was by Meredith (1983). Ormsbee and Wood (1986), Ormsbee (1986), and Ormsbee and Chase (1988) developed several other approaches that differed in the way they handled constraints.

Rather than explicitly incorporating the equations of conservation of mass and energy into the optimization routine, later approaches have simply called out to a standard hydraulic simulation program to evaluate the hydraulics of the solution (Ormsbee, 1989; and Lansey and Basnet, 1991). Then, the solution is passed back to the optimization routine, where the algorithm then computes the objective function, evaluates the constraints, and, if necessary, updates the decision variables. New values of the decision variables are then passed to the simulation routine, and the process is repeated until an acceptable calibration is obtained.

The stochastic search procedures, more commonly referred to as genetic algorithms (GA), also work by closely coupling an optimization routine with the hydraulic solver. GA optimization, based on the theory of genetics, works by generating successive populations of trial solutions, the "fittest" of which survive to breed and evolve into increasingly desirable offspring solutions (Savic and Walters, 1995, 1997; and Walters, Savic, Morley, de Schaetzen, and Atkinson, 1998).

Genetic algorithms work by evaluating the fitness of each potential solution consisting of values for the set of unknown network calibration parameters. Fitness is determined by comparing how well the simulated flows and pressures resulting from the candidate solution match the measured values collected in the field. Several steady-state simulations are run to simulate a variety of demand conditions, including the operating conditions for minimum, maximum, and average demands. At each measurement point and for each steady-state run, the differences between simulated and observed data (head and/or flow) are calculated, and the objective function (an overall error value for the network) is computed. Objective functions can be formulated in many different ways to achieve different goals. Usually a squared error or root mean square error criterion is adopted. Different weightings between head and flow measurements can also be incorporated within the objective function. The GA continues to spawn generations of potential solutions until comparison of solutions from successive generations no longer produce a significant improvement.

In addition to eliminating most of the routine and tedious aspects of the calibration process, GA will generally achieve better fits to the available data if the user can select the correct set of variables to be included in the solution and can establish the correct range of possible solutions.

Model Validation

Once a model is calibrated to match a given set of test data, the modeler can gain confidence in the model and/or identify its shortcomings by validating it using test data obtained under different conditions. In performing validation, system demands, initial conditions, and operational rules are adjusted to match the conditions at the time the test data was collected. For example, a model that was calibrated for a peak day may be validated by its ability to accurately predict average day conditions as well.

While it is desirable to validate every model, most utilities do not have the time or money required to perform a thorough verification of the entire system. Consequently, a modeler may want to perform a quick validation before applying the model to a new problem. For example, before a three-year-old model is applied to the study of a proposed water main on the east side of town, the utility may want to conduct a handful of fire flow tests or place some pressure recorders in the study area for use in validating the model in that portion of the system.

6.4 EPS MODEL CALIBRATION

Before beginning the calibration of an EPS model, the user needs to be confident that the steady-state model is calibrated correctly in terms of elevations, spatial demand distribution, and pipe roughness. Once calibration on that level is achieved, the EPS calibration procedure can begin and will consist primarily of the temporal adjustment of demands. Depending on the intended use of the model, the focus of the EPS calibration may vary. For example, for hydraulic studies, the comparison between field and model conditions will be centered around the prediction of tank water levels and flows at system meters. On the other hand, for an energy analysis, the ability of the model to predict pump station cycling and energy consumption will be the focus.

Parameters for Adjustment

Most EPS calibration deals with the examination of plots of observed versus modeled tank water levels. As a general rule of thumb, if the observed and modeled water levels are both heading in the same direction but at slightly different rates, then the water use in that pressure zone needs to be corrected. However, if the water levels in the tanks are going in opposite directions, then the on/off status at pumps or valves is usually the culprit. Data from chart recorders placed at key locations in the system can provide insights into what to adjust.

The magnitude of adjustment in demands can be approximated by the difference in tank storage volumes between modeled and observed conditions. For example, if the model and the observed tanks both contain 1.24 MG (46,939 m^3), but at the end of a one-hour time step the model tank contains 1.63 MG (61,702 m^3) while the real tank contains 1.57 MG (59,431 m^3), then the demands in the model may need to be increased by 0.06 MG (2271 m^3) during that hour (1000 gpm, 63 l/s). As always with calibration, such adjustments need to be logical and justifiable, and the calibration should result in a fairly smooth curve in agreement with the observed data.

Calibration Problems

Discrepancies between the model and observed values are not always a sign of model inaccuracies. Even though data may have come from a SCADA system with several digits of precision, it should not be assumed that the data are accurate to that level. A study done in Vancouver, Canada (Howie, 1999) documents difficulties in using SCADA data ranging from inconsistent data to problems involving time-logging. An EPS calibration done for the Wilkes-Barre/Scranton, Pennsylvania system documents additional problems, including improperly located tank level sensors, inaccurate logging of pump switches, and differences between instantaneous observations and time averaged data (Walski, Lowry, and Rhee, 2000).

In most modeling, it has been assumed that once an EPS model has been calibrated, then the diurnal curve could be used on other days with minor adjustments in the base demand. Walski, Lowry, and Rhee (2000) showed that demands in a given hour vary by up to 20 percent between days in which one would expect to have virtually identical demand patterns.

Calibration Using Tracers

While tracers are generally thought of as a tool used in calibrating water quality models, they are very helpful in calibrating EPS hydraulic models as well. For example, if a conservative tracer is used, the only parameters that a modeler has to adjust are those affecting the hydraulics of the system.

Before conducting a tracer study, it is best to use a model to simulate tracer movement in the system. The simulation helps to locate areas in which the tracer is sensitive to input parameters such as demand. These locations can then be used for monitoring the tracer.

The tracer selected should be inexpensive, safe, and easy to detect. In the case of a system with multiple sources, a water quality constituent present in one source at a concentration different than that of other sources may be a good tracer. For example, if one well contains water with a higher conductivity than other sources, conductivity (which is related to the concentration of total dissolved solids) could be used as the tracer. In other cases, turning off or adjusting the fluoride feed at a plant can create a disturbance that can be traced through the system.

The study is conducted by changing the tracer concentration and determining if the model can reproduce the fluctuations in concentration measured in the system. This type of analysis provides a great deal of information about the way that water moves through the system. It is very helpful in spatially allocating demands, identifying closed valves, and finding pipes with incorrect diameters. (It is not quite as helpful in identifying pipe roughness errors or pump curve errors, since these parameters do not significantly affect flow patterns.) More information on using tracer studies can be found in Grayman (1998).

Energy Studies

In calibrating models to be used for energy consumption studies, it is important to understand the nature of the data being used to calibrate the model. Pump stations not only require energy for pumping, but also for non-pumping functions such as lighting, SCADA, HVAC, etc. Because pump stations may have one power meter for all energy usage associated with the pump station, it may be necessary to subtract the non-pumping uses of energy from the total usage to get an accurate field estimate of power used by the pump.

For situations in which the electrical power rather than energy is measured, it is important to understand if actual power (in kW) or apparent power (in kVA) is being measured. The difference between the two is the reactive power used to induce the magnetic field within the motor (WEF, 1997). The ratio of the actual to apparent power is called the power factor.

$$PF = (actual\ power) / (apparent\ power) \qquad (6.8)$$

where PF = power factor

If only apparent power is measured, then the value must be converted to the actual power to make a comparison with the pump energy predicted by models.

Because of the complicated tariffs involved with converting power usage into power charges, comparisons between the model and the observed power usage should be made in terms of kilowatt-hours, not dollars.

6.5 CALIBRATION OF WATER QUALITY MODELS

Calibration is the process of adjusting a model so that the simulation reasonably predicts system behavior. The underlying philosophy of water quality calibration is the same as that for hydraulic calibration, though some methodological details of the approach differ. The goal of a water quality calibration is to capture the transient dynamic behavior of the network, making water quality calibration a more ill-defined problem than the notoriously ill-defined hydraulic calibration problem. As a result, expectations for agreement between simulations and real-world systems are considerably lower.

Source Concentrations

Constituent sources define boundary conditions for water quality simulations, just as tank and reservoir levels define boundary conditions for hydraulic simulations. For the purpose of water quality modeling, sources describe how a constituent enters the distribution system. For example, chlorine and fluoride typically enter a network from a water treatment plant or other source of finished water, such as an interconnection with an adjacent system. In the case of system contamination, a substance may be introduced at any point in the network, such as at a cross-connection or a contaminated storage tank. Water quality models typically allow reservoirs, tanks, or junction nodes to act as constituent sources for flexible modeling of different source types and scenarios.

Constituent sources can be modeled as a constant influx into the distribution system, or can exhibit variation over time. Patterns can be provided to model the dynamic behavior of constituent sources. Concentrations at sources can also behave like different simple feedback controllers (flow pacing or concentration set point control).

Initial Conditions

Unlike initial conditions in hydraulic simulations that dissipate quickly, initial conditions in water quality simulations can persist for the entire duration of a reasonably long simulation. Thus, when calibrating water quality models, the dynamics that result are always a function of the initial conditions. This increases both the importance and the difficulty of predicting initial conditions.

Initial conditions reflect the state of the network at the beginning of a water quality simulation. To model the dynamics of a real system that has been running continuously, events that have occurred prior to the start of the simulation must be accounted for (the history of system operations). For example, consider a scenario in which disinfectant additions made at a treatment plant 72 hours ago are just arriving at a node in the network periphery. The modeler could account for the effect of these historical additions by measuring and assigning an initial condition at the node. Initial conditions are a mathematical way of incorporating the historical chain of events that determine the state of the network at the beginning of a simulation.

Every pipe, junction, tank, and reservoir in the network can be assigned an initial condition related to the analysis being conducted. For constituent analyses, network components are assigned an initial concentration. For source trace and water age analyses, network components are assigned an initial percentage of water arriving from the source, or an initial water age, respectively. Initial conditions are assigned at nodes, tanks, and reservoirs, and an interpolation method is typically applied to assign them to pipes.

Predicting Initial Conditions. Assigning initial conditions using values determined in the field is extremely problematic for a number of reasons. For constituent analyses, measuring the disinfectant concentration at every node, tank, reservoir, and pipe is logistically impractical. In addition, measuring all of these concentrations at a single instant in time (the instant before the simulation is scheduled to start) is impossible. The same problem exists when determining initial conditions for hydraulic simulations. However, it is not as severe since hydraulic initial conditions are typically only measured to establish network boundary conditions. The smaller number of measurements greatly simplifies the logistical considerations associated with collecting them. Predicting initial conditions for water age analyses is also difficult because it is not a parameter that is easily measured in the field.

The dynamic behavior of the water quality model, however, can be used to eliminate the problems associated with assigning initial conditions. As water quality processes are modeled, they form a dissipative system. For example, disinfectant residuals assigned as an initial condition are present at the beginning of a simulation. As the simulation progresses, the effects of the initial conditions dissipate as disinfectant reacts and is removed from the network as hydraulic demands. The disinfectant initially present is removed from the system and is gradually replaced by disinfectant entering from source locations. Disinfectant concentrations in the network will eventually reach a dynamic equilibrium when concentrations become independent of initial conditions. Thus, if the simulation is allowed to run for a sufficiently long period of time, the values of the initial conditions assigned become irrelevant.

Setting Initial Conditions. This dissipative behavior of water quality models can be used to the modeler's advantage, eliminating the need to predict initial conditions by specifying long simulation times. The exact simulation time depends on network topology and hydraulics, but can run anywhere from 3 to 10 times the length of the diurnal demand pattern (typically, a 24-hour diurnal cycle is used). Essentially, the hydraulic scenario being modeled is assumed to repeat for all times into the future. To conduct a long simulation, it is necessary to balance the network hydraulics so that inflows equal outflows over the length of the demand pattern. Otherwise, tanks may drain empty or overfill as the simulation progresses, or disturbances may develop in what should appear as periodic pipe flows.

Once a model has been modified for a long-duration simulation, the initial conditions (at pipes and nodes) can then be set to any value, including 0.00 mg/l. The time it takes for concentrations in the distribution system to achieve equilibrium is influenced by the initial conditions set at tanks and reservoirs. Initial conditions within the tanks and reservoirs adjust very slowly. Conversely, initial conditions at junction nodes dissipate quickly, and thus initial conditions at junction nodes can safely be set to zero. Familiarity with a specific source operation scenario may allow the initial conditions within tanks and reservoirs to be set closer to their equilibrium values, significantly decreasing simulation times. If source operation or hydraulics change as alternative scenarios are evaluated, however, the equilibrium concentrations within the storage tanks are also likely to change.

Wall Reaction Coefficients

Finding wall reaction coefficients is much more difficult than establishing bulk reaction coefficients as discussed in Chapter 5 (see page 184). Wall reaction coefficients are similar to pipe roughness coefficients in that they can and do vary from pipe to pipe. Unfortunately, unlike the head loss test for pipe roughness values (see page 174), direct measurements of wall reaction coefficients are extremely difficult to make.

Reported values for wall reaction coefficients are in the range of 0 to 5 ft/day (0 to 1.524 m/day) (Vasconcelos, Rossman, Grayman, Boulos, and Clark, 1997). Because these values are difficult to measure, estimates can be based upon field concentration measurement and water quality simulation results as part of a calibration analysis. Vasconcelos, et al. (1997) postulated that the wall reaction coefficient is related to the pipe roughness according to the following equation.

$$k_w = \alpha / C \qquad (6.9)$$

where k_w = wall reaction coefficient (ft/day)

α = fitting coefficient

C = Hazen-Williams C-factor

The fitting coefficient is determined for a given system by trial and error during calibration. Assuming that a sufficient number of observed constituent concentrations have been collected at various locations throughout the system, initial values of wall reaction coefficients for each pipe can be estimated and the simulation performed. The observed constituent concentrations can then be compared to concentrations provided by the computer model. If the two values do not agree within reason, then the wall reaction coefficients should be adjusted until a suitable match is obtained.

6.6 ACCEPTABLE LEVELS OF CALIBRATION

Regardless of which approach to calibration is adopted, a realistic model should achieve some level of performance criteria. In the United Kingdom, certain performance criteria have been established, and designers strive to meet these standards (Hydraulic Research, 1983). The criteria for flow and pressure are shown in Table 6.2. Additional criteria also exist, including those for extended period simulations (WRc, 1989).

Table 6.2 Calibration criteria for flow and pressure

Flow Criteria
(1) Modeled trunk main flows (where the flow is more than 10% of the total demand) should be within ±5 % of the measured flows.
(2) Modeled trunk main flows (where the flow is less than 10% of the total demand) should be within ±10 % of the measured flows.
Pressure Criteria
(1) 85% of field test measurements should be within ±0.5 m or ±5 % of the maximum head loss across the system, whichever is greater.
(2) 95% of field test measurements should be within ±0.75 m or ±7.5 % of the maximum head loss across the system, whichever is greater.
(3) 100% of field test measurements should be within ±2 m or ±15 % of the maximum head loss across the system, whichever is greater.

For an EPS, in addition to pressures and flows, the volumetric difference between measured and predicted tank storage between two consecutive time steps should be ±5 % of the total tank turnover for significantly large tanks (tank turnover is taken to be total volume in plus total volume out between two time intervals).

No such guidelines exist in the United States; however, many modelers agree that the level of effort required to calibrate a hydraulic network model, and the desired level of calibration accuracy, will depend upon the intended use of the model (Ormsbee and Lingireddy, 1997; Cesario, Kroon, Grayman, and Wright, 1996; and Walski, 1995).

The true test of model calibration is that the end user (for example, the pipe design engineer or chief system operator) of the model results feels comfortable using the model to assist in decision-making. To that end, calibration should be continued until the cost of performing additional calibration exceeds the value of the extra calibration work.

Each application of a model is unique, and thus it is impossible to derive a single set of guidelines to evaluate calibration. The guidelines presented below give some numerical guidelines for calibration accuracy; however, they are in no way meant to be definitive. A range of values is given for most of the guidelines to reflect the differences among water systems and the needs of model users. The higher numbers generally correspond to larger, more complicated systems, while the lower end of the range is more relevant for smaller, simpler systems. The words "to the accuracy of elevation and pressure data" mean that the model should be as good as the field data. If the HGL is known to within 8 ft (2.5 m), then the model should agree with field data to within the same tolerance. It is important to remember that these guidelines need to be tempered by site-specific considerations and an understanding of the intended use of the model.

- **Master planning for smaller systems [24-in. (600-mm) pipe and smaller] -** The model should accurately predict hydraulic grade line (HGL) to within 5-10 ft (1.5-3 m) (depending on size of system) at calibration data points during fire flow tests and to the accuracy of the elevation and pressure data during normal demands. It should also reproduce tank water level fluctuations to within 3-6 ft (1-2 m) for EPS runs and match treatment plant/pump station/well flows to within 10-20 percent.

- **Master planning for larger systems [24-in. (600-mm) and larger] -** The model should accurately predict HGL to within 5-10 ft (1.5-3 m) during times of peak velocities and to the accuracy of the elevation and pressure data during normal demands. It should also reproduce tank water level fluctuations to within 3 to 6 ft (1-2 m) for EPS runs and match treatment plant/well/pump station flows to within 10-20 percent.

- **Pipeline sizing -** The model should accurately predict HGL to within 5-10 ft (1.5-3 m) at the terminal point of the proposed pipe for fire flow conditions and to the accuracy of the elevation data during normal demands. If the new pipe impacts the operation of a water tank, the model should also reproduce fluctuation of the tank to within 3-6 ft (1-2 m).

- **Fire flow analysis -** The model should accurately predict static and residual HGL to within 5-10 ft (1.5-3 m) at representative points in each pressure zone and neighborhood during fire flow conditions and to the accuracy of the elevation data during normal demands. If fire flow is near maximum fire flow such that storage tank sizing is important, the model should also predict tank water level fluctuation to within 3-6 ft (1-2 m).

- **Subdivision design -** The model should reproduce HGL to within 5-10 ft (1.5-3 m) at the tie-in point for the subdivision during fire flow tests, and to the accuracy of the elevation data during normal demands.

- **Rural water system (no fire protection) -** The model should reproduce HGL to within 10-20 ft (3-6 m) at remote points in the system during peak demand conditions, and to the accuracy of the elevation data during normal demands.

- **Distribution system rehabilitation study -** The model should reproduce static and residual HGL in the area being studied to within 5-10 ft (1.5-3 m) during fire hydrant flow tests, and to the accuracy of the elevation data during normal demands.

- **Flushing -** The model should reproduce the actual discharge from fire hydrants or distribution capability [such as the fire flow delivered at a 20 psi (138 kPa) residual pressure] to within 10-20 percent of observed flow.
- **Energy use -** The model should reproduce total energy use over a 24-hour period to within 5-10 percent; reproduce energy consumption on an hourly basis to within 10-20 percent; and reproduce peak energy demand to within 5-10 percent.
- **Operational problems -** The model should reproduce problems occurring in the system such that the model can be used for decision-making for that particular problem.
- **Emergency planning -** The model should reproduce HGL to within 10-20 ft (3-6 m) during situations corresponding to emergencies (for example, fire flow, power outage, or pipe out of service).
- **Disinfectant models -** The model should reproduce the pattern of observed disinfectant concentrations over the time samples were taken to an average error of roughly 0.1 to 0.2 mg/l depending on the complexity of the system.

In addition to these standards, the AWWA Engineering Computer Applications Committee (1999) posted some calibration guidelines on its web page. As mentioned previously in this section, however, each modeling application is unique and requires its own unique set of calibration requirements. The AWWA guidelines are merely examples of what could be written, and have not been accepted as standards.

In summary, a model can be considered calibrated when the results produced by the model can be used with confidence to make decisions regarding the design, operation, and maintenance of a water distribution system, and the cost to improve the model further cannot be justified.

REFERENCES

American Water Works Association Engineering Computer Applications Committee. (1999). "Calibration Guidelines for Water Distribution System Modeling." http://www.awwa.org/unitdocs/592/calibrate.pdf.

Bush, C. A., and Uber, J. G. (1998). "Sampling Design and Methods for Water Distribution Model Calibration." *Journal of Water Resources Planning and Management*, ASCE, 124(6), 334.

Califonia Section AWWA (1962). "Loss of Carrying Capacity of Water Mains." *Journal of the American Water Works Association*, 54(10).

Cesario, A. L., Kroon, J. R., Grayman, W., and Wright, G. (1996). "New Perspectives on Calibration of Treated Water Distribution System Models." *Proceedings of the AWWA Annual Conference*, American Water Works Association, Toronto, Canada.

Colebrook, C. F., and White, C. M. (1937). "The Reduction of Carrying Capacity of Pipes with Age." *Proceedings of the Institute of Civil Engineers*, 5137(7), 99.

Grayman, W.M. (1998). "Use of Tracer Studies and Water Quality Models to Calibrate a Network Hydraulic Model," *Essential Hydraulics and Hydrology*, Haestad Methods, Inc., Waterbury, Connecticut.

Herrin, G., (1997). "Calibrating the Model." *Practical Guide to Hydraulics and Hydrology*, Haestad Press, Waterbury, Connecticut.

Howie, D. C. (1999). "Problems with SCADA Data for Calibration of Hydraulic Models." *Proceedings of the ASCE Annual Conference of Water Resources Planning and Management*, American Society of Civil Engineers, Tempe, Arizona.

Hudson, W. D. (1966). "Studies of Distribution System Capacity in Seven Cities." *Journal of the American Water Works Association*, 58(2), 157.

Hydraulic Research (1983). *Tables for the Hydraulic Design of Pipes and Sewers*. Wallingford, England.

Lamont, P. A. (1981). "Common Pipe Flow Formulas Compared With the Theory of Roughness." *Journal of the American Water Works Association*, 73(5), 274.

Lansey, K., and Basnet, C. (1991). "Parameter Estimation for Water Distribution Networks." *Journal of Water Resources Planning and Management*, ASCE, 117(1), 126.

McBean, E. A., Al-Nassari, S., and Clarke, D. (1983). "Some Probabilistic Elements of Field Testing in Water Distribution Systems." *Proceedings of the Institute of Civil Engineers*, Part 2, 75-143.

Meier, R. W., and Barkdoll, B. D. (2000). "Sampling Design for Network Model Calibration Using Genetic Algorithms." *Journal of Water Resources Planning and Management*, ASCE, 126(4), 245.

Meredith, D. D. (1983). "Use of Optimization in Calibrating Water Distribution System Models." *Proceedings of the ASCE Spring Convention*, American Society of Civil Engineers, Philadelphia, Pennsylvania.

Muss, D. L. (1960). "Friction Losses in Lines with Service Connections." *Journal Hydraulics Division*, ASCE, 86(4), 35.

Ormsbee, L. E. (1986). "A Nonlinear Heuristic for Applied Problems in Water Resources." *Proceedings of the Seventeenth Annual Modeling and Simulation Conference*, University of Pittsburgh, Pittsburgh, Pennsylvania, 1117.

Ormsbee, L. E., and Wood, D. J. (1986). "Explicit Pipe Network Calibration." *Journal of Water Resources Planning and Management*, ASCE, 112(2), 166.

Ormsbee, L. E., and Chase, D. V. (1988). "Hydraulic Network Calibration using Nonlinear Programming." *Proceedings of the International Symposium on Water Distribution Modeling*, Lexington, Kentucky, 31.

Ormsbee, L. E. (1989). "Implicit Pipe Network Calibration." *Journal of Water Resources Planning and Management*, ASCE, 115(2), 243.

Ormsbee, L. E., and Lingireddy, S. (1997). "Calibrating Hydraulic Network Models." *Journal of the American Water Works Association*, 89(2), 44.

Ormsbee, L. E., and Lingireddy, S. (2000). "Calibration of Hydraulic Network Models." *Water Distribution Systems Handbook*, Mays, L. W., ed., McGraw-Hill, New York, New York.

Savic, D. A., and Walters, G. A. (1995). "Genetic Algorithm Techniques for Calibrating Network Models." *Report No. 95/12*, Centre For Systems And Control Engineering, School of Engineering, University of Exeter, Exeter, United Kingdom, 41.

Savic, D. A., and Walters, G. A. (1997). "Evolving Sustainable Water Networks." *Hydrological Sciences*, 42(4), 549.

Shamir, U., and Hamberg, D. (1988). "Schematic Models for Distribution System Design. I: Combination Concept." *Journal of Water Resources Planning and Management*, ASCE, 114(2), 129.

Vasconcelos, J. J., Rossman, L. A., Grayman, W. M., Boulos, P. F., and Clark, R. M. (1997). "Kinetics of Chlorine Decay." *Journal of the American Water Works Association*, 89(7), 54.

Walski, T. M. (1983). "Technique for Calibrating Network Models." *Journal of Water Resources Planning and Management*, ASCE, 109(4), 360.

Walski, T. M. (1986). "Case Study: Pipe Network Model Calibration Issues." *Journal of Water Resources Planning and Management*, ASCE, 109(4), 238.

Walski, T. M., Edwards, J. D., and Hearne, V. M. (1989). "Loss of Carrying Capacity in Pipes Carrying Softened Water with High pH." *Proceedings of the ASCE National Conference on Environmental Engineering*, American Society of Civil Engineers, Austin, Texas.

Walski, T. M. (1990). "Sherlock Holmes Meets Hardy Cross or Model Calibration in Austin, Texas." *Journal of the American Water Works Association*, 82(3), 34.

Walski, T. M. (1995). "Standards for Model Calibration." *Proceedings of the AWWA Computer Conference*, American Water Works Association, Norfolk, Virginia.

Walski, T. M. (2000). "Model Calibration Data: The Good, The Bad and The Useless." *Journal of the American Water Works Association*, 92(1), 94.

Walski, T. M., Lowry, S. G., and Rhee, H. (2000). "Pitfalls in Calibrating an EPS Model." *Proceedings of the Environmental and Water Resource Institute Conference*, American Society of Civil Engineers, Minneapolis, Minnesota.

Walters G.A., Savic, D. A., Morley, M. S., de Schaetzen, W., and Atkinson, R. M. (1998). "Calibration of Water Distribution Network Models Using Genetic Algorithms." *Hydraulic Engineering Software VII*, Computational Mechanics Publications, 131.

Water Research Center (WRc). (1989). *Network Analysis – A Code of Practice*. WRc, Swindon, England.

Water and Environment Federation (WEF). (1997). "Energy Conservation in Wastewater Treatment Facilities." *WEF Manual of Practice MFD-2*, Alexandria, Virginia.

DISCUSSION TOPICS AND PROBLEMS

Earn CEUs

Read Chapters 5 and 6 and complete the problems. Submit your work to Haestad Methods and earn up to 1.5 CEUs. See *Continuing Education Units* on page xiii for more information, or visit www.haestad.com/wdm-ceus/.

6.1 *English Units* - Calibrate the system shown in Problem 3.3 (see page 118) and given in Prob6-01.wcd so that the observed pressure of 63.0 psi at node J-5 is obtained. Adjust nodal demands by using the same multiplier for all demands (global demand adjustment).

a) By what factor must demands be adjusted to obtain the observed pressure?

b) Would you say that pressures in this system are sensitive to nodal demands? Why or why not?

SI Units - Calibrate the system shown in Problem 3.3 (see page 118) and given in Prob6-01m.wcd so that the observed pressure of 434.4 kPa at node J-5 is obtained. Adjust nodal demands by using the same multiplier for all demands (global demand adjustment).

a) By what factor must demands be adjusted to obtain the observed pressure?

b) Would you say that pressures in this system are sensitive to nodal demands? Why or why not?

6.2 Calibrate the system shown in Problem 4.1 (see page 152) so that the observed pressure of 54.5 psi is obtained at node J-4. Adjust the internal pipe roughness using the same multiplier for all pipes (global adjustment factor).

a) What is the global roughness adjustment factor necessary to obtain the pressure match?

b) Are the pressures in this system sensitive to pipe roughness under average day demands? Why or why not?

c) Would you say that most water distribution systems are insensitive to pipe roughness values under low flows?

d) Is it reasonable to expect that a field pressure can be read with a precision of ±0.5 psi? If not, what would you say is a typical precision for field-measured pressures?

e) What can contribute to the imprecision in pressure measurements?

6.3 Use the calibrated system found from Problem 6.2 and place a fire flow demand of 1,500 gpm at node J-4.

a) What is the pressure at node J-4?

b) Is a pressure of this magnitude possible? Why or why not?

c) If a pressure this low is not possible, what will happen to the fire flow demand?

d) What is the most likely cause of this low pressure?

6.4 Starting with the original pipe roughness values, calibrate the system presented in Problem 4.3 (see page 158) so that the observed pressure of 14 psi is obtained at node J-11. Close pipes P-6 and P-14 for this simulation. Assume that the area downstream of the PRV is a residential area.

Hint: Concentrate on pipe roughness values downstream of the PRV.

a) What pipe roughness values were needed to calibrate this system?

b) Would you consider these roughness values to be realistic?

c) A fire flow of 1,500 gpm is probably more than is needed for a residential area. A flow of 750 gpm is more reasonable. Using the uncalibrated model, determine if this system can deliver 750 gpm at node J-11 and maintain a minimum system-wide pressure of 30 psi?

6.5 Calibrate the system completed in Problem 4.4 (see page 161) and given in Prob6-05.wcd so that the observed hydraulic grade line elevations in the Central Tank (see the following table) are reproduced.

Hint: Focus on changing the multipliers in the diurnal demand pattern.

Time (hr)	Central Tank HGL (ft)
0.00	1,525
1.00	1,527
2.00	1,529
3.00	1,531
4.00	1,532
5.00	1,534
6.00	1,536
7.00	1,537
8.00	1,539
9.00	1,540
10.00	1,541
11.00	1,542
12.00	1,540
13.00	1,537
14.00	1,534
15.00	1,532
16.00	1,533
17.00	1,535
18.00	1,536
19.00	1,537
20.00	1,538
21.00	1,539
22.00	1,541
23.00	1,542
24.00	1,544

Fill in the table below with your revised diurnal demand pattern multipliers.

Time of Day	Multiplication Factor
Midnight	
3:00 a.m.	
6:00 a.m.	
9:00 a.m.	
Noon	
3:00 p.m.	
6:00 p.m.	
9:00 p.m.	
Midnight	

CHAPTER

7

Using Models for Water Distribution System Design

Engineers have designed fully functioning water distribution systems without using computerized hydraulic simulations for many years. Why then, in the last several decades, has the use of computerized simulations become standard practice for designing water distribution systems?

First, computerized calculations relieve engineers of tedious, iterative calculations, enabling them to focus on design decisions. Second, because models can account for much more of the complexity of real-world systems than manual calculations, they give the engineer increased confidence that the design will work once it is installed. Finally, the ease and speed with which models can be used gives the engineer the ability to explore many more alternatives under a wide range of conditions, resulting in more cost-effective and robust designs.

There is a price to pay for the extra capability that engineers now possess as a result of high-quality hydraulic simulation software. The easiest part of that price to quantify is the cost of the software itself. Another obvious cost is the time required to assemble data and construct a network model. Additionally, there are costs associated with training personnel to use a new tool and the time it takes to gain experience using it effectively. The total cost is small, however, compared to the value of the projects being considered and the repercussions of poor decisions.

A model that has been assembled properly is an asset to the water utility, much like a pipe or a fire hydrant. The model should therefore be maintained so that it is ready to be put to valuable use. The difficult part of valuing modeling lies in the fact that the costs of modeling are incurred mostly in model development, while the benefits are realized later in the form of quicker calculations and better decisions.

Because such a large investment in time and effort is needed to make a model usable, a common mistake is to not leave enough time in a study (whether it is creating a major master plan or checking the location of a proposed tank) to adequately analyze the design. To get the most out of a model, it is important to allow sufficient time to try different alternatives, and test these alternatives against a wide range of conditions. Although the time spent performing additional analyses may seem to cause a delay, good designs will save both time and money, provide insight into the workings of the system, and improve the performance of a project.

7.1 APPLYING MODELS TO DESIGN APPLICATIONS

Up to this point, the book has addressed how to build and calibrate models. The remainder focuses on using those models and the results they provide to build water systems and to assist in operating them. An overview of model application is shown in Figure 7.1. Each item in the figure is discussed in more detail below.

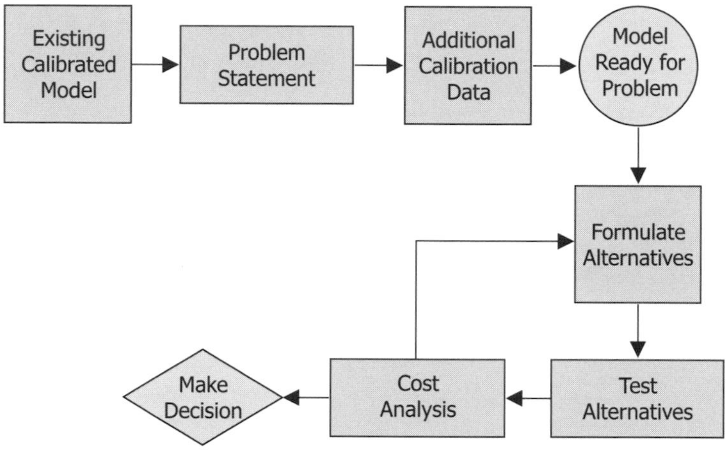

Figure 7.1 Overview of model application

Extent of Calibration and Skeletonization

Anyone who uses models regularly realizes that no model is ever perfectly calibrated (see Chapter 6). Therefore, before using a model to solve a particular problem, the engineer needs to verify that the model is sufficiently calibrated and has a high enough resolution to be useful for the problem under consideration. A single model may not work well for analyzing every problem without additional work. Therefore, it may be necessary to have slightly different versions of the model for performing different analyses. Care should be taken to keep all versions up to date.

For example, a model may predict peak flow and fire flow behavior in a given part of town very well, even though it is somewhat skeletonized. If the problem being considered involves determining what piping or storage must be added to ensure service in the event that the largest pipe supplying that section of town fails, the model may not contain sufficient detail. Numerous smaller pipes may need to be added to the model so that it more accurately represents the secondary paths that the water can take within the distribution system.

Depending upon the reason for the analysis, it may be worthwhile to install a few portable pressure recorders or run several hydrant flow tests in the area being considered, before getting too far into the analysis. Sometimes a detail important to a specific situation may be left out of a general model, even though the model as a whole appears well calibrated.

In other situations, the model may have far too much detail for the analysis being conducted. For example, a highly detailed model may be more than sufficient for setting control valves or evaluating pump cycling. Also, too much detail may give a false sense that the model will provide more accurate results simply because it contains more information.

A similar consideration exists with demands. The model may have been set up for a master planning study, with reasonable projected demands assigned to nodes; however, the question being posed may refer to a particular subdivision or new industrial customer. The previous master plan projections should be replaced by the more precise demand projections for this new customer or land development.

When using the model to assess the ability of the distribution system to serve a particular new customer, it is important to remember that the improvements being installed may also be required to serve future customers. Therefore, projected future demands must be accounted for in any sizing calculations. Often, the question then becomes one of how the cost of the new facilities will be divided between the new customer and the utility.

Design Flow

Ideally, each pipe, pump, and valve in a system has been sized using some design flow. The design flow used is typically the peak flow that the facility will encounter in the foreseeable future. In any study, the engineer must determine this flow for the facility being designed. The design flow is usually based on a prediction, which is problematic because it is almost always incorrect to some extent. Therefore, facilities should be sized to operate efficiently, accounting for uncertainty in design flow estimates.

Oversized facilities have pipes and pumps that are not fully utilized, with the associated inefficiencies and misallocations of capital resources. Oversized facilities may also be plagued with water quality problems due to long residence times. Conversely, undersized facilities are inadequate to meet demands, a situation that must later be corrected by paralleling, replacing, or retrofitting facilities to expand capacity.

To some extent, the decision on design flow acts as a self-fulfilling prophecy. If distribution capacity is installed, customers will eventually use that capacity. Today's "excess capacity" has a way of becoming a valuable resource that is quickly absorbed through development.

While design flow is a useful concept for specifying equipment, the model should also be used to simulate a large range of possible conditions and to ensure robust designs. EPS runs performed for a range of flows (such as current average day and year 2020 peak day) are particularly useful for evaluating how the system will respond under a variety of conditions.

Reliability Considerations

When designing or improving a system, the possibility that the system needs to function even when components are out of service (such as in the case of a pipe break, power outage, natural disaster, or off-line equipment) should be considered. The distribution system cannot be expected to perform without some degradation of service during an outage. However, when economically feasible, the system should be designed to at least meet appropriate minimum performance standards during reasonable emergencies and other circumstances in which facilities may be out of service.

To model the failure of a pipe, removing or closing off a single pipe link in a distribution model would be simple. The number of links and nodes removed, however, depends upon the locations of the valves necessary to close off that area or *segment* (the smallest portion of a system that can be isolated using valves). Seven water distribution segments are shown in the map in Figure 7.2(a). The effect of a break on the topology of the distribution model is shown for segments 1 and 2. For a break in segment 1, only a single pipe link is taken out of service [Figure 7.2(b)], while in segment 2, several pipe links and junction nodes are removed from the model [Figure 7.2(c)]. The effect of failures on facility operation is further described in Chapter 9 (see page 349).

Reliability analysis of entire water distribution systems has not yet proven to be workable partly because there are so many different ways of defining reliability (as summarized by Wagner, Shamir, and Marks, 1988a, 1988b). Mays (1989) summarized the state-of-the-art in reliability analysis in an ASCE Committee Report. More recently, Goulter, et al. (2000) provided an overview of reliability assessment methods includ-

"Fredric W. Desbrow & Son, plumbers."

ing 81 references. Walski (1993) pointed out that the problem is not simply a hydraulic analysis one, but that it is also highly related to operation and maintenance practices.

Figure 7.2
Distribution system segments

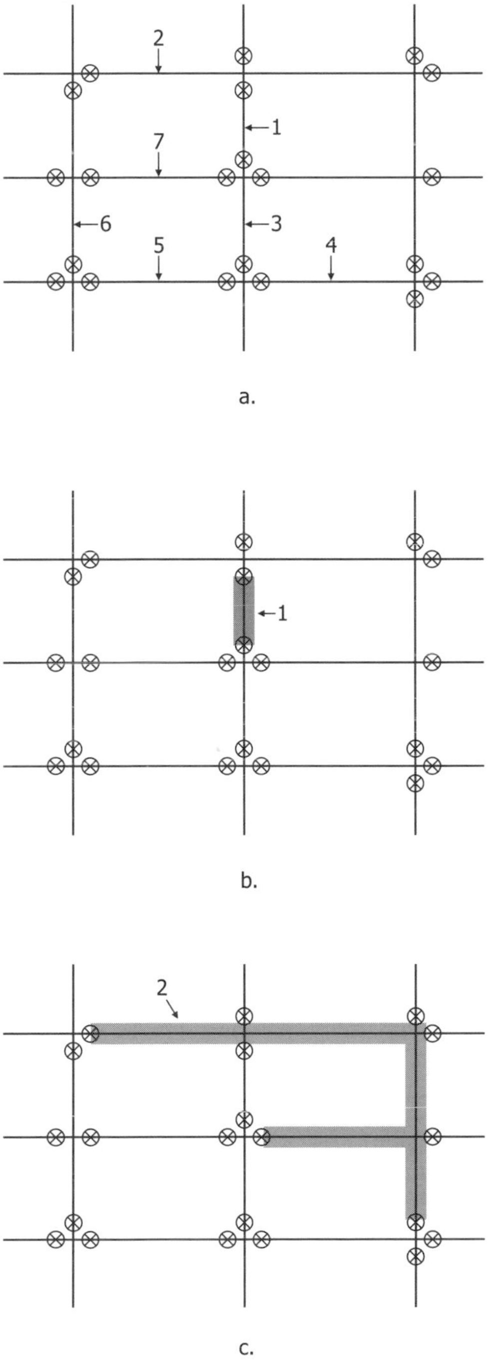

Key Roles in Design Using a Model

After the model is constructed and calibrated, it is ready to be used in design. There are two distinct roles in using a model. The first is that of the modeler who actually runs the program, while the second is that of the design engineer who must make the decisions regarding facility sizing, location, and timing of construction. In most cases, the models are sufficiently easy to use that both roles can be filled by a single individual. When two different individuals are involved, the task of the design engineer is to decide on the situations and design alternatives to be modeled. The modeler then runs the desired simulations.

To get the most benefit from the model, the designer should examine a broad range of alternatives. Background investigation prior to beginning the modeling process is often very helpful. A brainstorming session with utility employees can generate a consistent understanding of the nature of the problem, a review of the facts surrounding the problem, and most importantly, a wide range of alternative solutions. By involving others in this initial meeting, difficulties that can arise later (such as questions about why a particular alternative was not considered) can be prevented. A team approach also facilitates acceptance of designs that are developed using the model.

Types of Modeling Applications

There is no single correct way to use models. Walski (1995) described how model application for design purposes differs depending upon whether models are used for master planning, preliminary design, subdivision development, or system rehabilitation. Each type of model has a specific goal and related characteristics, as summarized below.

1. **Master planning -** Master planning models are used to predict what improvements and additions to the distribution system will be necessary to accommodate future customers. Therefore, these models have long planning horizons (on the order of 20 to 40 years). The designs are controlled by future demands, and emphasis is usually placed on larger transmission mains, pump stations, and storage tanks, as opposed to small neighborhood mains. Systems in master planning models can be highly skeletonized, and future pumps may be represented by constant head nodes (that is, modeled as reservoirs).
2. **Preliminary design -** In preliminary design, the engineer models the facilities that will be required to serve a particular area of, or addition to, the distribution system service area. For this type of modeling, the focus is limited to a small portion of the system. Actual pump curves should be included, but detailed calibration is only needed in the section of the model from the source to the project, while the remainder of the system can be highly skeletonized.
3. **Subdivision layout -** When designing a subdivision (particularly in the U.S.), fire flows usually dominate over customer demands, and the planning horizon is typically short (perhaps five years when the subdivision is built out). Calibration is only needed near the points of connection to the existing system, and although detail is required when modeling the pipes in the development, the remainder of the system can be highly skeletonized.

4. **Rehabilitation -** In a rehabilitation study of an area of a system, adequate capacity for fire flows is usually the most important consideration. Many more alternative scenarios are needed compared to designing new pipe, since a variety of possible solutions exist (for example, relining, paralleling, or looping). Detail is only needed for the part of the model that represents the study area; the remainder of the system model can be skeletonized.

Cesario (1995) reported that the most common application of water distribution modeling is *long-range planning* (referred to by some utilities as *master planning*, *capital budgeting*, or *comprehensive planning studies*). The next most common uses are fire flow studies and new development design. Models tend to be used more by planning and design personnel, rather than operations personnel. Of course, once a water utility's personnel become familiar with a model, the application is only limited by the time and imagination of the users.

Use of Optimization in System Design

Most applications of models involve running an analysis of the system given demands, operating parameters, and a physical description that includes pipe sizes, pump capacities, tank sizes, etc. The results of this analysis are then compared to pressure and flow constraints. A logical question is: Why will the computer not calculate pipe, pump, and tank properties when given a description of demands, costs, and target pressures?

This problem of solving for system component sizes is significantly more difficult than solving for flows and pressures alone. Instead of solving a system of n continuous equations with n unknowns (with n being the number of pipes or nodes in the network), optimization problems contain inequalities (such as pressure constraints), equalities (such as head loss equations), discrete variables (such as pipe sizes), and continuous variables (such as pump heads). Consequently, there are an incredibly large number of possible solutions, making optimization a much more complex problem than simply solving network equations. In terms of Figure 7.1, optimization models combine the tasks of "Formulate Alternatives," "Test Alternatives," "Cost Analysis," and "Make Decision" into a single step.

The earliest attempts at optimization date back to Babbitt and Doland (1931) and Camp (1939). The first computerized optimization was attempted by Schaake and Lai (1969). By 1985, Walski (1985) had documented nearly one hundred papers on the subject, and the number of papers has increased significantly since that time (Lansey, 2000). The methods used have included such techniques as linear programming, dynamic programming, mixed integer programming, heuristic algorithms, gradient search methods, enumeration methods, genetic algorithms, and simulated annealing. The models have been tested against standard modeling problems such as the New York tunnel problem (Schaake and Lai, 1969) and the Anytown problem (Walski, et al., 1987) and found to give reasonable answers; however, the answers are very sensitive to the way the model user interprets the problem.

Despite the research, optimization has not found its way into standard engineering practice. Part of the reason for this absence is that existing algorithms have not typi-

Perspectives on System Design

Part of the difficulty in applying optimization to water distribution design lies in the difficulty of describing the objectives, as different parties in the decision-making process have different perspectives, as summarized below:

Upper Management - "Provide adequate capacity but remain within the capital budget."

Planning - "Meet demands even though there is a great deal of uncertainty in forecasts."

Engineering - "When in doubt, make it big."

Construction - "If you're going to tear up a street and dig a hole, it doesn't cost much more to put in a big pipe."

Operations - "Give us flexibility and redundancy so we aren't hanging on a single pipe or pump."

Fire Protection - "Have you ever had to carry a body bag out of a building because you didn't have enough water to fight the fire? Give us plenty of water."

These different perspectives make it difficult to mirror the decision-making process with a computerized optimization.

cally been packaged as user-friendly tools. More significantly, existing algorithms require that the real problems of system design be modified to fit the algorithm, with the result being that the algorithms do not fully capture the design process (Walski, 2001). Most algorithms set up the optimization problem as one of minimizing costs subject to (1) hydraulic feasibility, (2) satisfaction of demands, and (3) meeting pressure constraints.

In reality, the problem faced by design engineers involves many more factors, including:

- Providing adequate capacity
- Meeting pressure constraints
- Dealing with highly uncertain demands
- Providing a reasonable level of redundancy and reliability
- Meeting budgetary constraints
- Evaluating tradeoffs between different objectives (for example, fire protection versus water quality)
- Formulating creative solutions

As Walski, Youshock, and Rhee (2000) pointed out using illustrative example problems, optimization models have not yet been able to address many of the above considerations. For this reason, most design engineers prefer to use a combination of steady state and EPS model runs and engineering judgment as they develop their designs.

Among the techniques that show promise, *genetic algorithms (GA)* are the most capable of meeting the needs of the design engineer without the necessity of contorting the problem to fit the algorithm (Dandy, Simpson, and Murphy, 1994; Savic and Walters,

1997; Walters, Halhal, Savic, and Ouazar, 1999). Because it is an enumeration technique, GA avoids many of the problems faced by optimization techniques using continuous variables. Nevertheless, while optimization may increasingly serve as a tool for design engineers, it is not likely to replace good engineering judgement.

7.2 IDENTIFYING AND SOLVING COMMON DISTRIBUTION SYSTEM PROBLEMS

Most water distribution systems share a number of common concerns. For example, the typical governmental standard for water system design is, "The system shall be designed to maintain a minimum pressure of 20 psi (138 kPa) at ground level at all points in the distribution system under all conditions of flow. The normal working pressure in the distribution system should be approximately 60 psi (414 kPa) and not less than 35 psi (241 kPa) (GLUMB, 1992)." Regulations do not typically spell out how to meet this requirement, leaving such decisions up to the design engineer, who will examine possible alternatives using modeling techniques.

In general, poor pressures tend to be caused by inadequate capacity in a pipe or pump, high elevations, or some combination of the two. Models are helpful in pinpointing the cause of the problem. Figure 7.3 shows how an EPS model can help determine if the low pressure is due to capacity or elevation problems. Customers at high elevations may experience constant problems with low pressure, while a capacity problem shows up only during periods of high demand. The "Typical" line in Figure 7.3 represents pressure fluctuations in a typical system; the "Capacity Problem" line shows pressures for a system with pump or main capacity problems; and the "Elevation Problem" line shows pressure fluctuations in a portion of a system where the utility is attempting to serve a customer at too high of an elevation.

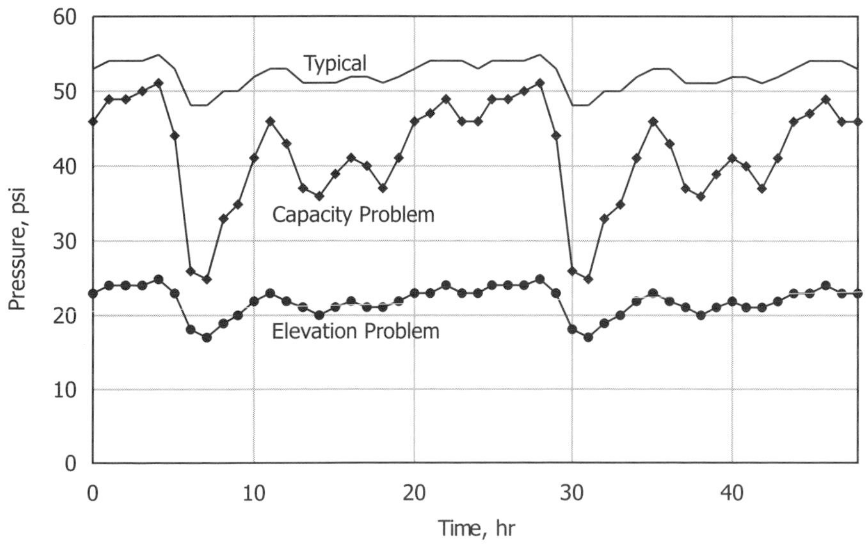

Figure 7.3
EPS runs showing low pressure due to elevation or system capacity

Undersized Piping

An undersized distribution main will not be easy to identify during average-day conditions, or even peak-day conditions, because demand and velocity are typically not high enough during those times to reveal the problem. If a pipe is too small, it may become a problem only during high-flow conditions such as fire flow. Fire flows are much greater than normal demands, especially in residential areas. Therefore, fire flow simulations are the best way to identify an undersized distribution main. If looking for sizing problems in larger pipes, such as those leaving treatment plants, the best time for diagnosing problems would likely be peak hour, or in some cases, during periods when tanks are refilling.

If undersized pipes are suspected, they can usually be found by looking for pipes with high velocities. These pipes can be located quickly by sorting model output tables by velocity or hydraulic gradient (friction slope), or color-coding pipes based on these parameters. It is important to note that when evaluating models for undersized pipes, it is better to evaluate based on hydraulic gradient then head loss. Although one pipe may have a much larger head loss than another, the hydraulic gradient may actually be lower, depending on the length of the pipes being compared.

There is no fixed rule regarding the maximum velocity in a main although some utilities do have guidelines), but pressures usually start to drop off (and water hammer problems become more pronounced) when velocities reach 10 ft/s (3 m/s). In larger pressure zones (several miles across), a velocity as low as 3 ft/s (1 m/s) may cause excessive head loss. Increasing the diameter of the pipe in the model should result in a corresponding decrease in velocity and increase in pressure. If not, then another pipe or pump may be the reason for poor pressures.

Inadequate Pumping

In a pressure zone that is served by a pump, pressures that drop off significantly may indicate a pump capacity problem. This drop will be most dramatic in situations in which most of the pumping energy is used for lift rather than for overcoming friction, or there is no storage in the pressure zone (or the storage is located far from the problem area). When the flow rate increases above a certain level, the head produced by the pump will drop off, and pressures will decrease by a corresponding amount.

At first, undersized pipes might be suspected as the cause of the problem, but increasing pipe sizes has little impact in this case. A comparison of the pump's production with its rated capacity [for example, a 600 gpm (0.037 m^3/s) pump trying to pass 700 gpm (0.044 m^3/s)] will indicate the problem. Installing a larger pump (in terms of flow, not head) or another pump in parallel will correct the problem if the pump flow capacity is the real cause.

When the pressure zone has enough storage, diagnosing problems caused by undersized pumps may be difficult. Undersized pumps will show up more clearly in EPS runs, however, because the tank water levels will not recover during a multi-day simulation.

What's the Maximum Permissible Velocity in a Pipe?

A frequently asked question in water distribution design is, "What is the maximum acceptable velocity in a pipe?" The answer to this question can make pipe design easier, since knowing the maximum velocity and the design flow, an engineer could calculate pipe diameter using

$$D = \sqrt{C_f Q / V}$$

where D = pipe diameter
Q = design flow
V = maximum velocity
C_f = unit conversion factor

There is no simple answer to this question because velocity is only indirectly the limiting factor in pipe sizing. It is really the head loss caused by the velocity, not velocity itself, that controls sizing. The problem is complicated by the fact that most water distribution systems are looped, so a sizing decision in one pipe affects the size, and therefore flow velocity, in all other pipes.

Technical papers going back to Babbitt and Doland (1931) and Camp (1939) discuss economically sound values for this maximum velocity. This work was extended by Walski (1983), who showed that the optimal velocity in pumped lines can range from 3 to 10 ft/s (1 to 3 m/s), depending on the relative size of the peak and average flow rates through the pipe and the relative magnitude of construction and energy costs.

Another factor to consider is that when velocity is high, changes in velocity are also high, and these accelerations can lead to harmful hydraulic transients (that is, water hammer). One approach to reducing transients is to reduce velocity.

With these multiple complicating factors, there cannot be a single maximum velocity that is optimal in every situation. On the contrary, designing pipe sizes for velocity alone is not the correct approach with water distribution systems. The velocities are useful only for spot-checking network model output when locating bottlenecks in the system (that is, pipes with very high velocities, and therefore high head losses). The real test of a design's efficiency is not velocity, but residual pressures in the system during peak demand times.

When checking designs for permissible velocities, some engineers use 5 ft/s (1.5 m/s) as a maximum, others use 8 ft/s (2.4 m/s), while still others use 10 ft/s (3.1 m/s). Because velocity is not the real design parameter, there is no simple answer. Rather, velocity is simply another parameter an engineer can use to check a design.

For most pump station designs, the pumps should meet design flow requirements, even with the largest pump out of service. For example, a three-pump station should be able to meet demands using any two of the pumps; otherwise, additional capacity may be needed.

Consistent Low Pressure

If pressures are consistently low in an area, then the problem is usually due to trying to serve customers at too high an elevation for that pressure zone. This problem is apparent even during low demand periods. Changing pipe sizes or pump flow capacity will not improve this situation. If this pressure zone has no storage tanks, it may be possible to increase the head for a fixed-speed pump, or increase the control point for a variable-speed pump (provided this increase does not over pressurize other portions of the system).

In many cases, the best solution is to move the pressure zone boundary so that those customers experiencing low pressures are now served from the next higher pressure zone. When a zone of higher pressure does not exist, one must be created (see page 269). If a new zone is established, the hydraulic grade line in that zone should serve a significant area, not just a few customers around the current pressure zone boundary. Each succeeding pressure zone should be approximately 100 ft (30.5 m) higher than the next lower zone. If they are less than 50 ft (15.2 m) apart in elevation, too many pressure zones may complicate operation. If they are more than 150 ft (45.7 m) apart in elevation, it will be difficult to serve the highest customers without overly pressurizing the lowest customers in that zone.

High Pressures During Low Demand Conditions

High pressures are usually caused by serving customers at too low an elevation for the pressure zone. Some utilities consider 80 psi (550 kPa) to be a high pressure, although most systems can tolerate 100 psi (690 kPa) before experiencing problems (for example, increased leakage, increased breaks, water loss through pressure relief valves, and increased load on water heaters and other fixtures). Portions of some distribution systems can bear significantly greater pressures because pipe having a high-pressure rating has been installed. When dealing with high pressures, PRVs can be used to reduce pressures for individual customers, although they may result in additional maintenance issues.

Usually, high pressures are easiest to evaluate with model runs at low demands (say 40 to 60 percent of average flow). This range corresponds to minimum night-time demands for a typical system. If the engineer feels that pressures are too high, the usual solution is to establish a new pressure zone for the lower elevation using system PRVs (as opposed to individual home PRVs).

When a constant-speed pump is moving a substantially lower flow than its design flow, high pressures within the pumped zone can result. Possible solutions include a variable speed pump, a storage tank, or a pressure relief valve that blows off water pressure to the suction side of the pump when the discharge pressure becomes too high.

Oversized Piping

Oversized piping can be difficult to identify because the system often appears to work well. The adverse effects are excessive infrastructure costs and potentially poor water quality due to long travel times. If a pipe is suspected of being too large during a design study, its diameter should be decreased and the model rerun for the critical condition for that pipe (peak hour or fire flow). If the pressures do not drop to an unacceptable range, the pipe is a candidate for downsizing.

Figure 7.4 shows a comparison of 6-in. (150-mm), 8-in. (200-mm), 12-in. (300-mm), and 16-in. (400-mm) pipes providing water to an area on a peak day. The pressure graph shows that a 6-in. pipe is too small to deliver good pressure during peak times, while the 8-in. pipe experiences an acceptable drop. Increasing the pipe size to 12 in. (300 mm) or 16 in. (400 mm) does not result in significantly improved pressure for the increased cost. This problem can also be viewed in terms of head loss (as in Figure 7.5), which shows there is virtually no head loss in the 12-in. (300-mm) or 16-in. (400-mm) pipe, while the loss in the 8-in. (200-mm) pipe is acceptable.

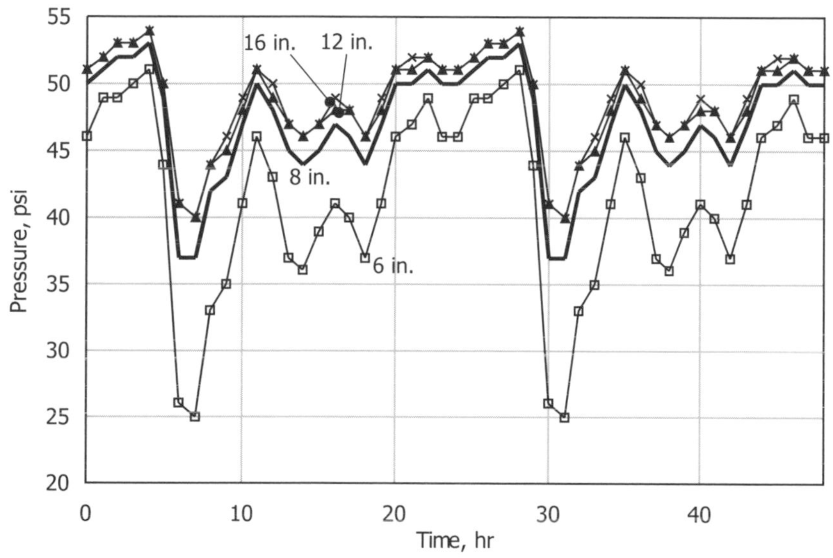

Figure 7.4
Pressure comparison for 6-, 8-, 12- and 16-in. pipes

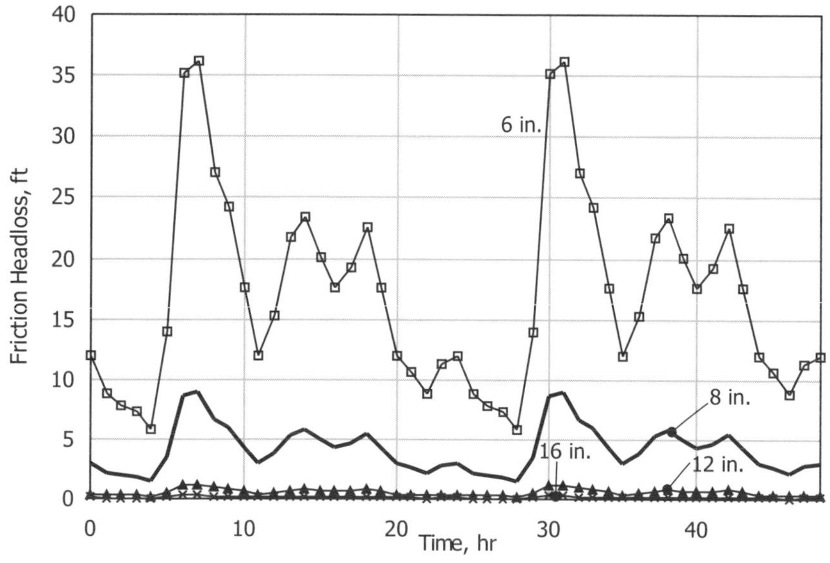

Figure 7.5
Head loss comparison for 6-, 8- and 16-in. pipes

7.3 PUMPED SYSTEMS

Most water distribution systems are fed through some type of centrifugal pump. From a modeling standpoint, the type of pump (for example, vertical turbine or horizontal split-case) does not make as much difference as do the pump head characteristics, the type of system in which the pump operates, and how the pump is controlled. Figure 7.6 shows some pumping configurations for various systems.

Figure 7.6
Pumping configuration alternatives

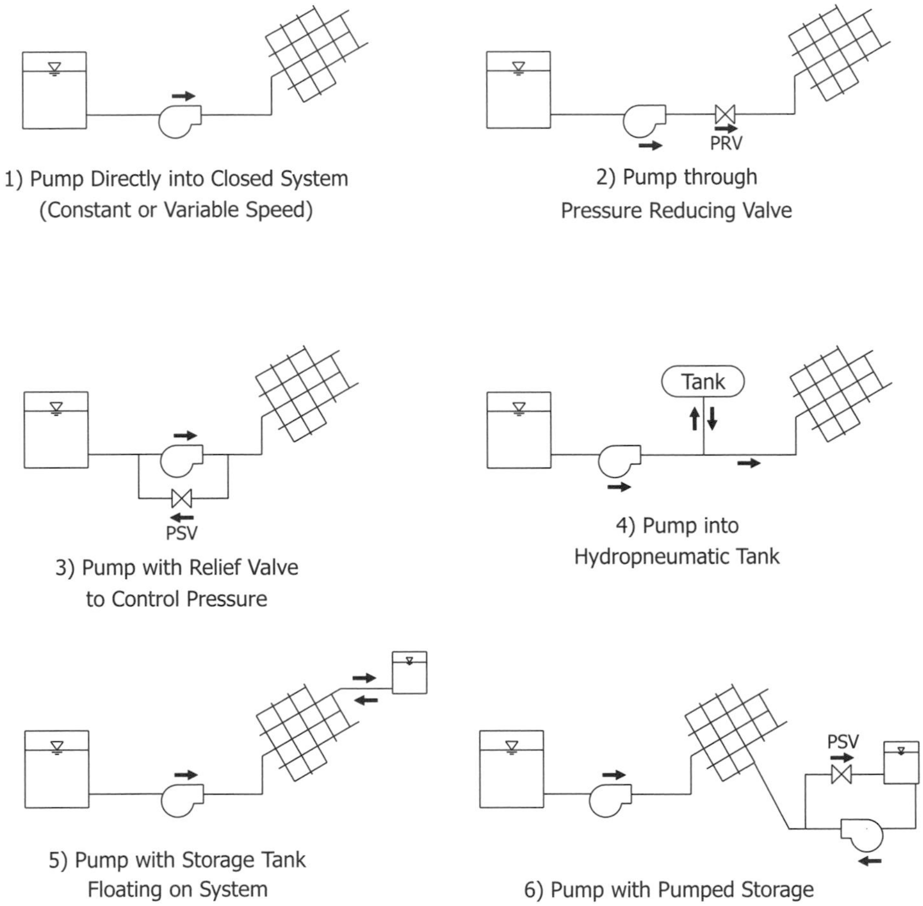

When serving a pressure zone through a pump station or by pumping directly from a well, a number of different methods of operation may be used:

1. Pump feeding directly into a closed system
2. Pump feeding through a PRV
3. Pump with a pressure relief valve
4. Pump feeding a system with a hydropneumatic tank
5. Pump feeding a system with a tank floating on the system
6. Pump feeding a system with a pumped storage tank (not floating on the system)

The early parts of this section refer to design problems in which the pumps will take suction from a source with an adequate and relatively constant HGL [less than 20 ft (6 m) variation], such as a tank or treatment plant clearwell. Situations in which the suction HGL can vary significantly, or the NPSH available (see page 49) is marginal, raise other issues that are addressed at the end of this section.

In the initial modeling of most pumped systems, the engineer may first want to represent the pump discharge as a known HGL elevation that the pump station will maintain (that is, model it as a reservoir). Steady-state runs for high-demand or fire flow conditions should be used to set this known HGL and to size pipes. The pipes should be sized so that the head loss during peak times is acceptable [for example, velocity less than 5 ft/s (1.5 m/s)], and the HGL set so that the pressures are within a desirable range of 40 psi (280 kPa) to 80 psi (550 kPa) [30 psi (200 kPa) to 100 psi (690 kPa) in hilly areas]. If a large range of elevations will be served, the system may be divided into more than one pressure zone (see page 270).

Figure 7.7
Pump station

Once the pump(s) are selected using system head curves (see page 278), the HGL in the model can be replaced with the actual pump curve data, and the suction side of the pump connected to the upstream system piping or boundary node. Then, a set of steady-state runs is made for minimum, average, and maximum day demands. Special consideration should be paid to situations in which the variability of flows is large, or new construction in the pressure zone is going to occur gradually. In such cases, the design may include specifying several pumps of different sizes, or choosing a pump station design with an empty slot so that an additional pump may be installed at a later time.

The design engineer is primarily concerned with selecting the correct pump(s), while pump control is an operational issue. However, the designer must have a good understanding of how the pumps may be operated to size them properly. An EPS run is the best way to understand the effect of pump controls and to study pump operation. If the system includes one or more tanks, the storage should be evaluated using EPS runs to check tank turnover and pump cycling. A few fire flow scenarios can be used to ensure that the tanks are able to recover relatively quickly after a high demand period or fire. The designer should also check pump suction pressures in the model. These pressures are especially critical in situations involving long suction lines.

In summary, to model a new water distribution system with a pump, follow the basic steps outlined below.

1. Choose an HGL elevation that will initially serve as the pump discharge head, and locate tank(s).
2. Using steady-state runs for high-demand or fire flow conditions, size the pipes to achieve acceptable head losses during high-demand conditions.
3. Develop system head curves from the steady-state runs, and select the pump(s) using these system head curves.
4. Replace the constant head node in the model with actual pump data.
5. Test the system using steady-state runs of minimum, average, and maximum day demands, and fire flow analyses.
6. If the system includes storage, also perform EPS runs for minimum, average day, and maximum day demands to check tank and pump cycling.
7. Perform fire flow EPS runs to check tank recovery, pump cycling, and pump suction pressures.

Pumping into a Closed System with No Pressure Control Valve

Most pressure zones contain some storage, or are fed by variable-speed pumps. Occasionally, there are too few customers, or there is not enough power consumption, to justify a tank or variable-speed pump. This situation may occur in small systems such as trailer parks, recreation areas, or isolated high points within larger distribution systems.

The simplest way to provide water to a closed pressure zone is by using a constant-speed pump and no storage. While this option is the least costly, the pump does not function efficiently much of the time and can easily over pressurize the system during low demand periods. For example, a pump selected to run efficiently at peak demand may run at an efficiency of 30 to 50 percent during periods of low demand. Therefore, constant speed, dead-end pumping tends to minimize capital costs but results in higher energy costs.

When designing a closed system with no pressure control, the engineer must pay special attention to ensure that the pump selected does not over pressurize or under pressurize the system. The pump should be selected such that the shutoff head is only slightly higher than the head at the pump's best efficiency point. Once the pump curve data have been entered into the model, system pressures should be checked at various usage levels. These pressures can be examined using either multiple steady state runs or a small set of EPS runs having a wide range of demand patterns.

After checking the pressures, the power consumption at various pump operating points should be examined. Using the power consumption and the cost of energy, the designer can estimate the cost of running the pump at each operating point. If the pump spends a great deal of time at inefficient operating points, then it may be cost-effective to install storage tanks or pressure controls to increase efficiency. Alternatively, the engineer may choose to use three smaller pumps rather than two larger ones. For example, if the peak flow is 200 gpm (0.0126 m^3/s), and the average flow is about 75 gpm (0.0047 m^3/s), then three 100 gpm (0.0063 m^3/s) pumps, or two 200 gpm (0.0126 m^3/s) pumps with a 75 gpm (0.0047 m^3/s) *jockey pump* (i.e. a small pump used to maintain pressure in a closed system) could be used instead of two 200 gpm (0.0126 m^3/s) pumps. The capital costs will be slightly higher, but operating costs will be lower, resulting in a net savings over the life of operation.

Pumping into a Closed System with Pressure Control

If the pumps tend to over pressurize the system during all but peak-use periods, then some type of pressure control may be needed. The first option is to install a pressure reducing valve (PRV) on the discharge side of the pumps. While doing so is wasteful in terms of energy, the initial costs are fairly low, and the downstream pressure will be corrected. This option is easily modeled by inserting a PRV onto the pump's discharge pipe, or, if there are multiple pumps in parallel, downstream of the node where the discharge pipes tie together.

A more effective solution may be to install a pressure relief valve that bleeds off water and pressure from the discharge side to the suction side of the pump during low demand periods. One advantage of this solution is that this valve can be much smaller than the PRV described above. For example, if the station pumps approximately 500 gpm (0.0316 m^3/s), a 4-in. (100-mm) to 6-in. (150-mm) PRV will be needed, but the relief valve can be as small as 2 in. (50 mm), and therefore less costly.

The relief valve can be modeled as a pressure sustaining valve (PSV) set to the pressure (or HGL) that is to be maintained on the discharge side of the pump. At high flow rates, the valve will stay shut, while at lower flow rates the valve will open enough to relieve pressure. Examining the range of pressures from an EPS run is a good way to check the valve operation. Different combinations of pump sizes and valve settings can be evaluated using the model to determine which works best. Figure 7.8 shows how pressures can climb in a system that does not have any storage or variable-speed pumping, compared to a system equipped with a pressure relief valve (modeled as a pressure sustaining valve).

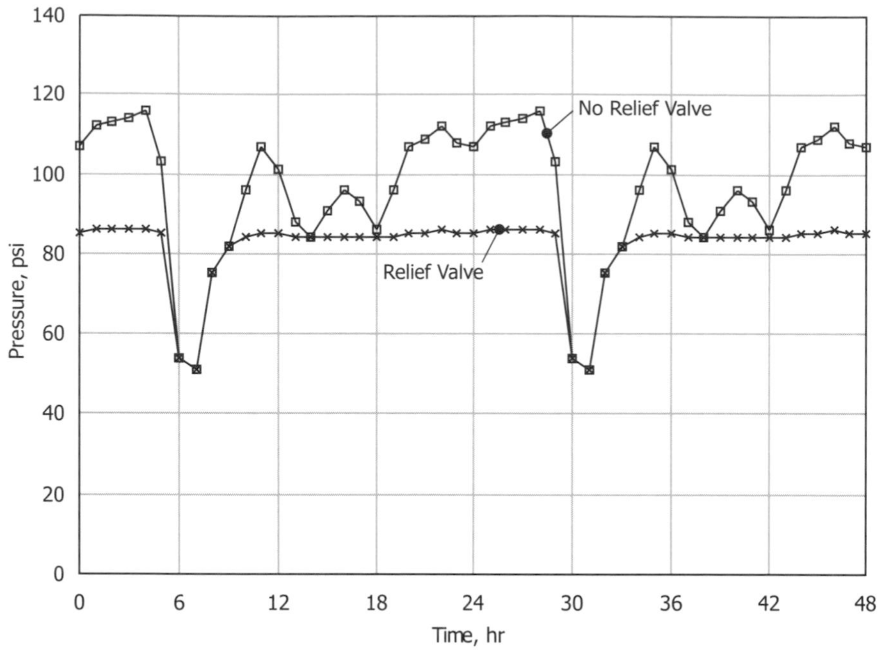

Figure 7.8
Pressures when pumping into a dead-end system (with and without a relief valve on the pump)

Variable-Speed Pumps

Variable-speed pumps are frequently used in systems that do not have adequate storage, and their use increases the initial capital cost of pumping stations, as well as maintenance expenses. Thus, the capital and operating costs must be compared to other alternatives. In smaller pressure zones, the expense of installing, maintaining, and operating a variable-speed pump is dwarfed by the cost of installing additional storage facilities. Furthermore, the shape of the pump curve for a variable-speed pump can be selected to reduce the energy costs associated with operation. Variable-speed pumps can prevent over pressurizing of the water distribution system in a pressure zone that has no storage floating on the system (that is, no tanks where the HGL in the tank is the same as the HGL in the system). A variable-speed pump can be reasonably efficient, although not as efficient as a properly sized constant-speed pump with a storage tank.

The model can help the designer to select the pump and determine the HGL (pressure) that the variable-speed pump will try to maintain. There are several ways to model variable-speed pumps. If the engineer is only analyzing this single pressure zone, the simplest way is to treat the pump as a constant head node, setting the head equal to the discharge HGL that the pump is trying to maintain. This approach works as long as the pump is never expected to reach 100 percent speed. If the pump is modeled in this fashion and achieves full speed, the model will not accurately account for the pump running out on its curve.

If the pump is going to reach full speed during some situations and is controlled by the pressure immediately downstream, then a corrected pump curve can be used to model the pump as long as the suction head does not change markedly. This *effective pump curve* is flat at low flows and curves downward once full speed is reached. The designer must select a pump that can deliver the maximum flow without a significant drop in pressure, and select the HGL to be maintained that will result in the best range of pressures.

Developing an effective pump curve for a variable-speed pump is illustrated with this example. Note that the full-speed pump curve is shown in Figure 7.9 as the dashed line. Assuming that the suction head is 708 ft (216 m), the pump station is located at an elevation of 652 ft (199 m), and the target discharge pressure set at the variable-speed control is 90 psi (610 kPa), the effective pump curve can be determined as the solid line using Equation 7.1. Beyond a flow rate of 200 gpm (12.5 l/s), the pump can no longer maintain 90 psi (610 kPa) so it behaves like a constant-speed pump, while below that flow rate, it maintains a constant discharge head independent of flow using the variable-speed drive. The total dynamic head (TDH) in the flat portion is determined as:

$$TDH = Z_{pump} + 2.31P_{set} - h_{suc} \qquad (7.1)$$

where TDH = total dynamic head in flat portion of effective curve (ft, m)
Z_{pump} = elevation of pump (ft, m)
P_{set} = discharge pressure setting (psi, kPa)
h_{suc} = suction head (ft, m)

For the case described above, TDH = 652 + 2.31(90) - 708 = 152 ft.

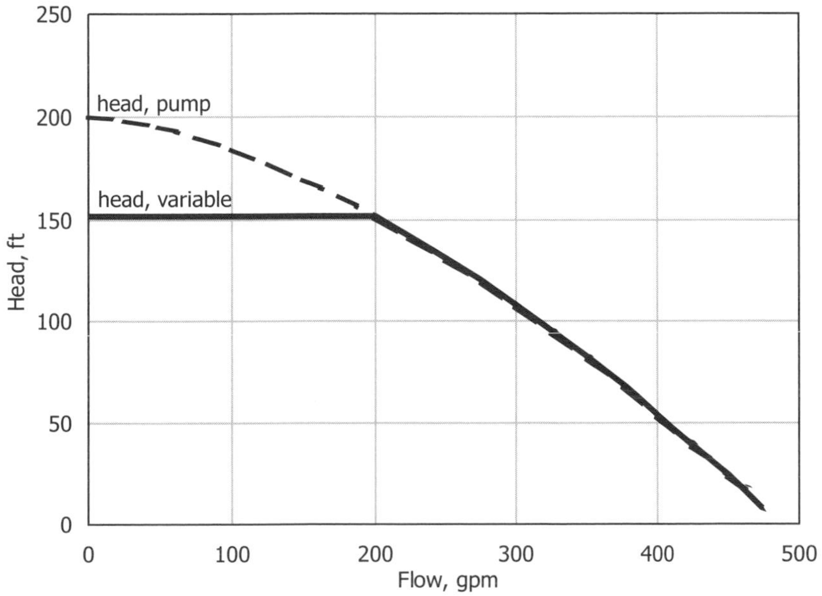

Figure 7.9
Effective pump curve

When the variable-speed pump is controlled by a tank water level or a pressure reading at a distant point in the system (rather than at a point directly downstream), the relative speed factors can control the speed of the pump in the model. A string of control statements, such as "Set speed to 80 percent if HGL is less than 540 ft (165 m)," can be used. The more statements included, the more precise the control will be. The controls need to be set up so that they will work whether the pump is ramping up or ramping down.

Alternatively, to simulate the behavior of variable-speed pumps, artificially high design, shutoff, and maximum operating heads can be specified. Then, a PRV downstream of the pump can be used to regulate the head to the setting of the variable-speed pump.

Pumping into a System with a Storage Tank

A storage tank is considered to be "floating on the system" if the HGL in the tank is generally the same as the HGL in the system. Pumping into a system with a storage tank that floats on the system, whether that tank is an elevated tank or a ground tank on a hill, usually represents very efficient operation.

A pump discharging into a closed system (meaning there is no storage) must respond instantaneously to changes in flow because there is no equalization storage. This immediate response is not necessary when pumping into a zone with a storage tank that floats on the system. In such cases, a more efficient and less costly constant-speed pump can be used. The pump can be selected to operate at its most efficient flow and pressure, thus eliminating the inefficiencies associated with variable-speed drives. Furthermore, if there is sufficient storage floating on the system, the pressure zone can respond to power outages without the need for a costly generator and transfer switch.

The pump should be selected so that the operating point will be very close to the best efficiency point of the pump. EPS runs can be used to determine how pump controls should be set, and to ensure that the pump is operating efficiently under virtually all conditions. EPS runs should be at least 48 hours in duration to show that the pumps can refill the storage tank even during a stretch of two or more maximum or near-maximum demand days. Performing EPS runs that show tank water levels recovering after a fire or power outage is also helpful. The tank water level should be able to recover within a few days of the emergency.

If there are several tanks in a single pressure zone, it may be difficult to efficiently operate the system in a way that takes full advantage of both tanks, without encountering a difficulty with preventing one tank from overflowing while keeping the other from draining. These operation problems are discussed further on page 275.

Pumping into Closed System with Pumped Storage

With pumped storage, the distribution storage (not the well or plant clearwell) has a head lower than the hydraulic grade line required by the system, so water must be pumped out of the tank to be used. An example would be a ground tank in flat terrain. Such tanks may be attractive in certain instances because they have a lower capital cost and less visual impact than elevated tanks. At times, this type of arrangement may be the only way of incorporating an existing tank into a larger system after annexation or regionalization.

In these cases, pumping is required to move water from the tank into the distribution system. Therefore, operating costs will be greater when compared to systems with tanks that float on the system. In addition, the expense of this type of tank configuration includes the capital and operating costs of a generator, transfer switch, valving, and controls so the system can operate during power outages. Because the HGL of the system is higher than the water surface elevation in the tank, filling the pumped storage tank wastes energy that must be added again when water is pumped out of the tank. The amount of energy lost depends on how much lower the water level in the tank is compared to the system HGL.

Running steady-state models of a pressure zone with pumped storage is complicated because there are really five different modes of operation, as presented in Table 7.1. In this table, the term *source pump* refers to the pump from the well, clearwell, or neighboring zone into the pressure zone where the storage facility is located. The pumped storage pump pressurizes water from the storage facility for delivery to the customers within the pressure zone.

Table 7.1 Pump operation modes when pumping into a closed system

Mode	Source Pump	Pumped Storage Pump	Notes
1	On	On	Peak demand period
2	Off	On	Storage providing water
3	On	Off	Pumped storage filling
4	On	Off	Pumped storage full or off-line
5	Off	Off	Alternative supply

Note that the fifth case above is only feasible if there is another storage tank floating on the system or an alternate water source (for example, a PRV from a higher zone); otherwise, turning both sets of pumps off will leave customers without water.

The above list of cases is an oversimplification, in that there may be numerous combinations of source pumps and pumped storage pumps in a real system. In some situations, there might not be a "source pump" at all, and the system may actually be fed by gravity, such as from a treatment plant on a hill or through a PRV from a neighboring pressure zone. In any case, areas of the system with very high or very low pressures must be identified to determine the required pump discharge heads. Unless there is floating storage, the pumps used in pumped storage systems are usually variable-speed pumps, and the designer needs to consider how to set the controls, as well as how to select the pumps.

The actual tank fill time is a very important consideration when planning the filling cycle of a pumped storage tank. If the tank fills up too quickly, it will depress the hydraulic grade line (and pressures) in its vicinity. Conversely, if the tank fills too slowly, water may not be available for pumping when it is needed. The tanks are usually fed through a pressure sustaining valve, as shown schematically in Figure 7.10. The engineer should experiment with different settings for the PSV to determine a setting that fills the tank at an adequate rate without adversely affecting pressure. Furthermore, the speed at which tanks fill and drain can have a significant impact on water quality within the tank volume.

Figure 7.10
Pumped storage tank fed through a PSV

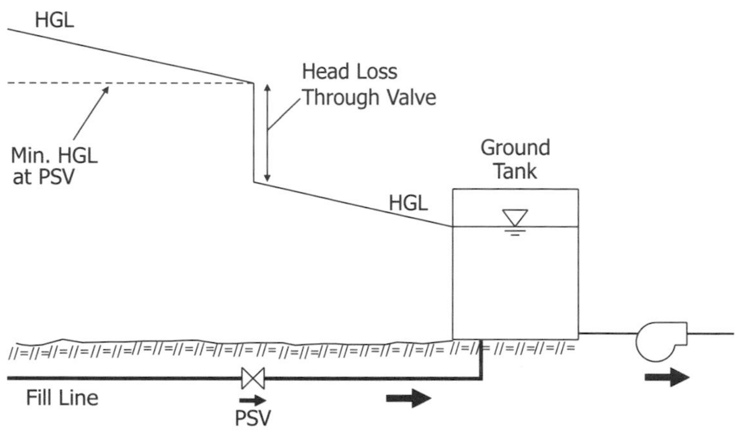

Once pumps, pump controls, and PSV settings have been specified, an EPS run can be performed for a duration of at least 48 hours, for both maximum and average day conditions, to guarantee that the system will work as designed. In particular, the operating points of the various pumps should be checked for problems. For example, a storage pump may run efficiently when operating alone, but if it runs with the source pump on, the elevated pressure on its discharge side may back it off to an inefficient point on the pump curve. Conversely, the storage pump may run correctly when running with the source pump, but may run out to a very high flow when the source pump shuts off. These inefficiencies can overload motors and waste energy.

Pumped storage systems are easy to run, but difficult to run efficiently. This inefficiency is due to the fact that the pumps may be working against one system head curve when they are running by themselves, and a much different system head curve when they are running with the other pumps. Selecting a pump that is sized according to the largest head and relying on the variable-speed drive to control the pump at other times is usually the best solution.

Pumping into Hydropneumatic Tanks

Hydropneumatic tanks are pressure tanks that can be used to store water at the correct HGL using pressure head rather than elevation head. Because pressure tanks are expensive, they are only used for small systems that are not required to meet fire flows. Capital costs for hydropneumatic tanks are high compared with variable-speed pumping or the installation of a pressure relief valve. Using this type of tank, however, allows pumps to operate more efficiently than when using no storage at all. A hydropneumatic tank also provides surge protection and additional storage in the event of a power outage.

Once a model for the hydropneumatic tank has been developed, it can help in selecting pumps, determining pump control settings, and evaluating the active storage volume in the tank. Other methods (available from tank manufacturers) are required to determine maximum and minimum air volumes in the tank.

EPS model runs allow the cycle times of pumps for various flow rates to be evaluated. One of the criteria for selecting pumps is the maximum number of starts per hour, and because hydropneumatic tank volumes are small, such criteria can be critical. Usually, the shortest cycle time occurs when the system demand is half of the pump production.

Well Pumping

Well pumping is similar to most of the other types of pumping previously described in this chapter. An important difference is that the pump suction head will vary due to the drawdown of the water table (piezometric surface) in the vicinity of the well as water is pumped from it. The greater the flow rate through the pump, the larger the drop in water table elevation.

In a model, a well is represented as a reservoir that is connected to a pump by a very short piece of suction pipe. In the actual well, the pump is submerged, so there is no suction pipe; however, pumps must be connected to a pipe for modeling purposes. The riser pipe that extends from the pump to the ground surface is usually smaller than the distribution piping, and can contribute significantly to head loss. A schematic showing how to model a well is shown in Figure 7.11.

Figure 7.11
Representing wells in the model

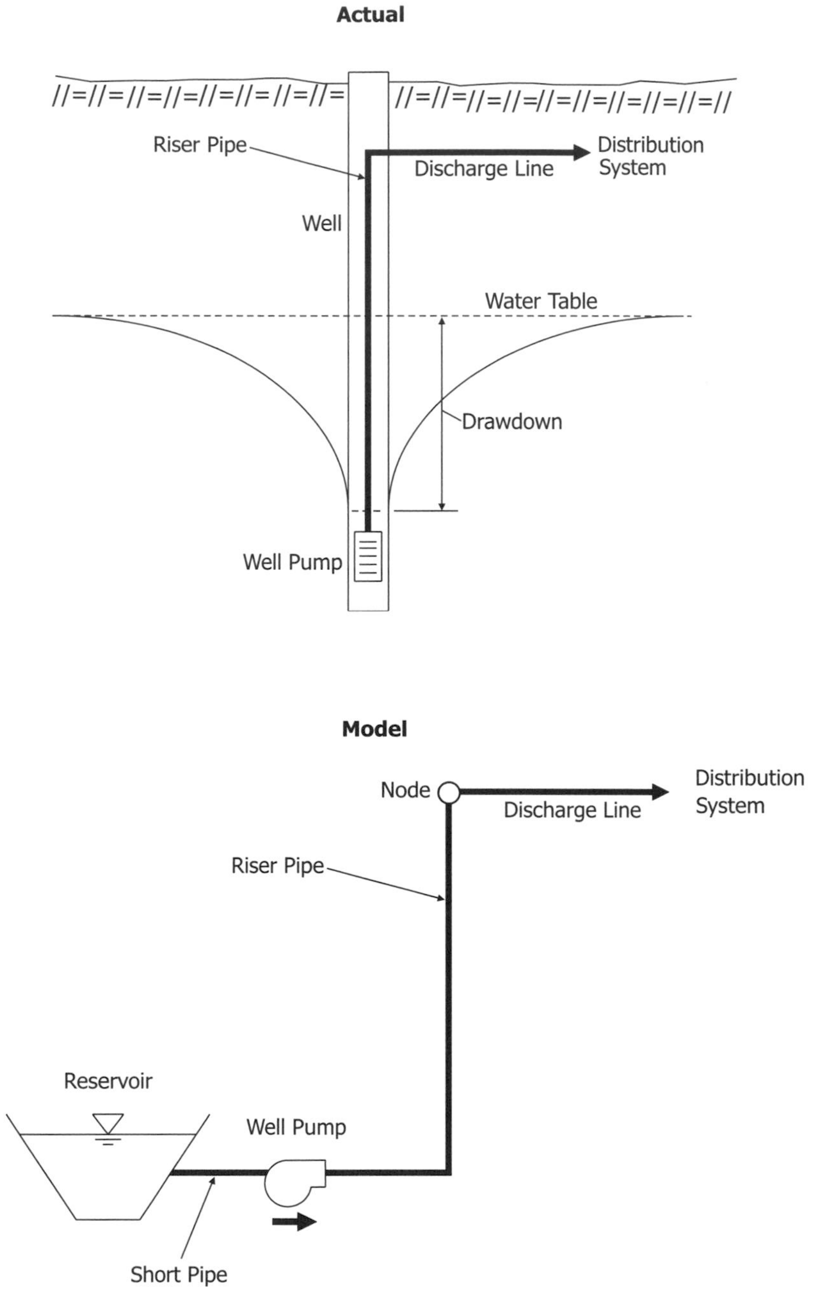

In very porous aquifers, the amount the water table will drop during pumping may be negligible, and the well can be represented by the reservoir alone. In most cases, however, the water level in the well will experience significant drawdown due to pumping, and this drawdown is relatively linear with respect to flow rate (that is, pump flow rate divided by well drawdown is equal to a constant). To model a drawdown situation, the pump curve is adjusted by subtracting the amount of drawdown from the pump curve to create a new "effective" pump curve for use in the model, as shown in Figure 7.12.

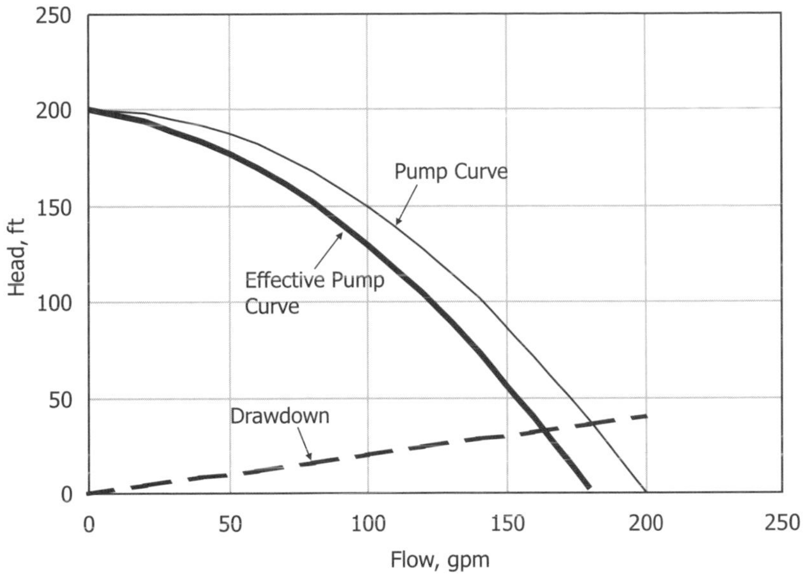

Figure 7.12
Adjustment of pump curve for well pumping

One problem with modeling wells is that groundwater tables can fluctuate for a wide variety of reasons. Seasonal variations in water usage and recharge and varying consumption rates of neighboring wells that use the same aquifer can contribute to fluctuations in groundwater tables. Regardless of the cause, the static groundwater table (or the model's reservoir level) must be adjusted for the situation being considered. For cases in which the groundwater table fluctuates significantly during the year [say, more than 20 ft (6 m)], the designer must use the model to check pumps against the full range of water table elevations. The pump that is selected needs to work with the lowest water table, and yet not overload the motor or over pressurize the distribution system when the water table is high. When the water table's elevation range is very large, the designer may want to install flow control valves and/or pressure regulating valves on the discharge piping from the well.

Usually, one of the key decisions in installing the well is whether to pump directly into the distribution system or into a ground or elevated tank (Figure 7.13). The ground tank alternative is more expensive because a tank and distribution pump are required in addition to the well pump. However, contact time requirements for disinfecting the water, if necessary, can be met through the use of ground tanks, eliminating the need for large buried tanks or pipes. Also, the ground tank can store more water for fire protection at a lower cost than an elevated tank. Using a ground tank with a well also provides some reliability in case the well should fail, because the distribution pumps at the tank can be placed in parallel. Because of the space constraints, well pumps cannot be placed in parallel without the construction of multiple wells.

Figure 7.13
Well pumped to ground storage tank

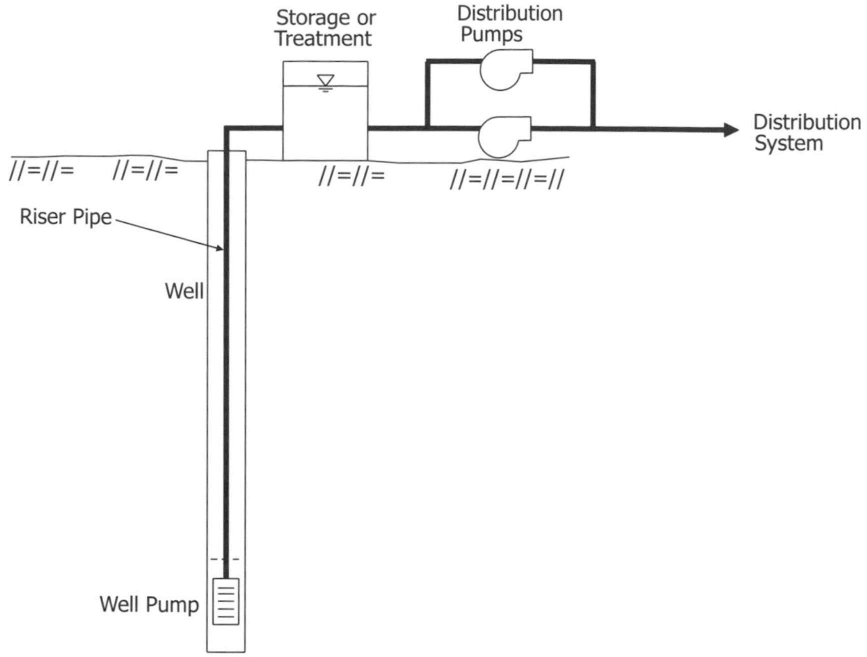

Pumps in Parallel

In general, pump stations should, at a minimum, be capable of meeting downstream demands when the largest pump is out of service. In smaller pump stations there are usually two pumps, either of which can independently meet demands. In larger stations, it is common to provide additional reliability and flexibility by having more than two pumps. If the pump station is to be operated such that different combinations of pumps will be run under different demand conditions, it is important that the pumps be selected to work efficiently when operating both alone and in parallel with the other pumps.

A major factor affecting pump efficiency is the capacity of the piping system upstream and downstream of the pump station. This capacity is reflected in the system head curve. A flatter slope on this curve for a given discharge reflects lower system head loss and ample pipe capacity. Conversely, when the slope of the curve is steep, the ability of the pump to supply adequate flows is limited by the system piping. The steepness of the system head curve determines the efficiency of running several pumps in parallel.

The simplest way to evaluate pumps in parallel is to run the model of the system for each different combination of pumps. For each combination, the operating point of each pump should be near its best efficiency point. If a pump's efficiency drops significantly, the utility may want to select different pumps or avoid running that combination.

Viewing the system head curves and pump head curves for parallel pump operation provides a better understanding of what occurs in the system. For example, Figure 7.14 shows two identical pumps in parallel. If there is ample piping capacity (that is, the system head curve is fairly flat), each pump can discharge 270 gpm when operating alone, and the pair running together can discharge 500 gpm. However, if piping capacity is limited, each pump will produce 180 gpm individually, and the two together will produce only 220 gpm. The reason for such a small increase in discharge when the second pump is added is a lack of capacity in the distribution piping, not a lack of pump capacity.

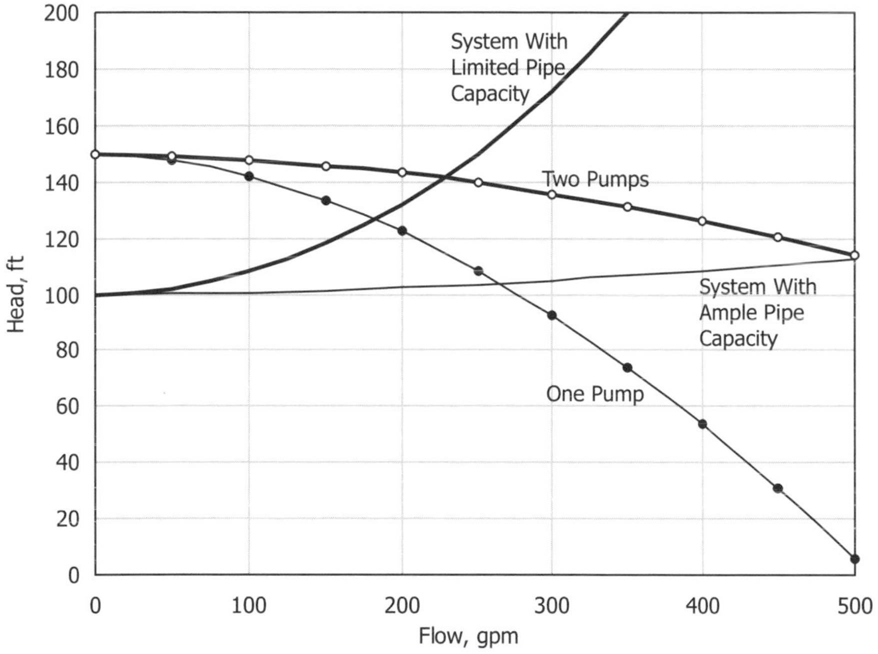

Figure 7.14
Two identical pumps in parallel

The problem becomes more complicated when the pumps are not identical, as shown in Figure 7.15. In this case, *Pump A* is run when high flows are needed, and *Pump B* is run during low-flow conditions. When the system head curve is flat, *Pump A* alone delivers 270 gpm, *Pump B* alone delivers 160 gpm, and the two together deliver 380 gpm. For the steeper system head curve, however, *Pump A* alone produces 180 gpm, *Pump B* alone produces 120 gpm, but the pair only produce 180 gpm. The reason for this lack of increase in discharge is that *Pump A* produces pressures in excess of *Pump B's* "shutoff head," so *Pump B* cannot contribute. Such a combination of system head characteristics and pumps should be avoided. The model run with these pumps will show a zero or very low discharge from *Pump B*.

Figure 7.15
Two different pumps in parallel

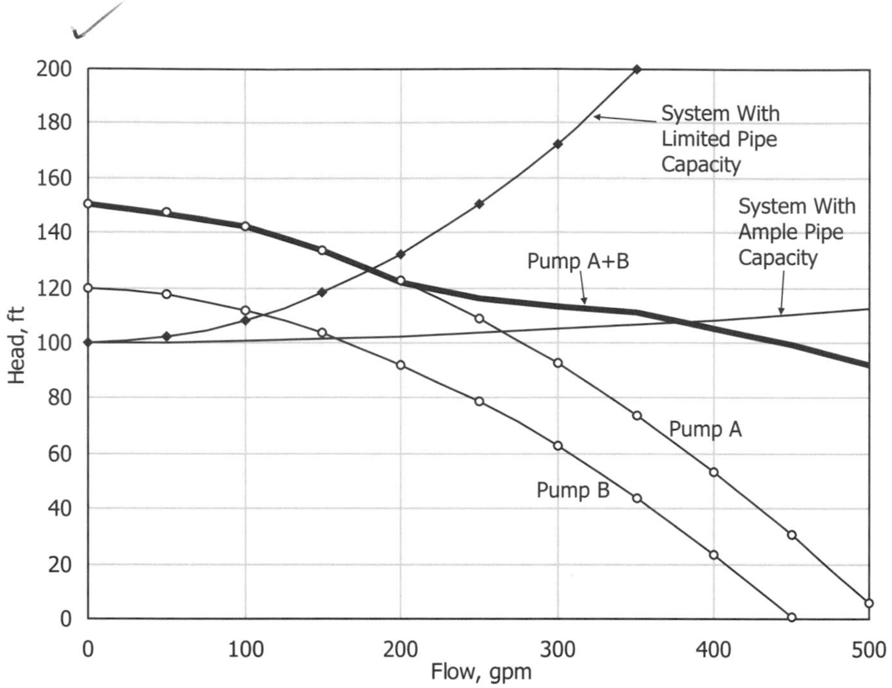

Head Loss on Suction Side of Pump

The discussion thus far in this section has centered on the hydraulics of pumps as controlled by the downstream system. Upstream piping is not usually as critical, because designers typically try to locate pumps near the storage facility or source from which they are drawing water to help reduce head losses. If the suction piping is long or lacks capacity, however, problems may occur due to the elevation of the pumps and the head losses in the suction piping. If the suction head is too low, the pump can experience problems with cavitation. Additionally, there could be difficulties keeping the pump primed.

The design of any pump requires that the suction head available be compared to the net positive suction head (NPSH) required. The NPSH available depends on the hydraulic grade elevation of the source, the elevation of the pump, and the head loss on the suction side of the pump. The NPSH required is a function of flow rate and pump properties as measured and documented by the manufacturer.

NPSH available is equal to the sum of atmospheric pressure at the pump and the static head (gage pressure) measured on the suction side of the pump, minus the water vapor pressure and the sum of the head and minor losses (velocity head is often negligible). For the simple situation in which the pump takes suction directly from a tank, the NPSH available is given by Tchobanoglous (1998).

$$NPSH_a = H_{bar} + H_s - H_{vap} - h_{loss} \qquad (7.2)$$

where $NPSH_a$ = net positive suction head available (ft, m)
H_{bar} = atmospheric pressure (at altitude of pumps) (ft, m)
H_s = static head (water elevation – pump elevation) (ft, m)
H_{vap} = water vapor pressure (corrected for temperature) (ft, m)
h_{loss} = sum of head and minor losses (from suction tank to pump) (ft, m)

For the situation in which the distance from the suction tank is large and the suction piping is complex, the model can be used to determine the (H_s - h_{loss}) term by subtracting the pump elevation from the HGL on the pump's suction side.

$$NPSH_a = h_{suc} - Z_{pump} + H_{bar} - H_{vap} \tag{7.3}$$

where h_{suc} = HGL at suction side of pump as calculated in model (ft, m)
Z_{pump} = elevation of pump (ft, m)

To determine the HGL on the suction side of the pump, it is helpful to model a node immediately upstream of the pump. The value of barometric pressure is primarily a function of altitude, although it also varies with weather. Vapor pressure is primarily a function of temperature. Standard values are listed in Tables 7.2 and 7.3 (Hydraulic Institute, 1979).

Table 7.2 Standard barometric pressures

Elevation (ft)	Elevation (m)	Barometric Pressure (ft)	Barometric Pressure (m)
0	0	33.9	10.3
1000	305	32.7	9.97
2000	610	31.6	9.63
3000	914	30.5	9.30
4000	1220	29.3	8.93
5000	1524	28.2	8.59
6000	1829	27.1	8.26
7000	2134	26.1	7.95
8000	2440	25.1	7.65

Table 7.3 Standard vapor pressures for water

Temperature (°F)	Temperature (°C)	Vapor Pressure (ft)	Vapor Pressure (m)
32	0	0.20	0.061
40	4.4	0.28	0.085
50	10.0	0.41	0.12
60	15.6	0.59	0.18
70	21.1	0.84	0.26
80	26.7	1.17	0.36
90	32.2	1.61	0.49
100	37.8	2.19	0.67

If the NPSH available is found to be less than the NPSH required, the designer must choose one of the following options to correct the problem and avoid cavitation:

- Lower the pump
- Raise the suction tank water level
- Increase the diameter of the suction piping to reduce head loss
- Select a pump with a lower NPSH requirement

The problem of meeting NPSH requirements can be particularly tricky when the suction line from the nearest tank is long. Using a model, the designer can try different piping and pump station location combinations to prevent NPSH problems from occurring in the real system.

7.4 EXTENDING A SYSTEM TO NEW CUSTOMERS

One of the most common water distribution system design problems is laying out and sizing an extension to an existing system. This section will focus on modeling new piping that will become part of an existing system (without a meter or backflow preventer), and that has a connection point that is not a tank or pump station. The new piping might be for a residential subdivision, industrial park, shopping mall, mobile home park, prison, school, or mixed-use land development.

Usually, the hydraulic demands placed on the new piping where the build-out is going to occur are known with greater certainty than master planning demand projections can provide. Frequently, when sizing new piping for a system extension, fire flow demands are more significant than peak hour demands.

Extent of Analysis

The difficult part of sizing new piping is that it cannot be sized independently of the existing distribution system. HGLs in a new extension are a function of existing piping and customer demands, as well as new and future customers in the same general area. Ignoring the existing network performance during the design process would yield poor results. Therefore, the best approach is to add the new piping to a calibrated model of the existing system.

Elevation of Customers

Before beginning the process of pipe sizing, the engineer needs to determine the elevations of the properties that will receive service to ensure that the water pressures there will be within a satisfactory range. Ideally, if a model of the existing system is available, EPS runs can help the designer to define the range of HGLs and pressures that may occur in the vicinity of the new piping. With or without a model, pressure readings should be taken where the new system will connect to the existing system so the general HGL can be determined. Knowing this range and the maximum and minimum acceptable pressures during non-fire situations, it is possible to approximate the elevation (Figure 7.16) of the highest and lowest customers that can be served using Equations 7.4 and 7.5.

$$El_{min} = HGL_{max} - C_f P_{max} \tag{7.4}$$

$$El_{max} = HGL_{min} - C_f P_{min} \tag{7.5}$$

where El_{min} = minimum allowable elevation of customers in zone (ft, m)
HGL_{max} = maximum expected HGL in pressure zone (ft, m)
P_{max} = maximum acceptable pressure (psi, kPa)
El_{max} = maximum allowable elevation of customers in zone (ft, m)
HGL_{min} = minimum expected HGL in pressure zone (ft, m)
P_{min} = minimum acceptable pressure (psi, kPa)
C_f = unit conversion factor (2.31 English, 0.102 SI)

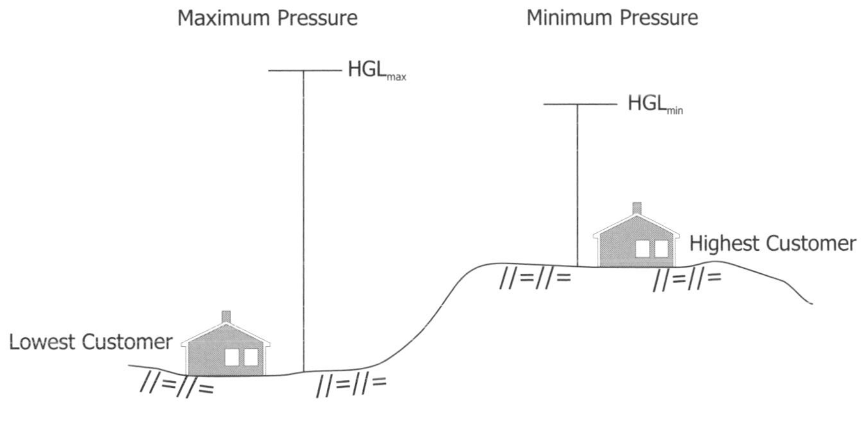

Figure 7.16 Limits of pressure zone

■ **Example** If the HGL in a pressure zone normally varies between 875 and 860 feet, the pressure varies between 35 and 100 psi, and the maximum pressure is 100 psi, what is the range of ground elevations that can be served?

$El_{min} = 875 - 2.31(100) = 644\ ft$

$El_{max} = 860 - 2.31(35) = 780\ ft$

If some of the area served is above the determined elevation range, then pumping or an alternative water source will most likely be required. Conversely, if some of the area is below the elevation range, a PRV or alternative source may be required (see page 343).

In Figure 7.17, suppose that the lowest customer is at an elevation of 700 ft and cannot have pressures above 100 psi. According to Equation 7.4, in order to experience these pressures, the HGL must be less than 931 ft. Suppose also that the highest customer is at an elevation of 890 ft and must have pressures greater than 30 psi. According-ing to Equation 7.5, in order to maintain this minimum pressure at this elevation, the HGL must be at least 960 ft. Since there is no value of HGL that is greater than 960 ft but less than 931 ft, the two customers must be served from different pressure zones.

Performing this calculation before modeling helps give the modeler an appreciation of the types of problems that are likely to be encountered. Thus, some alternatives can be immediately eliminated, such as trying to serve a customer at too high of an elevation for the pressure zone by using very large pipes. See page 270 for more information on creating new pressure zones.

Figure 7.17
Customers must be served from separate pressure zones

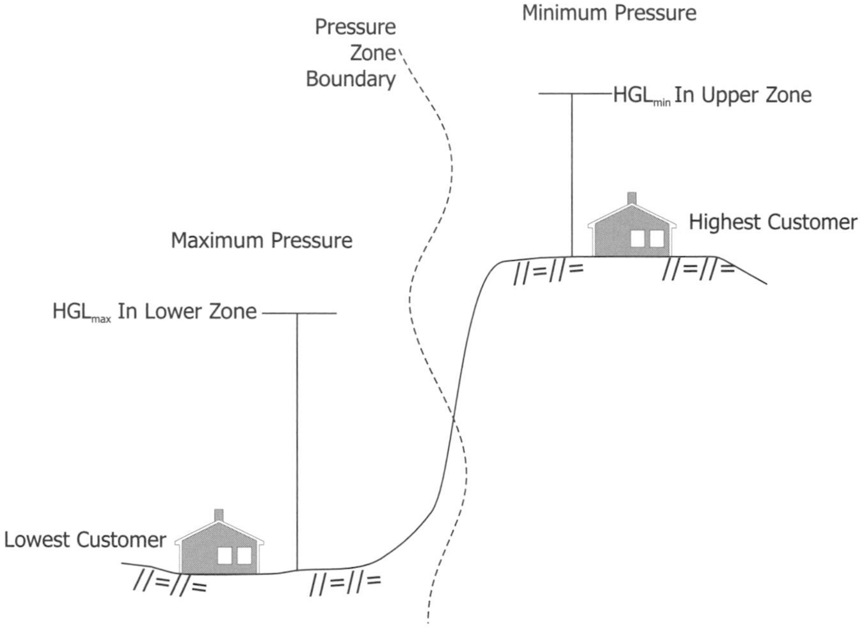

Assessing an Existing System

Because of the interaction between the new piping and the existing system, an important first step in analyzing a system extension is to conduct a hydrant flow test in the vicinity of the connection to the existing system. This test provides data for model calibration and a quick preliminary assessment of system strength. Performing a hydrant flow test is described in detail in Chapter 5 (see page 166), and in AWWA (1989).

A minimum of three values must be recorded during a hydrant flow test: static pressure (P_s), test pressure (P_t), and test flow(s) (Q_t). The pressures should be measured at the residual hydrant while the flows should be measured at the flowed hydrant. To convert the pressure to hydraulic grade line, the elevation of the residual hydrant must be accurately determined. In addition, it is helpful to record which pumps were running during testing, the tank water levels, and information regarding any special conditions in the system when the test was run (for instance, pipe breaks or fires).

The results of an example flow test are shown in Figure 7.18. The static pressure of the example flow test was 60 psi or 139 ft (614 kPa or 42 m), the hydrant flow was 500 gpm (31.5 l/s), and the residual pressure was 35 psi or 81 ft (241 kPa or 25 m). The flow value for the point where the graph intersects the horizontal axis (or any other pressure) can be determined from the following equation.

$$Q_o = Q_t\left(\frac{P_s - P_o}{P_s - P_t}\right)^{0.54} \tag{7.6}$$

where
Q_o = flow at pressure P_o (gpm, m^3/s)
Q_t = hydrant test flow (gpm, m^3/s)
P_s = static pressure during test (psi, kPa)
P_o = pressure at which Q_o is to be calculated (psi, kPa)
P_t = residual pressure during test (psi, kPa)

Note that this equation may be used with any units, as long as they are consistent (that is, all flow units and all pressure units are the same). By inserting $P_o = 0$ into the above equation the horizontal intercept can be back-calculated. The horizontal intercept is determined to be 802 gpm (50.6 l/s), as shown in Figure 7.18.

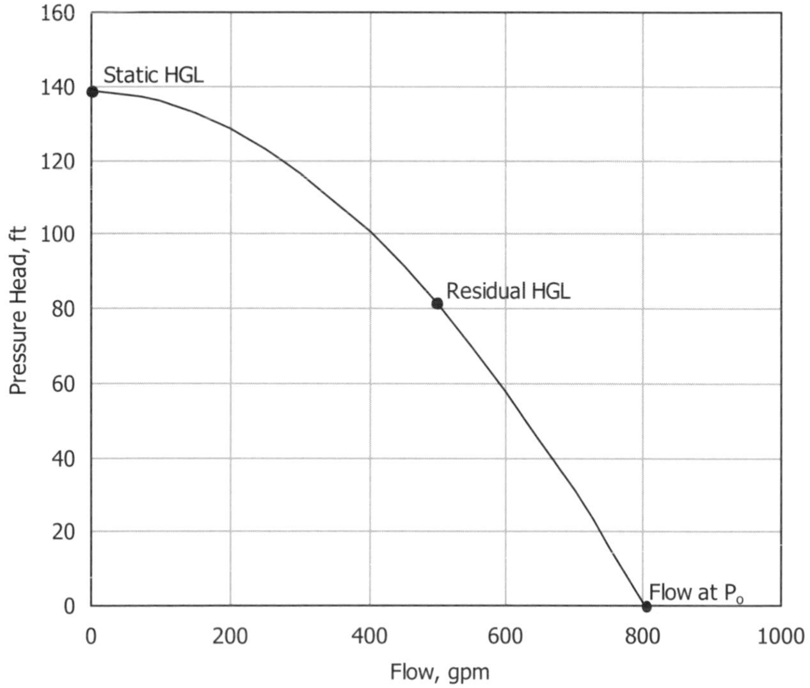

Figure 7.18
Plot of hydrant flow test data

Using a P_o value of 20 psi (140 kPa), the value of Q_o will give an indication of the strength of the system. The value of Q_o at 20 psi (140 kPa) should be significantly greater than the maximum demand for the new pipes. Otherwise, considerable improvements may be needed in the existing system.

When using hydrant tests to assess the existing system for expansion, the locations of the hydrants being tested are important. The residual hydrant should be located between the source and the flowed hydrant such that most of the water being discharged from the flowed hydrant passes by it [Figure 7.19(a)]. Otherwise, the results can be misleading, especially if the flowed hydrant is on a significantly larger main than the residual hydrant.

Figure 7.19
Reservoir/tank and pump approximation

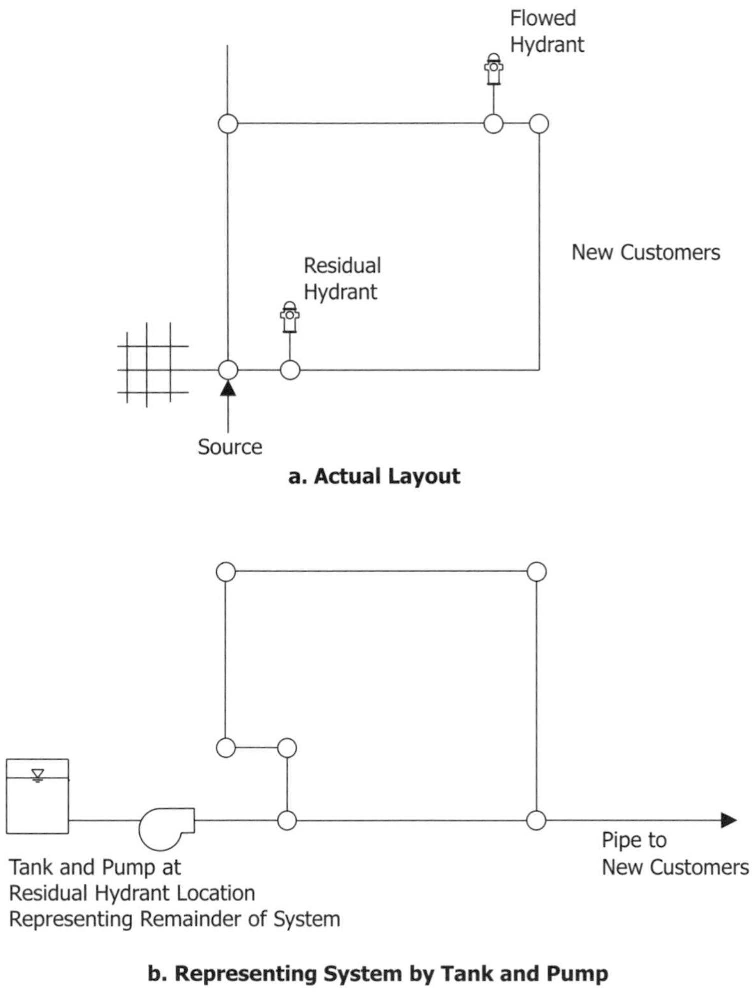

Once a fire hydrant flow test has been conducted, the data can be used to model the new piping using one of the three basic approaches listed below.

1. Add the proposed pipes to a current model of the existing system, or an appropriately skeletonized version of the model and verify the model with the fire flow test data.
2. Build a skeletal model of the existing system and add the proposed pipes onto it.
3. Use the hydrant flow test results to approximate the existing system by an equivalent reservoir and pump.

These approaches are detailed in the sections that follow. Note that setting an arbitrary HGL (based on a single pressure reading) where the system extension ties to the existing system is almost never the correct way to model the existing system.

Building onto an Existing Model. The best way to model an extension of a water system is to build the new pipes and customers into a calibrated model of the existing system. In this way, it is possible to model both the effect of the existing system operation on the new piping, and the effect of the new piping on the existing system. Having a calibrated model of the system also allows a wide variety of situations to be simulated, such as future year peak day demands, fires at various locations, and failures of important pipes.

The engineer designing the system extension, however, may have been hired by a land developer, and will probably not have much interest in studying the existing system. If the utility already has a calibrated model of the system, the most straightforward solution would be to make it available to developers to add on to the existing model. Unfortunately, it is often administratively difficult for the design engineer to utilize the existing model, either because of incompatible water distribution modeling software, or because the utility may not want to share its model. Because the utility can use information that the engineer does not have to evaluate the proposed system, several design and review iterations may be required to develop the best solution.

Skeletal Model of Existing System. If the model of the existing system cannot be made available to the design engineer, the designer should construct a skeletal model of the portion of the existing system affecting the new design. The skeletal model must begin at a real water source, such as the pump or tank, which will serve as the primary water source for the new extension pipes. It should be calibrated using the results of fire hydrant flow tests, especially the tests conducted near the location where the new extension will tie in.

This approach is not as accurate as using a more detailed existing model because of the high degree of skeletonization involved, and because assigning future demands to the model is a somewhat arbitrary process. For instance, the skeletal model probably will not be calibrated as well since a model that was used previously will have been tested under a wider variety of conditions. It is possible that the inherent inaccuracies of this method could lead to substantial modeling errors, even if the initial tests and calibration process indicated that the model seemed to be a reasonable representation of the system. If, for example, the engineer for the developer was not informed about planned projects and utility growth projections, the skeletonized model would yield little design value.

Approximating a System as a Pump Source. The simplest technique for modeling the existing system is to use a pump and reservoir to simulate conditions at the tie-in point, as shown in Figure 7.19(b). Referring back to Figure 7.18, notice how the results of a fire hydrant flow test look like a pump head curve. For modeling purposes, a reservoir node placed at the location of the residual hydrant from the flow test, with the hydraulic grade set to the hydrant's elevation, is sufficient for modeling an existing system. This reservoir is then connected to the new system through a short pipe and a pump. The pump is modeled using a three-point pump curve that is established using hydrant flow test data. Using notation similar to that used in Equation 7.6, the three points from the pump curve are shown in Table 7.4 below. Note that the value 2.31 converts the pressures (in psi) from the hydrant tests to head (measured in feet) for the pump curve.

Table 7.4 Points on simulated pump curve

Head (ft)	Flow (gpm)
$2.31P_s$	0
$2.31P_t$	Q_t
$2.31P_o$	Q_o

Flow Q_o is calculated by using Equation 7.6 with a given P_o, generally assumed to be 20 psi (140 kPa) (other reasonable values for pressure can also be used). The hydrant test can also be repeated with three different flow rates to obtain data from which to generate a curve.

For rural systems without fire hydrants, an approximate test can be conducted by opening a blow-off valve or flushing a hydrant and measuring the flow with a calibrated bucket and stopwatch. If this approach is not possible, then the best test that can be performed is to place a chart recorder at the connection point and monitor fluctuations in HGL. The model can then be calibrated to reproduce those conditions.

Using the pump approximation method can present problems because this approximation of the existing system only accounts for the exact boundary conditions and demands that existed at the time that the test was run (for example, the afternoon on an average day with one pump on at the source). Therefore, determining the effect of changing any of the demands or boundary conditions is difficult. An EPS that is performed using the pump approximation method will be less accurate, and may not provide reliable data regarding projected changes in consumption. The pump approximation approach only works well if the existing system is fairly built-out near the connection point, and the demand and operation conditions are expected to remain essentially the same in the long run. The hydrant flow test is useful for predicting changes in pressure when downstream demands change, but not for evaluating other types of system changes such as the addition of new pipes, or operational alternatives such as fire pumps starting up.

7.5 ESTABLISHING PRESSURE ZONES AND SETTING TANK OVERFLOWS

Selecting a tank overflow elevation is one of the most fundamental decisions in water distribution system design. This decision sets the limits of the pressure zone that can be served and the overall layout of the distribution system. Once a tank is constructed, the limits of the hydraulic grade line within a pressure zone are fixed. The only way to change the hydraulic grade line limits would be to replace, raise, or lower the existing tank (an expensive proposition).

Before developing a design, the engineer needs to look at the terrain being served with short-term and long-term usage projections in mind. The designer should consider what the distribution system may look like 20 to 50 years in the future when the area is completely built-out. This is true for dead-end systems that are served by pumps or pressure reducing valves, and especially true of new pressure zones with tanks.

Unlike PRVs that can be reset, or pumps that can be replaced easily, tanks are relatively permanent. Even for systems without tanks, customers become accustomed to a certain pressure, or, more importantly, industrial equipment and fire protection systems may have been designed and constructed to work with a given HGL. Any change to a network boundary condition like a tank overflow can change the dynamics of the system, and must therefore be carefully analyzed and designed.

Establishing a New Pressure Zone

The decision to create a new pressure zone may be triggered by:

- construction of a new isolated system;
- customers moving into an area with an elevation that is too high or too low to be adequately served from the existing pressure zone; or
- the utility wanting better control over an area.

Choosing the boundaries for the pressure zone is done manually before beginning to model the system. When laying out pressure zones, the designer should examine the elevations of the highest and lowest customers to be served. If customers are less than approximately 120 ft (37 m) apart vertically, then most likely a single pressure zone can serve them. If the elevation difference is significantly greater, more pressure zones are needed. In general, the elevation of the lowest and highest customers in the service area and the limits of the range of acceptable pressures are used to determine the HGL in a pressure zone. Equations 7.7 and 7.8 provide some useful guidelines for selecting a HGL:

$$HGL_{min} > (Elevation\ of\ highest\ customer) + C_f P_{min} \tag{7.7}$$

$$HGL_{max} < (Elevation\ of\ lowest\ customer) + C_f P_{max} \tag{7.8}$$

where HGL_{min} = minimum HGL (ft, m)
HGL_{max} = maximum HGL (ft, m)
P_{min} = minimum acceptable pressure (psi, kPa)
P_{max} = maximum acceptable pressure (psi, kPa)
C_f = unit conversion factor (2.31 English, 0.102 SI)

The first criterion (Equation 7.7) ensures that the highest customer will have at least some minimum pressure, while the second (Equation 7.8) ensures that the lowest customer will not experience excessive pressures. In flat terrain, there will usually be a band of possible HGL values that meet both criteria. In hilly terrain, however, because the elevations of the highest and lowest customers are very different, it may be impossible to find an HGL that satisfies both inequalities (see page 263). Usually, this much difference means that the proposed pressure zone should actually be two (or more) pressure zones, or the lowest customers will have pressures in excess of P_{max}.

The above rules pertain to pressures during normal conditions, not during fire flows when head loss becomes significant. Additional analysis is needed to size piping and ensure adequate pressures for such conditions. If there are only a small number of customers with excessive pressures, some utilities require the customer to install individual PRVs.

Laying Out New Pressure Zones

The need for pressure zones can be visualized as shown in Figure 7.20, which depicts how pressure zones can be set up along a hill 500 ft (152 m) high. In this example, the step size between pressure zones is set at 100 ft (30 m). Normally, the difference between pressure zones should be between 80 ft and 120 ft (24 m and 37 m). Large step sizes will either over pressurize the lower customers in a zone, or under pressurize the higher ones. Smaller step sizes require too many zones and, consequently, an excessive number of pumps, tanks, and PRVs.

The topography in most areas does not generally look like the smooth slope in Figure 7.20, but instead has ridges and valleys. A good way to get a feel for the layout of pressure zones is to choose the nominal HGLs of the pressure zones and identify the elevation contour that corresponds to the boundary between pressure zones. A sample of such a map is shown in Figure 7.21. The figure shows a topographic map with the high and low limits of a new pressure zone. The areas between the high and low pressure limits will be served by the zone. Those above the solid line will need to be served by a higher zone while those below the dashed line will need to be served by a lower zone. The boundary lines are not ironclad limits, but they give a suggestion of how the system should be laid out.

As with all the elements in a water distribution model, a naming convention should be developed for pressure zones. Some possibilities are:

- the part of town in which they are located;
- the nominal HGL (overflow level of the tank);
- the primary pump station/PRV serving the zone;
- the name of the tank in the zone; or
- the relative HGL in the zone.

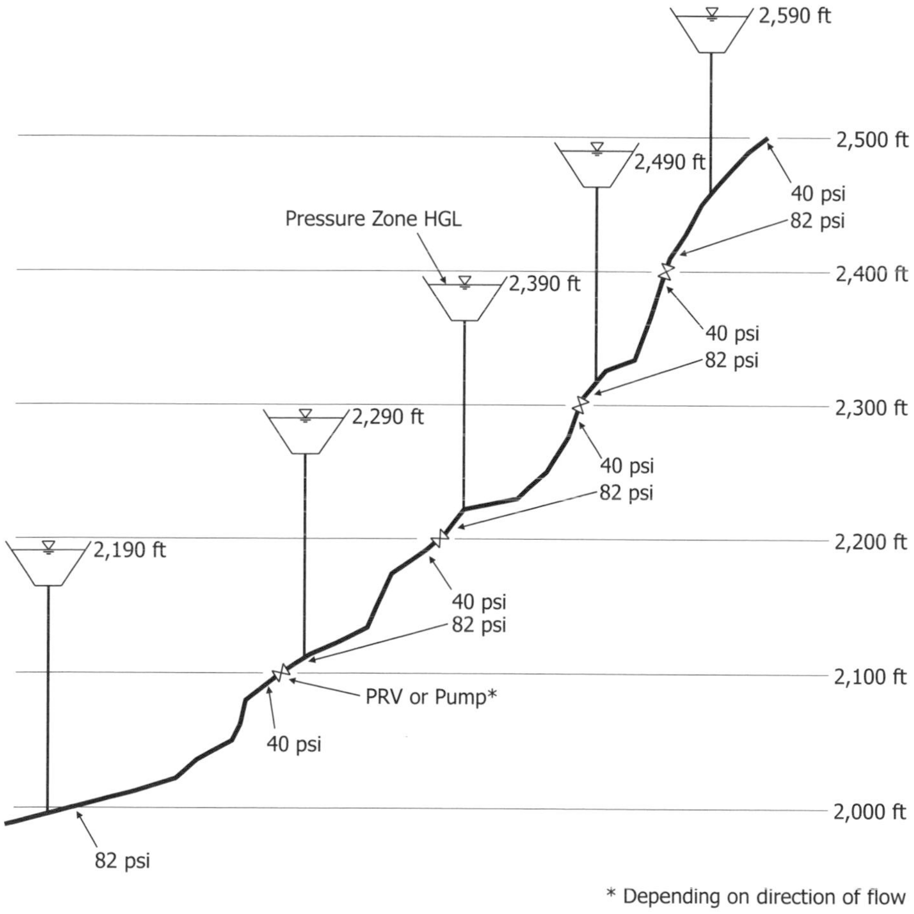

Figure 7.20
Profile of pressure zones

Table 7.5 provides some alternative naming schemes for the zones in Figure 7.20. It is important to be consistent with a naming convention in order to avoid confusion down the road. For example, suppose the Oakmont pump station takes suction from the Oakmont tank. In this case, is the Oakmont pressure zone the zone the pump discharges to or the zone the tank floats on?

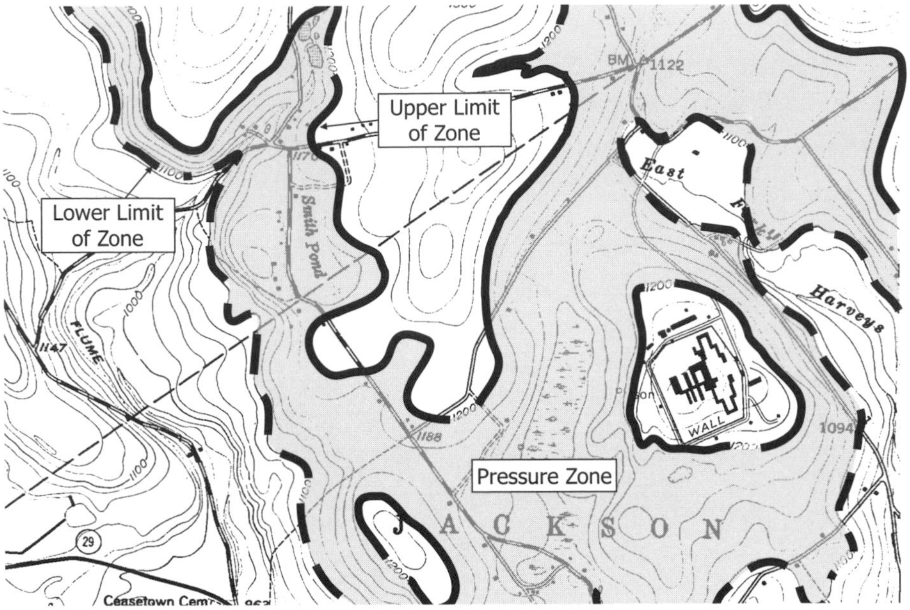

Figure 7.21
Pressure zone topographic map

Table 7.5 Alternative naming conventions for pressure zones

HGL	Part of Town	Tank Name	Pump/PRV Name	Relative HGL
2,190	South	Wilson St.	Mundy's Glen	Low Service
2,290	Central	Downtown	Hillside	Medium
2,390	North	Oakmont	Flat Road	High
2,490	Northwest	Liberty Hill	Oakmont	Very High
2,590	Far Northwest	Hanover Industrial Park	Rice Street	Top

With a map like Figure 7.21, the designer can begin to lay out transmission lines. Major transmission mains within a pressure zone (not including those connecting a zone to adjacent zones) should be laid roughly parallel to the contours and remain within the elevations that can be served by that pipe. Of course, the layout of roads and buildings may prevent this from actually occurring, but with a map such as this, the designer can roughly determine where the mains ought to be laid, thus avoiding having pipes far outside the defined pressure zones.

There will be situations in which it may be more economical to serve a new customer through a PRV or a pump from a different pressure zone, rather than from a tank in the same pressure zone. Figure 7.22 shows an example of a situation in which, at least in the short run, it is better to serve customers at the location labeled "New Development" from the higher pressure zone B, rather than from the lower pressure zone A. (Serving the area from zone A would require the costly installation of the long main labeled "proposed pipe".) Even though serving this area through the PRV wastes pumping energy, the PRV is necessary so that new customers in the development can be served at an HGL similar to that of pressure zone A. In this way, customers can be served at the "correct" pressure, without the expense of installing the proposed pipe.

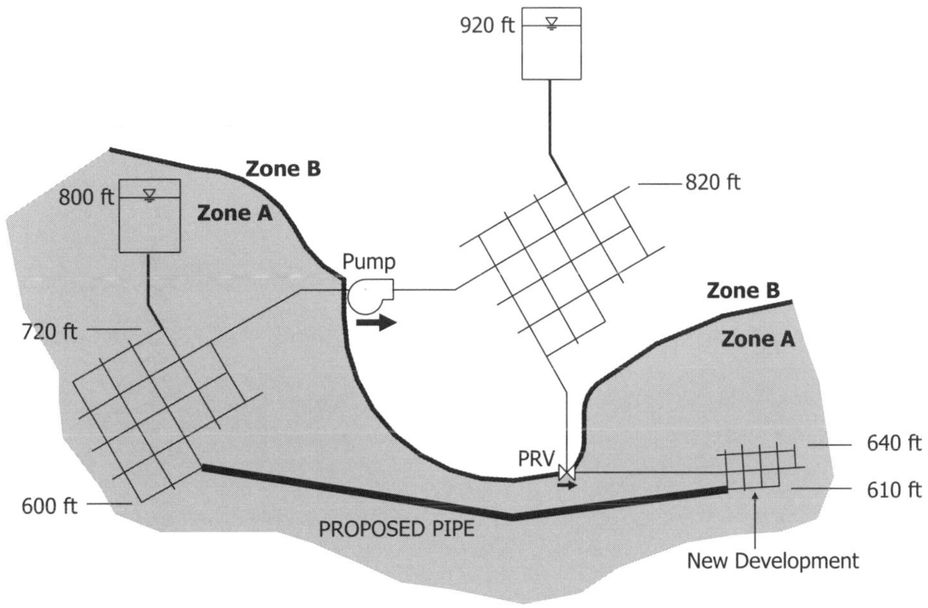

Figure 7.22
New development near "wrong" pressure zone

Tank Overflow Elevation

Once the tank overflow elevation is selected, the tank dimensions must be determined. First, tank height is set based on an appropriate water surface elevation range since this range has the greatest effect on defining the maximum and minimum pressures within the pressure zone. The upper and lower elevations are set such that adequate system pressures can be maintained at all tank levels. Because large fluctuations in tank water level correspond to similar fluctuations in pressure, most of the water in the tank should be stored within 20 to 40 ft (6 to 12 m) of the tank overflow. The analysis outlined here is the basis for determining the best location for a tank and what its overflow elevation should be. It is the role of the modeling analysis described later to determine if the piping is adequate to move the water through the pressure zone.

Consider the tank in Figure 7.23. If the water that is stored below an elevation of 869 ft (265 m) is used, the pressure will drop below 30 psi (207 kPa). If the water level drops below 846 ft (258 m), the water pressure will fail to meet the 20 psi (140 kPa) standard. Therefore, the storage volume below 846 ft (258 m) is "dead" storage, useful only in that it elevates a portion of the tank's volume to the acceptable elevation range. The water level cannot drop into that range without adversely affecting pressure. Furthermore, this excess volume can lead to long detention times and contribute to water quality problems.

To avoid water quality problems and wasted tank volume, storage must be placed at the correct elevation. In general, designers try to install all storage as "effective" storage that can provide pressures of at least 20 psi (140 kPa), and therefore favor elevated storage tanks. Although standpipes (see page 85) will cost less than elevated storage tanks with the same total storage volume, not all of the storage in a standpipe is useful. The existence of dead storage at the bottom of the tank can lead to water quality problems.

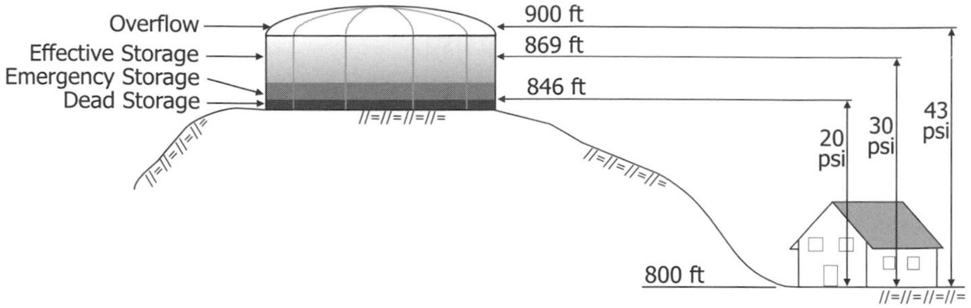

Figure 7.23
Tank profile

Tank Water Level Fluctuations. A calibrated hydraulic model can be used to check water level fluctuations in storage tanks. The pumps should have a design flow capacity such that peak day demand can be met even when the largest pump is out of service, and a head such that the band of system head curves for the pressure zone passes close to or through the best efficiency point of the pump.

The combination of pump, piping, and distribution tank is best evaluated using an EPS model. The EPS should be run based on projections for peak day, average day, and minimum day demands. If pumps fill the tanks, it is usually easy to cycle the pumps so that the tank operates in a reasonable range. It is important to run the model for at least 48 hours to determine if the tank can refill after a peak day. If the tank cannot recover, then the weak link in the system (either pumping or piping) needs to be upgraded.

If a distribution storage tank is filled from a plant clearwell, either by gravity or through a PRV, then it becomes more difficult to get the tank to fluctuate as desired. If the system is small, or the tank is close to the water source, the tank may not turn over sufficiently. The model can be used to simulate corrections for these conditions by simulating the closing or throttling of a valve for a few hours a day, or by switching to an alternate pilot valve to control the PRV for a few hours.

As the system and the head loss across the system become larger, the HGL tends to slope much more steeply during peak use periods. In terms of tanks, this lower HGL means that a tank with an overflow elevation selected to work well on a peak summer day may have too low of an elevation to work effectively during an average or minimal use winter day. The results of an EPS run for such a situation would look like Figure 7.24, which shows a tank that would operate in a different band during low, average, and maximum demand days. There are several possible solutions to this problem:

1. Operate the tank as pumped storage with the tank overflow below the HGL (this tends to be the most expensive solution as it wastes energy and needs a generator for reliability).

2. Construct a tall tank that operates in the upper range during the winter and the lower range during the summer (with large seasonal fluctuations in pressure).

3. Significantly increase piping capacity across the system so that the HGL does not drop as much during the summer (costly from a capital cost standpoint).

4. Construct the tank at an elevation that works well during a maximum use day. Use a control valve on the major system's main to control the filling rate on other days (to use this type of control effectively, a SCADA system is needed).

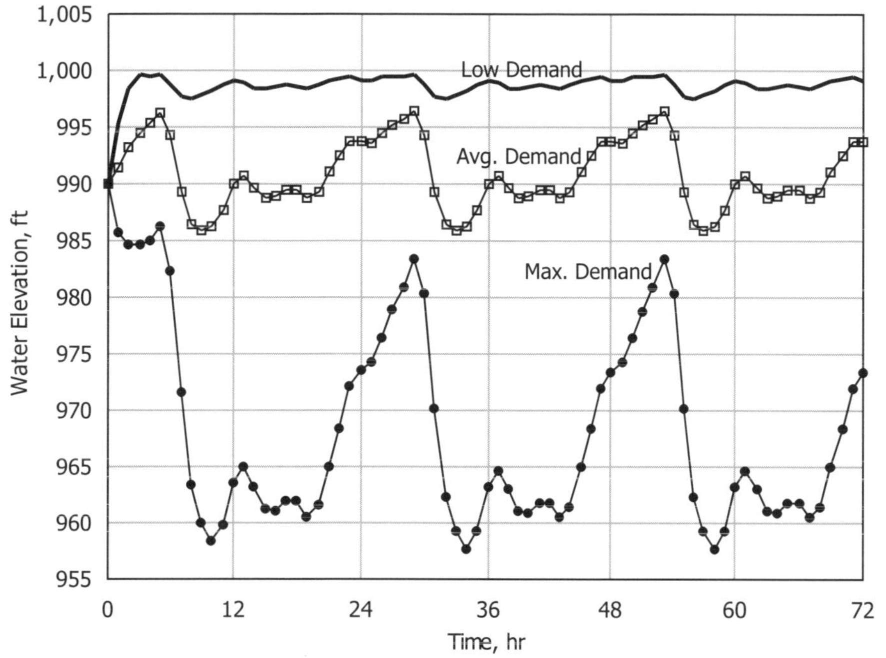

Figure 7.24 Tank water level fluctuations

An EPS model provides the designer with a tool to compare these approaches and determine how each could be used (for example, by finding the correct pipe size or effective control settings for a valve). Then, the benefits and costs of each solution can be compared.

Tank Behavior During Emergencies. Another design question relates to how well the tank can recover after a fire or power outage that draws the tank water level down. A tank cannot be expected to recover instantly, but it should not take more than a few days to bring water levels back to their normal cycle. While this is partly an operational problem, the designer needs to provide sufficient capacity for emergencies.

Multiple Tanks in a Pressure Zone. When there is more than one tank in a pressure zone, the problem of designing and operating the zone becomes much more complicated. For modeling purposes, it is difficult to get all of the tanks to fluctuate in the desired range. In general, all of the tanks in a pressure zone should be constructed with the same overflow elevation. In that way, the full range of each can be used. With multiple tanks, it is also helpful to construct each tank with an altitude valve. This is especially true for the tank that is hydraulically closer to the source, because the HGL will be higher in this area.

The usual problem is that the tank near the source fills up quickly and drains slowly, while the tank at the perimeter of the system fills more slowly and drains quickly. One solution is to fill the tank that is closer to the source using a throttle control valve to throttle the flow when the tank is nearly full, enabling more water to flow to the distant tank. The nearer tank should drain through a separate line with a check valve so that the tank can drain easily even if the power should fail while the control valve is in the throttled or closed position (Figure 7.25). This situation can be modeled with a check valve and a throttling control valve.

Figure 7.25
Multiple tanks in pressure zone

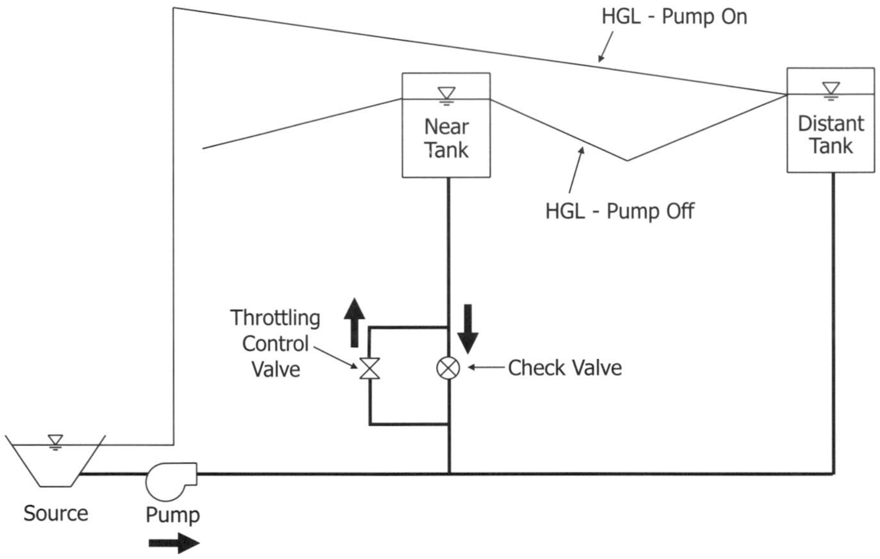

EPS models can be used to determine if there will be problems in pressure zones with multiple tanks, and to test alternative strategies for operating these zones. It is especially important to test the hydraulics under a wide range of demands. These demands should include seasonal variations and future projections, since a shift in the size or location of the population (for example, more demand in suburbs near a new tank) will change how the system will operate.

Regionalization. When water systems are combined, whether due to *regionalization*, *annexation*, or *acquisition*, the adjacent systems usually do not have the same HGL elevation; that is, they are in different pressure zones and cannot simply be connected. Therefore, integrating the distribution systems becomes problematic. The easiest way to integrate the systems is to install a pump or PRV at the boundary. Usually, one of the systems will no longer use its original source, or will use it only as a backup. Instead, it will use the other system as its source. Large pipes are usually needed at the connection point linking a system and its new water source. At points where two systems meet at their perimeters, the pipes are typically small. Substantial improvements consisting of pipe paralleling and/or replacement are usually required in one or both systems.

If new piping is going to be installed, the designer has a unique opportunity to establish pressure zones as they should be, rather than as they have evolved out of necessity. Usually, the sizes of the pipes near the interconnection points are the limiting factors, and paralleling or replacing those pipes becomes the focus of the modeling analysis.

Tank Volume Considerations. The discussion thus far has emphasized the importance of water level in a tank. The tank cross-section (and therefore volume) is also important. To a great extent, tank volume sizing can be done outside of the model by considering the amount of water that is needed for equalization storage, fire storage, and emergency storage. Too much storage, however, may contribute to water quality problems. Tank sizing requirements are described in more detail in the *Ten State Standards* (GLUMB, 1992) and by Walski (2000).

The volume of a tank is usually dictated by the volume needed for equalization and the larger of fire and emergency storage. These volumes can be viewed as areas under the curve as shown in Figure 7.26. The area between production and peak day demand is the volume needed for equalization, while the volume between the peak day demand and the peak day plus fire curves is the volume needed for fire protection. In some systems, emergency storage volumes exceed volumes needed for fire fighting and may predominate.

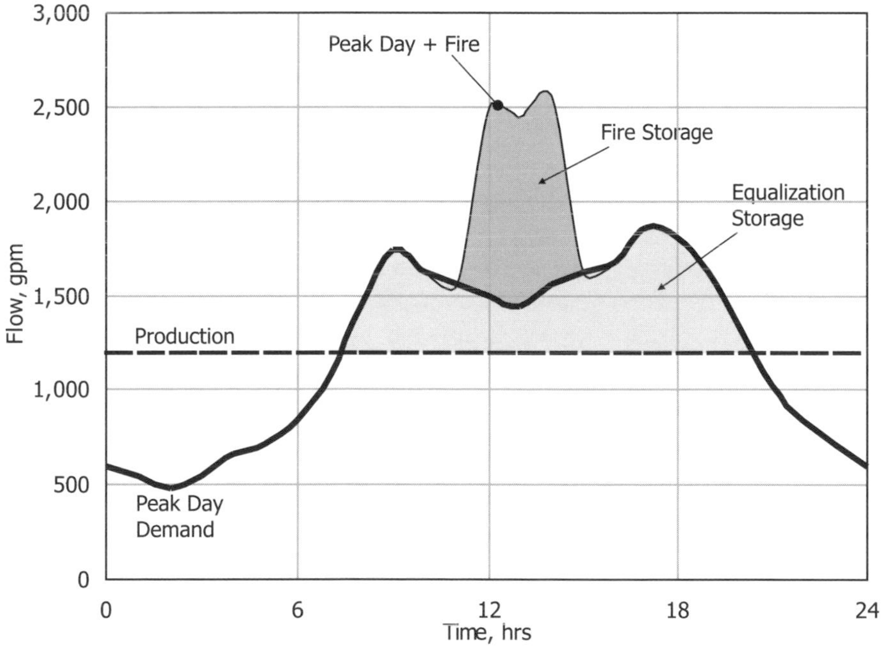

Figure 7.26
Determining tank volumes

The water level in a tank routinely fluctuates through a fill and drain cycle. Ideally, the tank water level should fluctuate by at least several feet during its cycle, whether that cycle is a full day or the time until the pump starts again. The EPS capability of modeling software is a valuable tool for predicting performance when comparing alternative tank and pipe sizes for various designs.

If the level does not drop much, the tank may be too large, or the pump may be set to cycle too frequently. If the tank water level drops very quickly during peak demands, then the tank may be too small. Increasing the volume of the tank to the next larger standard size may correct the problem. For the situation in which the tank cannot recover after maximum day or emergency conditions, the distribution system serving the tank may have insufficient capacity to satisfy demands. Several runs may be necessary to determine the problem (for example, an inadequate pump or a small pipe) and correct it.

The tank should not fully drain during emergency demand conditions [for example, a 2-hour, 1,500-gpm (0.095 m^3/s) fire]. If the tank drains completely during this time, then either the tank is too small or another source of water (such as a pump station or treatment plant) may not have performed as expected. Fire flow requirements can be found in AWWA M-31 (1998) and other sources from the fire insurance industry, as described on page 147.

If water quality problems due to chlorine decay are expected, then a water quality analysis should be conducted to determine whether or not the chlorine decay is due to the piping or the tank. When significant disinfectant decay is found to occur due to residence times within storage tanks, the volume may need to be reduced, or operating procedures may need to be modified (Grayman and Kirmeyer, 2000).

7.6 DEVELOPING SYSTEM HEAD CURVES FOR PUMP SELECTION/EVALUATION

The *system head curve* is a graph of head versus flow that shows the head required to move a given flow rate through the pump and into the distribution system. Prior to purchasing a pump, the system head curve that the pump will need to pump against must be determined. In a simple situation with a single pipe connecting two tanks, a system head curve can be generated without a model. When selecting a pump that will be used in a complicated water distribution system, especially one with looping and branching between the tanks on the suction and discharge sides of the pump, manual calculations only give a rough approximation to the system head curve. In such cases, a model is needed to derive a more exact solution.

The system head curve depends on tank water levels, the operation of other pump stations in the distribution system, the physical characteristics of the piping system, and the demands. Therefore, the system head curve uniquely reflects the system conditions at the time of the run. As a consequence, for any pump station, there is actually a band of multiple system head curves similar to those shown in Figure 7.27. The highest curves correspond to low suction-side tank levels, high discharge-side tank levels, low demands, other pumps/wells running, and possibly even throttled or closed valves. The lowest system head curves correspond to high suction-side tank levels, low discharge-side tank levels, no other sources operating, high demands (especially fire demands near the pump discharge), and all valves being open. For more information on system head curves, see Walski and Ormsbee (1989).

Figure 7.27
System head curves

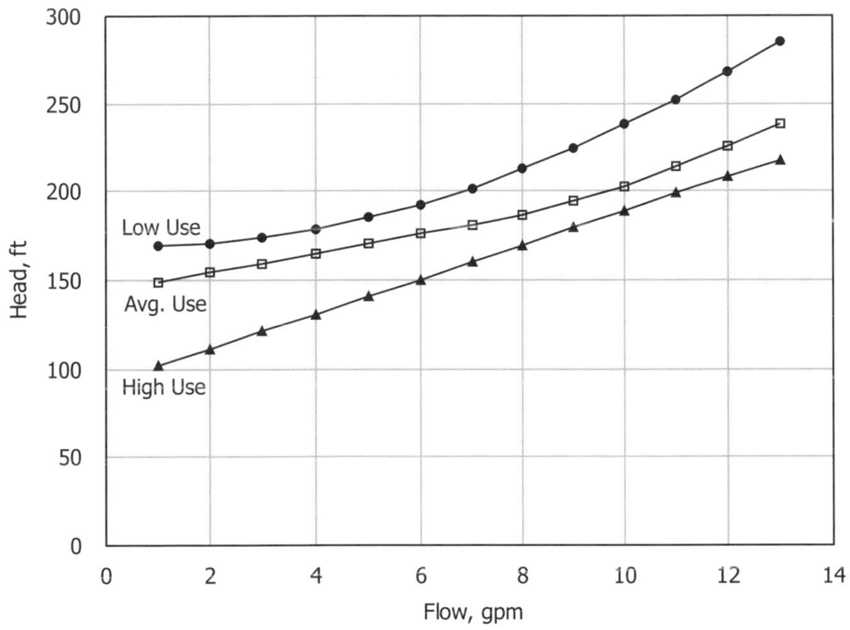

A single run of a water distribution model with a pump identifies a single point on a system head curve. Generating a system head curve for the full range of potential flows requires multiple steady-state runs of the model, with each steady-state run representing one point on the curve. The easiest way to arrive at the system head curve is to remove the proposed pump from the model, leaving the suction and discharge nodes in place, as shown in Figure 7.28. For the curve to be computed properly, a tank or reservoir must be present on each side of the pump.

Figure 7.28
Profile of system for system head curve

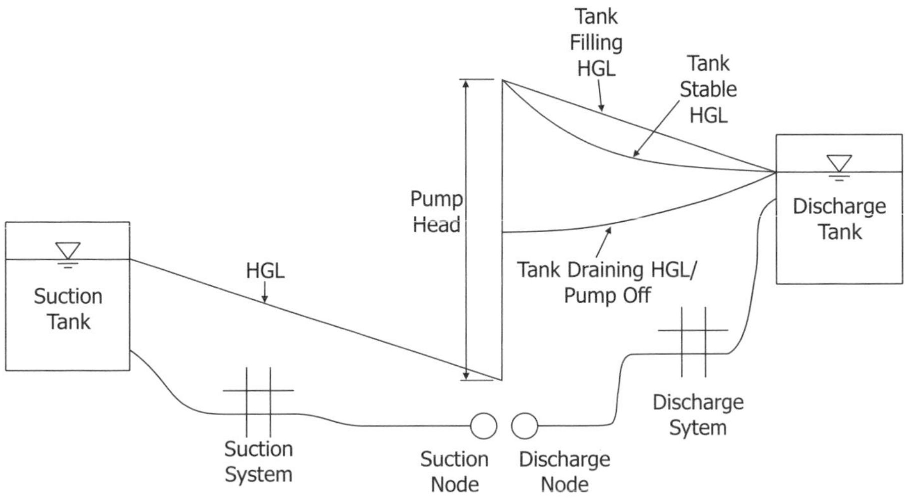

Generating a System Head Curve

1. Calibrate the model and identify suction and discharge nodes, but do not specify the pump between them yet.
2. Set the demands, tank water levels, and other operational conditions (for example, suction tank at 720 ft (220 m), discharge tank at 880 ft (270 m), average demands, well number 2 turned off).
3. Identify the range of flows that the pump may produce. For example, if selecting a 300 gpm (0.019 m^3/s) pump, use 0, 100, 200, 300, 400, and 600 gpm (0, 0.006, 0.013, 0.019, 0.025, 0.038 m^3/s).
4. Select the first flow and insert it as a demand on the suction node and an inflow on the discharge node.
5. Run the model and determine the HGL elevations at the suction and discharge nodes [for instance, the suction node HGL is 715 ft (218 m), and the discharge node HGL is 890 ft (271 m)].
6. Subtract the suction HGL from the discharge HGL to obtain the coordinates for a point on the system head curve [in this case, 100 gpm (0.006 m^3/s), and 175 ft (53 m)].
7. Repeat steps 4 through 6 until all the flow points have been generated.
8. Plot these points and connect them to obtain a system head curve.
9. If additional system head curves are desired, return to step 2 to set up new boundary conditions and demands, and repeat steps 3 through 8 until all desired curves are obtained.

The water that leaves the suction side pressure zone is identified as a demand on the suction node, while the water that enters the discharge side pressure zone is identified as an inflow (or negative demand) on the discharge node. The difference in head between the suction and discharge nodes as determined by the model is the head that must be added to move that flow rate through the pump (that is, between the two pressure zones). The flow rate at both the suction and discharge nodes is then changed and the model rerun to generate additional points on the curve, continuing until a full curve has been developed.

The curves should cover a reasonable range of conditions that the pump will experience. Once the system head curves are available, pump manufacturers can be contacted to determine which pumps (comparing model, casing, impeller size, and speed) will deliver the needed head at the desired flow rate with a high efficiency and sufficient net positive suction head (NPSH).

Overlaying the pump head curve that was obtained from the manufacturer with the system head curves will identify the pump operating points. The operating points can also be determined by inserting the proposed pump into the model and performing a series of runs for different conditions. The designer should check efficiency and NPSH for the range of operating points the pump is likely to encounter.

Usually, several pumps from different manufacturers will function properly. The decision about which one to buy will be based on a variety of factors, including the pump station floor plan, type of pump, operation and maintenance personnel preferences, cost, familiarity with a particular brand, and projected life-cycle energy cost. Calculating the energy cost is presented in Chapter 9. Once a pump has been selected, the designer should use EPS runs to determine how it will operate in the system over a variety of demands and emergency conditions.

7.7 SERVING LOWER PRESSURE ZONES

As a system expands into lower-lying areas, the customer elevations may not be within the serviceable range of the pressure zone containing the water source. Creating a lower pressure zone will prevent the delivery of excessive pressures to customers at low elevations. There is no consensus on the exact limit at which it becomes necessary to reduce pressure. However, for the majority of systems, the upper limit is set around 100 psi (690 kPa). Some systems, especially in hilly areas, may distribute water at up to 200 psi (1,380 kPa) and rely on PRVs in the service lines of individual customers to reduce pressures.

PRV Feeding into a Dead-end Pressure Zone

Installing a PRV to feed a dead-end zone is usually the easiest solution to controlling pressures in a low-elevation pressure zone. The key to this approach is to find a pressure (HGL) setting that will keep pressures within a reasonable range. Initially, the PRV is often installed to serve a small extension to the system. The PRV setting (or downstream pressure to be maintained) should be established, however, based on current projections of population growth and business development expected in the low area. The drop in pressure across the PRV should be approximately 40 to 60 psi, or 90 to 110 feet (275 to 413 kPa, or 27 to 34 m). A smaller cut in pressure will cause limitations on the size of the pressure zone to be served. Too large a cut may cause unacceptably high or low pressures for a band of customers along the divide.

The PRV should be located as close as possible to the contour line defining the boundary of the pressure zone. When the PRV is located far from the boundary, parallel pipes are often required to serve the two pressure zones. In this case, one parallel pipe would be located in the higher pressure zone, and the other parallel pipe would be in the neighboring, lower pressure zone.

Figure 7.29 shows the boundary line between a 1,810 ft (552 m) HGL zone and a 1,690 ft (515 m) HGL zone. The boundary is located at a ground elevation of 1,600 ft (488 m). If the PRV is placed exactly at 1,600 ft (488 m), then the upstream pressure will be 91 psi (627 kPa) and the downstream pressure will be 39 psi (269 kPa), both of which are reasonable pressures.

If the PRV is placed at 1,640 ft (500 m), the upstream pressure will be 74 psi (510 kPa) while the downstream pressure will be 22 psi (152 kPa). The lower pressure is only marginally acceptable, and with normal head losses, may prove unacceptable.

If the PRV is placed at 1,560 ft (475 m), the pressure will be cut from 108 psi (745 kPa) on the upstream side to 56 psi (386 kPa) on the downstream side. In this case, the pressure upstream of the valve is high enough that two pipes may be required in the street so that customers in this area can continue to be served by the lower pressure zone and not receive unacceptably high pressures.

Figure 7.29
Locating PRVs

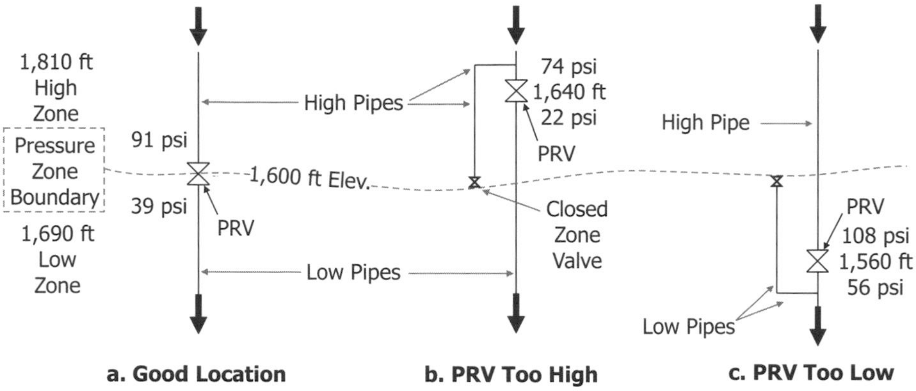

When selecting and modeling the PRV itself, it is important to note that a large PRV may not be able to precisely throttle small flows. Better control at low flow can be obtained by using a smaller PRV (for example, a 4-in. (100-mm) PRV for an 8-in. (200-mm) main). When a PRV has to pass much higher flows (to meet fire capacity requirements, for instance), the specifications should be checked to ensure that the smaller PRV will not significantly restrict flow. This restriction can also be examined by modeling the PRV's minor losses at high flow; however, some models do not account for a valve's minor losses when it is in the control (throttling) mode. When using such a model, the minor loss corresponding to the open PRV may be assigned to a pipe connecting to it. If the minor losses through the small PRV are too large at high flow, specifying a small PRV for normal flows and a larger PRV in parallel for higher flows can solve the problem.

In some cases, a PRV is used along a pipeline that carries water from a high source to a low area with few customers. The model may show that the PRV can successfully produce a very high pressure cut [say greater than 100 psi (690 kPa)], but it is important to check the specifications for the PRV to ensure that it can pass the flow rate with the required pressure cut without cavitating or eroding.

Lower Zone with a Tank

If there is a tank with its water level floating on the lower zone, setting the PRV becomes more difficult. If the PRV is set too high, the tank may overflow or be shut off by the altitude valve so that it no longer drains. If it is set too low, the tank may not fill adequately.

Usually, if the tank is far from the PRV, the head loss across the zone and the diurnal fluctuation in demand may be sufficient to make the tank cycle over the desired range. It may be necessary, however, to alter the PRV settings seasonally to achieve this range. The designer can find the right PRV settings and determine seasonal changes for those settings by using information obtained from EPS runs.

If the tank is close to the PRV, it will be virtually impossible to get the tank water level to fluctuate adequately using a single PRV setting. To get an adequate water level fluctuation, the designer could use a control valve, as described in the next section. Another option is to use a PRV with dual pilot controls, so that when the tank is in a "fill" mode, the higher setting prevails, and when the tank is in a "drain" mode, a lower setting prevails. The switching can be done using a timer so that the tank is in the fill mode when demands are low (typically at night). With this approach, there is no need for sophisticated programmable logic controllers; a simple timer will suffice. The model can check if the desired turnover of the tank can be achieved, and will calculate the amount of time it takes for the tank to refill. If the tank fills too quickly, the PRV can cause problems in the upstream pressure zone. If the tank fills too slowly, tank recovery may take longer than the designated time. The designer needs to check pressure fluctuations in the higher pressure zone and velocities in the transmission mains to ensure that they are acceptable.

Lower Zone Fed with Control Valves

If the utility desires controls that are more sophisticated than a PRV, a control valve can be used instead to regulate the filling and draining of the tank. A control valve can be programmed to operate based on fairly sophisticated logic by using information from the tank and other points in the system. The disadvantages of using a control valve are its reliance on expensive telemetry or SCADA equipment to provide information about tank water levels and its need for a distributed logic controller (or remote control by an operator) to operate the valve. Also, a backup power supply is required so that it can function properly during a power outage, whereas a PRV requires no power. The control valve also requires programming or alarming to handle any loss of signal or sensor, and is susceptible to lightning interference.

The control valve can have either a simple on/off control or an analog control. For example, the on/off control would open the valve when the tank is filling and close it when the tank is draining. In an analog control, the flow through the valve or the valve position is determined by tank level or some other analog input. The valve can be programmed to open wider as the tank water level falls. Conversely, the valve can hold a setting until the tank fills, and then switch to a more closed setting to enable the tank to drain. Using an on/off control is somewhat risky in the event that power should fail while the valve is shut. A throttled valve can at least pass some water during a power outage.

The controls can be tested by running simulations; however, valves are operated somewhat differently in models than they are in reality. With a real valve, the opening size is controlled (for example, it can be set at 40 percent open). In most models, though, the value that is controlled is the maximum flow, as with a flow control valve, or the minor loss coefficient, as with a throttling control valve.

Use of a flow control valve in the model to set a flow rate is the simplest approach to making sure that the piping and tank are sized correctly. This approach will not verify the sizing of the control valve, or be very helpful in selecting the valve opening that corresponds to a given set of conditions. To find this information, the valve should be modeled as a TCV with the minor loss coefficient being the variable controlled. The relationship between the minor loss coefficient and percent valve opening must be developed outside of the model using data supplied by the valve manufacturer.

Butterfly valves are usually used in this application because of their low cost and good throttling characteristics, provided the head loss in not too high. Ball valves are even better at control but are more expensive.

Conditions Upstream of the PRV or Control Valve

In some situations, the head loss in the upper zone above the boundary valve (whether it is a PRV or control valve) can become excessive [for example, if the demand of the lower zone is 500 gpm (0.032 m^3/s) and the water is delivered through a 6-in. (150-mm) pipe]. This head loss can cause pressures in the upper zone to drop to unacceptable levels. The long-term solution to this problem is to increase the carrying capacity of the pipes in the upper zone. This type of project is usually expensive, however, and an immediate solution may be necessary even if a large budget is not available.

The short-term solution may be the use of a combined PRV/PSV in the regulating vault. EPS runs can indicate what the PSV setting should be to adequately maintain pressures at the most critical (usually the highest) points in the upper zone. The combined PRV/PSV can be simulated in the model by placing a PSV immediately above the PRV. The designer should also look for any bottlenecks in the upper zone that can be inexpensively corrected to help feed the PRV.

7.8 REHABILITATION OF EXISTING SYSTEMS

Models are often used to assess the rehabilitation of older water distribution systems. The rehabilitation work may be necessary because of:

- The cumulative effect of tuberculation and scaling
- Increased demands due to new customers
- Excessive leakage
- Complete reconstruction of an area during system renewal
- Water quality problems

The problems associated with rehabilitation are somewhat more difficult than designing a new system, and include:

- Working with existing piping
- Numerous conflicts with other buried utilities
- The added importance of the condition of the paving
- The larger range of alternatives to be considered

The one way in which rehabilitation analysis is simpler than other design applications is that pressure zones and their boundaries are already defined, and are usually not being adjusted.

Instead of simply deciding on the size of pipe, the utility is faced with additional choices when performing rehabilitation. The utility can either replace existing pipes,

or keep them in place and parallel them for added capacity. In addition to new piping, the designer has a range of other options to choose from, including *pigging* (forcing a foam "pig" through the pipes using water pressure), cleaning with cement mortar or epoxy lining, installing inversion liners, sliplining, and pipe bursting. Each of these options will need to be modeled in a slightly different way, as described in the sections that follow.

Data Collection

Before modeling improvements, the designer needs to thoroughly analyze the existing system to determine its strengths and weaknesses. Because the system already exists, data are readily available. As was the case with model calibration, fire hydrant flow tests (see page 166) provide a great deal of information on the hydraulic capacity of the system. Other valuable tests include pipe roughness coefficient tests (see page 174) and the use of pressure recorders to obtain readings at key locations. The pipe roughness coefficient tests provide a view of the carrying capacity of individual pipes, while the chart recorders show how the system handles present day demand fluctuations. Any severe drops in pressure that occur during peak hours reveal capacity problems. More information on testing and calibration is available in Chapters 5 and 6.

Both the hydraulic capacity of the existing pipe and the structural integrity of the piping are important. If adequate metering is available, a water audit comparing water delivered to an area with metered water consumption can give an indication of the unaccounted-for water. A leak detection survey of the study area using sonic leak detection equipment, can also be conducted. A review of past work orders for pipe repairs and interviews with maintenance personnel can indicate if there are structural problems with the pipe. If a section of pipe must be excavated in that area for any reason, the designer should examine the inside of the pipe for tuberculation and scale, and the outside of the pipe for signs of corrosion damage. Graphitic corrosion of cast iron pipe may require scraping or even abrasive blast cleaning to reveal pits.

Records on service lines should also be assessed to determine if any service lines need to be replaced in conjunction with the mains, or if the old service lines can just be reconnected to the new mains. In some instances, it may be worthwhile to keep old mains in service simply to avoid the cost of renewing a large number of service lines. Other utilities have a policy of retiring old parallel mains and connecting old service lines to the new main when one has been installed.

Modeling Existing Conditions

With the results of fire flow and roughness coefficient tests, a detailed model of the study area can be calibrated. The calibration effort often reveals problems that are easily or inexpensively corrected, such as closed or partly closed valves. Clearly, opening a closed valve is very inexpensive compared with rehabilitation techniques or new piping.

The model of the existing system will also reveal which pipe segments are bottlenecks. These will usually be the segments with the highest velocities or highest hydraulic gradients. Field data should then be collected to corroborate the simulation results. Those segments that are bottlenecks will need to be replaced, paralleled, or rehabilitated. In general, peak hour demands and fire flow demands are the controlling conditions, and steady-state runs may be used to solve this type of problem.

Overview of Alternatives

Usually the decision to replace piping is the most expensive alternative, and should not be selected unless the existing piping is in poor structural condition. The decision of whether to parallel or rehabilitate the existing piping depends upon the design flow in the area. Rehabilitating the existing pipes will restore more of their original carrying capacity but will not greatly increase the nominal diameter of the pipe. Pipe bursting, a technique in which the old pipe is broken in place, allows a slightly larger pipe to be pulled through the opening where the old pipe once lay. If the future flows are going to be significantly greater than the original flows in the pipes, then rehabilitation will not provide sufficient capacity, and new pipes roughly paralleling the old system are needed. A schematic of the evaluation process recommended for replacement decisions is illustrated in Figure 7.30, and is discussed in the following sections.

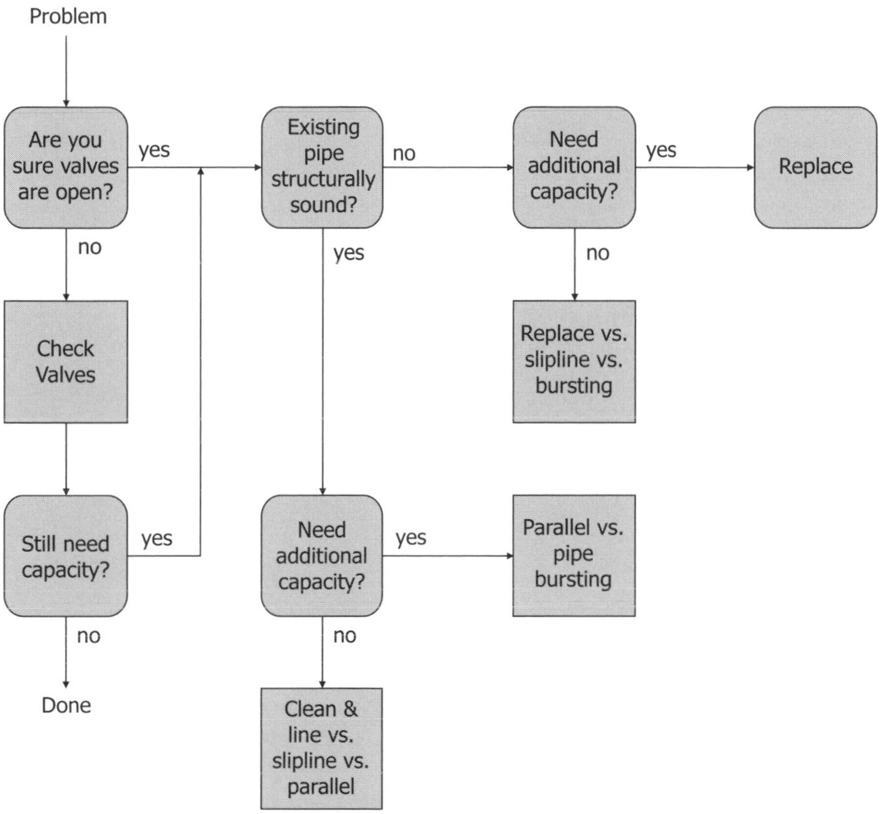

Figure 7.30
Overview of pipe rehabilitation options

Replacement. Most utilities will not have sufficient resources to replace large portions of the distribution system. With this limitation in mind, the designer must be extremely selective in identifying pipes for replacement. The model can answer questions as to which pipes are inadequate from a hydraulic standpoint. Information from the simulation needs to be combined with other information, such as which pipes have experienced breaks, leakage, and water quality problems in order to make informed decisions. In this way, the worst pipes in the system are identified for replacement. By examining fire flows at different points in the study area, the model will indicate those pipes with the most severe hydraulic limitations. In most cases, these will be old, unlined, 4-in. (100-mm) and 6-in. (150-mm) pipes. These pipes also tend to have the highest break rates because they have the lowest beam strength. The designer should selectively replace these pipes in the model and rerun it. Subsequent runs will then indicate the next worst bottlenecks. The designer should also be mindful that in some cases the worst hydraulic limitations may be outside of the study area.

Paralleling. If the existing piping is found to be in sound structural condition, pipes will not need to be replaced. The emphasis should then be placed on determining which lengths of pipe have the poorest hydraulic carrying capacities when compared with the required capacities. Fire hydrant flow tests can indicate which portions of the study area have problems, but the exact pipe(s) causing the problems is best determined through model runs.

Rather than paralleling or replacing pipes sporadically throughout the study area, the best solution will typically consist of installing a loop or a "backbone" of larger pipe [16-in. (400-mm)] through the heart of the study area. This new main will reduce the distance that water must travel from a large pipe to a fire hydrant. If the new parallel pipe is significantly larger than the existing pipe, hydrants should be transferred from the existing pipe to the new pipe to take advantage of the greater flow capacity. The designer also needs to remember that the available fire flow at a node in the model is not the same thing as the available fire flow from a hydrant near that node, because of the distance between the node and the hydrant and the associated losses (see page 173).

Pipe Cleaning and Lining (Non-Structural Rehabilitation). Pipe cleaning may be an economical and effective alternative to installing additional pipe to restore lost carrying capacity if:

- the pipe is structurally sound;
- future demands are not expected to be significantly greater than the demands for which the system was designed; and
- the loss in carrying capacity due to pipe tuberculation, scaling, or other deposits is significant.

For smaller pipe sizes [4-, 6-, and 8-in. (100, 150, and 200-mm) pipe], installing new pipe is usually only slightly more expensive than pipe rehabilitation. However, as pipe diameters increase, the economics of pipe rehabilitation by cleaning become very attractive. Pipe cleaning by scraping or pigging is most economical in situations in which the installation of new pipe is unusually expensive due to interference with other buried utilities or because of expensive pavement restoration costs.

The effects of pipe cleaning can be simulated by making the roughness factor of the cleaned pipe more favorable. Usually, the Hazen-Williams C-factor can be increased to values on the order of 100 to 120, with the higher values usually achieved in larger pipes. A C-factor increase from 90 to 110 will not justify the costs of pipe cleaning, but an increase from 40 to 110 is likely to correct a hydraulic deficiency at a reasonable cost.

Once the pipe is cleaned, the decision on whether to cement-line a main is usually based on water quality considerations. If the pipe is not expected to experience corrosion, scaling, or deposition problems in the future, the pipe may be left without a liner. In most cases, however, it is better to line the pipe to maintain the benefits of the cleaning. Cement mortar or epoxy, which does not decrease the inner diameter significantly, is typically the preferred lining material for distribution mains, but sliplining can also be used.

In modeling any kind of rehabilitation involving a liner, it is important to use the actual inner diameter of the liner pipe in any model runs.

Sliplining (Structural Rehabilitation). Several methods of rehabilitation that also increase the structural strength of the pipe are available. These include fold-and-form piping, swagelining, and sliplining. *Fold-and-form-pipes* are folded for easy insertion within the existing pipe, and then expanded once in place. *Swagelining* involves pulling the liner pipe through a die, temporarily reducing its size so that it can be easily inserted in the existing pipe. *Sliplining* is performed by pulling a slightly smaller pipe through the cleaned water main (Figure 7.31). *Inversion lining* (a type of sliplining) utilizes sock-like liners that must be cured in place. This procedure is usually practical only in low-pressure applications, because the thickness of the required inversion liner becomes excessive as pressures increase.

This liner used in sliplining is usually plastic and quite smooth (C-factor of 130). The diameter of the liner pipe, however, is somewhat different from the original pipe; thus, the actual inner diameter of the liner pipe must be used in the model. Structural rehabilitation is less attractive than cement-mortar lining for situations in which there are numerous services that must be reconnected to the pipe. Structural rehabilitation can be modeled by decreasing the effective roughness of the pipe and decreasing the diameter of the pipe being lined to coincide with the correct values for the liner.

Figure 7.31
Sliplining procedure

Pipe Bursting. Pipe bursting is the only rehabilitation technique that actually can increase the inner diameter of a pipe. In this technique, a mole is passed through a pipe made from a brittle material (cast iron or asbestos cement), and the pipe is burst. The fragments are forced into the surrounding soil and a liner pipe of the same size as the original pipe (or slightly larger) is then pulled through the resulting hole. Excavation work will be necessary if there are service lines that must be reconnected to the new pipe.

Evaluation

In distribution system rehabilitation studies, the number of alternative solutions tends to be much larger than in most other distribution design problems. Exploring all of the possibilities is the only way to ensure that the most cost-effective solution, based on whole life-cycle cost, is chosen. More than one alternative can solve a design problem, and each alternative has its own costs and benefits.

7.9 TRADEOFFS BETWEEN ENERGY AND CAPITAL COSTS

Near pumping stations, it may be worthwhile in some cases to use larger pipes in order to reduce head losses and, consequently, energy costs. The distribution system costs affected by pipe sizing include capital costs for piping and the present worth of energy costs. These costs can be given by Equation 7.9.

$$TC = \sum_{allpipes} f(D, x) + \frac{PW\int k_1 Qp(h_1 + k_2 D^{-4.87})}{e} \qquad (7.9)$$

where
TC = total life-cycle costs ($)
$f(D,x)$ = capital cost function
D = diameter (ft, m)
x = set of pipe-laying conditions
PW = present worth factor for energy costs
k_1 = unit conversion factor for energy
Q = actual flow over time (gpm, l/s)
p = price of energy ($/kW-hr)
h_1 = lift energy (ft, m)
k_2 = coefficient describing characteristics of system
e = wire-to-water efficiency (%)

The above equation cannot be solved analytically for a complex network. However, the problem can be simplified, since most of the pipes in a typical distribution system have only a negligible effect on energy costs. It is usually only the pipes from the pump stations to the nearest tanks that can have a significant impact on energy costs. For a series of pipes between two tanks, Walski (1984) provides an analytical solution for optimal pipe sizes. For the simplest case of a single pipe between two tanks, the solution can be viewed as shown in Figure 7.32.

Even though the present worth of total energy cost is fairly large when compared to construction costs, most of this energy is being used to overcome the difference in head between pressure zones (that is, it is used for static lift). Since only the energy cost used in overcoming friction losses is a function of pipe diameter, only this portion of the energy cost is involved in the trade-off with capital costs. Furthermore, the cost of the pump station itself, including the building, land, piping, valves, SCADA, and engineering are independent of head loss. The initial construction cost of pump stations is nor very sensitive to head loss, and need not be considered in this cost analysis.

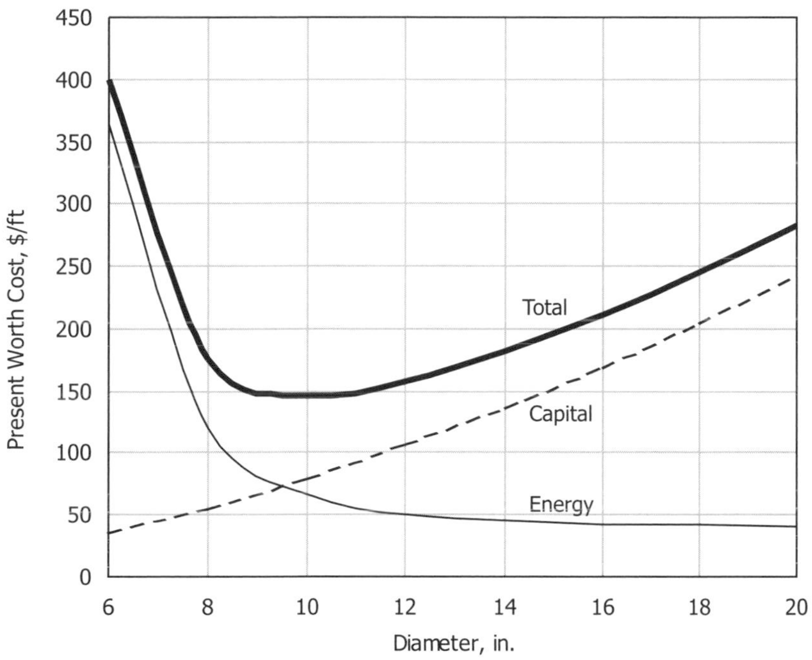

Figure 7.32 Example of relationship between capital and energy costs in a pumped pipeline

The optimal velocity to be used in pipe sizing depends on the relative costs of energy and construction, the interest rate, the efficiency of the pumps, and the ratio of peak flow in the pipes to average flow. For medium-size pumps [approximately 1,000 gpm (60 l/s)], Walski (1983) showed that the optimal velocity would be on the order of 6 ft/s (2 m/s) at peak flow when the ratio of peak flow to average flow is 2. For pipes with a ratio of peak to average flow of 1.25, the optimal velocity at peak flow would be on the order of 4.5 ft/s (1.5 m/s).

Several investigators (Murphy, Dandy, and Simpson, 1994; and Walters, Halhal, Savic, and Ouazar, 1999) have applied genetic algorithms to determine optimal pipe sizes in pumped systems.

REFERENCES

American Water Works Association. (1989). "Installation, Field Testing, and Maintenance of Fire Hydrants." *AWWA Manual M-17*, Denver, Colorado.

American Water Works Association. (1998). "Distribution System Requirements for Fire Protection." AWWA Manual M-31, Denver, Colorado.

Babbitt, H. E., and Doland, J. J. (1931). *Water Supply Engineering*. McGraw-Hill, New York, New York.

Camp, T. R. (1939). "Economic Pipe Sizes for Water Distribution Systems." *Transactions of the American Society of Civil Engineers*, 104, 190.

Cesario, A. L. (1995). *Modeling, Analysis, and Design of Water Distribution Systems*. AWWA, Denver, Colorado.

Dandy, G. C., Simpson, A. R., and Murphy, L. J. (1996). "An Improved Genetic Algorithm for Pipe Network Optimization." *Water Resources Research*, 32(2), 449.

Goulter, I. C., Walski, T. M., Mays, L. W., Sekarya, A. B. A., Bouchart, R., and Tung, Y. K. (2000). "Reliability Analysis." *Water Distribution Handbook*, Mays, L. W., ed., McGraw-Hill, New York, New York.

Grayman, W. M., and Kirmeyer, G. J. (2000). "Water Quality in Storage." *Water Distribution Handbook*, Mays, L. W., ed., McGraw-Hill, New York, New York.

Great Lakes and Upper Mississippi River Board of State Public Health & Environmental Managers (GLUMB). (1992). *Recommended Standards for Water Works*. Albany, New York.

Hydraulic Institute. (1979). *Engineering Data Book*. Hydraulic Institute, Cleveland, Ohio.

Lansey, K.E. (2000). "Optimal Design of Water Distribution Systems." *Water Distribution Systems Handbook*, Mays, L.W., ed., McGraw-Hill, New York, New York.

Mays, L.W., ed. (1989). *Reliability Analysis of Water Distribution Systems*. ASCE Task Committee on Risk and Reliability Analysis, New York, New York.

Murphy, L.J., Dandy, G.C., and Simpson, A.R. (1994). "Optimal Design and Operation of Pumped Water Distribution Systems." *Proceedings of the Conference on Hydraulics in Civil Engineering*, Australian Institute of Engineers, Brisbane, Australia.

Savic, D. A., and Walters G. A. (1997). "Genetic Algorithms for Least-Cost Design of Water Distribution Networks." *Journal of Water Resources Planning and Management*, ASCE, 123(2), 67.

Schaake, J. C., and Lai, D. (1969). "Linear Programming and Dynamic Programming Applied to Water Distribution Network Design." *MIT Hydrodynamics Lab Report 116*, Cambridge, Massachusetts.

Tchobanoglous, G. (1998). "Theory of Centrifugal Pumps." Sanks, R.L., ed., *Pumping Station Design*, Butterworth, Boston, Massachusetts.

Wagner, J., Shamir, U., and Marks, D. (1988a). "Water Distribution System Reliability: Analytical Methods." *Journal of Water Resources Planning and Management*, ASCE, 114(2), 253.

Wagner, J., Shamir, U., and Marks, D. (1988b). "Water Distribution System Reliability: Simulation Methods." *Journal of Water Resources Planning and Management*, ASCE, 114(2), 276.

Walski, T. M. (1983). "Energy Efficiency through Pipe Design." *Journal of the American Water Works Association*, 75(10), 492.

Walski, T.M. (1984). *Analysis of Water Distribution Systems*. Van Nostrand Reinhold, New York, New York.

Walski, T. M. (1985). "State-of-the-Art: Pipe Network Optimization." *Computer Applications in Water Resources*, Torno, H., ed., ASCE, New York, New York.

Walski, T. M., Brill, E. D., Gessler, J., Goulter, I. C., Jeppson, R. M., Lansey, K., Lee, H. L., Liebman, J. C., Mays, L. W., Morgan, D. R., and Ormsbee, L. E. (1987). "Battle of the Network Models: Epilogue." *Journal of Water Resources Planning and Management*, ASCE, 113(2), 191.

Walski, T. M., and Ormsbee, L. (1989). "Developing System Head Curves for Water Distribution Pumping." *Journal of the American Water Works Association*, 81(7), 63.

Walski, T. M. (1993). "Practical Aspects of Providing Reliability in Water Distribution Systems." *Reliability Engineering and Systems Safety*, Elsevier, 42(1), 13.

Walski, T. M. (1995). "Optimization and Pipe Sizing Decisions." *Journal of Water Resources Planning and Management*, ASCE, 121(4), 340.

Walski, T. M. (2000). "Water Distribution Storage Tank Hydraulic Design." *Water Distribution Handbook*, Mays, L. W., ed., McGraw-Hill, New York, New York.

Walski, T.M., Youshock, M., and Rhee, H. (2000). "Use of Modeling in Decision Making for Water Distribution Master Planning." *Proceedings of the ASCE EWRI Conference*, Minneapolis, Minnesota.

Walski, T.M. (2001) "The Wrong Paradigm—Why Water Distribution Optimization Doesn't Work," *Accepted for Journal of Water Resources Planning and Management*, ASCE, 127(2).

Walters, G.A., Halhal, D., Savic, D. and Ouazar, D (1999). "Improved Design of 'Anytown' Distribution Network Using Structured Messy Genetic Algorithms." *Urban Water*, 1(1), 23.

DISCUSSION TOPICS AND PROBLEMS

Earn CEUs — Read Chapters 7 and 8 and complete the problems. Submit your work to Haestad Methods and earn up to 1.5 CEUs. See *Continuing Education Units* on page xiii for more information, or visit www.haestad.com/wdm-ceus/.

7.1 *English Units* - For the system in Figure 7.33, find the available fire flow at node J-7 if the minimum allowable residual pressure at this node is 20 psi. Assume that pumps P1 and P2 are operating and that pump P3 is off. (This network is also given in Prob7-01.wcd.)

Hint: Connect a constant head (reservoir) node to junction node J-7 with a short, large-diameter pipe. Set the HGL of the constant head node to the elevation of node J-7 plus the required residual pressure head, and examine the rate at which water flows into it.

Figure 7.33

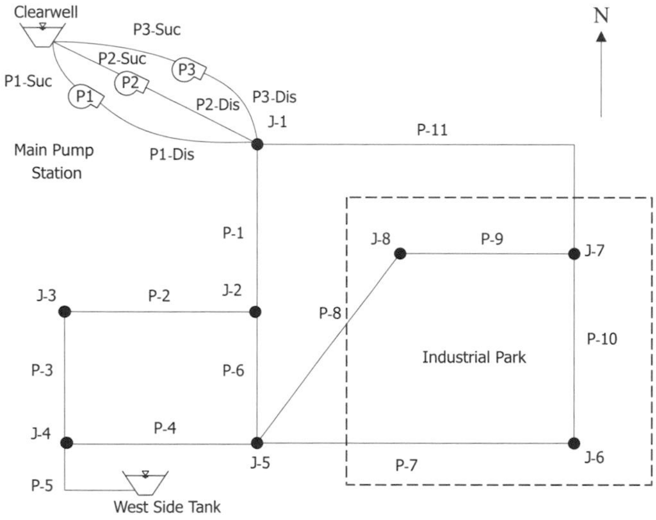

Node Label	Elevation (ft)	Demand (gpm)
Clearwell	630	N/A
West Side Tank	915	N/A
J-1	730	0
J-2	755	125
J-3	765	50
J-4	775	25
J-5	770	30
J-6	790	220
J-7	810	80
J-8	795	320
P1	627	N/A
P2	627	N/A
P3	627	N/A

Pipe Label	Length (ft)	Diameter (in.)	Hazen-Williams C-factor
P1-Suc	50	18	115
P1-Dis	120	16	115
P2-Suc	50	18	115
P2-Dis	120	16	115
P3-Suc	50	18	115
P3-Dis	120	16	115
P-1	2,350	12	110
P-2	1,500	6	105
P-3	1,240	6	105
P-4	1,625	12	110
P-5	225	10	110
P-6	1,500	12	110
P-7	4,230	6	105
P-8	3,350	6	105
P-9	2,500	6	105
P-10	2,550	6	105
P-11	3,300	4	85

Pump Curve Data

	P1		P2		P3	
	Head (ft)	Flow (gpm)	Head (ft)	Flow (gpm)	Head (ft)	Flow (gpm)
Shutoff	305	0	305	0	305	0
Design	295	450	295	450	295	450
Max Operating	260	650	260	650	260	650

a) Which node has the lowest pressure under the fire flow condition?

b) Is the available fire flow at node J-7 sufficient for the industrial park?

c) If the available fire flow is insufficient, what are the reasons for the low available fire flow?

d) Analyze alternatives for improving the available fire flow to node J-7.

SI Units - For the system in Figure 7.33, find the available fire flow at node J-7 if the minimum allowable residual pressure at this node is 138 kPa. Assume that pumps P1 and P2 are operating and that pump P3 is off. (This network is also given in Prob7-01m.wcd.)

Hint: Connect a constant head (reservoir) node to junction node J-7 with a short, large-diameter pipe. Set the HGL of the constant head node to the elevation of node J-7 plus the required residual pressure head, and examine the rate at which water flows into it.

Pipe Label	Length (m)	Diameter (mm)	Hazen-Williams C-factor
P1-Suc	15.2	457	115
P1-Dis	36.6	406	115
P2-Suc	15.2	457	115
P2-Dis	36.3	406	115
P3-Suc	15.2	457	115
P3-Dis	36.6	406	115
P-1	716.3	305	110
P-2	457.2	152	105
P-3	378.0	152	105
P-4	495.3	305	110
P-5	68.6	254	110
P-6	457.2	305	110
P-7	1,289.3	152	105
P-8	1,021.1	152	105
P-9	762.0	152	105
P-10	777.2	152	105
P-11	1,005.8	102	85

Node Label	Elevation (m)	Demand (l/s)
Clearwell	192.0	N/A
West Side Tank	278.9	N/A
J-1	222.5	0
J-2	230.1	7.9
J-3	233.2	3.2
J-4	236.2	1.6
J-5	234.7	1.9
J-6	240.8	13.9
J-7	246.9	5.0
J-8	242.3	20.2
P1	191	N/A
P2	191	N/A
P3	191	N/A

Pump Curve Data

	P1		P2		P3	
	Head (m)	Flow (l/s)	Head (m)	Flow (l/s)	Head (m)	Flow (l/s)
Shutoff	93.0	0	93.0	0	93.0	0
Design	89.9	28.4	89.9	28.4	89.9	28.4
Max Operating	79.2	41.0	79.2	41.0	79.2	41.0

a) Which node has the lowest pressure under the fire flow condition?

b) Is the available fire flow at node J-7 sufficient for the industrial park?

c) If the available fire flow is insufficient, what are the reasons for the low available fire flow?

d) Analyze alternatives for improving the available fire flow to node J-7.

7.2 *English Units* - A disadvantage associated with branched water systems, such as the one given in Problem 3.3, is that more customers can be out of service during a main break. Improve the reliability of this system by adding the pipelines in the table below. (This network can also be found in Prob7-02.wcd.)

Pipe Label	Start Node	End Node	Length (ft)	Diameter (in.)	Hazen-Williams C-factor
P-20	J-1	J-8	11,230	12	130
P-21	J-2	J-4	3,850	8	130
P-22	J-5	J-7	1,500	8	130
P-23	J-11	J-10	680	6	130

a) Complete the tables below for the new looped system.

Pipe Label	Flow (gpm)	Hydraulic Gradient (ft/1000 ft)
P-1		
P-2		
P-3		
P-4		
P-5		
P-6		
P-7		
P-8		
P-9		
P-10		
P-11		
P-12		

Node Label	HGL (ft)	Pressure (psi)
J-1		
J-2		
J-3		
J-4		
J-5		
J-6		
J-7		
J-8		
J-9		
J-10		
J-11		
J-12		

b) You can simulate a main break by closing a pipeline. Complete the tables below for the looped system if pipe P-3 is closed.

Pipe Label	Flow (gpm)	Hydraulic Gradient (ft/1000 ft)
P-1		
P-2		
P-3		
P-4		
P-5		
P-6		
P-7		
P-8		
P-9		
P-10		
P-11		
P-12		

Node Label	HGL (ft)	Pressure (psi)
J-1		
J-2		
J-3		
J-4		
J-5		
J-6		
J-7		
J-8		
J-9		
J-10		
J-11		
J-12		

SI Units - A disadvantage associated with branched water systems, such as the one given in Problem 3.3, is that more customers can be out of service during a main break. Improve the reliability of this system by adding the pipelines in the table below. (This network can also be found in Prob7-02m.wcd.)

Pipe Label	Start Node	End Node	Length (m)	Diameter (mm)	Hazen-Williams C-Factor
P-20	J-1	J-8	3422.9	305	130
P-21	J-2	J-4	1173.5	203	130
P-22	J-5	J-7	457.2	203	130
P-23	J-11	J-10	207.3	152	130

a) Complete the tables below for the new looped system.

Pipe Label	Flow (l/s)	Hydraulic Gradient (m/km)
P-1		
P-2		
P-3		
P-4		
P-5		
P-6		
P-7		
P-8		
P-9		
P-10		
P-11		
P-12		

Node Label	HGL (m)	Pressure (kPa)
J-1		
J-2		
J-3		
J-4		
J-5		
J-6		
J-7		
J-8		
J-9		
J-10		
J-11		
J-12		

b) You can simulate a main break by closing a pipeline. Complete the tables below for the looped system if pipe P-3 is closed.

Pipe Label	Flow (l/s)	Hydraulic Gradient (m/km)
P-1		
P-2		
P-3		
P-4		
P-5		
P-6		
P-7		
P-8		
P-9		
P-10		
P-11		
P-12		

Node Label	HGL (m)	Pressure (kPa)
J-1		
J-2		
J-3		
J-4		
J-5		
J-6		
J-7		
J-8		
J-9		
J-10		
J-11		
J-12		

7.3 Analyze the following changes to the hydraulic network for the system shown in Problem 4.3.

a) Increase the diameters of pipes P-16, P-17, and P-19 from 6 in. to 8 in. Are head losses in these lines significantly reduced? Why or why not?

b) Increase the head of the High Field pump to 120% of current head. Is this head increase sufficient to overcome the head produced by the Newtown pump? What is the discharge of the High Field pump station?

c) Decrease the water surface elevation of the Central Tank by 30 ft. Recall that the tank is modeled as a reservoir for the steady-state condition. How does the overall system respond to this change? Is the High Field pump station operating? Is the pump operating efficiently? Why or why not?

7.4 *English Units* - Analyze each of the following conditions for the hydraulic network given in Problem 4.2 (see page 155). Use the data provided in Problem 4.2 as the base condition for each of the scenarios listed below. Complete the table for these scenarios.

a) Increase the demand at nodes J-7, J-8, J-9, and J-10 to 175% of base demands.

b) Increase the demand at node J-6 to 300 gpm.

c) Change the diameter of all 6-in. pipes to 8 in.

d) Decrease the HGL in the West Carrolton Tank by 15 ft.

e) Increase the demands at nodes J-7, J-8, J-9, and J-10 to 175% of base demands, and change the diameter of all 6-in. pipes to 8 in.

f) Decrease the HGL in the West Carrolton Tank by 15 ft and increase the demand at node J-6 to 300 gpm.

g) Increase the demands at nodes J-7, J-8, J-9, and J-10 to 175% of base demands, change the diameter of all 6-in. pipes to 8 in., and drop the HGL in the West Carrolton Tank by 15 ft.

Scenario	Time (hr)	Pump Discharge (gpm)	Pressure at J-1 (psi)	Pressure at J-3 (psi)	Miamisburg Tank Discharge (gpm)
Part (a)	Midnight				
Part (b)	2:00 am				
Part (c)	7:00 pm				
Part (d)	Noon				
Part (e)	6:00 am				
Part (f)	9:00 pm				
Part (g)	Midnight				

SI Units - Analyze each of the following conditions for the hydraulic network given in Problem 4.2 (see page 155). Use the data provided in Problem 4.2 as the base condition for each of the scenarios listed below. Complete the table for each of the scenarios presented.

a) Increase the demand at nodes J-7, J-8, J-9, and J-10 to 175% of base demands.

b) Increase the demand at node J-6 to 18.9 l/s.

c) Change the diameter of all 152-mm pipes to 203 mm.

d) Decrease the HGL in the West Carrolton Tank by 4.6 m.

e) Increase the demands at nodes J-7, J-8, J-9, and J-10 to 175% of base demands, and change the diameter of all 152-mm pipes to 203 mm.

f) Decrease the HGL in the West Carrolton Tank by 4.6 m and increase the demand at node J-6 to 18.9 l/s.

g) Increase the demands at nodes J-7, J-8, J-9, and J-10 by 175%, change the diameter of all 152-mm pipes to 203 mm, and drop the HGL in the West Carrolton Tank by 4.6 m.

Scenario	Time (hr)	Pump Discharge (l/s)	Pressure at J-1 (kPa)	Pressure at J-3 (kPa)	Miamisburg Tank Discharge (l/s)
Part (a)	Midnight				
Part (b)	2:00 am				
Part (c)	7:00 pm				
Part (d)	Noon				
Part (e)	6:00 am				
Part (f)	9:00 pm				
Part (g)	Midnight				

7.5 *English Units* - Determine the available fire flows at node J-8 for each of the conditions presented below. Assume that the minimum system pressure under fire flow conditions is 20 psi. Use the system illustrated in Problem 7.1.

a) Only pump P1 running.

b) Pumps P1 and P2 running.

c) Pumps P1, P2, and P3 running.

d) The HGL in the West Side Tank increased to 930 ft and pumps P1 and P2 running.

e) Pipe P-11 replaced with a new 12-in. ductile iron line (C=120) and pumps P1 and P2 running.

f) Pipe P-11 replaced with a new 12-in. ductile iron line (C=120) and all pumps running.

Scenario	Available Fire Flow at Node J-8 (gpm)
Part (a)	
Part (b)	
Part (c)	
Part (d)	
Part (e)	
Part (f)	

SI Units - Determine the available fire flows at node J-8 for each of the conditions presented below. Assume that the minimum system pressure under fire flow conditions is 138 kPa. Use the system illustrated in Problem 7.1.

a) Only pump P1 running.

b) Pumps P1 and P2 running.

c) Pumps P1, P2, and P3 running.

d) The HGL in the West Side Tank increased to 283.5 m and pumps P1 and P2 running.

e) Pipe P-11 replaced with a new 305-mm ductile iron line (C=120) and pumps P1 and P2 running.

f) Pipe P-11 replaced with a new 305-mm ductile iron line (C=120) and all pumps running

Scenario	Available Fire Flow at Node J-8 (l/s)
Part (a)	
Part (b)	
Part (c)	
Part (d)	
Part (e)	
Part (f)	

7.6 *English Units* - A new subdivision is to tie in near node J-10 of the existing system shown in Figure 7.34. Use the information from the data tables below to construct a model of the existing system, or open the file Prob70-6.wcd. Answer the questions that follow.

Figure 7.34

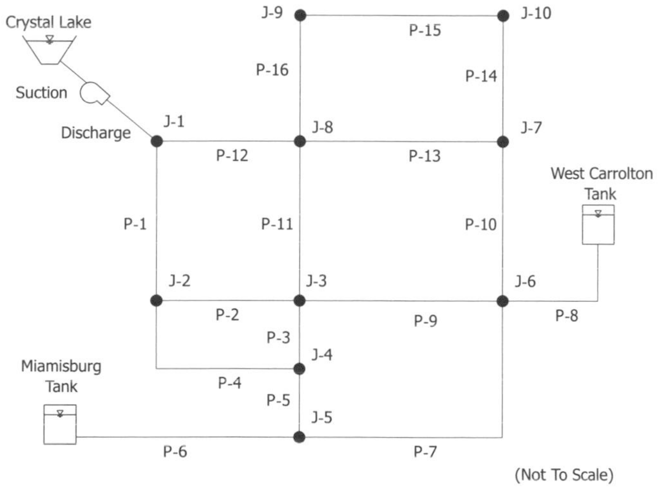

Pipe Label	Diameter (in.)	Length (ft)	Hazen-Williams C-factor
Discharge	21	220	120
Suction	24	25	120
P-1	6	1,250	110
P-2	6	835	110
P-3	8	550	130
P-4	6	1,010	110
P-5	8	425	130
P-6	8	990	125
P-7	8	2,100	105
P-8	6	560	110
P-9	8	745	100
P-10	10	1,100	115
P-11	8	1,330	110
P-12	10	890	115
P-13	10	825	115
P-14	6	450	120
P-15	6	690	120
P-16	6	500	120

Node Label	Elevation (ft)	Demand (gpm)
J-1	390	120
J-2	420	75
J-3	425	35
J-4	430	50
J-5	450	0
J-6	445	155
J-7	420	65
J-8	415	0
J-9	420	55
J-10	420	20

Tank Label	Minimum Elevation (ft)	Initial Elevation (ft)	Maximum Elevation (ft)	Tank Diameter (ft)
Miamisburg Tank	535	550	570	50
West Carrolton Tank	525	545	565	36

Reservoir Label	Elevation (ft)
Crystal Lake	320

Pump Curve Data

Pump Label	Shutoff Head (ft)	Design Head (ft)	Design Discharge (gpm)	Maximum Operating Head (ft)	Maximum Operating Discharge (gpm)
PMP-1	245	230	1,100	210	1,600

a) Determine the fire flow that can be delivered to node J-10 with a 20 psi residual.

b) Given the range of possible water level elevations in West Carrolton Tank, what is the approximate acceptable elevation range for nearby customers to ensure adequate pressures under normal (non-fire) demand conditions?

c) What can be done for customers that may be above this range?

d) What can be done for customers that may be below this range?

SI Units - A new subdivision is to tie in near node J-10 of the existing system shown in Figure 7.34. Use the information from the data tables below to construct a model of the existing system, or open the file Prob7-06m.wcd.

Pipe Label	Diameter (mm)	Length (m)	Hazen-Williams C-factor
Discharge	533	67.1	120
Suction	610	7.6	120
P-1	152	381.0	110
P-2	152	254.5	110
P-3	203	167.6	130
P-4	152	307.9	110
P-5	203	129.5	130
P-6	203	301.8	125
P-7	203	640.1	105
P-8	152	170.7	110
P-9	203	227.1	100
P-10	254	335.3	115
P-11	203	405.4	110
P-12	254	271.3	115
P-13	254	251.5	115
P-14	152	137.2	120
P-15	152	210.3	120
P-16	152	152.4	120

Node Label	Elevation (m)	Demand (l/s)
J-1	118.9	7.6
J-2	128.0	4.7
J-3	129.5	2.2
J-4	131.1	3.2
J-5	137.2	0.0
J-6	135.6	9.8
J-7	128.0	4.1
J-8	126.5	0.0
J-9	128.0	3.5
J-10	128.0	1.3

Tank Label	Maximum Elevation (m)	Initial Elevation (m)	Minimum Elevation (m)	Tank Diameter (m)
Miamisburg Tank	173.7	167.6	163.1	15.2
West Carrolton Tank	172.2	166.1	160.0	11.0

Reservoir Label	Elevation (m)
Crystal Lake	97.5

Pump Curve Data

Pump Label	Shutoff Head (m)	Design Head (m)	Design Discharge (l/s)	Maximum Operating Head (m)	Maximum Operating Discharge (l/s)
PMP-1	74.7	70.1	69.4	64.0	100.9

a) Determine the fire flow that can be delivered to node J-10 with a 138 kPa residual.

b) Given the range of possible water level elevations in West Carrolton Tank, what is the approximate acceptable elevation range for nearby customers to ensure adequate pressures under normal (non-fire) demand conditions?

c) What can be done for customers that may be above this range?

d) What can be done for customers that may be below this range?

7.7 A distribution system for a proposed subdivision is shown in Figure 7.35. Construct a model of the system using the data tables provided, or the file Prob7-07.wcd. This system will tie into an existing water main at node J-10. The water main hydrant flow test values measured at node J-10 are given below.

Fire Hydrant Number	Static Pressure (psi)	Residual Pressure (psi)	Pitot Pressure (psi)
2139	74	60	20

Figure 7.35

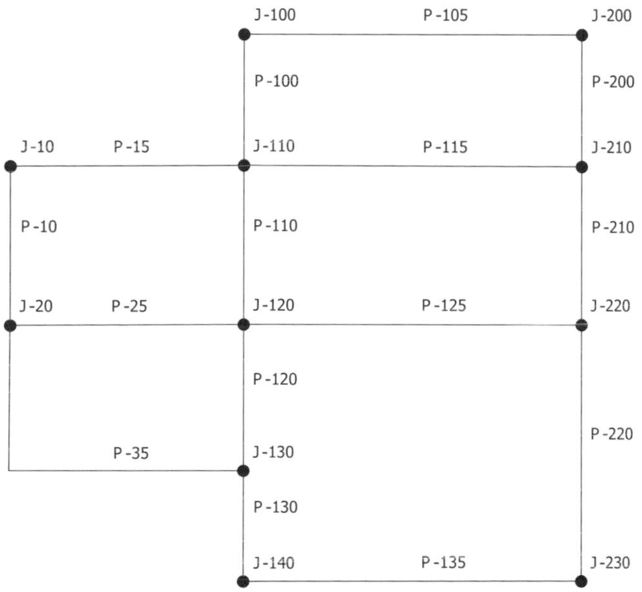

Determine if the new subdivision will have adequate pressures for a 750 gpm fire flow at each node. All pipes are new PVC with a Hazen-Williams C-factor of 150.

Model the existing system as a reservoir followed by a pump, with the elevation of the reservoir and the pump set to the elevation of the connecting node J-10. Use the results of the hydrant flow test as described on page 265 to generate a pump head curve for this equivalent pseudo-pump.

Node Label	Elevation (ft)	Demand (gpm)
J-10	390	20
J-20	420	20
J-100	420	20
J-110	415	20
J-120	425	20
J-130	430	20
J-140	450	20
J-200	420	20
J-210	425	20
J-220	445	20
J-230	460	20

Pipe Label	Diameter (in.)	Length (ft)
P-10	6	625.0
P-15	6	445.0
P-25	6	417.5
P-35	6	505.0
P-100	6	250.0
P-105	6	345.0
P-110	6	665.0
P-115	6	412.5
P-120	6	275.0
P-125	6	372.5
P-130	6	212.5
P-135	6	596.5
P-200	6	225.0
P-210	6	550.0
P-220	6	453.5

7.8 Given the two existing systems 2,000 ft apart shown in Figure 7.36, develop a system head curve to pump from a ground tank in the lower, larger system to the smaller, higher system. Data for this system has already been entered into Prob7-08.wcd.

Hint: To generate points on the system head curve, place a demand at the "Suction Node" and an inflow (or negative demand) of the same magnitude at the "Discharge Node." The difference in HGL between the two nodes is the head required at the pump for that flow rate. Repeat the process for a range of flows from 250 to 2,000 gpm.

Develop additional system head curves for water levels in the discharge tank of 1,170 ft and 1,130 ft.

Figure 7.36

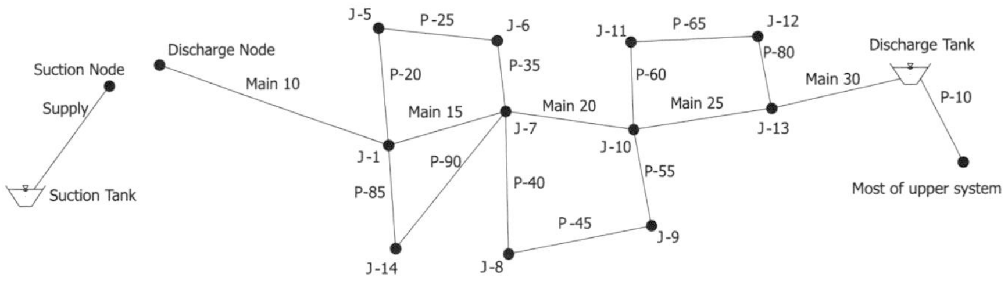

Pipe Label	Diameter (in.)	Length (ft)	Hazen-Williams C-factor
Main10	12	2,000	130
Main15	12	5,878	130
Main20	12	3,613	130
Main25	12	2,670	130
Main30	12	3,926	130
P-10	12	29	130
P-20	6	3,514	130
P-25	6	4,988	130
P-35	6	2,224	130
P-40	6	3,276	130
P-45	6	3,198	130
P-55	6	3,363	130
P-60	6	2,345	130
P-65	6	23	130
P-80	6	1,885	130
P-85	6	3,475	130
P-90	6	6,283	130
Supply	12	60	130

CHAPTER

8

Modeling Customer Systems

Most water distribution system modeling is done by or for water utilities. In some instances, there are entire water systems that are served by other water utilities through wholesale agreements, such that the water source is actually the neighboring system. This type of situation is shown in Figure 8.1 where the source water utility delivers to an adjacent customer water utility through a meter and a backflow preventer. Some examples are military bases, prisons, university campuses, and major industries. The systems can include domestic water use, industrial process water, cooling water, irrigation water use, and fire protection systems. Most water system design work is the same within a customer's system as it is within the water utility's system.

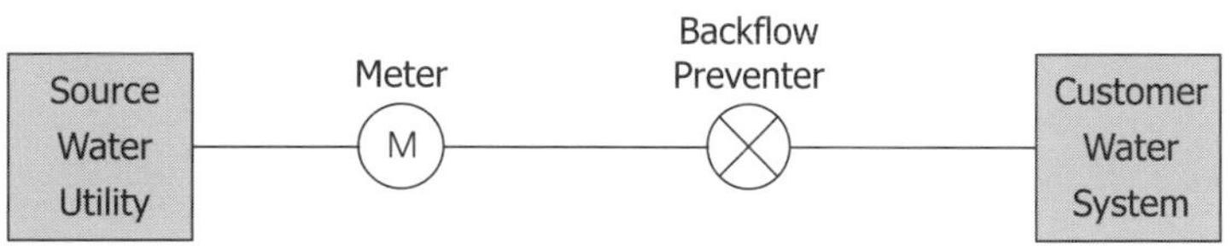

Figure 8.1
Customer water system using utility's system as a water source

There are several principal differences between working for a customer water system and a utility system. When working for a customer water system, the designer does not control the source of water, and therefore must model back into the utility system. More information regarding the extent to which the water utility's system must be modeled can be found in Chapter 7 (see page 262). In addition, the designer must account for head losses in meters and backflow preventers in the customer water system, which are usually not an issue for the utility engineer.

8.1 MODELING WATER METERS

A customer's water meter is usually a *positive displacement technology meter* used on lines sized from 5/8 in. to 2 in., or a *turbine technology meter* (Figure 8.2) for lines sized 1-1/2 in. to 20 in. For some applications in which the flow rate varies greatly, a *compound meter* is used. This meter houses a positive displacement element for the low flows and a turbine meter element for the high flows.

Figure 8.2
Turbine meter

6-in. (DN 150-mm) Cold Water Recordall ® Turbo Series Meter courtesy of Badger Meter Inc.

A single register meter can be represented in the model as a minor loss or an equivalent pipe; however, most meter manufacturers do not provide a minor loss coefficient (K_L) for use in modeling. Instead, they provide a curve relating pressure drop to flow rate, as shown in Figure 8.3. The designer must calculate the K_L by finding the flow and pressure drop for a point on the curve, and then substituting those values into the Equation 8.1. A point at the high end of the flow range is usually chosen.

$$K_L = C_f \Delta P D^4 / Q^2 \qquad (8.1)$$

where
K_L = minor loss coefficient
ΔP = pressure drop (psi, kPa)
D = diameter of equivalent pipe (in., m)
Q = discharge (gpm, m^3/s)
C_f = unit conversion factor (880 English, 1.22 SI)

Once K_L is determined for a given type of meter, it can be applied to different size meters of similar geometry. The following table lists some typical K_L values for several types of meters in representative sizes. Meter sizing is discussed in AWWA M-22 (1975).

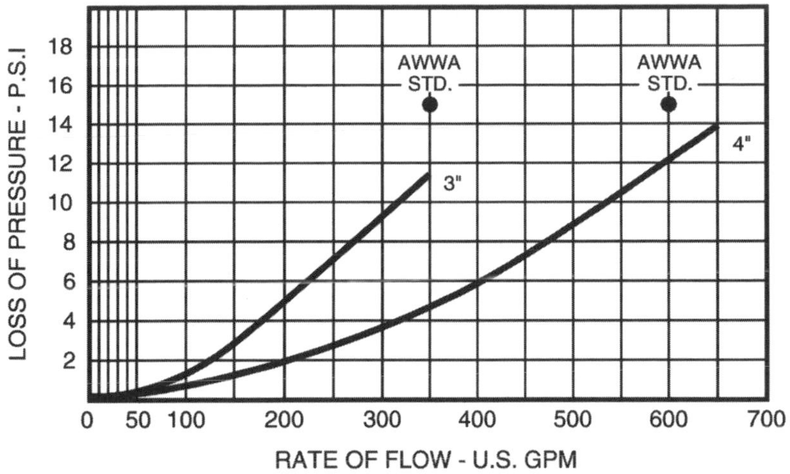

Courtesy of Hersey Products, Inc.

Figure 8.3 Manufacturer's water meter head loss curve

Table 8.1 Minor loss K_L values for various meter types

Type of Meter	Size (in.)	Minor Loss K_L
Displacement Meter	5/8	4.4
	2	8.3
	6	17.2
Turbine	1.5	6.7
	4	9.4
	12	14.9
Compound	2	3.9
	4	18.1
	10	33.5
Fire Service Turbine	3	4.1
	6	4.1
	10	4.3
Multi-jet	5/8	5.1
	1	5.3
	2	12.6

In the case of a compound meter, a single K_L value does not adequately describe the pressure drop versus flow relationship. When modeling high-flow conditions, the larger meter is in operation, and the diameter and K_L value for the larger meter are used. When an accuracy of 2 to 3 psi (13.7 to 20.6 kPa) is required for lower flow runs, the data for the smaller meter should be used instead. For example, when running simulations to look at tank cycling, pump operation, or energy consumption, the flow would typically be passing through the smaller meter. During a fire flow condition, the larger meter is active and should be used in the model so that head loss is not overestimated.

If accuracy over the full range of flows is necessary, the compound meter can be modeled as two parallel equivalent pipes using the appropriate sizes and K_L values. In the model, the pipe representing the smaller meter will always be open. For a steady-state run, the designer must specify whether the larger meter is also open. For an EPS run, the pipe representing the meter can be opened or closed based upon the flow rate through the pipe immediately upstream, or based upon the head loss across the small meter. For example, the controls could specify, "If the flow rate is greater than 30 gpm (0.002 m^3/s), or if the head loss is greater than 10 ft (3 m), then open the larger meter."

Figure 8.4 shows an approximation of an actual compound meter head loss curve, while Figure 8.5 shows how that meter can be represented in the model. An alternative approach to modeling compound meters is to use the generalized head loss versus flow curve definition capability available with some simulation software.

Figure 8.4
Approximation of compound meter head loss curve

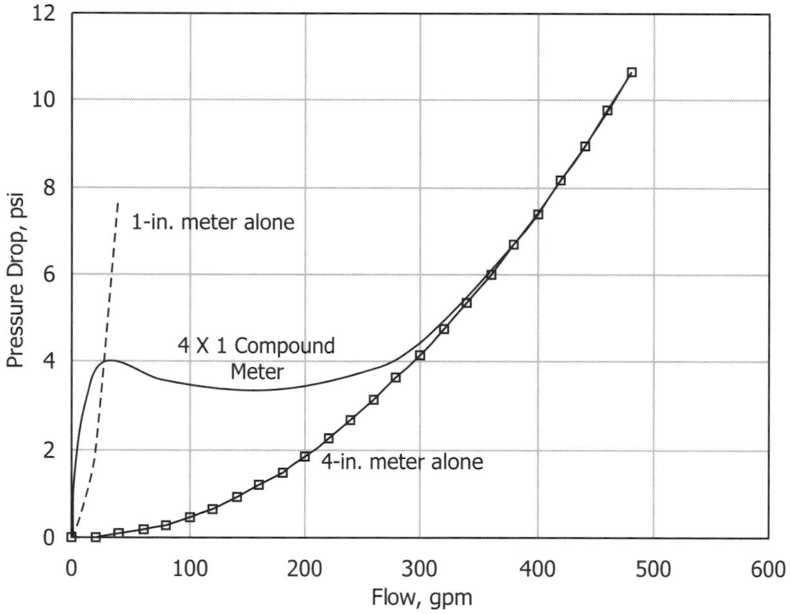

Figure 8.5
Model representation of compound meter

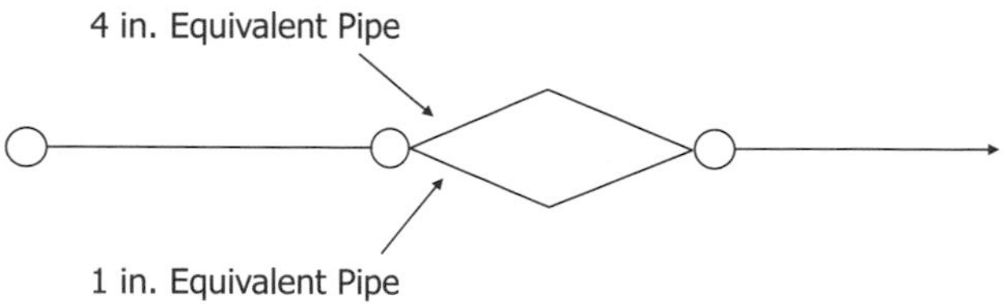

8.2 BACKFLOW PREVENTERS

A utility-approved backflow prevention assembly (Figure 8.6) is typically required for large customers to prevent cross-connections (AWWA M-14, 1990). The distinguishing feature of backflow preventers is that they require a fairly large pressure drop across the valve before they even begin to open. Consequently, the head loss through the device can be more significant, especially at low flow, than pipe friction losses in the service line or minor losses through meters.

Figure 8.6
Backflow preventer

Courtesy of CMB Industries, Inc.

A typical pressure drop curve for a reduced pressure backflow preventer or a double check backflow preventer is shown in Figure 8.7. Because of the significant drop in HGL required to open the valve, modeling backflow preventers is more complex than inserting a check valve on an equivalent pipe with an additional minor loss. There are several ways to model a backflow preventer.

The first technique is for models that support generalized head loss curves. In this case the modeler enters a table of head loss vs. flow. The second approach makes use of the fact that the shape of the valve's head loss curve is a great deal like the shape of an inverted pump curve. The backflow preventer can be modeled as a pump with negative heads as shown in Figure 8.8.

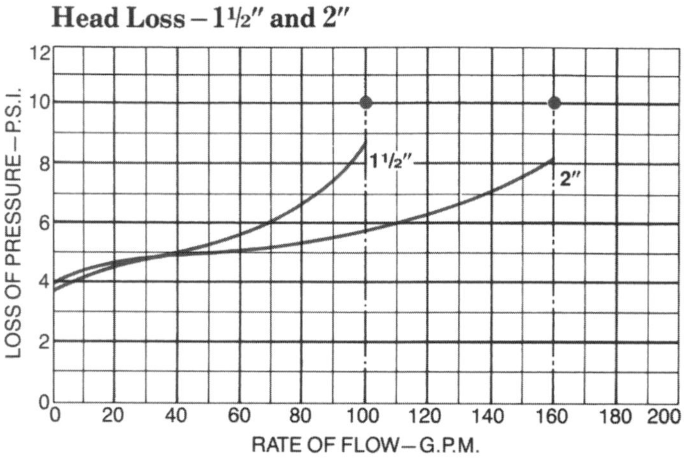

Courtesy of Hersey Products, Inc.

Figure 8.7
Pressure drop curve for reduced pressure backflow preventer

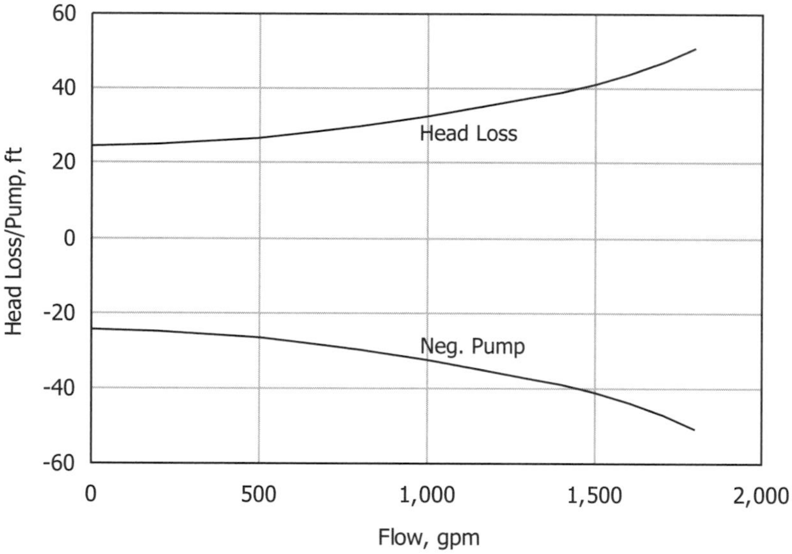

Figure 8.8
Modeling backflow preventer as negative pump

If the model does not permit negative heads in pump curves, the backflow preventer can be modeled as a pressure breaker valve with a head loss of P_{min} in series with an equivalent pipe that has a check valve and a minor loss coefficient (Figure 8.9). The minor loss coefficient is determined from the initial pressure drop plus a single representative point (Q, P) on the valve curve using the following equation.

$$k = C_f(P - P_{min})D^4/Q^2 \tag{8.2}$$

where P = pressure at representative point on curve (psi, kPa)
P_{min} = minimum pressure drop through backflow preventer (psi, kPa)
D = diameter of valve (in., m)
Q = discharge at representative point on curve (gpm, m^3/s)
C_f = unit conversion factor (880 English, 1.22 SI)

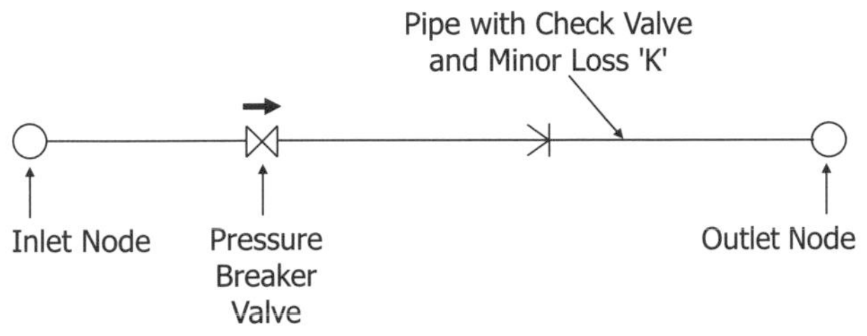

Figure 8.9
Model network representation of backflow preventer

The value of P_{min} is the point where the pressure drop curve intersects the vertical axis. The model approximation of the backflow preventer is shown in Figure 8.10. Backflow preventers with head loss curves that are difficult to approximate can be modeled using generalized user-defined head loss vs. flow relationships.

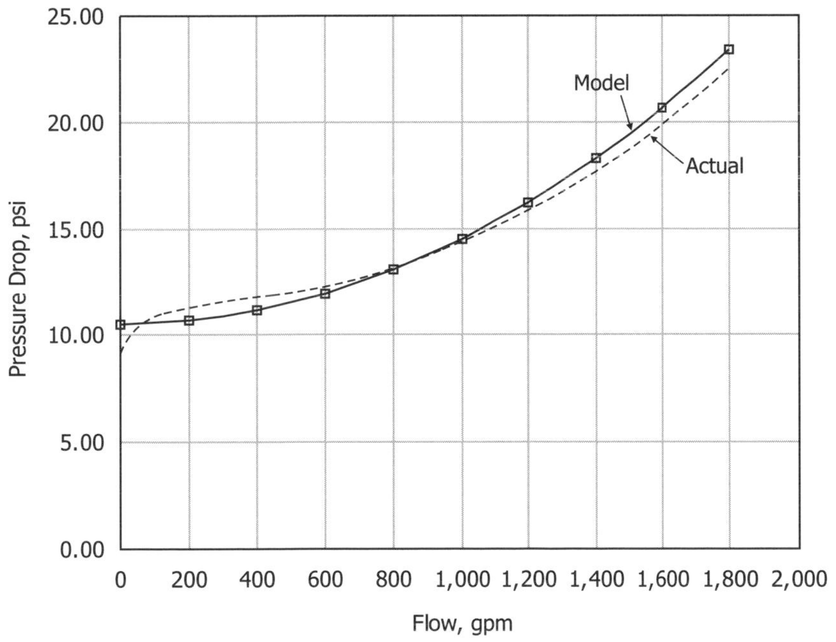

Figure 8.10
Model approximation of head loss for backflow preventer

8.3 REPRESENTING THE UTILITY'S PORTION OF THE DISTRIBUTION SYSTEM

As was the case with an ordinary extension to the distribution system, the model of a customer's system cannot simply start at an arbitrary point in the distribution system serving it. Unless the impact of the customer's load on the utility's system is negligible, the head loss from the source, tank, or pump station that controls pressure must be accounted for.

The best way to model the connection depends on the relative size of the customer's system compared to the size of the utility's system in the pressure zone providing service. If the customer uses half of the water in the source utility's system, and causes half of the head loss, then it is important to model the utility's system back to a reasonably known source. On the other hand, if the customer's system represents a negligible percent of the demand, then it may be possible to model the utility's system as a reservoir and pump, using the results of a hydrant flow test (see page 268). Of course, if fire flows are to be provided in the customer system, then the loads cannot be considered negligible.

8.4 CUSTOMER DEMANDS

The material on demand estimation in Chapter 4 is applicable to customer systems. When working with a customer's system, demands may be assigned more precisely than when modeling an entire system. For small industrial complexes, recent water usage rates can be determined directly using meter readings.

Commercial Demands for Proposed Systems

Engineers for commercial developments such as hotels and office buildings may also want to use modeling for their projects, but will not have data on existing customers as a water utility would. This problem was addressed by the National Bureau of Standards during the 1920s and 30s and resulted in the *Fixture Unit Method* for estimating demands (Hunter, 1940).

This method consists of determining the number of toilets, sinks, dishwashers, etc., in a building and assigning a *fixture unit value* to each. Fixture unit values are shown in Table 8.2. Once the total fixture units are known, the value is converted into a peak design flow using what is called a *Hunter curve* (Figure 8.11).

The basic premise of the Hunter curve is that the more fixtures in a building, the less likely it is that they will all be used simultaneously. This assumption may not be appropriate in stadiums, arenas, theaters, etc., where extremely heavy use occurs in a very short time frame, such as at halftime or intermission.

The values in Table 8.2 are somewhat out of date, as they were prepared before the days of low-flush toilets and low-flow shower heads, but a better method has not yet been developed. This technique is used in the Uniform Plumbing Code (International Association of Plumbing and Mechanical Officials, 1997) and a modified version is included in AWWA Manual M-22 (1975). While the fixture unit assigned may require some adjustment to reflect modern plumbing practice, the logic behind the Hunter curve still holds true.

Table 8.2 Fixture units

Fixture Type	Fixture Units	Fixture Type	Fixture Units
Bathtub	2	Wash sink (per faucet)	2
Bedpan washer	10	Urinal flush valve	10
Combination sink & tray	3	Urinal stall	5
Dental unit	1	Urinal trough (per ft)	5
Dental lavatory	1	Dishwasher (1/2")	2
Lavatory (3/8")	1	Dishwasher (3/4")	4
Lavatory (1/2")	2	Water closet (flush valve)	10
Drinking fountain	1	Water closet (tank)	5
Laundry tray	2	Washing machine (1/2")	6
Shower head (3/4")	2	Washing machine (3/4")	10
Shower head (1/2")	4	Kitchen sink (1/2")	2
Hose connection (1/2")	5	Kitchen sink (3/4")	4
Hose connection (3/4")	10		

Hunter, 1940

The peak demand as determined by the Fixture Unit Method must be increased to account for any sprinkler, cooling, and industrial process demands that are not otherwise included.

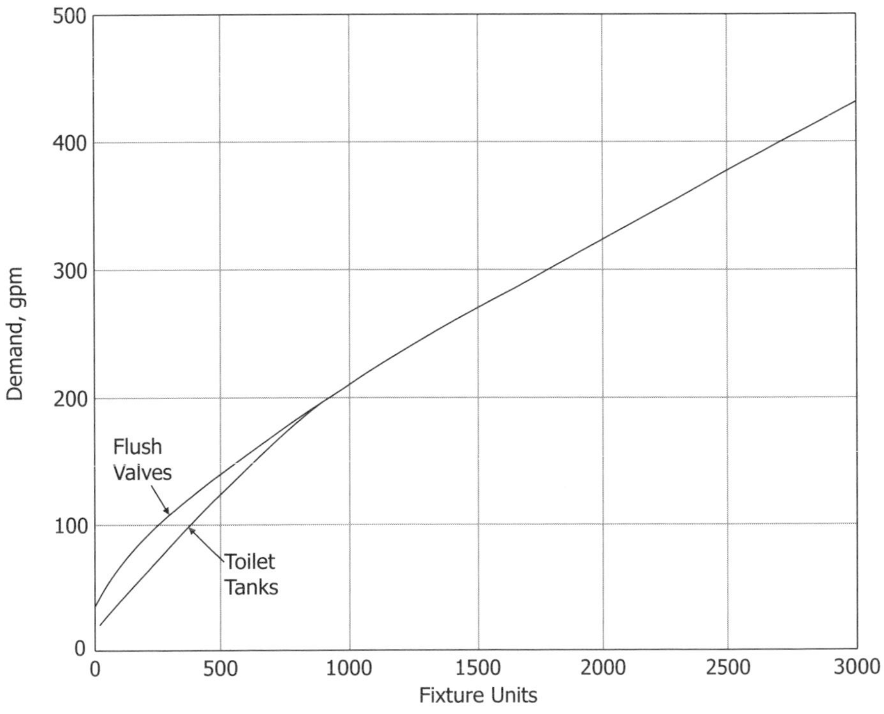

Figure 8.11
Determining peak demand from fixture units using a Hunter curve

"You need a new washer."

Additional work on residential and small commercial demands was conducted under the Johns Hopkins Residential Water Use Program in the 1950s and 60s (Linaweaver, Geyer, and Wolff, 1966; Wolff, 1961).

8.5 SPRINKLER DESIGN

Water distribution models can also be used to help design irrigation and fire sprinkler systems. The principal difference between modeling sprinklers and modeling a typical water distribution system is that pressure dictates what the sprinkler discharge will be (the demands are "pressure-based"), while in distribution systems, demands are typically modeled as if they are independent of pressure.

Starting Point for Model

One of the most important questions in sprinkler studies is where to start the model. For cases in which sprinklers are fed by pumps from wells, tanks, or ponds, the model should start at the source. Modeling a sprinkler system that is fed from a larger water distribution system is more complex. In such a situation, it may be difficult to determine if the model should begin at the main in the street, or be taken back to the actual source or tank that will be providing water. The key to this decision is determining the extent to which sprinkler flows, when combined with other demands, will draw down the hydraulic grade line in the distribution system. If the effect on pressures in the distribution system is significant, then it will be necessary to extend the model into the system. For further explanation on using fire hydrant flow tests to make this determination and modeling the customer's connection to the main, see page 268.

If a small pipe, such as a 2-in. (50 mm) rural water system main, feeds the sprinkler system, then it will almost certainly be necessary to include this pipe in the model, since the head loss at higher flows will be significant. If the sprinkler system is being fed from a typical water distribution system, then the meter and backflow prevention assembly must be included in the model using the techniques described previously in Section 8.1.

It is important to be conservative when estimating the pressure that will be available to operate a sprinkler system. The water distribution system can change over time as a result of tuberculation, additional customers, or changes in pressure zone boundaries. Water utilities cannot guarantee that they will maintain a specified pressure in the main permanently (AWWA M-31, 1998).

Sprinkler Hydraulics

Flow out of a sprinkler is governed by the equation for orifice flow.

$$Q = C_d A \sqrt{2gh} \tag{8.3}$$

where
Q = discharge (gpm, m^3/s)
C_d = discharge coefficient
A = orifice area ($in.^2$, m^2)
g = gravitational acceleration constant (32.2 ft/s^2, 9.81 m/s^2)
h = head loss across orifice (ft, m)

Rather than explicitly stating the area and discharge coefficient, sprinkler manufacturers usually employ a nominal size and a coefficient, K (not to be confused with the minor loss K_L). K is a function of the size and type of sprinkler and relates discharge and pressure according to:

$$Q = K\sqrt{P} \tag{8.4}$$

where
K = sprinkler coefficient
P = pressure (psi, kPa)

Table 8.3 shows head loss coefficients for fire sprinklers from Brock (1990). It is best to obtain sprinkler K-factors from the sprinkler suppliers. It is also possible to calculate K from a chart of pressure drop versus Q.

Table 8.3 Typical sprinkler K-factors

Size (in.)	K-factor
1/4	1.4
5/16	1.8 – 2.0
3/8	2.6 – 2.9
7/16	3.9 – 4.3
1/2	5.5 – 5.7
17/32	8.0 – 8.2

Brock (1990)

Choosing the Right Sprinkler System

Most sprinkler systems tend to be *wet-pipe systems* in which the system is always full of pressurized water. The individual sprinkler heads have fusible or frangible links that cause the sprinkler to open when exposed to heat. While this design works in the majority of situations, there are a number of variations to accommodate special conditions.

One common variation is a *deluge system*. In this type of system, the sprinkler heads are always open, and water is kept out of the piping by a main control valve. When a fire occurs, the main valve is opened manually, and all of the sprinklers discharge simultaneously. Deluge systems are typically used in places where heat from a fire is unlikely to cause a sprinkler to open, such as in a building with very high ceilings. When modeling this type of system, all sprinkler heads must be modeled as open.

A challenge often encountered in designing sprinkler systems is how to keep pipes from freezing in areas subject to cold temperatures. Two options available in this situation are antifreeze solutions and *dry-pipe systems*.

In *antifreeze systems*, the wet-pipe system is filled with a mixture of antifreeze and water. The antifreeze solutions recommended in systems that are connected back into a potable water system are chemically pure glycerine or propylene glycol. These systems are generally used to protect small, unheated areas.

Dry-pipe systems are filled with pressurized air. When heat causes a sprinkler to open, the air pressure in the system is reduced. This drop in pressure causes a dry-pipe valve to open, allowing pressurized water to travel through the system to the sprinkler heads. Because of the time delay in filling the sprinkler system piping, dry-pipe systems are not quite as efficient as wet-pipe systems in controlling fires. In a water distribution simulation, dry-pipe systems are modeled the same way as wet-pipe systems (that is, it is assumed that the system is already filled with water).

Approximating Sprinkler Hydraulics

Most water distribution system models do not explicitly account for sprinkler *K*-factors. Instead, the sprinkler must be modeled as an equivalent length of pipe discharging to the atmosphere. Atmospheric pressure downstream of the sprinkler can be represented as a discharge from the equivalent pipe into a reservoir, tank, or pressure source where the HGL setting of the downstream node is equal to the elevation of the sprinkler.

There are two ways of accounting for the effect of varying sprinkler sizes and *K*-factors. The preferred approach is to let the equivalent length of pipe account for losses through the sprinkler. The designer must assign a length, diameter, and roughness to the equivalent pipe representing the sprinkler. There are infinite combinations of *D*, *L*, and *C* that will give the same head loss for the sprinkler. One solution is to use a 1-in. (25 mm) diameter pipe with a length of 0.271 ft (0.083 m). With these dimensions, the C-factor for the pipe will equal the sprinkler *K* factor (Walski, 1995). This technique is shown schematically in Figure 8.12. More recent modeling software allows the user to model sprinklers using *flow emitter* elements. With a flow emitter, a modeler need only enter the sprinkler *K*-factor at a junction, and the model will determine discharge as a function of pressure at the node.

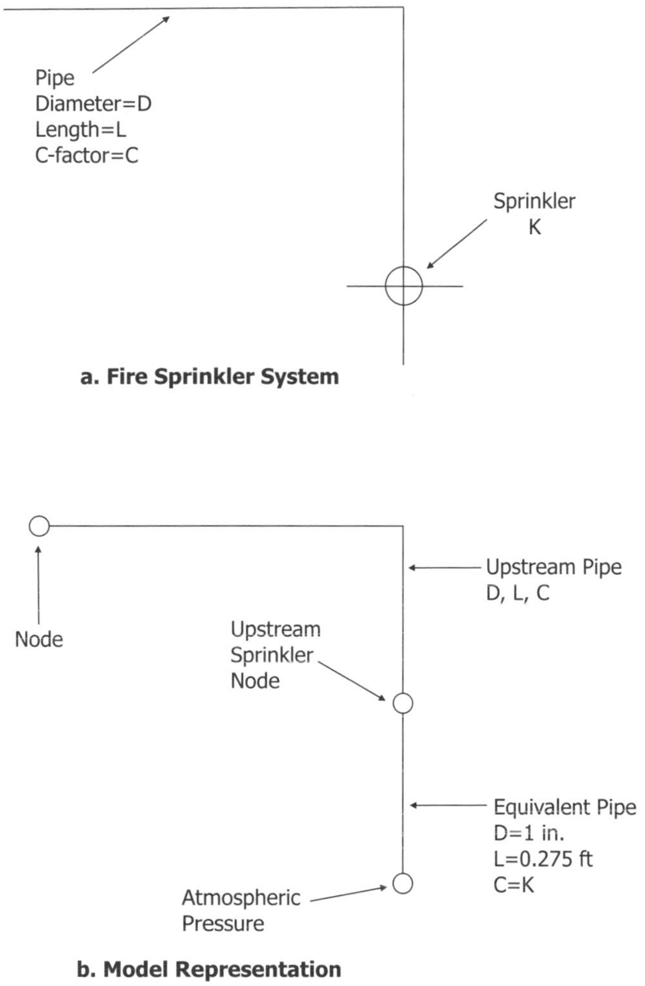

Figure 8.12
Model representation of sprinkler as equivalent pipe

Piping Design

To reduce costs, sprinkler systems are usually laid out in a branched, tree-like pattern. Looped water distribution systems use isolation valves to isolate individual segments. There are very few isolation valves in sprinkler systems. Unlike water distribution systems, if repairs are needed on sprinkler piping, the entire system can be shut down while repairs are made.

Velocities are usually higher in sprinkler system piping than in other distribution piping. Therefore, the minor losses from each valve and fitting in the system must be considered. Otherwise, discharge can be overestimated during design.

Sprinkler systems generally have small pipe diameters. With small pipe diameters, the difference between nominal diameter and actual internal diameter can be significant, depending on pipe material. For example, nominal 1-in. (250-mm) C901 HDPE pipe can have an inner diameter ranging from 0.860 in. to 1.062 in. (21.8 mm to 27.0 mm) depending on the *DR (diameter ratio)*, while copper tubing with the same nominal diameter can have an inner diameter ranging from 0.995 in. to 1.055 in. (25.2 to 26.8 mm) depending on the type. A 20 percent difference in inner diameter can result in a 40 percent difference in capacity. For this reason, it is important to use the actual internal diameter when performing sprinkler design.

Sprinkler heads do not require a great deal of pressure to operate. Pressures on the order of 10 psi (70 kPa) are usually sufficient. The designer should monitor the pressure at the upstream end of the equivalent pipe to determine if a particular set of pipe sizes results in adequate pressure. Because the pressure at the sprinkler is so critical in design, it is important to determine the exact elevation of the sprinkler heads when assigning the elevation of the nodes in the model.

The information covered up to this point on sprinkler hydraulics and design is applicable to both fire and irrigation sprinkler systems. While there are many similarities between these two types of systems, each also has unique features, as detailed in the next two sections.

Fire Sprinklers

National Fire Protection Association (NFPA) Standards 13 (1999) and 13D (1999) govern fire sprinkler design. Additional information is provided in NFPA (1999) and AWWA M-31 (1998).

Sprinklers are intended to control fires, not necessarily to completely extinguish them. Therefore, some allowance is made for hose stream flows from hydrants or fire trucks when determining sprinkler system performance requirements.

Sprinklers are usually laid out so that only a few need to open to control a fire. Designs should not be based on the assumption that all sprinklers will operate simultaneously, unless there is reason to believe this is the case. The spacing of sprinklers and the sprinkler demand are determined by the occupancy and size of the building.

Usually, sprinkler systems are modeled through a series of steady-state runs, each run corresponding to the operation of a different sprinkler or group of sprinklers. One or two sprinklers on the top floor at the far end of the building from the service line will typically control design calculations.

If the sprinkler system is not delivering sufficient flow, the engineer should first try to increase pipe sizes, thereby reducing head losses. If increasing pipe sizes is ineffective, the head at the supply main may not be sufficient to operate the system. In this case, the pressure to the sprinklers must be increased. In most instances, installing a fire pump in the building is usually simpler and less expensive than raising the pressure in the supply main.

Irrigation Sprinklers

Irrigation systems are operated frequently, and are designed so that more of the sprinklers can be used simultaneously. While irrigation sprinklers are different from fire sprinklers, they can still be modeled using orifice flow equations.

For larger systems, opening all of the sprinklers simultaneously will tend to use excessive water and require larger piping and meters. To reduce pipe and meter sizes, these systems are usually "zoned" so that only one set of sprinklers operates at a given time. If the water source is plentiful and storage volume is not an issue, then the operation of each zone can be modeled as a separate steady-state analysis. If the amount of storage is an issue (for instance, water is taken from a small pond), then an EPS run should be used in modeling to ensure that the water supply is adequate.

REFERENCES

American Water Works Association. (1975). "Sizing Service Lines and Meters." *AWWA Manual M-22*, Denver, Colorado.

American Water Works Association. (1990). "Recommended Practice for Backflow Prevention and Cross Connection Control." *AWWA Manual M-14*, Denver, Colorado.

American Water Works Association. (1998). "Distribution System Requirements for Fire Protection." *AWWA Manual M-31*, Denver, Colorado.

Brock, P. D. (1990). *Fire Protection Hydraulics and Water Supply*. Oklahoma State University, Stillwater, Oklahoma.

Hunter, R. B. (1940). "Methods of Estimating Loads in Plumbing Systems." *Report BMS 65*, National Bureau of Standards, Washington, DC.

International Association of Plumbing and Mechanical Officials. (1997). *Uniform Plumbing Code*. Los Angeles, California.

Linaweaver, F. P., Geyer, J. C., and Wolff J. B. (1966). *A Study of Residential Water Use: A Report Prepared for the Technical Studies Program of the Federal Housing Administration*. Department of Housing and Urban Development, Washington, DC.

National Fire Protection Association (NFPA). (1999). *Fire Protection Handbook*. Quincy, Massachusetts.

National Fire Protection Association (NFPA). (1999). "Sprinkler Systems in One- and Two-Family Dwellings and Manufactured Homes." *NFPA 13D*, Quincy, Massachusetts.

National Fire Protection Association (NFPA). (1999). "Standard for Installation of Sprinkler Systems." *NFPA 13*, Quincy, Massachusetts.

Walski, T. M. (1995). "An Approach for Handling Sprinklers, Hydrants, and Orifices in Water Distribution Systems." *Proceedings of the AWWA Annual Convention*, American Water Works Association, Anaheim, California.

Wolff, J. B. (1961). "Peak Demands in Residential Areas." *Journal of the American Water Works Association*, 53(10).

DISCUSSION TOPICS AND PROBLEMS

Earn CEUs — Read Chapters 7 and 8 and complete the problems. Submit your work to Haestad Methods and earn up to 1.5 CEUs. See *Continuing Education Units* on page xiii for more information, or visit www.haestad.com/wdm-ceus/.

8.1 The water system for an industrial facility takes water from the utility's system through a meter and reduced pressure backflow preventer. Figure 8.13 shows the industrial system piping connected to the skeletonized utility system. The head loss curves for the meter and the backflow preventer are given in Figure 8.14. The total head at the water source in the utility's system is 320 ft, and the elevation of the backflow preventer is 90 ft. The meter and backflow preventer are located on pipe P-C-1, a nominal 6-in. pipe. Construct a model of the system under normal demand conditions using the data provided below.

Figure 8.13

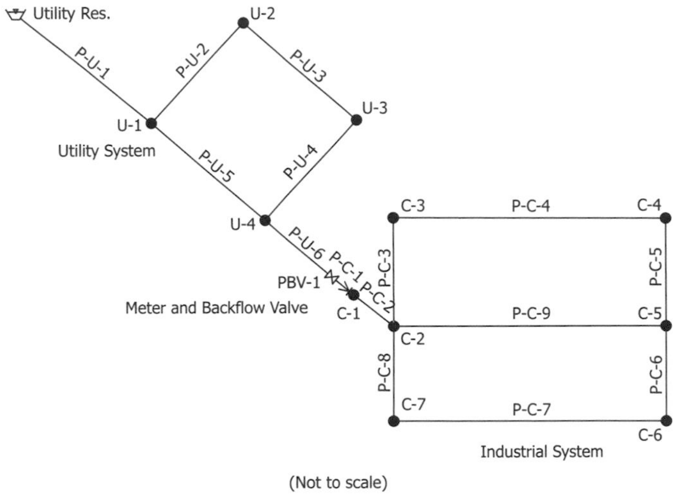

Node Label	Elevation (ft)	Demand (gpm)
C-1	90.0	0
C-2	120.0	5
C-3	100.0	5
C-4	135.0	5
C-5	140.0	5
C-6	135.0	5
C-7	130.0	5
U-1	100.0	200
U-2	95.0	500
U-3	80.0	700
U-4	100.0	200

Figure 8.14

Pipe Label	Length (ft)	Diameter (in.)	Hazen-Williams C-factor
P-C-1	1	6	130
P-C-2	50	6	130
P-C-3	500	6	130
P-C-4	500	6	130
P-C-5	500	6	130
P-C-6	500	6	130
P-C-7	500	6	130
P-C-8	500	6	130
P-C-9	500	6	130
P-U-1	3,000	16	130
P-U-2	2,000	12	130
P-U-3	2,000	12	130
P-U-4	2,000	12	130
P-U-5	2,000	12	130
P-U-6	100	12	130

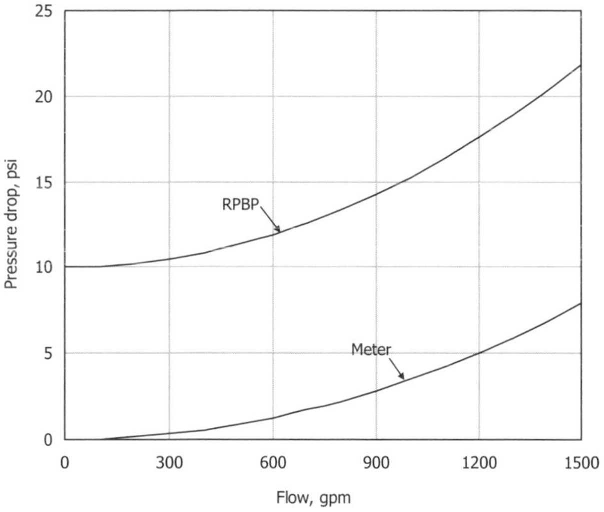

a) Determine the minor loss K-values for the meter and backflow preventer and P_{min} for the backflow preventer. Apply the minor losses to the pipe immediately downstream of the valve (P-C-1).

b) Determine the head immediately downstream of the backflow preventer and meter during normal demand conditions.

c) Add a 1,500 gpm fire demand to the normal demand at node C-4 and determine the residual pressure at this node. Under this demand condition, what is the HGL immediately downstream of the meter?

d) For the 1,500 gpm fire flow condition, determine the head loss (in feet) for the following portions of the system:

- Between the source and the meter/backflow preventer
- In the backflow preventer and meter
- Between the meter/backflow preventer and C-4

8.2 This problem uses the system from Problem 8.1. Suppose you do not want to model the utility's system at all, even as the skeletal system shown. Rather, you would like to model it as a constant head node located downstream of the meter and backflow preventer at node C-2. Using the HGL determined in part (b) of the previous problem, insert a reservoir attached to node C-1 through a 1-ft pipe with a 6-in. diameter and a Hazen-Williams C-factor of 130. Delete the valve and the utility part of the system from the model or disconnect the systems.

a) Using this HGL, what is the residual pressure at C-4 for a 1,500 gpm flow?

b) Does deleting the utility system, backflow valve, and the meter and instead modeling it as a constant head give an accurate representation of the system under fire demands?

8.3 An existing small irrigation system consists of five sprinklers in Area A, as shown in Figure 8.15. A new landscaped area (Area B) of roughly the same size is planned, requiring that an additional five sprinklers be installed.

Water for the existing irrigation system is pumped from a nearby pond. The owner would like to use the existing 1.5 hp pump to supply the additional sprinklers as well. Manufacturer pump curve data for this pump is provided in the following tables. The elevation of the pump is 97 ft.

Construct a steady-state hydraulic model of the sprinkler system if the pond water surface is at an elevation of 101 ft. Pipes M-3 and M-4 are both equipped with a 1-in. gate valve ($K = 0.39$) for isolating the system if necessary for repairs, etc., and a 1-in. anti-siphon valve ($K = 14$) to prevent contamination of the pond with substances such as chemical fertilizers.

To model the sprinklers, attach a reservoir with an HGL elevation equivalent to the sprinkler head elevation to the sprinkler node with an equivalent pipe.

According to the sprinkler manufacturer's information, a pressure of 30 psi is required at the sprinkler head to produce a discharge of 1.86 gpm. At this flow, the radius of the sprinkler coverage is 15 ft. The sprinkler spacing was determined based on this radius. Given this information, use Equation 8.4 to solve for the sprinkler coefficient, K, and determine the characteristics of the equivalent pipe as discussed in Section 8.2.

Figure 8.15

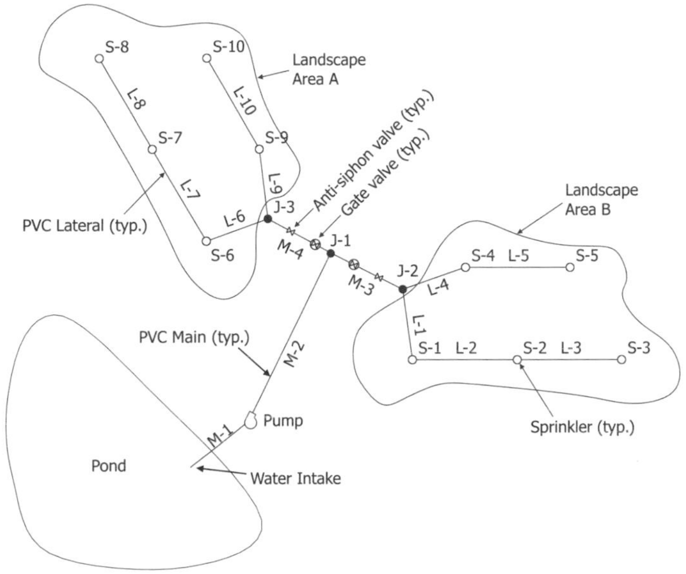

Sprinkler Label	Elevation (ft)
S-1	115.45
S-2	115.40
S-3	115.25
S-4	115.15
S-5	115.10
S-6	115.75
S-7	116.00
S-8	116.10
S-9	115.55
S-10	115.80

Node Label	Elevation (ft)
J-1	115
J-2	115
J-3	115

Main Label	Length (ft)	Hazen-Williams C-factor
M-1	19	150
M-2	80	150
M-3	12	150
M-4	12	150

Lateral Label	Length (ft)	Hazen-Williams C-factor
L-1	17	150
L-2	26	150
L-3	26	150
L-4	16	150
L-5	26	150
L-6	16	150
L-7	26	150
L-8	26	150
L-9	17	150
L-10	26	150

Pump Curve Data

	Head (ft)	Flow (gpm)
Shutoff	230	0
Design	187	10
Max Operating:	83	20

a) The existing system uses ¾-in. laterals and 1-in. mains. Run the model with only the existing system in operation (that is, close pipe M-3). Is the pump able to adequately supply all of the sprinklers? What is the minimum sprinkler discharge?

b) Re-run the model with all sprinklers (existing and proposed) open. Use ¾-in. laterals and 1-in. mains for both existing and proposed piping. Is the pump able to adequately supply all of the sprinklers? What is the minimum sprinkler discharge?

c) If you were designing the entire system from scratch (no pipes have been installed yet), what minimum size must the mains and laterals be to meet the minimum flow/pressure requirement? Assume all sprinklers are discharging simultaneously and the pump is the same as above.

d) The owner obviously prefers to continue using the existing piping, and would like to save on expenses by using smaller pipes in the new system as well. What could be done operationally to make such a design work?

8.4 This problem is a continuation of Problem 8.3. The irrigation system will be used to water the landscaped areas for 2.5 hours each day. A schedule is established such that Area A will be watered from 4:00 a.m. to 6:30 a.m., and Area B from 6:30 a.m. to 9:00 a.m. The pipe sizes to be used are ¾-in. laterals and 1-in. mains.

a) Using the existing pump and given the minimum system requirements from Problem 8.3, can adequate flow/pressure be supplied at all of the sprinklers?

b) You are concerned about whether the pond has enough water for irrigation during a dry spell. Volume data for the pond is provided in the following tables. Model the pond as a tank using this volume data, and run an EPS to determine the total volume of water used by the irrigation system in a daily cycle. Neglecting evaporation and infiltration, extrapolate this rate of consumption to determine how long could a dry spell last before the pond runs dry.

Pond Data

Total Pond Volume	10,000 ft^3
Maximum Pond Elevation	104 ft
Initial Pond Elevation	103 ft
Minimum Pond Elevation	98 ft

Pond Depth to Volume Ratios

Depth Ratio	Volume Ratio
0.0 (elev. = 98 ft)	0.0 (vol. = 0)
0.5 (elev. = 101 ft)	0.3 (vol. = 3,000 ft^3)
0.8 (elev = 102.8 ft)	0.7 (vol. = 7,000 ft^3)
1.0 (elev. = 104 ft)	1.0 (vol. = 10,000 ft^3)

8.5 For a building with an Ordinary Hazard Group 1 occupancy classification, the required minimum fire sprinkler capacity is 0.16 gpm/ft^2 for a 1500 ft^2 area. The coverage area for an individual sprinkler is 130 ft^2.

a) Compute the number of sprinklers required to provide coverage for a 1500 ft^2 area.

b) What is the minimum discharge required from each sprinkler to meet the capacity requirement for the 1500 ft^2 area?

c) If the type of sprinkler being used has a K-value of 4.0, what pressure must be supplied at the sprinkler head to deliver the required flow?

8.6 Use the fixture unit method to estimate the peak design flow for a commercial office complex with the following fixture totals:

-32 urinals (flush valve)

-60 water closets (flush valve)

-50 sinks

-2 shower rooms with 8 shower heads total

-16 drinking fountains

-2 dishwashers (¾-in.)

-4 kitchen sinks (¾-in.)

-4 hose connections (¾-in.)

The complex has lawn irrigation, but it does not operate during peak demand times. The fire service is through a separate line. Therefore, the fire and irrigation demands need not be included in the calculation.

Determine the total number of fixture units and the design flow. If you would like a velocity of 5 ft/s in the service line during peak flow, roughly what size pipe would you use?

CHAPTER

9

Operations

In the early days of water distribution computer modeling, simulations were primarily used to solve design problems. Since models were fairly cumbersome to use, operators preferred measuring pressures and flows in the field rather than working with a complicated computer program. Recent advances in software technology have made models more powerful and easier to use. As a result, operations personnel have accepted computer simulations as a tool to aid them in keeping the distribution system running smoothly.

Using a model, the operator can simulate what is occurring at any location in the distribution system under the full range of possible conditions. Gathering such a large amount of data in the field would be cost-prohibitive. With a model, the operator can analyze situations that would be difficult, or even impossible, to set up in the physical system (for example, taking a water treatment plant out of service for a day). A calibrated model enables the operator to leverage relatively few field observations into a complete picture of what is occurring in the distribution system.

9.1 THE ROLE OF MODELS IN OPERATIONS

Models can be used to solve ongoing problems, analyze proposed operational changes, and prepare for unusual events. By comparing model results with field operations, the operator can determine the causes of problems in the system and formulate solutions that will work correctly the first time, rather than resorting to trial-and-error changes in the actual system.

Physically measuring parameters such as flow in a pipe or HGL at a hydrant is sometimes difficult. If the operator needs to know, for instance, the flow at a location in the system where no flow meter is present, the location must be excavated, the pipe tapped, and a Pitot rod or other flow-measuring device installed (a substantial and costly undertaking). Also, since operators must deal with the health and safety of customers, they cannot simply experiment with the actual system to see what effects a change in, say, pressure zone boundaries will have on them. With a model, however, it is easy to analyze many types of operational changes and plan for unusual events.

Unlike design engineers working with proposed systems, operators can obtain field data from the actual system, including pressures, tank water levels, and flows. Solving operational problems involves the integrated use of this field data with simulation results. Some of the most useful types of data that will be referred to frequently in this chapter are hydrant flow tests, pressure chart recorders, and data collected through SCADA and telemetry systems.

Assuming that the model is well-calibrated, contradictions between field data and values computed by the model can indicate system problems and provide clues about how they may be solved. Problems that may be discovered by comparing field observations with model predictions include closed valves, water hammer, and pumps not operating as expected. The models discussed in this book do not explicitly examine short-term hydraulic transients (such as water hammer). However, when the other causes of unusual pressure fluctuations are ruled out, water hammer can be diagnosed through a process of elimination.

Models are also useful as training tools for operators. Just as pilots train on flight simulators, operators can train on a water distribution system simulation. It is much less costly to have an operator make mistakes with the model than the real system. In addition, operators can determine how to handle situations such as catastrophic pipe failures or fires before they occur. Cesario (1995) described how models can allow operators to attempt changes they might otherwise be reluctant to try.

Unusual situations that occur in a real system often give the modeler an opportunity to further calibrate the model against conditions that the operators purposely would not want to duplicate because of their disruptive and unwanted influence on the system. When these events occur, it is important to gather as much information as possible regarding pressures, system flows, consumer complaints, tank elevations, operator statements, etc. and record it before it is lost or forgotten. In many instances, experienced field crews and plant operators will log all the information while struggling with the problem, and then file or discard it after the crisis is over.

The following sections describe how a water distribution model can be used to address some operational problems. This chapter assumes that there is already an existing calibrated model of the system, and covers the following topics:

- Solutions to common operating problems
- Preparation for special events
- Calculation of energy efficiency
- Flushing
- Metering
- Water quality investigations
- Impact of operations on water quality

9.2 LOW PRESSURE PROBLEMS

The most frequently occurring operational problem associated with water distribution systems is low or fluctuating pressures. While confirming that the problem exists is usually easy, discovering the cause and finding a good solution can be much more difficult.

Identifying the Problem

Customer complaints, modeling studies, and field measurements obtained through routine checks can indicate that a portion of the system is experiencing low pressure. The pressure problem can be verified by connecting a pressure gage equipped with a data logging device or chart recorder to a hydrant or hose bib to continuously record pressure. Occasionally, a customer may report a low-pressure problem, but the pressure at the main is fine. In such cases, the low pressure may be due to a restriction in the customer's plumbing, or a point-of-use/point-of-entry device that is causing considerable head loss.

If measurements indicate that pressure in the main is low and a problem in the distribution system is suspected, the next step is to examine the temporal nature of the problem. If the test readings show that the pressure is consistently low, then the cause is probably that the elevation of the area is too high for the pressure zone serving it.

"This is going to be kind of a working lunch."

Pressure drops that occur only during periods of high demand are usually due to insufficient pipe or pump capacity, or a closed valve. If the problem occurs at off-peak times, nearby pumps may be shutting off once remote tanks have been filled, lowering pressure on the discharge side of the pumps.

Modeling Low Pressures

Once data are available, the problem can be re-created and simulated in the model. While steady-state runs with instantaneous pressure readings can be used, more information can be gained by attempting to reproduce a pressure-recording chart using an EPS.

Though some idea of the cause of the low-pressure problem (elevation, inadequate capacity, etc.) can be quickly gained from the chart recorder readings alone, the model is needed to accurately identify the weak system component causing the problem. For instance, to locate pipes potentially acting as bottlenecks in the system, the model can be checked for pipes with high velocities. The capacity of the high-velocity pipe(s) can then be increased in the model by adding parallel pipes, changing diameters, or adjusting roughness to see if the problem is then solved. If the problem is due to insufficient pump capacity, then pump curve data for a new pump or impeller size can be entered. If elevation is the culprit, then the pressure zone boundaries may need to be adjusted, or booster pumping added.

If a pressure problem only exists in a remote part of the system during peak demands, then adding a storage tank may be the solution. In urban situations, the need for storage is typically driven by fire fighting concerns, while in rural systems, it may be driven by peak hour demands. The need for storage is discussed further in Section 7.3.

Finding Closed Valves

Very often, the model does not agree with the chart recorder, especially during high water use periods or fire flow tests. The model may indicate a much smaller pressure drop than is observed. This discrepancy usually occurs when there is a closed or partially closed valve in the actual system that causes the system to have a significantly reduced capacity when compared to the model. The problem component can typically be located by measuring the HGL throughout the actual system and looking for abrupt changes that cannot be associated with pressure zone divides. If the HGL is significantly lower than model predictions downstream of a specific point, it is likely that a closed valve is located there.

As discussed previously, the HGL is equal to the sum of the elevation and the pressure head. Since HGL accounts for both elevation and pressure, it is easier to pinpoint closed valve locations by comparing HGLs rather than comparing pressures only.

Though the accuracy of the pressure gages affects the computed HGL, incorrect elevation is likely to contribute more significantly to error, since it is the most difficult of the two parameters to measure. Topographic maps usually have too large of a contour interval to provide the required accuracy and are not the most accurate source of data.

Elevations can be more accurately obtained using sewer system manhole elevations, altimeters, or global positioning systems (GPS) (Walski, 1998).

A good way to review the data is to compare plots of the measured and predicted HGLs from the water source (or nearby tank) to the area with the pressure problems. As previously noted, an abrupt drop in the measured HGL will indicate that there is a potentially closed valve.

Because head losses are smaller at lower flows, an abrupt drop in HGL may not occur under normal demand conditions (under normal conditions, the HGL may only slope one to two feet per thousand feet), making diagnosis of the problem difficult, as shown in Figure 9.1. Compounding this difficulty is the inaccuracy of the HGL values themselves, which may be off by more than five feet unless the elevations of the test locations were precisely determined through surveying or GPS. Therefore, the errors in measurement may be greater than the precision of data necessary to draw good conclusions.

Figure 9.1
Slope of HGL at lower flows

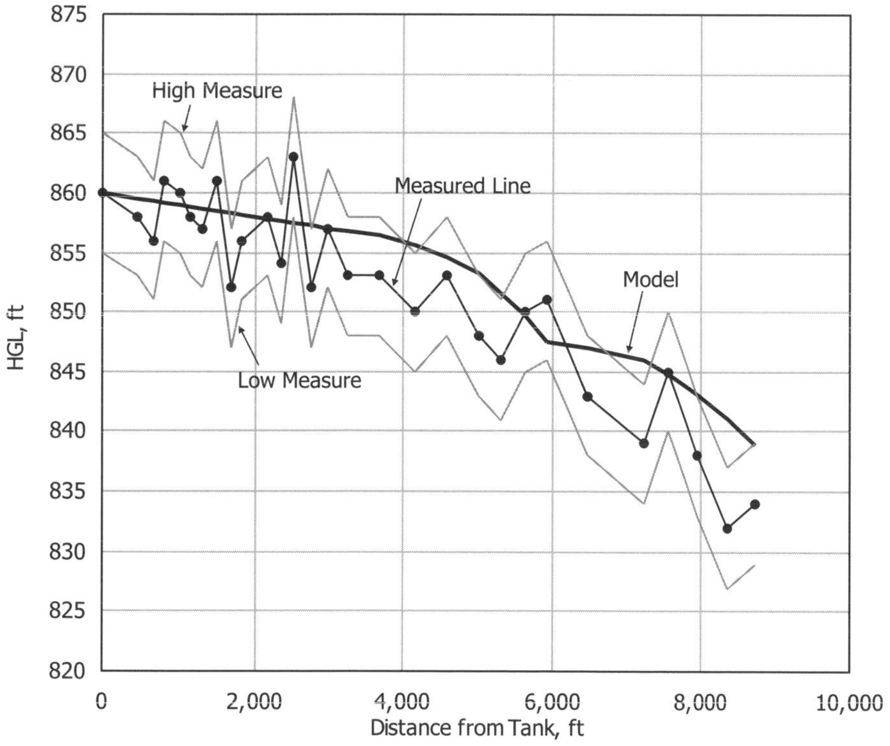

To overcome these inaccuracies, flow velocities in the pipes must be increased to produce a sufficiently large head loss. By opening a hydrant, or, if necessary, a blow-off valve, the head loss is increased so that the slope of the HGL is significantly greater than the measurement error, as shown in Figure 9.2. Even with the "noisy" data shown in the figure, the model and field data clearly diverge approximately 3,200 ft

(975 m) from the tank. For the rest of the range, the slope of the HGL is the same for both model and measured data. Therefore, either some type of restriction exists at around 3,200 ft (975 m), or the model has an error in that area.

Figure 9.2
Slope of HGL at higher flows

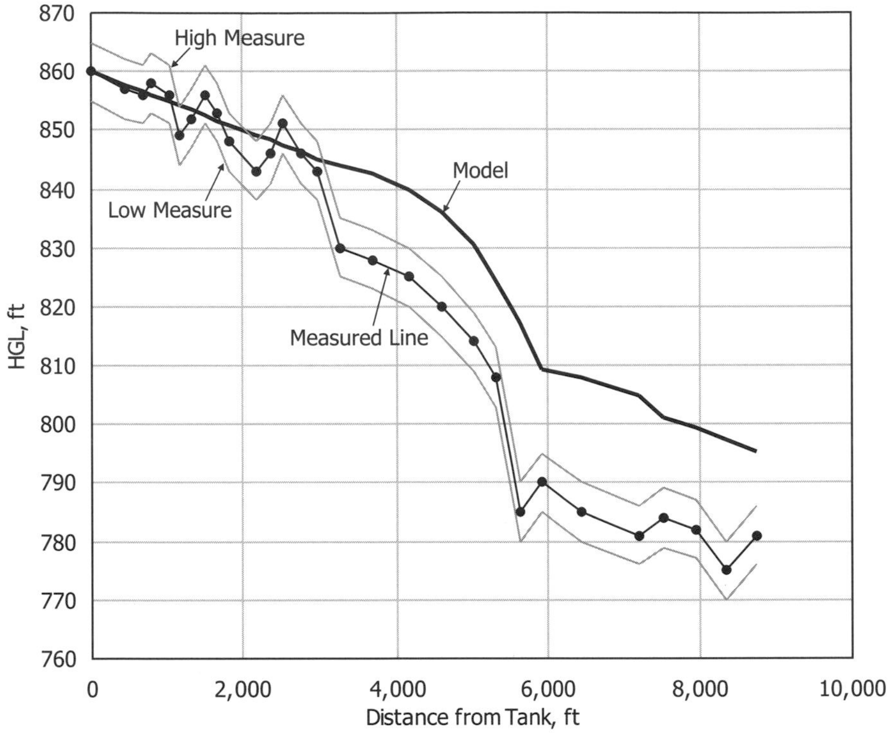

Because it is usually difficult to keep a hydrant or blow-off valve open for a long period of time while pressure gages are moved from location to location, it may be best to run several fire hydrant flow tests with the pressures at multiple residual hydrants being tested simultaneously. In this way, three tests can yield a significant number of data points. The same hydrant should be flowed at the same rate while pressures are taken at several residual hydrants.

Solving Low Pressure Problems

Once the cause of the pressure problem has been identified and confirmed, the possible solutions are usually fairly straightforward, and include the following:

- Making operational changes such as opening valves
- Changing PRV or pump control settings
- Locating and repairing any leaks
- Adjusting pressure zone boundaries
- Implementing capital improvement projects such as constructing new mains

- Cleaning and lining pipes
- Installing pumps to set up a new pressure zone
- Installing a new tank

Some pressure problems are difficult for the utility to resolve. For example, an industrial customer may demand a very high pressure, or a resident may experience low pressure due to the customer's own plumbing. When the utility cannot justifiably spend large sums of money making changes to the system to meet customer expectations or improve customer plumbing, the problem becomes one of customer relations.

Using the model, the utility can determine the cause of the problem, study ways of increasing pressure, better decide if the costs of system changes exceed the benefits, or identify that the problem is not in the utility's system. For example, a commercial customer who has installed a fire sprinkler system requiring 60 psi (414 kPa) to operate will be upset if the utility makes operational changes that cause the pressure to drop to 45 psi (310 kPa), even though this pressure meets normal standards. In another case, the model and field data may show 60 psi (414 kPa) in the utility system, but the customer has only 15 psi (103 kPa). The problem may be due to an undersized backflow preventer valve, meter, or a point-of-entry treatment unit with excessive head loss.

In some cases, customers near a pump station can become accustomed to high pressures, as shown in Figure 9.3. When a pump cycles off, those customers are fed water from a tank that may be some distance away. If the pump should cycle off during a high demand time, the pressure can drop significantly. The model can confirm this drop, and whether pump cycling is the cause. If so, it may be necessary to always run some pumps during periods of high demand, even if the tank is full.

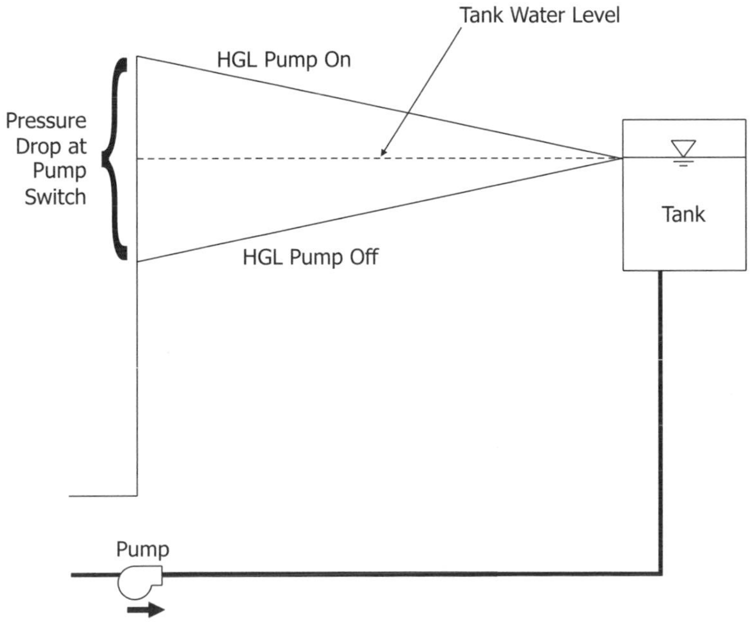

Figure 9.3
Effect of pump operation on customers near the pump

Problems with the model may also surface when trying to reproduce low pressure problems in the actual system. For instance, the model and field data may agree when pumps are off, but not when they are on, indicating that the pump performance curves may be incorrect in the model (for instance, a pump impeller may have been changed and not updated in the model). Another possible discrepancy between the model and field data is the control setting on the PRV. Settings can drift by themselves over time, or may be changed in the field but not in the model. To be useful, a model must reflect operating conditions current at the time the field data were collected.

Leak Detection. By evaluating the discrepancies between field data and computed results, a model can also be used to locate leakage. Unless demands are known very accurately, however, this approach is really only effective if the leakage is very large compared to demands [say, a 100 gpm (0.006 m^3/s) leak in a pressure zone with 200 gpm (0.013 m^3/s) usage]. In such cases, these large leaks will show up as surfacing water, making locating them using a model unnecessary.

As an exception to the above, modeling can be used to help locate leaks when very high nighttime demands are required to accurately reflect diurnal water usage in part of the system. Unless there are large nighttime water users, such as industries that operate at night, water use will typically drop to about 40 percent of average day consumption. Since leakage is not reduced at night, if very high nighttime usage is required for the model to match historical records, leakage can be suspected in that part of the system.

In some instances, the cause of low pressure is a large, non-surfacing water loss resulting from a pipe failure. In this case, the water may be lost through a large-diameter sewer, a stream, or a low area that is not easily observed. An indicator of this type of leak could be an increase in demand on a pump or an unusual drop in an elevated tank level if it is a very large loss or occurs near one of these facilities. If it is on one of the smaller grid mains, its effect would be felt over a smaller area and may not be noticed as an increase in demand. These leaks are generally found by checking sewer manholes for exceptional flows and/or listening on hydrants and valves.

9.3 LOW FIRE FLOW PROBLEMS

Low fire flows are another common operational problem. Solving this problem in an existing system is different than designing pipes for new construction, in that the utility cannot pass the cost of improvements onto a new customer. Rather, the operator must find the weak link in the system and correct it.

Identifying the Problem

The possible reasons for poor fire flows in an existing system are:

- Small mains
- Long-term loss of carrying capacity due to tuberculation and scaling
- Customers located far from the source
- Inadequate pumps

- Closed or partly closed valves (as discussed in Section 9.2)
- Some combination of the above

Fire flow tests can reveal the magnitude of the problem, but the model will help to determine and quantify the cause and possible solutions. Fire flow tests should first be used to more precisely calibrate the model in the area of interest. If the predicted pressures are higher than observed pressures during fire flow tests, the problem is usually due to closed valves (or occasionally pressure reducing valves failing to operate properly). Plotting the actual and modeled hydraulic grade line during high flow events can help locate and determine the reason for the low fire flows.

If the model can be calibrated and no closed valves are found, then the cause of the poor flows is either pipe capacity or distance between the problem area and the water source. The model provides the operator with a tool for examining velocity in each pipe. If velocities are greater than 8 ft/s (2.4 m/s) for long pipe runs, then the issue is small piping.

If the model requires a friction factor corresponding to extremely rough pipe (for instance, a Hazen-Williams C-factor of less than 60), and this value is verified by visual inspection of internal pipe roughness or through testing, then loss of carrying capacity due to tuberculation is to blame.

While the main size and roughness affect the slope of the HGL, the distance affects the magnitude of the pressure drop. For instance, it is possible to get a much larger flow through 100 ft (30.5 m) of old 6-in. (150 mm) main than through 10,000 ft (3,050 m) of the same pipe without significantly affecting pressure.

In models that have been skeletonized, it may be necessary to add pipes that have been removed back into the model to get an accurate picture of fire flow.

Solutions to Low Fire Flow

The best solutions to low fire flows depend on the problems as identified by the model and field data collection. In general, the solutions consist of some combination of:

- New piping
- Rehabilitation (cleaning and lining, sliplining, or pipe bursting)
- Booster pumping
- Additional storage near the problem area

Each of these options affects the system in different ways and has different benefits, so the comparison of alternatives should be performed based on a benefit/cost analysis as opposed to simply minimizing costs. The modeling for this evaluation can usually be performed with steady-state runs. Only if the volume of storage or the ability of the system to refill storage is in question should an EPS model be used.

New Piping and Rehabilitation. Sizing new piping and rehabilitating existing pipes flattens out the slope of the hydraulic gradient for a given flow rate, as shown in Figure 9.4. By allowing the modeler to examine the HGL, the model can help locate which individual pipes are bottlenecks in need of repair or rehabilitation.

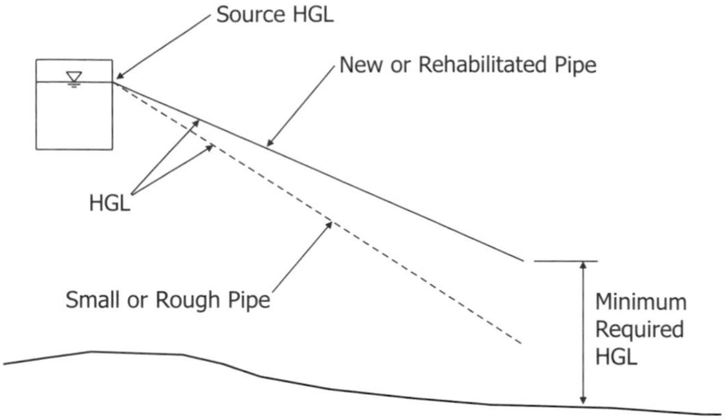

Figure 9.4
Effect of pipe improvements on HGL

Booster Pumping. Booster pumping is usually the least costly method of correcting low pressure problems from an initial capital cost standpoint. Booster pumps can significantly increase operation and maintenance costs, however, and do not allow as much flexibility in terms of future expansion as the other available options. Booster pumping increases the HGL at the pump location but does not reduce the hydraulic gradient, as shown in Figure 9.5. Therefore, booster pumps should, in general, only be used to transport water up hills, not to make up for pipes that are too small. Furthermore, booster pumps can over pressurize portions of the system and even cause water hammer, especially when there is no downstream storage or pressure relief.

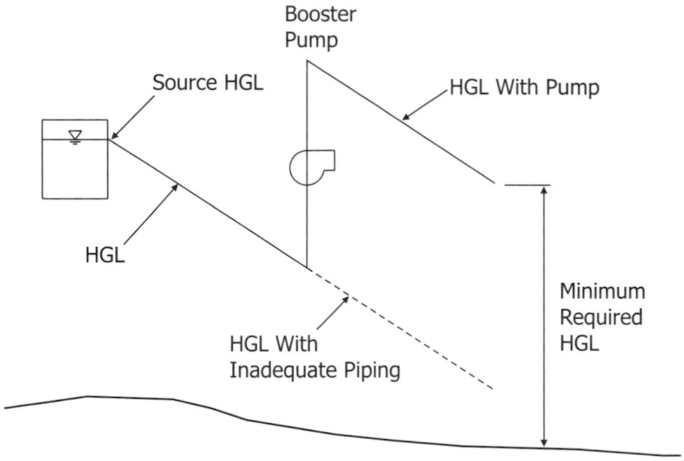

Figure 9.5
Increasing HGL using booster pumping

Adding Storage. Adding storage at the fringe of the system tends to be a costly alternative, but it provides the highest level of benefit. Storage greatly increases fire flows and pressure, because water can reach the fire from two different directions (both original and new sources). This splitting of flow significantly reduces velocities in the mains. Since head loss is roughly proportional to the square of the velocity, cutting the velocity in half (for example) reduces the head loss to one-quarter of its prior value, as shown in Figure 9.6. Storage also increases the reliability of the system in the event of a pipe break or power outage, and helps to dampen transients.

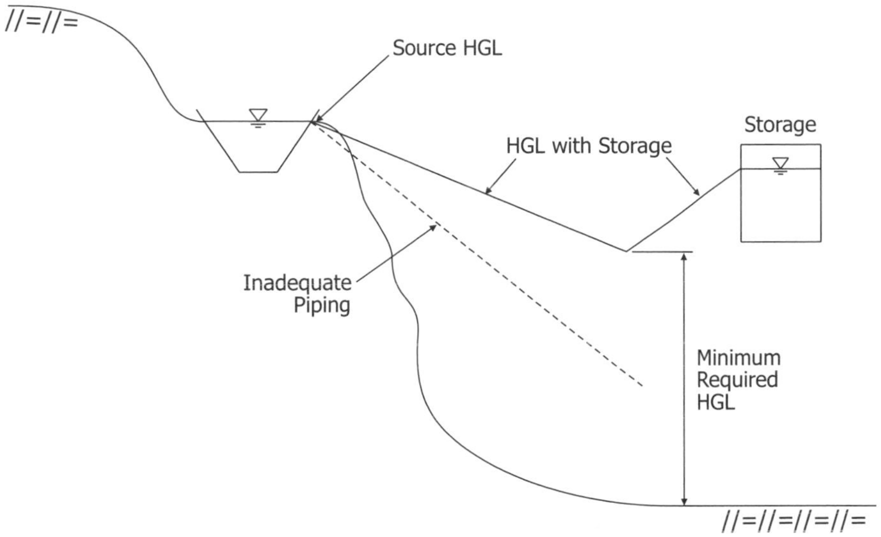

Figure 9.6
Effect of additional storage location on HGL

9.4 ADJUSTING PRESSURE ZONE BOUNDARIES

In spite of efforts to properly lay out water systems as discussed on page 269, utilities occasionally find themselves with pockets of very high or low pressures. Low pressure problems are usually identified and corrected quickly as described in Section 9.2 because of customer complaints. High pressure problems, on the other hand, can persist because most customers do not realize that they are receiving excessive pressures.

When it is determined that pressures are too high in an area, it is best to move the pressure zone boundary so that the customers receive more reasonable pressures from a lower zone. However, in some cases, this may not be a practical solution. For example, in Figure 9.7, the pocket of customers on the right may be too far from the low pressure zone on the left to economically be connected, so they must be served through a PRV from the higher zone. Reducing pressure should reduce leakage and improve the service life of plumbing fixtures. It is important that the performance of the PRV be modeled before installation to determine the impacts on existing customers and fire flows.

The utility may want to adjust the boundaries of the pressure zones to reduce the energy costs associated with pumping and avoid overpressurizing the system. The best way to start this work is to decide on the elevation contour that should be the boundary between pressure zones, and close valves in the model along that boundary.

For example, in Figure 9.8, the utility has selected the 1,200 ft (366 m) elevation contour as the boundary between pressure zones having HGLs of 1,300 ft and 1,410 ft (396 m to 430 m). The model can aid in pointing out problems that will result from closing valves in the system, and it can help the operator identify solutions. In this case, some of the customers between valves *B* and *D* should receive water from the higher pressure zone. However, the 12-in. (300-mm) pipe through the middle of the figure may be an important transmission main for the lower pressure zone. If valves *B* and *D* are closed, the pipe can no longer serve this purpose, so alternative solutions must be explored.

Figure 9.7
Serving high pressure pocket areas

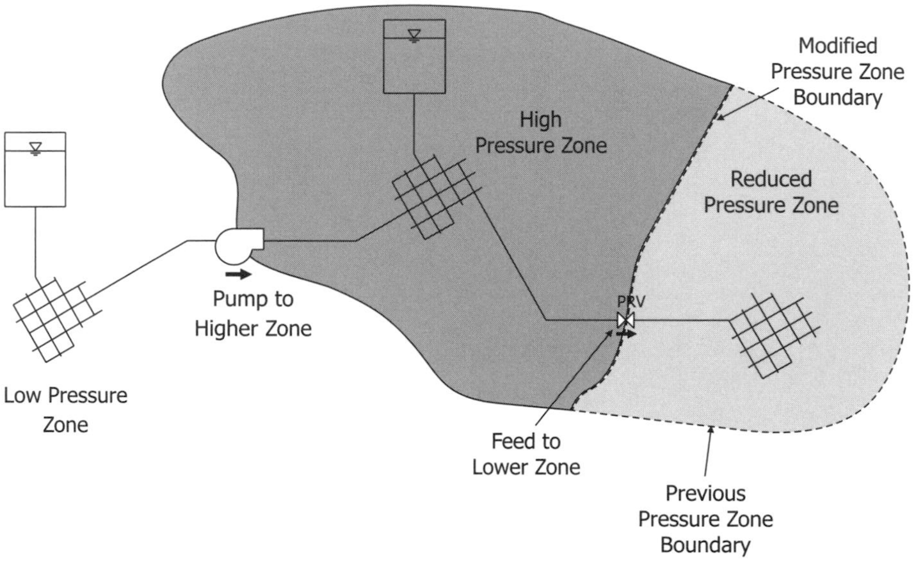

Figure 9.8
A single pressure zone

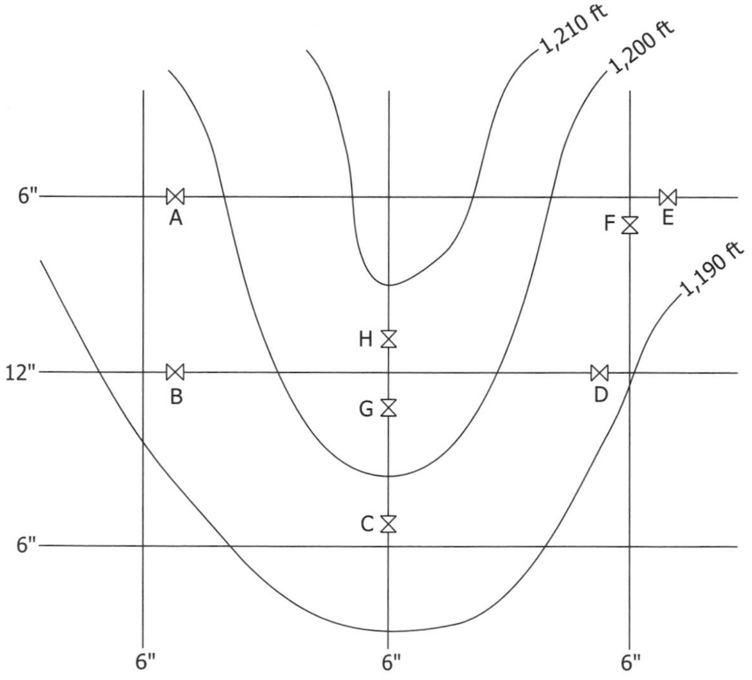

If the elevation of the area near valve *G* is only slightly higher than 1,200 ft (366 m), then it may be possible to simply move the pressure zone divide back to valve *H*, leaving valves *B*, *C*, and *D* open, as in Figure 9.9. If, however, this solution causes customers near *G* to receive pressures that are too low, then a crossover must be constructed between *G* and *H* (Figure 9.10). In addition, a small service line paralleling the 12-in. (300 mm) main and extending to the limits of the 1,410 ft (430 m) pressure zone will be necessary to serve the higher-elevation customers. Note that even though the pressure is lower, any hydrants near *G* should remain connected to the 12 in. (300 mm) line because of its greater capacity.

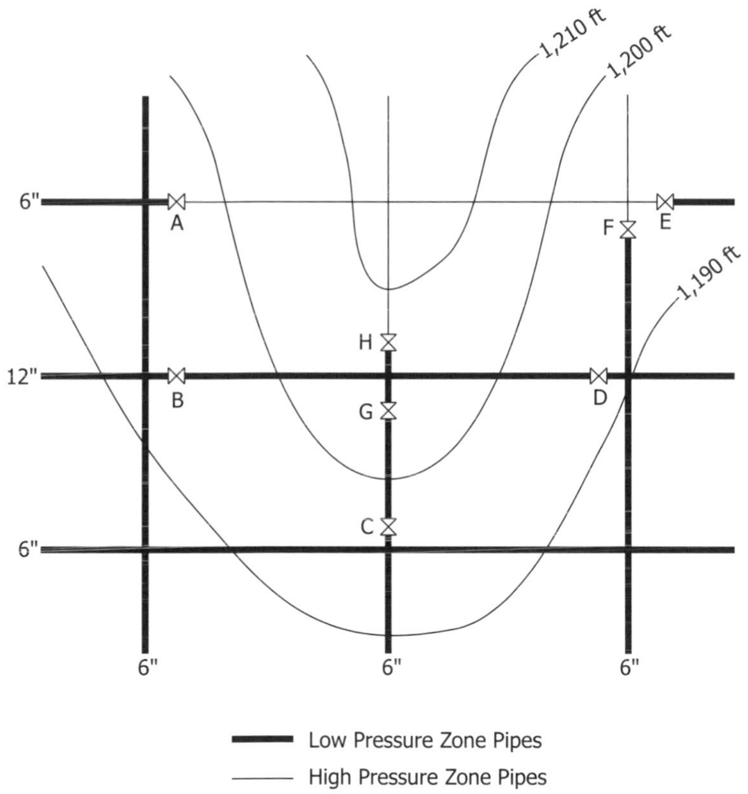

Figure 9.9
Relocating a pressure zone boundary

This example illustrates just how complex adjustments to pressure zone boundaries can become. The model is an excellent way to test alternative valving and determine the effects of the adjustments. If the model was originally skeletonized, it will be necessary to fill in the entire grid in the area being studied to obtain sufficient detail for the analysis. All pipes and closed valve locations along the pressure zone boundary are important. In Figure 9.10, for example, the node at the intersection near valves *E* and *F* is in the higher zone, while the valves themselves represent the ending nodes for two pipes in the lower zone.

Once the static runs have demonstrated that pressures are in a desirable range for a normal day, the results of hydrant flow simulations near the boundary are compared with actual hydrant test data. This comparison will identify any fire flow capacity problems resulting from a potential boundary change that may, for instance, reduce the number of feeds to an area. In some cases, it will be necessary to add pipes or to close loops. Also, PRVs and/or check valves can be installed between the zones to provide additional feeds to the lower zone, improving reliability.

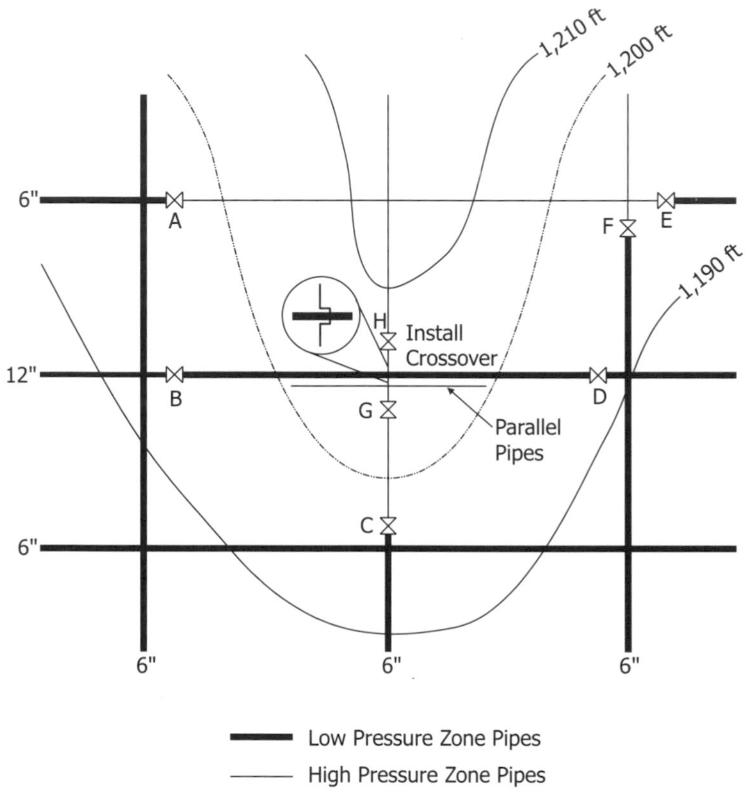

Figure 9.10
Isolating a pressure zone and installing a crossover pipe

Adjusting pressure zone boundaries may result in some long dead-end lines with little flow. These dead-ends should be avoided because of the potential for water quality problems. Blow-offs (bleeds) may need to be installed at the ends of such lines.

9.5 TAKING A TANK OFF-LINE

Occasionally, water distribution storage tanks must be taken off-line for inspection, cleaning, repair, and repainting. Even a simple inspection can cause a tank to be out of service for several days while the time-consuming tasks of draining, removing sediment, inspecting, disinfecting, and filling are completed.

Since tanks are so important to the operation of the system, taking one out of service markedly affects distribution system performance (see page 351 for information on the impact on pressures). The reduction in system capacity can be dramatic; conversely, the system can over pressurize during off-peak periods when demands fall well below pumping capacity.

Fire Flows

While tanks are important for flow equalization, their main purpose is to contribute capacity for peak hour demand and fire flows. Taking a tank out of service removes a major source of water for emergencies. Fire flows at several locations in the system should be analyzed using the model to determine what effect taking the tank out of service will have, and how much flow can be delivered from other sources (for example, the plant clearwell, pumps, or through PRVs).

If the loss of water for emergencies is significant, then the utility may wish to do one or more of the following:

- Install temporary emergency pumps
- Prepare to activate an interconnection with a neighboring utility, if necessary
- Install a pair of hydrants at a pressure zone divide so that a temporary fire pump can be connected in an emergency

These emergency connection alternatives can be simulated to determine the amount of additional flow provided. Sometimes, adding an emergency connection or pump may only provide a marginal increase in flow because of bottlenecks elsewhere in the system.

The utility can use the results of the simulations to better present the impacts of removing a tank from service on fire departments and major customers. In this way, fire departments can prepare for the tank to be out of service, and make appropriate arrangements to supply the water that may be needed if there is a fire in the affected area. For instance, the fire department may be prepared to use trucks to carry water in an emergency, rather than rely on the distribution system. Alternatively, they can research the feasibility of laying hose to hydrants in a neighboring pressure zone that has adequate storage.

Low Demand Problems

While problems meeting fire demands are most obvious when taking a tank off-line, problems can crop up even during times of normal or low water usage. When a pressure zone is fed by a pumping station with constant-speed pumps and no other storage, the pumps will move along their pump curves to match demand. In off-peak times, the pumps must deliver very low flow compared to design flow (for example, 40 percent of average), and this flow will therefore be delivered at a higher head. Depending on the shape of the pump curve, very high system pressures can result. The worst problems occur with deep well pumps designed to pump against very high heads (that is, their pump curves are very steep), since a slight change in demand can result in dramatic pressure changes.

An example of this situation is shown in Figure 9.11 and the corresponding data in Table 9.1. The figure shows pressures at a representative node in the system (for example, the pump discharge) and how pressures at other points vary with elevation. The comparatively low nighttime demands indicate that the system is probably experiencing very little head loss during this time, compounding the effect that the increased pump discharge head has on the system pressures. If the piping of an area normally operates at a pressure of 85 psi (586 kPa), a 15 psi (103 kPa) increase can cause marginal piping to break [pipes that could not withstand 85 psi (586 kPa) would have broken previously]. If a tank is off-line, the utility can ill afford a major pipe break.

Figure 9.11
Effect of a change in demand on a constant-speed pump in a closed system

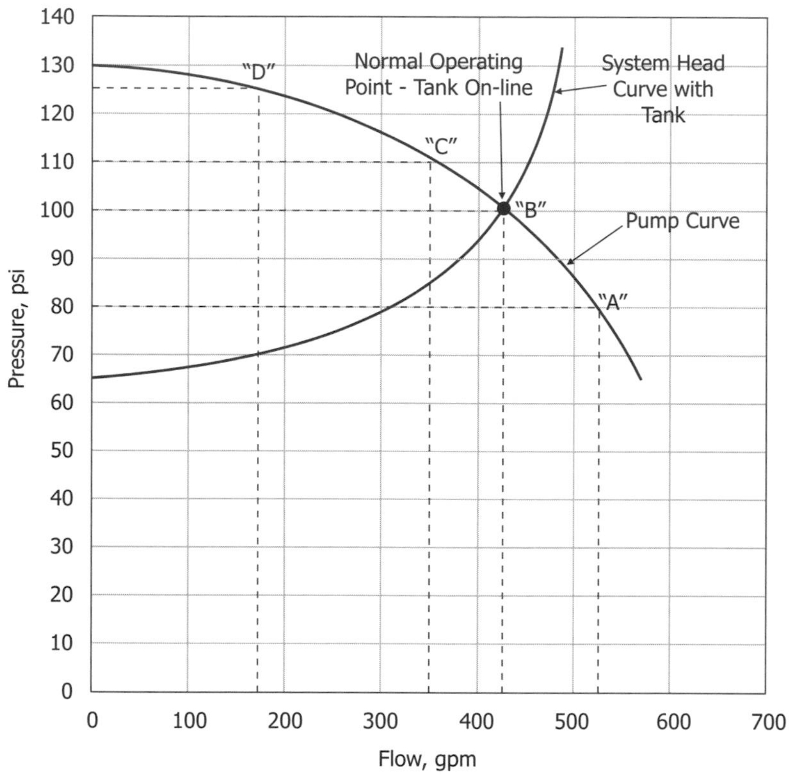

Table 9.1 Sample discharges and corresponding pressures for pump shown in Figure 9.11

Point	Demand	Pressure (psi)	Flow (gpm)
A	Peak demand	80	520
B	Normal operating point with tank	100	420
C	Average demand	110	350
D	Night-time demand	125	180

An EPS model can be used to simulate the pressures and flows that occur over the course of a day to determine if the pressures may be too high during off-peak demand hours, or too low during peak demand hours. If the pressures become too high, then a

PRV can be installed on the pump's discharge piping, or a pressure relief valve can be installed to release water back to the suction side of the pump when pressures get too high. The pressure relief valve can be modeled as a pressure sustaining valve set to open when the pressure exceeds a given setting. If the pressures are too low during peak times, then additional pumping or a modification of pump controls may be necessary.

9.6 SHUTTING DOWN A SECTION OF THE SYSTEM

Pipes are occasionally taken out of service to install a connection with a new pipe, repair a pipe break, or perform rehabilitation on a pipe section. Without a model, the modeler must either make an intelligent guess about the effect on system performance or perform a trial shutdown to see what happens. Simulations are an excellent alternative or supplement to these options.

Representing a Shutdown

The correct location of valves in the model is critical to determining the impact of a shutdown on distribution system performance. Figure 9.12 shows pipe P-140 connecting nodes J-37 and J-38. In shutdown scenario *A*, pipe P-140 is removed from service, along with nodes J-37 and J-38 and all pipes connected to these junctions. In shutdown scenario *B*, with valves *G* and *H* in service, only P-140 is taken out of service. Models are not usually set up to include small sections of pipe such as the one between valve *G* and node J-37, so the operator needs to carefully analyze how to modify the nodes and pipes to simulate the shutdown correctly. Most hydraulic simulation packages allow you to simulate pipe shutdowns as a function of the pipe instead of including all of the valves in the model.

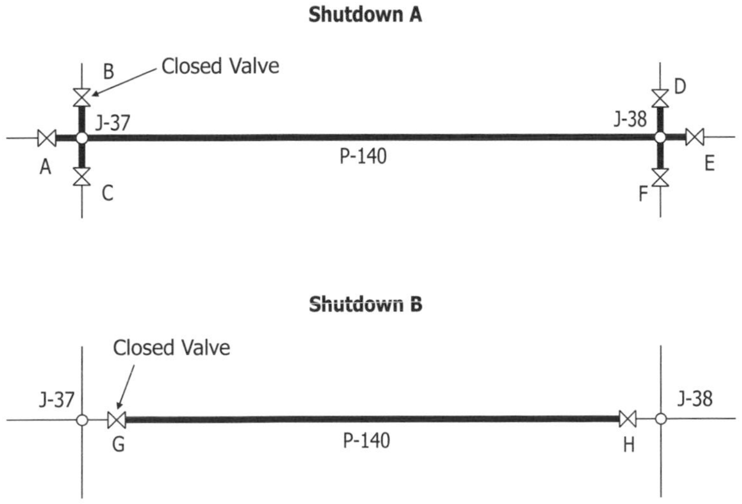

Figure 9.12
Simulating a pipe shutdown

When shutting down a large transmission main with many taps, the problem can be much more difficult. In this case, all smaller pipes that run parallel to the main must be included in the model, even if they have not been included under the current level of skeletonization (they may not have been considered important when the large main was in service). In Figure 9.13, the 6-in. (150-mm) pipe represented by the dashed line may have originally been excluded from the model. During a simulation of the shutdown of the 16-in. (400-mm) pipe, however, the smaller pipe becomes very important and must be included in the model.

Figure 9.13
Shutdown of a transmission main

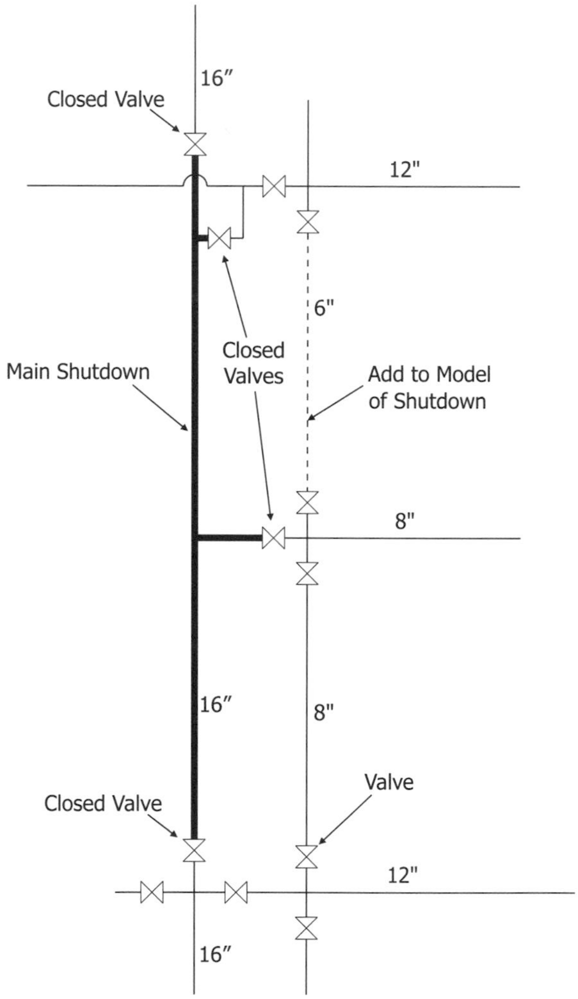

Simulating the Shutdown

Once the model is configured correctly, it can be used to simulate the shutdown. Prior to performing any EPS runs, steady-state simulations are used to determine if any customers will be immediately without water. This problem may show up in the model output as "disconnected node" warnings, or as nodes with negative pressures. Note that negative pressures do not actually exist in a water distribution system, rather they typically indicate that the specified demand cannot be met.

After the steady-state runs are successfully completed and it is clear which customers, if any, will be out of water, the operator will move on to EPS runs. An EPS run of the shutdown will show whether or not the affected portion of the system is being served with water from storage. A system that is living off of its storage can have tank water levels that drop quickly. In such cases, EPS runs are then used to study the range of tank water levels and their effect on system pressures.

Usually, in short-term shutdowns, the system can be supplied by storage. The model can determine how long it will take before storage is exhausted. If a long-term shutdown is required, the utility can identify the feasibility of alternative sources of water for the area using the EPS results.

This additional water supply may be provided by cracking open valves along pressure zone boundaries to obtain water from adjacent zones, opening interconnections with neighboring utilities, using portable pumps, or laying temporary pipes or hoses to transport water around the shutdown area. When a project is planned in which pipes will be out of service for cleaning and lining, temporary bypass piping laid on the ground (called *highlining*) can be used to transport water and supply customers in the area being taken out of service.

When modeling a tank shutdown, the effect that pressure has on demand needs to be considered. In actuality, water demands are a function of system pressure. When pressure drops below normal, less water is used and leakage decreases. When evaluating demands as a function of pressure drop, the model must be adjusted for this change in demand or the simulation results will be conservative. To quantitatively determine the amount to compensate for a change in demand, a model with pressure dependent-demands can be used (some hydraulic models allow you to specify demand as a function of pressure). In practice, however, demand is decreased by a factor related to the change in pressure, usually involving considerable judgment.

9.7 POWER OUTAGES

A power outage may affect only a single pump station, or it can impact the entire system. Typically, utilities attempt to tie important facilities to the power grid with redundant feeds in several directions. No electrical system is perfectly reliable, however, and power may be interrupted due to inclement weather or extreme power demands.

Most utilities rely on some combination of elevated storage, generators, or engine-driven pumps to protect against power outages. Generators may be permanently housed in pump stations, or temporarily stored elsewhere and transported to the area when they are needed. The generators located in pump stations may be configured to start automatically whenever there is a power outage, or they may require manual starting.

Modeling Power Outages

A power outage can be modeled by turning off all of the pumps that do not have a generator or engine. This action will probably result in nodes that are hydraulically disconnected from any tank or reservoir, or in negative pressures. A model that is structured this way will generate error messages and may not compute successfully. One possible way to work around this problem is to identify pressure zones that are disconnected and feed them from an imaginary reservoir (or fixed grade node) through a check valve at such a low head that all the pressures in the zone are negative. The negative pressures can then be used to indicate customers that will be without water.

Steady-state model runs of the power outage are performed before EPS runs. The steady-state runs identify the nodes that will immediately be without service. Once those problems have been addressed, EPS runs are used to study the effects of storage on service during a power outage. Zones with storage will first experience a drop in pressure as water levels fall, and then a loss of service once the tanks are empty. As with the case for systems with no tanks, each zone should have a reservoir at low head connected to the system through a very small pipe, so that nodes will not become disconnected in the model. Customers at lower elevations within a pressure zone may experience very little deterioration in service until the tank actually runs dry.

Demands will most likely decrease during a power outage. A factory that does not have power may have to shut down, and so will not use much water. Dishwashers and washing machines also do not operate during power outages. The modeler needs to estimate and account for this effect to the extent possible.

In areas where the utility uses portable generators to respond to power outages, the system will operate solely on storage for the amount of time that it takes to get the generator moved, set up, and running. Time-based controls can be set up in the model to turn on the pump after the time it would take to put the generator in place (probably a few hours after the start of the simulation).

Duration of an Outage

Estimating the duration of the power outage is one of the most difficult decisions in this type of analysis. Generally, the simulation should be based on the longest reasonable estimate of the outage duration (that is, model the worst-case situation). If the outage is shorter, the system performance will be that much better.

The EPS should be run for a duration that would give the tanks enough time to recover their normal water levels after the outage. Therefore, the EPS does not simply end at the time that the power is restored. Full tank level recovery may take hours or days. Although the system may have performed well up to this point, problems sometimes arise in the recovery period. For instance, because tank levels are lower there is less head to pump against, so the flow rate of the pumps may be too high, causing the motor to overload and trip. Also, after lengthy system-wide outages, recovery may be limited by source capacity.

9.8 POWER CONSUMPTION

One of the largest operating costs for most water utilities is the cost of energy to run pumps. Unfortunately, many utilities do not realize that an investment in a few small pump modifications or operational changes is quickly recovered through significant energy savings. Many pump stations provide an excellent opportunity for significant savings with minimal effort. Since so much energy is required for pumping, a savings of only one or two percent can add up to several thousand dollars over the course of a year. Some stations operate as much as 20 to 30 percent under optimal efficiency.

Common operational problems that contribute to high energy usage are:

- pumps that are no longer pumping against the head for which they were designed;
- pumps which were selected based upon a certain cycle time and are being run continuously; and
- variable-speed pumps being run at speeds that correspond to inefficient operating points.

In modeling pump operation, a highly skeletonized model can be used because only the large mains between the pump station and tanks are important in energy calculations. Adding detail usually has little impact on the results for this type of application.

In addition to the information in the following sections on using models for determining energy costs, publications with guidelines for minimizing energy costs are avail-

"Please help us reduce our garbage and improve our energy efficiency and our water quality. Help us to be eco-wise and—above all—to empower others."

able (Arora and LeChevallier, 1998; Hovstadius, 2001; Reardon, 1994; Walski, 1993). Numerous researchers have attempted to apply optimization techniques to energy management, with some success. Energy management continues to be a very active research area (Brion and Mays, 1991; Chase and Ormsbee, 1989; Coulbeck and Sterling, 1978; Coulbeck, Bryds, Orr, and Rance, 1988; Goldman, Sakarya, Ormsbee, Uber, and Mays, 2000; Lansey and Zhong, 1990; Ormsbee and Lingireddy, 1995; Ormsbee, Walski, Chase, and Sharp, 1989; Tarquin and Dowdy, 1989; and Zessler and Shamir, 1989).

Determining Pump Operating Points

Many pumps are selected based on what the operating points ought to be, but are run at operating points that can vary greatly over the course of a day. The simplest kind of analysis for a pump is to calculate pump production versus time of day and compare it with the flow rate at the pump's best efficiency point. Figure 9.14 shows pump discharge vs. time for a two-day period for a pump discharging into a pressure zone with no storage. If the pump's best efficiency point is approximately 400 gpm (0.025 m^3/s), then the pump is running efficiently. If however, the pump is a 600 gpm (0.038 m^3/s) pump, the pump is not being run efficiently and is wasting energy.

Figure 9.14
Pump discharge vs. time in closed system

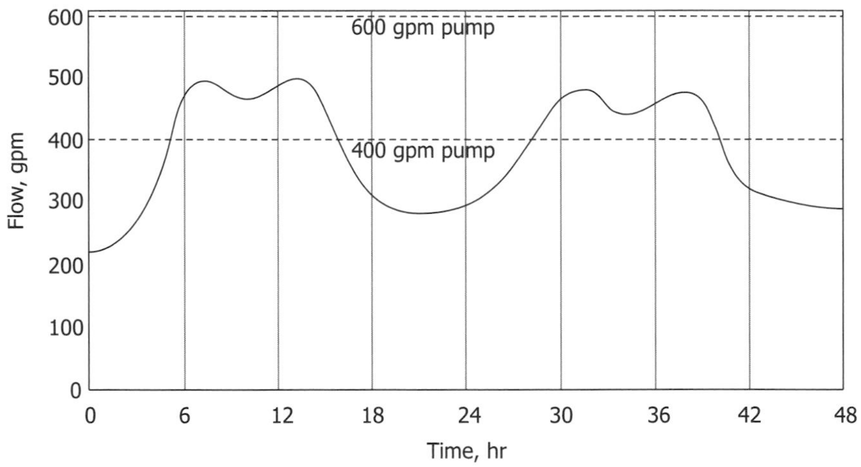

Variable-speed pumps do not run efficiently over a wide range of flows, as shown in Figure 9.15. For instance, a variable-speed pump discharging against 150 ft (46 m) of head may run efficiently at 500 gpm (0.032 m^3/s), but not at 250 gpm (0.016 m^3/s).

This type of analysis will help the operator determine whether the pump is operating efficiently. Operators will also want to know exactly how much money they are spending on a given pump versus a more efficient pump. The following sections explain the options to correct inefficiencies in pump operation and the calculations necessary to compute the associated costs.

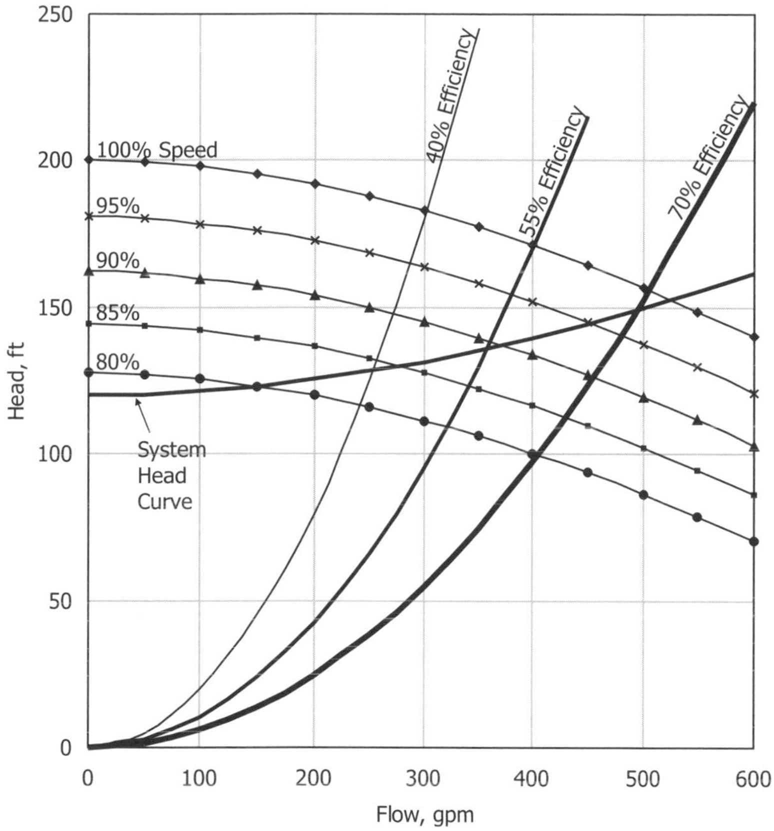

Figure 9.15
Method for determining pump operating points

Calculating Energy Costs

The cost of pumping depends on the flow, pump head, efficiency, price, and the duration of time that the pump is running. The cost for pumping energy over a given time period can be determined using the following equation:

$$C = C_f Q h_p p t / (e_p e_m) \tag{9.1}$$

where
C = cost over time duration t (\$)
Q = flow rate (gpm, l/s)
h_p = total dynamic head (TDH) of pump (ft, m)
p = price of energy (cents/kW-hr)
t = duration that pump is operating at this operating point (hrs)
e_p = pump efficiency (%)
e_m = motor efficiency (%)
C_f = unit conversion factor (0.0189 English, 1.019 SI)

To determine the daily and annual energy costs for continuously running pumps, use 24 hours and 8,760 hours, respectively for t. The product of pump efficiency and motor efficiency is generally referred to as the *wire-to-water efficiency* or *overall efficiency*, since it accounts for the efficiency of the motor and the pump combined, and is commonly measured directly in the field (see page 180).

Since most stations have a single pump running at a time, and if there is storage downstream it operates at roughly the same operating point over the course of the day, this equation can be used to estimate the energy consumption over a given time period. For example, to calculate the cost of running a pump for a day, t would represent the number of hours the pump is running per day, and C would be the daily energy cost. Determining the value of C can be complicated by the fact that some utilities pay different rates for power at different times of the day. If t is the number of hours that the pump is running per year, then C will be the annual energy cost.

■ **Example - Energy Costs** Consider a pump that discharges 600 gpm at a TDH of 230 ft (as determined by the model) and runs 12 hours per day. From the pump efficiency curve, we know that the pump efficiency is 62 percent. The motor is 90 percent efficient, and the power costs 8 cents per kW-hr. The energy cost equation (Equation 9.1) is applied as follows.

$$C\ (in\ \$/day) = (0.0189 \times 600\ gpm \times 230\ ft \times 8\ cents/kW\text{-}hr \times 12\ hours/day) / (62\% \times 90\%)$$

$$C = \$44.87/day$$

If the utility were to change to a 400 gpm pump that ran for 18 hours per day at a pump efficiency of 70 percent, and replace the motor with a premium efficiency motor having an efficiency of 95 percent, then the cost for energy would be $37.65/day. The annual savings would be $2,635, which may pay for the change in pumping equipment.

Multiple Distinct Operating Points

Some pumps do not stay on a single operating point when running, but will operate at several different operating points depending on tank water levels, demands, control valve settings, and the status of other pumps. The above equation would then be solved for each operating point by using the model to determine the Q and h for that operating point and the duration of time the pump will be running at that operating point.

As the flow changes over the course of a day, the head and efficiency of the pump change, affecting the amount of energy used. Therefore, each operating point and the duration the pump operates at that point must be considered separately when computing energy costs. The costs associated with each duration composing the period being studied are then totaled to arrive at the total cost for the time period.

For the example shown in Table 9.2, the total of all the individual durations during a day, including the time that the pump is not in operation, is 24 hours. For each operating point, the model will determine Q and h, and the pump efficiency curve will give a value for pump efficiency. The energy cost for the duration of each operating point is then determined. Costs are then summed to give daily or annual costs, as shown in Table 9.2 for a pump that can be approximated with three operating points.

Table 9.2 Example calculation of energy costs with different operating points

Given Information				Calculated Data (using Equation 9.1)	
Energy Price: $0.08 kW-hr		Motor efficiency: 92%			
Q (gpm)	h (ft)	e_p (%)	t (hrs/day)	C ($/day)	C ($/yr)
200	150	65	4	3.03	n/a
220	135	68	14	10.05	n/a
250	125	63	6	4.89	n/a
		TOTAL	24	17.97	6,561

Continuously Varying Pump Flow

For constant-speed pumps discharging into a dead-end system, the flow will vary continuously. These pumps do not have a single pump operating point, or even a handful of them. In determining energy costs associated with these pumps, each hour (or other time step) corresponds to a separate operating point. For example, if the table above were made for a pump with a continuously varying pump flow, it would have 24 operating points instead of three. A spreadsheet or a model that automatically computes energy costs then becomes the method of choice for the calculation. The time scale over which the flow varies would determine the time step size. For example, if there were large fluctuations within an hour, a smaller time step would be required.

The difficulty in using a spreadsheet is that the efficiency must be read from the pump curve for each flow in the spreadsheet. Ideally, a function could be developed relating flow to efficiency, as described in the next section.

Developing a Curve Relating Flow to Efficiency

A curve representing the relationship between pump discharge (Q) and pump efficiency (e_p) can usually be described by the equation for an inverted parabola as shown in Equation 9.2.

$$e_p = aQ^2 + bQ + c \tag{9.2}$$

The key, therefore, is to determine the values for the coefficients a, b, and c. The easiest way is to enter at least three pairs of Q and e values into a polynomial regression program (or spreadsheet), and have the program determine a, b, and c. This functionality is also available in some hydraulic models. For example, given the efficiency vs. flow data in the table below,

Q (gpm)	Efficiency (%)
200	55
400	85
600	60

a polynomial regression program can be used to produce the equation relating flow and efficiency as:

$$e_p = -0.00069\,Q^2 + 0.5625\,Q - 30$$

The graph of this equation is shown in Figure 9.16.

Figure 9.16
Flow vs. efficiency relationship

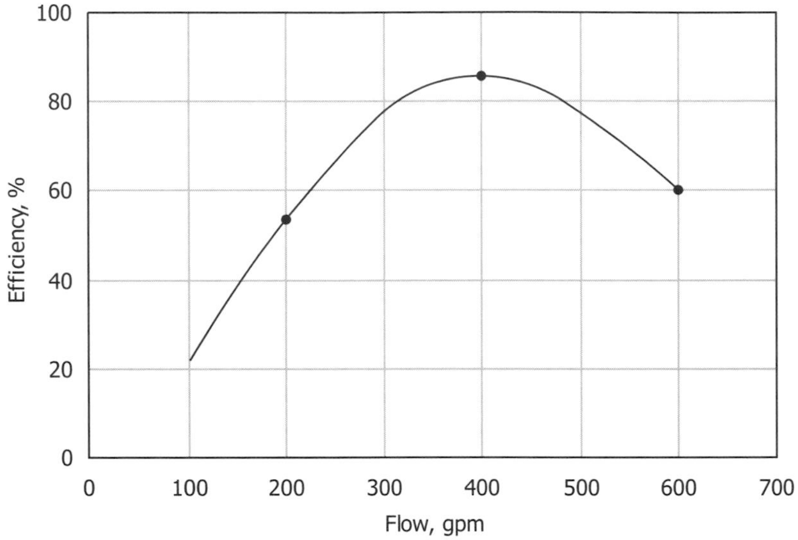

Variable-Speed Pumps

The procedure for computing the costs of variable-speed pumping is similar to the procedure for continuously-varying pumps, except that the relationship is not simply between flow and efficiency, but also a function of total dynamic head as well. The equation can be approximated by:

$$e_p = a(Q/n)^2 + b(Q/n) + c \tag{9.3}$$

where n = ratio of pump speed/pump test speed

A model can be used to determine a table of Q and h versus time of day. It is then possible to look up the efficiency for each time increment and use a spreadsheet program to sum up the costs for the entire period.

The results of these calculations usually surprise operators, who often assume that variable-speed pumps operate efficiently over the full range of speeds. Actually, variable-speed pumps are only slightly more efficient than a constant-speed pump when pumping into a dead-end zone. When considering both the cost of the variable-speed drive and the drive's energy costs, variable-speed pumping is not always a cost-effective option.

Extending Efficiency Curves

While centrifugal pumps can operate at rates that vary from no flow to flows well beyond the best efficiency point, most pump manufacturers only show the pump efficiency curve over a narrow range of flow rates. However, in performing energy calculations, the modeler may need to determine the efficiency of a pump at a very low or very high flow rate.

Plotting a curve of efficiency versus flow outside the range of the given efficiencies leaves a great deal of room for judgment, and therefore error. Fitting the points on the efficiency curve to a parabola and extrapolating that parabola provides a logical approximation of the data, but it is not necessarily correct.

Though manufacturers provide only a narrow range of efficiency data, they do provide head and power data over a much wider range of flows, usually all the way down to no flow. Pump efficiencies can be calculated from this data using the following equation:

$$e = \frac{100 C_f Q h_P}{BHP}$$

where
e = efficiency (%)
Q = flow rate (gpm, m^3/hr)
h_P = head added at pumps (ft, m)
BHP = brake horsepower (hp, kW)
C_f = unit conversion factor (2.53×10^{-4} English, 2.72×10^{-3} SI)

A plot of this equation should exactly match the manufacturer's efficiency data in the range provided, and it provides a means of computing efficiencies for points beyond the limits of this curve when necessary.

Using Pump Energy Data

The methods described previously will enable the operator to identify inefficient pumps and estimate the cost savings if they are replaced with pumps and motors that are more efficient. In some cases, the problem may be in the system rather than the pumps, so modifying the system can be the more cost-effective option. For example, it may be helpful to install a hydropneumatic tank in a small dead-end system so that the pump operates against a fairly steady head. Also, in a system with an existing hydropneumatic tank, changing the pump controls may save energy.

In general, pumps with a steady head on both the suction and discharge sides will be more efficient than pumps feeding a dead-end zone. Tanks (even hydropneumatic tanks in small systems) can be very helpful in reducing energy costs.

The model can be used to simulate various strategies. The energy costs associated with different pumps, operating points, and operating strategies are calculated by the simulation program, so that the most efficient and cost-effective solution can be chosen. Once the changes are instituted, energy savings pay back the utility year after year. The present worth of energy savings can be compared with the capital costs to achieve them.

Whenever there is a major change in the water distribution system, pumps must be reexamined. Installing a new parallel or larger pipe on the discharge side of a pumping station lowers the system head curve and moves the operating point to a higher flow rate. In some cases, this change can move the pump to a less efficient operating point. It may be necessary to counteract the change by trimming the impellers in some cases. Another alternative is to throttle valves to move the operating point to a more efficient location. The model can be used to determine the pump operating points before and after any changes.

Understanding Rate Structures

To get the most out of pump efficiency studies, it is essential for the utility to understand the power rate structure. Some power utilities have time of day energy pricing, especially during peak energy consumption periods. This pricing can be accounted for by using the applicable energy price for each time period. Others use a block rate for which the unit price drops as the total power consumed increases. Still others use block rates that change based on the peak energy consumption rate.

Not all energy costs are structured as described above. Some costs are *demand charges* or *capacity charges* related to the maximum rate at which the water utility uses energy. The time period on which the maximum rate is based may be the peak 15-minute period over the last three months, or the peak hour over the last year. It may be calculated meter-by-meter, by customer, or by some other criteria. The modeler can estimate the demand charge by simulating peak pumping periods and determining which one yields the highest power consumption rate. In some cases, total cost may be more sensitive to the peak demand than the energy use.

The water utility needs to understand this peaking charge and operate the system in a way that will minimize it. Often, the demand charge is set on a peak day or a day with a large fire. As a goal, the utility should try not to exceed peak day pumping rates.

The demand charge can be calculated using the peak flow rate in the following equation with the corresponding head and efficiencies.

$$Demand(kW) = C_f Q h_p / (e_m e_p) \tag{9.4}$$

where C_f = unit conversion factor (1.88 English, 0.0098 SI)

Note that time is not considered in the above equation, because the demand is a rate of energy usage, not the total energy used.

9.9 WATER DISTRIBUTION SYSTEM FLUSHING

Water distribution system *flushing* is an important tool for helping operators to control distribution system water quality. Flushing stirs up and removes sediments from mains and removes poor quality water from the system, replacing it with fresher water from the source. Procedures for flushing are discussed in detail in Antoun, Dyksen, and Hiltebrand (1999); California-Nevada AWWA (1981); Chadderton, Christensen, and Henry-Unrath (1992); Oberoi (1994); Patison (1980); and Walski (2000).

The term *directional flushing* or *uni-directional flushing* is used to describe operation of valves during flushing to maximize velocity and control flow direction.

Flushing is usually accomplished by opening one or more hydrants in a planned pattern. The usual rule of thumb for flushing is to always flush with clean water behind you, meaning that hydrants should be operated to pull the freshest water into the area being flushed. Flushing programs usually start at the source and move out through the system.

Unfortunately, operators conducting the flushing program cannot see what is occurring in the mains, or measure parameters like velocity or flow rate in pipes. Water distribution models provide a way to look into the pipes and obtain an indication of how a flushing program will work.

Modeling Flushing

Because every pipe can carry a good deal of water during flushing, all pipes in the area being flushed should be included in the model. If the pipe being flushed has a single directional feed, as in a branched system, a model is not needed to determine velocity; however, model runs can still help to identify the system's ability to maintain adequate service. In areas of a system with multiple sources or looping flow paths, determining the direction of flow and velocity is more challenging. Flow in pipes will often differ from what the operator anticipates in these cases, so analysis using a model is very helpful.

Representing a Flowed Hydrant

The easiest way to simulate flushing is to change the demand at the node being flowed to that expected during flushing, which can be called the *free discharge*. In concept, this approach is fairly simple. However, most utilities do not know the free discharge flow they can expect to get from each hydrant, so this value must be estimated. Closed valves can complicate the process of flow estimation, since valves are sometimes closed to facilitate directional flushing. Some utilities measure and keep a record of the discharge from each hydrant during flushing. This information can then be very helpful in future simulations, providing good estimates for nodal demands unless there have been significant changes in the system since the last flushing.

Estimating demand is also difficult because of the interrelationship of discharge and pressure. Pressure in the mains affects hydrant discharge, and hydrant discharge affects pressure. In larger mains, the flow is almost completely controlled by head losses in the hydrant lateral and the hydrant itself. In smaller mains, the distribution system may account for more head loss than the hydrant.

The hydrants must be modeled in a way that accounts for the pressure drop due to flushing. One way is to represent the hydrant discharging to the atmosphere as an equivalent pipe discharging to a reservoir located at the elevation of the hydrant. This representation is shown in Figure 9.17. The first step in this process is to estimate the head loss in the hydrant, and the conversion of static head to velocity head in the outlet. As a quick approximation, a 2½-in. (60-mm) hydrant outlet orifice can be represented by about 1,000 ft (305 m) of equivalent 6-in. (150-mm) pipe added to the hydrant lateral, while a 4½-in. (115-mm) outlet can be represented by 250 ft (76 m) of 6-in. (150-mm) pipe (Walski, 1995). Because the velocity is very high in the hydrant lateral, all minor losses must be accounted for, either by using minor loss *k*-factors or an equivalent pipe.

Figure 9.17
Representing a hydrant as a reservoir

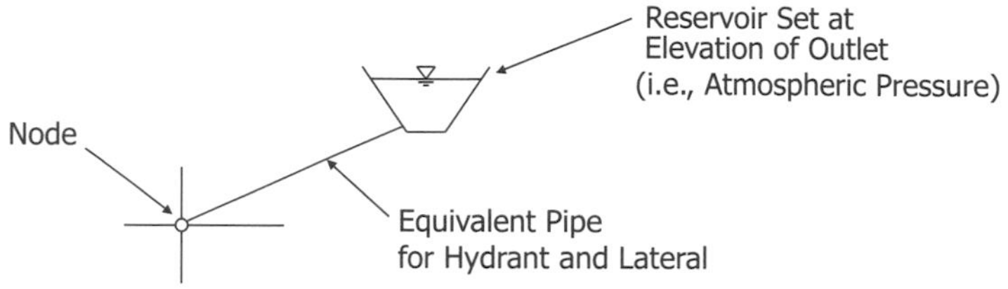

Using a reservoir with equivalent pipe increases the size of the model since each hydrant represents an additional pipe. The equivalent pipe representing the hydrant should be closed unless the hydrant is flowing. Provided the modeler uses appropriate equivalent lengths to represent the hydrant, this method can be more accurate than simply placing a demand on a node.

Hydrant Location Relative to Nodes

While hydrants are located close to intersections, they are usually not located precisely at model nodes. Therefore, modeling a hydrant flow by placing the flow at the model node is not entirely correct. Usually, this problem is only significant if the hydrant is on a small main close to a junction with a large main [for example, a hydrant located on a 6-in. (150-mm) pipe 30 ft (9 m) from a connection to a 24-in. (600-mm) main]. In the model, almost all of the flow will arrive at the hydrant from the 24-in. (600-mm) pipe. In reality, the flow must also travel through 30 ft (9 m) of 6-in. (150-mm) pipe before reaching the hydrant. Since the 6-in. (150-mm) pipe restricts the flow much more than the 24-in. (600-mm) pipe, it can have a significant effect on what the hydrant discharge will be.

In addition, when the utility is practicing directional flushing (that is, closing valves to control the direction of flow), differences between the actual position of the hydrant and the position of the hydrant model node may be significant. To complicate matters, there may be a closed valve between the hydrant and the node in the model during directional flushing. A hydrant that is close to a node may not be directly connected to the node, as shown in Figure 9.18. Placing the demand at the existing node may not be accurate, and another node might need to be added to depict the situation accurately. If the utility will be using directional flushing, then numerous additional nodes may be needed to accurately represent closed valves.

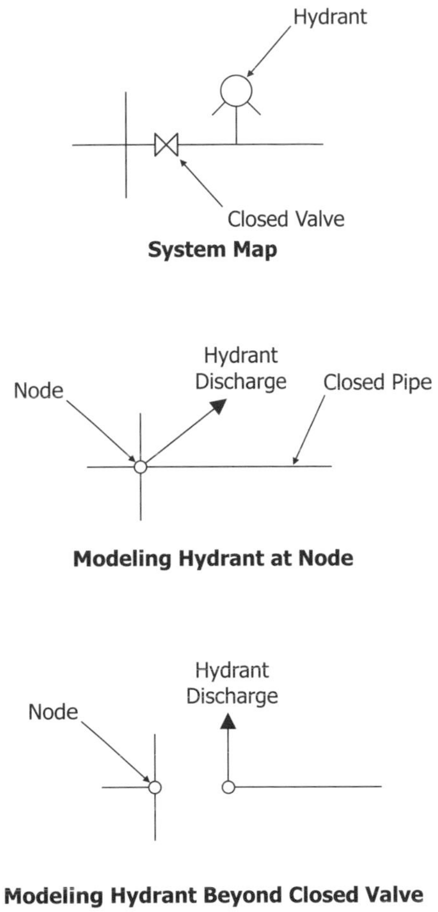

Figure 9.18
Accurately modeling a hydrant near a closed valve

Steady-State vs. EPS Runs

If the operator is only interested in velocities and is not trying to track water quality, then a steady-state run can be used to simulate each hydrant being flowed for flushing. The maximum velocity in each pipe over all of the steady-state simulations can then be used as an indicator in evaluating the effectiveness of flushing in increasing velocities and thereby cleaning the pipes. Individual water quality constituents can also be tracked using EPS runs to simulate flushing.

Some utilities do not fully open the fire hydrant for the entire flushing period. Instead, they fully open it to stir up sediment, and then back off the flow to remove the sediment from the pipe. This method is effective as long as the flow continues for a sufficient period of time, and continues in the same direction. When a hydrant is located between a tank and a pump, most of the flow may first come from the tank because the flow from the pump is limited by the pump curve. As the tank level drops and the hydrant flow backs off, however, more water may be delivered to the flowed hydrant from the pump rather than the tank. Therefore, the water stirred up during the higher flow period may not be removed effectively from the system, and may inadvertently enter the tank. This situation is shown in Figure 9.19. Model runs would show that it would be necessary to flush at a high rate or shut valves to control the direction of flow.

Figure 9.19
Effect on flushing of hydrant being located between pump and tank

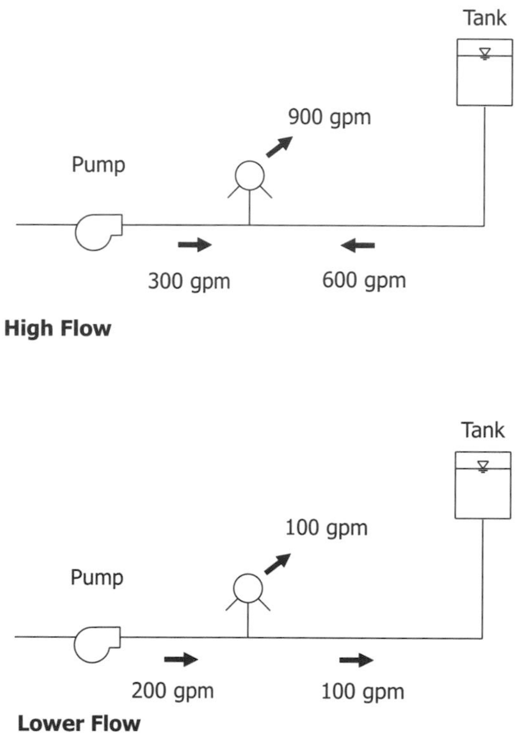

Indicators of Successful Flushing

When using simulations to determine the effectiveness of the flushing technique, the operator selects the parameters to use as indicators of success. The velocity is generally the best indicator of flushing effectiveness. There is no fast rule, however, for determining the velocity needed for successful flushing. In a neighborhood distribution grid of small pipes, a velocity of 2 ft/s (0.6 m/s) is considered a good value. However, raising velocity to values on the order of 5 ft/s (1.5 m/s) will result in even better flushing. It is difficult to achieve high velocities in large transmission mains, so flushing has little effect there.

Another important consideration is the change in velocity in a pipe relative to the pipe's normal velocity. For example, a pipe that normally experiences velocity of 2 ft/s (0.6 m/s) would require a substantially higher velocity for flushing. Any sediment in that pipe that could be suspended by a 2 ft/s (0.6 m/s) velocity has already been moved, and the material that is left is of a size and density that requires velocities greater than 2 ft/s (0.6 m/s) to be moved.

While velocity is the best indicator of flushing success, the flushing must be carried out for a long enough period of time to allow the water disturbed by flushing to be transported out of the system. Flushing can be tracked using the water quality tracing feature in a model, and the user can track chlorine as an indicator of how effective the flushing is.

Alternatively, the user can tag the water initially in the system and the tank with a concentration of 0.0 mg/l and tag the water at the source with a concentration of 100.0 mg/l and monitor how long it takes for the fresh water to move through the system during flushing (concentration in all pipes equal to 100 mg/l). Using a hydraulic simulation program's color-coding feature, the fresh water from the source can be represented by the color blue, while the water present in the pipes at the start of the simulation can be represented by red, and a spectrum of colors can be used for the concentrations in between. In this way, the model user can view the way in which the old water is displaced by the fresher water. This type of simulation can serve as an indication of how long the flushing needs to continue.

Ideally, the models would be able to track turbidity during flushing events. However, the affect of flushing on turbidity cannot be accurately predicted since turbidity does not conform to the law of conservation of mass (Walski, 1991). Some insights can be gained, however, by correlating turbidity with flushing velocity (Walski and Draus, 1996).

One of the problems in reviewing the results of flushing runs is determining the extent to which they were successful. When a hydrant is flowed, there are actually three levels of effectiveness that can be used to judge the success or failure:

1. Areas cleaned by flushing
2. Areas undisturbed by flushing
3. Areas that are stirred up but not successfully cleaned

The goal is to maximize the cleaned areas and minimize areas that are disturbed and not successfully cleaned. The latter areas contribute to turbidity complaints after flushing and are characterized by velocities that increase slightly over normal conditions, but not significantly enough to successfully be flushed; and by insufficient durations that prevent suspended sediment from making its way to the flushed hydrant. The model can help locate these areas and minimize them by adjusting the valving and sequence of flushing.

9.10 SIZING DISTRIBUTION SYSTEM METERS

Subsystem Metering

Many water systems have been constructed with little or no metering between the master meters at the treatment plant (or well) and the customer meters. System operators may like to have more information about distribution system flows at locations throughout the system to better understand water use, quantify available capacity in the system, and compute the amounts of unaccounted-for water in different parts of the system. Understanding unaccounted-for water on a basis can be helpful in managing leak detection and repair, and in instituting water main replacement programs. Once the meter is in place, it can also provide additional information used in fine-tuning model calibration. Subsystem metering is commonly practiced in the United Kingdom where individual customers are not universally metered.

Because of cost and difficulty of installation, system flow meters are only placed in a few select points throughout the system. Pump stations and PRV vaults at pressure zone boundaries are the most common locations for metering. Other key metering locations include pipelines that carry virtually all of the flow into an area.

Sizing the meters is primarily a problem of understanding the range of flows that the meter will experience. The meter needs to be selected to pick up both the high and the low ranges of flows. Unfortunately, unlike the situation with customer metering, there is no fixture unit method (see page 318) that can be used for large areas within the distribution system. The next section provides guidelines for using models to size meters.

Using Models for Meter Sizing

Before computerized modeling, the operator would estimate the range of flows based either on the number of customers or on readings from a temporary meter, such as a Pitot rod. Use of the Pitot rod required excavation to the top of the main and tapping the pipe. Even a less accurate clamp-on meter requires access to the pipe and long straight runs of pipe upstream of the meter, and when pipe wall properties are unknown, clamp-on meters need to be calibrated in place to have any validity. With temporary metering, the operator cannot be certain that the full range of flows has been captured because the temporary meter may not have been installed during the extreme event.

Running an EPS model can generate a demand pattern for any demand condition, including projected conditions. By making multiple runs of the model and plotting them, the operator can see the kinds of flows the meter is likely to encounter.

The meter can be sized based upon the pipe size and the type of meter. For example, once the range of flows is determined, the engineer can select the *Beta ratio* (the ratio of throat diameter to pipe diameter) for a venturi meter, or determine if the velocity is high enough for an electromagnetic meter. The flow patterns are usually quite different for a meter on a pipe that serves an area continuously (for example, a pipe from a PRV or a variable-speed pump with no storage) and a meter that is located at a pump that cycles on and off as it is discharging into a zone with storage. These different patterns are shown in Figure 9.20. Meters that are located at a pump in a system having storage can have a more limited range, while those on lines where flows must vary continuously to meet demands require a much greater range.

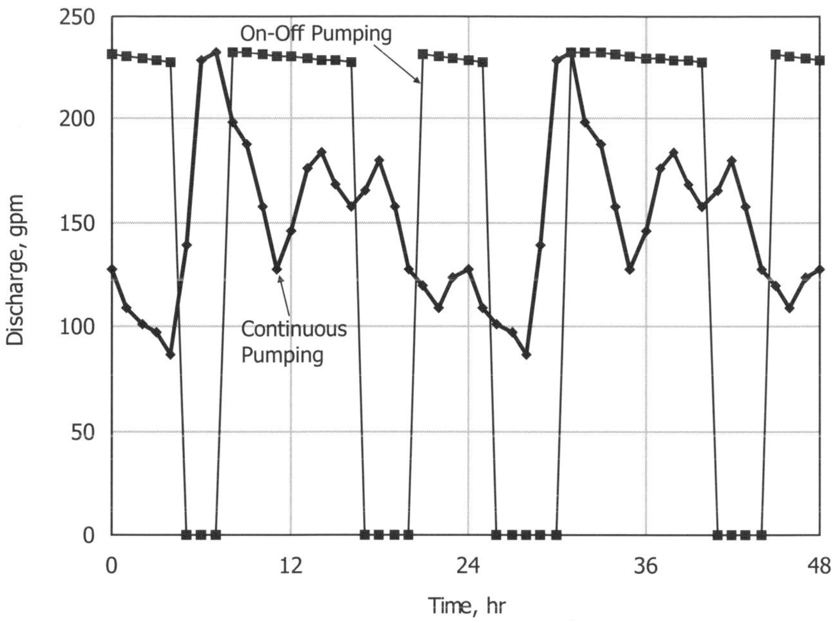

Figure 9.20
Variations in flow through meter to system with and without storage

Implications for Meter Selection

Once the range of flows has been estimated, the type of meter can be selected. Small flows, such as those on 4- or 6-in. (100 to 150-mm) pump discharge lines, can be metered by turbine meters equipped with some type of pulse counter that produces rate of flow information in analog form.

As flows become greater, the turbine meters are used less often than electromagnetic (mag) meters, differential head meters (venturi, orifice, flow tube, and nozzle types), or ultrasonic meters. Differential head meters are usually the most reliable and least expensive, and can be run without power. Unfortunately, they are limited (with some exceptions) to unidirectional flow and can produce significant head loss as the velocity increases. Also, recent advances in PRV technology have produced several types of PRVs that can also serve as flow meters.

Ultimately, the selection of a meter depends on the nature of the flow, the site, and the preference of the operator. The pipe network model can be used to provide information on the range of flows, and once the meter is in place, the model can be improved with information from the flow meter.

9.11 MODELS FOR INVESTIGATION OF SYSTEM CONTAMINATION

Models can also be used to analyze historical water system contamination events. Usually, when water distribution system contamination is suspected, there is not enough data to completely reconstruct the events. Using available data as a starting point, it is possible to reconstruct the events that caused contamination and identify locations in the system that received contaminated water using EPS models. Because it is not possible or desirable to recreate the actual contamination event(s), the modeler usually does not have all the data that would be available for modeling the current-day system, especially when the contamination events happened years earlier. The results will involve greater uncertainty than modeling current day conditions, but reasonable conclusions can nevertheless be drawn from the model.

The first application of water quality modeling to distribution systems was the now famous case of Woburn, Massachusetts. (Murphy, 1991; and Harr, 1995). The model was used to substantiate contamination that had happened years earlier. Therefore, several different versions of the model were needed to reflect how the system evolved over the time of the alleged contamination. Murphy also applied this type of modeling to San Jose, California.

The USEPA applied water quality modeling to investigate contamination first in Cabool, Missouri (*Esterichia coli* serotype 0157:H7) and Gideon, Missouri (*Salmonella typhimurium*). The Cabool outbreak involved 243 cases and 6 deaths and was attributed to two water line breaks (Geldreich, 1996). In Gideon, water quality modeling was used to identify contamination of a tank by bird droppings as the likely source (Clark, et al., 1996; Clark and Grayman, 1998). Of recent interest is the water system contamination in Walkerton, Ontario, Canada.

Kramer, Herwald, Craun, Calderon, and Juranek (1996) reported that 26.7 percent of waterborne disease outbreaks in the U.S. in 1993-94 were due to distribution system deficiencies. Among those cases due to source deficiencies, water quality models can be used to track the area of influence of each water source if the system has several sources.

Water quality models have also been used in forensic studies (also referred to as *hindcasting*) to identify responsible parties in litigation. While many such studies have been conducted, few have been published because of legal issues surrounding such applications. Two cases of forensic applications of water quality models are documented in Harding and Walski (2000) for Phoenix/Scottsdale, Arizona, and Maslia, et al. (2000) for Dover Township (Tom's River), New Jersey. The Phoenix study showed that contaminant concentrations can fluctuate widely at a particular location, both hourly and seasonally, due to changes in pump operation because of varying demands.

Forensic studies are different from most planning and design applications in that instead of running the EPS model for an average day or a peak day, the model must be run for a large number of actual days to reconstruct historical events. This type of modeling involves a great deal of research into how the system was being operated when the contamination is alleged to have occurred. Because the system evolved over many years, several versions of the model are required to reflect the different topology, facilities, and loading.

While typical water quality modeling studies reported in the literature have focused on disinfectant decay (Clark, Grayman, Goodrich, Deininger, and Hess, 1991; and Rossman, Clark, and Grayman, 1994), forensic studies can involve a variety of contaminants including VOCs, microbes, and inorganic chemicals. While behavior of these chemicals is often treated in the models as conservative (that is, there is no mechanism for volatile chemicals to leave a pipe), they can undergo a variety of transformations. For example, volatile chemicals can leave water stored in tanks. Walski (1999) determined that only a small portion of TCE (Trichlorethylene) is expected to be lost to the air in storage tanks because of the lack of turbulence in a tank.

Even when it is not possible to accurately model the behavior of a chemical or microbe in a distribution system, water quality models can provide a picture of how water moves in the system, and therefore which portions of the system are exposed to water from particular sources, tanks, or pipe breaks.

9.12 LEAKAGE CONTROL

Distribution system water losses can be split into two basic categories: losses due to pipe bursts and losses resulting from background leakage. Bursts are characterized by a sudden loss of water limited in duration to the time reported and unreported bursts are allowed to discharge. Background losses are characterized by a continual seeping of water from pipe fittings and from mains that are cracked or perforated through corrosion.

The quantity of leakage from a water distribution system is related to the system pressure, thus reducing pressures during off-peak hours can reduce leakage. While controlling leakage by reducing pressures is not common practice in North America, this approach is used in some European systems (Goodwin, 1980; Germanopoulos, 1995). Pressure reduction is accomplished through valve operation.

In addition to water pressure management, active leakage control involves the disaggregation of large networks into smaller areas (called District Metering Areas in the United Kingdom) that can be better monitored (Engelhardt, Skipworth, Savic, Saul, and Walters, 2000). *Water audits*, detailed accounting of water flow into and out of portions of the distribution system, are then used to identify areas having excessive leakage. Unfortunately, they do not provide specific information about the location of leaks. To pinpoint leaks, detection surveys are required.

Modeling can be used to help manage leak reduction by determining the effects that either the disaggregation of networks into smaller areas or the adjustment of the controlling valves has on pressure and flow through the system. The modeler should note that there is a practical limit to which pressure can be reduced before it adversely affects customers at higher elevations.

While predicting pressure as a result of valve operation is fairly straightforward, using a model to estimate the amount of leak reduction is far less precise. This estimation involves modeling leakage through the use of a flow emitter element or a reservoir connected to the system through a small pipe (see page 322 for information on a similar technique used for modeling sprinklers). A reduction in pressure results in a reduction in flow through this element. Whenever a leak is repaired, the coefficient of this element is then changed to reflect the reduced number of leaks.

Several studies have been conducted on leakage modeling using steady-state simulations (Martinez, Conejos, and Vercher, 1999; Pudar and Ligget, 1992; and Stathis and

Loganathan, 1999), but the hidden nature of leaks limits the precision. The use of inverse transient models to locate leaks has also been reported in literature (Tang, Brunone, Karney, and Rosetti, 2000; Kapelan, Savic, and Walters, 2000).

REFERENCES

Antoun, E. N., Dyksen, J. E., and Hiltebrand. (1999). "Unidirectional Flushing." *Journal of the American Water Works Association*, 91(7), 62.

Arora, H., and LeChevallier, M. W. (1998). "Energy Management Opportunities." *Journal of the American Water Works Association*, 90(2), 40.

Brion, L., and Mays, L. W. (1991). "Methodology for Optimal Operation of Pumping Stations in Water Distribution Systems." *Journal of Hydraulic Engineering*, ASCE, 117(11), 1551.

California-Nevada AWWA. (1981). *Distribution Main Flushing and Cleaning*. California-Nevada AWWA, Rancho Cucamonga, California.

Cesario, A. L. (1995). *Modeling, Analysis, and Design of Water Distribution Systems*. AWWA, Denver, Colorado.

Chadderton, R. A., Christensen, G. L., and Henry-Unrath, P. (1992). *Implementation and Optimization of Distribution Flushing Programs*. AWWARF, Denver, Colorado.

Chase, D. V., and Ormsbee, L. E. (1989). "Optimal Pump Operation of Water Distribution Systems with Multiple Tanks." *Proceedings of the AWWA Computer Conference*, American Water Works Association, 205.

Clark, R. M., Grayman, W. M., Goodrich, R. A., Deininger, P. A., and Hess, A. F. (1991). "Field Testing Distribution Water Quality Models." *Journal of the American Water Works Association,* 84(7), 67.

Clark, R. M., Geldreich, E. E., Fox, K. R., Rice, E. W., Johnson, C. H., Goodrich, J. A., Barnick, J. A., and Abdesaken, F. (1996). "Tracking a Salmonella Serovar Typhimurium Outbreak in Gideon, Missouri: Role of Contaminant Propagation Modeling." *Journal of Water Supply Research and Technology-Aqua*, 45(4), 171.

Clark, R. M., and Grayman, W. G. (1998). *Modeling Water Quality in Drinking Water Distribution Systems*. AWWA, Denver, Colorado.

Coulbeck, B., and Sterling, M. (1978). "Optimal Control of Water Distribution Systems." *Proceedings of the Institute of Electrical Engineers*, 125, 1039.

Coulbeck, B., Bryds, M., Orr, C., and Rance, J. (1988). "A Hierarchal Approach to Optimized Control of Water Distribution Systems." *Journal of Optimal Control Applications and Methods*, 9(1), 51.

Engelhardt, M.O., Skipworth, P.J., Savic, D.A., Saul, A.J., and Walters, G.A. (2000). "Rehabilitation Strategies for Water Distribution Networks: A Literature Review with a UK Perspective." *Urban Water*, Vol. 2, No. 2, 153-170.

Geldreich, E.E. (1996). *Microbial Quality of Water Supply in Distribution Systems*. Lewis Publishers, Boca Raton, Florida.

Germanopoulos, G. (1995). "Valve Control Regulation for Reducing Leakage." *Improving Efficiency and Reliability in Water Distribution Systems*, Kluwer Academic Press, London, United Kingdom, 165.

Goldman, F. E., Sakarya, B., Ormsbee, L.E., Uber, J., and Mays, L. (2000). "Optimization Models for Operations." *Water Distribution Systems Handbook*, Mays, L. W., ed., McGraw-Hill, New York, New York.

Goodwin, S.J. (1980). "The Results of the Experimental Program on Leakage and Leakage Control." *Technical Report TR 154*, Water Research Centre.

Harding, B.L., and Walski, T.M. (2000). "Long Time-series Simulation of Water Quality in Distribution Systems." *Journal of Water Resources Planning and Management*, ASCE, 126(4), 199.

Harr, J. (1995). *A Civil Action*. Vintage Books, New York, New York.

Hovstadius, G. (2001). "Pump System Effectiveness." *Pumps and Systems*, 9(1), 48.

Kramer, M.H., Herwald, B.L., Craun, G.F., Calderon, R.L., and Juranek, D.D. (1996). "Waterborne disease—1993 and 1994." *Journal of the American Water Works Association*, 88(3), 66.

Kapelan, Z., Savic, D.A., and Walters, G.A. (2000). "Inverse Transient Analysis in Pipe Networks for Leakage Detection and Roughness Calibration." *Water Network Modeling for Optimal Design and Management*, CWS 2000, Centre for Water Systems, Exeter, United Kingdom, 143.

Lansey, K. E., and Zhong, Q. (1990). "A Methodology for Optimal Control of Pump Stations." *Proceedings of the Water Resources Planning and Management Specialty Conference*, American Society of Civil Engineers, 58.

Martinez, F., Conejos, P., and Vercher, J. (1999). "Developing an Integrated Model of Water Distribution Systems Considering both Distributed Leakage and Pressure Dependent Demands." *Proceedings of the ASCE Water Resources Planning and Management Division Conference*, Tempe, Arizona.

Maslia, M. L., Sautner, J. B., Aral, M. M., Reyes, J. J., Abraham, J. E., and Williams, R. C. (2000). "Using Water-Distribution Modeling to Assist Epidemiologic Investigations." *Journal of Water Resources Planning and Management*, ASCE, 126(4), 180.

Murphy, P.J. (1991). *Prediction and Validation in Water Distribution Modeling*. AWWARF, Denver, Colorado.

Oberoi, K. (1994). "Distribution Flushing Programs: The Benefits and Results." *Proceedings of the AWWA Annual Conference*, American Water Works Association, New York, New York.

Ormsbee, L. E., Walski, T. W., Chase, D. V., and Sharp, W. (1989). "Methodology for Improving Pump Operation Efficiency." *Journal of Water Resources Planning and Management*, ASCE, 115(2), 148.

Ormsbee, L. E., and Lingireddy, S. (1995). "Nonlinear Heuristic for Pump Operations." *Journal of Water Resources Planning and Management*, ASCE, 121(4), 302.

Patison, P. L. (1980). "Conducting a Regular Main Flushing Program." *Journal of the American Water Works Association*, 72(2), 88.

Pudar, R.S., and Liggett, J.A. (1992). "Leaks in Pipe Networks." *Journal of Hydraulic Engineering*, ASCE, 118(7), 1031.

Reardon, D. (1994). "Audit Manual for Water-Wastewater Facilities." *CR-104300*, EPRI, St. Louis, Missouri.

Rossman, L. A., Clark, R. M., and Grayman, W. M. (1994). "Modeling Chlorine Residuals in Drinking-Water Distribution Systems." *Journal of Environmental Engineering*, ASCE, 120(4), 803.

Stathis, J.A., and Loganathan, G.V. (1999). "Analysis of Pressure-Dependent Leakage in Water Distribution Systems." *Proceedings of the ASCE Water Resources Planning and Management Division Conference*, Tempe, AZ.

Tang, K.W., Brunone, B., Karney, B., and Rossetti, A. (2000). "Role and Characterization of Leaks Under Transient Conditions." *Proceedings of the ASCE Joint Conference on Water Resources Engineering and Water Resources Management*, Minneapolis, Minnesota.

Tarquin, A., and Dowdy, J. (1989). "Optimal Pump Operation in Water Distribution." *Journal of Hydraulic Engineering*, ASCE, 115(2), 168.

Walski, T. M. (1991). "Understanding Solids Transport in Water Distribution Systems." *Water Quality Modeling in Distribution Systems*, AWWARF, Denver, Colorado.

Walski, T. M. (1993). "Tips for Energy Savings in Pumping Operations." *Journal of the American Water Works Association*, 85(7), 48.

Walski, T. M. (1995). "An Approach for Handling Sprinklers, Hydrants, and Orifices in Water Distribution Systems." *Proceedings of the AWWA Annual Conference*, American Water Works Association, Anaheim, California.

Walski, T. M., and Draus, S. J. (1996). "Predicting Water Quality Changes During Flushing." *Proceedings of the AWWA Annual Conference*, American Water Works Association, Toronto, Canada.

Walski, T. M. (1998). "Importance and Accuracy of Node Elevation Data." *Essential Hydraulics and Hydrology*, Haestad Press, Waterbury, Connecticut.

Walski, T.M. (1999) "Modeling TCE Dynamics in Water Distribution Tanks." *Proceedings of the 26th Water Resources Planning and Management Conference*, ASCE, Tempe, Arizona.

Walski, T.M. (2000). "Water Quality Aspects of Construction and Operation." *Water Distribution System Handbook*, Mays, L. W., ed., McGraw-Hill, New York, New York.

Zessler, M. L., and Shamir, U. (1989). "Optimal Operation of Water Distribution Systems." *Journal of Water Resources Planning and Management*, ASCE, 115(8), 735.

DISCUSSION TOPICS AND PROBLEMS

Earn CEUs — Read Chapter 9 and complete the problems. Submit your work to Haestad Methods and earn up to 3.0 CEUs. See *Continuing Education Units* on page xiii for more information, or visit www.haestad.com/wdm-ceus/.

9.1 Complete Problem 4.4 and add controls to the Newtown pump station so that the pump runs from midnight to 4:30 a.m., is off from 4:30 a.m. to 11:00 a.m., and then runs from 11:00 a.m. to midnight.

a) Produce a plot of HGL vs. time for the Central tank.

b) Produce a plot of discharge vs. time for the Newtown pump station.

c) Does the system work properly under these controls? If not, what is the problem with the system operation?

"A lot of homework?"

9.2 Complete Problem 4.4 and add the following pump station controls:

- The Newtown pump station enters service when the water elevation in the Central tank falls below 1,515 ft, and turns off when the water level in the tank reaches 1,535 ft.
- The High Field pump station enters service when the HGL in the tank falls below 1,510 ft, and turns off when the water elevation reaches 1,530 ft.

Initially, the Newtown pump station is running and the High Field pump station is off.

a) Produce a plot of HGL vs. time for the Central tank.

b) Produce a plot of discharge vs. time for the Newtown pump station.

c) Is it necessary to pump from the High Field reservoir to fill the tank under this typical daily demand condition?

9.3 Complete Problem 9.2 and add a fire flow of 2,250 gpm to node J-5. The fire demand begins at 11:00 am and lasts for three hours.

a) Plot HGL vs. time for the Central Tank.

b) Plot discharge vs. time for the Newtown pump station.

c) Plot discharge vs. time for the High Field pump station.

d) Plot pressure vs. time for node J-5.

e) Are pressures maintained within acceptable limits at J-5? Throughout the entire system?

f) Once the High Field pump station activates, how many hours does it take for the Central Tank to recover to its initial elevation at the start of the simulation (525 ft)?

9.4 The system shown in Figure 9.21 is the same system given in Problem 4.3. However, a PRV has been added to pipe P-6 and the status of pipe P-14 is closed. Note that adding a PRV to pipe P-6 will necessitate splitting the line into two pipes. The setting for the PRV in pipe P-6 is 74 psi. For this simulation, assume that both pumps are running.

Perform a fire flow analysis to find the maximum flow, in addition to the original demands, that can be supplied at each node in the system [that is, the fire flow will only be applied to one node at a time (in addition to the original demands), while the other nodes maintain their original demands]. The minimum allowable pressure anywhere in the system (other than on the suction side of a pump) is 30 psi.

Hint - If you are using WaterCAD, you can use the automated fire flow feature to automatically perform this analysis for all nodes in a single model run.

Figure 9.21

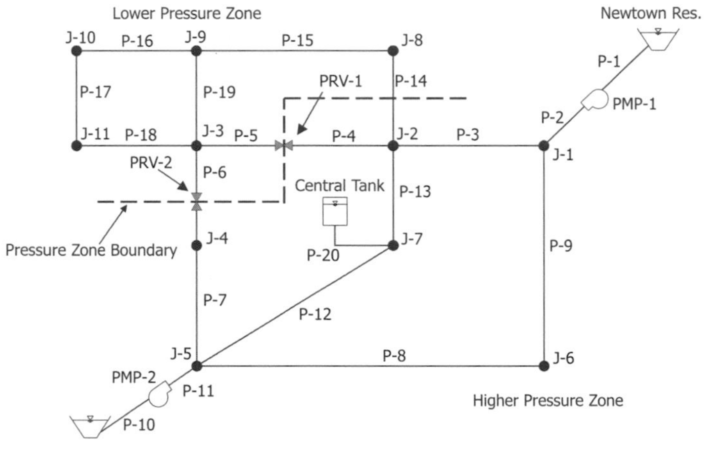

a) Complete the table below.

Node Label	Available Fire Flow (gpm)	Residual Pressure at Flowed Node (psi)
J-1		
J-2		
J-3		
J-4		
J-5		
J-6		
J-7		
J-8		
J-9		
J-10		
J-11		

b) Do you think this network is capable of meeting the fire flow requirements of a system that supplies water to a residential community and an industrial park? Assume the needed fire flow is 3,500 gpm.

c) How many fire hydrants have to be opened to deliver the available fire flow at node J-6? Assume that each fire hydrant can be represented by the system shown in Figure 9.17 and the hydrant opening size is 2 1/2 in. Also, recall that the HGL of the pseudo-reservoir must be set equal to the elevation of the node of interest, in this case, node J-6.

9.5 Given the layout of the system in Figure 9.22 and the data below (and in file Prob9-05.wcd), examine the tradeoffs between the two possible routes for a pipeline connecting the pump station with tank R-2. One route runs three miles along a highway with high backfilling and restoration costs. The alternative route is 3,000 ft longer, but the pipe can be laid in the shoulder of a back road at a lower cost.

Figure 9.22

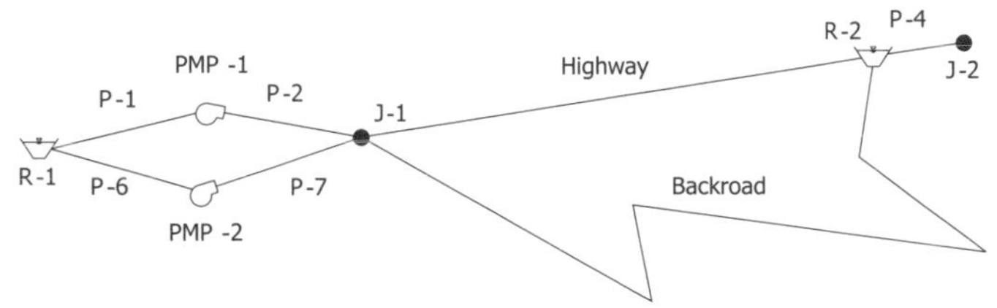

Node Label	Elevation (ft)	Demand (gpm)
J-1	980	500
J-2	950	1,200
R-1	1,000	N/A
R-2	1,100	N/A

Pump Curve Data

Pump Label	Shutoff Head (ft)	Design Head (ft)	Design Discharge (gpm)	Maximum Operating Head (ft)	Maximum Operating Discharge (gpm)
PMP-1	160	140	2,000	100	3,000
PMP-2	160	140	2,000	100	3,000

Pipe Label	Length (ft)	Diameter (in.)	Material	Hazen-Williams C-factor
P-1	40	12	Ductile Iron	130
P-2	40	12	Ductile Iron	130
P-4	25	12	Ductile Iron	130
P-6	40	12	Ductile Iron	130
P-7	40	12	Ductile Iron	130

With only one pump at the source running, determine whether to use a 12-, 14- or 16-in. pipe, and which route (highway or back road) is preferable. Information on energy and construction costs is provided below.

The fraction of time during which the pump is running can be calculated as:

$$f = Q_{demand} / Q_{pump}$$

where Q_{demand} = total demand in the system (gpm)
Q_{pump} = calculated pump flow rate (gpm)

For this system, the energy cost can then be calculated as:

$$C_{energy} = 0.22 \times Q_{pump} \times H_{pump} \times f$$

where C_{energy} = energy cost ($/year)
H_{pump} = calculated pump head (ft)

The present worth (PW, in $) of the energy cost over the next 20 years, assuming 7% interest per year, is given by:

$$PW = 10.6 \times C_{energy}$$

Use the values in the table below to compute construction costs for the pipe.

Pipe Size (in.)	Cost (in highway) ($/ft)	Cost (in back road) ($/ft)
12	90	60
14	95	65
16	100	70

Fill in the table below to give the construction cost and present worth of energy costs for each scenario.

Pipe Size (in.)	Route	Flow (gpm)	Head (ft)	f	Present Worth of Energy Cost ($)	Construction Cost ($)	Total Present Worth ($)
12	Back road						
14	Back road						
16	Back road						
12	Highway						
14	Highway						
16	Highway						

Which scenario is the most economical for the 20-year period being considered?

9.6 *English Units* - Find fractions of the water coming from the Miamisburg tank and the West Carrolton tank for the system presented in Problem 4.2 (see page 155). Add the following pump controls before conducting the simulation. The pump is initially on, but turns off at hour 8 of the simulation, and then back on at hour 16. Assume that the initial fraction at each junction node is zero. Complete the table below for conditions at hour 12 of the simulation.

Node Label	Fraction of Water from Miamisburg Tank	Fraction of Water from West Carrolton Tank
J-1		
J-2		
J-3		
J-4		
J-5		
J-6		
J-7		
J-8		
J-9		
J-10		

SI Units - Find the fractions of water from the Miamisburg tank and the West Carrolton tank for the system presented in Problem 4.2 (SI) (see page 155). Add pump controls before conducting the simulation. The pump is initially on, but turns off at hour 8 of the simulation, and back on at hour 16. Assume that the initial fraction at each junction node is zero. Complete the table below for conditions at hour 12 of the simulation.

Node Label	Fraction of Water from Miamisburg Tank	Fraction of Water from West Carrolton Tank
J-1		
J-2		
J-3		
J-4		
J-5		
J-6		
J-7		
J-8		
J-9		
J-10		

9.7 *English Units* - Determine the age of water in the system presented in Problem 4.2 (see page 155). Add pump controls before conducting the simulation. The pump is initially on, but turns off at hour 5 of the simulation, and back on at hour 12. Complete the table below for conditions at hour 12 of the simulation. The initial age of the water at each node is given below.

Node Label	Initial Age (hr)	Average Age (hr)
J-1	0.0	
J-2	0.0	
J-3	0.0	
J-4	0.0	
J-5	0.0	
J-6	0.0	
J-7	0.0	
J-8	0.0	
J-9	0.0	
J-10	0.0	
PMP-1	0.0	
Crystal Lake	10.0	N/A
Miamisburg Tank	15.0	
West Carrolton Tank	7.0	

SI Units - Determine the age of water in the system presented in Problem 4.2 (SI) (see page 155). Add pump controls before conducting the simulation. The pump is initially on, but turns off at hour 5 of the simulation, and back on at hour 12. Complete the table below for conditions at hour 12 of the simulation. The initial age of the water at each node is given below.

Node Label	Initial Age (hr)	Average Age (hr)
J-1	0.0	
J-2	0.0	
J-3	0.0	
J-4	0.0	
J-5	0.0	
J-6	0.0	
J-7	0.0	
J-8	0.0	
J-9	0.0	
J-10	0.0	
PMP-1	0.0	
Crystal Lake	10.0	N/A
Miamisburg Tank	15.0	
West Carrolton Tank	7.0	

9.8 *English Units* - Determine the concentrations of chlorine for the system presented in Problem 4.2 (see page 155). For this constituent, the bulk reaction rate is –2.6 day^{-1}, the wall reaction coefficient is –1.25 ft/day, and the diffusivity is 1.3 x 10^{-8} ft^2/s. The initial chlorine concentrations are 1.0 mg/l at each junction node, 2.3 mg/l at Crystal Lake reservoir, 0.7 mg/l at the Miamisburg Tank, and 0.9 mg/l at the West Carrolton Tank. Perform a 72-hour extended period simulation with the diurnal demands repeating each day. Complete the table below.

Node Label	Chlorine Concentration at 60 hr (mg/l)
J-1	
J-2	
J-3	
J-4	
J-5	
J-6	
J-7	
J-8	
J-9	
J-10	
Miamisburg Tank	
West Carrolton Tank	

SI Units - Determine the concentrations of chlorine for the system presented in Problem 4.2 (SI) (see page 155). For this constituent, the bulk reaction rate is –2.6 day^{-1}, the wall reaction coefficient is –0.38 m/day, and the diffusivity is 1.2 x 10^{-9}m^2/s. The initial chlorine concentrations are 1.0 mg/L at each junction node, 2.3 mg/l at Crystal Lake reservoir, 0.7 mg/l at the Miamisburg Tank, and 0.9 mg/l at the West Carrolton Tank. Perform a 72-hour extended period simulation with the diurnal demands repeating each day. Complete the table below.

Node Label	Chlorine Concentration at 60 hr (mg/l)
J-1	
J-2	
J-3	
J-4	
J-5	
J-6	
J-7	
J-8	
J-9	
J-10	
Miamisburg Tank	
West Carrolton Tank	

9.9 *English Units* - Given the network shown in Figure 9.23 and the model data given below or saved in file Prob9-09.wcd, determine if complaints of low pressure at node J-7 are due to limited capacity in the system or the elevation of the customer. Maintain a 35-psi residual pressure even during peak (non-fire) demands. To check the cause of the problem either:

- set up model runs with demand multipliers of 0.6, 1.0, and 1.33 to determine if the pressure drops; or
- set up an EPS run for a 24-hour period.

a) How much did the pressure and HGL change at J-7 from peak to low demand times? If an EPS run was made, what was the range of water level in the West Side tank?

b) Did the HGL (pressure) change markedly when demands changed, or was the pressure relatively insensitive to demands?

c) Was the pressure highly dependent on tank water level?

d) How many pumps need to be run to meet demands over the course of the day?

e) What recommendations would you make to improve pressures?

Figure 9.23

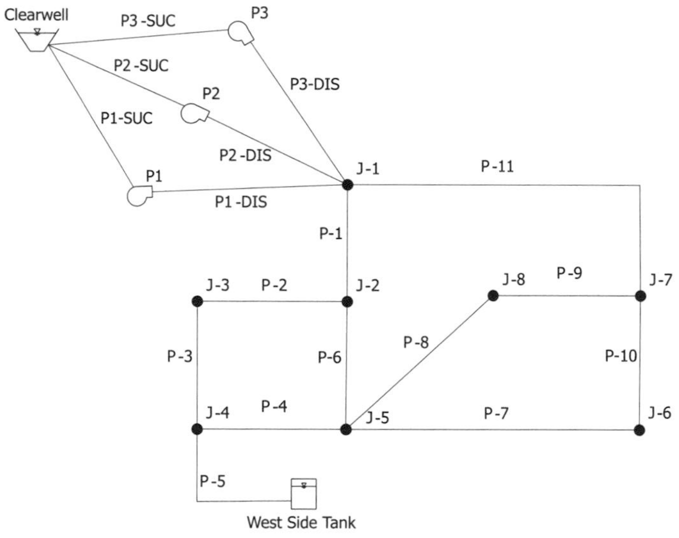

Pipe Label	Length (ft)	Diameter (in.)	Hazen-Williams C-factor
P1-Suc	50	18	115
P1-Dis	120	16	115
P2-Suc	50	18	115
P2-Dis	120	16	115
P3-Suc	50	18	115
P3-Dis	120	16	115
P-1	2,350	12	110
P-2	1,500	6	105
P-3	1,240	6	105
P-4	1,625	12	110
P-5	225	10	110
P-6	1,500	12	110
P-7	4,230	6	105
P-8	3,350	6	105
P-9	2,500	6	105
P-10	2,550	6	105
P-11	3,300	4	85

Node Label	Elevation (ft)	Demand (gpm)
J-1	730	0
J-2	755	125
J-3	765	50
J-4	775	25
J-5	770	30
J-6	790	220
J-7	810	80
J-8	795	320

Reservoir Label	Elevation (ft)
Clearwell	630

Tank Label	Minimum Elevation (ft)	Initial Elevation (ft)	Maximum Elevation (ft)	Tank Diameter (ft)
West Side Tank	900.0	917.0	920.0	50.0

Pump Curve Data

	P1		P2		P3	
Head (ft)	Flow (gpm)	Head (ft)	Flow (gpm)	Head (ft)	Flow (gpm)	Head (ft)
Shutoff	305	0	305	0	305	0
Design	295	450	295	450	295	450
Max Operating	260	650	260	650	260	650

Hydraulic Pattern (Continuous)

Time (hr)	Multiplier
0	0.60
3	0.75
6	1.20
9	0.90
12	1.15
15	1.00
18	1.33
21	0.90
24	0.60

Controls for Pump

	P1	P2	P3
Initial Setting	ON	ON	OFF
ON if West Side Tank is	Below 916.0 ft	Below 913.0 ft	Below 905.0 ft
OFF if West Side Tank is	Above 919.5 ft	Above 917.0 ft	Above 914.0 ft

SI Units - Given the network shown in Figure 9.23 and the model data given below or saved in file Prob9-09m.wcd, determine if complaints of low pressure at node J-7 are due to limited capacity in the system or the elevation of the customer. Maintain a 240 kPa residual pressure even during peak (non-fire) demands. To check the cause of the problem either:

- set up model runs with demand multipliers of 0.6, 1.0, and 1.33 to determine if the pressure drops; or
- set up an EPS run for a 24-hour period.

a) How much did the pressure and HGL change at J-7 from peak to low demand times? If an EPS run was made, what was the range of water level in the West Side tank?

b) Did the HGL (pressure) change markedly when demands changed, or was the pressure relatively insensitive to demands?

c) Was the pressure highly dependent on tank water level?

d) How many pumps need to be run to meet demands over the course of the day?

e) What recommendations would you make to improve pressures?

Pipe Label	Length (m)	Diameter (mm)	Hazen-Williams C-factor
P1-SUC	15.2	457	115
P1-DIS	36.6	406	115
P2-SUC	15.2	457	115
P2-DIS	36.6	406	115
P3-SUC	15.2	457	115
P3-DIS	36.6	406	115
P-1	716.3	305	110
P-2	457.2	152	105
P-3	378.0	152	105
P-4	495.3	305	110
P-5	68.6	254	110
P-6	457.2	305	110
P-7	1289.3	152	105
P-8	1021.1	152	105
P-9	762.0	152	105
P-10	777.0	152	105
P-11	1,006	102	85

Node Label	Elevation (m)	Demand (l/s)
J-1	222.50	0.0
J-2	230.12	7.9
J-3	233.17	3.2
J-4	236.22	1.6
J-5	234.70	1.9
J-6	240.79	13.9
J-7	246.89	5.0
J-8	242.32	20.2

Reservoir Label	Elevation (m)
Clearwell	192.0

Tank Label	Maximum Elevation (m)	Initial Elevation (m)	Minimum Elevation (m)	Tank Diameter (m)
West Side Tank	280.42	279.50	274.32	15.24

Pump Curve Data

Label	Shutoff Head (m)	Design Head (m)	Design Discharge (l/s)	Maximum Operating Head (m)	Maximum Operating Discharge (l/s)
P1	93.0	89.9	28.4	79.3	41.0
P2	93.0	89.9	28.4	79.3	41.0
P3	89.9	77.7	15.8	48.8	28.4

Hydraulic Pattern (Continuous)

Time (hr)	Multiplier
0	0.60
3	0.75
6	1.20
9	0.90
12	1.15
15	1.00
18	1.33
21	0.90
24	0.60

Controls for Pump

	P1	P2	P3
Initial Setting	ON	ON	OFF
ON if West Side Tank is	Below 279.2 m	Below 278.3 m	Below 275.8 m
OFF if West Side Tank is	Above 280.3 m	Above 279.5 m	Above 278.6 m

9.10 *English Units* - This problem uses the calibrated model from Problem 9.9. A customer near J-8 having an elevation of 760 ft complains of low water pressure. A pressure of 46 psi was measured at a hydrant near J-8. Is the problem in the distribution system or in the customer's plumbing?

a) Make an EPS run of the model and plot pressure at J-8 vs. time. Does a pressure of 46 psi look reasonable in that part of the system?

b) To get an idea of the cause of the problem, look at the HGL when the pressure is at its worst. Is it very different (>20 ft) from the HGL at the tank? What does that tell you about head loss?

c) To determine the source of the head loss, look at the velocities in the system at times of low pressure. Which pipes have the highest velocities?

d) Is there much that can be done operationally to correct the problem?

e) Is 46 psi a low pressure?

SI Units - This problem uses the calibrated model from Problem 9.9 (SI). A customer near J-8 having an elevation 231.65 m complains of low water pressure. A pressure of 317 kPa was measured at a hydrant near J-8. Is the problem in the distribution system or in the customer's plumbing?

a) Make an EPS run of the model and plot pressure at J-8 vs. time. Does a pressure of 317 kPa look reasonable in that part of the system?

b) To get an idea of the cause of the problem, look at the HGL when the pressure is at its worst. Is it very different (>6.1 m) from the HGL at the tank? What does that tell you about head loss?

c) To determine the source of the head loss, look at the velocities in the system at times of low pressure. Which pipes have the highest velocities?

d) Is there much that can be done operationally to correct the problem?

e) Is 317 kPa a low pressure?

9.11 A customer near J-6 in Figure 9.24 complains of low pressure, and pressure chart recorder data was collected as shown in Figure 9.25. Construct a model using the data tables below, or open Prob9-11.wcd.

a) Determine if the low pressure is due to elevation, inadequate pump capacity, undersized piping, or some large demand.

b) How would you use a model to confirm this problem? Perform the simulation to confirm it.

Figure 9.24

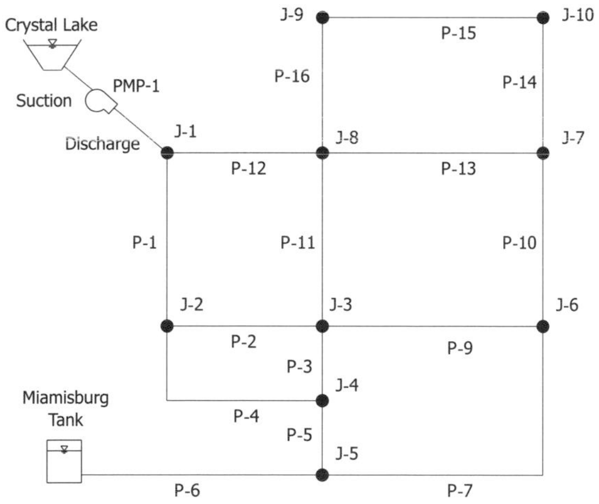

Figure 9.25

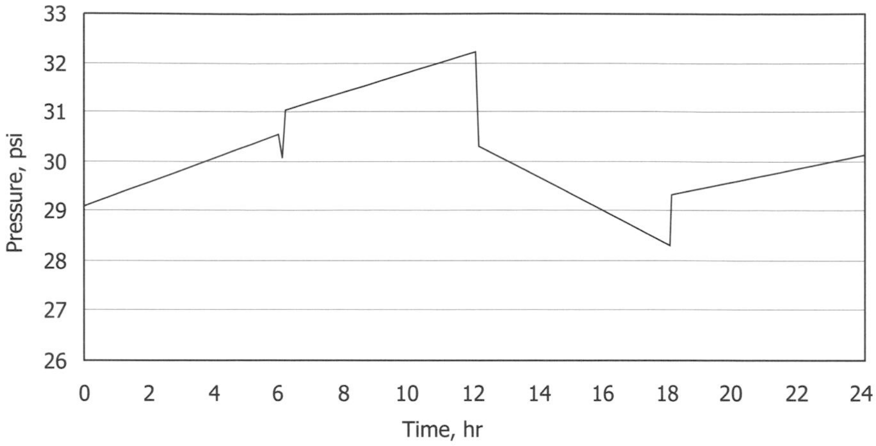

Node Label	Elevation (ft)	Demand (gpm)
J-1	390.00	120
J-2	420.00	75
J-3	425.00	35
J-4	430.00	50
J-5	450.00	0
J-6	485.00	155
J-7	420.00	65
J-8	415.00	0
J-9	420.00	55
J-10	420.00	20

Pipe Label	Length (ft)	Diameter (in.)
Discharge	220	21
Suction	25	24
P-1	1,250	6
P-2	835	6
P-3	550	8
P-4	1,010	6
P-5	425	8
P-6	990	8
P-7	2,100	8
P-9	745	8
P-10	1,100	10
P-11	1,330	8
P-12	890	10
P-13	825	10
P-14	450	6
P-15	690	6
P-16	500	6

Pump Curve Data

Pump Label	Shutoff Head (ft)	Design Head (ft)	Design Discharge (gpm)	Maximum Operating Head (ft)	Maximum Operating Discharge (gpm)
PMP-1	245	230.0	1,100	210.0	1,600

Reservoir Label	Elevation (ft)
Crystal Lake	320.0

Tank Label	Minimum Elevation (ft)	Initial HGL (ft)	Maximum Elevation (ft)	Tank Diameter (ft)
Miamisburg Tank	535.0	550.0	570.0	50.0

Hydraulic Pattern (Stepwise)

Time (hr)	Multiplier
0	1.00
6	0.75
12	2.00
18	1.20
24	1.00

9.12 If customers near J-5 in Figure 9.26 complain about having low pressures between 2:00 p.m. and 5:00 p.m. each day (hours 14 to 17 of the simulation), determine if their complaints are due to the utility's system. If so, use an EPS model run to formulate alternatives to improve the system. The customer has an alarm on a fire protection system that sounds when pressure drops below 37 psi. (This network can be found in Prob9-12.wcd)

Figure 9.26

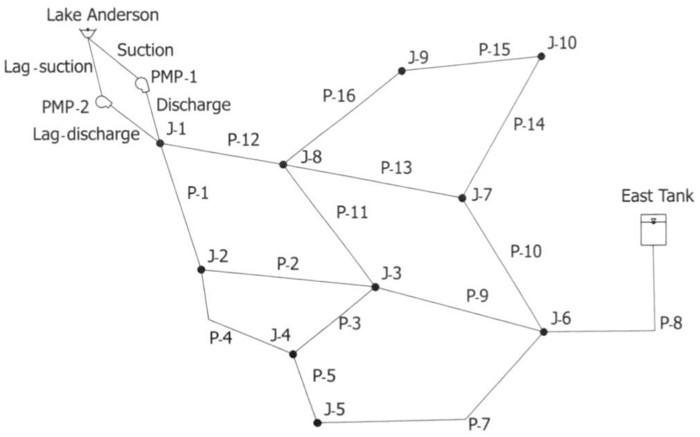

Node Label	Elevation (ft)	Demand (gpm)
J-1	390	120
J-2	420	75
J-3	425	35
J-4	430	50
J-5	460	20
J-6	445	155
J-7	420	65
J-8	415	0
J-9	420	55
J-10	420	20

Pipe Label	Diameter (in.)	Length (ft)	Hazen-Williams C-factor
P-1	6	1,250	110
P-2	6	835	110
P-3	8	550	130
P-4	6	1,010	110
P-5	8	425	130
P-7	8	2,100	105
P-8	12	560	110
P-9	8	745	100
P-10	10	1,100	115
P-11	8	1,330	110
P-12	10	890	115
P-13	10	825	115
P-14	6	450	120
P-15	6	690	120
P-16	6	500	120
Discharge	21	220	120
Suction	24	25	120
Lag-discharge	21	220	120
Lag-suction	24	25	120

Pump Curve Data

Pump Label	Shutoff Head (ft)	Design Head (ft)	Design Discharge (gpm)	Maximum Operating Head (ft)	Maximum Operating Discharge (gpm)
PMP-1	245	230	600	210	1,000
PMP-2	245	230	600	210	1,000

Controls for Pump

	PMP-1	PMP-2
Initial Setting	ON	OFF
ON if East Tank	Below 560 ft	Below 545 ft
OFF if East Tank	Above 564 ft	Above 555 ft

Tank Label	Maximum Elevation (ft)	Initial Elevation (ft)	Minimum Elevation (ft)	Tank Diameter (ft)
East Tank	565.0	553.0	525.0	54

Reservoir Label	Elevation (ft)
Lake Anderson	320.0

Hydraulic Pattern (Stepwise)

Time (hr)	Multiplier
0	1
6	0.75
12	2.0
18	1.2
24	1

9.13 Start with the same network used in Problem 9.12. Determine what kind of fire flows can be delivered with a 20 psi residual at every node at hour 8, first with the tank on-line, then with the tank off-line. Find the same information during peak demands at hour 12.

Hint - To use WaterCAD's automated fire flow feature for this problem, check the boundary and operational conditions in Problem 9.12 at the specified times. Create a steady-state run for these conditions, and set up and run the fire flow analysis.

Fire Flows at 20 psi at hour 8

Node Label	Tank On-line	Tank Off-line
J-1		
J-2		
J-3		
J-4		
J-5		
J-6		
J-7		
J-8		
J-9		
J-10		

Fire Flows at 20 psi at hour 12

Node Label	Tank On-line	Tank Off-line
J-1		
J-2		
J-3		
J-4		
J-5		
J-6		
J-7		
J-8		
J-9		
J-10		

9.14 Using the same model from Problem 9.12, determine how long it will be before the system reaches full recovery when there is a power outage from 2:00 pm to 8:00 pm, if hour 0 in the model represents midnight. Full recovery means that the tank level reaches the same level as before the power outage. With the data from Problem 9.12, simulate a power outage by controlling the open/closed status of the discharge pipes of the pumps at hour 14 and hour 20.

9.15 *English Units* - Given the existing small system shown in Figure 9.27, perform three runs to determine the impact on the pressure at node J-8 (highest elevation customer) if the pump is allowed to come on when the tank drops to levels of 25, 20, or 15 ft (relative to tank base elevation). Use the stepwise demand patterns shown in Figure 9.28. (This network can be found in Prob9-15.wcd)

Figure 9.27

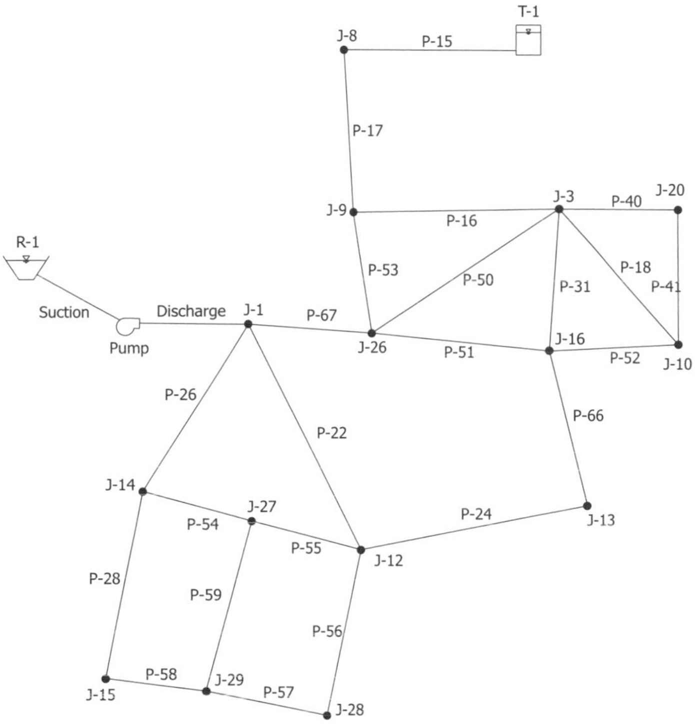

Node Label	Elevation (ft)	Demand (gpm)	Pattern
J-1	25.00	100	Residential
J-3	75.00	55	Residential
J-8	90.00	80	Commercial
J-9	80.00	15	Residential
J-10	65.00	18	Commercial
J-12	35.00	18	Residential
J-13	40.00	15	Commercial
J-14	20.00	20	Residential
J-15	10.00	20	Residential
J-16	55.00	10	Commercial
J-20	53.00	25	Commercial
J-26	60.00	25	Commercial
J-27	30.00	20	Commercial
J-28	20.00	15	Commercial
J-29	20.00	15	Residential

Pipe Label	Length (ft)	Diameter (in.)
Discharge	38	12
Suction	33	12
P-15	970	12
P-16	850	12
P-17	955	12
P-18	905	6
P-22	1,145	12
P-24	1,195	12
P-26	1,185	4
P-28	1,215	4
P-31	1,023	8
P-40	570	6
P-41	645	6
P-50	1,080	6
P-51	870	6
P-52	630	6
P-53	585	6
P-54	360	6
P-55	370	6
P-56	540	6
P-57	400	6
P-58	320	6
P-59	560	6
P-66	956	12
P-67	570	6

Pump Curve Data

Label	Shutoff Head (ft)	Design Head (ft)	Design Discharge (gpm)	Maximum Operating Head (ft)	Maximum Operating Discharge (gpm)
PUMP	210	160	600	100	900

Controls for Pumps

	PUMP
Initial Setting	ON
ON if T-1	Below 175.0 ft
OFF if T-1	Above 179.5 ft

Tank Label	Base Elevation (ft)	Maximum Elevation (ft)	Initial Elevation (ft)	Minimum Elevation (ft)	Tank Diameter (ft)
West Tank	150.0	180.0	176.0	150.0	40.0

Reservoir Label	Elevation (ft)
R-1	20.00

Figure 9.28
Hydraulic Patterns

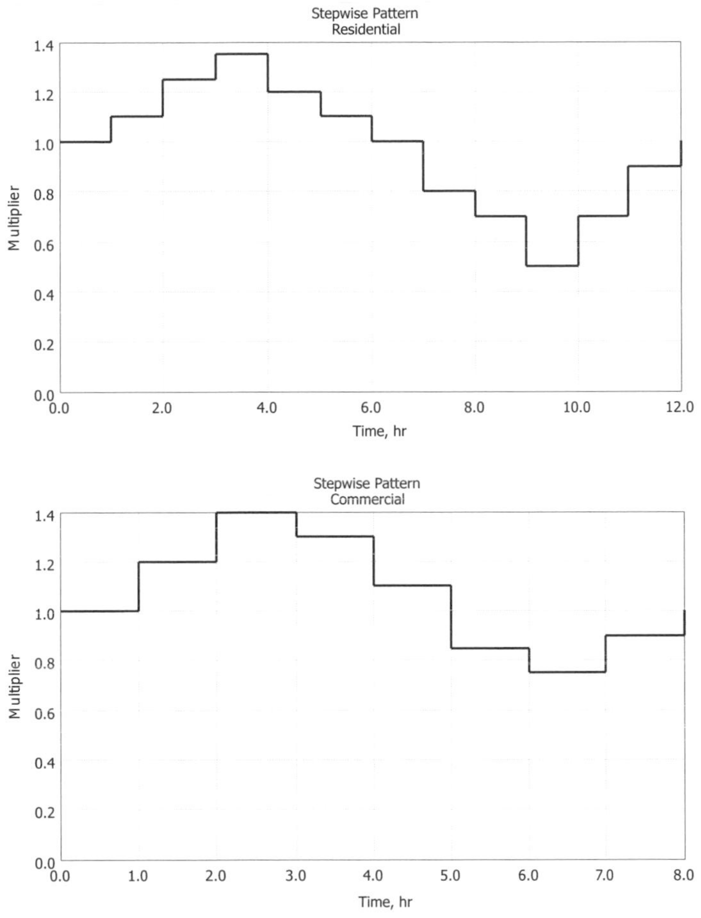

a) To observe the impact on J-8, prepare a plot of pressure vs. time at node J-8 for each pump control scenario.

b) Make a 480-hr (20-day) water quality run and graph the average water age in the tank vs. time for each operating alternative.

c) Based on your calculations, revise the initial water age in the tank to 60 hours and rerun the scenarios. Plot the minimum pressure at J-8 vs. average water age for each scenario, and consider the water pressure/quality tradeoffs.

d) How do you recommend this system be operated?

SI Units - Given the existing small system shown in Figure 9.27, perform three runs to determine the impact on the pressure at node J-8 (highest elevation customer) if the pump is allowed to come on when the tank drops to levels of 7.6, 6.1, or 4.6 m (relative to tank base elevation). Use the stepwise demand patterns shown in Figure 9.28. (This network can also be found in Prob9-15m.wcd)

Node Label	Elevation (m)	Demand (l/s)	Pattern
J-1	7.62	6.31	Residential
J-3	22.86	3.47	Residential
J-8	27.43	5.05	Commercial
J-9	24.38	0.95	Residential
J-10	19.81	1.14	Commercial
J-12	10.67	1.14	Residential
J-13	12.19	0.95	Commercial
J-14	6.10	1.26	Residential
J-15	3.05	1.26	Residential
J-16	16.76	0.63	Commercial
J-20	16.15	1.58	Commercial
J-26	18.29	1.58	Commercial
J-27	9.14	1.26	Commercial
J-28	6.10	0.95	Commercial
J-29	6.10	0.95	Residential

Pipe Label	Length (m)	Diameter (mm)
Suction	9.8	305
Discharge	11.9	305
P-15	295.7	305
P-16	259.1	305
P-17	291.1	305
P-18	275.8	152
P-22	349.0	305
P-24	364.2	305
P-26	361.2	102
P-28	370.3	102
P-31	311.8	203
P-40	173.7	152
P-41	196.6	152
P-50	329.2	152
P-51	265.2	152
P-52	192.0	152
P-53	178.3	152
P-54	109.7	152
P-55	112.8	152
P-56	164.6	152
P-57	121.9	152
P-58	97.5	152
P-59	170.7	152
P-66	291.4	305
P-67	173.7	152

Pump Curve Data

Pump Label	Shutoff Head (m)	Design Head (m)	Design Discharge (l/s)	Maximum Operating Head (m)	Maximum Operating Discharge (l/s)
PUMP	64.0	48.8	37.85	30.5	56.8

Controls for Pumps

	PUMP
Initial Setting	ON
ON if T-1	Below 7.62 m
OFF if T-1	Above 8.99 m

Tank Label	Minimum Elevation (m)	Initial HGL (m)	Maximum Elevation (m)	Diameter (m)
T-1	45.72	53.34	54.86	16.4

Reservoir Label	Elevation (m)
R-1	6.10

a) To observe the impact on J-8, prepare a plot of pressure vs. time at node J-8 for each pump control scenario.

b) Make a 480-hr (20-day) water quality run and graph the average water age in the tank vs. time for each operating alternative.

c) Based on your calculations, revise the initial water age in the tank to 60 hours and rerun the scenarios. Plot the minimum pressure at J-8 vs. average water age for each scenario, and consider the water pressure/quality tradeoffs.

d) How do you recommend this system be operated?

APPENDIX

A

Units and Symbols

Units

To accommodate all users, both sets of units - English and System International (SI) or metric - have been used throughout the text. Where numerical values have been given within the body of the text, the English units are displayed as the primary unit with the SI equivalent provided parenthetically. Where applicable, all formulas have been presented in both unit systems, with the appropriate conversion factors provided. For the case where formulas have been presented in their generic format, that is, they will work for either unit system provided that unit consistency is maintained; a generic unit system has been established as follows.

L = unit of length

M = unit of mass

T = unit of time

Symbols

The following is a list of the variables used throughout *Water Distribution Modeling*. Because there are far more parameters introduced than there are English letters and suitable symbols, some conflicts are unavoidable. However, whenever the same letter or symbol is used to represent two different parameters, the instances are far removed from each other to avoid confusion.

Typical units of measurement are provided in parentheses for both English and SI unit systems. Since different units are occasionally used in the text, the units are always displayed next to variable definitions for clarification. In some cases, the generalized units (explained on the previous page) are displayed below.

a = objective function unit conversion factor
a = rate of change in roughness height (in./year, mm/year)
A = correction factor
A = cross-sectional area (ft^2, m^2)
A = orifice area (in.^{2}, m^2)
A_i = cross-sectional area of pipe i (L^2)

$A_{i,t}$ = surface area of tank i during time step t (L^2)
A_{eq} = area of equivalent tank (ft^2, m^2)
A_1 = cross-sectional area of section 1(ft^2, m^2)
A_2 = cross-sectional area of section 2 (ft^2, m^2)
$\bar{A}$ = average area between section 1 and section 2 (ft^2, m^2)
b = objective function unit conversion factor
B = correction factor
$B_{i,j}$ = baseline demand for demand type j at junction i (L^3/T)
BHP = brake horsepower (hp, kW)
c = coefficient describing pump curve shape
C = cost over time duration t ($)
C = concentration (M/L^3)
C = Hazen-Williams C-factor
C_c = corrected value for C-factor
C_d = discharge coefficient
C_e = initial estimated value for C-factor
C_f = unit conversion factor (value changes from equation to equation)
C_i = concentration in pipe i (M/L^3)
$C_{i,l}$ = concentration in pipe i at finite difference node l (M/L^3)
$C_{i,np}$ = concentration entering junction node from pipe i (M/L^3)
C_k = concentration within tank or reservoir k (M/L^3)
C_{lim} = limiting concentration of the reaction (M/L^3)
C_o = reference C-Factor
C_{OUTj} = concentration leaving the junction node j (M/L^3)
C_v = valve coefficient ($gpm/(psi)^{0.5}$, $(m^3/s)/(kPa)^{0.5}$)
d = molecular diffusivity of constituent in bulk fluid (L^2/T)
$\frac{dV}{dy}$ = time rate of strain (1/T)
D = diameter (in. or ft, m or cm or mm)
e = efficiency (%)
$e_{w\text{-}w}$ = wire-to-water efficiency (%)
e_m = motor efficiency (%)
e_p = pump efficiency (%)
E_v = bulk modulus of elasticity (psi, kPa)
El_{max} = maximum allowable elevation of customers in zone (ft, m)
El_{min} = minimum allowable elevation of customers in zone (ft, m)
EP = electrical power (watts)
f = objective function to be minimized
f = Darcy-Weisbach friction factor
F = fire flow (gpm, m^3/s)
F = class of construction coefficient
g = gravitational acceleration constant (32.2 ft/s^2, 9.81 m/s^2)
h = depth of fluid above datum (ft, m)
h = head loss across orifice (ft, m)
h_{dis} = pump discharge head (m, ft)

h_l = static lift (ft, m)
h_L = head loss due to friction (ft, m)
Δh_L = error in measuring head loss due to friction (ft, m)
h_{loss} = sum of head and minor losses (from suction tank to pump) (ft, m)
h_m = head loss due to minor losses (ft, m)
h_o = cutoff (shutoff) head (pump head at zero flow) (L)
h_P = head added at pumps (ft, m)
h_{suc} = pump suction head (m, ft)
h_1 = measured head loss over test section, static conditions (ft, m)
h_1 = lift energy (ft, m)
h_2 = measured head loss over test section, flowed conditions (ft, m)
h_3 = modeled head loss over test section, static conditions (ft, m)
h_4 = modeled head loss over test section, flowed conditions (ft, m)
H = total head (ft, m)
H_{bar} = atmospheric pressure (at altitude of pumps) (ft, m)
H_i = water level in tank at beginning of i-th time step (ft, m)
$H_{i,t}$ = water level at beginning of times step t in tank i (L)
$H_{i,t+\Delta t}$ = water level at beginning of times step $t+\Delta t$ in tank i (L)
H_s = static head (water elevation – pump elevation) (ft, m)
H_{vap} = water vapor pressure (corrected for temperature) (ft, m)
HGL = hydraulic grade line (ft, m)
HGL_{max} = maximum HGL (ft, m)
HGL_{min} = minimum HGL (ft, m)
HGL_U = hydraulic grade at upstream fire hydrant (ft, m)
HGL_D = hydraulic grade at downstream fire hydrant (ft, m)
I = current averaged over all legs (amps)
IN_j = set of pipes entering node j
k = unit conversion factor depending on units used
k = reaction rate coefficient $((L^3/M)^{n-1}/T)$
k_1 = unit conversion factor for energy
k_2 = coefficient describing characteristics of system
k_b = bulk reaction coefficient (1/T)
k_w = wall reaction coefficient (L/T)
k_f = mass transfer coefficient, bulk fluid to pipe wall (L/T)
K = sprinkler coefficient
K = overall reaction rate constant (1/T)
K_L = minor loss coefficient (s^2/ft^5, s^2/m^5)
$\sum K_L$ = sum of individual minor loss coefficients (s^2/ft^5, s^2/m^5)
K_M = minor loss resistance coefficient
K_P = pipe resistance coefficient (s^z/ft^{3z-1}, s^z/m^{3z-1})
L = length of pipe (ft, m)
L = distance between section 1 and section 2 (ft, m)
L = leakage in future (L^3/T)
L_e = equivalent length of pipe (ft, m)

m = coefficient describing pump curve shape
M/A = corrected multiplier
$(M/A)_c$ = multiplier for consumptive users only
n = Manning roughness coefficient
n = reaction rate order constant
n = ratio of pump speed/pump test speed
n_i = number of finite difference nodes in pipe i
n_1, n_2 = pump speed (rpm)
N = number of phases
N = number of nodes at which head is known
N = perimeter of pipeline cross-section (ft, m)
NFF = needed fire flow (gpm)
$NPSH_a$ = net positive suction head available (ft, m)
O = occupancy factor
OH_n = observed head at n-th node (ft, m)
OQ_p = observed flow in p-th pipe (gpm, m^3/s)
OUT_j = set of pipes leaving node j
p = price of energy (cents/kW-hr or \$/kW-hr)
P = pressure (psi or lb/ft^2, kPa or Pa)
P = communication factor
P = number of pipes for which flow is known
ΔP = pressure drop (psi, kPa)
P_{abs} = absolute pressure (psi, Pa)
P_{atm} = atmospheric pressure (psi, Pa)
P_D = pressure at downstream fire hydrant (psi, kPa)
P_{dis} = discharge pressure (psi, kPa)
P_{DS} = pressure at downstream hydrant, static conditions (psi, kPa)
P_{DT} = pressure at downstream hydrant, flowed conditions (psi, kPa)
P_{gage} = gage pressure (psi, Pa)
PH_n = model-predicted head at n-th node (ft, m)
$P_{i,j,t}$ = pattern multiplier for demand type j at junction i at time t
P_{min} = minimum pressure drop through backflow preventer (psi, kPa)
P_{min} = minimum acceptable pressure (psi, kPa)
P_{max} = maximum acceptable pressure (psi, kPa)
P_o = pressure at which Q_o is to be calculated (psi, kPa)
PQ_p = model-predicted flow at p-th pipe (gpm, m^3/s)
P_s = static pressure during test (psi, kPa)
P_{set} = discharge pressure setting (psi, kPa)
P_{suc} = suction pressure (psi, kPa)
P_t = residual pressure during test (psi, kPa)
P_U = pressure at upstream fire hydrant (psi, kPa)
P_{US} = pressure at upstream hydrant, static conditions (psi, kPa)
P_{UT} = pressure at upstream hydrant, flowed conditions (psi, kPa)
P_1 = pressure at section 1(lb/ft^2, Pa)
P_2 = pressure at section 2 (lb/ft^2, Pa)

PF = power factor
PF = peaking factor between maximum day and average day demands
PW = present worth factor for energy costs
Q = pipe discharge (gpm or cfs, m^3/s)
Q = flow rate (cfs or gpm, l/s or m^3/s)
ΔQ = error in measuring Q (gpm, m^3/s)
Q_{avg} = average day demands (L^3/T)
Q_c = water use through customer meters in future (L^3/T)
Q_c = corrected value for demands (gpm, m^3/s)
Q_{demand} = average rate of demand (L^3/T)
Q_e = estimate of demand in area of test (gpm, m^3/s)
Q_i = flow into tank in i-th time step (cfs, m^3/s)
Q_{inflow} = average rate of production (L^3/T)
Q_i = inflow to node in i-th pipe (cfs, m^3/s)
Q_i = flow rate in pipe i (L^3/T)
Q_i = flow rate entering the node from pipe i (L^3/T)
$Q_{i,t}$ = total demand at junction i at time t (L^3/T)
Q_{max} = maximum day demands (L^3/T)
Q_o = flow at pressure P_o (gpm, m^3/s)
$Q_{outflow}$ = average outflow rate (L^3/T)
Q_P = pump discharge (L/T^3, cfs, m^3/s)
Q_t = hydrant test flow (gpm, m^3/s)
Re = Reynolds Number
R_H = hydraulic radius of pipeline (L)
S_H = Sherwood number
S_f = friction slope
t = duration that pump is operating at an operating point (hrs)
t = age of pipe (years)
Δt = time between volume measurements (T)
Δt = length of i-th time step (sec)
TC = total life-cycle costs ($)
TDH = total dynamic head (ft, m)
U = water usage at node (cfs, m^3/s)
U_j = concentration source at junction node j (M/T)
V = voltage (volts)
V = average fluid velocity (ft/s, m/s)
V_{dis} = velocity at point where discharge head is measured (ft/s, m/s)
V_{eff} = effective volume of tank (ft^3, m^3)
V_f = volume of fluid (ft^3, m^3)
$V_{i,t}$ = storage volume of tank i at time t (L^3)
$V_{i,t+\Delta t}$ = storage volume of tank i at time $t+\Delta t$ (L^3)
V_k = volume in tank or reservoir k (L^3)
V_o = reference value of velocity at which C_0 was determined (ft/s, m/s)
$\Delta V_{storage}$ = change in storage within the system (L^3)

V_{suc} = velocity at point where suction head is measured (ft/s, m/s)
$W_{n,p}$ = weighting factor for nodes and pipes
WP = water power (ML^2/T^3)
x = set of pipe laying conditions
X = vector of unknowns (roughnesses, demands, and elevations)
X = exposure factor
Δx_i = distance between finite difference nodes (L)
y = length (ft, m)
z = exponent on flow term
z = coefficient
Z = elevation (ft, m)
Z_D = elevation at downstream fire hydrant (ft, m)
Z_{pump} = elevation of pump (ft, m)
Z_U = elevation at upstream fire hydrant (ft, m)
Z_1 = elevation at section 1 (ft, m)
Z_2 = elevation at section 2 (ft, m)
α = fitting coefficient
α = angle of the pipe to horizontal
γ = fluid specific weight (lb/ft^3, N/m^3)
ρ = fluid density ($slugs/ft^3$, kg/m^3)
τ = shear stress (lb/ft^2, N/m^2)
μ = absolute viscosity ($lb\text{-}s/ft^2$, $N\text{-}s/m^2$)
ν = kinematic viscosity of fluid (L^2/T, ft^2/s, m^2/s)
τ_o = shear stress at pipe wall (lb/ft^2, N/m^2)
ε = index of internal pipe roughness (ft, m)
ε = absolute roughness (in., mm)
ε_o = roughness height of new pipe (t=0) (in., mm)
$\theta(C_i)$ = reaction term ($M/L^3/T$)
$\frac{dS}{dt}$ = change in storage (cfs, m^3/s)
$\theta(C_{i,l})$ = reaction term ($M/L^3/T$)
$\theta(C_k)$ = reaction term ($M/L^3/T$)
$\theta(C)$ = reaction term ($M/L^3/T$)

APPENDIX

B

Conversion Factors

To use the tables (compiled from ANSI, 1971) on the following pages, locate the "from" unit in the row and the "to" unit in the column and multiply the to conversion factor by the number you wish to convert. For example, to change kilometers to feet, look in the cell corresponding to the kilometer row and ft column to find 3,281, and multiply the number of kilometers by 3,281 to obtain the number of feet.

Length Conversion Factors

From/To	m	mm	km	in.	ft	yd	mi
meter (m)	1	1,000	0.001	39.37	3.281	1.094	0.0006215
millimeter (mm)	0.001	1	1.0E-06	0.03937	0.003281	0.001094	6.214E-07
kilometer (km)	1,000	1,000,000	1	39,370	3,281	1,094	0.6214
inch (in.)	0.0254	25.4	2.54E-05	1	0.08333	0.02778	1.578E-05
foot (ft)	0.3048	304.8	3.048E-04	12	1	0.3333	1.894E-04
yard (yd)	0.9144	914.4	9.144E-04	36	3	1	5.683E-04
mile (mi)	1,609	1,609,000	1.609	63,350	5,280	1,760	1

Volume Conversion Factors

From/To	m^3	l	ft^3	gal	Imp gal	ac-ft
cubic meter (m^3)	1	1,000	35.31	264.2	220.0	8.107E-04
liter (l)	0.001	1	0.03531	0.2642	0.2200	8.107E-07
cubic foot (ft^3)	0.02832	28.32	1	7.481	6.229	2.296E-05
gallon US	0.003785	3.785	0.1337	1	0.8327	3.069E-06
gallon Imp. (Imp gal)	0.004546	4.546	0.1605	1.201	1	3.686E-06
acre-foot (ac-ft)	1,233	1,233,000	43,560	325,900	271,300	1

Pressure Conversion Factors

From/To	Pa	kPa	bar	atm	psf	psi	ft H2O	mm H20	mm Hg
Pascal (Pa)	1	0.001	1.0E-05	9.869E-06	0.02089	1.451E-04	3.346E-04	0.1020	0.007501
kilopascal (kPa)	1000	1	0.01	9.869E-03	20.89	0.1450	0.3346	102.0	7.500
bar	1.00E+05	100	1	0.9869	2,089	14.50	33.46	10,200	750.0
atmosphere (atm)	1.01E+05	101.3	1.013	1	2,116	14.70	33.90	10,330	759.8
pounds per square foot (psf)	47.88	0.04788	0.0004788	4.725E-04	1	0.006944	0.01602	4.884	0.3591
pounds per square inch (psi)	6894	6.894	0.06894	0.06805	144.0	1	2.307	703.3	51.72
feet water (ft H2O)	2,986	2.986	0.02986	0.02948	62.43	0.4335	1	304.6	22.42
millimeters water (mm H2O)	9.803	0.009803	9.803E-05	9.677E-05	0.2047	0.001422	0.003283	1	0.07353
millimeters mercury (mm Hg)	133.3	0.1333	0.001333	0.001316	2.784	0.01934	0.04465	13.60	1

Flow Conversion Factors

From/To	m^3/s	l/s	m^3/hr	cfs	MGD	gpm	ac-ft/day
cubic meter/second (m^3/s)	1	1,000	1,440	35.32	22.83	15,850	70.08
liter/second (l/s)	0.001	1	1.440	0.03532	0.02283	15.85	0.07008
cubic meter/hour (m^3/hr)	0.0006944	0.6944	1	0.02453	0.01585	11.01	0.04866
cubic foot/second (cfs)	0.02831	28.31	40.77	1	0.6462	448.7	1.984
million gallon/day (MGD)	0.04381	43.81	63.09	1.548	1	694.4	3.070
gallon (US)/minute (gpm)	0.00006309	0.06309	0.09086	0.002229	0.001440	1	0.004421
acre-foot per day (ac-ft/day)	0.01427	14.27	20.55	0.5041	0.3257	226.2	1

Viscosity Conversion Factors

From/To	Pa-s	cP	lbf-s/ft^2
pascal-second (Pa-s)	1	1,000	0.02089
centipoise (cP)	0.001	1	2.089E-05
pound f-second/sq. ft (lbf-s/ft^2)	47.88	47,880	1

Kinematic Viscosity Conversion Factors

From/To	m^2/s	cS	ft^2/s
square meter/second (m^2/s)	1	1,000,000	10.76
centistoke (cS)	1.0E-06	1	1.080E-05
square feet/second (ft^2/s)	0.09290	9.290E+04	1

Velocity Conversion Factors

From/To	m/s	km/hr	fps	mph
meter/second (m/s)	1	3.600	3.281	2.237
kilometer/hour (km/hr)	0.2778	1	0.9114	0.6215
feet/second (fps)	0.3048	1.097	1	0.6819
miles/hour (mph)	0.4470	1.609	1.467	1

Power Conversion Factors

From/To	W	kW	hp	ft-lbf/s	BTU/hr
watt (W)	1	0.001	0.001341	0.7380	3.414
kilowatt (kW)	1000	1	1.340	738.0	3,414
horsepower (hp)	746	0.7460	1	550.6	2,547
foot pound f/sec (ft-lbf/s)	1.355	0.001355	0.001816	1	4.626
BTU/hour (BTU/hr)	0.2929	0.0002929	0.0003926	0.2162	1

APPENDIX

C

Tables

Density, viscosity, and kinematic viscosity of water

Temperature		Density		Viscosity		Kinematic Viscosity	
(°F)	(°C)	kg/m^3	$slugs/ft^3$	$N\text{-}s/m^2$	$lb\text{-}s/ft^2$	m^2/s	ft^2/s
32	0	999.8	1.940	1.781E-3	3.746E-5	1.785E-6	1.930E-5
39	4	1,000.0	1.941	1.568	3.274	1.586	1.687
50	10	999.7	1.940	1.307	2.735	1.306	1.407
68	20	998.2	1.937	1.002	2.107	1.003	1.088
86	30	995.7	1.932	0.798	1.670	0.800	0.864
104	40	992.2	1.925	0.547	1.366	0.553	0.709

Compiled from Bolz and Tuve (1973), Henry and Heinke (1996), Hughes and Brighton (1967), and Tchobanaglous and Schroeder (1985).

Standard vapor pressures for water

Temperature (°F)	Temperature (°C)	Vapor Pressure (ft)	Vapor Pressure (m)
32	0	0.20	0.061
40	4.4	0.28	0.085
50	10.0	0.41	0.12
60	15.6	0.59	0.18
70	21.1	0.84	0.26
80	26.7	1.17	0.36
90	32.2	1.61	0.49
100	37.8	2.19	0.67

Hydraulic Institute, 1979

Standard barometric pressures

Elevation (ft)	Elevation (m)	Barometric Pressure (ft)	Barometric Pressure (m)
0	0	33.9	10.3
1000	305	32.7	9.97
2000	610	31.6	9.63
3000	914	30.5	9.30
4000	1220	29.3	8.93
5000	1524	28.2	8.59
6000	1829	27.1	8.26
7000	2134	26.1	7.95
8000	2440	25.1	7.65

Hydraulic Institute (1979)

Reynolds Number for various flow responses

Flow Regime	Reynolds Number
Laminar	< 2000
Transitional	2000-4000
Turbulent	> 4000

Equivalent sand grain roughness for various pipe materials

	Equivalent Sand Roughness, ε	
Material	(ft)	(mm)
Copper, brass	$1x10^{-4}$ - $3x10^{-3}$	$3.05x10^{-2}$ - 0.9
Wrought iron, steel	$1.5x10^{-4}$ - $8x10^{-3}$	$4.6x10^{-2}$ - 2.4
Asphalt-lined cast iron	$4x10^{-4}$ - $7x10^{-3}$	0.1 - 2.1
Galvanized iron	$3.3x10^{-4}$ - $1.5x10^{-2}$	0.102 - 4.6
Cast iron	$8x10^{-4}$ - $1.8x10^{-2}$	0.2 - 5.5
Concrete	10^{-3} to 10^{-2}	0.3 to 3.0
Uncoated Cast Iron	$7.4x10^{-4}$	0.226
Coated Cast Iron	$3.3x10^{-4}$	0.102
Coated Spun Iron	$1.8x10^{-4}$	$5.6x10^{-2}$
Cement	$1.3x10^{-3}$ - $4x10^{-3}$	0.4 - 1.2s
Wrought Iron	$1.7x10^{-4}$	$5x10^{-2}$
Uncoated Steel	$9.2x10^{-5}$	$2.8x10^{-2}$
Coated Steel	$1.8x10^{-4}$	$5.8x10^{-2}$
Wood Stave	$6x10^{-4}$ - $3x10^{-3}$	0.2 - 0.9
PVC	$5x10^{-6}$	$1.5x10^{-3}$

Compiled from Lamont (1981), Moody (1944), and Mays (1999)

C-factors for various pipe materials

	C-factor Values for Discrete Pipe Diameters					
Type of Pipe	1.0 in. (2.5 cm)	3.0 in. (7.6 cm)	6.0 in. (15.2 cm)	12 in. (30 cm)	24 in. (61 cm)	48 in. (122 cm)
Uncoated cast iron - smooth and new		121	125	130	132	134
Coated cast iron - smooth and new		129	133	138	140	141
30 years old						
Trend 1 - slight attack		100	106	112	117	120
Trend 2 - moderate attack		83	90	97	102	107
Trend 3 - appreciable attack		59	70	78	83	89
Trend 4 - severe attack		41	50	58	66	73
60 years old						
Trend 1 - slight attack		90	97	102	107	112
Trend 2 - moderate attack		69	79	85	92	96
Trend 3 - appreciable attack		49	58	66	72	78
Trend 4 - severe attack		30	39	48	56	62
100 years old						
Trend 1 - slight attack		81	89	95	100	104
Trend 2 - moderate attack		61	70	78	83	89
Trend 3 - appreciable attack		40	49	57	64	71
Trend 4 - severe attack		21	30	39	46	54
Miscellaneous						
Newly scraped mains		109	116	121	125	127
Newly brushed mains		97	104	108	112	115
Coated spun iron - smooth and new		137	142	145	148	148
Old - take as coated cast iron of same age						
Galvanized iron - smooth and new	120	129	133			
Wrought iron - smooth and new	129	137	142			
Coated steel - smooth and new	129	137	142	145	148	148
Uncoated Steel - smooth and new	134	142	145	147	150	150
Coated asbestos cement - clean		147	149	150	152	
Uncoated asbestos cement - clean		142	145	147	150	
Spun cement-lined and spun bitumen-lined - clean		147	149	150	152	153
Smooth pipe (including lead, brass, copper, polyethylene, and PVC) - clean	140	147	149	150	152	153
PVC wavy - clean	134	142	145	147	150	150
Concrete - Scobey						
Class 1 - Cs = 0.27; clean		69	79	84	90	95
Class 2 - Cs = 0.31; clean		95	102	106	110	113
Class 3 - Cs = 0.345; clean		109	116	121	125	127
Class 4 - Cs = 0.37; clean		121	125	130	132	134
Best - Cs = 0.40; clean		129	133	138	140	141
Tate relined pipes - clean		109	116	121	125	127
Prestressed concrete pipes - clean				147	150	150

Lamont, 1981

Manning's roughness values

Material	Manning Coefficient
Asbestos cement	.011
Brass	.011
Brick	.015
Cast-iron, new	.012
Concrete	
Steel forms	.011
Wooden forms	.015
Centrifugally spun	.013
Copper	.011
Corrugated metal	.022
Galvanized iron	.016
Lead	.011
Plastic	.009
Steel	
Coal-tar enamel	.010
New unlined	.011
Riveted	.019
Wood stave	.012

Minor loss coefficients

Fitting	K_L	Fitting	K_L
Pipe Entrance		90° smooth bend	
Bellmouth	0.03-0.05	Bend radius/D = 4	0.16-0.18
Rounded	0.12-0.25	Bend radius/D = 2	0.19-0.25
Sharp-edged	0.50	Bend radius/D = 1	0.35-0.40
Projecting	0.78	Mitered bend	
Contraction - sudden		$\theta = 15°$	0.05
D_2/D_1=0.80	0.18	$\theta = 30°$	0.10
D_2/D_1=0.50	0.37	$\theta = 45°$	0.20
D_2/D_1=0.20	0.49	$\theta = 60°$	0.35
Contraction - conical		$\theta = 90°$	0.80
D_2/D_1=0.80	0.05	Tee	
D_2/D_1=0.50	0.07	Line flow	0.30-0.40
D_2/D_1=0.20	0.08	Branch flow	0.75-1.80
Expansion - sudden		Cross	
D_2/D_1=0.80	0.16	Line flow	0.50
D_2/D_1=0.50	0.57	Branch flow	0.75
D_2/D_1=0.20	0.92	45° Wye	
Expansion - conical		Line flow	0.30
D_2/D_1=0.80	0.03	Branch flow	0.50
D_2/D_1=0.50	0.08	Check valve - conventional	4.0
D_2/D_1=0.20	0.13	Check valve - clearway	1.5
Gate valve - open	0.39	Check valve - ball	4.5
3/4 open	1.10	Butterfly valve - open	1.2
1/2 open	4.8	Cock - straight through	0.5
1/4 open	27	Foot valve - hinged	2.2
Globe valve - open	10	Foot valve - poppet	12.5
Angle valve - open	4.3		

Walski, 1984

Bibliography

GENERAL WATER DISTRIBUTION HYDRAULICS

ASCE. (1975). *Pressure Pipeline Design for Water and Wastewater.* ASCE, New York, New York.

American Water Works Association. (1975). "Sizing Service Lines and Meters." *AWWA Manual M-22*, Denver, Colorado.

American Water Works Association. (1987). *Distribution System Maintenance Techniques*. Denver, Colorado.

American Water Works Association. (1989). "Distribution Network Analysis for Water Utilities." *AWWA Manual M-32*, Denver, Colorado.

American Water Works Association. (1996). "Ductile Iron Pipe and Fitting." *AWWA Manual M-41*, Denver, Colorado.

ASCE Committee on Pipeline Planning. (1992). *Pressure Pipeline Design for Water and Wastewater.* ASCE, Reston, Virginia.

ASCE/WEF. (1982). *Gravity Sanitary Sewer Design and Construction.* ASCE, Reston, Virginia.

Babbitt, H. E., and Doland, J. J. (1931). *Water Supply Engineering*. McGraw-Hill, New York, New York.

Benedict, R. P. (1910). *Fundamentals of Pipe Flow.* John Wiley and Sons, New York, New York.

Bernoulli, D. (1738). *Hydrodynamica*. Argentorati.

Buettner, C. F. (1980). *Practical Hydraulics and Flow Monitoring Workshop Notes.* Saint Louis, Missouri.

California-Nevada AWWA. (1981). *Distribution Main Flushing and Cleaning*. California-Nevada AWWA, Rancho Cucamonga, California.

Cesario, A. L. (1995). *Modeling, Analysis, and Design of Water Distribution Systems.* American Water Works Association, Denver, Colorado.

Chadderton, R. A., Christensen, G. L., and Henry-Unrath, P. (1992). *Implementation and Optimization of Distribution Flushing Programs.* AWWA Research Foundation, Denver, Colorado.

Colebrook, C. F., and White, C. M. (1937). "The Reduction of Carrying Capacity of Pipes with Age." *Proceedings of the Institute of Civil Engineers*, 5137(7), 99.

Crane Company. (1972). *Flow of Fluids through Valves and Fittings*. Crane Co., New York, New York.

Haestad Methods, Inc. (1997). *Computer Applications in Hydraulic Engineering*. Haestad Press, Waterbury, Connecticut.

Haestad Methods, Inc. (1997). *Practical Guide – Hydraulics and Hydrology.* Haestad Press, Waterbury, Connecticut.

Haestad Methods, Inc. (1999). *Essential Hydraulics and Hydrology.* Haestad Press, Waterbury, Connecticut.

Hauser, B. A. (1993). *Hydraulics for Operators*. Lewis Publishers, Ann Arbor, Michigan.

Hydraulic Institute. (1979). *Engineering Data Book*. Hydraulic Institute, Cleveland, Ohio.

Hydraulic Research. (1983). *Tables for the Hydraulic Design of Pipes and Sewers*. Wallingford, England.

Idelchik, I. E. (1999). *Handbook of Hydraulic Resistance*. 3rd edition. Begell House, New York, New York.

Lamont, P. A. (1981). "Common Pipe Flow Formulas Compared with the Theory of Roughness." *Journal of the American Water Works Association*, 73(5), 274.

Male, J. W., and Walski, T. M. (1990). *Water Distribution Systems—A Troubleshooting Manual*. Lewis Publishers, Chelsea, Michigan.

Mays, L.W., ed. (1989). *Reliability Analysis of Water Distribution Systems*. ASCE Task Committee on Risk and Reliability Analysis, New York, New York.

Mays, L.W., ed. (1996). *Water Resources Handbook*. McGraw-Hill, New York, New York.

Mays, L. W., ed. (1999). *Hydraulic Design Handbook*. McGraw-Hill, New York, New York.

Mays, L. W., ed. (2000). *Water Distribution Systems Handbook*. McGraw-Hill, New York, New York.

Miller, D. S. (1978). *Internal Flow Systems*. BHRA Fluid Engineering, Bedford, United Kingdom.

Nayar, M. L. (1992). *Piping Handbook*. McGraw-Hill, New York, New York.

Nikuradse (1932). "Gestezmassigkeiten der Turbulenten Stromung in Glatten Rohren." *VDI-Forschungsh*, No. 356 (in German).

Oberoi, K. (1994). "Distribution Flushing Programs: The Benefits and Results." *Proceedings of the AWWA Annual Conference*, New York, New York.

Olujic, Z. (1981). "Compute Friction Factors for Fast Flow in Pipes." *Chemical Engineering*, 91.

Patison, P. L. (1980). "Conducting a Regular Main Flushing Program." *Journal of the American Water Works Association*, 72(2), 88.

Rossman, L.A. (2000). *EPANET Users Manual*. Risk Reduction Engineering Laboratory, U.S. Environmental Protection Agency, Cincinnati, Ohio.

Rouse, H. (1980). "Some Paradoxes in the History of Hydraulics." *Journal of Hydraulics Division*, ASCE, 106(6), 1077.

Seidler, M. (1982). "Obtaining an Analytical Grasp of Water Distribution Systems." *Journal of the American Water Works Association*, 74(12).

Sharp, W. W., and Walski, T. M. (1988). "Predicting Internal Roughness in Water Mains." *Journal of the American Water Works Association*, 80(11), 34.

Stephenson, D. (1976). *Pipeline Design for Water Engineers*. Elsevier Scientific Publishing Company, New York, New York.

Streeter, V. L., Wylie, B. E., and Bedford, K. W. (1998). *Fluid Mechanics*. 9th edition, WCB/McGraw-Hill, Boston, Massachusetts.

Swamee, P. K., and Jain, A. K. (1976). "Explicit Equations for Pipe Flow Problems." *Journal of Hydraulic Engineering*, ASCE, 102(5), 657.

Task Committee on Design of Pipelines (1975). *Pressure Pipeline Design for Water and Wastewater*. ASCE, Reston, Virginia.

Wagner, J., Shamir, U., and Marks, D. (1988a). "Water Distribution System Reliability: Analytical Methods." *Journal of Water Resources Planning and Management*, ASCE, 114(2), 253.

Wagner, J., Shamir, U., and Marks, D. (1988b). "Water Distribution System Reliability: Simulation Methods." *Journal of Water Resources Planning and Management*, ASCE, 114(2), 276.

Walski, T. M. (1984). *Analysis of Water Distribution Systems*. Van Nostrand Reinhold, New York, New York.

Walski, T. M., Sharp, W., and Shields, F. D. (1988). "Predicting Internal Roughness in Water Mains." *Miscellaneous Paper EL-88-2*, U.S. Army Engineer Waterways Experiment Station, Vicksburg, Mississippi.

Walski, T. M., Edwards, J. D., and Hearne, V. M. (1989). "Loss of Carrying Capacity in Pipes Transporting Softened Water with High pH." *Proceedings of the National Conference on Environmental Engineering*, ASCE, Austin, Texas.

Williams, G. S., and Hazen, A. (1920). *Hydraulic Tables*. John Wiley & Sons, New York, New York.

GENERAL HYDRAULIC MODELING

ANSI, ASTM. (1971). *Metric Practice Guide*.

Bhave, P. R. (1991). *Analysis of Flow in Water Distribution Networks*. Technomics, Lancaster, Pennsylvania.

Collins, M. A. (1980). "Pitfalls in Pipe Network Analysis Techniques." *Journal of Transportation Division*, ASCE, 106(TE5), 507.

Cross, H. (1936). "Analysis of Flow in Networks of Conduits or Conductors." *Univ. Of Illinois Experiment Station Bulletin, No. 286*, Department of Civil Engineering, University of Illinois, Champaign Urbana, Illinois.

Dillingham, J. H. (1967) "Computer Analysis of Water Distribution Systems." *Water and Sewage Works*, 114(1), 1.

Epp, R., and Fowler, A. G. (1970). "Efficient Code for Steady State Flows in Networks." *Journal of Hydraulics Division*, ASCE, 96(HY1), 43.

Fishwick, P. A. (1995). *Simulation Model Design and Execution*. Prentice-Hall, Englewood Cliffs, New Jersey.

Chaudry M. H., and Yevjevich, V., eds. (1980). *Closed Conduit Flow*. Water Resources Publications, Littleton, Colorado.

Goodwin, S.J. (1980). "The Results of the Experimental Program on Leakage and Leakage Control." *Technical Report TR 154*, Water Research Centre.

Gupta, R., and Bhave, P. (1996). "Comparison of Methods for Predicting Deficient Network Performance." *Journal of Water Resources Planning and Management*, ASCE, 122(3), 214.

Jeppson, T. W. (1976). *Analysis of Flow in Pipe Network*. Ann Arbor Science Publishers, Ann Arbor, Michigan.

Larock, B. E., Jeppson, R. W., and Watters, G. Z. (1999). *Handbook of Pipeline Systems*. CRC Press, Boca Raton, Florida.

Moody, L. F. (1944). "Friction Factors for Pipe Flow." *Transactions of the American Society of Mechanical Engineers*, Vol. 66.

Muss, D. L. (1960). "Friction Losses in Lines with Service Connections." *Journal of Hydraulics Division*, ASCE, 86(4), 35.

Rao, H. S., and Bree, D. W. (1977). "Extended Period Simulation of Water Systems." *Journal of Hydraulics Division*, ASCE, 103(HY2), 97.

Salgado, R., Todini, E., and O'Connell (1987). "Comparison of the Gradient Method with Some Traditional Methods for the Analysis of Water Distribution Networks." *Proceedings of the International Conference on Computer Applications for Water Supply and Distribution*, Leicester Polytechnic, United Kingdom.

Shamir, U., and Howard, C. D. (1968). "Water Distribution Systems Analysis." *Journal of Hydraulics Division*, ASCE, 94(1), 219.

Todini, E., and Pilati, S. (1987). "A Gradient Method for the Analysis of Pipe Networks." *Proceedings of the International Conference on Computer Applications for Water Supply and Distribution*, Leicester Polytechnic, UK.

Walski, T. M., Gessler, J., and Sjostrom, J. W. (1990). *Water Distribution—Simulation and Sizing*. Lewis Publishers, Ann Arbor, Michigan.

Water Research Center (WRc). (1989). *Network Analysis – A Code of Practice*. WRc, Swindon, England.

Wood, D. J. (1980). *Computer Analysis of Flow in Pipe Networks*. University of Kentucky, Lexington, Kentucky.

Wood, D. J., and Charles, C. O. A. (1972). "Hydraulic Analysis Using Linear Theory." *Journal of Hydraulics Division*, ASCE, 98(7), 1157.

Wood, D. J., and Rayes, A. G. (1981). "Reliability of Algorithms for Pipe Network Analysis," *Journal of Hydraulics Division*, ASCE, 107(10), 1145.

Water Research Centre (WRc). (1989). *Network Analysis—A Code of Practice*. Water Research Centre. Swindon, United Kingdom.

APPLICATION OF MODELS

Basford, C., and Sevier, C. (1995). "Automating the Maintenance of Hydraulic Network Model Demand Database Utilizing GIS and Customer Billing Records." *Computers in the Water Industry*, AWWA, Denver, Colorado.

Bouchart, F., and Goulter, I. C. (1991). "Improvements in Design of Water Distribution Networks Recognizing Valve Location." *Water Resources Research*, 27(12), 3029.

Bowen, P. T., Harp, J., Baxter, J., and Shull, R. (1993). *Residential Water Use Patterns*. AWWARF, Denver, Colorado.

Buyens, D. J., Bizier, P. A., and Combee, C. W. (1996). "Using a Geographical Information System to Determine Water Distribution Model Demands." *Proceedings of the AWWA Annual Conference*, American Water Works Association, Toronto, Canada.

Cannistra, J. R. (1999). "Converting GIS Data for GIS." *Journal of the American Water Works Association*, 91(2), 55.

Carr, R. J., and Smith, N. A. (1995). "Useful or Useless – A Procedure for Maintaining Network Models." *Proceedings of the AWWA Annual Conference*, American Water Works Association, Anaheim, California.

Cesario, A. L. (1980). "Computer Modeling Programs: Tools for Model Operations." *Journal of the American Water Works Association*, 72(9), 508.

Cesario, A. L. (1991). "Network Analysis from Planning, Engineering, Operations and Management Perspectives." *Journal of the American Water Works Association*, 83(2), 38.

Dacier, N. M., Boulos, P. F., Clapp, J. W., Dhingra, A. K., and Bowcock, R. W. (1995). "Taking Small Steps Towards a Fully-Integrated Computer Based Environment for Distribution System Operation, Maintenance and Management." *Computers in the Water Industry*, AWWA, Denver, Colorado.

Davis, A. L., and Brawn, R. C. (2000). "General Purpose Demand Allocator (DALLOC)." *Proceedings of the Environmental and Water Resources Institute Conference*, American Society of Civil Engineers, Minneapolis, Minnesota.

Dustman, P. E., Beyer, D., Bialek, E. Z., and Pon, V. H. (1996). "Preserving the Existing Level of Service During Tank Outages." *Proceedings of the AWWA Annual Conference*, American Water Works Association, Toronto, Canada.

Engelhardt, M.O., Skipworth, P.J., Savic, D.A., Saul, A.J., and Walters, G.A. (2000). "Rehabilitation Strategies for Water Distribution Networks: A Literature Review with a UK Perspective." *Urban Water*, Vol. 2, No. 2, 153-170.

Eggener, C. L., and Polkowski, L. (1976). "Network Modeling and the Impact of Modeling Assumptions. *Journal of the American Water Works Association*, 68(4), 189.

ESRI. (2001). "What is a GIS?" http://www.esri.com/library/gis/abtgis/what_gis.html.

Germanopoulos, G. (1995). "Valve Control Regulation for Reducing Leakage." *Improving Efficiency and Reliability in Water Distribution Systems*, Kluwer Academic Press, London, United Kingdom, 165.

Goulter, I. C. (1987). "Current and Future Use of Systems Analysis in Water Distribution Network Design." *Civil Engineering Systems*, 4(4), 175.

Goulter, I. C., and Bouchart, F. (1990). "Reliability Based Design of Pumping and Distribution Systems." *Journal of Hydraulic Engineering*, ASCE, 116(2), 211.

Great Lakes and Upper Mississippi River Board of State Public Health & Environmental Managers (GLUMB). (1992). *Recommended Standards for Water Works*. Albany, New York.

Guihan, M. T., Irias, X. J., Swain, C., and Dustman, P. E. (1995). "Making the Case for the GIS Hydraulic Modeling Tool." *Computers in the Water Industry*, AWWA, Denver, Colorado.

Hudson, W. D. (1973). "Computerizing Pipeline Design." *Journal of Transportation Division*, ASCE, 99(1), 73.

Kaufman, M. M., and Wurtz, M. (1998). "Small System Maintenance Management Using GIS." *Journal of the American Water Works Association*, 90(7), 70.

Lee, J. H. (1998). "Case Study of a Water Distribution System by Computer Modeling." *Proceedings of the International Symposium on Computer Modeling*, University of Kentucky, Lexington, Kentucky.

Martin, D. C. (1987). "Professional Responsibilities Related to Computer-Aided Hydraulic Network Analysis." *Proceedings of the AWWA Annual Conference*, American Water Works Association, Kansas City, Missouri.

Martinez, F., Conejos, P., and Vercher, J. (1999). "Developing an Integrated Model of Water Distribution Systems Considering both Distributed Leakage and Pressure Dependent Demands." *Proceedings of the ASCE Water Resources Planning and Management Division Conference*, Tempe, Arizona.

Miller, T. C. (1988). "Application of Accurate Hydraulic Models." *Proceedings of the International Symposium on Computer Modeling*, University of Kentucky, Lexington, Kentucky.

O'Connell, K. M. C. (1992). "Allocation of Water System Demand in a Hydraulic Model for the City of Vancouver, BC." *Proceedings of the AWWA Annual Conference*, American Water Works Association, Vancouver, Canada.

Pudar, R.S., and Liggett, J.A. (1992). "Leaks in Pipe Networks." *Journal of Hydraulic Engineering*, ASCE, 118(7), 1031.

Shamir, U., and Howard, C. D. D. (1977). "Engineering Analysis of Water Distribution Systems." *Journal of the American Water Works Association*, 69(9), 510.

Shamir, U., and Hamberg, D. (1988). "Schematic Models for Distribution Systems Design I: Combination Concept." *Journal of Water Resources Planning and Management*, ASCE, 114(2), 129.

Shamir, U., and Hamberg, D. (1988). "Schematic Models for Distribution Systems Design II: Continuum Approach." *Journal of Water Resources Planning and Management*, ASCE, 114(2), 141.

Stathis, J.A., and Loganathan, G.V. (1999). "Analysis of Pressure-Dependent Leakage in Water Distribution Systems." *Proceedings of the ASCE Water Resources Planning and Management Division Conference*, Tempe, AZ.

Stern, C. T. (1995). "The Los Angeles Department of Water and Power Hydraulic Modeling Project: Combining GIS and Network Modeling Techniques." *Proceedings of the AWWA Computer Conference*, American Water Works Association, Norfolk, Virginia.

Tang, K.W., Brunone, B., Karney, B., and Rossetti, A. (2000). "Role and Characterization of Leaks Under Transient Conditions." *Proceedings of the ASCE Joint Conference on Water Resources Engineering and Water Resources Management*, Minneapolis, Minnesota.

Walski, T. M. (1983). "Using Water Distribution System Models." *Journal of the American Water Works Association*, 75(2), 58.

Walski, T. M., ed. (1987). *Water Supply System Rehabilitation*. ASCE, New York, New York.

Walski, T. M. (1993). "Practical Aspects of Providing Reliability in Water Distribution Systems." *Reliability Engineering and Systems Safety*, Elsevier, 42(1), 13.

Walski, T. M., and Lutes, T. L. (1994). "Hydraulic Transients Cause Low-pressure Problems." *Journal of the American Water Works Association*, 86(12), 24.

Walski, T. M. (1995). "An Approach for Handling Sprinklers, Hydrants, and Orifices in Water Distribution Systems." *Proceedings of the AWWA Annual Conference*, American Water Works Association, Anaheim, Calif.

Yanov, D. A., and Kotch, R. N. (1987). "A Modern Residential Flow Demand Study." *Proceedings of the AWWA Annual Conference*, American Water Works Association, Kansas City, Missouri.

PUMPING

Chase, D. V., and Ormsbee, L. E. (1989). "Optimal Pump Operation of Water Distribution Systems with Multiple Tanks." *Proceedings of the AWWA Computer Conference*, American Water Works Association, 205.

Hicks, T. G., and Edwards, T. W. (1971). *Pump Application Engineering*. McGraw-Hill, New York, New York.

Hovstadius, G. (2001). "Pump System Effectiveness." *Pumps and Systems*, 9(1), 48.

Hydraulic Institute. (1983). *Standards for Centrifugal, Rotary, and Reciprocating Pumps*. Cleveland, Ohio.

Hydraulic Institute. (2000). *Pump Standards*. Parsippany, New Jersey.

Karassik, I. J., ed. (1976). *Pump Handbook*. McGraw-Hill, New York, New York.

McPherson, M. B. (1966). "Distribution System Equalizing Storage Hydraulics." *Journal of Hydraulics Division*, ASCE, 92(6), 151.

Ormsbee, L. E., and Lingireddy, S. (1995). "Nonlinear Heuristic for Pump Operations." *Journal of Water Resources Planning and Management*, ASCE, 121(4), 302.

Sanks, R. L., ed. (1998). *Pumping Station Design*. 2nd edition, Butterworth, London, UK.

Tarquin, A., and Dowdy, J. (1989). "Optimal Pump Operation in Water Distribution." *Journal of Hydraulic Engineering*, ASCE, 115(2), 168.

Walski, T. M., and Ormsbee, L. (1989). "Developing System Head Curves for Water Distribution Pumping." *Journal of the American Water Works Association*, 81(7), 63.

Walski, T. M. (1993). "Tips for Energy Savings in Pumping Operations." *Journal of the American Water Works Association*, 85(7), 48.

CUSTOMER DEMANDS

Basford, C., and Sevier, C. (1995). "Automating the Maintenance of Hydraulic Network Model Demand Database Utilizing GIS and Customer Billing Records." *Proceedings of the AWWA Computer Conference*, American Water Works Association, Norfolk, Virginia.

Baumann D., Boland, J. and Hanemann, W. H., eds. (1998). "Forecasting Urban Water Use: Models and Application." *Urban Water Demand Management and Planning*, McGraw Hill. New York, New York.

Buchberger, S. G., and Wells, G. J. (1996). "Intensity, Duration, and Frequency of Residential Water Demands." *Journal of Water Resources Planning and Management*, ASCE, 122(1), 11.

Buchberger, S. G., and Wu, L. (1995). "A Model for Instantaneous Residential Water Demands." *Journal of Hydraulic Engineering*, ASCE, 54(4), 232.

Buyens, D. J., Bizier, P. A., and Combee, C. W. (1996). "Using a Geographical Information System to Determine Water Distribution Model Demands." *Proceedings of the AWWA Annual Conference*, American Water Works Association, Toronto, Canada.

Cesario, A. L., and Lee T. K. (1980). "A Computer Method for Loading Model Networks." *Journal of the American Water Works Association*, 72(4), 208.

Coote, P. A., and Johnson, T. J. (1995). "Hydraulic Model for the Mid-Size Utility." *Proceedings of the AWWA Computer Conference*, American Water Works Association, Norfolk, Virginia.

Dziegielewski, B., and Boland J. J. (1989). "Forecasting Urban Water Use: the IWR-MAIN Model." *Water Resource Bulletin*, 25(1), 101-119.

Hunter, R. B. (1940). "Methods of Estimating Loads in Plumbing Systems." *Report BMS 65*, National Bureau of Standards, Washington, DC.

Insurance Advisory Organization (IAO). (1974). *Grading Schedule for Municipal Fire Protection*. Toronto, Canada.

Insurance Services Office (ISO). (1980). *Fire Suppression Rating Schedule*. New York, New York.

International Association of Plumbing and Mechanical Officials. (1997). *Uniform Plumbing Code*. Los Angeles, California.

Linaweaver, F. P., Geyer, J. C., and Wolff J. B. (1966). *A Study of Residential Water Use: A Report Prepared for the Technical Studies Program of the Federal Housing Administration*. Department of Housing and Urban Development, Washington, DC.

Macy, P. P. (1991). "Integrating Construction and Water Master Planning." *Journal of the American Water Works Association*, 83(10), 44.

Male, J. W., and Walski, T. M. (1990). *Water Distribution: A Troubleshooting Manual*. Lewis Publishers, Chelsea, Florida.

Moore, M. (1998). "A Complete Integration of Water Distribution Computer Applications: Tomorrow's Water Utility." *Proceedings of the AWWA Information Management and Technology Conference*, American Water Works Association, Reno, Nevada.

Office of Water Services (Ofwat). (1998). *1997-98 Report on Leakage and Water Efficiency*. http://www.open.gov.uk/ofwat/leak97.pdf, United Kingdom.

Rhoades, S. D. (1995). "Hourly Monitoring of Single-Family Residential Areas." *Journal of the American Water Works Association*, 87(8), 43.

Vickers, A. L. (1991). "The Emerging Demand Side Era in Water Conservation." *Journal of the American Water Works Association*, 83(10), 38.

Water Research Centre (WRc). (1985). *District Metering, Part I - System Design and Installation*. Report ER180E, United Kingdom.

Wolff, J. B. (1961). "Peak Demands in Residential Areas." *Journal of the American Water Works Association*, 53(10).

MODEL CALIBRATION

American Water Works Association. (1989). "Installation, Field Testing, and Maintenance of Fire Hydrants." *AWWA Manual M-17*, Denver, Colorado.

American Water Works Association Engineering Computer Applications Committee. (1999). "Calibration Guidelines for Water Distribution System Modeling." http://www.awwa.org/unitdocs/592/calibrate.pdf.

Bhave, P. R. (1988). "Calibrating Water Distribution Network Models." *Journal of Environmental Engineering*, ASCE, 114(1).

Boulos, P., and Ormsbee, L. E. (1991). "Explicit Network Calibration for Multiple Loading Conditions." *Civil Engineering Systems*, 8, 153.

Brainard, B. (1994). "Using Electronic Rate of Flow Recorders." *Proceeding of the AWWA Distribution System Symposium*, American Water Works Association, Omaha, Nebraska.

Bush, C. A., and Uber, J. G. (1998). "Sampling Design and Methods for Water Distribution Model Calibration." *Journal of Water Resources Planning and Management*, ASCE, 124(6), 334.

California Section AWWA. (1962). "Loss of Carrying Capacity of Water Mains." *Journal of the American Water Works Association*, 54(10).

Cesario, A. L., Kroon, J. R., Grayman, W., and Wright, G. (1996). "New Perspectives on Calibration of Treated Water Distribution System Models." *Proceedings of the AWWA Annual Conference*, American Water Works Association, Toronto, Canada.

Coulbeck, B. (1984). "An Application of Hierarchical Optimization in Calibration of Large-Scale Water Networks." *Optimal Control Applications and Methods*, 6(31).

Datta, R. S. N., and Sridharan, K. (1994). "Parameter Estimation in Water Distribution Systems by Least Squares." *Journal of Water Resources Planning and Management*, ASCE, 120(4), 405.

DeOreo, W. B., Heaney, J. P., and Mayer, P. W. (1996). "Flow Trace Analysis to Assess Water Use." *Journal of the American Water Works Association*, 88(1), 79.

Duncan, C. T. (1998). "Maintaining the Simulation Quality of your Hydraulic Distribution Model Through Innovative Calibration Techniques." *Proceedings of the AWWA Information Management and Technology Conference*, American Water Works Association, Reno, Nevada.

Howie, D. C. (1999). "Problems with SCADA Data for Calibration of Hydraulic Models." *Proceedings of the ASCE Annual Conference of Water Resources Planning and Management*, Tempe, Arizona.

Hudson, W. D. (1966). "Studies of Distribution System Capacity in Seven Cities." *Journal of the American Water Works Association*, 58:2, 157.

Kapelan, Z., Savic, D.A., and Walters, G.A. (2000). "Inverse Transient Analysis in Pipe Networks for Leakage Detection and Roughness Calibration." *Water Network Modeling for Optimal Design and Management*, CWS 2000, Centre for Water Systems, Exeter, United Kingdom, 143.

Lansey, K., and Basnet, C. (1991). "Parameter Estimation for Water Distribution Networks." *Journal of Water Resources Planning and Management*, ASCE, 117(1), 126.

McBean, E. A., Al-Nassari, S., and Clarke, D. (1983). "Some Probabilistic Elements of Field Testing in Water Distribution Systems." *Proceedings of the Institute of Civil Engineers*, Part 2, 75-143.

McEnroe, B. M., Chase, D. V., and Sharp, W. W. (1989). "Field Testing Water Mains to Determine Carrying Capacity." *Miscellaneous Paper EL-89*, U.S, Army Engineer Waterways Experiment Station, Vicksburg, Mississippi.

Meier, R. W., and Barkdoll, B. D. (2000). "Sampling Design for Network Model Calibration Using Genetic Algorithms." *Journal of Water Resources Planning and Management*, ASCE, 126(4), 245.

Meredith, D. D. (1983). "Use of Optimization in Calibrating Water Distribution System Models." *Proceedings of the ASCE Spring Convention*, Philadelphia, Pennsylvania.

Morin, M., and Rajaratnam, I. V. (2000). *Testing and Calibration of Pitot Diffusers*. University of Alberta Hydraulics Laboratory, Alberta, Canada.

Ormsbee, L. E., and Wood, D. J. (1986). "Explicit Pipe Network Calibration." *Journal of Water Resources Planning and Management*, ASCE, 112(2), 166.

Ormsbee, L. E., and Chase, D.V. (1988). "Hydraulic Network Calibration using Nonlinear Programming." *Proceedings of the International Symposium on Water Distribution Modeling*, Lexington, Kentucky.

Ormsbee, L. E. (1989). "Implicit Pipe Network Calibration." *Journal of Water Resources Planning and Management*, ASCE, 115(2), 243.

Ormsbee, L. E., and Lingireddy, S. (1997). "Calibrating Hydraulic Network Models." *Journal of the American Water Works Association*, 89(2), 44.

Ormsbee, L. E., and Lingireddy, S. (1999). "Optimal Network Calibration Model Based on Algorithms." *Proceedings of the ASCE Annual Conference of Water Resources Planning and Management*, Tempe, Arizona.

Savic, D. A., and Walters, G. A. (1995). "Genetic Algorithm Techniques for Calibrating Network Models." *Report No. 95/12*, Centre For Systems And Control Engineering, School of Engineering, University of Exeter, Exeter, United Kingdom, 41.

Walski, T. M. (1983). "Technique for Calibrating Network Models." *Journal of Water Resources Planning and Management*, ASCE, 109(4), 360.

Walski, T. M. (1984). "Hydrant Flow Test Results." *Journal of Hydraulic Engineering*, ASCE, 110(6), 847.

Walski, T. M. (1985). "Correction of Head Loss Measurements in Water Mains." *Journal of Transportation Engineering*, ASCE, 111(1), 75.

Walski, T. M. (1986). "Case Study: Pipe Network Model Calibration Issues." *Journal of Water Resources Planning and Management*, ASCE, 109(4), 238.

Walski, T. M. (1988). "Conducting and Reporting Hydrant Flow Tests." *WES Video Report*, U.S. Army Engineer Waterways Experiment Station, Vicksburg, Mississippi.

Walski, T. M. (1990). "Sherlock Holmes Meets Hardy Cross or Model Calibration in Austin, Texas." *Journal of the American Water Works Association*, 82(3), 34.

Walski, T. M., and O'Farrell, S. J. (1994). "Head Loss Testing in Transmission Mains." *Journal of the American Water Works Association*, 86(7), 62.

Walski, T. M. (1995). "Standards for Model Calibration." *Proceedings of the AWWA Computer Conference*, American Water Works Association, Norfolk, Virginia.

Walski, T. M. (2000). "Model Calibration Data: The Good, The Bad and The Useless." *Journal of the American Water Works Association*, 92(1), 94.

Walski, T. M., Lowry, S. G., and Rhee, H. (2000). "Pitfalls in Calibrating an EPS Model." *Proceedings of the Environmental and Water Resource Institute Conference*, American Society of Civil Engineers, Minneapolis, Minnesota.

Walters G. A., Savic, D. A., Morley, M. S., de Schaetzen, W., and Atkinson, R. M. (1998). "Calibration of Water Distribution Network Models Using Genetic Algorithms." *Hydraulic Engineering Software VII*, Computational Mechanics Publications, 131.

OPTIMAL DESIGN

Alperovits, and Shamir, U. (1977). "Design of Optimal Water Distribution Systems." *Water Resources Research*, 13(6), 885.

Bhave, P. R. (1983). "Optimization of Gravity Fed Water Distribution Systems." *Journal of Environmental Engineering*, ASCE, 104(4), 799.

Camp, T. R. (1939). "Economic Pipe Sizes for Water Distribution Systems." *Transactions of the American Society of Civil Engineers*, 104, 190.

Dandy, G. C., Simpson, A. R., and Murphy, L. J. (1996). "An Improved Genetic Algorithm for Pipe Network Optimization." *Water Resources Research*, 32(2), 449.

Deb, A. K. (1976). "Optimization of Water Distribution Network System." *Journal of the Environmental Engineering Division*, ASCE, 102(4), 837.

DeNeufville, R., Schaake, J., and Stafford, J. (1971). "Systems Analysis of Water Distribution Networks." *Journal of Sanitary Engineering Division*, ASCE, 97(6), 825.

Eiger, G., Shamir, U., and Ben-Tal, A. (1994). "Optimal Design of Water Distribution Networks." *Water Resources Research*, 30(9), 2637.

Fujiwara, O., Jenchaimahakoon, B., and Edirisinghe, N. C. P. (1987). "A Modified Linear Programming Gradient Method for Optimal Design of Looped Water Distribution Networks." *Water Resources Research*, 23(6), 977.

Fujiwara, O., and Khang, D. B. (1990). "A Two-phase Decomposition Method for Optimal Design of Looped Water Distribution Networks." *Water Resources Research*, 26(4), 539.

Gessler, J. (1985). "Pipe Network Optimization by Enumeration." *Computer Applications in Water Resources*, Torno, H., ed., ASCE, New York, New York.

Goldberg, D. E. and Kuo, C. H. (1987). "Genetic Algorithms in Pipeline Optimization." *Journal of Computing In Civil Engineering*, 1(2), 128.

Loubser, B. F., and Gessler, J. (1994). "Computer Aided Optimization of Water Distribution Networks." *Proceedings of the AWWA Annual Conference*, American Water Works Association, New York, New York.

Morgan, D. R., and Goulter, I. C. (1985). "Optimal Urban Water Distribution Design." *Water Resources Research*, 21(5), 642.

Murphy, L.J., Dandy, G.C., and Simpson, A.R. (1994). "Optimal Design and Operation of Pumped Water Distribution Systems." *Proceedings of the Conference on Hydraulics in Civil Engineering*, Australian Institute of Engineers, Brisbane, Australia.

Ormsbee, L. E. (1986). "A Nonlinear Heuristic for Applied Problems in Water Resources." *Proceedings of Seventeenth Annual Modeling and Simulation Conference*, University of Pittsburgh, Pittsburgh, Pennsylvania.

Quindry, G. E., Brill, E. D., and Liebman, J. C. (1981). "Optimization of Looped Water Distribution Systems." *Journal of the Environmental Engineering Division*, ASCE, 107(4), 665.

Rowell, W. F., and Barnes, J. W. (1982). "Obtaining Layout of Water Distribution Systems." *Journal of Hydraulics Division*, ASCE, 108(1), 137.

Savic, D. A., and Walters, G. A. (1997). "Evolving Sustainable Water Networks." *Hydrological Sciences*, 42(4), 549.

Savic, D. A., and Walters G. A. (1997). "Genetic Algorithms for Least-Cost Design of Water Distribution Networks." *Journal of Water Resources Planning and Management*, ASCE, 123(2), 67.

Schaake, J. C., and Lai, D. (1969). "Linear Programming and Dynamic Programming Applied to Water Distribution Network Design." *MIT Hydrodynamics Lab Report 116*, Cambridge, Massachusetts.

Shamir, U. (1974). "Optimal Design and Operation of Water Distribution Systems." *Water Resources Research*, 10(1), 27.

Simpson, A. R., Dandy, G. C., and Murphy, L. J. (1994). "Genetic Algorithms Compared to Other Techniques for Pipe Optimization." *Journal of Water Resources Planning and Management*, ASCE, 120(4), 423.

Sonak, V. V., and Bhave, P. R. (1993). "Global Optimal Tree Solution for Single-Source Looped Water Distribution Networks Subject to a Single Loading Pattern." *Water Resources Research*, 29(7), 2437.

Stephenson, D. (1981). "The Design of Water Pipelines." *Journal of Pipelines*, 1(1), 45.

Swamee, P. K., Kumar, V., and Khanna, P. (1973). "Optimization of Dead End Water Distribution Systems." *Journal of the Environmental Engineering Division*, ASCE, 99(2), 123.

Torno, H., ed. (1985). *Computer Applications in Water Resources*. ASCE, New York, New York.

Varma, K. V. K., Narasimhan, S., and Bhallamudi, S. M. (1997). "Optimal Design of Water Distribution Systems Using NLP Method." *Journal of Environmental Engineering*, ASCE, 123(4), 381.

Walski, T. M. (1983). "Energy Efficiency Through Pipe Design." *Journal of the American Water Works Association*, 75(10), 492.

Walski, T. M. (1985). "State-of-the-Art: Pipe Network Optimization." *Computer Applications in Water Resources*, Torno, H., ed., ASCE, New York, New York.

Walski, T. M., and Gessler J. (1985). "Water Distribution System Optimization." *Technical Report EL-85-11*, U.S. Army Engineer Waterways Experiment Station, Vicksburg, Mississippi.

Walski, T. M., Brill, E. D., Gessler, J., Goulter, I. C., Jeppson, R. M., Lansey, K., Lee, H. L., Liebman, J. C., Mays, L. W., Morgan, D. R., and Ormsbee, L. E. (1987). "Battle of the Network Models: Epilogue." *Journal of Water Resources Planning and Management*, ASCE, 113(2), 191.

Walski, T. M., Gessler, J., and Sjostrom, J.W. (1988). "Selecting Optimal Pipe Sizes for Water Distribution Systems." *Journal of the American Water Works Association*, 80(2), 35.

Walski, T. M. (1995). "Optimization and Pipe Sizing Decisions." *Journal of Water Resources Planning and Management*, ASCE, 121(4), 340.

Walski, T.M., Youshock, M., and Rhee, H. (2000). "Use of Modeling in Decision Making for Water Distribution Master Planning." *Proceedings of the ASCE EWRI Conference*, Minneapolis, Minnesota.

Walski, T.M. (2001) "The Wrong Paradigm—Why Water Distribution Optimization Doesn't Work." *accepted for Journal of Water Resources Planning and Management*, ASCE, 127(2).

Walters, G.A., Halhal, D., Savic, D., and Ouazar, D (1999). "Improved Design of 'Anytown' Distribution Network Using Structured Messy Genetic Algorithms." *Urban Water*, 1(1), 23.

Watanatada, T. (1973). "Least Cost Design of Water Distribution System." *Journal of the Hydraulics Division*, ASCE, 99(9), 1497.

Wu, Z. Y., Boulos, P. F., Orr, C. H., and Ro, J. J. (2000). "An Efficient Genetic Algorithms Approach to an Intelligent Decision Support System for Water Distribution Networks." *Proceedings of the Hydroinformatics Conference*, Iowa.

Wu, Z. Y., and Simpson, A. R. (2000). "Evaluation of Critical Transient Loading for Optimal Design of Water Distribution Systems." *Proceedings of the Hydroinformatics Conference*, Iowa.

Wu, Z. Y., and Simpson A. R. (2000). "Competent Genetic Algorithm Optimization of Water Distribution Systems." *Accepted for Journal of Computing in Civil Engineering*, ASCE.

Simpson A. R., and Wu, Z. Y. (1997). "Optimal Rehabilitation of Water Distribution Systems Using a Messy Genetic Algorithm." *Proceedings of the AWWA 17th Federal Convention Water in the Balance,* Melbourne, Australia.

MODELING FOR ENERGY EFFICIENCY

Arora, H., and LeChevallier, M. W. (1998). "Energy Management Opportunities." *Journal of the American Water Works Association*, 90(2), 40.

Brion, L., and Mays, L. W. (1991). "Methodology for Optimal Operation of Pumping Stations in Water Distribution Systems." *Journal of Hydraulic Engineering*, ASCE, 117(11), 1551.

Chase, D. V. (1993). "Computer Generated Pumping Schedule for Satisfying Operational Objectives." *Journal of the American Water Works Association*, 85(7), 54.

Coulbeck, B., and Sterling, M. (1978). "Optimal Control of Water Distribution Systems." *Proceedings of the Institute of Electrical Engineers*, 125, 1039.

Coulbeck, B., and Orr, C. H., eds. (1988). *Computer Applications in Water Supply Vol 2: System Optimization and Control.* Research Studies Press Ltd., Leicester, United Kingdom.

Coulbeck, B., Bryds, M., Orr, C., and Rance, J. (1988). "A Hierarchal Approach to Optimized Control of Water Distribution Systems." *Journal of Optimal Control Applications and Methods*, 9(1), 51.

Lackowitz, G. W., and Petretti, P. J. (1983). "Improving Energy Efficiency Through Computer Modeling." *Journal of the American Water Works Association*, 75(10), 510.

Lansey, K. E., and Zhong, Q. (1990). "A Methodology for Optimal Control of Pump Stations." *Proceedings of the Water Resources Planning and Management Specialty Conference*, American Society of Civil Engineers, 58.

Ormsbee, L. E., Walski, T. W., Chase, D. V., and Sharp, W. (1989). "Methodology for Improving Pump Operation Efficiency." *Journal of Water Resources Planning and Management*, ASCE, 115(2), 148.

Ormsbee, L. E. (1991). "Energy Efficient Operation of Water Distribution Systems." *Research Report UKCE9104*, University of Kentucky, Lexington, Kentucky.

Reardon, D. (1994). "Audit Manual for Water-Wastewater Facilities." *CR-104300*, EPRI, St. Louis, Missouri.

Rehis, H. F., and Griffin, M. K. (1984). "Energy Cost Reduction Through Operational Practices." *Proceedings of the AWWA Annual Conference*, American Water Works Association, Dallas, Texas.

Sabel, M. H., and Helwig, O. J. (1985). "Cost Effective Operation of Urban Water Supply System Using Dynamic Programming." *Water Resources Bulletin*, 21(1), 75.

Sakarya, A. B. A., and Mays, L. W. (2000) "Optimal Operation of Water Distribution Pumps Considering Water Quality." *Journal of Water Resources Planning and Management*, ASCE, 126(4), 210.

Shamir, U. (1985). "Computer Applications for Real-time Operation of Water Distribution Systems." *Proceedings of the Water Resources Planning and Management Division Conference*, American Society of Civil Engineers, Buffalo, New York.

Sterling, M. J. H., and Coulbeck, B. (1975). "Optimization of Water Pumping Costs by Hierarchical Methods." *Proceedings of the Institute of Civil Engineers*, 59, 789.

Walski, T. M. (1980). "Energy Costs: A New Factor in Pipe Size Selection." *Journal of the American Water Works Association*, 72(6), 326.

Walski, T. M. (1993). "Tips for Saving Energy in Pumping Operations." *Journal of the American Water Works Association*, 85(7), 49.

Water and Environment Federation (WEF). (1997). "Energy Conservation in Wastewater Treatment Facilities." *WEF Manual of Practice MFD-2*, Alexandria, Virginia.

Zessler, M. L., and Shamir, U. (1989). "Optimal Operation of Water Distribution Systems." *Journal of Water Resources Planning and Management*, ASCE, 115(8), 735.

WATER QUALITY MODELING

American Water Works Association. (1990). "Recommended Practice for Backflow Prevention and Cross Connection Control." *AWWA Manual M-14*, Denver, Colorado.

American Water Works Association Research Foundation. (1991). *Water Quality Modeling in Distribution Systems*. Denver, Colorado.

Antoun, E. N., Dyksen, J. E., and Hiltebrand. (1999). "Unidirectional Flushing." *Journal of the American Water Works Association*, 91(7), 62.

APHA, AWWA, and WEF. (1998). *Standard Methods for Examination of Water and Wastewater.* 20th Edition, AWWA, Denver, Colorado.

Benjamin, M. M., Reiber, S. H., Ferguson, J. F, Vanderwerff, E. A., and Miller, M. W. (1990). *Chemistry of Corrosion Inhibitors in Potable Water.* AWWARF, Denver, Colorado.

Boccelli, D. L., Tryby, M. E., Uber, J. G., Rossman, L. A., Zierolf, M. L., and Polycarpou, M. M. (1998). "Optimal Scheduling of Booster Disinfection in Water Distribution Systems." *Journal of Water Resources Planning and Management*, ASCE, 124(2), 99.

Boulos, P. F., Altman, T., Jarrige, P. A., and Collevati, F. (1995). "Discrete Simulation Approach for Network Water Quality Models." *Journal of Water Resources Planning and Management*, ASCE, 121(1), 49.

Caldwell, D. H., and Lawrence, W. B. (1953). "Water Softening and Conditioning Problems." *Industrial Engineering Chemistry*, 45(3), 535.

Clark, R. M., Grayman W. M., and Males, R. M. (1988). "Contaminant Propagation in Distribution Systems." *Journal of Environmental Engineering*, ASCE, 114(4), 929.

Clark, R. M., and Cole, J. A. (1990). "Measuring and Modeling Variations in Distribution System Water Quality." *Journal of the American Water Works Association*, 82(8), 46.

Clark, R. M., Grayman, W. M., Goodrich, R. A., Deininger, P. A., and Hess, A. F. (1991). "Field Testing Distribution Water Quality Models." *Journal of the American Water Works Association,* 84(7), 67.

Clark, R. M., Grayman, W. M., Males R. M., and Hess, A. F. (1993). "Modeling Contaminant Propagation in Water Distribution Systems." *Journal of Environmental Engineering*, ASCE, 119(2), 349.

Clark, R. M., Geldreich, E. E., Fox, K. R., Rice, E. W., Johnson, C. H., Goodrich, J. A., Barnick, J. A., and Abdesaken, F. (1996). "Tracking a Salmonella Serovar Typhimurium Outbreak in Gideon, Missouri: Role of Contaminant Propagation Modeling." *Journal of Water Supply Research and Technology-Aqua*, 45(4), 171.

Clark, R. M., and Grayman, W. M. (1998). *Modeling Water Quality in Distribution Systems.* AWWA, Denver, Colorado.

Gagnon, J. L., and Bowen, P. T. (1996). "Supply Safety and Quality of Distributed Water." *Proceedings of the AWWA Computer Conference*, American Water Works Association, Chicago, Illinois, 287.

Gauthier, V., Besner, M. C., Barbeau, B., Millette, R., and Prevost, M. (2000). "Storage Tank Management to Improve Water Quality: Case Study." *Journal of Water Resources Planning and Management*, ASCE, 126(4), 221.

Geldreich, E. E. (1996). *Microbial Quality of Water Supply in Distribution Systems.* Lewis Publishers, Boca Raton, Florida.

Grayman, W. M., Clark, R. M., and Males, R. M. (1988). "Modeling Distribution System Water Quality: Dynamic Approach." *Journal of Water Resources Planning and Management*, ASCE, 114(3).

Grayman W. M., Deininger, R. A., Green, A., Boulos, P. F., Bowcock, R. W., and Godwin, C. C. (1996). "Water Quality and Mixing Models for Tanks and Reservoirs." *Journal of the American Water Works Association*, 88(7).

Harding, B. L. and Walski, T. M. (2000). "Long Time-series Simulation of Water Quality in Distribution Systems." *Journal of Water Resources Planning and Management*, ASCE, 126(4), 199.

Harr, J. (1995). *A Civil Action.* Vintage Books, New York, New York.

Hart, F. F., Meader, J. L., and Chiang, S. M. (1987). "CLNET—A Simulation Model for Tracing Chlorine Residuals in Potable Water Distribution Networks." *Proceedings of the AWWA Distribution System Symposium*, American Water Works Association, Denver, Colorado.

Kramer, M. H., Herwald, B. L., Craun, G. F., Calderon, R. L., and Juranek, D. D. (1996). "Waterborne Disease—1993 and 1994." *Journal of the American Water Works Association*, 88(3), 66.

Kroon, J. R., and Hunt, W. A. (1989). "Modeling Water Quality in a Distribution Network." *Proceedings of the AWWA Water Quality Technology Conference*, American Water Works Association, Denver, Colorado.

Islam, R., and Chaudhry, M. H. (1998). "Modeling Constituent Transport in Unsteady Flows in Pipe Networks." *Journal of Hydraulic Engineering*, ASCE, 124(11), 1115.

Langelier, W. F. (1936). "The Analytical Control of Anti-Corrosion in Water Treatment." *Journal of the American Water Works Association*, 28(10), 1500.

LeChevallier, M. W., Babcock, T. M., and Lee, R. G. (1987). "Examination of the Characterization of Distribution System Biofilms." *Applied and Environmental Microbiology*, 53(2), 714.

Liou, C. P., and Kroon, J. R. (1987). "Modeling Propagation of Waterborne Substances in Distribution Networks." *Journal of the American Water Works Association*, 79(11), 54.

Maddison, L. A., and Gagnon, G. A. (1999). "Evaluating Corrosion Control Strategies for a Pilot-Scale Distribution System." *Proceedings of the Water Quality Technology Conference*, American Water Works Association, Denver, Colorado.

Males, R.M., Clark, R.M., Wehrman, P.I., and Gates, W.E. (1985). "An Algorithm for Mixing Problems in Water Systems," *Journal of Hydraulic Engineering*, ASCE, 111(2).

Maslia, M. L., Sautner, J. B., Aral, M. M., Reyes, J. J., Abraham, J. E., and Williams, R. C. (2000). "Using Water-Distribution Modeling to Assist Epidemiologic Investigations." *Journal of Water Resources Planning and Management*, ASCE, 126(4), 180.

Mau, R. E., Boulos, P. F., Clark, R. M., Grayman, W. M., Tekippe, W. M., and Trussel, R. R. (1995). "Explicit Mathematical Model of Distribution Storage Water Quality." *Journal of Hydraulic Engineering*, ASCE, 121(10), 699.

McNeil, L. S., and Edwards, M. (2000). "Phosphate Inhibitors and Red Water in Stagnant Iron Pipes." *Journal of Environmental Engineering*, ASCE, 126(12), 1096.

Merrill, D. T., and Sanks, R. L. (1978). *Corrosion Control by Deposition of $CaCO_3$ Films*. AWWA, Denver, Colorado.

Mullen, E. D., and Ritter, J. A. (1974). "Potable-Water Corrosion Control." *Journal of the American Water Works Association*, 66(8), 473.

Murphy, P. J. (1991). *Prediction and Validation in Water Distribution Modeling*. AWWARF, Denver, Colorado.

Rossman, L. A., Boulos P. F., and Altman, T. (1993). "Discrete Element Method for Network Water Quality Models." *Journal of Water Resources Planning and Management*, ASCE, 119(5), 505.

Rossman, L. A. (1994). *EPANET Users Manual*. U.S. Environmental Protection Agency, Cincinnati, Ohio.

Rossman, L. A., Clark, R. M., and Grayman, W. M. (1994). "Modeling Chlorine Residuals in Drinking-Water Distribution Systems." *Journal of Environmental Engineering*, ASCE, 120(4), 803.

Rossman, L. A., and Boulos, P. F. (1996). "Numerical Methods for Modeling Water Quality in Distribution Systems: A Comparison." *Journal of Water Resources Planning and Management*, ASCE, 122(2), 137.

Shah, M. and Sinai, G. (1988). "Steady State Model for Dilution in Water Networks." *Journal of Hydraulic Engineering*, ASCE, 114(2), 192.

Sharp, W.W., Pfeffer, J., and Morgan, M. (1991). "In Situ Chlorine Decay Rate Testing." *Proceedings of the AWWARF/EPA Conference on Water Quality Modeling in Distribution Systems*, Cincinnati, Ohio.

Summers, R. S., Hooper, S. M., Shukairy, H. M., Solarik, G., and Owen, D. (1996). "Assessing DBP Yield: Uniform Formation Conditions." *Journal of the American Water Works Association*, 88(6), 80.

Tryby, M. E., Boccelli, D., Koechling, M., Uber, J., Summers, R. S., and Rossman. L. (1999). "Booster Chlorination for Managing Disinfectant Residuals." *Journal of the American Water Works Association*, 91(1), 86.

Vasconcelos, J. J., Rossman, L. A., Grayman, W. M., Boulos, P. F., and Clark, R. M. (1996). *Characterization and Modeling of Chlorine Decay in Distribution Systems*. AWWA Research Foundation, Denver, Colorado.

Vasconcelos, J. J., Rossman, L. A., Grayman, W. M., Boulos, P. F., and Clark, R. M. (1997). "Kinetics of Chlorine Decay." *Journal of the American Water Works Association*, 89(7), 54.

Volk, C., Dundore, E., Schiermann, J., LeChevallier, M. (2000). "Practical Evaluation of Iron Corrosion Control in a Drinking Water Distribution System." *Water Research*, 34(6), 1967.

Walski, T. M. (1991). "Understanding Solids Transport in Water Distribution Systems." *Water Quality Modeling in Distribution Systems*, AWWARF, Denver, Colorado.

Walski, T. M., and Draus, S. J. (1996). "Predicting Water Quality Changes During Flushing." *Proceedings of the AWWA Annual Conference*, American Water Works Association, Toronto, Canada.

Walski, T. M. (1999) "Modeling TCE Dynamics in Water Distribution Tanks." *Proceedings of the 26th Water Resources Planning and Management Conference*, American Society of Civil Engineers, Tempe, Arizona.

Welker, R., Sakamoto, K., LeFebre, W., and Hanna, Y. (1995). "The Application of a Calibrated Water Quality Model in a System-wide Disinfection Study." *Computers in the Water Industry*, American Water Works Association, Denver, Colorado.

FIRE PROTECTION

American Water Works Association. (1998). "Distribution System Requirements for Fire Protection." *AWWA Manual M-31*, Denver, Colorado.

Boulos, P. F., Rossman, L. A., Orr, C. H., Heath, J. E., and Meyer, M. S. (1997). "Fire Flow Computation with Network Models." *Journal of the American Water Works Association*, 89(2), 51.

Brock, P. D. (1990). *Fire Protection Hydraulics and Water Supply.* Oklahoma State University, Stillwater, Oklahoma.

Circulaire des Ministreres de l'Intériur et de l'Agriculture du Février. (1957). *Protection Contre l'incendie dnas les Communes Rurales.* Paris, France

Circulaire du Ministrere de l'Agriculture du Auout. (1967). *Réserve d'eau Potable. Protection Contre l'incendie dans les Communes Rurales.* Paris, France.

Circulaire Interministérielle du Décembre. (1951). *Alimentation des communes en eau potable - Lutte contre l'incendie.* Paris, France.

DVGW. (1978). "DVGW W405 Bereitstellung von Löschwasser durch die Öffentliche Trinkwasserversorgung." *Deutscher Verein des Gas - und Wasserfaches*, Franfurt, Germany.

Hickey, H. E. (1980). *Hydraulics for Fire Protection.* National Fire Protection Association, Quincy, Massachusetts.

Insurance Service Office (ISO). (1963). *Fire Flow Tests.* New York, New York.

Insurance Services Office (ISO). (1998). *Fire Suppression Rating Schedule.* New York, New York.

National Fire Protection Association (NFPA). (1992). "Standard for Inspection, Testing and Maintenance of Water Based Fire Protection Systems." *NFPA 25*, Quincy, Massachusetts.

National Fire Protection Association (NFPA). (1999). *Fire Protection Handbook.* Quincy, Massachusetts.

National Fire Protection Association (NFPA). (1999). "Sprinkler Systems in One- and Two-Family Dwellings and Manufactured Homes." *NFPA 13D*, Quincy, Massachusetts.

National Fire Protection Association (NFPA). (1999). "Standard for Installation of Sprinkler Systems." *NFPA 13*, Quincy, Massachusetts.

SNIP. (1985). *Water Supply Standards* (in Russian). 2.04.02-84, Moscow, Russia.

Walski, T. M., and Lutes, T. L. (1990). "Accuracy of Hydrant Flow Tests Using a Pitot Diffuser." *Journal of the American Water Works Association*, 82(7), 58.

Water UK and Local Government Association. (1998). *National Guidance Document on the Provision of Water for Fire Fighting.* London, United Kingdom.

TRANSIENTS

Almeida, A. B., and Koelle, E. (1992). *Fluid Transients in Pipe Networks*. Elsevier Applied Science, Southampton, UK.

Chaudhry, M. H. (1987). *Applied Hydraulic Transients*. Van Nostrand Reinhold, New York.

Liggett, J. A., and Chen, L. C. (1994). "Inverse Transient Analysis in Pipe Networks." *Journal of Hydraulic Engineering*, ASCE, 120(8), 934.

Thorley, A. R. D. (1991). *Fluid Transients in Pipeline Systems*. D&L George Ltd., United Kingdom.

Wylie, E. B., and Streeter, V. L. (1993). *Fluid Transients in Systems*. Prentice-Hall, New York.

Index

A

B

C

D

E

F

G

H

I

J

K

L

M

N

O

P

Q

R

S

T

U

V

W

Z

NOTES

NOTES

NOTES

NOTES

NOTES

NOTES